The INTERNATIONAL CRITICAL COMMENTARY on the Holy Scriptures of the Old and New Testaments

GENERAL EDITORS

G. I. DAVIES, F.B.A.
Emeritus Professor of Old Testament Studies in the University of Cambridge
Fellow of Fitzwilliam College

AND

C. M. TUCKETT
Professor of New Testament in the University of Oxford
Fellow of Pembroke College

CONSULTING EDITORS

J. A. EMERTON, F.B.A.
Emeritus Regius Professor of Hebrew in the University of Cambridge
Fellow of St John's College, Cambridge
Honorary Canon of St George's Cathedral, Jerusalem

AND

C. E. B. CRANFIELD, F.B.A.
Emeritus Professor of Theology in the University of Durham

FORMERLY UNDER THE EDITORSHIP OF

G. N. STANTON
General Editor of the New Series

S. R. DRIVER
A. PLUMMER
C. A. BRIGGS
Founding Editors

A CRITICAL AND EXEGETICAL COMMENTARY

ON

ISAIAH 56–66

BY

JOHN GOLDINGAY

David Allan Hubbard Professor of Old Testament,
Fuller Theological Seminary, Pasadena, California

BLOOMSBURY
LONDON • NEW DELHI • NEW YORK • SYDNEY

Bloomsbury T&T Clark
An imprint of Bloomsbury Publishing Plc

50 Bedford Square
London
WC1B 3DP
UK

1385 Broadway
New York
NY 10018
USA

www.bloomsbury.com

First published 2014
Paperback edition published in 2025

British Library Cataloguing-in-Publication Data
A catalogue record for this book is available from the British Library.

ISBN: HB: 978-0-56756-962-2
PB: 978-0-56771-694-1

Library of Congress Cataloging-in-Publication Data
A catalog record for this book is available from the Library of Congress.

Typeset by Forthcoming Publications

CONTENTS

General Editors' Preface		vii
Preface		ix
Abbreviations		xi
Works Consulted		xv
INTRODUCTION		1
COMMENTARY		59
I.	56.1-8	61
II.	56.9–57.21	94
	(a) 56.9–57.2	104
	(b) 57.3-13	116
	(c) 57.14-21	134
III.	58.1–59.8	150
	(a) 58.1-14	162
	(b) 59.1-8	186
IV.	59.9-15a	204
V.	59.15b-21	219
VI.	60.1-22	240
VII.	61.1-9	286
VIII.	61.10–62.12	319
IX.	63.1-6	354
X.	63.7–64.11 [12]	376
XI.	65.1–66.17	426
	(a) 65.1-7	440
	(b) 65.8-25	453
	(c) 66.1-17	478
XII.	66.18-24	509

GENERAL EDITORS' PREFACE

Much scholarly work has been done on the Bible since the publication of the first volumes of the International Critical Commentary in the 1890s. New linguistic, textual, historical and archaeological evidence has become available, and there have been changes and developments in methods of study. In the twenty-first century there will be as great a need as ever, and perhaps a greater need, for the kind of commentary that the International Critical Commentary seeks to supply. The series has long had a special place among works in English on the Bible, because it has sought to bring together all the relevant aids to exegesis, linguistic and textual no less than archaeological, historical, literary and theological, to help the reader to understand the meaning of the books of the Old and New Testaments. In the confidence that such a series meets a need, the publishers and the editors are commissioning new commentaries on all the books of the Bible. The work of preparing a commentary on such a scale cannot but be slow, and developments in the past half-century have made the commentator's task yet more difficult than before, but it is hoped that the remaining volumes will appear without too great intervals between them. No attempt has been made to secure a uniform theological or critical approach to the problems of the various books, and scholars have been selected for their scholarship and not for their adherence to any school of thought. It is hoped that the new volumes will attain the high standards set in the past, and that they will make a significant contribution to the understanding of the books of the Bible.

G.I.D
C.M.T

PREFACE

In the preface to *Isaiah 40–55*,[1] we outlined the background to our writing that commentary and our method of proceeding. David Payne is now long since retired and thus I alone am responsible for this commentary. I am grateful to Fuller Theological Seminary for its encouragement to faculty writing projects and for the magnificent support of the library. I am again grateful to Graham Davies for his careful comments on the manuscript, which drew attention to many slips, and for his suggestions about exegesis.

In this volume, in referring to the Hebrew text I use the term ‘chapter’ to denote a perasha petucha (‘open division’, one that originally left the rest of the line blank) and the term ‘paragraph’ to denote a perasha setuma (‘closed division’, one that originally involved a space in the midst of the line). In MT mss, the former is marked by a *p*, the latter by an *s*. For much of the information on the location of these, I rely on *HUB*; Maori, ‘מסורתת ה"פסקאות" בכתבי יד עבריים קדומים: מגילות מקרא ופרשים מספר ישעיהו מקומראן’; Oesch, *Petucha und Setuma*; and Olley, ‘“Hear the Word of Yhwh”’. In referring to my own understanding of divisions in the text, I use the term ‘section’ to refer to the twelve major divisions listed in the Contents, and the term ‘subsection’ to refer to units within those sections.

My approach to questions about the text appears in the introduction to the commentary on Isaiah 40–55.[2] Here, I do need to add information on the Qumran manuscripts relating to chapters 56–66.[3] These are as follows:

1QIs[a]	complete for chapters 56–66
1QIs[b]	56.1–57.4; 57.17–59.8; 59.20–61.2; 62.2–64.1; 64.6-8; 65.17–66.24
4QIs[b]	61.1-3; 64.5–65.1; 66.24
4QIs[c]	66.20-24
4QIs[d]	57.9–58.3; 58.5-7
4QIs[e]	59.15-16
4QIs[i]	56.7-8; 57.5-8
4QIs[m]	60.20–61.1; 61.3-6
4QIs[n]	58.13-14

[1] Goldingay and Payne, *Isaiah 40–55*, I, pp. ix-x.

[2] Goldingay and Payne, *Isaiah 40–55*, I, pp. 8-17.

[3] GID draws my attention to Armin Lange, *Handbuch der Textfunde vom Toten Meer. 1, Die Handschriften biblischer Bücher von Qumran und den anderen Fundorten* (Tübingen: Mohr, 2009), esp. pp. 257-96, as a valuable guide to the contents and the nature of the text in these manuscripts.

ABBREVIATIONS

1QH	The Qumran Cave 1manuscript Hodayot (Thanksgivings)
1QIs^{a}	The 'a' manuscript of Isaiah from Qumran Cave 1
1QIs^{b}	The 'b' manuscript of Isaiah from Qumran Cave 1
4QIs$^{a\text{-}r}$	The manuscripts of Isaiah from Qumran Cave 4, subtitled 'a' to 'r'
1QS	The Qumran Cave 1 manuscript Serek haYahad (Community Rule)
ANET	James B. Pritchard (ed.), *Ancient Near Eastern Texts Relating to the Old Testament*. Princeton: Princeton University Press, 3rd edn, 1969
Aq	Aquila's Greek translation
ASTI	*Annual of the Swedish Theological Institute*
B.	Babylonian Talmud
BASOR	*Bulletin of the American Schools of Oriental Research*
BDB	Francis Brown with the co-operation of S. R. Driver and Charles A. Briggs, *A Hebrew and English Lexicon of the Old Testament*, 1906. Reprinted with corrections, Oxford: Oxford University Press, 1962
BJRL	*Bulletin of the John Rylands University Library of Manchester*
BN	*Biblische Notizen*
BSac	*Bibliotheca sacra*
BZ	*Biblische Zeitschrift*
CAD	*The [Chicago] Assyrian Dictionary.* Chicago: Oriental Institute; Glückstadt: Augustin, 1964–
CBQ	*Catholic Biblical Quarterly*
CD	Cairo manuscript of the Damascus Document (cf. 1QS)
D	The Deuteronom[istic]ic source in the Pentateuch, as traditionally identified
DCH	D. J. A. Clines and others (eds.), *The Dictionary of Classical Hebrew*. 8 volumes. Sheffield: Sheffield Academic Press (vols. 1–5), Sheffield Phoenix Press (vols. 6–8), 1993–2011
DG	John C. L. Gibson, *Davidson's Introductory Hebrew Grammar—Syntax*. Edinburgh: T. & T. Clark, 1994
dittog.	dittography (accidental repetition of a letter, word, or phrase)
DTT	Marcus Jastrow, *A Dictionary of the Targumim, the Talmud Babli and Yerushalmi, and the Midrashic Literature.* New York: Choreb; London: Shapiro, 1926
E	The Elohistic strand in the Pentateuch, as traditionally identified
ET	English Translation
f.	feminine
GID	Suggestions by G. I. Davies in editing the commentary

GK	*Gesenius' Hebrew Grammar*. Reprint. Oxford: Oxford University Press, 2nd edn, 1966. ET from Wilhelm Gesenius, *Hebräische Grammatik*. Edited and enlarged by E. Kautzsch. Leipzig: Vogel, 28th edn, 1909
H	The Holiness Code (Lev 17–26) in the Pentateuch, as traditionally identified
HALOT	Ludwig Koehler, Walter Baumgartner and others, *The Hebrew and Aramaic Lexicon of the Old Testament*. Reprint. Leiden: Brill, 2001. ET from *Hebräisches und Aramäisches Lexicon zum Alten Testament*. Leiden: Brill, 3rd edn, 1967–95
haplog.	haplography (accidental omission of a letter, word, or phrase that was repeated)
HAR	*Hebrew Annual Review*
HUB	Moshe H. Goshen-Gottstein (ed.), *The Book of Isaiah*. The Hebrew University Bible. Jerusalem: Magnes, 1995
HUCA	*Hebrew Union College Annual*
IBHS	Bruce K. Waltke and M. O'Connor, *An Introduction to Biblical Hebrew Syntax*. Winona Lake, IN: Eisenbrauns, 1990
JBL	*Journal of Biblical Literature*
JJS	*Journal of Jewish Studies*
J	The Yahwistic strand in the Pentateuch, as traditionally identified
JE	The Yahwistic–Elohistic strand in the Pentateuch, as traditionally identified
JM	Paul Joüon, *A Grammar of Biblical Hebrew*. Translated and revised by T. Muraoka. Rome: Pontifical Biblical Institute, 1991
JPSV	*JPS Hebrew–English Tanakh*. Philadelphia: Jewish Publication Society, 2nd edn, 1999
JQR	*Jewish Quarterly Review*
JSOT	*Journal for the Study of the Old Testament*
JSS	*Journal of Semitic Studies*
JTS	*Journal of Theological Studies*
K	kethiv
KJV	King James (Authorised) Version
LXX	Septuagint
m.	masculine
ms(s)	manuscript(s)
MT	Masoretic Text
NEB	New English Bible
NRSV	New Revised Standard Version
n.s.	new series
OG	Old Greek
OL	Old Latin
OTE	*Old Testament Essays*
OTS	*Oudtestamentische Studiën*
P	The Priestly strand in the Pentateuch, as traditionally identified
PBH	Post-biblical Hebrew
PG	Patrologia Graeca
PL	Patrologia Latina

pl.	plural
Q	qere
R.	Rabbah (following a biblical book, e.g., Gen. R. = Genesis Rabbah)
RB	*Revue Biblique*
sg.	singular
SJOT	*Scandinavian Journal of the Old Testament*
Sym	Symmachus's Greek translation
Syr	Syriac
TDOT	G. Johannes Botterweck and others (eds.), *Theological Dictionary of the Old Testament*. Grand Rapids: Eerdmans, 1974–. ET from *TWAT*
Tg	Targum
Th	Theodotion's Greek translation
THAT	Ernst Jenni and Claus Westermann (eds.), *Theologisches Handwörterbuch zum Altes Testament*. 2 vols. Munich: Kaiser, 1971, 1976
TLOT	Ernst Jenni and Claus Westermann (eds.). *Theological Lexicon of the Old Testament*. 3 vols. Peabody, MA: Hendrickson, 1997. ET from *THAT*
TNIV	Today's New International Version
TTH	S. R. Driver, *A Treatise on the Use of the Tenses in Hebrew and Some Other Syntactical Questions*. Oxford: Oxford University Press, 3rd edn, 1892
TWAT	G. Johannes Botterweck and others (eds.), *Theologisches Wörterbuch zum Alten Testament*. 8 vols. Stuttgart: Kohlhammer, 1970–95
UF	*Ugarit-Forschungen*
v.	verse
Vg	Vulgate
Vrs	Versions
VT	*Vetus Testamentum*
WTJ	*Westminster Theological Journal*
WW	*Word and World*
ZAW	*Zeitschrift für die alttestamentliche Wissenschaft*

WORKS CONSULTED

In the footnotes in this volume, I give the full information on works that relate primarily to that one section. Where I refer subsequently in that section to such a work, I use a short title, sometimes adding the annotation '(see above)' to indicate that the information on the work will be found earlier in that section of the commentary.

The bibliography that follows here gives information on more general works to which the footnotes refer by a short title. Primary sources are listed here under Goshen-Gottstein, Kittel, and Thomas (MT), Burrows, Cross, Parry and Qimron, Steck, and Ulrich (1QIs[a]), Sukenik and Ulrich (1QIs[b]), Ulrich (4QIs), Sperber and Stenning (Targum), Rahlfs and Ziegler (Greek), Field (Hexapla), Vööbus (Syro-Hexapla), Brock (Syriac), Gryson and Weber (Latin), and Derenbourg (Arabic).

Abel, F.-M. 'Le commentaire de Saint Jérôme sur Isaïe'. *RB* 25 (1916), pp. 200-25.

Abernethy, Andrew, and others (eds.). *Isaiah and Imperial Context.* Eugene, OR: Pickwick, 2013.

Abramowski, Rudolf. 'Zum literarischen Problem des Tritojesaja'. *Theologische Studien und Kritiken* 96/97 (1925), pp. 90-143.

Achtemeier, Elizabeth. *The Community and Message of Isaiah 56–66.* Minneapolis: Augsburg, 1982.

Ackroyd, Peter R. 'Isaiah', in Charles M. Laymon (ed.), *The Interpreter's One-Volume Commentary on the Bible*. Nashville: Abingdon, 1971, pp. 329-71.

—*Studies in the Religious Tradition of the Old Testament.* London: SCM, 1987.

—'Theological Reflections on the Book of Isaiah'. *King's Theological Review* 4 (1981), pp. 53-63; 5 (1982), pp. 8-13, 43-48.

Albert the Great. *Postilla super Isaiam*. c. 1250. Reprinted in *Opera omnia,* XIX, pp. 1-632. [Münster:] Aschendorff, 1952.

Albertz, Rainer. *Religionsgeschichte Israels in alttestamentlicher Zeit.* 2 vols. Göttingen: Vandenhoeck & Ruprecht, 1992. ET *A History of Israelite Religion in the Old Testament Period.* 2 vols. London: SCM; Louisville: Westminster John Knox, 1994.

Alexander, Joseph Addison. *The Later Prophecies of Isaiah.* New York: Wiley, 1847. Revised edn reprinted in *Commentary on the Prophecies of Isaiah.* Edinburgh: Elliot, 1865.

Alonso Schökel, L. *A Manual of Hebrew Poetics*. Rome: Pontifical Biblical Institute, 1988.

Alonso Schökel, L., and J. L. Sicre Diaz. *Profetas I: Isaias, Jeremias.* Nueva biblia española. Madrid: Cristiandad, 1980.

Armstrong, James F. 'A Study of Alternative Readings in the Hebrew Text of the Book of Isaiah'. Diss. Princeton, 1958.

Baer, David A. *When We All Go Home: Translation and Theology in LXX Isaiah 56–66.* Sheffield: Sheffield Academic Press, 2001.

Banwell, B. O. 'A Suggested Analysis of Isaiah xl–lxvi'. *Expository Times* 76 (1964–65), p. 166.

Barker, Margaret. 'Isaiah', in James D. G. Dunn and John W. Rogerson (eds.), *Eerdmans Commentary on the Bible*, pp. 489-542. Grand Rapids: Eerdmans, 2003.

Barth, Karl. *Die Kirchliche Dogmatik*. Zurich: Evangelischer Verlag, 1932–70. ET *Church Dogmatics*. Edinburgh: T. & T. Clark; New York: Scribner's, 1936–69.

Barthélemy, Dominique. *Critique textuelle de l'Ancien Testament 2: Isaïe, Jérémie, Lamentations*. Göttingen: Vandenhoeck & Ruprecht, 1986.

Baumgärtel, Friedrich. 'Die Septuaginta zu Jesaja das Werk zweier Übersetzer', in Johannes Herrmann and Friedrich Baumgärtel, *Beiträge zur Entstehungsgeschichte der Septuaginta*, pp. 20-31. Berlin: Kohlhammer, 1923.

Bedford, Peter Ross. *Temple Restoration in Early Achaemenid Judah*. Leiden: Brill, 2001.

Beegle, Dewey M. 'Proper Names in the New Isaiah Scroll'. *BASOR* 123 (1951), pp. 26-30.

Begg, Christopher T. 'The Absence of *YHWH ṣebāʾôt* in Isaiah 56–66'. *BN* 44 (1988), pp. 7-14.

—'Foreigners in Third Isaiah'. *The Bible Today* 23 (1985), pp. 98-102.

Bentzen, A. *Jesaja II*. Copenhagen: Gads, 1943.

Berges, Ulrich. *Das Buch Jesaja*. Freiburg: Herder, 1998.

Berquist, Jon L. *Judaism in Persia's Shadow*. Minneapolis: Fortress, 1995.

—'Reading Difference in Isaiah 56–66'. *Method and Theory in the Study of Religion* 7 (1995), pp. 23-42.

Beuken, W. A. M. *Jesaja: Deel III A; Deel III B*. Nijkerk: Callenbach, 1989.

—'The Main Theme of Trito-Isaiah: "The Servants of Yahweh"'. *JSOT* 47 (1990), pp. 67-87.

—'Trito-Jesaja', in F. García Martínez, C. H. J. de Geus, and A. F. J. Klijn (eds.), *Profeten en Profetische Geschriften*, pp. 71-85. A. S. van der Woude Festschrift. Kampen: Kok, 1987.

—'The Unity of the Book of Isaiah: Another Attempt at Bridging the Gorge Between its Two Main Parts', in J. C. Exum and H. G. M. Williamson (eds.), *Reading from Right to Left*, pp. 50-62. D. J. A. Clines Festschrift. London: Sheffield Academic Press, 2003.

Birks, T. R. *Commentary on the Book of Isaiah*. London: Church of England Book Society, 2nd edn [?1878].

Birnbaum, S. A. 'The Date of the Incomplete Isaiah Scroll from Qumrân'. *Palestine Exploration Quarterly* 92 (1960), pp. 19-26.

Blank, Sheldon H. *Prophetic Faith in Isaiah*. New York: Harper, 1958.

Blenkinsopp, Joseph. *Isaiah 56–66*. New York: Doubleday, 2003.

—*Opening the Sealed Book: Interpretations of the Book of Isaiah in Late Antiquity*. Grand Rapids: Eerdmans, 2006.

Bonnard, P.-E. *Le Second Isaïe*. Paris: Gabalda, 1972.

Bourguet, Daniel. 'Pourquoi à-t-on rassemblé des oracles si divers sous le titre d'Esaïe?' *ETR* 58 (1983), pp. 171-79.

Box, G. H. *The Book of Isaiah*. London: Pitman; New York: Macmillan, 1909.

Bredenkamp, C. J. *Der Prophet Jesaia*. 2 vols. Erlangen: Deichert, 1887.

Briggs, Charles Augustus. *Messianic Prophecy*. New York: Scribner's, 1886.

—'An Analysis of Isaiah 40–62', in R. F. Harper, F. Brown, G. F. Moore (eds.), *Old Testament and Semitic Studies in Memory of William Rainey Harper*, I, pp. 65-111. Chicago: University of Chicago, 1908.

Brock, S. P. (ed.). *Isaiah*. The Old Testament in Syriac According to the Peshiṭta Version. Part III/1. Leiden: Brill, 1987.

Brockington, L. H. 'The Greek Translator of Isaiah and his Interest in δοξα'. *VT* 1 (1951), pp. 23-32.

—*The Hebrew Text of the Old Testament: The Readings Adopted by the Translators of the New English Bible*. [Oxford]: Oxford University Press; [Cambridge]: Cambridge University Press, 1973.

Brownlee, William H. *The Meaning of the Qumrân Scrolls for the Bible with Special Attention to the Book of Isaiah*. New York: Oxford University Press, 1964.

Broyles, Craig C., and Craig A. Evans (eds.). *Writing and Reading the Scroll of Isaiah*. 2 vols. Leiden: Brill, 1997.

Brueggemann, Walter. *Isaiah*. 2 vols. Louisville: Westminster John Knox, 1998.

—*Using God's Resources Wisely: Isaiah and Urban Possibility.* Louisville: Westminster John Knox, 1993.
Budde, K. 'Das Buch Jesaia Kap. 40–66', in E. Kautzsch and A. Bertholet (eds.), *Die Heilige Schrift des Alten Testaments: Erster Band*, pp. 653-720. Tübingen: Mohr, 4th edn, 1922.
—'Zum hebräischen Klagelied'. *ZAW* 11 (1891), pp. 234-47.
Burrows, Millar. 'Orthography, Morphology, and Syntax of the St. Mark's Isaiah Manuscript'. *JBL* 68 (1949), pp. 195-211.
—'Variant Readings in the Isaiah Manuscript'. *BASOR* 111 (1948), pp. 16-24; 113 (1949), pp. 24-32.
—'Waw and yodh in the Isaiah Dead Sea Scroll'. *BASOR* 124 (1951), pp. 18-20.
—and others (eds.). *The Isaiah Manuscript and the Habakkuk Commentary*. New Haven: American Schools of Oriental Research, 1950.
Calmet, Augustin. *Le Prophète Isaïe.* Paris: Emery, 1714.
Calov, Abraham. *Biblia Testamenti Veteris illustrata.* Tomus secundus. Frankfurt: Wustius, 1672.
Calvin, John. *Commentarii in Iesaiam prophetam*. Amsterdam: Schipper, 1671. ET *Commentary on the Book of the Prophet Isaiah.* 4 vols. Reprinted Grand Rapids: Eerdmans, 1956.
Carr, David M. 'Reaching for Unity in Isaiah'. *JSOT* 57 (1993), pp. 61-80. Repr. in Philip R. Davies (ed.), *The Prophets*, pp. 164-83. Sheffield: Sheffield Academic Press, 1996.
Carroll, Robert P. 'Twilight of Prophecy or Dawn of Apocalyptic?' *JSOT* 14 (1979), pp. 3-35.
Cassuto, Umberto. 'On the Formal and Stylistic Relationship between Deutero-Isaiah and Other Biblical Writers', in Cassuto, *Biblical and Oriental Studies*, I, pp. 141-71. Jerusalem: Magnes, 1973. ET from *Rivista Israelitica* 8 (1911), pp. 191-214; 9 (1912), pp. 81-90; 10 (1913), pp. 1-13.
Cheyne, T. K. *The Book of Isaiah Chronologically Arranged.* London: Macmillan, 1870.
—*The Book of the Prophet Isaiah.* New York: Dodd, Mead; London: Clarke, 1898.
—*Critica Biblica.* London: Black, 1904.
—'Critical Problems of the Second Part of Isaiah'. *JQR* 3 (1891), pp. 587-603; 4 (1892), pp. 102-28.
—*Introduction to the Book of Isaiah.* London: Black, 1895.
—*The Mines of Isaiah Re-explored.* London: Black, 1912.
—*Notes and Criticisms on the Hebrew Text of Isaiah.* London: Macmillan, 1868.
—*The Prophecies of Isaiah.* 2 vols. London: Kegan Paul, 1880–82; rev. edn, 1886.
Childs, Brevard S. *Introduction to the Old Testament as Scripture*. Philadelphia: Fortress; London: SCM, 1979.
—*Isaiah.* Louisville: Westminster John Knox, 2001.
—*The Struggle to Understand Isaiah as Christian Scripture.* Grand Rapids: Eerdmans, 2004.
Chilton, Bruce D. *A Galilean Rabbi and His Bible*. Wilmington, DL: Glazier, 1984.
—*The Glory of Israel: The Theology and Provenience of the Isaiah Targum*. Sheffield: JSOT, 1983.
—*The Isaiah Targum*. Wilmington: Glazier, 1987.
Clark, David J. 'The Influence of the Dead Sea Scrolls on Modern Translations of Isaiah'. *The Bible Translator* 35 (1984), pp. 122-30.
Clements, R. E. 'Isaiah: A Book without an Ending?' *JSOT* 91 (2002), pp. 109-26.
—'A Light to the Nations: The Central Theme of the Book of Isaiah', in J. W. Watts and P. R. House (eds.), *Forming Prophetic Literature*, pp. 57-69. John D. W. Watts Festschrift. Sheffield: Sheffield Academic Press, 1996.
—'The Unity of the Book of Isaiah'. *Interpretation* 36 (1982), pp. 117-29. Repr. in Clements, *Old Testament Prophecy*, pp. 93-104. Louisville: Westminster John Knox, 1996.
Clericus, Johannes [Jean Le Clerc]. *Veteris Testamenti prophetae ab Esaia ad Malachiam.* Amsterdam: Westenios, 1731.
Clifford, Richard J. 'Isaiah 40–66', in James L. Mays *et al.* (eds.), *Harper's Bible Commentary*, pp. 571-96. San Francisco: Harper, 1988.
Cobb, William Henry. 'The Language of Isaiah xl–lxvi'. *BSac* 38 (1881), pp. 658-86; 39 (1882), pp. 104-32.

—'The Integrity of the Book of Isaiah'. *BSac* 39 (1882), pp. 519-54.
—'Where Was Isaiah xl–lxvi Written?' *JBL* 27 (1908), pp. 48-64.
Cocceius, Johannes. 'Synopsis Prophetiae Jesaiae', in *Commentarii in prophetiam Jesaiae*, pp. 3-56. Cocceius, Opera omnia theologica, exegetica, didactica, polemica, philologica, 2. Amsterdam: Johannes Van Someren, 1673.
—'Curae majores in prophetiam Esaiae', in *Commentarii in prophetiam Jesaiae*, pp. 57-438. Cocceius, Opera omnia theologica, exegetica, didactica, polemica, philologica, 2. Amsterdam: Johannes Van Someren, 1673.
Coffin, Henry S. 'The Book of Isaiah: Chapters 40–66: Exposition', in George A. Buttrick *et al.* (eds.), *The Interpreter's Bible*, V, pp. 381-773. Nashville: Abingdon, 1956.
Coggins, R. 'Isaiah', in John Barton and John Muddiman (eds.), *The Oxford Bible Commentary*, pp. 433-86. Oxford: Oxford University Press, 2007.
Collins, J. J. *Isaiah*. Collegeville: Liturgical, 1986.
Condamin, Albert. *Le Livre d'Isaïe*. Paris: Victor Lecoffre, 1905.
Conrad, Edgar W. *Reading Isaiah*. Minneapolis: Fortress, 1991.
Cook, Johann. 'The Orthography of Some Verbal Forms in 1QIsa^{a}', in *New Qumran Texts and Studies* (eds. G. J. Brooke with F. García Martínez), pp. 133-47. Leiden: Brill, 1994.
Croatto, J. Severino. *Imaginar el futuro. Estructura retórica y querigma del Tercer Isaías*. Buenos Aires: Lumen, 2001.
Cross, F. M., and others. 'The Great Isaiah Scroll (1QIs^{a})', in *Scrolls from Qumrân Cave 1*, pp. 13-123. Jerusalem: The Albright Institute of Archaeological Research, 1972.
Cyril of Alexandria. Ἐξήγησις ὑπομνηματικὴ εἰς τὸν προφήτην Ἡσαΐαν. PG 70, cols. 9-1450.
Daniel, Suzanne. *Le vocabulaire du culte dans la Septante*. Paris: Klincksieck, 1966.
Darr, Katheryn Pfisterer. *Isaiah's Vision and the Family of God*. Louisville: Westminster John Knox, 1994.
Davies, Andrew. *Double Standards in Isaiah*. Leiden: Brill, 2000.
Delekat, Lienhard. 'Die Peschitta zu Jesaja zwischen Targum und Septuaginta'. *Biblica* 38 (1957), pp. 185-99, 321-35.
—'Die syropalästinische Jesaja-Übersetzung'. *ZAW* 71 (1959), pp. 165-201.
Delitzsch, Franz. *Biblischer Commentar über den Propheten Jesaia*. Leipzig: Döffling & Franke, 2nd edn, 1869. ET from the 3rd edn, *Isaiah*. 2 vols. in 1. Reprinted Grand Rapids: Eerdmans, 1975.
Derenbourg, J. 'Version d'Isaïe de R. Saadia'. Part Two. *ZAW* 10 (1890), pp. 1-84.
Dillmann, August. *Der Prophet Jesaia*. Leipzig: Hirzel, 5th edn, 1890.
—*Der Prophet Jesaja*. Revised by Rudolf Kittel. Leipzig: Hirzel, 6th edn, 1898.
Dodson, M. *A New Translation of Isaiah*. London: Society for Promoting the Knowledge of the Scriptures, 1790.
Doederlein, Jo. Christoph. *Esaias*. Rev. ed., Altorf: Schüpfel, 1780.
Drechsler, Moritz. *Der Prophet Jesaja*. Completed by Heinrich August Hahn and Franz Delitzsch. 3 vols. Berlin: Schlawitz, 1845, 1849, 1857.
Driver, G. R. 'Hebrew Notes on Prophets and Proverbs'. *JTS* 41 (1940), pp. 162-75.
—'Isaianic Problems', in Gernot Wiessner (ed.), *Festschrift für Wilhelm Eilers*, pp. 43-57. Wiesbaden: Harrassowitz, 1967.
—'Linguistic and Textual Problems: Isaiah xl–lxvi'. *JTS* 36 (1935), pp. 396-406.
—'Notes on Isaiah', in J. Hempel and L. Rost (eds.), *Von Ugarit nach Qumran*, pp. 42-48. O. Eissfeldt Festschrift. Berlin: Töpelmann, 1958.
Driver, S. R. *Isaiah*. London: Nisbet, 1888; New York: Randolph [?1888].
—*A Treatise on the Use of the Tenses in Hebrew and Some Other Syntactical Questions*. Oxford: Oxford University Press, 3rd edn, 1892.
Duhm, Bernhard. *Das Buch Jesaia*. Göttingen: Vandenhoeck & Ruprecht, rev. edn, 1902.
Dumbrell, William J. 'The Purpose of the Book of Isaiah'. *Tyndale Bulletin* 36 (1985), pp. 111-28.

Eaton, J. H. 'The Isaiah Tradition', in R. J. Coggins, A. Phillips, and M. Knibb (eds.), *Israel's Prophetic Tradition*, pp. 58-76. P. R. Ackroyd Festschrift. Cambridge: Cambridge University Press, 1982.

—'The Origin of the Book of Isaiah'. *VT* 9 (1959), pp. 138-57.

Ehrlich, Arnold B. *Randglossen zur hebräischen Bibel*, IV. Leipzig: Hinrichs, 1912.

Eichhorn, Johann Gottfried. 'Jesaias', in *Einleitung in das Alte Testament*, III, pp. 56-116. Leipzig: Weidmann, rev. edn, 1803.

Eitan, Israel. 'A Contribution to Isaiah Exegesis'. *HUCA* 12-13 (1937–38), pp. 55-88.

Elliger, Karl. *Deuterojesaja in seinem Verhältnis zu Tritojesaja*. Stuttgart: Kohlhammer, 1933.

—*Die Einheit des Tritojesaia*. Stuttgart: Kohlhammer, 1928.

—'Der Prophet Tritojesaja'. *ZAW* 49 (1931), pp. 112-41.

Elliott, Mark W. (ed.). *Isaiah 40–66*. Ancient Christian Commentary on Scripture: Old Testament XI. Downers Grove, IL: IVP, 2007.

Emmerson, Grace I. *Isaiah 56–66*. Sheffield: Sheffield Academic Press, 1992.

Eusebius of Caesarea. *Der Jesajakommentar*. Edited by Joseph Ziegler. Berlin: Akademie, 1975.

Evans, Craig A. 'On the Unity and Parallel Structure of Isaiah'. *VT* 38 (1988), pp. 129-47.

Everson, A. Joseph, and Hyun Chul Paul Kim (eds.). *The Desert Will Bloom: Poetic Visions in Isaiah*. Atlanta: SBL, 2009.

Ewald, Heinrich. *Die Propheten des Alten Testaments*. 2 vols. Stuttgart: Krabbe, 1840 and 1841. ET *Commentary on the Prophets of the Old Testament*. 5 vols. London: Williams & Norgate, 1875–81.

Fekkes, Jan. *Isaiah and the Prophetic Traditions in the Book of Revelation*. Sheffield: Sheffield Academic Press, 1994.

Feldmann, Franz. *Das Buch Isaias*. 2 vols. Münster: Aschendorff, 1925 and 1926.

Field, Frederick. *Origenis Hexapla quae supersunt*, II. Oxford: Oxford University Press, 1874. Reprinted Hildesheim: Ohms, 1964.

Firth, David G., and H. G. M. Williamson (eds.). *Interpreting Isaiah*. Nottingham, UK/Downers Grove, IL: IVP, 2009.

Fischer, Johann. *Das Buch Isaias*. 2 vols. Bonn: Hanstein, 1937 and 1939.

—*In welcher Schrift lag das Buch Isaias den LXX vor?* Giessen: Töpelmann, 1930.

Fishbane, Michael A. *Biblical Interpretation in Ancient Israel*. Oxford: Oxford University Press, 1985.

Fitzgerald, Curtis W. 'A Rhetorical Analysis of Isaiah 56–66'. Diss. Dallas Theological Seminary, 2003.

Flint, Peter W., and Nathaniel N. Dykstra. 'Newly Identified Fragments of 1QIsa^{b}'. *JJS* 60 (2009), pp. 80-89.

Fohrer, G. *Das Buch Jesaja Kapitel 40–66*. Zurich: Zwingli, 1964.

Fritsch, Charles T. 'The Concept of God in the Greek Translation of Isaiah', in J. M. Myers, O. Reimherr, and H. N. Bream (eds.), *Biblical Studies in Memory of H. C. Alleman*, pp. 155-69. Locust Valley, NY: Augustin, 1960.

Garbini, Giovanni. '1QIsa^{b} et le texte d'Esaïe'. *Henoch* 6 (1984), pp. 17-21.

Gaster, Theodore H. 'Notes on Isaiah', in A. I. Katsh and L. Nemoy (eds.), *Essays on the Occasion of the Seventieth Anniversary of the Dropsie University*, pp. 91-107. Philadelphia: Dropsie University, 1979.

Gesenius, Wilhelm. *Philologisch-kritischer und historischer Commentar über den Jesaia*. 2 vols. Leipzig: Vogel, 1821.

Ginsberg, H. L. 'Some Emendations in Isaiah'. *JBL* 69 (1950), pp. 51-66.

Glahn, Ludvig. 'Quelques remarques sur la question du Trito-Esaïe et son état actuel'. *Revue d'histoire et de philosophie religieuses* 12 (1932), pp. 34-46.

Glahn, Ludvig, and Ludwig Köhler. *Der Prophet der Heimkehr*. Giessen: Töpelmann, 1934.

Glazebrook, M. G. *Studies in the Book of Isaiah*. Oxford: Clarendon, 1910.

Goldingay, John. *Isaiah*. Peabody, MA: Hendrickson; Carlisle: Paternoster, 2001.

—*The Message of Isaiah 40–55*. London: T&T Clark International, 2005.
Goldingay, John, and David Payne. *A Critical and Exegetical Commentary on Isaiah 40–55*. 2 vols. London: T&T Clark International, 2006.
González, Angel. 'La lengua y la base lingüística del Rollo de Isaías'. *Estudios bíblicos* 19 (1960), pp. 237-44.
Goshen-Gottstein, M. H. *Text and Language in Bible and Qumran*. Tel Aviv: Orient, 1960.
Gosse, Bernard. *Structuration des grands ensembles bibliques et intertextualité à l'époque perse*. Berlin: de Gruyter, 1997.
Goulder, Michael. *Isaiah as Liturgy*. Aldershot: Ashgate, 2004.
Graetz, H. *Emendationes in plerosque Sacrae Scripturae Veteris Testamenti libros*. Fascicle 1. Breslau: Schlesische; New York: Stechert, 1892.
Gray, G. Buchanan. 'The Greek Version of Isaiah: Is It the Work of a Single Translator?' *JTS* 12 (1910–11), pp. 286-93.
Gray, Mark. *Rhetoric and Social Justice in Isaiah*. New York: T&T Clark International, 2006.
Gressmann, Hugo. *Ueber die in Jes. C. 56-66 vorausgesetzten zeitgeschichtlichen Verhältnisse*. Göttingen: Dieterich, 1898.
Grotius, Hugo. *Annotationes in Vetus Testamentum*. 3 vols. Halle: Johann Jacob Curt, 1775, 1776, 1776.
Gryson, Roger (ed.). *Esaias capita 40–66*. Vetus Latina 12, ii. Freiburg: Herder, 1993.
—'Les anciennes versions latines du livre d'Isaïe'. *Revue théologique de Louvain* 17 (1986), pp. 22-37.
Hagelia, Hallvard. *Coram Deo: Spirituality in the Book of Isaiah, with Particular Attention to Faith in Yahweh*. Stockholm: Almqvist, 2001.
Hanson, Paul D. *The Dawn of Apocalyptic*. Philadelphia: Fortress, 1975.
—*Isaiah 40–66*. Louisville: Westminster John Knox, 1995.
Haymon of Halberstadt (778–853). *Commentariorum in Isaiam libri tres*. PL 116, cols 715-1086.
Hempel, Johannes. *Hebräisches Wörterbuch zu Jesaja*. Berlin: Töpelmann, 1965.
Henderson, E. *The Book of the Prophet Isaiah*. London: Hamilton Adams, 1840.
Hendewerk, Carl Ludwig. *Des Propheten Jesaja Weissagungen*. 2 vols. Königsberg: Gebrüder Bornträger, 1838 and 1843.
Hensler, Christian Gotthilf. *Jesaias*. Hamburg: Bohn, 1788.
Herbert, A. S. *The Book of the Prophet Isaiah*. 2 vols. Cambridge: Cambridge University Press, 1973 and 1975.
Hitzig, Ferdinand. *Der Prophet Jesaja*. Heidelberg: Winter, 1833.
Höffken, Peter. *Jesaja: Der Stand der theologichen Diskussion*. Darmstadt: Wissenschaftliche, 2004.
Hollerich, Michael J. *Eusebius of Caesarea's* Commentary on Isaiah. Oxford: Oxford University Press, 1999.
Hoppe, Leslie J. 'The School of Isaiah'. *The Bible Today* 23 (1985), pp. 85-89.
Houbigant, Charles-François. *Notae criticae in universos Veteris Testamenti libros*. 2 vols. Frankfurt: Varrentrapp, 2nd edn, 1777.
de Hulster, Isaac K. *Iconographic Exegesis and Third Isaiah*. Tübingen: Mohr, 2009.
Ibn Ezra, Abraham. *The Commentary of Ibn Ezra on Isaiah*. Translated by M. Friedländer. Reprint. New York: Feldheim, 1964.
Jain, Eva. 'Die materielle Rekonstruktion von *1QJes^b* (*1Q8*) und einige bisher nicht edierte Fragmente dieser Handschrift'. *Revue de Qumran* 20 (2001–2002), pp. 389-409.
Jenkins, R. G. 'The Biblical Text of the Commentaries of Eusebius and Jerome on Isaiah'. *Abr-Nahrain* 22 (1983–84), pp. 64-78.
—'Some Quotations from Isaiah in the Philoxenian Version'. *Abr-Nahrain* 20 (1981–82), pp. 20-36.
Jenni, Ernst. *Das hebräische Pi'el*. Zurich: EVZ, 1968.

Jenni, Ernst, and Claus Westermann (eds.). *Theologisches Handwörterbuch zum Altes Testament*. 2 vols. Munich: Kaiser, 1971, 1976. ET *Theological Lexicon of the Old Testament*. 3 vols. Peabody, MA: Hendrickson, 1997.
Jeppesen, Knud. 'From "You, My Servant" to "the Hand of the Lord Is With My Servants"'. *SJOT* 1 (1990), pp. 113-29.
Jerome (Sophronius Eusebius Hieronymus). *Commentariorum in Isaiam prophetam libri duodeviginti*. PL 24, cols. 17-678.
Jones, Douglas R. 'Isaiah—II and III', in M. Black and H. H. Rowley (eds.), *Peake's Commentary on the Bible*, pp. 516-36. London: Nelson, 1962.
—*Isaiah 56–66 and Joel*. London: SCM, 1964.
Kahana, Rab. *Pesiqta deRab Kahana*. Translated by Jacob Neusner. 2 vols. Atlanta: Scholars, 1987.
Kaufmann, Yehezkel. *The Babylonian Captivity and Deutero-Isaiah*. New York: Union of American Hebrew Congregations, 1970. ET from תולדות האמונה הישראלית, IV. Tel Aviv: Bialik, ?1956.
Kedar-Kopfstein, Benjamin. 'Divergent Hebrew Readings in Jerome's Isaiah'. *Textus* 4 (1964), pp. 176-210.
Kellermann, Ulrich. 'Tritojesaja und das Geheimnis des Gottesknechts'. *BN* 58 (1991), pp. 46-82.
Kelley, Page H. 'Isaiah'. *The Broadman Bible Commentary*, V, pp. 149-374. Nashville: Broadman, 1971.
Kennett, Robert H. *The Composition of the Book of Isaiah*. London: Oxford University Press, 1910.
Kessler, Werner. *Gott geht es um das Ganze: Jesaja 56–66 und 24–27*. Stuttgart: Calwer, 1960.
—'Zur Auslegung von Jesaja 56–66'. *Theologische Literaturzeitung* 81 (1956), cols. 335-38.
Kidner, Derek. 'Isaiah', in D. A. Carson *et al.* (eds.), *New Bible Commentary: 21st Century Edition*, pp. 629-70. Reprint. Leicester/Downers Grove, IL: IVP, 2002.
Kissane, Edward J. *The Book of Isaiah*. 2 vols. Dublin: Browne & Nolan, 1941 and 1943.
Kittel, Rudolf (ed.). 'Jesaia. ישעיה', in Kittel (ed.), *Biblia hebraica*, pp. 609-702. Stuttgart: Württembergische Bibelanstalt, 1937.
Klostermann, A. *Deuterojesaia*. Munich: Beck, 1893.
—'Jesaja Kap. 40–66'. *Zeitschrift für die gesammte lutherische Theologie und Kirche* (1876), pp. 1-60.
Knabenbauer, Joseph. *Commentarius in Isaiam prophetam*. 2 vols. Paris: Lethielleux, rev. edn, 1922 and 1923.
Knight, George A. F. *The New Israel: A Commentary on the Book of Isaiah 56–66*. Grand Rapids: Eerdmans; Edinburgh: Handsel, 1985.
Knobel, August. *Der Prophet Jesaia*. Reprint. Leipzig: Hirzel, 1872.
Koch, Dietrich-Alex. *Die Schrift als Zeuge des Evangeliums*. Tübingen: Mohr, 1986.
Koch, Klaus. *Die Propheten II*. Stuttgart: Kohlhammer, 1980. ET *The Prophets Volume Two*. London: SCM; Philadelphia: Fortress, 1983.
Köhler, Ludwig. *Der Prophet der Heimkehr*. [see under Glahn].
König, E. *Das Buch Jesaja*. Gütersloh: Bertelsmann, 1926.
—*The Exiles' Book of Consolation*. Edinburgh: Clark, 1899.
Koenen, Klaus. *Ethik und Eschatologie im Tritojesajabuch*. Neukirchen: Neukirchener, 1990.
—'Textkritische Anmerkungen zu schwierigen Stellen im Tritojesajabuch'. *Biblica* 69 (1988), pp. 564-73.
Koenig, Jean. *L'herméneutique analogique du Judaïsme antique d'après les témoins textuels d'Isaïe*. Leiden: Brill, 1982.
Koole, J. L. *Jesaja III*. Kampen: Kok, 1995. ET *Isaiah Part III*. Leuven: Peeters, 2001.
Koppe, Johann Benjamin (ed.). *D. Robert Lowth's Jesaias*. 4 vols. Leipzig: Weidmann, 1779–81.
Kosters, W. H. 'Deutero- en Trito-Jezaja'. *Theologisch Tijdschrift* 30 (1896), pp. 577-623.
Kraus, Hans-Joachim. 'Die ausgebliebene Endtheophanie'. *ZAW* 78 (1966), pp. 317-32. Repr. in Kraus, *Biblisch-theologische Aufsätze*, pp. 134-50. Neukirchen: Neukirchener, 1972.
—*Das Evangelium der unbekannten Propheten: Jesaja 40–66*. Neukirchen: Neukirchener, 1990.

Kuhl, Cuhl. 'Schreibereigentümlichkeiten: Bemerkungen zur Jesajarolle (DSIa)'. *VT* 2 (1952), pp. 307-33.

Kutscher, E. Y. הלשון והרקע הלשוני של מגילת ישעיהו השלמה ממגילות ים המלח. Jerusalem: Magnes, 1959. ET *The Language and Linguistic Background of the Isaiah Scroll (1 Q Isa*[a]*)*. Leiden: Brill, 1974.

Laato, Antti. *'About Zion I Will Not Be Silent'*. Stockholm: Almqvist, 1998.

Lack, Rémi. *La Symbolique du Livre d'Isaïe*. Rome: Biblical Institute Press, 1973.

Lagarde, Paulus de. *Prophetae chaldaice*. Leipzig: Teubner, 1872.

Lambert, Roger Lee. 'A Contextual Study of *yd'* in the Book of Isaiah'. Diss. Fuller Theological Seminary, 1982.

Lau, Wolfgang. *Schriftgelehrte Prophetie in Jes 56–66*. Berlin: de Gruyter, 1994.

Lee, Archie C. C. 'Returning to China'. *Biblical Interpretation* 7 (1999), pp. 156-73.

Leslie, Elmer A. *Isaiah*. Nashville: Abingdon, 1963.

Leupold, H. C. *Exposition of Isaiah*. 2 vols. Grand Rapids: Baker, 1968 and 1971.

Ley, Julius. *Historische Erklärung des zweiten Teils des Jesaia*. Marburg: Elwert, 1893.

Liebreich, Leon J. 'The Compilation of the Book of Isaiah'. *JQR* 46 (1955–56), pp. 259-77; 47 (1956–57), pp. 114-38.

Lim, Bo H. *The 'Way of the Lord' in the Book of Isaiah*. London: T&T Clark International, 2010.

Lipschits, Oded, Gary N. Knoppers, and Manfred Oeming (eds.). *Judah and the Judeans in the Achaemenid Period*. Winona Lake, IN: Eisenbrauns, 2011.

Lipschits, Oded, and Manfred Oeming (eds.). *Judah and the Judeans in the Persian Period*. Winona Lake, IN: Eisenbrauns, 2006.

Littmann, Enno. *Über die Abfassungszeit des Tritojesaia*. Freiburg: Mohr, 1899.

Loewinger, Samuel. 'The Variants of DSI II'. *VT* 4 (1954), pp. 155-63.

Lowth, Robert. *Isaiah*. London: Dodsley, 1779; London: Tegg, 12th edn, 1837.

Lubsczyk, Hans. *Das Buch Jesaja Teil II*. Düsseldorf: Patmos, 1972.

Luther, Martin. *In Esaiam prophetam enarraciones*. 1527-30. Reprinted in *Werke*, Band 31/2, pp. 1-585. Weimar: Böhlaus, 1964. ET *Lectures on Isaiah Chapters 1–39* and *Lectures on Isaiah Chapters 40–66*. St Louis: Concordia, 1972.

Luzzatto, Samuel D. 'Animadversiones in Jesajae vaticinia', in Ernst F. C. Rosenmüller, *Scholia in Jesajae Vaticinia*, pp. vi-xl. Leipzig: Barth, 1835.

—ספר ישעיהו *Il profeta Isaia*. Padua: Bianchi, 1867.

Ma, Wonsuk. *Until the Spirit Comes: The Spirit of God in the Book of Isaiah*. Sheffield: Sheffield Academic Press, 1999.

Maass, Fritz. '"Tritojesaja"?', in Maass (ed.), *Das ferne und nahe Wort*, pp. 153-63. L. Rost Festschrift. Berlin: Töpelmann, 1967.

Maori, Yeshayahu. 'מסורתת ה"פסקאות" בכתבי יד עבריים קדומים: מגילות מקרא ופרשים מספר ישעיהו מקומראן'. *Textus* 10 (1982), pp. א-נ, 134-35.

Margoliouth, G. 'Isaiah and Isaianic'. *Expositor* VII/9 (1910), pp. 525-29.

Marti, Karl. *Das Buch Jesaja*. Tübingen: Mohr, 1900.

Martin, Malachi. *The Scribal Character of the Dead Sea Scrolls*. 2 vols. Louvain: Publications Universitaires, 1958.

—'The Use of Second Person Singular Suffixes in 1QIs[a]'. *Le muséon* 70 (1957), pp. 127-44.

Martin, W. J. *The Dead Sea Scroll of Isaiah*. London: Westminster Chapel, 1954.

Maurer, Franz. *In Jesaiam Commentarius*. Leipzig: Volckmar, 1836.

McCullough, W. S. 'A Re-examination of Isaiah 56–66'. *JBL* 67 (1948), pp. 27-36.

McGinnis, Claire Mathews, and Patricia K. Tull (eds.). *'As Those Who Are Taught': The Interpretation of Isaiah from the LXX to the SBL*. Atlanta: SBL, 2006.

McKenzie, John L. *Second Isaiah*. Garden City, NY: Doubleday, 1968.

Melugin, Roy F., and Marvin A. Sweeney (eds.). *New Visions of Isaiah*. Sheffield: Sheffield Academic Press, 1996.

Michaelis, J. D. 'Anzeige der Varianten in Jesaia', in Michaelis, *Orientalische und exegetische Bibliothek* 14, pp. 99-155; 14a, pp. 3-223. Frankfurt: Johann Gottlieb Garbe, 1779.
Michel, Diethelm. 'Zur Eigenart Tritojesajas'. *Theologia Viatorum* 10 (1966), pp. 213-30. Repr. in Michel, *Studien zur Überlieferungsgeschichte alttestamentlicher Texte*, pp. 181-97. Gütersloh: Kaiser, 1997.
Middlemass, Jill. *The Troubles of Templeless Judah*. Oxford: Oxford University Press, 2005.
Miscall, Peter D. *Isaiah*. Sheffield: Sheffield Academic Press, 1993.
—'Isaiah: New Heavens, New Earth, New Book', in D. Nolan Fewell (ed.), *Reading between Texts*, pp. 41-56. Louisville: Westminster John Knox, 1992.
Morgenstern, Julius. 'The Loss of Words at the Ends of Lines in Manuscripts of Biblical Poetry'. *HUCA* 25 (1954), pp. 41-83.
Morrow, Francis James. 'The Text of Isaiah at Qumran'. Diss. Catholic University of America, Washington, 1973.
Motyer, J. Alec. *The Prophecy of Isaiah*. Leicester, UK/Downers Grove, IL: IVP, 1993.
Mowinckel, Sigmund. 'Neuere Forschungen zu Deuterojesaja, Tritojesaja und dem ʿÄbäd-Jahwä-Problem'. *Acta orientalia* 16 (1938), pp. 1-40.
Muilenburg, James. 'The Book of Isaiah: Chapters 40–66: Introduction and Exegesis', in George A. Buttrick *et al.* (eds.), *The Interpreter's Bible*, V, pp. 381-773. Nashville: Abingdon, 1956.
—'The Linguistic and Rhetorical Usages of the Particle כִּי in the Old Testament'. *HUCA* 32 (1961), pp. 135-60.
Muraoka, T. *Emphatic Words and Structures in Biblical Hebrew*. Jerusalem: Magnes; Leiden: Brill, 1985.
—'On Septuagint Lexicography and Patristics'. *JTS* n.s. 35 (1984), pp. 441-48.
Murtonen, A. 'Third Isaiah—Yes or No?' *Abr-Nahrain* 19 (1980–81), pp. 20-42.
Musculus, Wolfgang. *In Esaiam prophetam commentarii locupletissimi*. Basle: Officina Hervagiana, 1570.
Naegelsbach, C. W. Eduard. *Der Prophet Jesaja*. Bielefeld: Belhagen, 1877. ET *The Prophet Isaiah*. Edinburgh: T. & T. Clark; New York: Scribner's, 1884.
Neusner, Jacob. *Isaiah in Talmud and Midrash*. 2 vols. Lanham, MD: University Press of America, 2007.
Nicholas of Lyra. *Postillam super totam Bibliam: Secunda Pars*. Strasbourg: Mentelin, 1492.
Nötscher, F. 'Entbehrliche Hapaxlegomena in Jesaia'. *VT* 1 (1951), pp. 299-302.
Nurmela, Risto. *The Mouth of the Lord Has Spoken: Inner Biblical Allusions in Second and Third Isaiah*. Lanham, MD: University Press of America, 2006.
Obara, Elżbieta M. *Le strategie di Dio*. Rome: Gregorian Biblical Press, 2010.
O'Connell, Robert H. *Concentricity and Continuity: The Literary Structure of Isaiah*. Sheffield: Sheffield Academic Press, 1994.
Odeberg, Hugo. *Trito-Isaiah*. Uppsala: Lundquist, 1931.
Odendaal, Dirk H. *The Eschatological Expectation of Isaiah 40–66 with Special Reference to Israel and the Nations*. Nutley, NJ: Presbyterian and Reformed, 1970.
Oesch, Josef M. *Petucha und Setuma*. Göttingen: Vandenhoeck & Ruprecht, 1979.
Olley, John W. '"Hear the Word of Yhwh": The Structure of the Book of Isaiah in 1QIsa[a]'. *VT* 43 (1993), pp. 19-49.
—*'Righteousness' in the Septuagint of Isaiah*. Missoula, MT: Scholars, 1979.
Oort, H. 'Kritische Aanteekeningen op Jez. 40–66'. *Teologisk Tidsskrift* 25 (1891), pp. 461-77.
von Orelli, C. *Der Prophet Jesaja*. Munich: Beck, 3rd edn, 1904. ET from the first ed., *The Prophecies of Isaiah*. Edinburgh: T. & T. Clark, 1889.
Orlinsky, Harry M. 'The Treatment of Anthropomorphisms and Anthropopathisms in the Septuagint of Isaiah'. *HUCA* 27 (1956), pp. 193-200.
Orlinsky, Harry M., and Norman H. Snaith. *Studies on the Second Part of the Book of Isaiah*. Leiden: Brill, 1967.
Oswalt, John N. *The Book of Isaiah*. 2 vols. Grand Rapids: Eerdmans, 1986 and 1998.

Ottley, R. R. *The Book of Isaiah according to the Septuagint*. 2 vols. Cambridge: Cambridge University Press, 1906.
Park, Kyung-Chul. *Die Gerechtigkeit Israels und das Heil der Völker*. Frankfurt: Lang, 2003.
Parry, Donald W., and Elisha Qimron. *The Great Isaiah Scroll (1QIsa[a])*. Leiden: Brill, 1999.
Parry, Donald W. *et al.* (eds.). *Qumran Cave 1 Revisited*. Leiden: Brill, 2010.
Paul, Shalom M. ישעיה פרקים מ-סו. 2 vols. Tel Aviv: Am Oved, 2008. ET *Isaiah 40–66*. Grand Rapids: Eerdmans, 2012.
Pauritsch, Karl. *Die neue Gemeinde: Gott sammelt Ausgestossene und Arme (Jesaia 56–66)*. Rome: Biblical Institute Press, 1971.
Payne, D. F. 'Characteristic Word-play in "Second Isaiah"'. *JSS* 12 (1967), pp. 207-29.
Penna, Angelo. *Isaia*. Turin: Marietti, 1958.
—'La Volgata e il manoscritto 1QIs[a]'. *Biblica* 38 (1957), pp. 381-95.
Perles, Felix. *Analekten zur Textkritik des Alten Testaments*. Munich: Ackermann, 1895.
—*Analekten zur Textkritik des Alten Testaments: Neue Folge*. Leipzig: Engel, 1922.
Petersen, David L. *Late Israelite Prophecy*. Missoula, MT: Scholars, 1977.
Polan, Gregory J. *In the Ways of Justice toward Salvation: A Rhetorical Analysis of Isaiah 56–59*. New York: Lang, 1986.
—'Salvation in the Midst of Struggle'. *The Bible Today* 23 (1985), pp. 90-97.
—'Still More Signs of Unity in the Book of Isaiah: The Significance of Third Isaiah', in *Society of Biblical Literature 1997 Seminar Papers*, pp. 224-33. Atlanta: Scholars, 1997.
Porúbčan, Štefan. *Il Patto nuovo in Is. 40–66*. Rome: Pontifical Biblical Institute, 1958.
Praetorius, F. 'Zum Text des Tritojesajas'. *ZAW* 33 (1913), pp. 89-91.
Procopius of Gaza (475–528). Ἐπιτομή τῶν εἰς τὸν προφήτην Ἡσαΐαν καταβεβλημένων διαφόρων ἐξηγήσεων. PG 87/2, cols. 1801-2718.
Pulikottil, Paulson. *Transmission of Biblical Texts in Qumran*. Sheffield: Sheffield Academic Press, 2001.
Qimchi, David. 'ישעיה', in מקראות גדולות. Reprinted New York: Pardes, 1993. Partial ET in A. J. Rosenberg, *Isaiah*. 2 vols. New York: Judaica, 1982 and 1983.
Qimron, Elisha. *The Hebrew of the Dead Sea Scrolls*. Atlanta: Scholars, 1986.
Rabin, Chaim. *The Zadokite Documents*. Oxford: Oxford University Press, 2nd edn, 1958.
Radday, Yehuda T. *The Unity of Isaiah in the Light of Statistical Linguistics*. Hildesheim: Gerstenberg, 1973.
Rahlfs, Alfred (ed.). *Septuaginta*. 2 vols. Repr., Stuttgart: Württembergische Bibelanstalt, 9th edn, 1971.
Ramis Darder, Francesc. *Isaías 40–66*. [Bilbao:] Desclée De Brouwer, 2008.
Rashi (Solomon ben Isaac). 'ישעיה', in מקראות גדולות. Reprinted New York: Pardes, 1993. Partial ET in A. J. Rosenberg, *Isaiah*. 2 vols. New York: Judaica, 1982 and 1983.
Rendtorff, Rolf. 'The Book of Isaiah—A Complex Unity', in *Society of Biblical Literature 1991 Seminar Papers*, pp. 8-20. Atlanta: Scholars, 1991. Rev. ed. in Melugin and Sweeney (eds.), *New Visions of Isaiah*, pp. 32-49. Further rev. ed. in Yehoshua Gitay (ed.), *Prophecy and Prophets*, pp. 109-28. Atlanta: Scholars, 1997.
Reuss, Edouard. *Les Prophètes*. Paris: Sandoz, 1876.
Ridderbos, J. *De Profeet Jesaja*. 2 vols. Kampen: Kok, 1926. ET *Isaiah*. Grand Rapids: Regency, 1985.
Roberts, Bleddyn J. 'The Second Isaiah Scroll from Qumrân'. *BJRL* 42 (1959–60), pp. 132-40.
Roodenburg, Pieter C. *Israël, de knecht en de knechten*. Meppel: Krips [1974].
Rooker, Mark F. 'Dating Isaiah 40–66'. *WTJ* 58 (1996), pp. 303-12.
Rosenbloom, Joseph R. *The Dead Sea Isaiah Scroll*. Grand Rapids: Eerdmans, 1970.
Rosenmüller, Ernst F. C. *Scholia in Jesajae Vaticinia*. Leipzig: Barth, 2nd edn, 1835.
Rowlands, E. R. 'The Targum and the Peshiṭta Version of the Book of Isaiah'. *VT* 9 (1959), pp. 178-91.
Rubinstein, Arie. 'Conditional Constructions in the Isaiah Scroll'. *VT* 6 (1956), pp. 69-79.

—'Formal Agreement of Parallel Clauses in the Isaiah Scroll'. *VT* 4 (1954), pp. 316-21.
—'Notes on the Use of the Tenses in the Variant Readings of the Isaiah Scroll'. *VT* 3 (1953), pp. 92-95.
—'Singularities in Consecutive-tense Constructions in the Isaiah Scroll'. *VT* 5 (1955), pp. 180-88.
—'The Theological Aspect of Some Variant Readings in the Isaiah Scroll'. *JJS* 6 (1955), pp. 187-200.
Ruiten, J. van, and M. Vervenne (eds.). *Studies in the Book of Isaiah.* W. A. M. Beuken Festschrift. Leuven: Leuven University Press, 1997.
Running, Leona G. 'An Investigation of the Syriac Version of Isaiah'. *Andrews University Seminary Studies* 3 (1965), pp. 138-57; 4 (1966), pp. 37-64, 135-48.
Ruszkowski, Leszek. *Volk und Gemeinde im Wandel. Eine Untersuchung zu Jesaja 56–66.* Göttingen: Vandenhoeck & Ruprecht, 2000.
Saadia Gaon. [see under Derenbourg].
Sawyer, John F. A. *The Fifth Gospel.* Cambridge: Cambridge University Press, 1996.
—*Isaiah.* 2 vols. Edinburgh: St Andrew; Philadelphia: Westminster, 1984 and 1986.
Scholz, Anton. *Die alexandrinische Uebersetzung des Buches Jesaja.* Würzburg: Woerl, 1880.
Schleusner, Johann Friedrich. *Opuscula critica ad versiones graecas Veteris Testamenti pertinentia.* Leipzig: Weidmann, 1812.
Schramm, Brooks. *The Opponents of Third Isaiah.* Sheffield: Sheffield Academic Press, 1995.
Scullion, John. *Isaiah 40–66.* Wilmington: Glazier, 1982.
—'Some Difficult Texts in Isaiah cc.56–66'. *UF* 4 (1973), pp. 105-28.
Seccombe, David. 'Luke and Isaiah'. *New Testament Studies* 27 (1981), pp. 252-59.
Secker, Thomas. Annotations to his copy of J. H. Michaelis's *Biblia hebraica* (2 vols; Halle: Orphanotropheus, 1720) (Lambeth Palace Library ms 2578).
Seeligmann, Isac Leo. *The Septuagint Version of Isaiah.* Leiden: Brill, 1948. Reprinted in *The Septuagint Version of Isaiah and Cognate Studies.* Tübingen: Mohr, 2004.
Sehmsdorf, Eberhard. 'Studien zur Redaktionsgeschichte von Jesaja 56–66'. *ZAW* 84 (1972), pp. 517-76.
Seitz, Christopher R. 'The Book of Isaiah 40–66', in Leander E. Keck *et al.* (eds.), *The New Interpreter's Bible*, VI, pp. 307-552. Nashville: Abingdon, 2001.
—*Word without End.* Grand Rapids: Eerdmans, 1998.
Seitz, Christopher R. (ed.). *Reading and Preaching the Book of Isaiah.* Philadelphia: Fortress, 1988. Reprint, Eugene, OR: Wipf & Stock, 2002.
Sekine, Seizo. *Die Tritojesajanische Sammlung (Jes 56–66) redaktionsgeschichtlich untersucht.* Berlin: de Gruyter, 1989.
Sheppard, Gerald T. 'The Book of Isaiah: Competing Structures according to a Late Modern Description of its Shape and Scope', in *Society of Biblical Literature 1992 Seminar Papers*, pp. 549-82. Atlanta: Scholars, 1992.
—'Isaiah as a Scroll or Codex within Jewish and Christian Scripture', in *Society of Biblical Literature 1996 Seminar Papers*, pp. 204-24. Atlanta: Scholars, 1996.
Shum, Shiu-Lun. *Paul's Use of Isaiah in Romans.* Tübingen: Mohr, 2002.
Simon, Uriel. 'Ibn Ezra between Medievalism and Modernism: The Case of Isaiah xl–lxvi'. *Congress Volume: Salamanca 1983*, pp. 257-71. Leiden: Brill, 1985.
Skarsaune, Oskar. *The Proof from Prophecy.* Leiden: Brill, 1987.
Skehan, Patrick W. 'Isaias and the Teaching of the Book of Wisdom'. *CBQ* 2 (1940), pp. 289-99.
—'The Text of Isaias at Qumrân'. *CBQ* 17 (1955), pp. 158-63.
Skinner, J. *The Book of the Prophet Isaiah Chapters XL–LXVI.* Cambridge: Cambridge University Press, Revised edn, 1922.
Slotki, I. W. *Isaiah.* London: Soncino, 1949.
Smart, James D. *History and Theology in Second Isaiah.* Philadelphia: Westminster, 1965.
Smith, George Adam. *The Book of Isaiah.* 2 vols. London: Hodder, 1890.
Smith, P. A. *Rhetoric and Redaction in Trito-Isaiah.* Leiden: Brill, 1995.

Snaith, Norman H. 'Isaiah 40–66', in Harry M. Orlinsky and Norman H. Snaith, *Studies on the Second Part of the Book of Isaiah*, pp. 135-264. Leiden: Brill, 1967.

Sommer, Benjamin D. *A Prophet Reads Scripture: Allusion in Isaiah 40-66*. Stanford: Stanford University Press, 1998.

—'The Scroll of Isaiah as Jewish Scripture', in *Society of Biblical Literature 1996 Seminar Papers*, pp. 225-42. Atlanta: Scholars, 1996.

Sperber, Alexander. *The Latter Prophets According to Targum Jonathan*. Leiden: Brill, 1962.

Steck, Odil Hannes. 'Bemerkungen zur Abschnittgliederung der ersten Jesajarolle von Qumran (1QIs^{a}) im Vergleich mit redaktionsgeschichtlichen Beobachtungen im Jesajabuch', in B. Kollmann, W. Reinbold, and A. Steudel (eds.), *Antikes Judentum und Frühes Judentum*, pp. 12-28. H. Stegemann Festschrift. Berlin: de Gruyter, 1999.

—*Die erste Jesajarolle von Qumran (1QIs^{a})*. 2 vols. Stuttgart: Verlag Katholisches Bibelwerk, 1998.

—'Gottesvolk und Gottesknecht in Jes 40–66', in *Volk Gottes, Gemeinde und Gesellschaft*, pp. 51-75. *Jahrbuch für Biblische Theologie* 7 (1992).

—'Der sich selbst aktualisierende "Jesaja" in Jes 56,9–59,21', in Wolfgang Zwickel (ed.), *Biblische Welten*, pp. 215-30. Martin Metzger Festschrift. Göttingen: Vandenhoeck & Ruprecht, 1993.

—*Studien zu Tritojesaja*. Berlin: de Gruyter, 1991.

Stenning, J. F. *The Targum of Isaiah*. Oxford: Clarendon, 1949.

Stromberg, Jacob. *An Introduction to the Study of Isaiah*. London: T&T Clark International, 2011.

—*Isaiah after Exile*. Oxford: Oxford University Press, 2011.

Stummer, Friedrich. 'Einige keilschriftliche Parallelen zu Jes. 40–66'. *JBL* 45 (1926), pp. 171-89.

Sukenik, E. L. (ed.). *The Dead Sea Scrolls of the Hebrew University*. Jerusalem: Magnes, 1955.

Sweeney, Marvin A. *Form and Intertextuality in Prophetic and Apocalyptic Literature*. Tübingen: Mohr, 2005.

—*Isaiah 1–4 and the Post-Exilic Understanding of the Isaianic Tradition*. Berlin: de Gruyter, 1988.

—'On Multiple Settings in the Book of Isaiah', in *Society of Biblical Literature 1993 Seminar Papers*, pp. 267-73. Atlanta: Scholars, 1993. Repr. in *Form and Intertextuality in Prophetic and Apocalyptic Literature*, pp. 28-35.

Talmon, Shemaryahu. 'Aspects of the Textual Transmission of the Bible in the Light of Qumran Manuscripts'. *Textus* 4 (1964), pp. 95-132. Repr. in Talmon, *The World of Qumran from Within*, pp. 71-116.

—'Observations on Variant Readings in the Isaiah Scroll', in Talmon, *The World of Qumran from Within*, pp. 117-30. ET from *Elias Auerbach Festschrift*, I, pp. 147-56. Jerusalem: Kiryat Sepher, 1956.

—*Text and Canon of the Hebrew Bible*. Winona Lake, IN: Eisenbrauns, 2010.

—*The World of Qumran from Within*. Jerusalem: Magnes; Leiden: Brill, 1989.

Talstra, E., and A. L. H. M. van Wieringen (eds.). *A Prophet on the Screen: Computerized Description and Literary Interpretation of Isaianic Texts*. Amsterdam: VU University Press, 1992.

Tate, Marvin E. 'The Book of Isaiah in Recent Study', in J. W. Watts and P. R. House (eds.), *Forming Prophetic Literature*, pp. 22-56. J. D. W. Watts Festschrift. Sheffield: Sheffield Academic Press, 1996.

Theodore of Heraclea. 'Εκ τῆς εἰς 'Ησαΐαν ἐξηγησέως. PG 18, cols. 1307-78.

Theodoret of Cyrrhus. 'Ερμηνεία εἰς τὸν προφήτην 'Ησαΐαν. ET *Commentaire sur Isaïe*. 3 vols. Paris: Cerf, 1980, 1982, 1984.

Thexton, S. Clive. *Isaiah 40–66*. London: Epworth, 1959.

Thomas, D. Winton. 'Jesaia ישעיה'. Biblia hebraica stuttgartensia 7. Stuttgart: Württembergische Bibelanstalt, 1968.

Thomas Aquinas. 'In Isaiam prophetam expositio'. Reprinted in *Opera omnia* XVIII, pp. 668-821; XIX, pp. 1-65. Paris: Bibliopola, 1871.

Tomasino, Anthony J. 'Isaiah 1.1–2.4 and 63–66, and the Composition of the Isaianic Corpus'. *JSOT* 57 (1993), pp. 81-98.

Tiemeyer, Lena-Sofia. *Priestly Rites and Prophetic Rage: Post-Exilic Prophetic Critique of the Priesthood.* Tübingen: Mohr, 2006.
Torrey, Charles Cutler. *The Second Isaiah.* Edinburgh: T. & T. Clark; New York: Scribner's, 1928.
—'Some Important Editorial Operations in the Book of Isaiah'. *JBL* 57 (1938), pp. 109-39.
Trakatellis, Demetrius. 'Theodoret's Commentary on Isaiah', in B. Nassif (ed.), *New Perspectives on Historical Theology*, pp. 313-42. J. Meyendorff Memorial. Grand Rapids: Eerdmans, 1996.
Troxel, Ronald L. *LXX-Isaiah as Translation and Interpretation.* Leiden: Brill, 2008.
Uhlig, Torsten. *The Theme of Hardening in the Book of Isaiah.* Tübingen: Mohr, 2009.
Ulrich, Eugene. 'Light from 1QIsa[a] on the Translation Technique of the Old Greek Translator of Isaiah', in Anssi Voitila and Jutta Jokiranta (eds.), *Scripture in Transition*, pp. 193-204. Raija Sollamo Festschrift. Leiden: Brill, 2008.
—*Qumran Cave 4. X: The Prophets.* Discoveries in the Judaean Desert 15. Oxford: Oxford University Press, 1997.
Eugene, Ulrich, and Peter W. Flint, with a contribution by Martin G. Abegg. *Qumran Cave 1. II: The Isaiah Scrolls.* 2 vols. Discoveries in the Judaean Desert 32. Oxford: Oxford University Press, 2010.
Vande Kappelle, Robert P. 'Evidence of a Jewish Proselytizing Tendency in the Old Greek (Septuagint) Version of the Book of Isaiah'. Diss. Princeton Theological Seminary, 1977.
Van der Meer, Michaël N., *et al.* (eds.). *Isaiah in Context.* A. van der Kooij Festchrift. Leiden: Brill, 2010.
Van der Kooij, Arie. 'Accident or Method?' *Bibliotheca orientalis* 43 (1986), pp. 366-76.
—*Die alten Textzeugen des Jesajabuches.* Freiburg: Universitätsverlag, 1981.
—'The Old Greek of Isaiah in Relation to the Qumran Texts of Isaiah', in G. J. Brooke and B. Lindars (eds.), *Septuagint, Scrolls and Cognate Writings*, pp. 195-213. Atlanta: Scholars, 1992.
Van der Kooij, Arie, and Michaël N. van der Meer (eds.). *The Old Greek of Isaiah.* Leuven: Peeters, 2010.
Van Wieringen, Archibald L. H. M., and Annemarieke van der Woude (eds.). *'Enlarge the Site of Your Tent': The City as Unifying Theme in Isaiah.* Leiden: Brill, 2011.
Vermeylen, J. *Du prophète Isaïe à l'apocalyptique.* 2 vols. Paris: Gabalda, 1977 and 1978.
Vermeylen, J. (ed.). *The Book of Isaiah: Le Livre d'Isaïe.* Leuven: Leuven University Press, 1989.
Vitringa, Campegius. *Commentarius in librum prophetiarum Jesaiae.* 2 vols. Herborn: Johann Nicolaus Andreae, 1715 and 1722.
Volz, Paul. *Jesaja II.* Leipzig: Deichert, 1932.
Vööbus, Arthur. *The Book of Isaiah in the Version of the Syro-hexapla: A Facsimile Edition of Ms. St. Mark 1 in Jerusalem.* Louvain: Peeters, 1983.
de Waard, Jan. *A Handbook on Isaiah.* Winona Lake, IN: Eisenbrauns, 1997.
—'Old Greek Translation Techniques and the Modern Translator'. *The Bible Translator* 41 (1990), pp. 311-19.
Wade, G. W. *The Book of the Prophet Isaiah.* London: Methuen, 1911.
Wagner, J. Ross. *Heralds of the Good News: Isaiah and Paul 'In Concert' in the Letter to the Romans.* Leiden: Brill, 2002.
Wallis, Gerhard. 'Gott und seine Gemeinde: Eine Betrachtung zum Tritojesaja-Buch'. *Theologische Zeitschrift* 27 (1971), pp. 182-200.
Watson, W. G. E. *Classical Hebrew Poetry.* Sheffield: JSOT, 1984.
—'Fixed Pairs in Ugaritic and Isaiah'. *VT* 22 (1972), pp. 460-68.
—*Traditional Techniques in Classical Hebrew Verse.* Sheffield: Sheffield Academic Press, 1994.
Watts, John D. W. *Isaiah.* 2 vols. [Nashville]: Nelson, rev. edn, 2005.
Webb, Barry G. *The Message of Isaiah.* Leicester/Downers Grove, IL: IVP, 1996.
—'Zion in Transformation', in D. J. A. Clines, S. E. Fowl, and S. E. Porter (eds.), *The Bible in Three Dimensions*, pp. 65-84. Sheffield: Sheffield Academic Press, 1990.

Weber, Robert (ed.). *Biblia sacra iuxta vulgatam versionem*. Stuttgart: Deutsche Bibelanstalt, 3rd edn, 1983.

Wells, Roy. D. 'The Statements of Well-Being in Isaiah 60–62'. Diss. Vanderbilt, 1968.

Wernberg-Moller [*sic*], P. 'The Contribution of the *Hodayot* to Biblical Textual Criticism'. *Textus* 4 (1964), pp. 133-75.

Wernberg-Møller, P. 'Studies in the Defective Spellings in the Isaiah-scroll of St Mark's Monastery'. *JSS* 3 (1958), pp. 244-64.

Westermann, Claus. *Das Buch Jesaja Kapitel 40–66*. Göttingen: Vandenhoeck & Ruprecht, 1966. ET *Isaiah 40–66*. London: SCM; Philadelphia: Westminster, 1969.

Whitehouse, Owen C. *Isaiah xl–lxvi*. Reprint. London: Caxton [c. 1911].

Whybray, R. N. *Isaiah 40–66*. London: Oliphants, 1975; Grand Rapids: Eerdmans, 1981.

Wilk, Florian. *Die Bedeutung des Jesajabuches für Paulus*. Göttingen: Vandenhoeck & Ruprecht, 1998.

Wilken, Robert Louis, and others (eds.). *Isaiah Interpreted by Early Christian and Medieval Commentators*. Grand Rapids: Eerdmans, 2007.

Williamson, H. G. M. *The Book Called Isaiah*. Oxford: Oxford University Press, 1994.

—*Variations on a Theme: King, Messiah and Servant in the Book of Isaiah*. Carlisle: Paternoster, 1998.

Wright, G. Ernest. *Isaiah*. Richmond: Knox, 1964; London: SCM, 1965.

Wutz, Franz. *Die Transkriptionen von der Septuaginta bis zu Hieronymus*. Stuttgart: Kohlhammer, 1933.

Young, Edward J. *The Book of Isaiah*. 3 vols. Grand Rapids: Eerdmans, 1965, 1969, 1972.

—*Studies in Isaiah*. Grand Rapids: Eerdmans, 1954; London: Tyndale, 1955.

Zapff, Burkard M. *Jesaja 56–66*. Würzburg: Echter, 2006.

Ziegler, Joseph. *Isaias*. Vetus Testamentum Graecum Auctoritate Societatis Litterarum Gottingensis editum 14. Reprint. Göttingen: Vandenhoeck & Ruprecht, 1967.

—*Sylloge: Gesammelte Aufsätze zur Septuaginta*. Göttingen: Vandenhoeck & Ruprecht, 1971.

—*Untersuchungen zur Septuaginta des Buches Isaias*. Münster: Aschendorf, 1934.

van Zijl, Jan. 'Errata in Sperber's Edition of Targum Isaiah'. *ASTI* 4 (1965), pp. 189-91.

—'The Root פרק in Targum Isaiah'. *Journal of Northwest Semitic Languages* 2 (1972), pp. 60-73.

—'A Second List of Errata in Sperber's Edition of Targum Isaiah'. *ASTI* 7 (1970), pp. 132-34.

Zillessen, Alfred. 'Bemerkungen zur alexandrinischen Übersetzung des Jesaja (c. 40–66)'. *ZAW* 22 (1902), pp. 238-63.

—'"Tritojesaja" und Deuterojesaja'. *ZAW* 26 (1906), pp. 231-76.

Zimmerli, Walther. 'Zur Sprache Tritojesajas'. *Schweizerische theologische Umschau* 20 (1950), pp. 110-22. Repr. in *Festschrift für Ludwig Köhler*, pp. 62-74. Bern: Büchler, 1950. Repr. in Zimmerli, *Gottes Offenbarung*, pp. 217-33. Munich: Kaiser, 1963.

Zwingli, Ulrich. *Complanationis Isaiae prophetae foetura prima*. Repr. in Corpus Reformatorum 101, pp. 1-412. Zurich: Berichthaus, 1959.

INTRODUCTION*

It was at one stage planned that the International Critical Commentary would treat Isaiah in three volumes covering chapters 1–27, 28–48, and 49–66.[1] Such a contravening of the traditional critical division of the book would have been a suggestive anticipation of subsequent renewed interest in the unity of the book called Isaiah[2] and in the interrelationship of its various parts. Yet treating Isaiah 56–66 in an independent volume separate from Isaiah 1–39 and 40–55 is not a mere convenience related to the length of the book of Isaiah. It presupposes the correctness of that traditional critical view that the book by its own nature does divide into two unequal parts comprising chapters 1–39 and 40–66 (though chapters 34–39 also link forwards with chapters 40–66), and it also accepts the traditional critical view that Isaiah 40–66 then divides into two unequal parts, with chapters 40–55 comprising material that addressed a Judahite community during the Babylonian period and chapters 56–66 material that addressed a community in Judah during the Persian period.

This latter aspect of the traditional critical view is not universally held. There have been scholars who have argued that the whole of Isaiah 40–66 comes from one prophet[3] or that the proper distinction is between Isaiah

* This Introduction incorporates material from my articles 'About Third Isaiah…', in James Aitken and others (eds.), *On Stone and Scroll* (G. I. Davies Festschrift; Berlin: de Gruyter, 2011), pp. 375-89; 'Poetry and Theology in Isaiah 56–66', in Stanley E. Porter and Matthew R. Malcolm (eds.), *Horizons in Hermeneutics* (A. C. Thiselton Festschrift; Grand Rapids: Eerdmans, 2013), pp. 15-31; 'The Theology of Isaiah', in Firth and Williamson (eds.), *Interpreting Isaiah*, pp. 168-90; 'Isaiah 56–66: An Isaianic and a Postcolonial Reading', in Abernethy and others (eds.), *Isaiah and Imperial Context*, pp. 151-66; and 'How Important is Isaiah 1–55 to Isaiah 56–66?' (forthcoming in a symposium).

[1] See Goldingay and Payne, *Isaiah 40–55*, pp. ix-x.

[2] H. G. M. Williamson's nice phrase which provides the title for *The Book Called Isaiah*.

[3] See, e.g., Torrey, *The Second Isaiah*; König, *Das Buch Jesaja*; Glahn and Köhler, *Der Prophet der Heimkehr*; Kaufmann, *The Babylonian Captivity and Deutero-Isaiah*; Smart, *History and Theology in Second Isaiah*; Menaḥem Haran, 'The Literary Structure and Chronological Framework of the Prophecies in Is. xl–xlviii', in *Congress Volume: Bonn 1962* (Leiden: Brill, 1963), pp. 127-55 (148-55); Maass, 'Tritojesaja?'; recently William L. Holladay, 'Was Trito-Isaiah Deutero-Isaiah After All?', in Broyles and Evans (ed.), *Writing and Reading the Scroll of Isaiah*, I, pp. 193-217; Sommer, *A Prophet Reads Scripture*; Paul, ישעיה פרקים מ-סו.

40–53 and 54–66[4] or Isaiah 40–54 and 55–66[5] or Isaiah 40.1–56.9 and 56.10–66.24.[6] In *Isaiah 40–55* we sought to show that chapters 40–55 form a coherent and relatively independent collection in the sense that they have a beginning and end and a structure of their own with a distinctive argument, whether or not they ever existed independently of their relationship with some form of Isaiah 1–39. My study of Isaiah 56–66 has led me to agree with the common view that the same applies to Isaiah 56–66. One evidence is the chapters' concentric arrangement;[7] they form a chiasm or stepped structure or inverted pyramid, along the following lines:

Preface and postscript: the place of foreigners in the service of Yhwh	
56.1-8	66.18-24
Yhwh's challenges concerning the Jerusalem community's life	
56.9–59.8	65.1–66.17
Prayers for Yhwh's forgiveness and restoration	
59.9-15a	63.7–64.11
Visions of Yhwh acting in judgment	
59.15b-21	63.1-6
Visions of Jerusalem restored	
60.1-22	61.10–62.12
The prophet's commission	
61.1-9	

While there is room for debate about the details of this understanding,[8] in outline it reflects concrete features of the text and it has thus been recognized by scholars of varying redaction-critical views. The outline helps illuminate the nature of the chapters' message. At their centre is the prophet's account of his call; there is a certain logic about its location here in a chiasm, whereas in a more linear structure such as that of Isaiah 40–55 an equivalent account comes at the beginning. Outside that centre are visions of the restored Jerusalem that repeat in more glorious technicolor the kind of promises that appear in Isaiah 40–55, with their concomitant promise of Yhwh's acting in judgment on the people's oppressors. Outside these visions are prayers that essentially plead with Yhwh to do what the visions portray. Outside these prayers is a series of challenges and warnings about the community's life in both its social and

[4] So Seitz, 'The Book of Isaiah 40–66', p. 474.

[5] So Watts, *Isaiah*, p. 816.

[6] So Penna, *Isaia*, p. 367.

[7] The first exposition of the arrangement known to me is that of Étienne Charpentier, *Jeunesse du Vieux Testament* (Paris: Fayard, 1963), p. 79. See subsequently, e.g., Bonnard, *Le Second Isaïe*, pp. 318-19; Lack, *La Symbolique du Livre d'Isaïe*, pp. 125-34; Emmerson, *Isaiah 56–66*, pp. 18-20.

[8] O'Connell (*Concentricity and Continuity*, pp. 216-21) and Fitzgerald ('A Rhetorical Analysis of Isaiah 56–66', pp. 35-97) review various accounts of the chiasm and present their own detailed understandings of the chapters in light of it.

worship aspects. Finally, the opening and closing verses concern themselves with the status of foreigners in relation to Yhwh's people. This structured arrangement is a formal pointer towards the coherence and relative independence of Isaiah 56–66.

In itself this need not suggest that chapters 56–66 come from a different context from that of chapters 40–55, but I also accept this standard critical view. Chapters 40–55 refer several times to Babylon (43.14; 46.1; 47.1; 48.14, 20) in a way that suggests Babylon is still the imperial power but that its fall is imminent. The chapters refer to the Persian king Cyrus (44.28; 45.1) in a way that suggests he is to be the agent of this event. These prophecies make sense as addressed to Judahites living in Babylon, though it is possible to imagine them as addressed to people living in Judah, who are also Babylon's underlings. Either way, they make sense in the context of the exilic period. Chapters 56–66 speak of issues related to the building and worship of the temple (e.g. 56.1-8; 66.1-6) and critique the community for forms of worship and for abuses of community relationships that are comparable to practices in Judah critiqued by earlier prophets (e.g. 56.9–59.8). As it is possible to imagine the promises in Isaiah 40–55 addressed to people in Judah, so it is possible to imagine the promises about the restoration of Jerusalem (e.g. 60.1–62.12) addressed to people living in Babylon, for whom Jerusalem remains a focus, but these latter promises make most sense as addressed to people who especially 'mourn Zion' (61.3) because they live there. There are perhaps later prophecies incorporated into chapters 40–55, and its redacting and arranging might be later, but the vast bulk of the material belongs before the fall of Babylon. We shall see that there are perhaps earlier prophecies incorporated into chapters 56–66, but the vast bulk of the material comes from Judah in the Persian period.

Jon L. Berquist has commented that Isaiah 56–66 'resists analysis from almost any methodological perspective'.[9] I have come to the conclusion that paying attention to the structured arrangement of chapters 56–66, outlined above, is a key strategy for understanding them, though there are several other illuminating methods of approach. I do see Berquist's observation as applying to two methodological perspectives that have dominated scholarly work on the chapters at the end of the twentieth century and the beginning of the twenty-first.

1. *A Redaction-historical Reading*

One such approach seeks to trace the process whereby the chapters developed and reached the form they now have. There is a small-scale aspect to this investigation, in which one looks at individual units and seeks to discern the layering within them. There is also a large-scale

[9] 'Reading Difference in Isaiah 56–66', p. 23.

aspect whereby one seeks to discern how the whole came together, perhaps through the combining of the layers that run through the individual units. The possibility of tracing this process promises much insight, but the problem is that analysts who attempt it come to quite different conclusions.

When Bernhard Duhm definitively asserted the distinction between Isaiah 40–55 and Isaiah 56–66 and entitled the latter 'Third Isaiah' over against 'Second Isaiah', integral to his understanding was the conviction that this Third Isaiah lived a century after the Second Isaiah, in the time of Ezra and Nehemiah.[10] Subsequent scholars such as Karl Budde, Rudolf Abramowski, Paul Volz, Jacques Vermeylen, and Odil Hannes Steck believed that actually the material did not come from a single 'Third Isaiah' but from a number of authors working over some centuries.[11] Isaiah 40–66 or 56–66 thus belongs to a period when prophecy has become a collective or community phenomenon.[12]

In a different contrast, Karl Elliger accepted Duhm's view that Isaiah 56–66 comes from one period and could thus have been the work of a person whom we can call 'Third Isaiah', but located this prophet in the early Persian period rather than in the time of Ezra and Nehemiah.[13] While a number of scholars have followed Elliger in his earlier dating of much of the material, they have generally followed those other scholars in thinking that the chapters reflect the work of a number of prophets or theologians. Their differences from scholars such as Budde, Volz, Vermeylen and Steck is that they see them as mostly working during the opening decades of the Persian period rather than over a period of centuries. This is true of R. N. Whybray,[14] Paul D. Hanson,[15] and P. A. Smith.[16] A further, mediating view sees the material as developing over the

[10] See Duhm, *Das Buch Jesaia*; so also Marti, *Das Buch Jesaja*. In contrast, Kennett (*The Composition of the Book of Isaiah*) dated all eleven chapters in the second century, while W. S. McCullough ('A Re-examination of Isaiah 56–66') dated them in the early decades of the exile.

[11] Budde dated much of it rather earlier than Duhm did, though some a little later: see 'Das Buch Jesaia Kap. 40–66'. Abramowski's study 'Zum literarischen Problem des Tritojesaja' focused on the diverse style and perspective of the material, concluding that 57.14–63.6 and 63.7–66.5 are the main redactional units (p. 138). Volz dated some of it before or during the exile, and some in the Hellenistic period: see *Jesaja II*, esp. p. 200. Such approaches have been taken more recently by Vermeylen (see *Du prophète Isaïe à l'apocalyptique*, esp. II, pp. 503-17) and Steck (see especially the essays collected in his *Studien zu Tritojesaja*; also 'Autor und/oder Redaktor in Jesaja 56–66', in Broyles and Evans [ed.], *Writing and Reading the Scroll of Isaiah*, I, pp. 219-59).

[12] Cf. Hanson, *The Dawn of Apocalyptic*, p. 41; Schramm, *The Opponents of Third Isaiah*, p. 34.

[13] See *Die Einheit Tritojesaja*; 'Der Prophet Tritojesaja'; *Deuterojesaja in seinem Verhältnis zu Tritojesaja*, pp. 278-303.

[14] *Isaiah 40–66*, pp. 42-43.

[15] *The Dawn of Apocalyptic* and *Isaiah 40–66*.

[16] *Rhetoric and Redaction in Trito-Isaiah.*

century between the beginning of the Persian period and the time of Ezra and Nehemiah: so, for instance, Seizo Sekine,[17] Klaus Koenen,[18] and Joseph Blenkinsopp.[19]

In a number of these studies of Isaiah 56–66 a motif recurs. Hanson, for instance, noted (first) that there was nothing approaching a consensus on the date and authorship of the material. It lacks reference to explicitly identifiable historical events, and the history of the period it addresses is shrouded in darkness, so scholars are reduced to reconstructing the history on the basis of the oracles and interpreting the oracles within the context of this reconstructed history.[20] But then (second) he said that he had discovered the way through this impasse. He thus went on (third) to expound his solution, which was to base dating on his view of the development of poetic structure and metre in the material (the more poetic oracles are earlier, the more prosaic ones later), of the development of types of prophetic oracle or genres, and of the beliefs among different groups in the community concerning how Yhwh's purpose for the community would find fulfillment.[21]

Yet Hanson's solution has not been accepted by subsequent scholars such as Sekine, Koenen and Blenkinsopp,[22] so that Brent Strawn takes up the problem in similar terms to Hanson as he once more notes that 'the historical and linguistic arguments regarding Trito-Isaiah are at something of an impasse. A way forward, furthermore, does not seem to be forthcoming.'[23] He thereby repeats what Hanson had said thirty years previously, and like him goes on to affirm that he has an alternative solution. His suggestion is to look for further external data, which he does in comparing Isaiah 60 with reliefs from Darius I's palace at Persepolis that may provide background to the portrayal of Jerusalem in Isaiah 60. The construction of Persepolis was begun at the same time as that of the Second Temple, though it went on for some decades.

Blenkinsopp, too, notes that 'we simply do not have the information to locate the composition of these chapters within an absolute chronology with any degree of precision' (in my view, this statement markedly

[17] *Die tritojesanische Sammlung (Jes 56–66) redaktionsgeschichtlich untersucht.*

[18] *Ethik und Eschatologie im Tritojesajabuch.*

[19] *Isaiah 56–66.*

[20] *The Dawn of Apocalyptic*, p. 33.

[21] See *The Dawn of Apocalyptic*, e.g., pp. 29, 104.

[22] In addition, see Schramm, *The Opponents of Third Isaiah*, p. 86, on Hanson's view of the development of prosody that he believes can be perceived within Isa 56–66, which is a subordinate aspect of his understanding, and which 'places Hanson into what Kugel has described as 'the Syllable-Counting Text-Rewriting school of biblical prosody' (Schramm refers to J. L. Kugel, *The Idea of Biblical Poetry* [New Haven: Yale University Press, 1981], p. 296). In contrast, Elizabeth Achtemeier in *The Community and Message of Isaiah 56–66* takes for granted Hanson's perspective without hinting that it is simply a scholarly theory.

[23] Brent Strawn, '"A World under Control"', in Jon L. Berquist (ed.), *Approaching Yehud* (Atlanta: SBL, 2007), pp. 85-116 (86, 87).

understates the case). He goes on, 'for the most part, therefore, commentators are reduced to proposing dates based on the way they reconstruct the process of formation of these chapters…, on which there are practically as many hypotheses as there are commentators'.[24] Unlike Hanson and Strawn he does not claim to have a solution to the impasse, and it is therefore surprising to find him going on to allocate and date the material.[25]

Aware of the difficulty that there are many plausible but different analyses of the redactional development of Isaiah 56–66 and of its historical and/or sociological background, in an even more recent study Jacob Stromberg[26] proceeds by beginning from the broad consensus view that Isaiah 60–62 is the oldest material in the chapters and is of distinct origin over against what stands on either side. But is even that consensus secure? Those chapters have been seen as a later insertion.[27] The consensus view is based in part on theological tensions between Isaiah 60–62 and the blocks of material on either side, yet the eventual compiler of Isaiah 56–66 could evidently live with this tension, so why could a single author not have done so? The consensus view also bases itself on the assumption that the dependence of Isaiah 60–62 on Isaiah 40–55 means it is near to those chapters in date. But this inference does not follow: I understand Daniel 7 to be dependent on Daniel 2, but I take them to be centuries apart in date, and the Revelation to John is dependent on the Prophets, but they are centuries older.

The consensus view that Isaiah 60–62 is the oldest material in Isaiah 56–66 may be correct, but the revolutions in the study of Isaiah and of the Pentateuch over the past half-century show the problem with consensus views; today's consensus is tomorrow's out-of-date scholarship. Reviewers of monographs sometimes include a closing comment that the work in question will have to be taken into account in future study of the issue it studies. This observation raises the question whether scholarly research on a subject like the origin of Isaiah 56–66 is merely an intertextual conversation among scholars that does not correspond to anything in the external world, a conversation that is never going to reach conclusions. We may choose to try to look behind Isaiah 56–66 and ask after the process whereby it came into being, but it is not clear that this inquiry is asking questions that can be answered.

My working assumption is that there is indeed less basis for thinking of Third Isaiah as an individual person responsible for all or most of the material in Isaiah 56–66 than there is for thinking than Second Isaiah was

[24] *Isaiah 56–66*, p. 42.

[25] Isaiah 60–62 belongs to the beginning of the Persian period; broadly speaking, 56.9–59.21 and 63.1–64.12 belong to the time between 516 and 458; 56.1-8 and 65.1–66.24 belong to the time of Ezra and Nehemiah.

[26] *Isaiah after Exile*.

[27] So Anneli Aejmelaeus, 'Der Prophet als Klageliedsänger: Zur Funktion des Psalms Jes 63,7–64,11 in Tritojesaja', *ZAW* 107 (1995), pp. 31-50 (36-37).

such a person (though this latter assumption has also become subject to questioning). It may be safer to see Isaiah 56–66 as a compilation of material issuing from a number of prophets and preachers, which in a variety of ways takes forward agenda and perspectives expressed in Isaiah 40–55 and elsewhere, and which accumulated gradually, at least over some decades at the beginning of the Persian period. I work with this view because I need some assumption about the question, not because I think we have concrete information that helps us to know. Unlike the other major parts of the book, Isaiah 56–66 indeed refers to no specific people or events, and in this sense provides no indications of the historical contexts to which it relates. Its comments on political and social conditions and on the religious situation could fit many contexts. We cannot realistically attempt to locate individual sections historically in any specific period or periods. While for the most part we can safely read the chapters against the background of the Second Temple, we cannot read them on the basis of relating them to particular periods within these parameters.

Brevard S. Childs argued that the compilers of Isaiah 40–55 employed the material available to them in such a way as to 'eliminate almost entirely' the concrete features that indicated a link with a particular historical situation and to 'subordinate the original message to a new role within the canon'. He then drew a contrast with the concrete historical references in Amos.[28] Yet Isaiah 40–55 does refer to Babylon and to Cyrus, and actually the only difference between Isaiah 40–55 and Amos or other prophetic books is that Isaiah 40–55 has no superscription, a difference that relates to its being linked to the preceding material. Its message is not subordinated to a new role within the canon; it is subordinate to a role within the larger book of Isaiah, because of its links with the material that appears earlier in the book. Childs's comment would be more apposite in connection with Isaiah 56–66. Here indeed there are no concrete historical references; hence (in part) the unresolved debate about the period(s) to which the chapters belong. When we seek to set these prophecies in a historical context, we are working against the grain of the material, which declines to provide the information that would help us date them. The situation is similar to attempts to date psalms.

More general study of the Persian period in Judah is a subject of lively interest in the scholarly world, and it is possible that in due course such historical study may offer illumination on Isaiah 56–66 and vice versa, but oddly, works that have issued from this study make little reference to Isaiah 56–66.[29] Conversely, any attempt to write the history of the Second

[28] *Introduction to the Old Testament as Scripture*, p. 327. John N. Oswalt sees the vagueness of the chapters as an indication that they derive from the eighth century ('Who Were the Addressees of Isaiah 40–66?', *BSac* 169 (2012), pp. 33-47 (34).

[29] See, e.g., Lipschits and Oeming (eds.), *Judah and the Judeans in the Persian Period*, and Lipschits, Knoppers, and Oeming (eds.), *Judah and the Judeans in the Achaemenid Period*.

Temple period will need to try to date the material, but a concern with dating cannot be central to interpreting Isaiah 56–66 itself. Focusing on this question means not seeking to read Isaiah 56–66, but to read behind it in a way that remains speculative.

The standard title for each volume in the series to which this commentary belongs describes it as 'A critical and exegetical commentary'. The juxtaposition of 'critical' and 'exegetical' in that expression is a happy one. It fits with John Barton's argument that the aim of biblical criticism is to get at the plain meaning of the biblical text.[30] If that is its aim, why is it called criticism? Critical study began as critique of the way Scripture had been interpreted, though it eventually became criticism of Scripture itself. Barton's argument helps nuance this point. Criticism, he contends, seeks to take an open-minded approach to the question of what kind of text one is reading. It is concerned with 'the recognition of genre in texts and with what follows from this about their possible meaning'.[31] Criticism often begins from an awareness of difficulties in a text, which has been a major interest of the study of Isaiah 56–66; the presence of tensions in the chapters has been a stimulus to redaction-critical study. There are tensions over questions such as the relationship between Yhwh's commitment to Jerusalem and its community and Yhwh's concern for the nations, between the future's dependence on Yhwh's promises being fulfilled and its dependence on the community's obedience, between the importance of religious observances such as the Sabbath and the importance of relieving the needy.

Redaction-critical study seeks to offer a kind of explanation of such tensions, but it cannot do so. The material hides the evidence that would enable us to trace the process whereby it came into existence. It is a consequence of this fact that there are as many redaction-critical theories as there are redaction-critics. One learns from their work; they are heuristically productive. They enable us to see things, even if their historical explanations are wrong or unprovable (and even if sometimes one learns from their work by being stimulated into thinking 'that can't be right, so what is right?'). Reading the text as it is, without attending to the process that led to its reaching the form that we have, might produce flat readings. But the opposite may be the case: 'obvious tensions' in a document 'can be easily solved by multiplying authors and life situations in which they wrote' but this process may generate a historical reconstruction 'containing a string of flat positions. It is religiously and intellectually more profitable to explore the rich relief of the existent text'.[32] The text itself

[30] John Barton, *The Nature of Biblical Criticism* (Louisville: Westminster John Knox, 2007), p. 3.

[31] Barton, *The Nature of Biblical Criticism*, p. 5.

[32] So Miroslav Volf, 'Johannine Dualism and Contemporary Pluralism', in Richard Bauckham and Carl Mosser (ed.), *The Gospel of John and Christian Theology* (Grand Rapids: Eerdmans, 2008), pp. 19-50 (21). He is thus referring to John's Gospel, but the point transfers to other works.

apparently made sense to someone or to the Jewish community in some context,[33] and the material invites us to read it as it is with its tensions, not to think that we 'solve' the 'problem' of the tensions by locating them in different contexts or attributing them to different groups.

P. A. Smith observes on the first page of his study of the redaction of Isaiah 56–66 that 'the primary question concerning the majority of commentators' on these chapters 'has been whether these chapters should be regarded as the work of one author or of a multiplicity of authors over a greater or lesser period of time'.[34] If it has been their primary focus, this observation points to something unfortunate. In interpretation, everything depends on the interests, assumptions, and questions that interpreters bring to the text. 'The crucial question, which is prior to questions of method and sets the context for them, is that of purpose and goal. To put it simply, *how we use the Bible depends on why we use the Bible*. In practice, many of the disagreements about how are, in effect, disagreements about why, and failure to recognize this leads to endless confusion.'[35] In the study of Isaiah 56–66 to which I have referred, the interests, assumptions, and questions are historical ones. The scholarly interest lies in tracing the history of events and movements in the Second Temple period, its assumption is that we can establish when the chapters came into being, and its questions concern the nature of that process. But the history of scholarship over the past century and in particular over the past forty years shows that the assumption that we can establish how the chapters came into being is fallacious. While the material invites interpretation against the background of life in Judah sometime after the fall of Babylon to the Persians, understanding Isaiah 56–66 involves recognizing that we do not know more precisely when the material originated. We cannot base an interpretation on such knowledge, and we have to ask how we may work with this situation. To say 'we do not know' is then not a gloomy admission of defeat but an acknowledgment that opens up the possibility of focusing our study on questions that we might be able to answer.

2. *A Sociological Reading*

Redaction-critical approaches to Isaiah 56–66 characteristically read the text in the light of conflicts within the Second Temple community. There certainly were such conflicts in Judah, as Ezra–Nehemiah makes clear, and Isaiah 56–66 gives considerable space to confronting groups within the community. This feature distinguishes Isaiah 56–66 from Isaiah 40–55. In dealing with the problems it identifies in the community it

[33] Cf. Wallis, 'Gott und seine Gemeinde', p. 182.

[34] *Rhetoric and Redaction in Trito-Isaiah*, p. 1.

[35] R. W. L. Moberly, *The Old Testament of the Old Testament* (Minneapolis: Fortress, 1992), p. 2.

addresses and with the issues it needs to face, Isaiah 40–55 treats this community as one whole, characterized in its entirety by the problems it identifies. From the beginning, Isaiah 56–66 deals with problems and tensions internal to the community's life. Some of these issues and questions (such as the status of certain religious practices) are ones with which we are familiar from Isaiah 1–39 and elsewhere in pre-exilic prophecy, though others (such as the position of eunuchs and foreigners in the community) are new and reflect the Second Temple context.

A related approach to the redaction-historical reading of these chapters in the late twentieth and early twenty-first centuries has thus sought to link them to the sociological contexts of the Second Temple community with its conflicts, which they reflect and address.[36] The very opening of the chapters in 56.1-8 points to such a conflict, as it urges that both foreigners who acknowledge Yhwh, and also eunuchs, should be able to view themselves as full members of the community; it implies a tension between more rigorous or purist and more liberal or permissive groups (I intend these as descriptive terms that imply no positive or negative evaluation of the groups and their practices). Over this first issue, the prophetic word identifies with the more liberal.[37]

The following section, 56.9–57.21, offers a contrast with this stance. More explicitly reflecting tensions in the community, the prophecy here attacks people who observe the traditional religious practices of Canaan, in continuity with the practice of many Judahites in the monarchic period. In this section the prophecy identifies with the purist group and with earlier figures such as Jeremiah who opposed such practices. From the prophecy's viewpoint the liberal group is syncretistic or heterodox while the purists are orthodox. The prophecy implies that in the context to which 56.9–57.21 belongs, power in the community lies with the liberal group. Isaiah 58.1–59.21 can then be seen as continuing to reflect the views of a rigorist but powerless group over against a group it sees as oppressive in lifestyle as well as liberal in religious practice. The antithesis resumes in 65.1–66.17, where the prophecy describes the rigorist group as 'Yhwh's servants'—a term previously used for the community as a whole (e.g. 54.17; 56.6; 63.17). Here the prophecy speaks most explicitly about conflict between the permissive and the purist; the former are in a position to repudiate and exclude the latter. This might mean they are excluding them from the temple and from citizenship, or that they are excluding them from leadership or ministry.

[36] See, e.g., the discussion of views in Daniel L. Smith, 'The Politics of Ezra', in Philip R. Davies (ed.), *Second Temple Studies I* (Sheffield: Sheffield Academic Press, 1991), pp. 73-97, reprinted in Charles E. Carter and Carol L. Meyers (ed.), *Community, Identity and Ideology* (Winona Lake, IN: Eisenbrauns, 1996), pp. 537-56.

[37] Cf. Joachim Schaper, 'Torah and Identity in the Persian Period', in Knoppers and Lipshits (eds.), *Judah and the Judeans in the Achaemenid Age*, pp. 27-38 (34).

The people for whom the chapters themselves speak identify with the prophetic tradition represented by the book of Isaiah, oppose worship practices such as consulting the dead, expect to see Yhwh miraculously restore Jerusalem and bring about the world's acknowledgment, and urge commitment to the needy within the community and to the Sabbath. On its account, there are other people who engage in those other worship practices and ignore or take advantage of the position of the needy in the community. If we look outside Isaiah 56–66 to Ezra–Nehemiah, we see parallel evidence of a divide in the community, again described from the perspective of a conservative rather than a permissive group. Malachi further instances the concerns of a conservative group.

The views expressed in Isaiah 56–66 seem sometimes to be those of people who present themselves as a minority within a larger whole or as people without power within the wider community; as a dissenting group, it dissociates its beliefs from those of the people in power and it has been in some sense excommunicated by it. Conversely, it sometimes pictures itself as the real people of God within which alone Yhwh's blessing is to be expected, and it expects adherence to a distinctive code of behaviour and form of worship. On some definitions, that makes it a sect.[38] Yet a feature that raises questions about the designation 'sect' is that both Haggai and Zechariah and Ezra–Nehemiah presuppose that it is the purists who are in power in their respective periods. Further, calling it a sect seems odd in that its views appear not within a document that represents a sect's position over against that of the larger or more powerful group but within a document that represents the views of the mainstream community—within the book of Isaiah and within the Torah, the Prophets, and the Writings.[39] 'Remarkably, the text *preserves* the losing voices in the struggle.'[40]

Admittedly, it is difficult to relate the features of the conflict that Isaiah 56–66 reflects to the written sources for the early Second Temple period. In Ezra–Nehemiah, ethnic considerations interweave with religious considerations in defining the different communities, but there is no indication that the people behind Isaiah 56–66 can be identified with people who returned from exile as opposed to people who had not gone into exile (or vice versa), or with Judahites over against Samarian worshippers of Yhwh in the old territory of Ephraim. Ezra–Nehemiah indicates that both purist and liberal groups include people who have come from Babylon and people whose families had remained in Judah. The only explicit criterion for belonging to the group with which Isaiah 56–66

[38] But see, e.g., Joseph Blenkinsopp, 'A Jewish Sect of the Persian Period', *CBQ* 52 (1990), pp. 5-20, on the problem of defining the notion of a sect.

[39] As Joseph Blenkinsopp notes in a closing footnote to 'The Servant and the Servants in Isaiah and the Formation of the Book', in Broyles and Evans (ed.), *Writing and Reading the Scroll of Isaiah*, I, pp. 155-75 (175).

[40] Berquist, 'Reading Difference in Isaiah 56–66', p. 37.

identifies is an adherence to Yhwh that excludes the traditional religious practices condemned by the Torah (though the chapters never refer to 'the Torah'); indeed, 56.1-8 might imply that the group over against which it distances itself was more inclined to emphasize ethnic distinctiveness.

Other Second Temple documents suggest that there were priests on both sides of the conflict (Hag 1–2; Zech 3; 6.11, 13; Ezra 1–8; Neh 3; 7–12; 13.3; but Mal 2; Ezra 9–10; Neh 13.4, 28-29), and also prophets on both sides of the conflict (cf. Neh 6.14). It would not be surprising if there were prophets among the people Isaiah 56–66 attacks, the kind of people who could speak in the terms of Isaiah 66.5b. So the two groups cannot be identified as prophetic and priestly.[41] Zechariah supports the position of the high priest and neither the Ezekiel tradition nor Haggai and Zechariah can be identified as offering support to the position of the permissive group as described in Isaiah 56–66 or in Ezra–Nehemiah. While there would likely be priests among the people that Isaiah 56–66 critiques, none of the references to priests in Isaiah 56–66 are negative, and there would also be lay people among the objects of the critique. Isaiah 56–66 can be anti-establishment without being anti-cultic.[42] While the divisions within the community may reflect issues concerning possession of and power over the temple, the chapters make only a limited number of explicit references to the temple, which suggests at least that these issues are not central to the chapters (reference to Zion constitutes reference to the city not the temple).[43] Conversely, when they speak of divisions, they do not refer to the temple.

To understate the point, then, 'which are the groups who are fighting each other in Trito-Isaiah…is not, I think, an easy problem to solve'.[44] The scholarly world has generated two main sociological accounts of the conflict in the Second Temple community, which one might especially associate with Morton Smith[45] and Paul Hanson.[46] Smith speaks of the

[41] Against Tiemeyer, *Priestly Rites and Prophetic Rage*.

[42] See Joachim Schaper, 'Rereading the Law', in Bernard M. Levinson and Eckart Otto (eds.), *Recht und Ethik im Alten Testament* (Münster: Lit, 2004), pp. 125-44 (137).

[43] Cf. Jill Middlemass, 'Divine Reversal and the Role of the Temple in Trito-Isaiah', in John Day (ed.), *Temple and Temple Worship in Biblical Israel* (London: T&T Clark International, 2005), pp. 164-87. See further Bedford, *Temple Restoration in Early Achaemenid Judah*, for critique of the idea that the key to understanding early Second Temple history is conflict between groups struggling for socio-economic and political power.

[44] Jeppesen, 'From "You, My Servant" to "the Hand of the Lord Is With My Servants"', p. 128.

[45] See Morton Smith, *Palestinian Politics and Parties that Shaped the Old Testament* (New York: Columbia University Press, 1971; reprinted London: SCM, 1987); also Bernhard Lang, 'Die Jahwe-allein-Bewegung', in Lang (ed.), *Der einzige Gott* (Munich: Kösel, 1981), p. 47-83; ET in Lang, *Monotheism and the Prophetic Minority* (Sheffield: Almond, 1983), pp. 13-56.

[46] See *The Dawn of Apocalyptic*.

two groups as the 'Yahweh-alone party' and the 'syncretistic party';[47] their difference focused on whether other gods could be worshipped alongside Yhwh. While the analysis in terms of religious conviction fits a number of the elements in Isaiah 56–66 just noted, the material in Isaiah 56–66 need not require that the permissive group consciously worshipped deities other than Yhwh, and a passage such as 66.5 may imply that they were firm in adherence to Yhwh alone. They may have believed that they could worship other beings without compromising Yhwh's supremacy, and/or their permissiveness may have lain in the forms of worship that they believed appropriate in the context of a commitment to Yhwh. In reporting that Yhwh had not commissioned or even contemplated the sacrifice of one's offspring, Jeremiah 7.31 implies that such sacrifice was made to Yhwh.

Hanson's approach has been the more influential in recent decades, but a consideration of its outworking suggests that it parallels the attempt to link the material in Isaiah 56–66 to specific historical contexts in not seeming able to deliver as much insight as one might have hoped. While 'there is a wealth of literature on the socioeconomic and political situation of Yehud' during the Persian period,[48] this burgeoning study is in inverse proportion to the amount of hard data available for it. A sociological approach to the material aims to offer aid in precisely such a situation, by beginning from modern sociological theory and looking at the text in the light of it. The procedure is a reasonable one that may issue in enabling the enigmatic to become intelligible, but in this case it seems to impose an alien interpretation on the text.

Hanson's key for understanding the conflicts in the Second Temple community comes from the sociology of knowledge; he refers to one of its key early texts, Karl Mannheim's *Ideology and Utopia*.[49] From Mannheim Hanson takes the insight that it is common for communities to include a ruling group who as such are happy with how things are in the community and a group who are alienated from power, dissatisfied with how things are, and looking for a future realization of how things should be. Hanson sees Isaiah 60–62 as the dreams of such visionaries, whereas Ezekiel 40–48 is the blueprint of hierocratic realists or pragmatists.[50] The visionaries are people who cannot see God's vision for the community coming to fulfillment through human action because the people in a position to take the appropriate action are working against it; they therefore

[47] E.g. Smith, *Palestinian Politics and Parties that Shaped the Old Testament*, p. 112 (= pp. 84-85).

[48] Raymond de Hoop, 'The Interpretation of Isaiah 56:1-9', *JBL* 127 (2008), pp. 671-95 (689).

[49] *Ideologie und Utopie* (Bonn: Cohen, 1929); expanded ET, *Ideology and Utopia* (London: Routledge; New York: Harcourt, 1936).

[50] See *The Dawn of Apocalyptic*, pp. 71-72, where he associates this distinction with Mannheim's 'ideology' and 'utopia'; also pp. 211-20.

look for God to bring about the fulfillment of that vision in a miraculous way. The hierocrats are people in a position of power, specifically in the temple, who are committed to acting so that their understanding of God's vision is indeed implemented. Their practical plans for doing so appear in the Torah.

In substance, Hanson's analysis also links with that of Otto Plöger, who emphasizes a similar distinction within the Second Temple community.[51] A difference is that Hanson works forwards from the exile and Isaiah 40–55, whereas Plöger works backwards from the crisis in the time of Antiochus Epiphanes and Daniel, and considers Isaiah 24–27, Zechariah 12–14, and Joel; in a preface to the English translation of his monograph he notes that it would be possible to incorporate Isaiah 56–66 into his account.[52] Plöger thus anticipates Hanson and recalls Mannheim, though Hanson refers to Plöger only once in a footnote relating to Chronicles and Daniel, and Plöger does not refer to Mannheim or to the sociology of knowledge.

In principle an analysis of Isaiah 56–66 in the light of conflicts in the community should be illuminating, though a bipolar understanding of the community may be too simple.[53] Hanson's contrast between Ezekiel 40–48 and Isaiah 56–66 immediately raises questions. Ezekiel 40–48 is, after all, not exactly a realistic blueprint, and it is part of prophetic tradition. Similar difficulties are raised by any suggestion that an eschatological orientation is a distinguishing characteristic of the group whose beliefs are expressed in Isaiah 56–66, since most Judahite groups seem likely to have had an eschatological orientation; the exceptions would be those represented by Ecclesiastes and Chronicles (indeed, many scholars would attribute one even to Chronicles, though this view has to be inferred from the text; it is not explicit). Ezekiel 40–48 certainly manifests one.[54] While the people whom the Isaiah 56–66 group see as opposed to them may have emphasized Yhwh's involvement in the present more than Yhwh's promises for the future, a stance represented in Chronicles though not in Ezra–Nehemiah, Isaiah 66.5 attributes a future-oriented perspective (albeit a sardonic one) to them.

[51] *Theokratie und Eschatologie* (Neukirchen: Neukirchener, 1959; 2nd edn, 1962); ET *Theocracy and Eschatology* (Oxford: Blackwell, 1968; Richmond: Knox, 1969).

[52] *Theocracy and Eschatology*, p. vi. Alexander Rofé ('The Onset of Sects in Postexilic Judaism', in Jacob Neusner *et al.* [eds.], *The Social World of Formative Christianity and Judaism* [H. C. Kee Festschrift; Philadelphia: Fortress, 1988, pp. 39-49]) similarly sees in Isaiah 56–66 background to the later tension between Pharisees and Sadducees, but there seems insufficient correspondence between these groups' positions and those evidenced in Isa 56–66.

[53] See the discussion in Albertz, *Religionsgeschichte Israels in alttestamentlicher Zeit*, esp. II, pp. 461-68 (ET II, pp. 437-43). Berquist offers a more complex but speculative one in *Judaism in Persia's Shadow*, pp. 73-80.

[54] Perhaps we should rather think in terms of different eschatologies (cf. Robert P. Carroll, 'Twilight of Prophecy or Dawn of Apocalyptic?', *JSOT* 14 [1979], pp. 3-35 [26]).

In considering the background of Isaiah 56–66 in community conflicts, Hanson sees the chapters as giving a key role to a new form of prophetic address, the 'salvation-judgment oracle', which he sees as warning some people of judgment that is to come on them and promising deliverance to others.[55] The designation 'salvation-judgment oracle' is useful, though it would be more natural to call it a judgment-salvation oracle.

In Hanson's view, chronologically 58.1-12 is the first example of such an oracle. The problem with his understanding of this passage is twofold. First, 58.1-12 actually addresses 'my people…the household of Jacob'; and second, it gives no indication that the warning and the promise address different groups. Far from the juxtaposition of vv. 2-5 and 6-12 implying a division of the people into the wicked and the righteous,[56] it implies that the wicked had better become the righteous, and that they can then enjoy Yhwh's deliverance. Hanson says that here the dichotomy between the two groups is incomplete;[57] actually, it is non-existent, as he implicitly grants in speaking of the prophecy 'leaving the *possibility* of salvation open to the *whole* nation'.[58] The second example of a judgment-salvation oracle, 59.1-20, similarly offers no indication that there are two groups in the community.

The third example, 65.1-25, also concerns itself with a 'nation', a 'people', but then contrasts this 'nation' or 'people' with 'my servants' and sets contrasting destinies before them.[59] It is a plausible view that 'my servants' here and in the fourth example (66.1-17) refers to the faithful within the community, and this judgment-salvation oracle indeed promises judgment and salvation to different groups, though it is not clear that the phenomenon needs interpreting sociologically or positivistically rather than rhetorically. The last possibility may be supported by the fact that the last of the judgment-salvation oracles (in Hanson's ordering), 56.9–57.13, includes no indication of the existence of an 'alternative community' and mentions only the possibility that the individual who takes refuge with Yhwh 'will own the land, will possess my holy mountain'. Likewise the context suggests that the warnings to the wicked in 57.19-20 confront the community as a whole rather than presupposing a division within it.[60] 'The servants of Yhwh' (in the plural) has been seen as a key motif in Isaiah 56–66, but if it is, it is odd that eight of the ten occurrences of the expression occur in the last two chapters (seven of them in Isa 65; one in Isa 56.6 refers to foreigners, and one in 63.17 refers to the community as a whole). It is an expression that comes into

55 E.g. *The Dawn of Apocalyptic*, pp. 106-7.

56 *The Dawn of Apocalyptic*, p. 108.

57 *The Dawn of Apocalyptic*, p. 107.

58 *The Dawn of Apocalyptic*, p. 108.

59 See, e.g., Beuken, 'Trito-Jesaja', pp. 78-83.

60 As Hanson assumes, *The Dawn of Apocalyptic*, pp. 78-79; cf. Westermann, *Jesaja Kapitel 40–66*, p. 263 (ET pp. 330-31).

its own only in connection with the chapters' closing talk in terms of a division between the real people of God and the people who exclude themselves.

According to Brooks Schramm, Isaiah 56–66 is concerned 'to identify and to define who the people are who will be allowed to participate in this salvation' and who will not.[61] But passages such as Isaiah 59 make clear that the prophet's polemic relates to a whole community issue; it is not a basis for dividing the community. The same is true about the community's brokenness in 57.14-21 and its oppressiveness in 58.1-14; both passages envisage the possibility of restoration for the whole community, not just for a group within it. In addition, when the prophecies might be critiquing elements within the community, they do not emphasize a link with the question of participation in the restoration. The focus of a passage such as 56.9–57.13 lies on critique. Only in a half-verse at the end does it refer to the fact that 'the person who takes refuge with me will own the land, will possess my holy mountain'.

If a division within the community is implicit throughout the chapters, however, what is the nature of this division? According to Hanson's typology, the prophecy critiques the people who control the temple, whom he refers to as the Zadokites, the people whose views are expressed in Ezekiel 40–48 and in the Torah itself. This raises a difficulty in relation to the confrontation in Isaiah 56–66. These chapters critique people who sacrifice children, engage in observances designed to make contact with dead family members, worship by means of images (of Yhwh and/or of other deities), and eat pork and other food forbidden by the Torah (57.5-13; 65.3-4; 66.17). Much of the detailed interpretation of this critique is difficult, but there is no doubt regarding its central features. What it makes clear is that the practices the prophecy attacks cannot be identified with anything that would be affirmed by the people whose views are represented anywhere in the Torah or in Ezekiel. Indeed, they are identical to the practices attacked by Ezekiel, by the Torah, and by prophets such as Isaiah and Jeremiah in the period before the exile. Hanson's way of approaching these passages is therefore to take their language as 'symbolical' and 'hyperbolical'. It '*equates* the cult of those attacked with Canaanizing sacrificial practices'.[62] Now this is a possible interpretation of the allusive language in 66.3-4, which might be declaring that God takes the same view of people who make proper offerings as God does of people who make forbidden ones; so 1QIs[a], which adds the preposition *k* to make the point (cf. LXX, Tg, Vg). But the openness of the elliptical language in Isaiah 66 then contrasts with that in Isaiah 57 and 65, where there is nothing to point to a metaphorical understanding. Ironically, Hanson notes that the material in Isaiah 56–66 'is ambiguous enough to be amenable to most any hypothesis, given an ample amount of

[61] Schramm, *The Opponents of Third Isaiah*, p. 82.
[62] *The Dawn of Apocalyptic*, p. 147 (my emphasis).

eisegesis'.[63] Importing an interpretation into the text from his sociological model is exactly what one might see Hanson as doing.[64]

Again, let us for a moment grant the possibility that the attacks in Isaiah 57 and 65 are expressed metaphorically. Are there any passages where they are expressed literally? Hanson finds one in Isaiah 66.1-2: 'What is this house which you would build for me…? All of these things my hand has made…. But upon this one I will look, the humble, who is broken in spirit and trembles at my word.'[65] 'From 66:1-4', Hanson says, 'it is clear that chapters 56–66 of Isaiah stem from a group that have no faith in the temple rebuilding program of the dominant priestly party, the Zadokites'.[66] The problem with this understanding is its conflict with the relative enthusiasm for the temple that runs through the chapters' other references to the temple: see 56.7; 57.13; 60.7, 13; 64.11; 65.11.[67] 'If one interprets Isa. 66.1-2 either as a rejection of temple building as such…or merely as a rejection of Haggai's temple, then one must also claim that Isa. 66.1-2 stands in contradiction with the rest of Third Isaiah!'[68]

Sociological theory obscures Isaiah 56–66 more than it illuminates. Whereas the scholarly world took the sociological turn in the study of the Second Temple period in the hope that it could provide a way of circumventing some impasses of traditional historical study, it has rather led to the building of hypothesis upon hypothesis regarding a question such as the nature of the conflict that lies at the back of the material in Isaiah 56–66. Hanson's thesis has led to lively discussion, but that is all, because it involves too speculative a construction on the basis of too small a collection of data, and furthermore a construction that has to ignore some of the data.

In taking conflict within the community as key to understanding Isaiah 56–66, Hanson's understanding parallels Duhm's. It was intrinsic to Duhm's understanding of Isaiah 56–66 that its background lay in the time of Ezra and Nehemiah and specifically in intra-community conflict in that period, conflict between the godly and the schismatics.[69] Hanson thus has a different understanding of the parties in the conflict, but agrees that conflict is key to understanding the chapters. Duhm has had an extraordinary wide and lasting influence on the study of the prophets, perhaps wider and more long-lasting than Julius Wellhausen's influence on the study of the Pentateuch.[70] It seems to be another aspect of this astonishing

[63] *The Dawn of Apocalyptic*, p. 32.

[64] Cf. Schramm, *The Opponents of Third Isaiah*, p. 88.

[65] Hanson's translation, *The Dawn of Apocalyptic*, p. 164.

[66] Hanson, *Isaiah 40–66*, p. 199.

[67] Blenkinsopp, *Isaiah 56–66*, p. 294.

[68] Schramm, *The Opponents of Third Isaiah*, p. 164.

[69] *Das Buch Jesaia*, p. 379.

[70] I think I owe this observation to my student Joseph Henderson. Clements in 'Isaiah: A Book without an Ending?' questions basic assumptions of Duhm's view.

influence that he made division in the community the key to understanding prophecy in Second Temple times. On this assumption, Isaiah 56–66 presupposes a divided community in a way that preexilic prophecy did not.

The idea that the Second Temple community was divided and that Isaiah 56–66 represents the stance of one of the groups within it is unexceptionable. We possess various writings from Second Temple Jerusalem, such as the retelling of Israel's distant history in Chronicles, the narrative of episodes in its recent history in Ezra–Nehemiah, the reflection in Ecclesiastes, and the orientation to what Yhwh will do in the future in the Prophets, which can itself take various forms. In some sense the recension of the Torah and of both the Former and Latter Prophets belongs in this context. These works represent theological convictions standing in tension with one another. It is easy to imagine their adherents arguing as keenly as Christian groups do today and contending for control in the Jerusalem community. Yet all these works found acceptance with the community that affirmed the material that came to be known as the Torah, the Prophets, and the Writings. Further, this material itself indicates that these works by no means represented the full range of faith convictions within the community. Interpreted literally, Isaiah 56–66 itself gives indication of other convictions within the community, in its attacks on observances designed to make contact with family members who had passed. The convolutions within the Anglican Communion or the Presbyterian Church are nothing compared with these disagreements.

All this is unexceptionable. What is puzzling is the suggestion that there is something new in this situation. A cursory read of 1 and 2 Kings, Isaiah 1–39, Jeremiah, Ezekiel, and other prophets makes clear that it had always been so (as for that matter is the case with the Anglican Communion and the Presbyterian Church). The community centred on Jerusalem had always been divided into groups with contrary faith positions that were battling for control of Jerusalem's temple and soul. Isaiah 56–66 gives the same impression as the one suggested by preexilic prophecy, where a prophet and a possibly small group of supporters stand over against the community as a whole. 'Like the old prophets, Trito-Isaiah tears open a gulf where one was not hitherto seen, and separates Israel from Israel.'[71] While conflict is an important reality in the Second Temple community, there is nothing distinctive about that community in this respect.

[71] Gerhard von Rad, *Theologie des Altes Testaments Band II* (Munich: Kaiser, 1960), p. 293 (ET *Old Testament Theology* [Edinburgh: Oliver & Boyd, 1965], II, p. 280).

3. *A Textual Reading*

'Isaiah 56–66 does not constitute what most people today would recognize as a literary work. To the extent that it exhibits coherence and unity, the effect is the result of redactional rather than authorial activity.'[72] In this respect, it is typical of the Old Testament; Blenkinsopp's comment would apply to the book of Isaiah as a whole, to the Pentateuch, to the Psalter and Proverbs, to Ezra and Nehemiah. There are few books in the Old Testament that one can discuss in terms of authorial activity and that fit Western conceptions of the nature of a literary work (Jonah? Ruth? Esther?). While the quest for coherence and unity in terms of the activity of an individual author may be inappropriate, therefore, the formulation implies that there could be another version of the quest, in redactional terms. Blenkinsopp himself describes the opening and closing paragraphs of Isaiah 56–66 as a pair of 'brackets' around material that is 'in some respects one text with a distinctive point of view'.[73]

Redactional study of Isaiah 56–66 has been concerned with the redactional *process*, in keeping with the implications of the second half of the word *Redaktionsgeschichte*. It has not been so interested in the text that has resulted from this process. Yet it would be natural for interpretation to concern itself with this actually existent text and not merely with the hypothetical process of how it came into being. Instead of taking redaction-historical theories or sociological theories as key to understanding Isaiah 56–66, it is therefore possible to ask about the form of the chapters themselves and to read them in the textual form in which they appear. I noted at the beginning of this Introduction the presence of indications that Isaiah 56–66 forms a structured work, a chiasm or stepped structure or inverted pyramid. These in particular make it natural to ask after the meaning, coherence, and unity of this eventual text.

In *Isaiah 40–55*[74] we do not assume or conclude that all the material in those chapters comes from the same prophet. Although I suspect that at least the vast bulk of it does, the chapters as a whole have assembled diverse materials in order to make it a coherent argument. I do not know whether or not the arrangement comes from the prophet who generated most or all of the material. Isaiah 56–66 also represents a coherent arrangement of diverse material, but both the arrangement and the diversity have different profiles. It may represent more diversity of date. There is more diversity about the material than is the case in Isaiah 40–55, in style and in content or emphases, which might reduce the basis for inferring that most or all the material comes from the same prophet,[75] yet

[72] Blenkinsopp, *Isaiah 56–66*, p. 37.

[73] *Isaiah 56–66*, p. 132; Hanson (*Isaiah 40–66*, p. 196) makes a similar observation and compares the way Isaiah 40–55 is framed by 40.1-11 and 55.1-13.

[74] Goldingay and Payne, *Isaiah 40–55*.

[75] But contrast Elliger, *Die Einheit des Tritojesaja*; 'Der Prophet Tritojesaja'.

there is not the degree of diversity that would rule out this possibility. The movement between promises and condemnation, for instance, is not a basis for seeing separate authors or different addressees, especially given that the former may be designed to encourage repentance on the part of the people who are condemned, who might thus see the promises fulfilled.[76] The distinction between prose and verse in the chapters likewise need not preclude authorship by one person; people who compose poetry also compose prose. As is the case in Isaiah 1–39 and 40–55, there is a prophetic 'I' that speaks in Isaiah 56–66 (59.21; 61.1). While this fact might seem to imply that all eleven chapters issue from that individual, it need not do so; the person or group that put the chapters together might have incorporated material of other origins in the conviction that it expressed one mission or outlook. It seems best simply to ignore the question of authorship; as is the case with the question of date, the material fails to provide data on the basis of which we could come to a view on the question.

The intricate concentric arrangement of Isaiah 56–66 does suggest that these eleven chapters as a whole provide a significant interpretative context for the units within it. In this respect it parallels other parts of the book such as chapters 1–12 or 13–23 or 40–55, which are in varying ways arranged; they do not comprise a series of unstructured anthologies.

Further, the structured nature of the chapters invites us to read the material in the order in which the text itself unfolds. In treating Isaiah as a drama, John D. W. Watts offers an interpretation that deals with the text sequentially, but his understanding seems arbitrary on both the macro- and the micro-scale. On his account, in much of Isaiah 56–58 (for instance) the speakers alternate between 'the heavens' and 'the earth', and the addressee is the Persian king Darius I,[77] but the text gives no indication that speakers alternate, that the heavens and the earth are the speakers, or that Darius is the addressee.

In contrast, Smith (for instance) reads the material in the light of the order in which he thinks it was composed rather than in the order in which the text unfolds. So 56.1-8 'takes up' terms and themes from 60.1–63.6 'in order to clarify, or possibly correct' the statements there about the place of proselytes in the new community.[78] Isaiah 58.1–59.20 'responds to a question or complaint raised by the people' concerning why Yhwh takes no notice of their fasting (58.3) and 'responds to the complaint by reinterpreting the preaching of TI [Trito-Isaiah] (60:1–63:6) in the light of the criteria set out in 56:1-8'.[79] As a whole, Isaiah 56–59 function to prepare for the promises in 60.1–63.6, which come from the preceding two decades, the first years of the Persian period.

[76] Cf. Tiemeyer, *Priestly Rites and Prophetic Rage*, p. 36.
[77] Watts, *Isaiah 34–66*, pp. 811-46.
[78] Smith, *Rhetoric and Redaction in Trito-Isaiah*, p. 59.
[79] Smith, *Rhetoric and Redaction in Trito-Isaiah*, p. 101.

It may be that historically Isaiah 60–62 came first and that historically 56.1-8 is responding to it, and that 58.1–59.20 is reinterpreting those same chapters, but even if that is so, reading Isaiah 56–66 involves working with the fact that Isaiah 56–59 comes before Isaiah 60–62. When we come to Isaiah 60–62 we could consider the relationship of substance between them and what has preceded, but to reverse the process of interpretation by systematically reading Isaiah 56 and 58–59 in the light of Isaiah 60–62 is to put the cart before the horse. To make the point in another way, a commentary is different from a monograph such as Smith writes; the latter is freer than the former to subordinate the text to questions the author brings to the text.

In contrast to Isaiah 1–12, 13–23, and 40–55, only chapters 56–66 have a systematically concentric structure. In this respect the rhetorical dynamic of Isaiah 56–66 contrasts in particular with that of Isaiah 40–55, which works in a linear way. Isaiah 40–55 is a little like a narrative with a plot. One cannot fully understand the significance of (for instance) 41.8-10 without considering 42.1-4, or that of 42.1-4 without considering 42.18-25, and so on. Earlier passages raise questions that later passages answer or at least take up again. I have argued for a linear reading of Isaiah 56–66, in the sense that we should read Isaiah 56 before Isaiah 60. But paradoxically, a linear reading reveals to readers that while the chapters initially go somewhere, they then come back again. It thus uncovers a key aspect of their burden. They are like Isaiah 40–55 in that any particular passage needs to be seen in the light of the way the whole subsequently unfolds;[80] but the linear reading reveals that this unfolding is circular or spiral rather than linear. By its nature, a concentric structure has a different dynamic from a linear one. It looks as if it is going somewhere but it turns out to be doing something more ambiguous. Its second half may indeed take the argument forward, as the second of two cola within a poetic line characteristically goes beyond the first in some way. There will thus be a little linearity about the structure; it is more like a spiral than a circle. But formally, at least, Isaiah 56–66 ends up coming back to where it started.

Linearly, chapters 60–62 could seem the proper ending to the book of Isaiah. Isaiah 60

> resumes and summarizes the book's most central theme which concerns Jerusalem and its destiny.... It brings to a resolution problems and issues regarding the city's place among the nations of the world which occupy a

[80] Cf. Claire R. Mathews's arguments in 'Apportioning Desolation: Contexts for Interpreting Edom's Fate and Function in Isaiah', in *Society of Biblical Literature 1995 Seminar Papers* (Atlanta: Scholars, 1997), pp. 250-66. Indeed, Ibrahim Taha argues that the interpretation of a text has to start from the end, 'since only then is the reader required to invest concentrated effort in the interpretation of the entire text' ('Semiotics of *Ending* and *Closure*', *Semiotica* 138 [2002], pp. 259-77 [265], as quoted by Emmanuel Uchenna Dim, *The Eschatological Implications of Isa 65 and 66 as the Conclusion of the Book of Isaiah* [Bern: Lang, 2005], p. 3).

> central role in the book from the beginning. If we are looking for a skilfully planned *inclusio* of the kind that corresponds with the issues that repeatedly rise and fall throughout the intervening chapters, then this is very clearly evident between chs. 5 and 60 (62). It is ch. 60 that conveys what Frank Kermode (1967) has called 'the sense of an ending' appropriate to the scroll's beginning in ch. 1.... The chapters, chs. 63–66, that follow scarcely provide a suitable ending at all for the book since they undermine the very certainties and finalities that ch. 60 has established.[81]

The fact that the book of Isaiah does not end with chapters 60–62 but continues in the way it does constitutes a telling indication of the thesis that emerges from it, and in particular from Isaiah 56–66. As Isaiah 1–55 and then 56.1 announce, the book as a whole and these closing chapters expound two chief convictions, that Jerusalem needs to face Yhwh's challenges about its life (see 56.9–59.8; 65.1–66.17) and that Yhwh is committed to its glorious restoration (see 60.1–62.12). But the last eleven chapters, like their opening verse, do not establish the relationship between these two convictions. They simply juxtapose them. They do suggest that it is an oversimplification to say that the vital thing is for Jerusalem to repent and that its restoration will then follow, but they also suggest that neither is it the case that Yhwh's act of restoration will take place irrespective of Jerusalem's stance in relation to Yhwh.

As the genius of Isaiah 40–55 is to expound issues by means of a linear argument, the genius of Isaiah 56–66 is to expound issues by means of a chiasm. These strategies are contextual and not interchangeable. The thrust of Isaiah 40–55 could not be expressed as a chiasm, whereas the thrust of Isaiah 56–66 could not be expressed by a linear sequence. It expounds the irresolvable tensions between challenge, prayer, and promise, between an interest in the nations that focuses on their blessing and one that focuses on Israel's blessing, and between judgment and restoration. It is a highly multivalent text.[82] Such significance in a chiasm emerges when one contrasts it with a text open to deconstruction. There are texts that emphasize either divine action or human action, and it is not then surprising if readers can see the other emphasis lurking somewhere beneath the surface of the text. Indeed, this is so in Isaiah 40–55.[83] The genius of a chiasm (or is it the cowardice of a chiasm?) is to avoid deconstruction by being upfront with the two assertions that stand in tension with each other.[84] To put it another way,

[81] Clements, 'Isaiah: A Book without an Ending?', pp. 109-10, 114; he refers to Clements, 'A Light to the Nations', and to Frank Kermode, *The Sense of an Ending: Studies in the Theory of Fiction* (Oxford: Oxford University Press, 1967).

[82] See further Berquist, 'Reading Difference in Isaiah 56–66'.

[83] See Goldingay, 'Isaiah xl–lv in the 1990s: Among Other Things, Deconstructing, Mystifying, Intertextual, Socio-critical, and Hearer-involving', *Biblical Interpretation* 5 (1997), pp. 226-46.

[84] But see Berquist, 'Reading Difference in Isaiah 56–66', for a deconstructionist approach to Isa 56–66 at other levels than the macro-structure of the section.

while Isaiah 40–55 is amenable to deconstruction without inviting it, Isaiah 56–66 wears its deconstruction on its sleeve. It thereby engages its audience in reflecting on the relationship between its affirmations and in forming an attitude to the questions they raise.

Brevard Childs opposes appeal to the concentric structure of Isaiah 56–66 as a key to its interpretation, even though this structure is an aspect of the canonical form of the text, to which Childs is committed to paying attention.[85] Childs's opposition stems from an ambiguity about the significance of this concentric structure. He sets his view over against that of Claus Westermann, who describes chapters 60–62 as the *Kern* or nucleus of the message of Isaiah 56–66.[86]

The image of a nucleus can have at least three implications. (a) The nucleus of something is the originating centre from which it develops. (b) The nucleus is the object's control centre; nothing develops in the cell that is not determined by the nucleus. The kernel image has similar implications; a kernel or seed is or contains the embryo from which a plant grows. (c) The nucleus of something is its structural centre.

With regard to Isaiah 56–66, implication (a) is that the chapters gradually accumulated around Isaiah 60–62. Roughly speaking, the chiasm then reflects their historical origin. Isaiah 60–62 is the oldest material; 56.1-8 and 66.18-24 is the youngest; the intervening material comes from in between.[87] While Westermann accepts all three implications of the 'nucleus' image, his emphasis on Isaiah 60–62 especially relates to his interest in tracing the redaction history of the material. It is in this connection that Childs believes that interpreting the material in the light of its concentric structure yields too much to speculative historical-critical theories.

Implication (c), that a nucleus is the structural centre of something, is the one reflected in the concentric structure of the chapters as we have them. But implication (b), that the nucleus or kernel is the control centre, does not hold. First, Westermann himself sees much of Isaiah 56–57 as preexilic in origin and much of Isaiah 63–64 as exilic in origin, so that here the so-called nucleus was attracting foreign material to itself rather than generating material. Second, Westermann then notes that further material such as 65.1-16a has other distinctive features than those which characterize chapters 60–62. We have already noted its assumption that the community can be divided into the faithful and the rebels, and that

85 *Isaiah*, pp. 448-49.

86 *Das Buch Jesaja Kap. 40–66*, p. 237 (ET p. 296). Maass uses a parallel image in speaking of the material having a *Grundbestand* or basic element comprising 57.14-19; 58.1-12; 59.1-3, 9-21; 60.1–62.12; 66.1-16, which was then expanded; see '"Tritojesaja"?', p. 163.

87 For variants on this approach, nuancing it in different ways, see (e.g.) Sekine, *Die tritojesajanische Sammlung (Jes 56–66) redaktionsgeschichtlich untersucht* and Steck, *Studien zu Tritojesaja*. Lau associates the original form of 66.18-24 with an earlier stage (*Schriftgelehrte Prophetie in Jes 56–66*, pp. 143-51).

only the former will enjoy Yhwh's act of restoration; such a division does not appear in Isaiah 60–62. Further, the offences that 65.1-16a attacks mostly involve the world of worship, which Westermann sees as not a preoccupation in Isaiah 60–62. In Isaiah 65, then, the so-called nucleus is not generating material but provoking what one might call a hostile growth. Third, Westermann then sees passages such as 58.1-12 as corresponding to Isaiah 60–62 in addressing the whole community but as contrasting with those chapters in making its restoration conditional on the people's response to its challenge. Westermann ascribes 58.1-12 to the author of Isaiah 60–62, but it also seems to involve some evolution in a direction that cannot be traced to the nucleus's DNA. Fourth, an oracle of judgment against a foreign nation such as 63.1-6 is then 'appended to the nucleus itself, chs. 60–62. The intention is perfectly plain; the attitude towards the nations expressed in chs. 60–62 is amended [*korrigierend*] by the addition of "but thereafter God begins his great battle with them to destroy them!"'[88] The nature of the material that accumulates around chapters 60–62 is thus more to raise a series of questions about it than to reinforce the 'message of salvation and nothing but salvation' (*reine Heilsbotschaft*) that Westermann finds there.[89]

A parallel ambiguity attaches to Blenkinsopp's description of chapters 60–62 as 'the central core' and 'central panel' of Isaiah 56–66. These two images have different implications. In a triptych, the central panel is simply the central panel. But the core of something is its densest part. 'The central panel presents the ideal situation in programmatic form, a kind of best-case scenario for the future' which then stands in contrast with the real situation in the community portrayed on either side.[90] So chapters 60–62 are the central panel, but they are not really the core.

These considerations point to another reason for surprise at Childs's reluctance to focus on the concentric shape of Isaiah 56–66, or they at least point to an irony in that reluctance. Reading the material as structurally embodying tensions over theological questions has theological implications that are congenial to Childs's emphasis on the way the chapters hold together theological perspectives that necessarily stand in tension. Attaching exegetical priority to the final form of the text, he notes, does not imply a harmonizing approach, 'because often the retention of elements of tension within the canonical text has been judged to be essential to Israel's authoritative scriptures'.[91] In connection with

[88] *Das Buch Jesaja Kap. 40–66*, p. 243 (ET pp. 304-5).

[89] *Das Buch Jesaja Kap. 40–66*, p. 237 (ET p. 296). Westermann sees this feature as a link with Isa 40–55, which prompts the remark that his need to see elements in Isa 40–55 as later than the work of the main prophecy, in light of his conviction that Second Isaiah preaches 'salvation and nothing but salvation', is a sign that his understanding deconstructs; Isa 40–55 holds together the same two emphases as Isa 56–66, though it does not hold them in such equal tension.

[90] Blenkinsopp, *Isaiah 56–66*, pp. 38-39.

[91] Childs, *Isaiah*, p. 441.

56.9–57.13, for instance, he comments that the similarity of the passage's critique to that of preexilic prophecy suggests that it confronts 'the theological problem that turned on the continuing presence of the old along with the very real experience of the new'. The relation between the two is 'ontological, not just chronological, in essence'. The new age is coming but the old will remain.[92] We may again note that, while Isaiah 40–55 is amenable to deconstruction without inviting it, Isaiah 56–66 wears its deconstruction on its sleeve. We have noted further that the presence of ontological questions here, in that the chapters involve an inherently complex substantial theological issue, suggests that theological tensions in the chapters need not point to diversity of authorship. The chapters may reflect a wrestling with questions that a single prophet or theologian could recognize were complex.

In discussing the chapters' interpretation, Childs appeals to their 'canonical' form, but it seems best to avoid the word 'canonical' in this connection. 'Canonical interpretation' has many different meanings, even for Childs himself. Further, it is inclined to suggest confessional and churchly; canonical interpretation is important for people who want to read Isaiah 'as Scripture'.[93] (Admittedly it is odd that this expression does not sound 'ridiculously tautological', given that the book of Isaiah only ever existed as a book of Jewish, then Christian Scripture.[94]) As a consequence the word 'canonical' resembles the word 'evolution' in being a hurrah word for some people and a boo word for others. It does not trigger people into cool-headed study.

For this reason, while I am asking questions about what Childs would call the canonical form of the text, I avoid using this language. Asking about the inherent meaning of Isaiah 56–66 as we have it has nothing intrinsically to do with the text's canonical status. It is equivalent to asking questions about the meaning of a Shakespeare play. We do not expect Shakespeare commentators to stop at analysing the sources the dramatist used, the historical events the play refers to, the contemporary events it reflects, or the process whereby it reached its final form. We expect them to explicate the text before us, starting at the beginning and working through it, and thus helping us to appreciate it. Such a task is appropriate to the study of Isaiah 56–66. I draw the analogy with Shakespeare in order further to make clear that I am not arguing for a canonical interpretation of Isaiah in the sense that the argument has something to do with Isaiah being a scriptural text (and the fact that Shakespeare is part of the literary canon does not affect the point). In reading Shakespeare or Plato as texts, as works, we ask about their structure and the way their drama develops, and consider the ideas they put forward. In doing so, we

92 *Isaiah*, p. 463.

93 See the title of Childs's *Introduction to the Old Testament as Scripture*.

94 Sheppard, 'Isaiah as a Scroll or Codex within Jewish and Christian Scripture', pp. 206-7.

do not see ourselves as involved in canonical or final-form or synchronic or theological interpretation. It is just—interpretation. I here use the expression 'textual interpretation' and speak of taking a textual approach to the material, because reflecting on options in Old Testament study, where approaches are conflicting, requires an adjective in front of the word 'interpretation', though 'textual interpretation' is close to a tautology.

Asking historical questions of Isaiah 56–66 does not work very well because the people who compiled the book of Isaiah were not interested in them, so that working with our historical focus means reading against the grain of the text's focus and seeking to guess at what lies between the lines. We are like people studying Shakespeare in order to discover the history of Henry VIII or to trace the process whereby John Fletcher may have collaborated in writing the play or may have revised it. Isaiah 56–66 does not cooperate with us by answering our historical questions. As such questions do not open up the interpretation of Shakespeare's play, neither do they for the interpretation of Isaiah. Our preoccupation with providing historical contexts for the material in Isaiah 56–66 suggests that we are in the same bondage as my students who in reading the Psalms have a hard time weaning themselves from wanting to know when David wrote them.[95]

While there is a pragmatic reason for focusing on the text itself rather on its prehistory or the events it refers to (the fact that we cannot uncover the prehistory or the events and will never be able to do so), there is also a reason of principle. Some propriety or wisdom attaches to interpreting a work in the light of its own nature. Isaiah is a religious, ethical, and theological text. It talks about the way people relate to God, about what they think it is right and wrong to do, and about how they think of God and of the relationships between God, Israel, and other peoples. If we are to be 'competent readers' of Isaiah, if we are to be the readers it 'implies',[96] we need to adopt the position of people interested in religion, ethics, and theology. In this connection, an alternative to speaking in terms of canonical interpretation is to speak in terms of theological interpretation, though this term, too, has many different meanings, and it, too, is inclined to suggest something confessional, something important for people who reckon that the book of Isaiah can tell them what to believe. Since the rise of biblical criticism, commentators have been wary of theological readings of the text. But stating the text's own theology is part of exegesis, especially if theology is important to it. While every text has

[95] Cf. Roy F. Melugin's argument in 'Isaiah in the Worshipping Community', in M. P. Graham, R. R. Marrs, and S. L. McKenzie (eds.), *Worship and the Hebrew Bible* (J. T. Willis Festschrift; Sheffield: Sheffield Academic Press, 1999), pp. 244-64.

[96] The phrase 'competent readers' comes from Jonathan Culler; see, e.g., *Structuralist Poetics* (London: Routledge; Ithaca: Cornell University Press, 1975). The phrase 'implied reader' comes from Wolfgang Iser, *The Implied Reader* (Baltimore: The Johns Hopkins University Press, 1978).

an implicit theology and a theological reading of any text (we may again instance Shakespeare) could be apposite, in biblical texts questions about God are near the centre of its agenda.

While the book of Isaiah occasionally refers explicitly to historical figures and events, because at these points its questions about religion, ethics, and theology are formulated in various kinds of connection with such figures, even here it is those questions that are its concern and those questions that competent readers of the book will focus on. Isaiah 56–66 in particular refers to no such figures and events, and this omission is significant both as part of the explanation for the difficulty involved in interpreting it by reference to history and also as a clue to its actual concern. Our problem in the study of Isaiah 56–66 is that our study is not historical or critical. If our study were historical it would work with the nature of the document it seeks to study. If it were critical it would analyse and critique its own presuppositions and assumptions.

The notion of theological reading raises another question that arises out of the fact that Isaiah 56–66 is (part of) a document with religious significance for the people who brought it into being and needs to be read in the light of its nature as a religious document. In Isaiah 58, for instance, one of 'the two most important critical issues' is 'the exact nature of the distinction between genuine and nongenuine piety'.[97] Now one commentator spells out this distinction by declaring that genuine religion is that which is of the heart,[98] another by describing it as that which takes action to set people free.[99] This difference of interpretation instances the way we easily read texts in the light of perspectives from outside without realizing that we are doing so—more conservative or more liberal ones. One reason for the importance of a critical approach to interpretative questions is the need to critique commentators' contrasting views.

A theological reading can mean consciously bringing a perspective from outside. Presupposing that God is real and that the text says something true about God fosters engagement with the text; it recognizes that the text invites a religious and theological response. But the actual text may not be the object of this engagement. One influential form of theological interpretation argues that 'the Nicene tradition…provides the proper basis for the interpretation of the Bible as Christian Scripture…, the lens through which to view the heterogeneity and particularity of the biblical texts'.[100] There are a number of problems with this view. It clashes with the view of the churches that formulated apostolic or Nicene doctrine, in that they assumed that Scripture needed to interpret them

[97] Childs, *Isaiah*, p. 476. The other is the relation of vv. 13-14 to what precedes.

[98] So Oswalt, *The Book of Isaiah Chapters 40–66*, p. 494.

[99] So Westermann, *Jesaja Kapitel 40–66*, p. 268 (ET pp. 337).

[100] R. R. Reno, in Matthew Levering, *Ezra & Nehemiah* (Grand Rapids: Brazos, 2007), p. 12.

rather than the other way around. It assumes that apostolic and Nicene tradition has an absolute authority rather than being a particular cultural embodiment of Christian faith. And it gives up the task of discovering the theological freight of the text itself.

From a different perspective, Blenkinsopp comments that 'for both Childs and Seitz, it seems to be *theologically* necessary for biblical books to be coherent, well thought-out units so that if it could be shown that a biblical book such as Isaiah is a compilation of disparate materials, *mixtum compositum*...it would be impossible to extract theological meanings, or at least the proper canonical meaning, from its components'.[101] We have noted comments by Childs that suggest he does not take this view;[102] likewise in his comments on Isaiah Seitz has questioned the assumption that 'theological coherence involves a single point of view'.[103] Ironically, Blenkinsopp can give the impression that he takes this view; at least he does not seek to extract theological or canonical meanings from these components.

There is a further irony that historical-critical readers themselves do bring theological perspectives from outside to their reading of the text. This works in the favour of Isaiah 56–66 in the sense that such readers prefer the attitude to outsiders expressed in 56.3-8 to the one expressed in Deuteronomy or Ezra–Nehemiah,[104] but against Isaiah 56–66 when the readers come to a passage such as 63.1-6 or 66.24. With regard to the last of these, commentators commonly assume the activity of the Isaianic equivalent to 'that uncomplaining old scapegoat, the ecclesiastical redactor' who in connection with John's Gospel gets 'saddled with most of the passages in the Gospel that for one reason or another modern interpreters find theologically reprehensible'.[105] John Barton has commented that biblical criticism is practised by people who love their texts; otherwise they would not bother.[106] It is not always evident from the work of critics that this is so, and a critic might offer as the reasonable rationale for their work that a book such as Isaiah is a significant cultural artifact, something with a similar status as Plato or Shakespeare, whose influence one might see as not always beneficent and whose authority one might want to test or undermine. But commentators' positive or negative attitude to material can seem simply to reflect the unargued assumptions of modern Western readers.

[101] *Isaiah 56–66*, p. 29, referring to Childs, *Isaiah*, Seitz, 'The Book of Isaiah 40–66', and Lau, *Schriftgelehrte Prophetie in Jes 56–66*, p. 5.

[102] See his comments on the 'retention of elements of tension within the canonical text' earlier in this section.

[103] *Word without End*, p. 120.

[104] See, e.g., Westermann, *Jesaja Kapitel 40–66*, pp. 248-51 (ET pp. 311-14).

[105] John Ashton, *Understanding the Fourth Gospel* (Oxford: Oxford University Press, 1991), p. 513.

[106] See *The Nature of Biblical Criticism*, p. 89.

It would be inappropriate to suggest that readers must ultimately agree with a text that they read, but readers owe texts the ethical commitment of seeking to understand them, in their own terms and not merely within our own framework, before we disagree with them. Likewise it would be inappropriate to suggest that it is possible to come to texts with a mind that resembles a blank slate; in this sense an objective reading of texts is impossible. But reading texts on their own terms, in a way that seeks to get under the skin of their author or their community, is worth more of a try than commentators may be inclined to give it.

The reading strategy I wish to adopt seeks to read with the grain of the material in the sense that it reads the text as it is. This need not imply that one agrees with what one finds (though in the interests of full disclosure I acknowledge that I intend to do so). It does imply that one wants to discover what by their nature the chapters say and what sense the community that affirmed them might have made of them in the light of their setting among other works that they affirmed. While reading with the grain may be 'harnessed to an ideologically conservative program of reaffirming classical texts and values',[107] reading against the grain may simply be harnessed to another set of values,[108] and critical study involves being as wary about absolutizing the values one already affirms as one is about absolutizing a different set. It is at least wise initially to read closely with the grain.[109] Critical study has to be self-critical, and it is for this reason that it involves foreswearing reading strategies that clash with the nature of the material, and adopting reading strategies that correspond to it.

4. *A Poetic Reading*

In modern Hebrew and English Bibles, most of Isaiah 56–66 is printed as poetry, but some of the closing verses and a few others are printed as prose. Yet there is difference between editions and translations over distinguishing poetry and prose. JPSV and Thomas's edition in *Biblia hebraica stuttgartensia* lay out 66.22-24 as verse, TNIV as prose, while NRSV lays out just 66.22-23 as verse and 66.24 as prose. These differences may reflect the fact that distinguishing between prose and verse is a Western practice, going back to Hellenistic writers[110] but then encouraged

[107] George Aichele *et al.*, *The Postmodern Bible* (New Haven: Yale University Press, 1995), p. 166.

[108] For an example, see Katharine Doob Sakenfeld's comments on the work of Archie C. C. Lee (see section 5 of this Introduction, 'A Postcolonial Reading').

[109] Cf. Gray, *Rhetoric and Social Justice in Isaiah*, p. 10. Aichele (*The Postmodern Bible*, p. 166) indeed notes that with-the-grain reading needs to be 'radically self-reflexive'.

[110] Jed D. Wyrick notes that they distinguish two categories of authors, poets (*poiētai*) and prose writers (*sungrapheis*): see *The Ascension of Authorship* (Cambridge, MA: Harvard University Press, 2004), p. 17.

by the invention of the printing press. Further, the two are ideal types; the distinction between them is real, but fuzzy. Poetry can be prosaic and prose can be poetic. Hortatory sentences and poetic prophecies occupy different places on a spectrum that includes both prose and verse. It can therefore be a judgment call whether one sees particular units or lines as one or the other.[111]

As ideal types, one could say that Old Testament prose regularly incorporates longer and more complex sentences, uses more straightforward and literal description, and provides more aids to understanding such as the relative particle *ʾăšer*, suffixes, and the object marker *ʾet*. Poetry makes more use of imagery such as simile, metaphor and symbol, which enable it to say things that cannot be said by means of straightforward statements, are indispensable to our being able to make statements about God, and add to the communicative depth of its statements. It omits many of those syntactical and grammatical aids to understanding, and this omission contributes to its being characterized by greater denseness, a capacity to use fewer words yet to say more than prose. It makes less use of *w*-consecutive than prose, and thus often leaves the relationship between clauses less clear. Whereas prose seeks to make things as easy as possible for its listeners and appeals to the left side of the brain, poetry focuses more on engaging its audience and making it think and feel, and it appeals to the right side of the brain. It has to be read slowly and attentively, and it involves its readers in discerning its meaning and significance at several levels and not just the analytical.

English poetry and Old Testament poetry share the characteristics of denseness and the use of imagery. Old Testament poetry has a third key characteristic that is more distinctive. It commonly expresses itself in units or lines that are shorter than regular prose sentences, comprising about six words, and that divide roughly into two halves in which the second repeats, intensifies, clarifies, contrasts with, or simply completes the first. These two-part lines or bicola often constitute complete sentences, though it is also possible for one or more lines to be syntactically subordinate to a preceding or following line. While 'parallelism' is not a very accurate term to describe the interrelationship of the two-part lines that characterize Old Testament poetry, it is a useful shorthand expression.[112] Parallelism compares and links with the device of hendiadys, in which two terms form a single compound expression. An example is the expression *mišpāṭ ûṣᵉdāqâ* or *ṣᵉdāqâ ûmišpāṭ*, conventionally 'justice and righteousness'. Parallelism also compares with the way larger textual units can form chiasms in which an earlier and a later element within a composition form a pair. Like imagery, parallelism and hendiadys can

[111] See further the commentary on 56.1-8 below.

[112] See further James Kugel, *The Idea of Biblical Poetry* (New Haven: Yale University Press, 1981).

feature in prose, but they find their natural home in the two-part lines that characterize Old Testament poetry. Similarly, chiasms appear in prose, but find their natural home in poetry.

Parallelism features in the opening verse of Isaiah 56–66:

> Guard *mišpāṭ*, act in *ṣᵉdāqâ*,
> Because my *yᵉšûʿâ* is near to coming, my *ṣᵉdāqâ* to appearing. (Isa 56.1)

Each of these lines is a bicolon (2-2 and 3-2 in MT).[113] Each is characterized by parallelism. The combination of the terms *mišpāṭ* and *ṣᵉdāqâ* in the first line recurs in 58.2; 59.4, 9, 14. The fact that these two nouns appearing in parallel cola can elsewhere form a hendiadys encourages us to take them as a compound expression, which serves to articulate a complex theological and ethical idea. *Mišpāṭ* suggests the making of decisions by the exercise of legitimate power. *Ṣᵉdāqâ* suggests people doing right by one another in light of the relationships between them; it connotes doing the right thing by people. I thus translate the two words by words such as 'government' and 'faithfulness'. The compound expression associates power with right relationships in the community. Utilized in the context of poetic parallelism, it illustrates how poetic form facilitates the expression of compound theological ideas. If it is an overstatement to see hendiadys as an implicitly poetic device, the way parallelism encourages the separation of the elements in the hendiadys highlights the separate yet related nature of the two expressions.

The second line in 56.1 points to the related link between *yᵉšûʿâ* and *ṣᵉdāqâ*, deliverance and faithfulness (cf. 59.16, 17; 61.10; 62.1; 63.1) and thus offers another instance of parallelism's capacity to express the binary relationship of ideas. Faithfulness suggests the basis for Yhwh's acts, which lies in Yhwh's relationship with Israel; deliverance suggests the nature of the action.

The interrelationship of the two lines in 56.1 points to a further feature of poetry. While *ṣᵉdāqâ* has similar meaning each time, it has different reference; the first line alludes to human *ṣᵉdāqâ*, the second to divine *ṣᵉdāqâ*. What is the relationship between these two commitments to *ṣᵉdāqâ*, God's and ours? This relationship is mysterious and impossible to articulate in unambiguous, univocal prose. The poetry does not make clear which understanding is correct, which is not a weakness of thinking but a strength.[114]

In 57.15, Yhwh goes on to declare,

> I dwell on high and holy, and with the crushed and low in spirit.

[113] I treat the opening 'Yhwh has said this' as extra-metrical.

[114] See further the comments on the verse in section 6 of this Introduction, 'An Isaianic Reading'.

On one hand, the transcendent God dwells in a heavenly realm, as a king lives in a palace to which ordinary people do not have access. On the other hand, whereas the king may not make a habit of visiting people in their ordinary homes in the city, Yhwh does associate with ordinary people, especially with people who are hurt. Parallelism compares with and facilitates the expression of Yhwh's two-sided nature as both holy and involved. Perhaps parallelism has intrinsic theological significance: the very existence of parallelism points to the binary (not dualistic) nature of reality (e.g. divine and human, creator and creation, corporate and individual).

Subsequently, the prophet testifies to a commission,

> To proclaim the year of acceptance by Yhwh, the day of redress by our God. (61.2)

Whereas 49.8 referred to 'a time of acceptance' and 'a day of deliverance', in 61.2 'deliverance' becomes 'redress'. The two terms 'acceptance' and 'redress' recognize the twofold significance of Yhwh's act. The line's parallelism enables its cola to offer two ways of describing the same occasion: a year becomes a day, Yhwh becomes our God, and acceptance becomes redress. Yhwh later similarly declares,

> A day of redress was in my mind, my year of restoration had come. (63.4)

Here 'day of redress' is balanced by 'year of restoration', the 'negative' and 'positive' phrases appearing in the reverse order compared with 61.2.

The phrase 'day of redress' recalls the expression 'day of Yhwh'. Traditionally people had expected Yhwh's day to be an occasion when they would experience blessing and when redress would be exacted of their enemies; it is the expectation that Amos 5.18-20 subverts. Isaiah 61.2 and 64.8 reverse the expectation again, reaffirming the traditional assumption about the day. As 47.3 has promised God's redress on Babylon, and as Jesus will speak of God's redress on his people's adversaries, and also on the people itself (Lk 18.7-8; 21.22), so 61.2 and 63.4 promise God's redress on Judah's current overlords. Acceptance/restoration and redress are complementary aspects of the meaning of Yhwh's act. One might compare this with the way the Old Testament sees the dominant side of Yhwh's moral character as love and mercy; while wrath and a willingness to exact judgment are also part of that character, they are less central to it.

As well as facilitating expression of the binary aspects of reality, parallelism facilitates expression of the more complex nature of other key theological matters. In 58.1 Yhwh bids the prophet,

> Tell my people about their rebellion, the household of Jacob about their offences.

Isaiah 59.12 talks about waywardness as well as about rebellion and offence. These three terms have a prominent place in the range of the Old Testament's expressions for sin. Yet formulating the point in that way implies that there is something that we can adequately term 'sin'. While it is convenient to have a summarizing expression of this kind, the Old Testament does not imply the view that one term such as 'sin' can adequately convey the nature of the reality to which it refers. It rather uses a variety of terms such as rebellion, offence, and waywardness to convey this reality. All seem to have started off life as metaphors from everyday life (even if Old Testament writers have forgotten the metaphorical origin of some of them)—hence my translating *ḥaṭṭāʾt* 'offence' rather than 'sin'. In the *Symbolism of Evil*,[115] Paul Ricoeur sees defilement, sin, and guilt as the primary symbols of evil; in *The Conflict of Interpretations* he speaks of shame in these terms.[116] It is doubtful whether the Old Testament suggests that there are primary symbols of evil, given that it has a broader range of images for evil without implying that one is primary, though it is true of this range of images that 'symbol gives rise to thought'.[117] All help us articulate conceptually the nature of evil or sin.

Each of the images constitutes a compressed story, as is characteristic of images. For convenience, one can express them as similes. Sin is like rebelling against a superior authority (*pāšaʿ*), like turning one's back on a relationship (*šûb*), like betraying a friendship (*bāgad*), like getting dirty (*ṭāmēʾ*), like wandering off the road (*ʿāwôn*), like transgressing a law (*ʿābar*), like failing to achieve something one should have achieved and thus offending someone (*ḥāṭāʾ*), like trespassing on someone's rights or property or honour (*māʿal*). Within Isaiah 56–66, prominence attaches to sin as rebellion (57.4; 58.1; 59.12, 13 20; 66.24), sin as offence (58.1; 59.2, 12; 64.5 [4]; 65.20), and sin as wandering off the road (57.17; 59.2, 3, 12; 64.6, 7, 9 [5, 6, 8]; 65.7). Sin as turning away and sin as getting dirty occur once (57.17; 64.6 [5]). The chapters do not refer to sin as betrayal, as transgression, or as trespassing on someone's rights.

An adequate grasp of the significance of human wrongdoing requires the use of a variety of images. Each encapsulates an aspect of its significance; further, the body of images acts as a constraint on the narrowness of each individual image and guards against inappropriate inference from an individual image. In the parallelisms in Isaiah 56–66, then, rebellion and offence are juxtaposed in 58.1 (also in parallel lines in 59.2), rebellion, offence, and waywardness in 59.12a, rebellion and waywardness in 59.12b. Poetic parallelism encourages the juxtaposition of such images, enriches the prophet's statements, and safeguards against narrowness or the inference that theological statements are univocal, analytic, and conceptual.

[115] New York: Harper, 1967; reprinted Boston: Beacon, 1969. See pp. 1-157.

[116] Evanston: Northwestern University Press, 1974. See p. 289.

[117] *The Conflict of Interpretations*, p. 288; *The Symbolism of Evil*, p. 347.

One significance of metaphor is to suggest points of connection between things. Isaiah 60.1-3 urges,

> Get up, be alight, because your light has come; Yhwh's splendour has shone forth upon you.
> Because there: darkness will cover the earth, pitch dark the peoples,
> But upon you Yhwh will shine forth, his splendour will appear upon you.
> Nations will walk to your light, kings to your shining brightness.

Prosaically put, at present Judah and other peoples live under the oppressive domination of an imperial power, but God intends to bless and restore Jerusalem; its task and privilege is to let that blessing and restoration be seen by the other peoples so as to draw them to Jerusalem to share in the blessing and restoration. Working with the image of light and darkness not only makes the prophet's message express that prospect with greater rhetorical force. It fulfills a theological function by suggesting a link between the nations' calamity, Yhwh's blessing, Jerusalem's vocation, and the nations' response. Whereas darkness suggests the gloom of defeat, loss, oppression, and disaster, light suggests deliverance, healing, restoration, and blessing. The city will be able to shine out its light because its light will have dawned upon it. The opening verse's second colon heightens and sharpens the point of the first. 'Yhwh's splendour' suggestively heightens 'your light'. The light that dawns will be no ordinary light but something supernaturally bright, because it is not natural light but divine light. The city will mirror Yhwh's own shining brilliance. Its restoration will not be something that can be humanly generated but something that issues from and reflects divine action. The city's being able to 'lighten up' will be a response to light having shone out on it. A paronomasia is involved,[118] and the paronomasia is not simply a literary device; it implies a theological point.

Isaiah 60 goes on to illustrate how the prevalence of metaphor in prophetic poetry also relates to the fact that prophecy often speaks about the ultimate future. By the ultimate future I mean not so much an imminent historical event such as the fall of Jerusalem that was imminent in the time of Jeremiah and Ezekiel (though they also use metaphor to convey its significance, not least the way it anticipates the ultimate future) but the coming consummation of God's purpose, which may or may not be imminent, but which either way may be less amenable to literal description.[119]

Prophecies commonly stand somewhere on a line between promising or warning of a concrete event whose fulfillment can be seen on the earthly plane (see, e.g., Jer 28.16-17) and promising or warning of an event whose fulfillment requires or presupposes the introduction of a new

[118] Cf. Lau, *Schriftgelehrte Prophetie in Jes 56–66*, p. 27.

[119] See the comments on 'eschatology' in the 'Conclusion' to the commentary on Isaiah 60 and on Isaiah 66.17-24.

world order, such as has not yet come about even two and a half millennia after the prophet's day (see, e.g., Rev 21). Isaiah 40–55 and Isaiah 60–62 stand on that line, respectively nearer the former and the latter end. Isaiah 60 speaks of the actual city of Jerusalem and its actual temple, of actual Judahite exiles and contemporary peoples, but describes events in terms that are figurative and larger than life. The rebuilding of temple and city and the return of many exiles form a partial fulfillment of its promises, but the figurative and larger-than-life aspect to the promises is one reason why they stand open to reformulation in later contexts, as still-instructive statements of God's ultimate intent. Isaiah 60 thus resembles Ezekiel 40–48 (prose, but not prosaic) in being imaginative and visionary without this characteristic implying that the prophets have no hopes or expectations regarding something to happen in the community's experience. Poetry makes it possible to describe the indescribable. The Bible thus characteristically speaks poetically when speaking of the Beginning (creation) as well as the End (it is failure to recognize that Genesis 1, though formally prose, is poetry-like that leads to a mistaken literalism in approaching the Bible's first creation account).[120]

Christian lectionaries set the beginning of Isaiah 60 for Epiphany and thus link the chapter with the story of eastern sages bringing Jesus gold, incense, and myrrh (Matt 2.1-12). While the recurrence of reference to gold and incense constitutes a formal link between the two passages, there is insufficient correspondence between prophecy and event to make it possible to see Isaiah 60 as a 'prediction' of which that event is the 'fulfillment'. The New Testament itself does not relate the prophecy and the event; it rather links the sages' coming with Micah 5.1-3 [2-4]. Yet the subsequent explicit Christian juxtaposing of Isaiah 60 and Matthew 2 does better justice to the nature of Isaiah 60 than does a reading that envisages Isaiah 60 as essentially describing the way a prophet expects political events to unfold at the end of the sixth century or in the fifth. The chapter is poetic, lyrical, and hyperbolic in its language, not prosaic. It is typical of Isaiah 56–66 in not relating its promises to specific political contexts or events, though it links with a particular historical context in the sense that it emerges from some such context and reflects it. But both the attempt to see it as envisaging fulfillment in a specific imminent context and the understanding of it as a prediction of a particular event six centuries later miss the significance of its poetic nature. It is questionable whether establishing its precise historical context 'does very much at all to explain its character and intention'.[121]

[120] I here take up a comment by Patrick D. Miller at the session during the Society of Biblical Literature 2010 Annual Meeting at Atlanta, Georgia, at which I read the paper on 'Poetry and Theology in Isaiah 56–66' referred to at the beginning of this Introduction.

[121] Ronald E. Clements, '"Arise, Shine; for Your Light Has Come"', in Broyles and Evans (ed.), *Writing and Reading the Scroll of Isaiah*, I, pp. 441-54 (446).

Its character and intention do relate to the broad context of the Second Temple period rather than the period of the exile or the monarchy or an earlier time. Patrick D. Miller argues that decontextualization is a characteristic feature of biblical poetry, as of poetry in general. 'Poetry in nearly all instances stands in some fashion on its own.'[122] With regard to the Old Testament, while this comment is appropriate to the Psalms and the Wisdom Books, it does not seem to apply to biblical poetry generally, and specifically to the Prophets. Within Isaiah, the prose material does not seem more overtly contextual than the poetic material; indeed, a prose passage such as 30.19-26 is harder to position contextually than the poetic material earlier in that chapter. The point applies more broadly to Jeremiah. Isaiah 56–66 is indeed the least overtly contextual of the major units in the book of Isaiah in the sense that it makes no reference to concrete historical events or people. But this fact links with the theological message reflected in its concentric structure. It sees the tension between promise and challenge as a dominant feature of the relationship between God and Israel in the period following that to which Isaiah 40–55 overtly belongs, when Cyrus was on his way to throwing down the Babylonian Empire and making it possible for Judahites in Babylon to go home. The partial decontextualization of the poetry of Isaiah 56–66 links with the theological significance of the period; decontextualization is not inherent in biblical poetry. 'We cannot generalize about the role of propositions, metaphors, or poetry in the Biblical writings as a whole. The issues depend on what genre the writer is using, the purpose of the passage in question, and whether a "closed" or "open" text is under consideration.'[123] Closed texts (ones that invite readers to a particular interpretation) are more likely to derive their significance from contextual considerations; open texts (ones that invite various interpretations on the part of readers) are less likely to do so. Isaiah 60 is not an open text in the way that the Psalms are.

The genius of prose is a capacity to make things clear. The genius of poetry is a capacity to obscure them. Why would prophets want to obscure their statements? Sometimes their delivering of their message is designed as an act of punishment; it utilizes, confirms, and deepens the people's willful stupidity (see Isa 6.9-10, taken up by Jesus in Mark 4.11-12). But in addition, their enigmatic poetic utterances have the potential to make people think and (in combination with their use of imagery) even to get them to yield to their message before they quite understand the nature of this message (as might also be true of Jesus' parables). Poetry attacks the mind not frontally (like prose) but indirectly and subversively.

[122] "The Theological Significance of Biblical Poetry," in Samuel E. Balentine and John Barton (ed.), *Language, Theology, and the Bible* (James Barr Festschrift; Oxford: Oxford University Press, 1994), pp. 213-30 (224); reprinted in Miller, *Israelite Religion and Biblical Theology* (Sheffield: Sheffield Academic Press, 2000), pp. 233-49 (244-45).

[123] Anthony Thiselton, *The Hermeneutics of Doctrine* (Grand Rapids: Eerdmans, 2007), p. 78.

At one level this is a point about rhetoric rather than about theology, but these two are closely related. The use of rhetoric presupposes a theology. This aspect of the use of poetry implies the assumption that the prophets' message will not be welcome and that its hearers will need to be won.[124] That is so whether the prophet is critiquing people who think they are in the right or seeking to encourage people who think there is no hope. Prophetic poetry draws attention to humanity's resistance to God. It presupposes that the people of God are inherently resistant to listening to God's word through a prophet.

Isaiah 56.9-11 speaks of the community's leaders:

> All you animals of the wild, come on and eat, all you animals in the forest!
> Its lookouts are blind, all of them; they do not know.
> All of them are dumb dogs, they cannot bark.
> They are snoozing, bedding down, loving to doze.
> But the dogs—they are mighty in appetite; they do not know 'enough'.
> Those people—they are shepherds who do not know how to be discerning.
> All of them have directed themselves to their own way, each one to his own ill-gotten gain, every last part of him.

With whom is the prophet seeking to communicate? The intended audience might be the leaders themselves, or the people who follow them, or the community as a whole. At one level the answer becomes clearer in the material that follows, in Isaiah 57, where the prophet directly addresses the segment of the community that engages in religious observances that the prophet disdains. Yet the difference in the Prophets between the audience on the stage and the audience in the house may mean that the prophet's own direct audience is the segment of the community that does not engage in such practices. Either way, in 56.9-11 the prophet seeks to get the audience to look at the leadership in a new way, and does so by means of a series of metaphors. Prosaically put, the prophet declares that the community's leaders do not recognize the danger that threatens it and thus do not warn the community, and that they are failing in this respect because of their self-indulgence. The poetic imagery presupposes that the community does not recognize that this is so. The people with whom the prophet identifies do not see it, the other members of the community do not see it, and the leaders themselves do not see it.

Many aspects of a passage such as 56.9–57.13 now raise difficulties of understanding. Our exegetical study often implies we assume that these difficulties would disappear if we possessed better information on the meaning of the passage's words or could gain access to a version of the text that was closer to the original. While this assumption may be

[124] Cf. Yehoshua Gitay's discussion of 'Why Metaphors? A Study of the Texture of Isaiah', in Broyles and Evans (ed.), *Writing and Reading the Scroll of Isaiah*, I, pp. 57-65.

appropriate to a number of the passage's difficulties, other difficulties were likely inherent in the text from the beginning. While some of them may reflect the prophet's unintentional failure to be clear and the use of words and formulation of sentences that were obscure only by accident, others may reflect a deliberate desire to be compressed and dense so as to compel listeners to wrestle with the prophecy in order to come to an understanding. That very process requires listeners to engage with its content in a more self-involving way than is necessary if the prophecy has the immediate clarity that more commonly attaches to prose. At the same time it gives listeners the opportunity to avoid engaging with the prophecy, and thereby to avoid their last state being worse than their first by virtue of the fact that they have had God's message made clear to them and have rejected it. In both respects the significance of using poetry includes its drawing attention to the way the people of God characteristically resist God's message.

In varying ways, then, parallelism, hendiadys, paronomasia, chiasm, imagery, ambiguity, and obscurity in the poetry in Isaiah 56–66 suggest the complexity, depth, interrelatedness, intelligibility, and unacceptability of the ideas that run through the chapters.

5. *A Postcolonial Reading*

Alongside questions about the way the text of Isaiah 56–66 works textually and poetically or rhetorically one can ask about its ideological significance in the sense of whose interests it seeks to serve. We have considered one aspect of this question in asking about the sociology of the community whose views it represents, and seen that it represents a rigorous 'Yhwh-alone' group that is intolerant of people who are more liberal in their attitude to traditional religious practices but more tolerant regarding outsiders who are prepared to commit themselves to Yhwh. It is a group that has little power in the community and thus little scope to enforce acceptance of its commitments.

The oddness of the community's coming to accept these prophecies into the book of Isaiah may reflect the fact that they may have been strikingly useful over against the foreign powers that controlled Judah. Like other parts of the Bible, Isaiah 56–66 is the product of an imperial context, and one might have wondered whether the eventual acceptance of Isaiah as a book implies imperial patronage. Yet the contents of the book (and specifically of Isaiah 56–66) look more like the vision of prophets who seek to bolster the faith and stimulate the imagination of a subaltern people. Mark Gray sees his study of Isaiah with its focus on chapters 1 and 58 as text-based and rhetorical but also as postcolonial and as designed to further a concern with ethics, justice and mission.[125]

[125] *Rhetoric and Social Justice in Isaiah*, pp. 1-18.

Katharine Doob Sakenfeld makes a parallel point about the significance of Isaiah 56–66 in particular. Commenting on a paper that read the chapters in light of the situation of the people of Hong Kong after its return to China in 1997, she notes that this paper made virtually no reference to God but focused on democratization, hybridization, and inclusiveness that can embrace plurality. Yet the chapters themselves speak a great deal about God and about what God desires, so she asks whether the Bible can be used theologically in the consideration of a way forward in a postcolonial situation.[126]

In a study written in South Africa, Wilhelm J. Wessels characterized Nahum as resistance literature, which he compared with anti-apartheid literature.[127] Nahum invites people in Judah to believe that the Assyrian Empire will fall. In the years after it has done so, the actual book of Nahum invites subsequent generations to believe that the same truth applies to the empire of their day, such as Babylon as Assyria's successor. Isaiah 40–55 indeed picks up the promises of Nahum in declaring that Babylon is about to fall (see, e.g., 40.9-11; 52.1, 7-10). The form of the prophecies in Nahum encourages this process by means of the paucity of their specific references to Nineveh or Assyria (modern translations are inclined to add to these references). The paucity of specific references to Babylon in Isaiah 40–55 has the same effect in its context. The entire absence of specific references in Isaiah 56–66 makes the point even more strongly. In the sequence of empires, a pattern in Yhwh's dealings with the world keeps asserting itself.

It is not surprising that Western scholarship has dismissed Nahum as nationalistic. Its declarations about the fate of the empire constitute a threat to the imperial powers to which scholars in Britain and the United States belong. The same dynamics appear in scholarly responses to Isaiah 56–66, where scholars like the 'universalism' of passages such as 56.1-8 but dislike the 'nationalism' of passages such as chapter 60. They especially dislike the bloodthirsty nature of the visions in chapter 59 and 63.1-6.[128]

In broad terms, one could describe Judah as a colonial entity for the entirety of its life in Old Testament times. It was always under some form of control by a bigger power. Only during one period was Israel something like an imperial power, according to the Old Testament story, the time of David and Solomon, and it is not clear that we have any material in the Old Testament from this period that could tell us of the ideological underpinnings or subversions of its position as an empire (I assume there

[126] 'Social Location in the Hebrew Bible and Hong Kong', *Biblical Interpretation* 7 (1999), pp. 186-91 (191), commenting on Lee, 'Returning to China'.

[127] Wilhelm J. Wessels, 'Nahum', *Old Testament Essays* 11 (1998), pp. 615-28.

[128] See, e.g., Paul D. Hanson, 'Third Isaiah: The Theological Legacy of a Struggling Community', in Seitz (ed.), *Reading and Preaching the Book of Isaiah*, pp. 91-103 (99-100).

is no basis for dating J in this period or for thinking that Solomon wrote any wisdom books; possibly there are psalms that come from this time). In the preceding centuries, if we can say anything about Israel's existence it is that Israel was an underling of Egypt and/or of peoples in Canaan. From the eighth century onwards, it was an underling of Assyria, Babylon, Persia, and Greece, until the second century. In the Persian period Judah was more like a colony in a stricter sense. While it did not have a community of people from the imperial centre living in its midst, it was a subordinate part of an empire that projected itself as benign and benevolent and allowed Judah to have some control of internal affairs, but it did not have its own king and it lived under the oversight of a governor responsible to the imperial administration, to which it paid taxes. It lived in Persia's shadow.[129]

Like the rest of Isaiah, and like other prophetic books, Isaiah 56–66 does not urge Judah to rebel against the superpower. While it speaks of violent action that will bring about the downfall of Judah's overlords, this action is explicitly Yhwh's and not that of any human agent, imperial or colonial. Whereas Isaiah 13 has spoken of the Medes bringing destruction upon Babylon, when Isaiah 56–66 speaks of the destruction of 'the nations', it attributes this event to direct action by Yhwh, who is, indeed, aggrieved that there is no would-be next superpower itching to take Persia's place that he can use as he used Assyria, Babylon, and Persia itself (see 59.15b-19; 63.1-6). Whereas a prophet in the 540s had Cyrus to envisage as the means whereby Yhwh's will could be fulfilled, and Yhwh could work by means of him, there is no such power emerging in the period to which Isaiah 56–66 belongs. (For all the references to Yhwh's raising up Assyria, Babylon, or Persia, their emergence is entirely explicable in historical terms; no supernatural intervention was involved. Yhwh usually works via historical processes.)

One could call Isaiah 56–66 quietist in stance. While it does not explicitly stress trust in the manner of Isaiah 1–39, it implies the same stance. The restoring of Jerusalem will come about, but by Yhwh's action. Nahum does not urge rebellion on Judah, but does believe that a process of conscientization or consciousness-raising needs to happen, whereby the colonized people can cut the imperial power down in its thinking, pending the day when Yhwh cuts it down politically. Isaiah 56–66 has a similar aim. All it does is encourage hope and encourage prayer, but these are frightening actions.

The chapters' nature as resistance literature is not in tension with their being poetic, lyrical, and hyperbolic in their language. The central chapters of Isaiah 56–66, and especially chapter 60, illustrate how (again like Nahum) poetic form contributes to encouragement and consciousness-raising. Powerful poetry often emerges from oppressed societies.

[129] Cf. the title of Berquist's *Judaism in Persia's Shadow*.

The imagery and hyperbole of the chapters in describing the transformation of Jerusalem and the reversal of positions between its people and its overlords creates before people's imagination a different world from the one people currently experience and promises that this world will become a reality. The prophet 'does not consider Israel the heir of the pagan world empire' but implicitly 'rejects empire, in the sense of rule of one nation over another.... There will be no Israelite empire.'[130] There will be a reversal of the situation whereby 'the nations'—which in the Prophets commonly denotes the superpower of the day—lord themselves over Judah, exile its people, and arrogate its resources, but it is the city of Jerusalem as the location of Yhwh's temple that the empire will come to serve.

In late sixth and fifth centuries, it would again be easy for Judah to believe that Yhwh had forgotten it and was not after all the kind of faithful God who put things right in the world. Isaiah 56–66 declares that Yhwh is that God. Unlike Nahum, this prophecy does not see Judah's imperial overlord as a great oppressor. Perhaps it recognizes the ambiguity of its overlord, in keeping with that overlord's shrewd policy. According to Ezra–Nehemiah, people in Judah did complain about the crippling tax burdens imposed by the imperial authorities, but it was those same imperial authorities that facilitated the return of Judahites to Jerusalem, the rebuilding of the temple, the mission of Ezra, and the mission of Nehemiah, and also supported Judah's independence over against surrounding provinces of the Persian Empire. The imperial policy of divide and rule and of playing both good cop and bad cop worked well.

The vision of the empire's future in Isaiah 56–66 thus has a different profile from that in Isaiah 1–55 or other Prophets. In Isaiah 56–66 'The empire writes back' as it does in Nahum, but not so much 'with a vengeance' (the title of an article by Salman Rushdie in the London *Times*, July 3, 1982), as it does in Nahum. As is the case in Nahum, further, Isaiah 56–66 does not write back 'to the centre' (as an adapted version of the phrase goes on), like an author such as Rushdie writing for British consumption. It writes for its own community. The chapters presuppose the classic colonial experiences of powerlessness and the exaction of resources, and promise that these experiences will not go on forever. They resist any pressure to use the empire's language (contrast Isa 36.11!—and Ezra?). As far as Persia is concerned, the province centring on Jerusalem is called Yehud, the name that usually appears on coins from the period[131] as well as in the Aramaic of Daniel and Ezra, and also in Western scholarly study,[132] which—ironically—often shares criticism's

[130] Kaufmann, *The Babylonian Captivity and Deutero-Isaiah*, p. 189.

[131] See, e.g., Charles E. Carter, *The Emergence of Yehud in the Persian Period* (Sheffield: Sheffield Academic Press, 1999), pp. 142, 268-69.

[132] See, e.g., Diana V. Edelman and Ehud Ben Zvi (eds.), *The Production of Prophecy: Constructing Prophecy and Prophets in Yehud* (London: Equinox, 2009); Jeremiah W. Cataldo, *A Theocratic Yehud?* (New York: T&T Clark International, 2009).

instinct to 'master' and 'imperialize' rather than respecting otherness[133] even when it is being postcolonial. Isaiah 56–66 refers once to Judah, eleven times to Jerusalem, never to Yehud. The chapters hold onto the Judahites' own way of looking at Judah and Jerusalem.

As well as containing no encouragement to rebellion, the chapters contain no exhortation to bring about the transformation of the city themselves; they thus differ in their stance from Haggai and Nehemiah. They simply promise that what must have seemed impossible will become actual. In the context of a postcolonial reading of the chapters, particular significance attaches to the similarities we have noted between the portrayal of Jerusalem's restoration and the reliefs in the palace that Darius I began to build at his new capital, Persepolis, in the last decades of the sixth century, which portray peoples bringing tribute to the king.[134] Whereas Judah had to pay tribute to the king of Persia, the prophet declares that Persia is going to be paying tribute to Yhwh. It is an aspect of the great reversal whereby the superpower and its kings turn from contempt to obeisance.

Here and in other chapters, Isaiah 56–66 recognizes the tensions in perspective between different groups within the colonial entity.[135] In the twenty-first century world, many people from former colonies all over the world (including many of their most able) migrate to North America and Europe and thus leave their home countries without the resources they could have contributed to these countries' development. In addition, many of these postcolonial countries are riven by strife, partly issuing from divisions that go back to the work of the imperial powers that created artificial nations out of diverse groups. Isaiah 56–66 recognizes parallel realities. Many (most?) exiles from Judah had not seized the opportunity to return to this backwater of the empire. Isaiah 60–62 promises that they will do so. Judah is riven by strife between people with different religious commitments; Isaiah 56–59 and 65–66 promises not that they will come to live in peace but that the situation will not continue. This religious perspective links with another aspect of the vision of a restored Jerusalem that we have noted, that resources come to the city not simply to beautify it as a capital but to resource the worship of its temple, the worship of the true God (60.7, 13).

In the central chapter of the central complex of chapters in Isaiah 56–66, the prophet declares himself to be someone 'anointed' by Yhwh. It is an unexpected expression, because anointing is a rite applied to kings and priests as holders of an office. Being a prophet is not an office, and prophets were not anointed. There were special reasons for the testing of this rule in 1 Kings 19.16 (Elijah is to have an official successor, and the

[133] Cf. Anthony C. Thiselton, *Thiselton on Hermeneutics* (Grand Rapids: Eerdmans, 2006), e.g. p. 8.

[134] See Strawn's paper noted in section 1 of this Introduction.

[135] Cf. Lee's comments in 'Returning to China' from a Hong Kong perspective.

language of anointing is here used metaphorically—1 Kings does not speak of Elijah actually anointing Elisha), and there are special reasons for its testing here. The last anointed king was Cyrus (45.1), so for the prophet to claim an anointing constitutes a 'strong rereading'[136] of the commendation of Cyrus in Isaiah 40–55. This prophet has a part to play in the fulfilling of the role destined for the Persian deliverer who has become the Persian overlord. The description of Yhwh's servant as destined for spectacular anointing, in 52.14,[137] was perhaps the previous strong rereading of 45.1, and possibly Isaiah 61 also sees the prophet in light of that vision.

The prophet is commissioned to bring good news to people who are afflicted, broken in spirit, captives, and prisoners, to people who mourn Zion. The last phrase is likely an objective genitive not a partitive genitive. It refers not to the people who mourn in Zion (as if there were some who did not) but to the Jerusalem community as a whole that mourns the state of its city. It promises that they will have reason for joy, and perhaps that they will be able to take up the work of rebuilding the city. The passage is ambiguous about whether they are the people who will do the building or whether it is simply the case that some people will—the prophecy earlier envisaged foreigners doing so (60.10). The significant point is that the work will be done. Once again there is a link with Cyrus, who was earlier the person destined to do the work (45.13).

In the decades and centuries that followed, the people of Yhwh did not see these promises much more fulfilled than they had been through the work of Cyrus, which was one reason why it was possible for Jesus to take up chapter 61, a favourite passage in his day. Pre-critical Christian commentaries naturally assume that Isaiah 61 is a prophecy of the Messiah; indeed, Jürgen Moltmann declares that here 'Trito Isaiah, finally, sees the coming messiah as quintessential bearer of the Spirit'.[138] Jesus indeed tells the people in the Nazareth synagogue that 'today this scripture is fulfilled in your ears'. But his statement is more suggestive and allusive than is often assumed. 'Fulfilled' is πληρόω, which is not a kind of technical term like the English word 'fulfill' but the ordinary Greek word for 'fill'. While 'filling' a passage of Scripture might mean fulfilling it, it might also imply something like filling it out. The use of πληρόω need not imply that the passage in question was a prediction or promise with a one-to-one relationship to a subsequent event. Indeed, what Jesus is doing with Isaiah 61 is something not unlike what Isaiah 61 was doing with passages from Isaiah 40–55. He is using scriptural material to interpret his own significance and to make a claim for that

136 Harold Bloom's term in *The Anxiety of Influence* (Oxford: Oxford University Press, revised edn, 1997).

137 See Goldingay and Payne, *Isaiah 40–55*, and Goldingay, *The Message of Isaiah 40–55*, on the passage.

138 *Der Geist des Lebens* (Munich: Kaiser, 1991), pp. 66-67; ET *The Spirit of Life* (Minneapolis: Fortress, 1992), p. 53.

significance, at least as much as using his own significance to interpret Isaiah 61.

Jesus' ministry did not result in the fulfillment of these promises in Isaiah 60–62, and liberty of the kind that the prophet envisaged has no more been enjoyed by the church than it has been enjoyed by Israel. On the other hand, it is not the case that nothing of this kind took place in Second Temple Judaism and then during Jesus' ministry and in the life of the church. Here again we see the pattern whereby the proclamations of prophets do not find complete fulfillment but do find some fulfillment. Like other prophecies, Isaiah 61 represents a re-expression of God's ultimate purpose for Israel and for the world, for which the Judahites of the prophet's day could expect to see some fulfillment (as they did), but of which they might not be surprised to find they did not see the complete fulfillment.

Reading Isaiah 56–66 in the light of Jesus thus illumines some aspects of the chapters, but encourages us to ignore many aspects of their inherent theological significance. A postcolonial reading brings out theological significance in the chapters that we might otherwise not note. It suggests insight on the relationship of colonial peoples to the imperial centre and adds to the considerable material in the Old Testament that offers illumination on God's attitude to superpowers, a question that could have been of crucial importance to peoples such as Britain and the United States, but that Christian interpretation has missed.

6. *An Isaianic Reading*

There is another framework within which one might formulate questions about whether Isaiah 56–66 is a work.[139] The scholarly world currently recognizes that Isaiah 56–66 needs to be understood in relation to the rest of the book of Isaiah. Fervent redaction-critics such as Steck emphasize that the chapters' development is as an aspect of the redaction of the book as a whole and that Isaiah 56–66 came into being as part of the process that brought Isaiah 1–55 into being; it never existed as a self-standing collection. Jacob Stromberg suggests that the person behind Isaiah 56–66 was the very person who brought into being the book of Isaiah as we know it.[140]

Whether or not that is so, there is no such thing as 'the book of Trito-Isaiah', as these chapters are sometimes called.[141] Even if all eleven chapters come from a single author, they are not a book but part of a

[139] See the opening of section 3 of this Introduction.

[140] See *Isaiah after Exile*, summarized in *An Introduction to the Study of Isaiah*, pp. 48-53.

[141] E.g. Westermann, *Das Buch Jesaja Kap. 40–66*, p. 245 (ET p. 306); cf. Pauritsch, *Die neue Gemeinde*; Koenen, *Ethik und Eschatologie im Tritojesajabuch*.

book. Within this book, any individual prophecy does have a series of diachronic contexts for its interpretation: the prophet's life and ministry, the life of the community it addressed, the redactional layer to which it belongs, the major unit where it comes to appear, and the composition of the eventual book of Isaiah. But it also has a series of synchronic contexts: what immediately precedes and follows it, the major unit of which it is part, and the entire book. The formal nature of Isaiah 56–66 as part of a larger whole is complemented by the more substantial point that it often takes up motifs, issues, and phrases from Isaiah 1–55. The importance of this link should not be exaggerated; like Isaiah 40–55, Isaiah 56–66 has significant links with other prophetic material, particularly in Jeremiah (see, e.g., 56.3, 9; 57.14-21; 58.12; 60.12; 61.4; 62.4-5; 65.6-9, 15-16, 19, 22).[142] But its being part of the same work as Isaiah 1–55 gives an extra level of significance to its links with those fifty-five chapters. Part of its meaning lies in its taking up, affirming, modifying, supplementing, and ignoring earlier material in the book.

The fact that chapters 40–55 and 56–66 form structured wholes does not exclude their being material that derives from the same prophet. If chapters 56–66 come from the late sixth century, they may come from within the lifetime of the prophet whose work lies behind chapters 40–55. On the assumption that the exilic Isaiah lived in Babylon, I think I recall my first Old Testament mentor, John Austin Baker, saying that the prophet would surely have been among the exiles who returned to Jerusalem after the fall of Babylon if he had had to crawl all the way on broken glass. The prophet could then have continued a ministry in Jerusalem. While the way Isaiah 56–66 takes up material from chapters 40–55 and from Jeremiah may make this unlikely, it cannot be excluded, though it does not seem a possibility worth focusing on in interpreting the chapters.

While there have been practical reasons for dividing up the book of Isaiah in order to write a commentary, it has also implied and encouraged the assumption that its different parts could be considered in relative isolation from each other. In reading Isaiah 56–66 in particular, the location of the chapters at the end of the book called Isaiah has not been prominent in efforts to understand them. Yet notwithstanding its recognizable divisions, the book of Isaiah is a single work. It contains no markers dividing it into five parts, in the manner of the Psalter. Still less does it comprise five separate works in the manner of the Torah as we have it. Nor is its being a single work an accident, as would be implied if Isaiah 40–66 was originally credited to Jeremiah or if its author was someone who also happened to be called Isaiah or if it was added to Isaiah 1–39 because someone had a scroll of a convenient length or if it was so added to give it the authority of the great Isaiah.[143] The links between chapters 40–66 and 1–39 raise fatal difficulties for such theses.

[142] Cf. Sommer, *A Prophet Reads Scripture*.

[143] See Goldingay and Payne, *Isaiah 40–55*, p. 1.

Thus the end of the twentieth century saw renewed awareness of the links between the book's different parts and caused some tempering of the assumption that they could be interpreted as if the other parts did not exist. Isaiah 40–55 takes up from Isaiah 1–39, and in turn Isaiah 56–66 takes up from Isaiah 40–55.[144] It does so in ways that are in turn distinctive to it; there is more frequently a direct textual relationship between the last two parts of the book than there is between the first two parts, and Isaiah 56–66 can be called an exercise in scriptural interpretation.[145] 'The period of the fresh outpouring of the prophetic spirit yields to the studied reapplication of the words of former prophecy',[146] and Isaiah 56–66 constitutes the 'rhetorical culmination' of the book as a whole.[147] When John Oswalt suggests that the phenomena in Isaiah 56–66 point to a need to take a theological approach to this material,[148] he has in mind the relationship between the issues it raises and the issues raised in the rest of the book of Isaiah.

How far does Isaiah 1–55 set the agenda for Isaiah 56–66? In reconsidering the conviction that Isaiah 40–66 could be read quite separately from Isaiah 1–39 and Isaiah 56–66 from Isaiah 40–55, much energy has gone into showing how the different parts of the book interrelate in the sense that lines or phrases or motifs from one part reappear in another part. In a metaphorical sense one might see the later parts of the book (and for that matter much of Isaiah 1–39 itself) as issuing from the work of disciples of Isaiah, though the phenomenon of quotation suggests a textual discipleship rather than the existence of an Isaianic community or a series of personal relationships.[149]

Yet even the idea of a writer quoting from an earlier part of a book or reworking an earlier part, with deliberate precision or with deliberate modification, makes more sense in the age of the codex or of the internet than in the age of the scroll.[150] The passages in Isaiah 56–66 that might

[144] See initially Zillessen, '"Tritojesaja" und Deuterojesaja', who first traced in detail the links between Isaiah 40–55 and Isaiah 56–66, which was a sequel or continuation of those preceding chapters; then Odeberg, *Trito-Isaiah*; Zimmerli, 'Zur Sprache Tritojesajas'; Michel, 'Zur Eigenart Tritojesajas'. All examined quotations and reminiscences, and noted that the nuances or implications of phrase that recurred were often different from those that attached to the earlier use. Elliger (*Deuterojesaja in seinem Verhältnis zu Tritojesaja*) saw more continuity between chapters 40–55 and 56–66. Among commentaries, see especially Beuken, *Jesaja IIIA* and *IIIB*.

[145] 'Schriftgelehrte Auslegung' (Michel, 'Zur Eigenart Tritojesaja', p. 197); cf. Beuken, 'Trito-Jesaja'.

[146] Hanson, *The Dawn of Apocalyptic*, p. 69.

[147] O'Connell, *Concentricity and Continuity*, p. 215 (though he is referring to chapters 54–66).

[148] See Oswalt, *The Book of Isaiah Chapters 40–66*, p. 452.

[149] On this question, see J. Vermeylen, 'L'unité du livre d'Isaïe', in Vermeylen (ed.), *The Book of Isaiah: Le Livre d'Isaïe*, pp. 11-53 (16-17), and his references.

[150] This question needs further study analogous to that surveyed in respect of Paul's reading of Romans in Wagner, *Heralds of the Good News*, pp. 20-28.

evidence something like quotation may more likely be based on memory than issuing from direct poring over a scroll. More important, they comprise only a minute proportion of the book as a whole or of any part of it. Much traditional study of the Prophets assumes that the most important element within them is the prophecies of the Messiah, but even if one grants a messianic understanding of all the passages that have been seen as messianic, these comprise only one or two percent of the prophetic books; they can hardly be the key to understanding the Prophets. The same is true of quotations and allusions in Isaiah 56–66 to the preceding chapters.

We have noted that Isaiah 40–55 take the form of a linear argument, while Isaiah 56–66 take the form of a chiasm. The latter structure with its related statement is the way the section as a whole fulfills its function in connection with chapters 1–55. Rolf Rendtorff made a decisive observation in this connection in suggesting that 56.1 is a key to the composition or formation of the book of Isaiah.[151] Whether or not this is so, the verse is significant in connection with the statement made by the book as we have it.[152]

'Yhwh has said this', the chapters begin, 'observe *mišpāṭ*, do *ṣ*e*dāqâ*, because my *y*e*šû'â* is near to coming, my *ṣ*e*dāqâ* to revealing itself'.[153] The imperative phrases 'observe *mišpāṭ*, do *ṣ*e*dāqâ*' sum up the thrust of Isaiah 1–39. The declaration 'My *y*e*šû'â* is near to coming, my *ṣ*e*dāqâ* to revealing itself' sums up the thrust of Isaiah 40–55.[154] When these two pairs of expressions are juxtaposed, they make more evident a question that is also raised by the material they summarize. What is the relationship between the imperatives and the declarations? Isaiah 1–39 implies that Jerusalem's failure to observe *mišpāṭ* and do *ṣ*e*dāqâ* means it does not experience *y*e*šû'â* and *ṣ*e*dāqâ*. Isaiah 40–55 implies that Yhwh will bring about its *y*e*šû'â* and will manifest *ṣ*e*dāqâ* irrespective of the people's action.[155] At first sight it might seem that interposing the conjunction

[151] See 'Jesaja 56,1 als Schlüssel für die Komposition des Buches Jesaja', in Rendtorff, *Kanon und Theologie* (Neukirchen: Neukirchener, 1991), pp. 172-79; ET 'Isaiah 56:1 as a Key to the Formation of the Book of Isaiah', in Rendtorff, *Canon and Theology* (Minneapolis Fortress, 1993), pp. 181-89.

[152] Compare the comments in section 3 of this Introduction on the place of chapters 60–62 in the redactional development of Isaiah 56–66 over against their place in the eventual form of Isaiah 56–66.

[153] I leave the words *mišpāṭ* and *ṣ*e*dāqâ* untranslated both because we do not have English words to translate them without being misleading and because the effect of the passage depends in part on its making use of two significances of *ṣ*e*dāqâ*. 'Deliverance' is a perfectly adequate translation of *y*e*šû'â*, but as I am not translating the first two Hebrew nouns, it seems natural to leave this one untranslated.

[154] On the use of the two pairs of words in Isaiah, see Polan, 'Still More Signs of Unity in the Book of Isaiah'.

[155] On the different connotations of *ṣ*e*dāqâ* in the different parts of the book, see Rolf Rendtorff's earlier paper, 'Zur Komposition des Buches Jesaja', *VT* 34 (1984), pp. 295-

'because' between the imperatives and the declarations resolves the tension between these two stances, but it does not do so. The new statement could mean 'Observe *mišpāṭ*, do *ṣᵉdāqâ*, because such action is necessary if I am to fulfill my promise, so that my *yᵉšûʿâ* is near to coming, my *ṣᵉdāqâ* to revealing itself'. Obedience to the command is a condition of the fulfillment of the promise. Or it could mean 'Observe *mišpāṭ*, do *ṣᵉdāqâ*, because such action is the only appropriate response to the fact that my *yᵉšûʿâ* is near to coming, my *ṣᵉdāqâ* to revealing itself'. If we have to choose, then the second understanding seems more plausible; but there is indeed some ambiguity about the relationship between the imperatives and the declarations.

The chapters that follow underline the ambiguity of this opening rather than resolving it. The whole of 56.2–59.15a is dominated by critique of the community and by the laying down of expectations, closing with a prayer that constitutes an acknowledgment to Yhwh that this critique is fair. The expectations relate both to religious life and to ethical life. One could say that they are the outworking of what it means to observe *mišpāṭ* and do *ṣᵉdāqâ*. The whole of 59.15b–63.6 then constitutes promises that Yhwh intends to take action against his enemies, who are also Jerusalem's enemies, and to restore Jerusalem and make it the world's focus. When we reach 63.6, we might conclude that the ambiguity about the relationship of the imperatives and the declarations is solved. First put your life right; then the promises will be fulfilled. But it transpires that 63.6 is not the end of the book or of the unit begun at 56.1, because there follows a further prayer that constitutes an acknowledgment of the critique's fairness (though it goes on to ask Yhwh to have mercy), and then the two final chapters dominated by further critique of the community and by the laying down of expectations. Thus 63.7–66.24 as a whole balances 56.2–59.15a, and dissolves any sense that the ambiguity of 56.1 has been resolved. The first and last major parts of Isaiah 56–66 stand in irresolvable tension with the central part. The first and last parts correspond to the thrust of Isaiah 1–39; the central part corresponds to the thrust of Isaiah 40–55.

The chiastic structure of Isaiah 56–66 thus makes a theological point. The material's omission to resolve the tension at issue is not a failure but a recognition of a question that by its nature cannot be resolved. Attempts to resolve it lead either to a contractual understanding of the relationship between humanity and God (we do right, then God will do so) or give the impression that human responsibility is dispensable (God will deliver us whether or not we do the right thing). In reality, the relationship between God and humanity is neither conditional nor unconditional. The legal or contractual framework for understanding the relationship does not work. A more illuminating model for understanding the relationship implied by

320 (312-14), repr. Rendtorff, *Kanon und Theologie*, pp. 141-61 (155-57); ET *Canon and Theology*, pp. 146-69 (162-64).

the book of Isaiah is that of marriage, at least as often understood in the West. When two people marry, from a legal angle they enter into a contract with one another, but they do not normally see this as the central understanding of their relationship, as if they were saying to each other, 'I commit myself to you on condition that you commit yourself to me'; if the couple think in terms of conditional commitment, they need to postpone the wedding to give them time to talk things through with a therapist. But neither are they saying, 'I commit myself to you whether or not you commit yourself to me'. Both parties undertake an act of commitment that presupposes that the other is doing the same, yet do so on the basis of trust and a willingness to risk oneself to the other person. The mutuality of commitment is a kind of logical necessity or definitional necessity rather than a legal necessity. In the relationship between God and Israel, both misunderstandings are avoided and complexity is recognized by the ambiguity of the prophet's words. The concentric or chiastic structure of Isaiah 56–66 as a whole fulfills the same function as the juxtaposition of the two lines in 56.1; it preserves mystery and ambiguity, and leaves irresolvable questions unresolved.

In general terms, then, Isaiah 56–66 serves to articulate the inherent tension between Isaiah 1–39 and Isaiah 40–55, and not to resolve it. How may one express more specifically the relationship between the agenda of the first two parts of the book and that of the last part?

First, how does Isaiah 1–39 spell out the nature of observing *mišpāṭ* and doing *ṣᵉdāqâ*, the exercise of authority in a way that is expressive of faithfulness? Isaiah 5.7 indicates it involves the opposite of the shedding of blood and the encouraging or ignoring of cries of distress. Isaiah 5 goes on to suggest that neglect of *mišpāṭ* and *ṣᵉdāqâ* issues in the way successful people accumulate land and enlarge their homes, engage in bribery and the fixing of court cases in this connection, indulge themselves in the excess of their eating and drinking, and behave on the assumption that they can retain their position of importance and ignore the possibility that Yhwh will do anything. Related passages refer to the associated neglect of the needs of needy people such as orphans and widows (e.g. 1.11-23; 10.1-4), and to other forms of self-indulgence (e.g. 3.16–4.1; 28.1-8).

A second major emphasis in Isaiah 1–39 is trust in Yhwh rather than in one's own importance, capacities, or political resources (1.6-22; 7.1-17; 9.7-9 [8-10]; 28.14-22; 30.1-17; 31.1-3; 36.1–37.20). To judge from Isaiah 28.17, operating on the basis of trust in Yhwh rather than in political alliances is a further expression of *mišpāṭ* and *ṣᵉdāqâ*. The motif is one concern underlying the prophecies about other nations in Isaiah 13–23; people are to trust Yhwh rather than trusting alliances with other nations or being afraid of other nations. A third but much lesser emphasis in Isaiah 1–39 is worship of Yhwh alone, worship of a kind that avoids certain traditional and foreign forms of worship (e.g. 1.29; 2.6-8, 22; 8.19-22; 31.6-7).

In Isaiah 56–66, the critique of the community's leadership and their self-indulgence (56.9–57.2) and of people's twisting of judicial procedures in way that leads to the death of the innocent (59.1-15a) compares with that in Isaiah 1–39. Its critique of fasting (58.1-12) compares with the critique of worship at the beginning of the book (1.10-20); both relate to the community's failure to live by *mišpāṭ* and *ṣᵉdāqâ* (58.2). On the other hand, Isaiah 56–66 does not directly take up the motif of trust that is important in Isaiah 1–39, nor the royal promises. It does manifest a distinctive stress on openness to individual foreigners and eunuchs, and on the Sabbath (56.2-8; 58.13-15), and it places much greater emphasis than Isaiah 1–39 on the wickedness of certain traditional worship practices and of the worship of other deities (57.3-13; 65.1-12; 66.1-4, 17).

The agenda of Isaiah 56–66 as it spells out 'observe *mišpāṭ*, do *ṣᵉdāqâ*' thus overlaps with the agenda of Isaiah 1–39, but does so only in part and not in a way that distinguishes the relationship of Isaiah 56–66 to Isaiah 1–39 compared with its relationship to (for instance) Jeremiah or Zechariah.[156] Perhaps it is indeed the parallels of specific phrases and lines between Isaiah 1–39 and Isaiah 56–66 that form the link between the first and last parts of the book rather than any distinctive theological link, though even these parallels do not radically distinguish the connection between these two units over against a link with Jeremiah.

How does the agenda of Isaiah 40–55 compare with that of Isaiah 56–66? The summary of the agenda of Isaiah 1–39 presented above omitted its occasional use of the words *mišpāṭ* and *ṣᵉdāqâ* in connection with divine actions (1.27; 5.16; 9.6 [7]; 32.16; 33.5). While the precise hendiadys *mišpāṭ ûṣᵉdāqâ* does not appear in Isaiah 40–55 (51.5-6 does have *mišpāṭ* and *ṣedeq*), the chapters do use the two words separately with reference to divine action. The combination of *yᵉšûʿâ* or related words with *ṣᵉdāqâ* or *ṣedeq* is more characteristic of Isaiah 40–55 (45.8; 46.12-13; 51.5, 6, 8; cf. also 45.22-24). It is this combination that appears in 56.1; in other words, the opening verse of Isaiah 56–66 does make a good link with what precedes. The combination reappears in the central parts of Isaiah 56–66, the material that focuses on Yhwh's promises concerning Jerusalem's future (59.9, 14, 16, 17; 61.10; 62.1; 63.1). There are other ways in which these promises compare with Isaiah 40–55. They portray Yhwh the warrior at last stirring himself in order to take violent action against his foes, and thus acting in *qinʾâ* (59.17) in order to effect *nāqām* (59.17; 61.2; 63.4), acting as Zion's *gōʾēl* (59.20; 60.16). They speak of Yhwh's exercise of *mišpāṭ*, sometimes in association with *ṣᵉdāqâ* (59.9, 11, 14, 15). They describe at great length the restoration and transformation of Zion, the wondrous return of its peoples from all over the world, and its recognition by the world's peoples, whose attitude to

156 Cf. Sommer, 'The Scroll of Isaiah as Jewish Scripture', pp. 228-29.

Zion is thus reversed from what it had been when Zion had been the nations' victim. The image of Yhwh as creator is of key importance in Isaiah 40–55 and appears briefly in Isaiah 56–66 (57.19; 65.17-18). The understanding of the prophet's own role in 61.1-9 compares with that of the prophet's role in 49.1-6; 50.4-9, as does the absence of any concern with a future Davidic ruler.

Like Isaiah 1–39, however, Isaiah 40–55 has other agenda that is not picked up by Isaiah 56–66, even where the latter expounds its declaration that Yhwh's *yᵉšûʿâ* is near to coming, its *ṣᵉdāqâ* near to arriving. While it is possible that Isaiah 56–66 is preoccupied with an awareness that Yhwh's promises have not been fulfilled and is concerned to explain why this is so and to declare that the promises will be fulfilled, this theme is at most implicit. In contrast, Isaiah 40–55 overtly focuses on the need to convince the community that Yhwh really is going to restore Jerusalem, indeed that Yhwh is in the midst of doing so, and that the fall of one superpower and the rise of another is Yhwh's means of bringing about that restoration. Much of its argument is directly concerned to confront the community's disbelief and resistance to the prophet's understanding of Yhwh's activity, and to encourage it not to be afraid. These concerns do not feature overtly in Isaiah 56–66. The assertion that Yhwh alone is God, the argument that Yhwh's speaking and then acting is evidence of that fact, the associated polemic against images of Yhwh or of other gods, and the polemic against the significance of other gods are missing from Isaiah 56–66. So is the description of Israel as Yhwh's servant and the developed account of the servant in 52.13–53.12.

How important, then, is Isaiah 1–55 to Isaiah 56–66? Isaiah 1–55 provides Isaiah 56–66 with a theological framework, a stress on Yhwh as Israel's Holy One, a stress on the importance of Zion, a stress on *mišpāṭ* and *ṣᵉdāqâ* and on *yᵉšûʿâ* and *ṣᵉdāqâ*. But Isaiah 56–66 is not merely an exposition of the statements expressed earlier in the book any more than it is an exposition of actual texts from earlier in the book. As a whole it is not a 'strong (re)reading' of Isaiah 1–55, maybe not even a rereading. It is a partial reading, an expansive reading, and a reading that reflects on some of the issues that the earlier chapters raise.

The relationship between Isaiah 1–55 and Isaiah 56–66 resembles the one a Christian might perceive in the relationship between the two Testaments. The New Testament has a generally similar understanding of God and of humanity to that of the earlier Scriptures and it occasionally quotes them, but more broadly it disregards much of the agenda of the earlier Scriptures and it has an agenda of its own arising out of its own context, one that is not incompatible with the agenda of the earlier Scriptures but is distinctive over against them. The relationship of Isaiah 56–66 to Isaiah 1–55 is comparable.

A question raised by Isaiah 56–66 and its relation to what precedes is as follows. The material may come from varied historical contexts, overlapping with those of Isaiah 1–55 but substantially issuing from later ones. What is the significance of the way this undated material has been placed after the material that contains concrete historical references? It has been suggested that Isaiah 1–39 represents a critique of ideology, Isaiah 40–55 a public embrace of pain that leads to hope, and Isaiah 56–66 a release of social imagination,[157] but the agenda of the parts of the book seem more complex than this summary implies, and their interrelationship more subtle.

Isaiah 1–39 embodies Yhwh's reaction to the situation in Judah in the eighth century and announces the divine intention in regard to it, while Isaiah 40–55 embodies Yhwh's reaction to the situation among Judahites (in Jerusalem and/or Babylon) in the mid-sixth century.[158] Located between the historical contexts to which these two blocks of material refer, the fall of Jerusalem and the exile to Babylon constitute both the solution to the problem set up by Isaiah 1–39 and the problem for which Isaiah 40–55 offers the solution. With Isaiah 55 the chapters thus come to a happy ending. The book could stop there. There is no need for anything else. Yet apparently there is. Historically we can properly interpret that need in light of the experience of Judah in the Persian period and see Isaiah 56–66 as speaking to that context. But the chapters' lack of concrete reference and their bringing together material whose origin is not confined to this context suggest that there is more going on here. The chapters make a general point about the nature of Yhwh's involvement in the world and the nature of Yhwh's people. In this respect they might seem to have something in common with parts of Isaiah 40–55; there are no references to Babylon or to Cyrus through 40.1–43.13 or 49.1–55.13, though that fact is qualified by the concrete historical references in 43.14–48.22 which point to a concrete context for understanding the material on either side.

Isaiah 56–66 acknowledges that Yhwh's activity is something whose consummation remains in the future (though appeal to the word 'eschatological' does not help clarity) and for which Yhwh's people pray urgently. Yhwh's people are characterized by faithlessness in relation to one another and to Yhwh, and they thus need to be urged to faithfulness and hope. The chapters' lack of concrete historical reference perhaps directly implies that these are ongoing facts about the people; at least it opens itself to that inference. One could then see the book called Isaiah as encapsulating the three-part nature of the Scriptures themselves. Chapters 1–39 correspond to the Torah with its focus on the past, chapters 40–55 to the Prophets with their focus on the future, chapters 56–66 to the Writings with their focus on the present. A symbol of this fact is the way

[157] Walter Brueggemann, 'Unity and Dynamic in the Isaiah Tradition', *JSOT* 29 (1984), pp. 89-107, repr. Brueggemann, *Old Testament Theology* (Minneapolis: Fortress, 1992), pp. 252-69.

[158] I do not imply that all the material in either section comes from these periods, but they are the material's starting point and the ones to which it explicitly refers.

Isaiah 1–39 as well as Isaiah 40–55 is largely structured linearly,[159] while Isaiah 56–66 is structured chiastically. In Isaiah 56–66 there is no progress. The people of Yhwh mark time as they await the consummation of Yhwh's purpose.

Isaiah 40–55 promises an act of God via a named imperial power that will bring a judgment on the present imperial power and will be simply the fulfillment of Yhwh's purpose. It will benefit the Judahites as a whole and it is not exactly dependent on their response, though that response (of expectancy) is required. Isaiah 56–66 promises a direct act of God unmediated by an imperial power and emphasizes the importance of the Judahites' faithfulness to Yhwh and to one another, with the implication that a failure of faithfulness will mean the act of God does not arrive. It promises a judgment on the present imperial power and on the faithless within Judah; not all Judah will benefit from Yhwh's act.

J. J. M. Roberts has remarked that 'If there is any one concept central to the whole Book of Isaiah, it is the vision of Yahweh as the Holy One of Israel'.[160] An understanding of Yhwh as the holy one indeed runs through the entire book, yet this vision is not as prominent in chapters 56–66 as it is in chapters 1–55; that distinctive Isaianic phrase 'the Holy One of Israel' comes only in 60.9, 14. In chapters 56–66 a more prominent theme is the destiny of Jerusalem-Zion. Israel's holy one is mentioned as the one who has glorified the city (60.9), which is indeed characterized as 'Zion of Israel's holy one' (60.14). From this starting-point one might nominate Jerusalem-Zion as the motif that most consistently runs through the book.[161]

The opening 'vision' in Isaiah concerns 'Judah and Jerusalem', and while the expression 'holy city' does not yet have all the resonances it will later gain, it is noteworthy that the phrase first comes in Isaiah (48.2; 52.1; the other Old Testament occurrences are Neh 11.1, 18 and Dan 9.24). Further, in 51.16 Zion is uniquely described as 'my people'. In Isaiah, Jerusalem-Zion (like 'servant') is a tensive symbol, capable of having more than one referent. It can denote a location, or a physical city, or the people who live in the city, or the corporate personality of the city (it is possible to talk in similar terms of London or New York). That corporate personality can also be seen as a metaphysical entity that in some sense exists independently of its population; indeed, it is possible

[159] Which does not mean entirely chronologically: cf. Mathews's comments in 'Apportioning Desolation' (see section 3 of this Introduction). Even where Babylon precedes Assyria in Isa 13–14, the argument proceeds linearly.

[160] J. J. M. Roberts, 'Isaiah in Old Testament Theology', *Interpretation* 36 (1982), pp. 130-43 (131).

[161] Cf. Dumbrell, 'The Purpose of the Book of Isaiah'; van Wieringen and van der Woude (eds.), *'Enlarge the Site of Your Tent': The City as Unifying Theme in Isaiah*; Webb, 'Zion in Transformation' (though he links with this theme the idea of the remnant); Gosse, *Structuration des grands ensembles bibliques et intertextualité à l'époque perse*, pp. 22-26; Laato, *'About Zion I Will Not Be Silent'*.

that the term ‘Zion’ can even apply to the people of the city who are living elsewhere but who identify with it (whereas ‘Jerusalem’ can be used as a down-to-earth geographical term, ‘Zion’ is always a more dominantly religious or theological term, especially to denote the place where Yhwh lives).

Isaiah 1 introduces major aspects of this theme. It starts as bad news. After the desolating of Judah as a whole by Sennacherib, ‘Maiden Zion has survived like a shelter in a vineyard, like a hut in a melon field’, almost as devastated as Sodom and Gomorrah (1.8-9). Yet this is nothing compared with the devastation that will come with the city’s fall in 587, which is unrecorded in the book but presupposed by Isaiah 40–55 and still a reality in Isaiah 56–66.

The bad news regarding the city’s experience has at its background the bad news regarding its life. Its Sodom-like experience matches its Sodom-like life (1.10-23). Jerusalem-Zion is significant because the temple is there, and the people have been faithful in their worship in that temple, bringing offerings, celebrating festivals, and praying fervently. Isaiah does not accuse them of offering merely formal worship. They meant every hallelujah and every urgent cry for deliverance; there was no mismatch between their inner feelings and the outward expression of their worship. But there was a mismatch between the fervency of their worship and the life the city lived outside worship. When their hands were raised in fervent praise, what Yhwh saw was the blood on these hands. While few people would be directly guilty of murder, the capital city ran the affairs of Judah in a way that enabled it to live well by skilful manipulation of the systems of taxation, law, migration, and landholding, ignoring the rights of orphans and widows and depriving subsistence farmers of their means of livelihood, and abandoning any conviction that Yhwh was involved in political events in their day and any attentiveness to Yhwh’s teaching or word (cf. 5.8-25). So ‘truthful town’, the place where ‘faithfulness used to stay’, has become immoral in its unfaithfulness to Yhwh and the place where murderers live (1.21).

Notwithstanding the fervency of their praise and prayer, they have kept their heart far from Yhwh; their reverence is a learned human command (29.13). While their heart in the English sense, their emotions, may have been in their worship, there was a disjunction between their heart in the Old Testament sense, their mind, attitude or will, and God’s heart. They were familiar with the words of the worship material but that was as far as their reverence for Yhwh went. Isaiah 56–66 similarly critiques the city’s people for having recourse to Yhwh for guidance and blessing, and for fasting in this connection, but accompanying their fasting by exploiting fellow-members of their own community, so that Yhwh pays no attention to their worship. Better to share their food (and their homes and clothes) than forgo their food (58.1-7).

How, then, is Yhwh to handle the sin of Jerusalem? Does Yhwh's commitment to the city mean it can always be sure of pardon? Or does Yhwh's commitment to righteousness mean it is bound to be abandoned and destroyed?

The book's opening chapter suggests an interim answer. The country and city have experienced terrible devastation, but the city has finally been preserved. Yhwh acts in anger against Jerusalem to exact redress for wrongdoing (1.24), as to Sodom, but notwithstanding its failure to wash the blood off its hands (1.16), some leftovers survive; the parallel with Sodom breaks down. The narrative in Isaiah 36–37 fills out this story, which shows Yhwh fulfilling a promise: 'I will protect this city and deliver it for my sake and for the sake of David my servant' (37.35)—not because of the deserve of its present occupants. Hezekiah himself fills out the argument that lies behind the basis for that promise (e.g. 37.15-20).

The prophecies in Isaiah 29 and 31 nuance this understanding. In light of its wrongdoing, Yhwh declares the intention to camp against Jerusalem as David once had (29.1-4), notwithstanding the way it keeps the festivals year by year, or perhaps even because it keeps the festivals year by year (cf. 29.13). The city looks doomed to fall to Yhwh as it once fell to David. But there is a great reversal, and Yhwh 'attends to' Jerusalem in a positive way. Suddenly the strangers attacking the city disappear like dust or chaff or like a bad dream (29.5-6). To put it another way, Yhwh will descend on Mount Zion like a lion or vulture pouncing on its prey, but will turn out to shield and rescue it (31.4-5).

These deliverances cannot and will not be the end of the story. Jerusalem escaped because of Yhwh's mercy not its deserve. It had regard to its defences and looked to its water supply, 'but you did not have regard to the one who did it, you did not look to the one who shaped it long before'. Yhwh had summoned people to mourning (at their losses, at the waywardness that caused these, at the further danger this waywardness put them in), but instead they were rejoicing (at their escape, at Yhwh's deliverance, at Yhwh's presence with them) like people who did not acknowledge that another disaster might be on its way tomorrow (22.8-13). 'If this waywardness could be expiated for you before you die…', Yhwh continues, with the terrible solemnity of an oath that leaves the consequences unstated. The only thing that makes cleansing and reconciliation impossible is the denial that there is a problem and a consequent refusal to have it dealt with. Therefore you have to turn back to Yhwh (31.6).

Then the people of Jerusalem will not continue to weep because Yhwh will show great grace at the sound of their crying out (30.19-26; both 'weep' and 'show grace' are repeated). And whenever they leave the path they will hear a voice behind saying, 'this is the way, follow it', and they will abandon their images. The rains will fall, crops grow, cattle flourish, brooks flow, sun and moon shine preternaturally; and all on the day of slaughter when towers fall, the day when Yhwh bandages the people's injuries. The image of new growth already appeared in 4.2-6, leading into the further promise that the survivors of Yhwh's devastation will be counted as holy. Yhwh in person will have washed the bloodstains off Jerusalem. The burning it has gone through will be a refining. Henceforth the city will be protected. Its chastisement turns out to be not merely punitive but also restorative (1.21-31). Its silver has become slag (1.22) but the turning of Yhwh's hand against it is designed to smelt away this slag. More literally, Yhwh will restore its leadership and re-establish it as 'faithful city, truthful town' (1.26-27).

Isaiah 12 lays out songs for 'the population of Zion' to sing 'in that day', the day of Yhwh's restoration. Zion is called to give thanks to Yhwh for its deliverance in such a way that all the nations hear. Isaiah 26.1-6 provides another song to sing about Judah's strong city. In the prophet's vision, the city lacks literal walls, but 'deliverance is what he makes walls and rampart': who then needs walls? (cf. Zech 2.5-9 [1-5]). The city does have gates, but they are present in the vision in order to be opened for 'the faithful nation, the one that guards truthfulness. [Its] intention held firm, you guard it in peace, in peace because it is trustful in you' (26.3). 'Yhwh founded Zion; in it the weak of his people can take refuge' (14.32). 'The moon will know shame, the sun will know disgrace, when Yhwh Armies has begun to reign, on Mount Zion and in Jerusalem, and before his elders will be splendour' (24.21-23).

We have noted that the destruction of Jerusalem in 587 is unrecorded but presupposed in the book of Isaiah; it provides the answer to the question whether Yhwh would stay long-tempered forever. But that catastrophe, too, cannot be the end of the story. After fifty years of the city's devastation and the exile of many of its people, Yhwh declares that the time of its chastisement is over; the time for its comfort has come. Yhwh intends to return to the city, along with its exiled residents. The people is withered like grass by Yhwh's searing wind; but Yhwh's word stands forever. Thus there is good news to be proclaimed to Zion-Jerusalem (40.1-11). But meanwhile, Zion says to itself, 'Yhwh left me; my Lord forgot me' (49.14). While the actual people of Jerusalem (whether in exile or in Judah) can be envisaged lamenting thus, it is the corporate entity existing as a person independently of the people who happen to live there at a particular moment that the prophet imagines lamenting. Yhwh denies the charge of putting Zion out of mind and points to the way its exiles are gathering, like her bridal garments. Instead of being short of inhabitants, she will be overwhelmed by them (49.15-26). If Yhwh had divorced Zion and sold its children into servitude, then they could not complain, because there was good reason (50.1). But Yhwh's continuing interest in Zion's children (which contrasts with their unresponsiveness) suggests that divorce is not the right image for what happened to the relationship. Yhwh is still committed to delivering them and has the power to put down the powers of oppression (50.1-3). The city is in a hopeless situation as a result of being the victim of Yhwh's wrath, but Yhwh is now transferring that wrath to its oppressors. It has to believe that fact and act like it (51.17–52.6). Its God has begun to reign and is returning (52.7-10). It can shout for joy because it is about to spread right and left, its fear and shame abolished (54.1-16a). Yhwh admits having abandoned it but did so only for a short time and is now re-establishing it, and promises not to abandon it again. Yhwh's commitment and covenant will now stand forever. The situation parallels the one after the flood, when Yhwh promised not to flood the earth again. The city will become like a woman bejewelled. Its people will now be Yhwh's disciples and will all enjoy well-being and security.

While Jerusalem-Zion is implicitly the background of the confrontations in Isaiah 56–59, the first explicit reference in chapters 56–66 comes in 59.20. There the prophecy promises that Yhwh will come as restorer to Zion, which is glossed as the location of the people in Jacob who turn from rebellion. In the context, being restorer implies being the one who will exact redress from the attackers who have shed the blood of the city's people. The prayer in 63.7–64.11 [12] appeals for such promises to become a reality, against the contrasting background of Zion-Jerusalem's current wilderness-like, devastated state (64.9 [10]).

At the centre of Isaiah 56–66, chapters 60–62 expound the restoration in glorious terms. The world is in darkness but Yhwh's light has dawned on Zion, so that nations can walk by it. Its children are coming from afar. So is the wealth of the nations coming for Zion's sake, to declare Yhwh's praise and to bring offerings, which will benefit the city and glorify Yhwh. These foreigners will build the city's walls and the city will be splendidly appointed. All nations and kings are to serve it. This is 'Zion of Israel's holy one'. It will know Yhwh as its deliverer and restorer and be characterized by well-being and faithfulness rather than violence and ruin. Yhwh will be its light, night and day (60.1-22). At the moment Zion is an object of mourning, characterized by weakness, wounding, captivity, and grief, but then, foreigners will look after its people's flocks and crops while Judahites function as Yhwh's priests and servants. Their great shame will be replaced by great wealth and Yhwh will make a permanent covenant commitment to them (61.1-7). Zion-Jerusalem will be a beautiful crown in Yhwh's hand, no longer neglected, forsaken, and desolate, but delighted in and espoused by Yhwh (62.1-5). Once again Yhwh commissions the clearing of a way for people to come back to Zion and for Yhwh to come as deliverer (62.10-11).

How could the future of the city be envisioned in any more glorious terms? By picturing it as the creation of a new heavens and new earth (65.17-25). The context indicates that the prophet is not referring to a literal new cosmos but to a whole new world for this city. 'The sound of weeping and the sound of a cry will not make itself heard there again', in contrast to 5.7. People will live out their lives instead of having them cut off. They will build houses and live in them, plant vineyards and enjoy their fruit, rather than having them destroyed by enemies. Thus 'they will not toil to no purpose, they will not bear children to terror'. They will have a relationship of living, instant communication with Yhwh, one in which the new creation vision of 11.6-9 will be realized. Jerusalem will be a whole new world, indeed.

The point is re-expressed in 66.7-14a, which takes up the image of Zion as mother and pictures her giving birth to a whole new family. In other words, Jerusalem is to become once more a populated, bustling city, and a place of well-being, rejoicing, and comfort. Here, it has been said, 'the theology of Zion in the second half of the book of Isaiah…reaches its highpoint'.[162] Yet the footnote in 66.20-21 is hardly to be underestimated. The way Zion will become mother of many children is through foreign nations bringing all the relatives of the present population of Judah to Jerusalem as an offering to Yhwh. It will even be the case that these nations not only share in the everyday tasks of farming while Israelites fulfill the sacred duties, but share the role of priests. The image of Zion is a means both of affirming Yhwh's commitment to Israel in particular and of declaring that all the world will come to acknowledge Yhwh.

[162] Beuken, *Jesaja IIIB*, p. 120.

COMMENTARY

I

ISAIAH 56.1-8

Translation and Notes

1 Yhwh has said this:
'Guard the exercise of judgment,// act in faithfulness,
Because my deliverance is near to coming,// my faithfulness to manifesting'.
2 The good fortune of the one who does this,// the person who holds fast to it:
Who guards the Sabbath rather than profaning it,[1]// guards his hand[2] rather than doing any wrong.

3 So[3] the foreigner is not to say,// the one who has attached himself[4] to Yhwh, saying,
'Yhwh will definitely separate me// from among his people'.
And the eunuch is not to say,// 'Ah, I am a dry tree'.

4 Because Yhwh has said this:
'To[5] the eunuchs who guard my Sabbaths// and choose[6] what I delight in,// those who hold fast to my covenant:[7]
5 I will give to them[8]// within my house, within my walls,
A memorial and a name// better than sons and daughters.
I will give to him[9] a lasting name,// one that will not be cut off.

[1] מחללו: unusually, שבת is treated as m., perhaps under the influence of the fuller יום שבת. 1QIs^{a} corrects to מחללה.

[2] 1QIs^{a} has pl.; cf. Vrs.

[3] 1QIs^{a} lacks the ו (so also LXX).

[4] One would expect the participial pointing הַנִּלְוֶה (Vrs have a participle); MT's pointing is that of the qatal. On the article used as a relative, see GK 138i, j, k.

[5] The ל does not indicate that Yhwh is speaking (directly) 'to' the eunuchs, because the eunuchs are in the third person. The 'to' anticipates the 'to' in v. 5. Nor does the ל mean 'as for', since one would then expect the preposition also to appear on the word for 'foreigners' in v. 6.

[6] For MT's *w*-consecutive ובחרו, 1QIs^{a} has PBH conjunctive ו, ויבחורו.

[7] The transition from finite verbs to a participle is unusual; the transition normally takes the opposite form (see the discussion in Sekine, *Die Tritojesajanische Sammlung*, pp. 34-35, 38-39). Thus the participial expression parallels the subject 'the eunuchs' and likely does not belong to the relative clause, as MT's soph pasuq hints, and as is the case in v. 6.

[8] The w-consecutive follows on the extraposed clause. Scullion ('Some Difficult Texts in Isaiah cc.56–66', pp. 105-6) translates 'put'; but this is more difficult when נתן is followed by ל, esp. in v. 5b.

[9] For MT לו (cf. 1QIs^{b}), 1QIs^{a} has pl. להמה (cf. Vrs), assimilating to the first line.

6 ‘And the foreigners who attach themselves to[10] Yhwh,// to minister to him
and to dedicate themselves to[11] Yhwh’s name,// to be servants to him,
Every one who guards[12] the Sabbath rather than profaning it,[13]// and those
who hold fast to my covenant:
7 I will bring them[14] to my holy mountain// and let them rejoice in my prayer
house,
Their whole offerings and their sacrifices[15]// acceptable on my altar,
Because my house will be called// a prayer house, for all peoples.[16]
8 The declaration of the Lord Yhwh,// who gathers together[17] the scattered of
Israel:
‘I will gather together yet more towards it, to its gathered ones’.

Introduction

‘Though conventionally regarded as the beginning of “Trito-Isaiah” there are few signs of a new start here.’[18] In v. 1, the message formula and the change of subject from Isaiah 55 do mark the opening of a section. Most MT manuscripts have chapter or paragraph markers before vv. 1, 3, 4, 6, and 10, but they have none before v. 9; nor do 1QIs[a, b]. But the declaration formula at v. 8 and the change of subject at v. 9 mark the end of the section and the beginning of another. The central theme is Yhwh’s welcoming foreigners and eunuchs into membership of the community. In relation to this theme, however, the opening verse stands out for its general nature, and it looks like an introduction to Isaiah 56–66 as a whole.[19] Conversely, the lines that open with v. 2 would stand quite happily on their own; ‘the good fortune of’ often begins a unit (e.g. Pss 1; 32; 119; 128). Further, v. 2 is an exclamation that begins a human statement, so that it marks a transition from Yhwh’s words to the prophet’s. At the same time, the verbs ‘guard’ and ‘act’ in v. 1 reappear in v. 2 (the second is there translated ‘do’, twice). Guarding *mišpāṭ* and acting in

[10] The preposition changes from the usual אל (v. 3) to the uncommon על. 1QIs[a] repeats אל (1QIs[b] has על both times).

[11] 1QIs[a] has the more familiar ולברך for the unusual ולאהבה (Kutscher, הלשון והרקע הלשוני של מגילת ישעיהו השלמה, pp. 29, 171 [ET pp. 37, 225-26]).

[12] LXX has pl., assimilating to the context; so also 1QIs[a] as part of a broader different reading of the line, which seeks to safeguard against ascribing too significant a role to foreigners (see Pulikottil, *Transmission of Biblical Texts in Qumran*, pp. 181-84).

[13] 1QIs[a] corrects to מחללה as at v. 2.

[14] The *w*-consecutive again follows on the extraposed clause.

[15] One would expect a verb such as יעלו ‘will go up’ as in 60.7, which 1QIs[a] provides; cf. also Tg. LXX provides ‘will be’.

[16] More precisely, in the Hebrew word order, ‘Because my house a prayer house// will be called for all peoples’.

[17] Here and in the next line, resultative piel (Jenni, *Das hebräische Pi῾el*, pp. 187-88).

[18] Coggins, ‘Isaiah’, p. 479.

[19] See the ‘Conclusion’ to 56.1-8 below.

ṣ^e^dāqâ are spelled out in guarding the Sabbath and not doing any wrong. The repetition of the verb 'guard' points to this being a key theme in vv. 1-8. Verse 8, too, would be quite capable of standing on its own, though in terms of theme it fits with vv. 2-7. The passage has been dated in the exile,[20] the late sixth century,[21] the fifth,[22] and the third,[23] and its redactional history has been analysed in a number of ways.[24] Perhaps v. 1 was composed to lead into what follows, and/or v. 2 was composed to link v. 1 and what follows,[25] or separate units that had words in common were juxtaposed, and/or perhaps v. 8 was of separate origin from what precedes and was appended to it because of its compatibility of theme; whatever their redactional history, vv. 1-8 link together.

The verses have some verbal links with Isaiah 54.17b–55.13: both passages speak of someone or something being 'near', both refer to a covenant, both refer to rejoicing, both refer to Israel's relationship with other peoples, both refer to a name that will be lasting and will not be cut off, both refer to Yhwh's 'servants'.[26] 1QIs[a] provides a *ky*ʾ (because) to link the chapters; so also a medieval piyyut, a synagogue lyric.[27] But drawing attention to these links also draws attention to the two sections' distinctiveness. In 54.17b–55.13 Yhwh is near, the covenant is the covenant with David extended to Israel, the rejoicing is Israel's, the peoples are the objects of David's commanding and Israel's summoning, the transformation of nature will issue in the name that will not be cut off, and 'the servants of Yhwh' is a term for the people's entire relationship with Yhwh. In 56.1-8, Israel's deliverance is near, the covenant is one to which eunuchs and foreigners hold fast, the nations are the ones rejoicing, they are the objects of Yhwh's encouragement and acceptance, it is the eunuchs who will have a name that will not be cut off, and 'servants to him' refers to involvement in worship. While 56.1-8 makes verbal links with 54.17b–55.13, then, it harnesses them to a different message.[28]

[20] E.g. Feldmann, *Das Buch Isaias*, II, p. 197.

[21] E.g. Smith, *Rhetoric and Redaction in Trito-Isaiah*, pp. 54-60.

[22] E.g. Fohrer, *Jesaja*, III, pp. 185-86.

[23] So Steck, *Studien zu Tritojesaja*, pp. 244-48.

[24] See, e.g., Michel, 'Zur Eigenart Tritojesajas', pp. 187-93; Sekine, *Die Tritojesajanische Sammlung*, pp. 37-41; Steck, *Studien zu Tritojesaja*, pp. 244-48. Jonathan Schaper ('Rereading the Law', in Bernard M. Levinson and Eckart Otto [eds.], *Recht und Ethik im Alten Testament* [Münster: Lit, 2004], pp. 125-44 [132]) comments, 'the list of literary-critical, form-critical, redaction-critical, and other analyses that have been suggested for Isa 56:1-8 is virtually endless'.

[25] Cf. Park, *Die Gerechtigkeit Israels und das Heil der Völker*, pp. 72-75.

[26] See, e.g., Beuken, *Jesaja IIIA*, pp. 19-39. Indeed (for instance), Penna (*Isaia*, pp. 404, 555) sees 56.1-8 as the end of the section of the book that begins at 40.1 and thus sees 56.9 as the beginning of the book's third major section, 56.9–66.24, while Goulder (*Isaiah as Liturgy*, pp. 133-34) treats 55.1–56.8 as a section within 49.1–57.21

[27] So Meir Wallenstein, 'The Piyyuṭ', *BJRL* 34 (1951–52), pp. 469-76 (475).

[28] Cf. D. W. Van Winkle, 'Isaiah lvi 1-8', in *Society of Biblical Literature 1997 Seminar Papers* (Atlanta: Scholars, 1997), pp. 234-52 (245-46).

Verses 1-8 are conventionally printed as verse, but their verse is mostly of a prosaic kind; one could, indeed, rather describe them as elevated prose. In form they are quite complex. They begin as a prophetic exhortation and promise (v. 1) and close as another prophetic promise, whose addressees would seem to be the community as a whole. But after the opening, they become a declaration of good fortune, and that understanding can apply to the whole of vv. 2-7. They are not directly a piece of instruction, a kind of regulation.[29] They are very different in form from a piece of prophetic instruction such as Ezekiel 44.9-24 or Zechariah 7–8, as well as from Deuteronomy 23, passages that are all related in subject matter. Indeed, arguably 'the secret to proper interpretation of this unit lies in the degree of caution one exercises in using other biblical texts to reconstruct the sociohistorical context in which it allegedly fits'.[30] It is not a speech of warning or a call to conversion.[31] It is more like the kind of prophetic exhortation (not something designed to suggest a regulation) that appears in Isaiah 1.10-20; 58.9b-14.[32] It might be called a sermon.[33]

Comment

56.1 Yhwh has said this:
Guard the exercise of judgment,// act in faithfulness,
Because my deliverance is near to coming,// my faithfulness to manifesting.

Isaiah 56–66 as a whole begins with the message formula, more literally 'Thus [has] Yhwh said', the form of words used by a messenger relaying the words of a king; for the literal usage, see 36.4, 14, 16. The formula emphasizes the kingly authority asserted for what follows. EVV follow LXX and Vg in translating the qatal verb by means of a present tense verb, 'says'. The background in the expression's literal usage indicates why this is misleading. The messenger is not declaring what the king is saying now but what he said in commissioning the messenger. There are a number of occurrences of the message formula in Isaiah 56–57 and in Isaiah 65–66 but none in Isaiah 58–64; there were many instances in

[29] So, e.g., Duhm, *Jesaia*, p. 380. Theodor Lescow sees vv. 1-7 as an example of a three-stage torah, comprising a generalizing introduction, a core of cultic/ethical material, and a conclusion ('Die dreistufige Tora', *ZAW* 82 [1970], pp. 362-79 [370]).

[30] Seitz, 'The Book of Isaiah 40–66', p. 484.

[31] Against K. Arvid Tångberg, *Die prophetische Mahnrede: Form- und traditionsgeschichtliche Studien zum prophetischen Umkehrruf* (Göttingen: Vandenhoeck & Ruprecht, 1987), pp. 121-25.

[32] Cf. Jones, 'Isaiah–II and III', p. 529. They are not among the passages discussed by Joachim Begrich, 'Die priesterliche Tora', in *Gesammelte Studien zum Alten Testament* (Munich: Kaiser, 1964), pp. 232-60 (he does refer frequently to Isa 1.10-17).

[33] So Michael Fishbane, 'The Hebrew Bible and Exegetical Tradition', in Johannes C. de Moor (ed.), *Intertextuality in Ugarit and Israel* (Leiden: Brill, 1998), pp. 15-30 (26).

Isaiah 43–52.[34] The formula thus makes a link with what precedes, at least with the hindsight that the rest of the verse will provide.[35] While the rest of v. 1 'merely' summarizes the implications of the message of Isaiah 1–55, it does so as a divine word and not as a mere piece of scholarly scriptural interpretation.[36]

After the message formula, v. 1 comprises two linked pairs of neat bicola (2-2, 3-2), each internally parallel. In the first pair, 'do faithfulness' (to be more literal) nuances 'guard the exercise of judgment'. The two brief clauses are one exhortation divided into two in order to form parallel cola. The sequence recurs in Psalm 106.3; the unusual nature of the expression 'guard *mišpāṭ*', which comes only in these two passages, may mean that the prophet echoes the psalm. To put the prophet's point more prosaically, 'Act with care in exercising judgment with faithfulness'.[37] Dividing the linked words between the cola produces an odd expression; 'guard the exercise of judgment' does not make very good sense on its own. The phrase recurs in Hosea 12.7 [6], and also very often elsewhere with plural *mišpāṭîm*; the singular, in combination with *ṣᵉdāqâ*, indicates that the prophet is referring to a broad issue rather than adherence to a set of specific regulations. Verse 2b will take up the potential in the use of the odd expression here.

The exercise of judgment and faithfulness, *mišpāṭ* and *ṣᵉdāqâ*, are a word-pair in the Old Testament, and within Isaiah in 1.27; 5.7, 16; 9.6 [7]; 28.17; 32.16; 58.2; 59.9, 14. Both appear in 54.17, but in separate connections, and their absence otherwise in Isaiah 40–55 stands in contrast to their more frequent appearance in the first and last parts of the book. It reflects a difference in emphasis between its different parts, of which the first and last give considerable space to challenging the community about *mišpāṭ* and *ṣᵉdāqâ*.

Neither word has a close English equivalent. *Mišpāṭ* refers to the exercise of authority or power. This connotation links with that of the verb *šāpaṭ*, which means to exercise rule or authority or power or leadership in such a way as to restore order to a community when it has been disturbed.[38] In a legal context this entails giving a judgment (hence here LXX's κρίσις, Vg's *iudicium*), but neither the verb nor the noun is confined to legal contexts; further, in English judging commonly has negative connotations. For *mišpāṭ* here and elsewhere, modern translations have expressions such as 'justice', which contrasts with judgment in being abstract rather than concrete and in having inherently positive

[34] On the marking of divine speech in Isa 56–66, see Samuel A. Meier, *Speaking of Speaking* (Leiden: Brill, 1992), pp. 253-57.

[35] Cf. Childs, *Isaiah*, p. 453, though his form of words could imply that the phrase is not a marker of the beginning of a passage in Isa 40–55; as his examples show, it does function thus.

[36] Cf. Childs, *Isaiah*, p. 455.

[37] Cf. Pauritsch, *Die neue Gemeinde*, p. 39.

[38] Cf. G. Liedke, *THAT*, II, p. 1001 (ET *TLOT*, III, p. 1393).

connotations, but both these characteristics make it a misleading translation for *mišpāṭ*. While ideally this authority will be exercised with justice, the value notion is not inherent in the word. Leviticus 19.15, 35 find it necessary to forbid people to exercise *mišpāṭ* in a manner that involves wrong (*ʿāwal*), while Habakkuk 1.4 laments a situation is which *mišpāṭ* goes out twisted or bent or crooked (*meʿuqqāl*). Further, the word's concrete connotation is intrinsic to it. B. Johnson notes some contexts in Isaiah where the term 'tends in the direction of God's active intervention',[39] and this nuance of active intervention fits here. The prophet certainly presupposes that God's active intervention is exercised in the cause of what is right, and in English when we speak about the importance of the exercise of authority or leadership, or the necessity to take a decision or the need of governmental action, we presuppose that authority, leadership, authority, and government will be exercised in a proper way, but that implication is not written into the meaning of these words, and neither is it written into the word *mišpāṭ*. The need for *mišpāṭ* to be exercised in a proper way is conveyed precisely through complementing it with a word such as *ṣedāqâ*; the power word is nuanced by the value word. But perhaps it should be acknowledged here that nearly all interpreters assume, like modern translations, that the word has inherent moral implications and thus translate it something like 'justice'.[40]

For *ṣedāqâ*, LXX has δικαιοσύνη, Vg *iustitia*, which again suggest 'justice', but this implies that *ṣedāqâ*, too, is a legal expression, or at least that it focuses on the notion of fairness. *Ṣedāqâ* rather suggests doing the right thing by people with whom one is in a relationship, the right thing by the people in one's community. In *Isaiah 40–55* we translated it 'right'; I here render it 'faithfulness'.[41] 'Above all...*ṣedāqâ* refers to Yahweh's positive and beneficent intervention.'[42] So the hendiadys *mišpāṭ* and *ṣedāqâ* suggests something like faithful exercise of authority. 'It is equivalent to right government of the people.'[43] This exhortation concerning the exercise of authority is addressed to the community as a whole, but responsibility for making sure that power is exercised in a way that does honour community relationships will rest especially with people who have authority in the community. Even when Ezekiel 18 speaks of individuals doing *mišpāṭ* and *ṣedāqâ*, its illustrations show it has in mind

[39] *TWAT*, V, p. 102 (*TDOT*, IX, p. 93); see also Goldingay and Payne, *Isaiah 40–55*, I, pp. 214-16.

[40] See further B. Johnson's discussion of *mišpāṭ* in *TWAT*. Johnson begins by noting that the equivalent word occurs in Ugaritic and Phoenician with the meaning 'government, authority', which is an interesting fact, though my argument is based on the use of the word and its parent verb in Hebrew.

[41] G. A. F. Knight ('Is "Righteous" Right?', *Scottish Journal of Theology* 41 [1988], pp. 1-10) notes that 'righteousness' is a misleading translation of *ṣedāqâ* but seems to have no alternative translation. K. Koch defines *ṣdq* as *gemeinschaftstreu*, 'to be communally faithful' (*THAT*, II, p. 507 [ET *TLOT*, II, p. 1046]).

[42] B. Johnson, *TWAT*, VI, p. 913 (ET *TDOT*, XII, p. 253).

[43] Odeberg, *Trito-Isaiah*, p. 33.

people in positions of authority. The line's assumption is that it is easy not to guard or keep or act with faithful authority or faithfulness in governing. If one needed more than regular human experience in order to affirm this fact, then Isaiah 1–39 has made it clear, but Isaiah 56–66 will further underline the point. In the context of the Persian period, a passage such as Nehemiah 5 illustrates it. The fact that *ṣᵉdāqâ* comes to suggest love expressed in almsgiving facilitates Rabbi Judah's comment on this verse, 'Great is charity, because it brings redemption nearer'.[44]

In v. 1b, 'because is near' opens the line and applies to both cola; 'my faithfulness to manifesting' in turn nuances 'my deliverance to coming'. Whereas the previous line concerned the community's faithfulness, this line concerns Yhwh's faithfulness, Yhwh's doing the right thing by the community. And whereas the previous line's links were with Isaiah 1–39 (as well as with subsequent sections within Isaiah 56–66), this line's links are with Isaiah 40–55 (again, as well as with subsequent sections). Whereas *mišpāṭ* and *ṣᵉdāqâ* form a word pair in Isaiah 1–39 but do not appear as a word pair in Isaiah 40–55, deliverance and faithfulness (*yᵉšûʿâ* and *ṣᵉdāqâ*) do not appear in Isaiah 1–39 but form a word pair in Isaiah 51.6, 8, and in 59.17; 62.1; compare faithfulness and deliverance (*ṣedeq* and *yešaʿ*) in 45.8; 51.5; also faithful and deliverer in 45.21. Indeed, 51.5 declared that Yhwh's faithfulness 'is near' and that Yhwh's deliverance has gone forth, while 40.5 and 53.1 spoke of Yhwh's splendour and Yhwh's arm 'manifesting', and 46.13 spoke of Yhwh's faithfulness being near. So the meaning of *ṣᵉdāqâ* on its first occurrence follows its meaning in Isaiah 1–39, while its meaning on its second occurrence follows that in Isaiah 40–55 ('language and translation really matter here'[45]). Indeed, this last line in v. 1 summarizes the message of Isaiah 40–55 as the preceding line sums up the message of Isaiah 1–39.[46] More immediately, the two lines provide an initial statement of a synthesis that will be expounded over the next four chapters, Isaiah 56–59.[47] But whereas the implication of such declarations in Isaiah 40–55 is simply

44 B. Baba Batra 10a.

45 Andreas Schuele, 'Isaiah 56:1-8', *Interpretation* 66 (2012), pp. 286-88 (288). Cf. Payne, 'Characteristic Word-play in "Second Isaiah"', p. 210. On the usage of the words in Isa 40–55 and 56–66, see earlier Karl Cramer, 'Der Begriff צדקה bei Tritojesaja', *ZAW* 27 (1907), pp. 79-99; more recently John J. Scullion, '*ṣedeq-ṣedaqah* in Isaiah cc. 40-66', *UF* 3 (1971), pp. 335-48.

46 See Rolf Rendtorff, 'Jesaja 56,1 als Schlüssel für die Komposition des Buches Jesaja', in Rendtorff, *Kanon und Theologie* (Neukirchen: Neukirchener, 1991), pp. 172-79; ET *Canon and Theology* (Minneapolis: Fortress, 1993), pp. 181-89. See also Bernard Gosse, 'Isaïe 56–59', *Henoch* 19 (1997), pp. 267-81 (276-78); John S. Oswalt, 'Righteousness in Isaiah', in Broyles and Evans (eds.), *Writing and Reading the Scroll of Isaiah*, I, pp. 177-91; Polan, 'Still More Signs of Unity in the Book of Isaiah: The Significance of Third Isaiah'.

47 Cf. Bernard Gosse, 'L'évolution des rapports entre le salut (*yšwʿh*) et le jugement (*mšpṭ*) dans les rédactions d'ensemble du livre d'Isaïe et du Psautier, et le rôle des cantiques bibliques', *RB* 109 (2002), pp. 323-42; also 'Deux usages du Psaume 96', *OTE* 12 (1999), pp. 266-78.

that people must pay heed (46.12-13), the implication in 56.1 when this promise follows on 'guard *mišpāṭ* and act in *ṣᵉdāqâ*' is that in light of the promise they must act in the proper way.[48]

'Deliverance' suggests an extraordinary rescue from forces that would otherwise continue to overwhelm forever. In Isaiah 40–55 those forces are embodied in Babylonian overlordship. The Babylonians are now gone, but the domination of the Persians in their place (even though they made it possible for people to return to Judah and for the temple to be restored), the pressure of the other Persian provinces around Judah, and the still devastated circumstances of Jerusalem mean that the need for deliverance has by no means passed; Yhwh reaffirms the promise that it will come. Thus at one level the reference of 'deliverance' is indicated by what has preceded in Isaiah 40–55; at another level it will be indicated by what follows in Isaiah 56–66.

LXX renders the second phrase τὸ ἔλεός μου ἀποκαλυφθῆναι, 'my mercy to being revealed'. Only here in Isaiah does it render *ṣᵉdāqâ* by ἔλεός (it does three times use ἐλεημοσύνη, and it is fond of the word ἔλεός in other connections, 'to express every possible form of God's merciful aid').[49] One influence on LXX in translating *ṣᵉdāqâ* by a different word from the one used in the previous line may be LXX's dislike of repetitions,[50] but the change does bring out the change in the meaning of *ṣᵉdāqâ*, and the word ἔλεός does bring out the relational rather than merely legal implications of *ṣᵉdāqâ*. On the other hand, something of the significance of the verse is also lost by translating the word differently in the two lines; contrast Vg, which has *iustitia* both times. The act of deliverance will be an expression of Yhwh's faithfulness; it will implement the commitment Yhwh has to the community. There will be nothing 'just' about it. Justice would point to Yhwh's simple abandonment of Judah, which has done nothing to make Yhwh's deliverance appropriate. The necessity for this deliverance emerges from within Yhwh as one who entered into a relational commitment to Judah and must honour it, notwithstanding Judah's not being very responsive on its part. Deliverance emerges from Yhwh's faithfulness. EVV follow LXX also in translating *higgālôt* with a passive verb, 'be revealed', but intransitive or reflexive is more intrinsically the connotation of the niphal. Once again the second verb nuances the first, as happens with the nouns: not only will Yhwh's faithful deliverance come, it will manifest itself in glory. The use of a word such as revelation[51] assumes the idea that God's revelation lies in God's acts (especially the acts of faithfulness), though the way in which the divine act is preceded by the prophetic word also assumes the idea that acts in themselves are not revelatory; it is the

[48] Cf. Westermann, *Jesaja Kapitel 40–66*, p. 247 (ET p. 309).

[49] Seeligmann, *The Septuagint Version of Isaiah*, p. 98.

[50] Cf. Olley, *'Righteousness' in the Septuagint of Isaiah*, p. 71.

[51] Thus in Obara's study, *rivelazione* is a key word (e.g. *Le strategie di Dio*, pp. 62-87, 139-87).

prophetic word and the divine act that makes revelation actual. Further, while 'come' and 'manifest' occur in parallelism only here, they seem to be a common pairing in Ugaritic to describe a person arriving/showing up,[52] which points to the personal nature of the manifesting/coming in this verse. It is the deliverer who is coming, the faithful one who is becoming manifest.

56.2 The good fortune of the one who does this,// the person who holds fast to it:
Who guards the Sabbath rather than profaning it,// guards his hand rather than doing any wrong.

Poetically, v. 2a (3-3) works in a similar way to v. 1b: 'the good fortune of' applies to both cola, which are closely parallel in comprising subject then yiqtol verb then object, and 'holds fast to it' adds weight to 'does this'. Within v. 2b (3-4) the participial verb is repeated, and in each colon it is followed by a direct object and then by a 'rather than' expression. Such repetition is very unusual, but its unusual nature is qualified by the verb's having different shades of meaning in the two cola. The line thus makes us think it is being uncharacteristically repetitive but turns out in substance not to be. Nevertheless 'guarding the hand' nuances 'guarding the Sabbath', while 'doing any wrong' reexpresses 'profaning'. The parallelism also means that the reference to the Sabbath carries over from the first colon into the second, which thus does not refer to doing wrong in general but to acting in a way that constitutes profaning the Sabbath.[53]

LXX renders *ʾašrê* ('the good fortune of') by the adjective μακάριος, Vg by *beatus*, but the Hebrew expression is an exclamation, and an intensive plural. 'It is not a wish and not a promise.... It is a joyful cry and a passionate statement.'[54] The expression is characteristic of the Psalms and Proverbs. In a passage such as Psalm 1, such a declaration is an implicit challenge. Here, it will turn out to be what it seems, a promise. It introduces the spelling out of the implications of Yhwh's words in v. 1; the force of speaking in Yhwh's name carries over to v. 2, a little in the manner of a preacher speaking 'in the name of the Father, the Son, and the Holy Spirit' and then speaking the preacher's own words.[55] The Greek and Latin words do have the advantage of avoiding any split between outward and inward, material and spiritual. The expression points to the whole of life working out well. The standard English translation 'blessed' may suggest the spiritual, though as it happens, in this context it is spiritual blessing that the prophet will focus on.

[52] Cf. Hans-Jürgen Zobel, *TWAT*, I, p. 1023 (ET *TDOT*, II, p. 481).
[53] Cf. Theodoret of Cyrrhus, *Commentaire sur Isaïe* 171a (III, pp. 188-91).
[54] Martin Buber, *Right and Wrong* (London: SCM, 1952), p. 51, U.S. edition *Good and Evil* (New York: Scribner's, 1952), p. 53.
[55] Cf. Dirk U. Rottzoll, 'Die *kh ʾmr* ...-Legitimationsformel', *VT* 39 (1989), pp. 323-40 (337).

The verb 'does' takes up from v. 1 (but there, I translated *ʿāśâ* 'act with'); the repeated 'guards' in v. 2b will do the same. This would suggest we take 'this' as retrospective; it refers to guarding *mišpāṭ* and acting in *ṣᵉdāqâ*. MT's section division (linking vv. 1-2 and breaking the section after v. 2) also points in this direction. Yet the move from v. 1 to v. 2 involves a significant move from plural addressees to singular subject. It will be a feature of some chapters of Isaiah 56–66 to assume a distinction within the community between the faithful and the faithless. The opening two verses thus introduce the tension between Yhwh's involvement with the people as a whole and the challenge to individuals to offer Yhwh the response that ensures they belong to the faithful.

The move from v. 2a to v. 2b is then surprising, as the 'guarding' and 'doing' of v. 1 are given concrete expression in 'guarding' and not 'doing' any wrong on the Sabbath. The way Isaiah 56–66 immediately moves from the general to the concrete further distinguishes these chapters from Isaiah 40–55.[56] Guarding (*śāmar*) already points to the awareness that the Sabbath needs some protecting; it can easily be profaned. The notion of profanation starts from the fact that there are things that are holy, taken out of ordinary use. In terms of time, that applies to the Sabbath. The instructions for building the wilderness dwelling emphasize the antithesis of guarding the Sabbath and profaning it (Exod 31.12-17 [P]); Yhwh had made the Sabbath holy, taken it out of ordinary use, after completing the original work of creation on this day (Gen 2.1-3 [P]). Both these parts of the Torah were likely written in the same general period as Isaiah 56. Again at about this period, Nehemiah 13.15-22 gives a vivid concrete description of what it looks like to profane the Sabbath or do wrong on the Sabbath, and what it looks like to exercise *mišpāṭ* and *ṣᵉdāqâ* so as to make it holy. But whereas Nehemiah thus focuses on the Sabbath as a community obligation and therefore one that as governor he has some responsibility for, the prophecy goes on to focus on the Sabbath as an obligation that individuals are responsible to guard in their own lives.

The parallel with Nehemiah 13 also helps clarify why the general exhortation to guard *mišpāṭ* and act in *ṣᵉdāqâ* can be spelled out in terms of observing the Sabbath. In Jeremiah 17.19-27 and Ezekiel 20, neglect of the Sabbath is a key reason why Yhwh will bring about the destruction of Jerusalem and the exile. In Babylon, it would not be surprising if observance of the Sabbath was a key distinguishing mark expected to be shown by the Judahite community, and in the Second Temple period, passages such as Nehemiah 13 make explicit that this is so over against Judah's neighbour communities. It is a mark of being truly committed to Yhwh and of being actually a distinct and distinctive people (see further Isa 58.1-14). Nehemiah 9.13-14 similarly implies that the Sabbath is the

[56] Cf. Ramis, *Isaías 40–66*, p. 250.

key command at Sinai,[57] a synecdoche for the whole.[58] Whereas Genesis 17 [P] makes circumcision the sign of the covenant, and elsewhere in the Torah it is the key requirement of a foreigner who is to identify with Israel, perhaps circumcision can be taken for granted in the Second Temple community as Sabbath-keeping cannot.

56.3 So the foreigner is not to say,// the one who has attached himself to Yhwh, saying,
'Yhwh will definitely separate me// from among his people'.
And the eunuch is not to say,// 'Ah, I am a dry tree'.

The first two cola (2-3) are again internally parallel, with forms of the verb 'say' bracketing them and the second colon importantly nuancing the first. The middle line can be treated as 3-2 but the second colon simply completes the first and the line marks a transition to more prosaic prosody. The single line comprising v. 3b (2-4) then parallels the two lines comprising v. 3a as a whole, with its first colon repeating the first colon of v. 3a except for the necessary change of subject.

Initially v. 3 would seem to have changed the subject, but it will become clear in v. 4 that it does not do so. It concerns whether that joyful exclamation applies to everyone, and raises the question whether it applies to two groups who might have thought it did not apply to them, and to whom other members of the community might think it did not apply. It articulates something like a lament on the part of representative individuals from the two groups, a lament that the exclamation indeed does not apply to them. But it is not the typical lament issuing a protest and plea to God but one that simply externalizes the unhappiness of the speaker rather than being a protest addressed to someone. It speaks of Yhwh rather than to Yhwh (cf. 40.27).

The question of foreigners 'attaching themselves' (*lāwâ* niphal) to Yhwh surfaces from time to time in Old Testament narratives referring to people such as Jethro, Rahab, Ruth, Uriah, and Ebed-Melech, though these narratives do not involve the use of this verb. In the context of a promise of the fall of Babylon it was used of people attaching themselves to Israel in 14.1 and also of Israelites attaching themselves to Yhwh in Jeremiah 50.5: this verse adds the phrase 'in a lasting covenant'. The reference to a covenant in Isaiah 56.1-8 increases the likelihood that the Jeremiah passage lies behind the reference here, which underlines the contrasting emphasis on the fact that here it is foreigners who are attaching themselves to Yhwh,[59] as well as the contrast over against 14.1-2 where the foreigners become Israel's servants and underlings.

[57] Cf. Schramm, *The Opponents of Third Isaiah*, pp. 119-20.

[58] So Roman Halas, 'The Universalism of Isaias', *CBQ* 12 (1950), pp. 162-70 (169).

[59] In this connection Park (*Die Gerechtigkeit Israels und das Heil der Völker*, pp. 115-62) emphasizes the theme of the covenant's significance for the whole world in the book of Isaiah.

The presence of individual foreigners in Israel in Old Testament narratives seems to be quite uncontroversial. Regulations in the Torah presuppose that the resident alien, the *gēr*, may indeed become a member of the worshipping community. Yet it is significant that the passage does not concern itself with the *gēr* but with foreigners in general, with the *ben-hannēkār*.[60] Elsewhere the Old Testament does worry about the neither-one-thing-nor-the-other status of a foreigner who does not become a member of the worshipping community. Thus Exodus 12.43 (P) prohibits participation in the Passover on the part of a foreigner (*ben-nēkār*), who is implicitly someone who does not want to make that full commitment, does not want to become attached to Yhwh. In the early Second Temple period, this question seems uncontroversial to others. Zechariah 2.15 [11] envisages many nations 'attaching themselves' to Yhwh and becoming Yhwh's people; Zechariah 8.20-23 then pictures peoples, inhabitants of cities, individuals, and groups doing so.

The fear expressed in v. 3aγδ seems odd in light of such texts. Presumably it links with another strand of attitude to foreigners that appears in Isaiah 52.1; Deuteronomy 23.4-9 [3-8]; and Ezra–Nehemiah. Deuteronomy 23 places severe constraints on admitting to Yhwh's congregation Ammonites, Moabites, and Edomites (who are prominent among the communities of Second Temple times). Whatever the date and background of Deuteronomy 23, Nehemiah 13.1-3 indicates that it was appealed to and made the basis of action in Nehemiah's day. In the time of Ezra and Nehemiah Judah was a small and beleaguered community that could feel that in more than one way it was in danger of being engulfed by surrounding communities, with its culture and its vocation to serve Yhwh thereby being compromised or overwhelmed.

'Separation' is the language in Ezra 6.21; 9–10; Nehemiah 9–10; 13.3, used in connection with the community's need to separate itself from those communities. Theologically, behind this expectation is Yhwh's having separated Israel from the peoples of Canaan (Lev 20.24-26 [H]; 1 Kgs 8.53). In v. 3 a hypothetical foreigner reworks the language of separation in yet another way in speaking of Yhwh separating a foreigner from Israel. The language will be reused in another negative way in 59.2. Given that Yhwh's election of Israel can be spoken of as a separation, the foreigner is implicitly expressing anxiety about being de-selected.[61]

In Leviticus and in Ezra the concern about other peoples is not so much ethnic as religious; perhaps a better way to put it is to recognize that societies usually associate the ethnic and the religious. The concern of the Torah and of Ezra is that those other peoples do not lead Israel into sharing their religious practices (for which Israel has usually been quite ready). The point is not explicit in Deuteronomy 23.4-9 [3-8] or in

[60] Cf. Croatto, *Imaginar el futuro*, p. 26.

[61] Cf. Benedict Otzen, *TWAT*, I, p. 520 (ET *TDOT*, II, p. 3).

Nehemiah. The prophet would agree that the community cannot accept foreigners who want to join it without giving up their present religious commitment (as is implicitly the case with the foreign women whom Judahites marry according to Ezra, and perhaps in Deuteronomy 23 and Nehemiah). In v. 6 the prophet will address this concern further, but here the significant point is the vital refining of 'foreigner' by 'who attaches himself to Yhwh'. Thus there is not a real tension between the more liberal view of Isaiah 56.1-8 and the more exclusivist attitude expressed subsequently in the chapters that divide the community into people who are really Yhwh's servants and people who are not,[62] because the basis for that distinction is whether or not people who belong ethnically to Israel are actually adhering to Yhwh. In this respect the Old Testament attitude is not so different from one that would obtain among people such as the Hittites and the Greeks.[63] The expression 'his people' surely refers to the community as a whole and not just 'the "pious" impoverished lower class'.[64]

Yet in light of the stance illustrated in Ezra and Nehemiah, the hypothetical foreigner who in the manner of those preexilic figures wanted to join Yhwh's people would have good reason for expecting to be spurned. Indeed, it is common to see Isaiah 56.1-8 as expressing a stance that contrasts with that in Deuteronomy[65] and/or Ezekiel[66] and/or Ezra–Nehemiah[67]. The prophet believes that the qualifications for membership of the community should be social and ethical markers rather than purity or reproductive ability.[68] Or one might see the passage as implying a compromise between segregationists (like Ezra and Nehemiah) and

[62] See, e.g., Christophe Nihan, 'Ethnicity and Identity in Isaiah 56–66', in Lipschits, Knoppers, and Oeming (eds.), *Judah and the Judeans in the Achaemenid Period*, pp. 67-104 (69).

[63] Cf. B. Lang, *TWAT*, V, p. 458 (ET *TDOT*, IX, p. 427); Meyer Fortes, 'Strangers', in Fortes and S. Patterson (eds.), *Studies in African Social Anthropology* (I. Schapera Festschrift; London: Academic, 1975), pp. 229-53.

[64] Against Albertz, *Religionsgeschichte Israels in alttestamentlicher Zeit*, II, p. 552 (ET p. 505).

[65] See, e.g., F. J. Stendebach, 'Überlegungen zum Ethos des Alten Testaments', *Kairos* 18 (1976), pp. 273-81 (280-81); Bernd Jørg Diebner, 'Jes 56,1-8 entsprechend Jes 66,18-24 und die prophetische Überbietung des Torah', in A. von Dobbeler, K. Erlemann, and R. Heiligentha (eds.), *Religionsgeschichte des Neuen Testaments* (Klaus Berger Festschrift; Tübingen: Franke, 2000), pp. 31-42. Knabenbauer (*Commentarius in Isaiam* 2, p. 387) heads the section, 'The limits of the Mosaic law are removed'.

[66] See Steven S. Tuell, 'The Priesthood of the "Foreigner"', in John T. Strong and Steven S. Tuell (eds.), *Constituting the Community* (S. D. McBride Festschrift; Winona Lake, IN: Eisenbrauns, 2005), pp. 183-204.

[67] See, e.g., J. Blenkinsopp, 'Second Isaiah—Prophet of Universalism', *JSOT* 41 (1988), pp. 83-103 (93-97), reprinted in P. R. Davies (ed.), *The Prophets* (Sheffield: Sheffield Academic Press, 1996), pp. 186-206 (199-204).

[68] See Clinton E. Hammock, 'Isaiah 56:1-8 and the Redefining of the Restoration Jewish Community', *Biblical Theology Bulletin* 30 (2000), pp. 46-57.

assimilationists.[69] Even if Ezra and Nehemiah themselves presuppose a religious rather than an ethnic bar on the acceptance of foreigners, it is easy to see that this could seem a subtle difference to many people in the community. It has been argued that 'foreigners' in Ezra and Nehemiah covers any people who are not returning exiles, including such as Samarians and Judahites who had not gone into exile.[70] If that is so here is in Isaiah 56.3, then *a fortiori* they are covered by its declaration. The non-occurrence of the word *gēr* ('resident alien') in Isaiah 56–66 as in Ezra–Nehemiah might support the idea that 'foreigner' would cover people such as Samarians.

A eunuch (v. 3b) is a man who has been rendered impotent and/or sterile by an act such as tying off or crushing his testicles, a recognized practice in the Middle East and the Greek world. It would render royal servants incapable of sexual involvement with women at court, or at least of procreating children by them, but also of of procreating other children and thus creating a potential alternative dynasty that might compete with the king's.[71] A eunuch is thus a dry tree as opposed to a green and flourishing one that is capable of producing fruit. In Matthew 19.12 the Greek word ἐυνοῦχος may also cover men who by nature lack heterosexual feelings, but there are no examples of this usage in the Old Testament.[72] Some occurrences of the word *sārîs* refer to officers at the royal court who were not eunuchs (e.g. Gen 40.2). Indeed, etymologically *sārîs* denotes 'official', and this seems to be the only passage that 'refers to the condition of a eunuch as a merely physical phenomenon'.[73] EVV assume that Isaiah 39.7 envisages some of Hezekiah's descendants becoming eunuchs in the palace in Babylon, and it would not be surprising if the exile meant this happened to a number of Judahites.[74] Nor would it be surprising if their return to Jerusalem raised the question whether they could still be a proper part of the community, given the regulation in Deuteronomy 23.2 [1]. Thus Isaiah 56–66 begins where Isaiah 1–39 ends.[75]

[69] S. David Sperling, 'Rethinking Covenant in Late Biblical Books', *Biblica* 70 (1989), pp. 50-73 (69-72).

[70] So Sara Japhet, *From the Rivers of Babylon to the Highlands of Judah* (Winona Lake, IN: Eisenbrauns, 2006) e.g., p. 114.

[71] See further Jacob L. Wright and Michael J. Chan, 'King and Eunuch: Isaiah 56:1–8 in Light of Honorific Royal Burial Practices', *JBL* 131 (2012), pp. 99-119.

[72] Augustine (*De sancta virginitate* 24-25) assumes that the eunuchs here in Isaiah are people who have made themselves eunuchs because of the kingdom of heaven, as in Matt 19.12. Elsewhere (*Contra Faustum Manicaeum* 14.1, 13) he takes up the tension between Isa 56 and the obligation to raise up seed in Israel (Deut 25.5-10) and comments, 'the same God spoke by Moses and Isaiah'; one needs to distinguish between begetting children in marriage and begetting spiritual children.

[73] B. Kedar-Kopfstein, *TWAT*, V, pp. 951-52 (ET *TDOT*, X, p. 347).

[74] See further Hayim Tadmor, 'Was the Biblical *sārîs* a Eunuch', in Z. Zevit, S. Gitin, and M. Sokoloff (eds.), *Solving Riddles and Untying Knots* (J. C. Greenfield Festschrift; Winona Lake, IN: Eisenbrauns, 1995), pp. 317-25.

[75] Frederick Gaiser, 'A New Word on Homosexuality?', *WW* 18 (1994), pp. 280-93 (286-88).

As we have noted, Nehemiah 13.1-3 indicates that Deuteronomy 23.4-5 [3-4] was appealed to and made the basis of action in Nehemiah's day. It would not be surprising if those other verses in the context were assumed to apply to men who had been made eunuchs in the exile and thus that Isaiah 56 should in effect declare that these verses do not in fact apply to them.[76] Eunuchs could naturally think of themselves and be seen by others as second-class citizens. Given the reduced state of the community, having children would be a key way that people contributed to its future and thus to its fulfilment of its vocation; the community can no more fulfil its vocation if it dies out than it can if it assimilates to the peoples around. The eunuch is pictured as recognizing that someone who cannot have children cannot do the thing the community most needs. The prophet affirms that neither foreign proselyte nor Israelite eunuch need fear Yhwh's rejection.

It will emerge that Isaiah 56–66 is concerned that many members of the Judahite community do not properly observe the Sabbath, and that this is not the only problem about their commitment to Yhwh's covenant. Yet it is not implausible to imagine these people being strict about the exclusion of eunuchs and foreigners from worship of Yhwh; they could easily make a case from the Torah for such a stance. The present passage thus turns their stance on its head. Jesus will make a similar point when he speaks of prostitutes and sinners entering God's realm ahead of the religious leaders of his day (Matt 21.31). The passage speaks in this way notwithstanding the importance later chapters will attach to the promise that the people's offspring and thus name will endure (66.23, in the passage that corresponds to 56.1-8 at the close of chapters 56–66).[77]

56.4 Because Yhwh has said this:
'To the eunuchs who guard my Sabbaths// and choose what I delight in,//
those who hold fast to my covenant:
5 I will give to them// within my house, within my walls,
A memorial and a name// better than sons and daughters:
I will give to him a lasting name,// one that will not be cut off.

Although vv. 2-3 were implicitly set in the context of the words of Yhwh in v. 1, it is the nature of clauses beginning 'The good fortune of' to be human speech. A resumptive message formula in v. 4 thus marks a transition back to explicitly divine speech; the rest of the line is a tricolon (4-3-2). The declaration that 'Yhwh has said this' makes for a contrast with what v. 3 has reported that the foreigner and eunuch might be inclined to say, but must not say.[78] But the message does not address the groups whose representatives have just spoken. Rather, its addressees are

[76] Cf. Sommer, *A Prophet Reads Scripture*, p. 279.
[77] Cf. Porúbčan, *Il Patto nuovo in Is. 40–66*, p. 233.
[78] Cf. Fitzgerald, 'A Rhetorical Analysis of Isaiah 56–66', p. 115.

the same as those of the words introduced by the opening message formula. It is the community as a whole that needs to hear what Yhwh says about eunuchs and foreigners. So the argument is: You must live in faithfulness in light of Yhwh's coming act of deliverance (v. 1); your living in faithfulness must be expressed in keeping Sabbath (v. 2); and you must treat eunuchs and foreigners who keep Sabbath as embraced by Yhwh's promise (vv. 3-8). For the eunuchs and foreigners themselves, it is perhaps at least as good to hear Yhwh addressing the community about them as hearing Yhwh directly address them. If they were to claim that Yhwh had spoken to them in words such as the ones the prophet goes on to relate, it might carry no weight with the community. If God speaks about them to the community, they get both things they need: a reassurance from Yhwh and a word to the community. It is not exactly the case that Yhwh is issuing a statute, for instance to supersede the one in Deuteronomy 23.[79] Yhwh's words do not have the form of a statute, and 'the two texts do *not* share a single term in common', as they do with Ezra–Nehemiah and Ezekiel 44.[80] But as a prophetic word, they would have the effect of countering any claim that Deuteronomy 23 excluded either eunuchs or foreigners who attach themselves to Yhwh.

In substance vv. 3-8 work in abb′a′ order: v. 3 spoke of the fears of foreigners then eunuchs, but in responding to these fears vv. 4-5 speaks first of eunuchs. Indeed, one could see the verses as an abcb′a′ chiasm, in which the declaration 'because Yhwh has said this' stands at the centre with some emphasis.[81] The prosaic nature of the speech is marked by the occurrences of 'who', 'what', and the object marker in v. 4 (*ʾăšer* twice, *baʾăšer*, *ʾet*; further instances in v. 5), which in poetry would regularly be omitted (contrast v. 2). At the same time, the three cola describing the eunuchs are parallel depictions such as might naturally feature in verse.

It is v. 4 that begins to indicate that there has been no change of subject in v. 3. In effect v. 3 has declared that in the context of the prophet's and the community's life, guarding faithfulness is expressed by guarding the Sabbath. Yhwh now goes on to assure the eunuchs (indirectly) that if they do guard the Sabbath, this overrides the significance of their being unable to make that other contribution to the community's future, by fathering children. Yhwh (also indirectly) instructs the community not to look askance at eunuchs who keep the Sabbath (unlike some of its members?).

[79] So Herbert Donner, 'Jesaja lvi 1-7: ein Abrogationsfall innerhalb des Kanons', in J. A. Emerton (ed.), *Congress Volume: Salamanca 1983* (Leiden: Brill, 1985), pp. 81-95; it is on this basis that Gaiser sees the passage as providing a precedent for accepting same-sex relationships ('A New Word on Homosexuality').

[80] Nihan, 'Ethnicity and Identity in Isaiah 56–66' (see above), p. 75. Duhm (*Jesaia*, p. 382) assumes that in any case Deut 23.2-9 [1-8] comes from later.

[81] So Fitzgerald, *A Rhetorical Analysis of Isaiah 56–66*, p. 106. Berges (*Das Buch Jesaja*, p. 510) sees vv. 1-8 as a whole as a chiasm, but the links between vv. 1-2 and 8 are not strong.

Yhwh first heightens the earlier reference to 'guarding the Sabbath' by speaking of 'guarding my Sabbaths'; the use of this verb with the plural noun, which is then suffixed, recurs elsewhere (e.g. Exod 31.13 [P]; Lev 19.3, 30; 26.2 [H]), and both the plural and the suffix serve to underline the point. As was the case in v. 2b, the general statements that follow, concerning choosing and holding fast to the covenant, actually explicate that first statement. In Isaiah 58.13 Yhwh speaks of the necessity for people to turn their feet from the Sabbath, from 'doing what you delight in on my holy day'. The Sabbath is Yhwh's territory; they are not to trample on it.[82] Paradoxically, choosing what Yhwh delights in or likes rather than what they delight in or like means choosing to do nothing, or at least choosing not to work. The prophet is not referring to what we would call pleasure activities but to what we would see as things we like to choose to do, which in a Western context could well be work activities, as they would be for the prophet's community (see Neh 10.32 [31]; 13.15-22). The employment of the verb 'choose' with a human being as subject and something to do with God as object is the reverse of the more usual Old Testament usage; it correspondends to the occurrence in Deuteronomy 30.19 where 'choose becomes an act of religious confession' from which Israel's existence derives. The word suggests more the making of a decision to serve Yhwh than an act that involves weighing different options.[83]

Even more strikingly, guarding the Sabbath and choosing to do what Yhwh says on that day is then characterized as holding fast to Yhwh's covenant.[84] The verb picks up from v. 2a. While Exodus 31.16 links Sabbath and covenant by requiring Israel to guard the Sabbath as a lasting covenant, this identifying of Sabbath-keeping with covenant-keeping is unparalleled.[85] Yhwh implies that observing the Sabbath is the key principle of the covenant, the marker of whether someone does keep the covenant. Whereas in Exodus 31 profaning Yhwh's Sabbaths rather than keeping them is the basis for Israelites being cut off from the community, here keeping Yhwh's Sabbaths rather than profaning them is the basis for foreigners and eunuchs not being cut off from the community.[86] Further,

[82] But perhaps plural 'Sabbaths' includes the Sabbath Year and the Jubilee (so Mark Brett, 'Imperial Imagination in Isaiah 56–66', in Abernethy and others (eds.), *Isaiah and Imperial Context*, pp. 170-84.

[83] Horst Seebass, *TWAT*, I, p. 607 (ET *TDOT*, II, p. 86). See further the comment on 65.12.

[84] Polan's suggestion that the *w* on the verb is explicative and that this marks the colon as a summarizing explanatory statement (*In the Ways of Justice toward Salvation*, pp. 69-70) may be right, but the *w* explicative in itself does not look very different from those in vv. 1a, 1b, 2a, and 2b.

[85] Cf. Lau, *Schriftgelehrte Prophetie in Jes 56–66*, p. 267.

[86] Cf. Lezek Ruszkowski, 'Der Sabbat bei Tritojesaja', in Beat Huwyler and H.-P. Mathys (eds.), *Prophetie und Psalmen* (K. Seybold Festschrift; Münster: Ugarit, 2001), pp. 61-74 (72).

the link between Sabbath and sanctuary in vv. 4-5 parallels the link between keeping Yhwh's Sabbaths and revering Yhwh's sanctuary in Leviticus 19.30; 26.2 (as well as the link in Exod 31). 'Holiness has both a spatial and a temporal dimension'.[87]

Part of the background will again be that this expectation regarding the Sabbath is under particular pressure in the context, when the surrounding communities are keen to do business in Jerusalem seven days a week and the Judahites are under economic pressure themselves that makes it hard to 'waste' a day when they could be safeguarding their future. This statement about eunuchs will thus also give the rest of the community something to think about.

In v. 5a, Yhwh's actual undertaking comprises two bicola (2-2, 2-3) with some internal parallelism within cola (within my house/walls, a memorial/name, my sons/daughters) that would have made it easy to incorporate parallelism into the lines, but the prophet did not do so. Verse 5b picks up the verb 'give' from v. 5a (though in a different form) and the word 'name', and the line as a whole constitutes a refining of v. 5a through the addition of 'lasting' and 'that will not be cut off'. In addition the singular 'him' complements the plural 'them' and takes up the singulars of vv. 2-3, individualizing the point (LXX changes to plural, smoothing the text). So the relationship between the two halves of the verse is like that of parallelism.

Yhwh's declaration concerning the eunuchs may suggest that the question about them concerns their possible second-class status within Israel rather than their total exclusion from the community. First, it presupposes the issue of their status within the temple—'my house' and 'my walls'. The reduced state of the community, a few thousand people gathered over a few square miles around Jerusalem, would mean that for the Judahite community the temple was a more significant focus than it had been in Israel's heyday. A larger people was then spread over hundreds of square miles with many towns and villages; Jerusalem and its temple were less pivotal to most people's lives. Now they are central. Yhwh is therefore making a significant promise when declaring that eunuchs will receive 'a memorial and a name' there, *yād wāšēm* (the phrase provides the Jerusalem Holocaust Memorial with its name). The use of *yād* (usually 'hand') to mean memorial is established: see 1 Samuel 15.12 and especially 2 Samuel 18.18, which relates to a man who dies childless.[88] So one might take the phrase to denote a 'memorial stele'.[89] While LXX apparently did not recognize that *yād* could mean

[87] Jacob Milgrom, *Leviticus 17–22* (New York: Doubleday, 2000), p. 1699.

[88] Cf. Robert Gordis, 'A Note on *yad*', *JBL* 62 (1943), pp. 341-44; he suggests that here it means offspring.

[89] D. W. Van Winkle, 'The Meaning of *yād wāšēm* in Isaiah lvi 5', *VT* 47 (1997), pp. 378-85. See further de Hulster, *Iconographic Exegesis and Third Isaiah*, pp. 151-68.

'monument', it rightly takes the phrase as a hendiadys,[90] 'a named place', implying 'an honoured place', 'a place of distinction'.[91] For eunuchs to have a place at all would be a significant statement, given the possibility that the Torah might be thought to exclude them.

The basis for this extended meaning of *yād* is not clear. One understanding arises from the possibility that *yād* can be a euphemism for penis (e.g. 57.8, 10);[92] perhaps a monument had phallic significance, so that it is significant that it is a eunuch who is promised a *yād*. This *yād* might then come from a different root from the word meaning 'hand'.[93] Another understanding arises from the occasional portrayal of hands on steles; perhaps the hand signifies prayerful supplication. There are a number of parallels to the idea that someone might erect such a monument in a temple,[94] though not in connection with the temple at Jerusalem. Metaphorically speaking, sons and daughters would normally give a man a memorial and a place of honour in the community. They keep his name alive. Thus name and offspring are often associated (e.g. 48.19; 66.22). Metaphorically speaking, Yhwh will act in this way for the eunuchs.[95] They will have an assured place with Yhwh, and thus in the temple. The promise might link with the negative attitude to religious practices in connection with dead people that will surface in Isaiah 57.[96] Yhwh will keep the eunuchs' name alive. He will behave in the manner of a king honouring his servants, and specifically the eunuchs among them.[97]

[90] Cf. H. A. Brongers, 'Yād wāšēm', in *Übersetzung und Deutung* (A. R. Hulst Festschrift; Nijkerk: Callenbach, 1977), pp. 35-37.

[91] Dodson, *Isaiah*, p. 342. Compare Gnana Robinson's suggestion ('The Meaning of יָד in Isaiah 56 5', *ZAW* 88 [1976], pp. 282-84) that *yād* means a share in the land; cf. Sara Japhet, 'יד ושם (Isa 56:5)', *Maarav* 8 (1992), pp. 69-80. Τόπος is one of LXX's recourses for words it is puzzled by (Troxel, *LXX-Isaiah*, pp. 115-16); cf. also Tg, Vg, Syr.

[92] See possibly Cant 5.4 and certainly 1QS 7.13; *yd* can have this meaning in Ugaritic. See, e.g., Shalom M. Paul, 'The "Plural of Ecstasy" in Mesopotamian and Biblical Love Poetry', in Zevit, Gitin, and Sokoloff (eds.), *Solving Riddles and Untying Knots* (see above), pp. 585-97 (593).

[93] See M. Delcor, 'Two Special Meanings of the Word יד in Biblical Hebrew', *JSS* 12 (1967), pp. 230-40 (234-40).

[94] See, e.g., Scullion, 'Some Difficult Texts in Isaiah cc.56–66', p. 107; Judith M. Hadley, 'The Khirbet el-Qom Inscription', *VT* 37 (1987), pp. 50-62 (60-62); Yigael Yadin, *Hazor* (London: Oxford University Press, 1972), pp. 71-74; but these references show that this interpretation of the steles is itself speculative and controverted.

[95] Cf. Oswald Loretz, 'Stelen und Sohnespflicht im Totenkult Kanaans und Israels', *UF* 21 (1989), pp. 241-46; Shemaryahu Talmon, 'Yad wašem', *Hebrew Studies* 25 (1984), pp. 8-17.

[96] Cf. Francesca Stavrakopoulou, *Land of Our Fathers* (London: Continuum, 2010), pp. 121-26. But the further suggestion that the passage's promises to foreigners and eunuchs imply a grant of land rights and thus the dispossession of others surely reads agenda into the text, which is concerned with rights in connection with worship.

[97] See Wright and Chan, 'King and Eunuch' (see above).

How will their memorial be better than that given by sons and daughters? If we assume that there were no memorials in the temple itself, then Yhwh's giving the eunuchs their assured place there is one aspect of its superiority. In the manner of parallelism, v. 5b (3-3) likely adds to that point. It will mean a lasting name. 'Everlasting' might overstate the implication of *ʿôlām* in connection with the eunuch's name; in itself the word could indicate simply that the name will last until the end of the eunuch's life. Who knows whether a person's sons and daughters will survive to constitute his memorial? Absalom's sons apparently did not do so; hence the memorial he erects. The eunuchs could have feared that they would indeed be cut off from Israel (among many examples of this verb, see, e.g., Lev 18.29 [H]); being excluded from the temple might have that implication. Yhwh promises that their name and thus they themselves will not be cut off, and this promise could go beyond that indicated by *ʿôlām*. They will be remembered, and in this sense will live on.[98] Both in wording and in substance the line is thus close to 48.19 as well as 55.13. If *yād* does or could mean penis, the declaration that the eunuch's name will not be cut off might raise a smile.

This passage about eunuchs played a part in the spirited debate among Christians in the second century concerning celibacy; Christians who regarded virginity as a higher state than marriage and rejected both marriage and procreation claimed its support.[99] Karl Barth also comments on the passage's significance in connection with commitment to a single life for God's sake, seeing the promise to eunuchs as an anticipation of the New Testament's positive vision for single life.[100]

56.6 And the foreigners who attach themselves to Yhwh,// to minister to him and to dedicate themselves to Yhwh's name,// to be servants to him,
Every one who guards the Sabbath rather than profaning it,// and those who hold fast to my covenant:
7 I will bring them to my holy mountain// and let them rejoice in my prayer house,
Their whole offerings and their sacrifices// acceptable on my altar,
Because my house will be called// a prayer house, for all peoples.

Verse 6 returns to the foreigners, completing the abb'a' treatment of foreigners and eunuchs; more space is given to foreigners than to eunuchs both in the 'good fortune' statement (v. 3) and in the divine word (vv. 4-5 and 6-8). After the resumptive opening taking up the terms of v. 3a but making them plural, as vv. 4-5 made the eunuchs plural, the main part of

[98] See Stanley Brice Frost, 'The Memorial of a Childless Man', *Interpretation* 26 (1972), pp. 437-50.

[99] See Wilken and others (eds.), *Isaiah Interpreted by Early Christian and Medieval Commentators*, pp. 450-58; Elliott (ed.), *Isaiah 40–66*, pp. 193-94.

[100] Barth, *Die Kirchliche Dogmatik* III/4, pp. 157-58 (ET p. 142); cf. Mark S. Gignilliat, *Karl Barth and the Fifth Gospel* (Farnham, UK: Ashgate, 2009), pp. 134-36.

v. 6a again comprises three parallel statements about the foreigners that explicate what attaching themselves to Yhwh implies. It thus parallels the three statements about the eunuchs that expand on what guarding Yhwh's Sabbaths implies. Although v. 6a (a tricolon, 4-4-3) refers to Yhwh in the third person, there is no need to infer that Yhwh has stopped speaking or that we should emend the text so that the verse becomes wholly first-person.[101] Indeed, the transition back to first-person speech at the end of the verse supports the idea that we should see Yhwh as self-referring throughout v. 6 and thus throughout vv. 4-7 after the message formula. Of course the prophet actually formulates Yhwh's words, and we can imagine the prophet moving unselfconsciously between speaking *as* Yhwh and speaking *of* Yhwh; the dynamic differs from the one involved in the use of the message formula, or the declaration formula in v. 8, when the prophet is conscious of speaking as prophet and not as mouthpiece for Yhwh's own words.

First, attaching oneself to Yhwh involves 'ministering to him'. While *šārat* can denote service of a non-religious kind, it more often denotes service in a worship setting, and this fits the present context (see also 60.7, 10; 61.6); Aq, Sym, Th thus have λειτουργεῖν. This ministry can be of a more down-to-earth and practical kind, the ministry of Levites, or of the more eminent kind exercised by priests. Either way, it suggests a more specialized activity than the commoner *ʿābad*, not unlike the English word 'minister' as opposed to 'serve', and it gives the foreigners a position of importance in connection with the worship of Yhwh. In 61.6 'ministers' and 'priests' appear in parallelism as descriptions of the position and function of the Israelites as a whole over against foreigners, who support them by fulfilling everyday practical tasks in the manner of the other clans that support the Levites. By anticipation, the declaration here broadens out the possibilities open to foreigners. Read in light of 61.6 and of 66.18-24 with its other links to this opening passage in Isaiah 56–66, these ministers' work could well be of a priestly kind. This might explain the replacement of the word by 'servants' in 1QIs[a], and also explain both LXX's δουλεύειν and Vg's *colant*; MT's verb could seem scandalously implausible.[102] Ezekiel 44 excludes foreigners from the sanctuary, though it makes a point of referring to them as 'uncircumcised', which might be a sign that (like the passages from Ezra noted in connection with v. 3) it is concerned about people who have not made a commitment to Yhwh rather than with a purely ethnic question. It is difficult to imagine that the prophet whose message appears in Isaiah 56

[101] So, e.g., Budde, 'Jesaia Kap. 40–66', p. 695.

[102] Cf. Roy D. Wells, '"Isaiah" as an Exponent of Torah: Isaiah 56.1-8', in Melugin and Sweeney (eds.), *New Visions of Isaiah*, pp. 140-55 (147-48); Dwight W. Van Winkle, 'An Inclusive Authoritative Text in Exclusive Communities', in Broyles and Evans (eds.), *Writing and Reading the Scroll of Isaiah*, I, pp. 423-40; Daniel, *Le vocabulaire du culte dans la Septante*, pp. 98-100.

would think that people could 'attach themselves to Yhwh' without being circumcised.[103] Both would agree with Nehemiah's action reported in Nehemiah 13.4-9.

Second, attaching oneself to Yhwh involves dedicating oneself to Yhwh's name. While both the verb and the idea of Yhwh's 'name' are Deuteronomic emphases, the combination of the two otherwise comes only in Psalms 5.12 [11]; 69.37 [36]; 119.132. All three passages assume that this dedication is (ideally) a description of all Israelites. The verb is *ʾāhēb*, commonly translated 'love', but it is a word that denotes commitment and not just feelings. Dedication to Yhwh's name implies a commitment to honouring it. 1QIs[a] has *brk* 'worship'.

The third explication does introduce the notion of being Yhwh's 'servants'. LXX nicely gender-inclusivizes the noun, translating δούλους καὶ δούλας, perhaps following 14.2,[104] but like the variant treatments of *šārat*, the double translation may be designed to rule out any idea that the line refers to service in worship.[105] Whereas Isaiah 40–55 uses the singular term 'servant' to identify Israel (the plural comes only in 54.17), Isaiah 63–66 uses the plural. Like the converse move from plural to singular in vv. 1-3, it indicates the awareness in Isaiah 56–66 that people need to make their own commitment to Yhwh. And the verse points to the way in which arguably 'service' is the Bible's 'comprehensive... concept of the active life' which complements the idea of life as a gift from God.[106]

While some references to 'Yhwh's servants' are open to referring to people within Israel who *really* serve Yhwh, the term is designed to be one that describes all Israel. The absence of an 'and' before the last phrase in this line has the effect of binding together the two expressions. It is then noteworthy that 'his servants' appears in parallelism with people who are 'dedicated to his name' in Ps 69.37 [36]. This double reference comes in a promise that Yhwh will deliver Zion and build up the cities of Judah so that the offspring of Yhwh's servants will possess it and all who are dedicated to Yhwh's name will live there. Once again, the prophecy is indicating that foreigners can share in Israel's privileges.

The verse introduces us to 'a fundamentally different use of the language of servanthood' from that in Isaiah 40–55,[107] though it is an

[103] Contrast Schaper, 'Rereading the Law' (see above), p. 135. We have noted in the comment on v. 2 that it might be intelligible that circumcision could be taken for granted, while Sabbath has become *the* distinguishing mark of belonging to the covenant community.

[104] Cf. Ziegler, *Untersuchungen zur Septuaginta des Buches Isaias*, p. 77.

[105] Cf. Rubinstein, 'The Theological Aspect of Some Variant Readings in the Isaiah Scroll', pp. 189-90.

[106] So Barth, *Die Kirchliche Dogmatik* III/4, p. 543; on p. 545 he refers to v. 6 (ET pp. 474, 476).

[107] Joseph Blenkinsopp, 'The Servant and the Servants in Isaiah', in Broyles and Evans (eds.), *Writing and Reading the Scroll of Isaiah* 1, pp. 155-75 (166); cf. Knud Jeppesen,

exaggeration to say that the central theme of Isaiah 56–66 is 'Who are the servants of Yhwh'.[108] Even here it is a subordinate motif, applied only to the foreigner and not to the eunuch, and it does not surface again until Isaiah 63. To support the thesis regarding its centrality by positing the presence of the theme when the term is absent confuses the question. One can indeed note that it is a central theme of the entire Bible, but this argument would obscure the significance of these chapters' use of the actual term 'servants of Yhwh'.[109] It is indeed striking that the expression appears in this opening section of Isaiah 56–66; Numbers Rabbah 8.2 notes how systematically vv. 6-7 apply to proselytes terms that are elsewhere characteristically used of Israel.[110]

Four of the terms in v. 6a have resonances from the Torah.[111] It prohibits 'foreigners' from eating Pesah (unless they have decided to join Israel properly, by implication) (Exod 12.43). It calls the Levites people who 'attach themselves' to Aaron (Num 18.1-6 [P]), as their name hints; we do not know whether historically the name *lēwî* and the verb *lāwâ* are connected, but Genesis 29.34 shows that Israelites made the link. It speaks much of the 'ministry' that priests and Levites exercise and of the 'service' of the wilderness dwelling (both terms also come in Num 18.1-6).[112] All this serves to turn on its head the idea that Yhwh might want to 'separate' foreigners from Israel, which is also an idea the Torah would raise for readers (e.g. Lev 20.22-26 [H]). On the contrary, they will be able to bring the whole offerings and sacrifices that the Torah prescribes. Not only will they be like Israelites; they will be like Levites.

'From "You, My Servant" to "The Hand of the Lord Is with My Servants"', *SJOT* 1 (1990), pp. 113-29. Mark S. Gignilliat (*Paul and Isaiah's Servants* [New York: T&T Clark International, 2007], pp. 112-31) sees the move from 'servant' in Isa 40–55 to 'servants' in Isa 40–66 as significant background to 2 Cor 5.14–6.10.

[108] Against (e.g.) Beuken, 'Trito-Jesaja', pp. 78-83. Ulrich Berges in 'Who Were the Servants?' (in Johannes C. de Moor and Harry F. van Rooy [eds.], *Past, Present, Future* [Leiden: Brill, 2000], pp. 1-18) develops a further thesis that these servants played a key role in bringing the book of Isaiah into being, and that we need to relate them to 'the servants of Yhwh' in the Psalter.

[109] John D. Oswalt does argue that 'servanthood' is 'the single most dominating theme of the present book of Isaiah' ('The Kerygmatic Structure of the Book of Isaiah', in J. E. Coleson and V. H. Matthews (eds.), *'Go to the Land I Will Show You'* (D. W. Young Festschrift; Winona Lake: Eisenbrauns, 1996), pp. 143-57 (156).

[110] Cf. M. A. Beek, 'De vreemdeling krijgt toegang', in H. H. Grosheide *et al.* (eds.), *De Knecht: Studies rondom Deutero-Jeseja* (J. L. Koole Festschrift; Kampen: Kok, 1978), pp. 17-22 (19).

[111] For what follows, see Fishbane. 'The Hebrew Bible and Exegetical Tradition' (see above), pp. 27-28.

[112] Elsewhere Fishbane comments that 'Ezek. 44 and Isa. 56 provide explicit testimony of contesting exegesis of one common Scripture: Num. 18', though he notes that Deut 23 also played a role in this debate (*Biblical Interpretation in Ancient Israel*, p. 142).

The description of the foreigners indicates they are people who in later terms would count as proselytes, though the use of the word may be anachronistic.[113] Shaye Cohen comments about texts from the Persian period:

> With the destruction of the temple, the disappearance of the tribal system, the emergence of a diaspora, the weakening of the connection between the people and the land, and the gradual elaboration of non-temple-oriented forms of religiosity comes the beginning of the idea that gentiles could somehow attach themselves to the people of Israel by attaching themselves to Israel's God. Here then are the harbingers of the idea of conversion, in both its religious and its social sense, but the idea itself is not yet in evidence.[114]

Volker Haarmann suggests another basis for seeing the word 'proselytes' as inappropriate for the people to whom the passage refers, the fact that they do not become members of Israel. They attach themselves to Yhwh, not to Israel.[115] Everything depends on whether one uses the word *proselyte* to denote an adherent of a religion or a person who joins a people. While this distinction is harder to make in a traditional society than in a Western society, Isaiah 56.1-8 does speak of people joining Yhwh, not joining Israel. The temple can become a house of prayer for all peoples without Israel's ethnic distinctiveness being abolished. A different form of 'attachment to Yhwh' will indeed develop in the newer socio-religious context to which Cohen refers, but in the period to which 56.1-8 belongs, not all these features have emerged. On the other hand, it is hardly appropriate to see the prophecy as relating to the eschatological age,[116] if this implies that a foreigner could not expect to join in the worship of Yhwh in the present. Rather it implies that Yhwh's eschatological intent has implications for now. We have noted that the idea that foreigners might 'attach themselves' to Yhwh is a familiar one at all periods of Israel's history, and that at least some of the stories about such foreigners appear in writings commonly thought to come from the Persian period, though one can imagine the idea being under pressure in Judah in that period.

[113] Wolfgang Kraus ('Contemporary Translation of the Septuagint' in W. Kraus and R. G. Wooden [eds.], *Septuagint Research* [Atlanta: SBL, 2006], pp. 63-83 [76-77]) makes this point on the basis of MT's not using the word *gēr*.

[114] *The Beginnings of Jewishness* (Berkeley: University of California Press, 1999), p. 122; cf. Joachim Schaper, 'Torah and Identity in the Persian Period', in Lipschits, Knoppers, and Oeming (eds.), *Judah and the Judeans in the Achaemenid Period*, pp. 27-38 (29); earlier, Kaufmann, *The Babylonian Captivity and Deutero-Isaiah*, pp. 52-58, 164-68.

[115] *JHWH-Verehrer der Völker* (Zurich: Theologischer Verlag Zürich, 2006), pp. 206-46.

[116] Against Cohen, *The Beginnings of Jewishness*, p. 122 (cf. p. 250); Park, *Die Gerechtigkeit Israels und das Heil der Völker*, pp. 77-79.

Verse 6b (3-2) explicates the point further, in part applying specifically to the foreigners what v. 2 said in general terms and in part applying to the foreigners the phraseology that appeared in v. 4 in connection with eunuchs. As v. 5 moved from plural to singular concerning eunuchs, so does v. 6 concerning foreigners, thus making explicit in the first colon the implication that the promise applies to each one of them. As the expectation of the foreigners in v. 6 corresponds to the expectation of the eunuchs in v. 4, so the promises to the foreigners in vv. 7-8 correspond to the promises to the eunuchs in v. 5, though we have noted that both expectations and promises for foreigners are more extensive than those for eunuchs.

Verse 7 begins with a neat pair of parallel cola (3-3), each comprising a first-person *w*-consecutive qatal verb (one hiphil, one piel) with third-person suffix and a prepositional construct phrase, but there is nothing very poetic about the second and third lines in v. 7 (they can be read as 2-2, 3-2). The first two lines offer complementary and closely related promises; the third line provides their theological background.

The first, double, promise is a notably personal one. Yhwh in person will bring these foreigners to Jerusalem, 'my holy mountain'. Perhaps there is an implication that they need not worry about Israel being hesitant or dilatory about doing so if Yhwh intends to take this action. But the words are reminiscent of those in 52.1, which reassure 'the holy city' that the uncircumcised and unclean will no more 'come' (*bôʾ* as here) into it;[117] so perhaps the words reassure them that they need not worry about that earlier promise imperilling their coming. It is less plausible that the occurrence of this common verb links with the occurrence in v. 1 in a different sense and that this recurrence also links with the use of the verb in Deuteronomy 23.2-9 [1-8].[118]

Once more the foreigners overhear God telling the Judahites something they need to note. 'Letting them rejoice' in the temple then takes further and makes more explicit the idea of 'bringing' them there, given that the very nature of worship at the sanctuary is to involve 'rejoicing before Yhwh' (e.g. Deut 12.7, 12, 18). The promise also makes a link with Ezra 6.21-22, where Yhwh causes the community to rejoice at the restoration of the temple; that community comprised people who had returned from the exile along with all the people who had 'separated themselves' from the impurity of the local peoples. The expression 'my holy mountain' recurs in the opening and closing sections of Isaiah 56–66 (see 56.7; 57.13; 65.11, 25; 66.20). The phrase involves the adjectival use of the noun *qōdeš*, which is more broadly characteristic of chapters 56–66 in further references to holy day, holy courtyards, holy people, holy spirit,

[117] Cf. Christopher T. Begg, 'The Peoples and the Worship of Yahweh in the Book of Isaiah', in Graham, Marrs, and McKenzie (eds.), *Worship and the Hebrew Bible*, pp. 35-55 (49).

[118] Contrast Schaper, 'Rereading the Law' (see above), p. 135.

holy eminence, holy cities, and holy house (58.13; 62.9, 12; 63.10, 11, 15, 18; 64.9, 10 [10, 11]).[119] Earlier in the book 'holy mountain' comes only at 11.9 (elsewhere at Ezek 20.40; Joel 2.1; 4.17 [3.17]; Obad 16; Zeph 3.11). Elsewhere, Psalm 43.3 speaks of being brought to Yhwh's holy mountain; the presence of other verbal links between the psalm and the verse in Isaiah may mean the prophet is echoing the psalm.[120] The talk of rejoicing in connection with the temple also reflects the Old Testament assumption that rejoicing is something outward and not merely internal. It refers to celebration, not merely to joyful feelings but to 'articulated expressions of joy', involving 'external (vehement) movement'.[121]

In turn, 'my holy mountain' is given precision by the reference to 'my prayer house'. The description of the temple as a prayer house comes only here, though it follows the emphasis on prayer in and toward the temple in Solomon's temple dedication prayer (1 Kgs 8; 2 Chr 6–7). Further, the place where people pray the prayers in the Psalter would commonly be the temple. For Christians, who dissociate prayer and offerings, the move from talk of the temple as a prayer house to talk of offerings is a surprise,[122] but prayer is regularly an accompaniment of offerings and offerings are regularly an accompaniment of prayer. While the exile and the cessation of its regular worship may have meant that prayer gained in prominence as the rationale for having a temple, evidently the prophet does not assume that offerings are now unnecessary. Neither prayer nor offering is complete without the other. Prayer makes explicit what an offering is about; an offering avoids being cheap in reaching out to Yhwh.

Whole offerings and sacrifices cover offerings in general (see Lev 1–3). 'Whole offerings' are made in their entirety to Yhwh as an act of worship, in particular at daybreak and dusk on behalf of the people as a whole; these times are then also the regular daily times of prayer. 'Sacrifices' are shared by offerer and Yhwh; they are more occasional and often express gratitude for prayers that Yhwh has answered. Israel's disdain for what Yhwh expected of it could mean that its whole offerings and sacrifices were not acceptable or welcome (*l^erāṣôn*, as also in Jer 6.20; and compare the verb *rāṣâ* in Amos 5.22; Mic 6.7; Mal 1.10; Ps 51.18 [16]). They would not then have the desired effect of further cementing Israel's relationship with Yhwh or encouraging Yhwh to answer its prayers. Conversely, Yhwh could decide that other peoples' offerings and sacrifices were acceptable and could have those effects. A similar phrase

[119] See H. Ringgren, *TWAT*, VI, pp. 1195-96 (ET *TDOT*, XII, pp. 536-37).

[120] Cf. Nurmela, *The Mouth of the Lord Has Spoken*, pp. 90-91.

[121] G. Vanoni, *TWAT*, VII, p. 814 (ET *TDOT*, XIII, p. 149).

[122] Ruszkowski (*Volk und Gemeinde*, p. 143) calls v. 7aβ a 'foreign body'. His positing a contrast in Prov 15.8 is surely mistaken, as that aphorism's parallelism implies an association of prayer and sacrifice: Yhwh repudiates both on the part of the faithless but accepts both on the part of the upright.

will recur in 60.7, where foreigners' flocks and rams 'will come up for acceptance on my altar' (*'al-rāṣôn mizbᵉḥî*); the verse even describes the animals as 'ministering' (cf. v. 6), though they are ministering to Jerusalem rather than directly to Yhwh.

The third line provides the theological background to this decision by Yhwh; or one might call the *kî* clause a result clause.[123] It is Yhwh's intention that the temple should be a prayer house not just for Israel but for all peoples, such as Ammonites, Moabites, Edomites, and Samarians, people with whom Judah had tense relationships in Second Temple times. The comma in the translation recognizes an oddity about the word order in the 3-2 line: literally, 'For my house a prayer-house will be called for all peoples'. The possibility of foreigners praying towards the temple is also flagged in Solomon's prayer (1 Kgs 8.41-43; 2 Chr 6.32-33), though this declaration goes much further in making foreigners actual members of the congregation.[124] The idea of resident aliens bringing offerings is recognized in the Torah, which specifies that the same regulations apply to them as to Israelites (Lev 17.8-12; 22.17-20 [H]; Num 15.14-16 [P]).

56.8 The declaration of the Lord Yhwh,// who gathers together the scattered of Israel:
'I will gather together yet more towards it, to its gathered ones'.

Again, there is nothing very poetic about this closing verse, though it might be understood as a 3-3-4 tricolon. The opening phrase functions resumptively to introduce and add emphasis to the promise that will follow in the second line (as in 55.8; 66.22). It is a common alternative formulation to 'Yhwh has said this', though it more usually appears after the words to which it refers (e.g. 54.17; 59.20; 66.2, 17; LXX takes it so here). Isaiah 1.24 compares with this instance. It commonly functions to add force to some strong statement that people need to be urged to take with absolute seriousness on the basis of the fact that Yhwh actually said it and means it with absolute seriousness.[125] The unusual prefixing of the word 'Lord' to the name Yhwh in this expression, which comes only here in Isaiah 40–66, also underlines the point.

Its elaboration by a phrase describing Yhwh is also unusual. Appended to 'Yhwh has said this', such phrases provide further anticipatory undergirding for the subsequent message. Here the phrase's relationship with what follows is less straightforward, even somewhat ironic. The fact that Yhwh is the one who gathers together the scattered of Israel would naturally undergird some promise to Israel; a promise to gather together

123 So Obara, *Le strategie di Dio*, p. 111, referring to *IBHS* 38.3b.
124 Cf. Christoph Bultmann, *Der Fremde im antiken Juda* (Göttingen: Vandenhoeck & Ruprecht, 1992), p. 210.
125 See F. Baumgärtel, 'Die Formel *nᵉʾum jahwe*', *ZAW* 73 (1961), pp. 277-90.

the scattered of Israel (using the same expression as here) appears in 11.12. It is noteworthy that the line uses the term Israel to denote people dispersed over the world as well as people in Judah.[126] If v. 8 stood on its own as an independent promise (as it has been suggested it originally did), its significance would indeed be as a promise about the gathering of the community. In a context where many Judahites in Babylonia had not jumped at the opportunity to 'return' to Judah, this characterization of Yhwh is significant for the Jerusalem community. Yet here it leads into a promise that raises people's eyes higher.

The second line is oddly expressed, though its point is clear enough. The oddness of the expression may link with the way it recalls Deuteronomy 30.4, which promises that even if your 'scattered' is at the end of the world, Yhwh will 'gather you together'('scattered' and 'you' are here singular). Verse 8 implicitly takes up this promise but extends it. Yhwh's 'gathering' is not confined to Israel; in welcoming the foreigners, Yhwh will be gathering yet more to Israel. The preposition is *ʿal*, the Hebrew preposition with most varied meaning. I take *l*ᵉ*niqbāṣāyw* as in apposition to *ʿālāyw*, whose interpretation can then be related to that final expression. Yhwh's gathering of scattered Israel is not the end of Yhwh's gathering. Tg does assume that the extra ones Yhwh gathers are more Israelites, which makes entire sense in itself and corresponds to promises expressed elsewhere. But in the context the extra ones must be the foreigners of whom vv. 6-7 have spoken. To the already gathered Israelites Yhwh will gather yet more, from those foreigners. For *l*ᵉ*niqbāṣāyw*, LXX's suggestive rendering is simply συναγωγήν.

Conclusion

The opening verse in Isaiah 56–66 sets agenda for the chapters as a whole. It challenges the Judahite community to live in the light of Yhwh's promises concerning its coming restoration, which will be an expression of Yhwh's faithfulness, and it challenges this community (and by implication in particular its leadership, the people with most responsibility for *mišpāṭ*) also to live in faithfulness in its own community life. Isaiah 56–66 is 'permeated through and through by the conviction that a healthful relationship to Yhwh depends on continuous *ṣ*ᵉ*dāqâ* towards one's fellow-countrymen'.[127] Yet the verse makes no mention of the

[126] The use reappears in 66.20 in a passage that pairs with 56.1-8; the only other occurrences of 'Israel' in Isa 56–66 are two in the phrase 'Israel's holy one' (60.9-14), one referring to the 'household of Israel' over the centuries (63.7), and one referring to the individual Jacob-Israel (63.15); cf. H. G. M. Williamson, 'The Concept of Israel in Transition', in R. E. Clements (ed.), *The World of Ancient Israel* (Cambridge: Cambridge University Press, 1989), pp. 141-61 (150-51). This supports the possibility that v. 8 is dependent on 11.12 (Stromberg, *Isaiah after Exile*, pp. 82-86).

[127] Koch, *Die Profeten II*, p. 159 (ET p. 155).

Judahite community itself and thus sets a pattern for Isaiah 56–66 in suggesting that its exhortation applies to the people of God in any context.

Summarizing as they do much of the thrust of Isaiah 1–39 and 40–55, the two lines in v. 1aβb form an effective overture[128] to Isaiah 56–66, with a number of implications. One is that nothing has changed. The fact that Isaiah 1–39 repeatedly challenged the community to take *mišpāṭ* and *ṣᵉdāqâ* more seriously does not mean that this exhortation can now be taken for granted. Further, neither does it mean that the challenge is so historically located that it ceases to be significant for a later generation. On the contrary; its placement there in the earlier Isaiah tradition, which was likely in written form for this prophet, makes it capable of addressing future generations of Israel, so that it both opens up the possibility and imposes the necessity of a future generation heeding it. Indeed, the fact that the earlier community had not heeded this message (and had paid the penalty) places a more demanding obligation on the present and future community to do so.

Likewise the fact that Isaiah 40–55 made extravagant promises to the community of the exilic period concerning *yᵉšûʿâ* and *ṣᵉdāqâ* does not mean that these notions have lost their importance. Indeed, it increases their importance. As is typical with prophetic promises (and warnings), the promises in Isaiah 40–55 have received some measure of implementing, but nothing like as radical an implementing as one might have expected. While Yhwh has seen to the conquest of Babylon by Cyrus and to Cyrus's encouraging Judahites to return to rebuild the temple, Judah now lives under the dominion of another imperial power and the city still stands in a devastated state. The chapters do not show any sense of let down about this or of much great overt anxiety about it, perhaps rather less than appears in Ezra and Nehemiah. There is no indication that 'the failure of prophecy was keenly felt among the followers of Second Isaiah' or that this underlies the critique of the community that will follow in 56.9–59.8.[129] 'There is no hint that there has been any delay in the realization of Second Isaiah's promises concerning the restoration.'[130] Isaiah 56.1-8 does not give any indication that its promise responds to disappointment with the non-fulfilment of the promises in Isaiah 40–55. Talk about God's action being 'near' recurs in the Psalms (e.g. 75.2 [1]; 85.10 [9]; 119.151; 145.18); it does not belong to one particular context. The present passage does not give any indication of a psychological motivation. 'The prophetic promise functions exclusively on the theological level' in holding together in necessary fashion God's promise and the need for the people's response.[131] This is not merely an argument from

[128] Cf. Obara, *Le strategie di Dio*, p. 43.

[129] Against R. P. Carroll, 'Second Isaiah and the Failure of Prophecy', *Studia theologica* 32 (1978), pp. 119-31 (129-30).

[130] Schramm, *The Opponents of Third Isaiah*, p. 119.

[131] Childs, *Isaiah*, p. 456.

silence, because both Isaiah 40–55 and Isaiah 56–66 show a distinctive capacity to express in no uncertain terms their disappointment with Yhwh's action. But in the circumstances, alongside the importance of repeating the challenge to 'guard *mišpāṭ* and act in *ṣᵉdāqâ*', it is important to repeat the promises, as will happen in glorious technicolor in subsequent chapters. The promises' partial fulfilment makes their reaffirmation both necessary and possible.

The collocation of the two lines also exposes an irresolvable question about their interrelationship, which the 'because' does nothing to settle.[132] They make for an interesting comparison and contrast with the two summaries of Jesus' preaching in Matthew 3.2 and Mark 1.15 (and with Isa 60.1),[133] which provoke reflection on the same question. Is it the case that people must pay attention to *mišpāṭ* and *ṣᵉdāqâ* because Yhwh is about to act in *yᵉšûʿâ* and *ṣᵉdāqâ*? In other words, is a life of *mišpāṭ* and *ṣᵉdāqâ* a response to a divine commitment to *yᵉšûʿâ* and *ṣᵉdāqâ*?[134] Or is it the case that people must pay attention to *mišpāṭ* and *ṣᵉdāqâ* because only then will Yhwh act in *yᵉšûʿâ* and *ṣᵉdāqâ*? In other words, is Yhwh's *yᵉšûʿâ* and *ṣᵉdāqâ* a response to a human commitment to *mišpāṭ* and *ṣᵉdāqâ*?[135] The consequences that follow from accepting either answer to the question show why it is irresolvable. The first answer is open to implying that Yhwh is committed to acting in *yᵉšûʿâ* and *ṣᵉdāqâ* irrespective of the community's attitude, even though the prophet does look for a response on their part. The second answer is open to implying that the community's *mišpāṭ* and *ṣᵉdāqâ* is the decisive consideration in determining whether Yhwh acts in *yᵉšûʿâ* and *ṣᵉdāqâ*, so that the relationship between the people and Yhwh becomes a transactional or contractual one. When two people commit themselves to each other in marriage, their commitment presupposes that it is mutual; yet we would not say either 'I commit myself to you without knowing whether you are committing yourself to me' or 'I commit myself to you on condition that you commit yourself to me'. Rather the relationship is covenantal in the sense that both parties make a commitment that presupposes the commitment of the other without being exactly dependent on it. This is also the nature of the relationship between Yhwh and Israel.

132 See further the comments on 56.1 in section 6 of the Introduction to this commentary, above.

133 Cf. Kessler, *Gott geht es um das Ganze*, p. 21.

134 Thus Hans-Joachim Kraus calls the *kî* causal rather than conditional ('Die ausgebliebene Endtheophanie', *ZAW* 78 [1966]: 317-32 [327], repr. Kraus, *Biblisch-theologische Aufsätze* [Neukirchen: Neukirchener, 1972], pp. 134-50 [146]).

135 E.g. Koenen gives as a heading to his treatment of 56.1 'Righteousness as Condition of Salvation' (*Ethik und Eschatologie im Tritojesajabuch*, p. 11), while José Severino Croatto speaks of the promise of salvation in v. 1b as 'conditional on the realization of the program in v. 1a' ('La inclusión sociale en el programa del Tercer Isaías: Exégesis de Isaías 56, 1-8 y 66, 17-24', *Revista Bíblica* 60 [1998], pp. 91-110 [95]; cf. Paul, ישעיה פרקים מ-סו, II, p. 405 [ET p. 447]).

The opening and closing verses of vv. 1-8 imply that the entire section addresses the Judahite community as a whole; the foreigner and eunuch are not the direct addressees. They might be among those who heard the prophet or might be expected to hear about what the prophet says, one way or another, but the prophet addresses the community as a whole with a view (among other things) to shaping its attitude to the foreigners and eunuchs in its midst. In relation to the community in Babylon, v. 8 might imply an exhortation to the Judahite exiles to bring foreigners and eunuchs back with them to the land; they are not to be left behind.[136] The section then implies 'a circle that has accommodated the Babylonian experience into its identity discourse and has therefore resolved to be open to accept foreigners, even Babylonians, to the worship services of the community'.[137] The section's concrete comments about the (individual) foreigner and eunuch imply that it is making not promises about Yhwh's ultimate intention but declarations with implications for community life in the present. It is both encouraging to the minorities of which it speaks and challenging to the broader community and/or the leaders whom it implicitly addresses. In it the prophet 'is doing a balancing act between a defined community with strict requirements and rules and an undefined community with no limits or borders'.[138]

There is a sense in which this section sets forth a universalist perspective, which Paul's declaration that there is neither Jew nor Greek (Gal 3.28) takes up.[139] Indeed, wording like that of v. 1, *ṣidqātî lᵉhiggālôt*, appears in Paul's summary of his gospel in Romans 1.17, 'God's righteousness is revealed' in that gospel.[140] A patristic commentator such as Cyril of Alexandria thus sees Christ as the fulfilment of the promise in v. 1.[141] The language also reappears in a passage such as Romans 13.11 when Paul speaks of salvation now being nearer, and when Jesus speaks of a coming time when redemption will be near (Lk 21.28). Isaiah 40–55 has declared that Yhwh is gathering his sheep and bringing them home (40.11; cf. 43.5; 49.18; 54.7); it has also had the nations gathering (43.9; 45.20). Isaiah 40–55 has often declared that all the nations are to recognize Yhwh, most recently in 55.5. Isaiah 56.1-8 works out the details. If the vision is eschatological,[142] this is so in the sense that it implies the fulfilment of God's ultimate purpose in a way that goes beyond human accomplishment, not that it is far-off or associated with an end to this-worldly life.

[136] Cf. Delitzsch, *Jesaia*, p. 572 (ET II, p. 363).
[137] Lee, 'Returning to China', p. 168.
[138] Miscall, *Isaiah*, p. 129.
[139] Cf. Sawyer, *Isaiah*, II, pp. 161.
[140] Cf. Alonso Schökel and Sicre Diaz, *Profetas*, I, p. 349.
[141] See Ἐξήγησις ὑπομνηματική εἰς τὸν προφήτην Ἡσαΐαν, col. 1240.
[142] So Polan, *In the Ways of Justice toward Salvation*, p. 77.

Yet the sense in which the passage is universalist needs careful stating and it is doubtful whether it is any more universalist than other parts of the Old Testament, or any more missionary.[143] It is not universalist in the sense that it simply accepts all nations as they are but in the sense that it accepts individual foreigners who commit themselves to the covenant.[144] Openness to other peoples lies in welcoming them if they accept Israel's own key marker of identity. In constituting 'Trito-Isaiah's programmatic introduction to YHWH's covenant', Isaiah 56.1-8 'points to Shabbat observance as the overriding concern, which is developed more fully in subsequent chapters'.[145] To take the Sabbath as a figure for the 'rest' we find in Christ (Heb 4.9), rather than focusing on the literal Sabbath, is not to miss the reality for the type[146] but to miss the reality. There are a number of reasons for the importance of the Sabbath. Any community needs distinctive practices such as Sabbath, as markers of its identity.[147] While such observances are meaningless if they are not the signs and accompaniments of more profound commitments (Isa 1.13), if they are indeed associated with moral and social commitments and form part of a broader way in which a community manifests its distinctiveness, then they buttress this identity. Further, in the case of Sabbath, they are by their nature markers of such commitments. Sabbath is not a random observance parallel to wearing ones clothes or hair in a certain way. It is a means of making sure that people have time to rest and that they are not consumed by consumption.[148] It is not merely a signal but a sign. It is an embodiment of *mišpāṭ* and *ṣᵉdāqâ*. 'The sabbath, as a social institution, made a deep impression on the pagan environment.... The pagan world knew of no day of rest for the laborer.... The sabbath became the very special symbol of the social-moral quality of the religion of Israel. It was in a sense the gospel of the good God and of the love of man.'[149]

Sabbath, identity, and universalism go together.[150] Nor should we think of Israel becoming a religious community rather than a political entity, or an entity based on personal choice rather than ethnic identity, or think of

[143] Contrast Hans Klein, 'Die Aufnahme Fremder in die Gemeinde des Alten und des Neuen Bundes', *Theologische Beiträge* 12 (1981), pp. 21-34 (29).

[144] Orlinsky, in *Studies on the Second Part of the Book of Isaiah*, p. 37.

[145] Marvin A, Sweeney, 'The Reconceptualization of the Davidic Covenant in Isaiah', in Ruiten and Vervenne (eds.), *Studies in the Book of Isaiah*, pp. 41-61 (51).

[146] Cocceius, 'Synopsis Prophetiae Jesaiae', p. 48.

[147] Cf. Coffin, 'The Book of Isaiah', p. 655.

[148] Cf. Brueggemann, *Using God's Resources Wisely*, p. 50.

[149] Kaufmann, *The Babylonian Captivity and Deutero-Isaiah*, p. 42.

[150] Cf. Bernard Gosse, 'Sabbath, Identity and Universalism Go Together after the Return from Exile', *JSOT* 29 (2005), pp. 359-70, repr. *OTE* 17 (2004), pp. 231-41; also 'Loi et sanctuaire à Jérusalem au retour de l'exil', *Transeuphratène* 28 (2004), pp. 91-115 (91-102). Cf. also Friedrich Delitzsch, *Die Grosse Täuschung* (Stuttgart: Deutsche, reprinted 1921), II, pp. 19-20; Jill Middlemas, 'Trito-Isaiah's Intra- and Internationalization', in Lipschits, Knoppers, and Oeming (eds.), *Judah and the Judeans in the Achaemenid Period*, pp. 105-25.

relationships with Yhwh being individual rather than communal.[151] The Old Testament would view all these antitheses as false. Foreigners are still foreigners, but they are free to share Israel's relationship with Yhwh. Isaiah 60–62 will work out the implications of v. 8 in a way that puts more emphasis on the way it is good news for Israel itself. Isaiah 56.1-8 by anticipation makes it impossible for anyone to read Isaiah 60–62 in a way that imperils the position of other peoples.[152]

[151] See, e.g., Volz, *Jesaja II*, p. 200.
[152] Cf. Smith, *Rhetoric and Redaction in Trito-Isaiah*, pp. 50-66.

II

ISAIAH 56.9–57.21

Translation and Notes

9 All you animals of the wild,[1]// come on and eat,// all you animals in the forest!
10 Its lookouts[2] are blind, all of them;// they do not know.[3]
All of them are dumb dogs,// they cannot bark.[4]
They are snoozing,[5] bedding down,// loving to doze.[6]
11 But the dogs—they are mighty in appetite;// they do not know ‘enough’.
Those people—they are shepherds[7]// who do not know how to be discerning.

[1] חיתו is an anomalous construct (see JM 93r). The recurrence later in the line may also be a construct, though there it is followed by ב, not by an absolute noun, and the accent indicates that MT took it as an absolute noun (cf. David B. Freedman and Miles B. Cohen, ‘The Masoretes as Exegetes’, *1972 and 1973 Proceedings IOMS* [Masoretic Studies 1; Missoula, MT: Scholars, 1974], pp. 35-46 [37]). 1QIs[a] has the more regular חיות both times (it might be sg. or pl.). שדי is also an unusual and poetic form over against שדה.

[2] Following Q צפיו (cf. 1QIs[a], Tg, Vg, Aq, Sym, Th). If ‘its’ has a grammatical antecedent, it must be ‘Israel’ in v. 8, but more likely the suffix presupposes an ellipse; the verbs in the previous line have an implicit object (in Jer 12.9 it is ‘my people’) to which the suffix refers. K’s צפו might be imperative (‘look out [they are blind…]’; cf. LXX), assimilating to the imperative in the preceding line, though the subject is different; or it might be qatal (‘they [who] looked out are blind’; cf. Bonnard, *Le Second Isaïe*, p. 349), assimilating to the qatal verb that follows (cf. *HUB*). Syr *ṣpyn* perhaps implies absolute צפים (Hanson, *The Dawn of Apocalyptic*, p. 192). Other suggestions are צֹפַי, ‘my lookouts’ (e.g. Duhm, *Jesaia*, p. 385), or צפי עמי, ‘my people’s lookouts’ (cf. Elliger, *Die Einheit des Tritojesaia*, p. 8).

[3] LXX ‘they do not know how to think’ perhaps arises from unease at the absolute use of ידע and consequently assimilates to the construction in v. 10aβb (cf. H. A. Brongers, ‘Jes lvi 10a’, *VT* 25 [1975], pp. 791-92).

[4] On the verb נבח, see Harold R. Cohen, *Biblical Hapax Legomena in the Light of Akkadian and Ugaritic* (Missoula, MT: Scholars, 1978), pp. 114-15.

[5] On this word, see the comment.

[6] For the MT idiom whereby the construct precedes a preposition, אהבי לנום, 1QIs[a] substitutes the more usual אוהבים לנואם (cf. Kutscher, הלשון והרקע הלשוני של מגילת ישעיהו השלמה, p. 340 [ET p. 429]).

[7] Cf. 1QIs[a], Aq, Th. LXX, Sym, Syr, Tg have ‘evil’, taking the word as from רע rather than רעה. It would be nice to suppose that the prophet said the רֹעִים were רָעִים; cf. Budde, ‘Jesaia Kap. 40–66’, p. 696. For the difficult expression והמה רעים Dillmann (*Jesaia* [1890 edn], p. 484) suggests והם הרעים. 1QIs[a] has והמה הרועים. Praetorius (‘Zum

All of them have directed themselves to their own way,// each one to his own ill-gotten gain, every last part of him.[8]
12 'Come on, I'll get[9] wine,// we'll quaff drink.
And tomorrow will be[10] the same,// abundantly, exceedingly great!'[11]
57.1 The faithful person—he has perished,[12]// and there is no one giving heed,[13]
People of commitment—they are gathered up,// while there is no one discerning
That it is from the presence of calamity// that the faithful has been gathered up.
2 He goes in peace as they rest on their beds,// the person who walks straight.[14]

3 But you, draw near,// children of a diviner,
Offspring of an adulterer[15] and of one who acts immorally,[16]// 4 in whom do you revel?

Text des Tritojesajas', pp. 89-90) takes the phrase as a gloss based on passages such as Jer 12.10; Ezek 34.2.

[8] Lit., 'from his end', that is, from the whole of him. Vg, Sym understand 'every last one of them', but the suffix is sg. (cf. Syr; Motyer, *Isaiah*, p. 469). Gen 19.4 and Jer 51.31 parallel the use of the noun, though lacking the suffix; the latter more closely parallels the usage here in having a sg. referent. For the second colon LXX has an abbreviated text (with variation between manuscripts: contrast Rahlfs, *Septuaginta*, II, p. 642, with Ziegler, *Buch Isaias*, p. 332, also Ziegler, *Untersuchungen zur Septuaginta des Buches Isaias*, pp. 158-59); it then lacks v. 12 altogether.

[9] Whereas 1QIs[a] has pl. נקחה (cf. Vrs), the sg. verb (so also 1QIs[b], Aq) continues the move between sg. and pl. that ran through 56.1-8.

[10] For MT's *w*-consecutive והיה, 1QIs[a] has PBH-style *w*-conjunctive ויהי.

[11] For גדול יתר מאד, Vg, Sym have 'much more' (Tg has the comparative note in the first colon), but it is doubtful whether the comparative is justified by the words. In 1QIs[a], גדול was omitted then added above the line. Talmon ('Aspects of the Textual Transmission of the Bible in the Light of Qumran Manuscripts', p. 119, repr. *The World of Qumran from Within*, pp. 100-1) suggests that MT preserves a doublet (cf. also Hans Kosmala's comments in 'Form and Structure in Ancient Hebrew Poetry', *VT* 14 [1964], pp. 423-45; 16 [1966], pp. 152-80 [reprinted in Kosmala, *Studies, Essays, and Reviews* (Leiden: Brill, 1977), I, pp. 84-135]). The effect in MT is to underline the mocking critique in the verses as a whole.

[12] 1QIs[a] has participle אובד 'is perishing'; 1QIs[b] corresponds to MT.

[13] Lit., 'putting on mind'.

[14] LXX paraphrases v. 2, 'His burial will be in peace; he has been taken from their midst'. Perhaps it finds the line hard to interpret (Blenkinsopp, *Isaiah 56–66*, p. 149), though *HUB* sees some messianic exegesis here, which would fit a reading of 57.1 in light of 52.13–53.12. Theodoret of Cyrrhus thus sees vv. 1-2 as referring to Jesus, and to the first Christian martyr, Stephen: see *Commentaire sur Isaïe* 171b (3.196-99); cf. Cyril of Alexandria, Ἐξήγησις ὑπομνηματική εἰς τὸν προφήτην Ἡσαΐαν, col. 1256; Eusebius of Caesarea, *Der Jesajakommentar*, p. 351; Jerome, *Commentariorum in Isaiam prophetam libri duodeviginti*, col. 546; Cyprian, *Treatises* 3.14. There are indications that the verses belonged to a collection of Old Testament passages believed to refer to Jesus (see, e.g., Skarsaune, *The Proof from Prophecy*, pp. 30-31, 160-61, on references in Justin Martyr).

[15] There is no reason to emend m. מנאף to f. מנאפת (e.g. Klostermann, *Deuterojesaia*, p. 72).

[16] Or 'one who has acted immorally' (cf. *TTH* 117). 1QIs[a] has pl. ותזנו. The construction is idiomatic and it is doubtful if the simpler constructions in Vrs indicate an alternative text such as וְזֹנָה or that we need to hypothesize that MT's verb form is actually masculine

At whom do you open your mouth wide,// put out your tongue?
Are you not rebellious children,// deceitful offspring?—
5 You who inflame yourselves among the oaks,// under every verdant tree,[17]
Who slaughter children among the canyons,// under the clefts in the crags.
6 Among the canyon's deceptions is your share;// they, they are your allocation.
Yes, to them you have poured a libation,// presented an offering;// in view of these things, should I relent?[18]
7 On a high and lofty mountain// you have put[19] your bed,
Yes, there you have gone up// to offer sacrifice,
8 And behind the door and the doorpost// you have set your memorial.
For from me you have gone away[20] and gone up,// you have opened your bed wide.
You have sealed things[21] for yourself from them, you have loved their bed;[22]// you have beheld their love.[23]
9 You have come to see[24] the King in your oils,[25]// you have multiplied your perfumes.[26]
You have sent off[27] your envoys far,// sent down as far as Sheol.[28]
10 Though you became weary with the length of your journey,// you have not said 'It's futile'.

(so Mitchell Dahood, 'Third Masculine Singular with Preformative *t*- in Northwest Semitic', *Orientalia* 48 [1979], pp. 97-106 [100]).

[17] On the prepositions, see Jonas C. Greenfield, 'The Preposition b….. taḥat….. in Jes 57 5', *ZAW* 73 (1961), pp. 226-28, and Watson, 'Fixed Pairs in Ugaritic and Isaiah', pp. 461, 467.

[18] Tg 'Should my word turn back?'; Tg often uses תוב to render נחם. Aq, Sym, Th have 'be consoled'; but this usage normally refers to taking comfort as one recovers from some grief. BDB takes the verb to denote getting relief by taking vengeance, as in 1.24, but LXX, Vg 'should I not be angry?' indicate that the verb then needs a negative. On the treatment of this verb here and elsewhere in the Vrs, see Raphael Loewe, 'Jerome's Treatment of an Anthropopathism', *VT* 2 (1952), pp. 261-72. It has been suggested that the colon should be deleted or moved elsewhere because it 'disturbs' the metre (e.g. Budde, 'Das Buch Jesaia Kap. 40–66', p. 697).

[19] LXX 'there' reads שׂמת as שׁמה. OL, Aq, Sym, Th correspond to MT.

[20] See the comment.

[21] On the verb, see the comment. The m. ותכרת is odd, but Ibn Ezra (*The Commentary of Ibn Ezra on Isaiah*, p. 261) compares Jer 3.5. 1QIs[a] has the expected f. ותכרותי. Duhm (*Jesaia*, p. 389) emends וַתִּכְרִי 'you bought', as in Hos 3.2, while G. R. Driver suggests that MT is a composite reading combining that with וְכָרִית, 'you buy' ('Problems of the Hebrew Text and Language', in *Alttestamentliche Studien Friedrich Nötscher* [Bonn: Hanstein, 1950], pp. 46-61 [49]).

[22] Ginsberg ('Some Emendations in Isaiah', p. 60) repoints to אַהֲבַת מִשְׁכָּבִם, '[in] love for beds/sexual acts'.

[23] The force of the suffix on 'bed' carries forward here.

[24] On this verb, see the comment.

[25] Literally 'in oil'; the suffix on 'perfumes' also applies here.

[26] LXX 'those far from you' reads a form from רחק rather than from רקח.

[27] Resultative piel (see Jenni, *Das hebräische Pi'el*, pp. 193-96).

[28] *IBHS* 14.5b takes this as an instance of the superlative: 'You debased yourself even to hell'. LXX, Aq, Sym, Th, Vg also understand the verb as an inwardly transitive hiphil.

You found life for your strength;// therefore you have not weakened.[29]

11 For whom have you felt awe and reverence,// that[30] you act deceptively?[31]
Of me you have not taken thought;// you have not given heed to me.[32]
Have I not been silent,[33] yes from of old,[34]// but to me you show no reverence?[35]

12 I am the one who will declare your faithfulness;// your works[36]—they will not avail you.

13 When you cry out, your abominable gatherings[37] can rescue you;// a wind will carry all of them off, a breath of air[38] will take them.
But the person who takes refuge with me will own the land,// will possess my holy mountain.

14 And someone says[39], Build up, build up,[40] clear a road,// lift high the stumbling-block from my people's road.

[29] LXX, Aq, Vg have 'you have not asked [for relief]', the meaning of חלה II. But Th has 'you were not wounded', implying חלל I (GID).

[30] In a question such as this the כי underlines the sense of surprise or deprecation; see A. Schoors, 'The Particle כי', in A. S. van der Woude (ed.), *Remembering All the Way...* (Leiden: Brill, 1981), pp. 240-76 (262-63).

[31] The piel perhaps suggests concrete acts of deception rather than simply being false (cf. Jenni, *Das hebräische Pi'el*, p. 171).

[32] Lit., 'put [me] on your mind' (cf. v. 1); 'me' carries over from the first colon. 1QIs[a] rather adds אלה 'these things'.

[33] On LXX's 'and I seeing you', see *HUB*.

[34] For ומעלם LXX, Vg imply וּמַעְלִם 'and hiding' from עלם, as in Ps 10.1 (either presupposing 'my eyes' as object, or inwardly transitive hiphil); MT might be assimilation to 42.14. But 1QIs[a], 4QIs[d], Syr, Tg correspond to MT.

[35] Vg 'see' suggests it understands the verb as a form of ראה rather than ירא.

[36] The parallelism suggests that this phrase begins the second colon (cf. MT's accent). The lack of את before צדקה also suggests that ואת marks a new beginning; the phrase is then extraposed before the *w*-verb (against T. Muraoka, *Emphatic Words and Structures in Biblical Hebrew* [Jerusalem: Magnes, 1985]), p. 153). LXX has 'evil deeds', but Aq, Sym, Th, Vg have simply 'deeds'. Tg has a double reading. 1QIs[a] adds קובציך, anticipating the next line and implying '...your faithfulness and your works, and your abominable gatherings will not avail you'.

[37] Marti (*Jesaja*, p. 370) emends קבוציך to שקוציך (cf. Budde, 'Das Buch Jesaja Kap. 40–66', p. 698). Nötscher emends in the other direction, by keeping the root rather than the vowels and reading וקבציך 'those who care for you' ('Entbehrliche Hapaxlegomena in Jesaia', p. 300). LXX 'in your affliction [they must rescue you]' implies בצוקיך for קבוציך (Fischer, *In welcher Schrift lag das Buch Isaias den LXX vor?*, p. 63; cf. Patrick W. Skehan, 'Some Textual Problems in Isaia', *CBQ* 22 (1960), pp. 47-55 (55); and see *HALOT*. On the basis of Aramaic קְבַע (cf. PBH קָבַע) meaning 'fix', G. R. Driver suggests 'statues' ('Studies in the Vocabulary of the Old Testament viii', *JTS* 36 [1935], pp. 293-301 [294]). Klaus Koenen emends to בקציך 'at your end' ('Zum Text von Jesaja lvii 12-13a', *VT* 39 [1989], pp. 236-39).

[38] Cf. Sym. LXX has 'tempest', Aq 'emptiness', Tg 'nothing'.

[39] For MT's *w*-consecutive ואמר, 1QIs[a] has PBH-style *w*-conjunctive ויואמר.

[40] 1QIs[a] adds המסלה 'the ramp' as in 62.10 (Kutscher, הלשון והרקע הלשוני של מגילת ישעיהו השלמה, p. 434 [ET p. 543]).

15 For the one who is high and towering has said this,// the one who dwells forever,[41] whose name is 'Holy one':[42]
'I dwell[43] on high and holy,[44]// and with the crushed and low in spirit,
In enlivening the spirit of the people who are low,// enlivening the heart of the people who have been crushed.
16 For I do not always contend,// I am not irate[45] forever.[46]
For before me the spirit would faint,[47]// the breathing beings I myself made.
17 At the waywardness of its ill-gotten gain[48] I was irate;// I would hit it,[49] hiding[50]—I would be irate.[51]

[41] On the basis of Ugaritic, one could hypothesize a Hebrew word עַד meaning 'throne' (see *DCH*, VI, pp. 269-70, 852-53) of which this could be an instance (so M. Dahood, 'Hebrew–Ugaritic Lexicography vii', *Biblica* 50 [1969], pp. 337-56 [347]). Cheyne (*The Mines of Isaiah Re-explored*, p. 167) emends to ער, which he then takes as an abbreviation for ערב and relates to his theory about the north Arabian background of the material, which is the basis for many textual emendations in Isa 56–66 (see further his *Critica Biblica*, pp. 46-49).

[42] Or 'For the one whose name is "high and towering"', 'the one who dwells forever", "holy one", has said this'; cf. Francis I. Andersen, *The Sentence in Biblical Hebrew* (The Hague: Mouton, 1974), p. 21.

[43] 1QIs[a] and 4QIs[d] continue the third-person verb construction, as does Tg. LXX and Vg continue the participial construction, which LXX then maintains through v. 15.

[44] 1QIs[a] במרום ובקודש makes the expressions nouns rather than adjectives and provides prepositions for both, following the more familiar usage (cf. Kutscher, הלשון והרקע הלשוני של מגילת ישעיהו השלמה, p. 308 [ET p. 406]); cf. Vg (and on their relationship, Kedar-Kopfstein, 'Divergent Hebrew Readings in Jerome's Isaiah', pp. 199-200; van der Kooij, *Die alten Textzeugen des Jesajabuches*, p. 314). LXX also implies a noun for the second expression, but Tg has the adjective. Some of these variants may reflect 'doxological' instincts (*HUB*; cf. Seeligmann, *The Septuagint Version of Isaiah*, p. 102, with Troxel's comments, *LXX-Isaiah*, pp. 155-56).

[45] Rooker ('Dating Isaiah 40—66', pp. 309-10) sees the use of קצף as an indication of preexilic linguistic usage in Isa 40–66.

[46] LXX adds 'with you' in both cola, applying the text to its audience (Baer, *When We All Go Home*, p. 63).

[47] For 'faint' (BDB's עטף III), LXX, Vg, Syr have 'go forth', so that the two cola are more closely parallel, but perhaps in theological dependence on Ps 104.30 (Ziegler, *Untersuchungen zur Septuaginta des Buches Isaias*, p. 129); the LXX version features in controversy over the origin of the soul, and in debate with Vincentius Victor, Augustine (*A Treatise on the Soul and its Origin* 1.21) takes it to refer to the Spirit's proceeding from the Father. Tg has Yhwh 'restoring' the spirits of the dead. Both understandings apparently assume the verb is עטף I, whose Syriac cognate meaning 'turn back' is more common (though Syr itself uses the verb *npq*); but see further Baer, *When We All Go Home*, pp. 103-5. Aq and Sym assume BDB's עטף II 'clothe oneself [with the body]' (cf. Jerome, *Commentariorum in Isaiam prophetam libri duodeviginti*, cols. 557-58), also presupposed by 3 Enoch 43.3 (cf. Odeberg *Trtto-Isaiah*, p. 105) and Calvin (*In Iesaiam prophetam*, p. 367 [ET IV, p. 215]). But either of these requires substantial inference.

[48] The suffix refers back to עמי in v. 14. R. Bergmeier ('Das Streben nach Gewinn', *ZAW* 81 [1969], pp. 93-97) sees בצע as here neutral in its reference to gain; the negative judgment comes in pointing to the waywardness with which the people sought gain. More likely it keeps its usual negative connotation, applied earlier in the section in 56.11 (Tg's expansion makes this explicit). See further P. J. Harland, 'בצע', *VT* 50 (2000), pp. 310-22. LXX may imply בעוונו בצע 'at its waywardness briefly [I was irate]' (cf.

It lived turning to the way of its own heart;[52]// 18 I have seen its ways, but I will heal it.[53]

I will lead it[54] and restore all comfort[55] to it;[56]// for its mourners,[57] 19 as the fruit[58] of lips I am creating well-being,

Well-being for the far and for the near',// Yhwh has said, 'I will heal it'.

Lowth, *Isaiah*, p. 376; Torrey, *Isaiah*, p. 436). But for the thought, cf. 54.7-8, which LXX may be following here, and in its expansion on 'turning away' in the next colon (cf. *HUB*); on LXX in the verse as a whole, see further Baer, *When We All Go Home*, pp. 105-6. Th, Aq, Sym, Vg, Syr, Tg correspond to MT.

[49] The simple ו implies that this hitting is another way of speaking of the ire rather than a consequence. On the yiqtol, see further the note below on ואקצף, the further simple *w*-yiqtol which closes the line.

[50] The infinitive is used adverbially. 1QIs[a] and 4QIs[d] simplify to a finite verb; Vrs also have a sequence of finite verbs. Morrow ('The Text of Isaiah at Qumran', p. 152) calls this the better reading; it is a nice theory that one form of the tradition had two finite verbs, one two infinitives (cf. Aare Rubinstein, 'Isaiah lvii 17', *VT* 4 [1954], pp. 200-1), but the evidence is thin.

[51] The simple *w*-yiqtol verb again suggests an action contemporary with the verbs that precede. Lau (*Schriftgelehrte Prophetie in Jes 56–66*, p. 123) refers to GK107h; cf. *DG* 85c, which has similar implications. We should hardly emend these distinctive verbs to regular *w*-consecutives. LXX makes the transition to a third-person verb here, suggesting that Israel responded with vexation to Yhwh's vexation.

[52] For MT לבו 1QIs[a] has לבי, perhaps influenced by the coming declaration of Yhwh's healing.

[53] Through v. 18 MT has simple *w*-yiqtol verbs, implying that these are promises, while LXX, Vg have past tense verbs, implying *w*-consecutives, under the influence of the opening qatal verb.

[54] For MT's hiphil from נחה, LXX and Syr have 'console', Tg 'have compassion'. This may suggest the pointing וָאֲנִחֵהוּ, hiphil from נוח, 'I will give them rest', or וָאֲנַחֲמֵהוּ, 'I will comfort them'. 1QIs[a] omits the word, and the overlap between 'I will comfort them' and 'I will restore all comfort to them' may suggest that these are parallel variants (so Talmon, 'Aspects of the Textual Transmission of the Bible in the Light of Qumran Manuscripts', pp. 122-23 = pp. 104-5). But Rowlands ('The Targum and the Peshiṭta Version of the Book of Isaiah'), p. 190) suggests that LXX, Syr, and Tg shared a common lexical approach rather than a common different text from MT. Shalom Paul ('Polysensuous Polyvalency in Poetic Parallelism', in M. Fishbane and E. Tov [eds.], *Sha'arei Talmon* [S. Talmon Festschift; Winona Lake, IN: Eisenbrauns, 1992], pp. 147-63 [157]) suggests that the prophet intended both meanings.

[55] Literally, 'comforts'.

[56] On the placing of לו and its repetition in 1QIs[a], see Talmon, 'Aspects of the Textual Transmission of the Bible in the Light of Qumran Manuscripts', p. 115 = pp. 94-95.

[57] LXX's ἀληθινήν (qualifying 'comfort') suggests it has connected ולאבליו with אבל 'in truth' (Ottley, *Isaiah according to the Septuagint*, II, p. 358).

[58] K and 4QIs[d] have נוב, Q and 1QIs[a] ניב. On the basis of Arabic, Godfrey R. Driver derives from a different root נוב and translates 'What drops from the lips' ('Hebrew Roots and Words', *Die Welt des Orients* 1 [1947–52], pp. 406-15 [407]). M. Dahood in *Proverbs and Northwest Semitic Philology* (Rome: Pontifical Biblical Institute, 1963), p. 20, takes it to mean 'flow', but in 'Ugaritic Lexicography vi' (*Biblica* 49 [1968], pp. 355-69 [362]) suggests that נִיב actually means 'speech'.

20 But the faithless: they are like the sea tossing,[59]// because[60] to be still: it cannot.[61]
Its waters toss[62] muck and mud;// 21 'there is no well-being' (my God has said) 'for the faithless'.

Introduction

We have noted that notwithstanding the chapter and paragraph divisions in MT and 1QIs[a, b], 56.8 closes off 56.1-8. Verse 9 moves to different imagery, and to a more directly confrontational tone. Both MT's chapter or paragraph division after 56.9 (MT mss vary over which they provide) and the medieval Christian division after 56.12 imply an interpretation of vv. 9-12 like that of Tg, where v. 8 promises the return of more exiled Israelites and vv. 9-12 promise a concomitant victory over Jerusalem's attackers.[63] On this understanding, the medieval chapter division is appropriate; 57.1 marks a transition to confrontation of Israel's faithlessness. In contrast, neither MT nor 1QIs[a, b] has either a chapter or a paragraph marker at 57.1, which fits the fact that 56.9-12 more likely confronts Israel's own leadership and thus leads more directly into chapter 57.

Most MT manuscripts do have a paragraph marker before 57.3, though the Leningrad manuscript does not; 1QIs[a] has a chapter marker here. 1QIs[a] and 4QIs[d] then have a chapter break after 57.13, but MT's next 'agreed' break comes after 57.14, though there the manuscripts again vary over whether it is a paragraph marker or a chapter marker. Oddly, this break is again a verse 'too late'; 1QIs[a] and 4QIs[d] suggest a more appropriate understanding of the relationship between the units. MT's lack of a break after 57.13 does draw attention to the fact that 57.14, like 57.3, begins with a *w*, which does not encourage us to locate breaks at these points. Indeed, in the actual wording of the material in 56.9–57.21 there are no formal pointers to the beginning and end of sections, such as 'Yhwh has said this', unless we count the 'and someone said' at 57.14. After 57.14, MT's next marker comes after 57.21. In most manuscripts it is a chapter marker, as it is in 1QIs[a] (1QIs[b] has a paragraph marker), and

[59] 1QIs[a] has qatal pl. נגרשו, applying directly to the faithless rather than within the simile (cf. LXX). 1QH has a form of רגש 'be in tumult', and both the partial reading in 1QIs[b] and Tg's טרד suggest the same reading (see Wernberg-Moller, 'The Contribution of the *Hodayot* to Biblical Text Criticism', p. 169).

[60] EVV translate 'that', but I assume that כי keeps its common causal connotation.

[61] For 'it cannot be still', the usual construction involves infinitive construct; a number of passages use infinitive absolute when the infinitive comes first, suggesting emphasis (GK 113d; JM 123b). 1QIs[a] has לאשקוט, the ל being the result of correction (Parry and Qimron, *The Great Isaiah Scroll*, p. 95).

[62] For MT's qal, 1QIs[a] has hitpael ויתגרשו. For the two occurrences of the verb in this verse Georg Hoffmann emends to forms from גדש (heap up) ('Versuche zu Amos', *ZAW* 3 [1883], pp. 87-126 [122]).

[63] Cf. Chilton, *Targum of Isaiah*, p. 109.

the Christian chapter division comes at the same point. The break follows the declaration that 'There is no well-being (my God has said) for faithless people', which is succeeded by a new divine commission to proclaim a message to the people. So 57.21 does look like an ending and it is succeeded by a new beginning. I thus treat 56.9–57.21 as a section.[64]

The section combines confrontation and encouragement, in that order, in the first two subsections, then in the reverse order in the third subsection. This suggests an aba′b′b″a″ outline for 56.9–57.21 along the following lines:[65]

56.9-12		Warning to leaders	
	57.1-2		Consolation for people who are faithful
57.3-13a		Warning to people involved in false worship	
	57.13b		Promise for people who trust in Yhwh
57.14-19		Encouragement for people who are broken	
	57.20-21		Warning to people who are faithless.

Seeing the section in this way is not to imply that the material was composed in this form and with these interrelationships. It could have been constructed from prophecies that were originally separate. Specifically, the first pair of subsections (56.9-12 and 57.1-2) might have been self-standing, though in isolation they look truncated as well as lacking any forms of introduction or conclusion. With regard to the second pair, 57.3-13a would be capable of standing alone, though 57.13b will then more likely be a subsequent addition rather than a self-contained, independent line. While the difference in the form of address between 57.3-5 (mostly plural masculine) and 57.6-13 (mostly singular feminine) does raise the question whether these are of separate origin,[66] both parts focus on unfaithfulness expressed in child sacrifice and offerings to the dead, and it is as plausible to think that the whole subsection addresses the same people in the two different ways.[67] With regard to the third pair, the recurrence of the motif of *šālôm* might suggest that they are inherently linked or might indicate that they have been brought together on that basis.

Alongside these general considerations are the instances of repetition and paronomasia in the material. In 56.9, a voice bids the wild animals, 'come' and eat; in 56.12, a representative shepherd bids, 'come' and drink

[64] So, e.g., Berges, *Das Buch Jesaja*, pp. 466-73; Bonnard, *Le Second Isaïe*, pp. 349-67; Penna, *Isaia*, pp. 555-67. Other scholars see 56.9–57.13 and 57.14-21 as separate sections (e.g. Bentzen, *Jesaja II*, pp. 120-29; Pauritsch, *Die neue Gemeinde*, pp. 51-73; Sekine, *Die Tritojesajanische Sammlung*, pp. 105-20) or see 56.9–57.2, 57.3-13, and 57.14-21 as three sections (e.g. Lau, *Schriftgelehrte Prophetie in Jes 56–66*, pp. 118-26, 151-68, 229-39); for other understandings see, e.g., Blenkinsopp, *Isaiah 56–66*, pp. 148-73; Westermann, *Jesaja Kapitel 40–66*, pp. 252-63 (ET pp. 316-31).

[65] Cf. Bonnard, *Le Second Isaïe*, pp. 353-54; Alonso Schökel and Sicre Diaz, *Profetas* 1, p. 354.

[66] Cf. Volz, *Jesaja II*, p. 208; he links 57.3-5 with 56.9–57.2.

[67] Cf. Koenen, *Ethik und Eschatologie im Tritojesajabuch*, p. 37.

(both times *ʾētāyû*, not a form from the more usual *bôʾ*). These biddings form an *inclusio* around 56.9-12. In the intervening lines, three times the prophet laments, 'they do not know', 'they do not know', 'they do not know', and three times laments 'all of them', 'all of them', 'all of them'. Within v. 9, the opening and closing vocative phrases repeat each other. The repetitions convey an expression of 'taut anger'.[68] The last occurrence of 'they do not know' is completed by the verb 'how to give heed', and then in 57.1-2 the phrases 'there is no one giving heed' and 'there is no one discerning' correspond to the content and/or the words of expressions just noted in 56.9-12.

Within 57.3-13, none of these expressions recur, but other words do: there is a series of references to 'children' and 'offspring' (vv. 3, 4, 5) and three occurrences of *śamt* (vv. 7, 8, 11). More distinctive are the instances of paronomasia: *hannēḥāmîm* and *ʾennāḥēm* (opening and closing vv. 5-6), *nᵉḥālîm, naḥal,* and *nāḥal* (vv. 5, 6, 13); *ḥalqê* and *ḥelqēk* (v. 6). In addition, the passage may hint at the double meanings of the words *ʿōnᵉnâ* (with its similarity to *ʿāwōn*, v. 3), *ʾēlîm* (terebinths/oaks and gods, v. 5), *gālâ*/*gillâ* (go into exile and expose, v. 8), *yād* (hand, power, memorial, penis, love, vv. 8, 10), and *qibbûṣayik* (with its resemblance to *šiqqûṣayik*, v. 13).

Within 57.14-21, a number of yet further words or roots recur, notably *derek, rûm, šāpal, rûaḥ, qāṣap, rāpāʾ* as well as *šālôm*. The fourfold occurrence of the common verb *ʾāmar* might not be noteworthy except for the fact that it did not come at all in 56.9–57.13.

In themselves these data suggest that each pair of subsections (56.9–57.2; 57.3-13; 57.14-21) belong together, but they do not exclude the possibility that the three pairs are of separate origin; the *w* at 57.3 and 14 might then be a secondary link emerging from the assembling of the material into the form that we have. But as well as the repetition and paronomasia within the subsections, between the three subsections there are also significant verbal links. These include *šākab* and *miškāb* (56.10; 57.2, 7, 8); *hāzâ* and *ḥāzâ* (56.10; 57.8); the phrase 'not give heed', literally 'not put on mind' (57.1, 11); *ṣaddiq and ṣᵉdāqâ* (57.1, 12); 'all of them' (56.10, 11; 57.13); 'a lofty and towering mountain', 'my holy mountain', and 'the high and towering one…whose name is holy' (57.7, 13, 15); *šāpal* (57.9, 15 twice); *biṣʿô* (56.11; 57.17); *nāḥam* and *niḥumîm* (57.6, 18); and *šālôm* (57.2, 19, 21).

These data preclude the view that the units have been juxtaposed on a random basis. They could suggest that the whole of 56.9–57.21 was composed together and that the individual units had no existence outside this context; the composition has then used different rhetorical techniques in the different parts while also binding the whole with repetitions. This would fit the sophistication of the rhetoric that can be seen at various points. It would also fit the relationship of the various subsections to

[68] Motyer, *Isaiah*, p. 468.

traditional forms of speech, such as the way a prophet may critique the behaviour of the community and declare the punishment that Yhwh is bringing on it, and the way a psalm may protest at oppressive treatment of faithful people. This composition then reflects such traditional forms of speech yet uses them in innovative ways (it does not have marks of a liturgy[69]). Alternatively, the data could suggest that a number of units that worked rhetorically in rather different ways have been brought together partly on the basis of verbal links that were originally matters of chance (or by a process that involved some provision of extra verbal links) and have been provided with the syntactical links between 56.9–57.2, 57.3-13 and 57.14-21. While I incline to the view that the first is the more economical understanding, it is not possible to pontificate about the question. Either way, the section as a whole is designed to be read as a whole.

Whereas 56.1-8 suggested a Second Temple context, the warnings in 56.9–57.13 parallel the language and concerns of preexilic prophets (the encouragement sections also link with the Psalms); this prophet's 'social criticism does not fall behind Amos in ferocity'.[70] It has been dated in the preexilic period[71] as well as in the late sixth century,[72] the fifth century,[73] and the fourth.[74] In the arrangement of the book, however, it gives more concrete expression to what is involved in guarding *mišpāṭ* and acting in *ṣᵉdāqâ*, and urges the community to the kind of conversion these imperatives imply.[75]

In 57.14-21 language from 40.1-11 and from 6.1-13 reappears. Indeed, the entire section 56.9–57.21 has concrete links with material in Isaiah 1–9; 33; and 40, which suggests that one aspect of its significance is that here both the Isaiah and the Yhwh who speak in those earlier chapters are

69 Against Fohrer, *Jesaja*, 3.190; he compares 24.1–27.13, but the latter does involve movement between prophetic address and praise. Budde ('Zum hebräischen Klagelied', pp. 239-41) analyses 56.9–57.13 in light of the form of a lament, but this involves substantial emending of the text, which rather confirms that the passage uses traditional forms but does so in an independent way.

70 Koch, *Die Profeten II*, p. 158 (ET p. 154).

71 E.g. Ewald, *Die Propheten des Alten Bundes*, II, pp. 459-63 (ET IV, pp. 321-25). For more recent such argument regarding Isa 56–66 as a whole, see J. Barton Payne, 'Eighth Century Israelitish Background of Isaiah 40–66', *WTJ* 29 (1966–67), pp. 179-90; 30 (1967–68), pp. 50-58, 185-203. Dating it in the seventh century, S. D. Luzzatto reckons it the single passage in Isaiah that postdates Isaiah ben Amoz; see Shmuel Vargon, 'Isaiah 56:9–57:13', *Jewish Studies Quarterly* 6 (1999), pp. 218-33. Luzzatto sees 57.1 as referring to Isaiah's death in the reign of Manasseh (ספר ישעיהו *Il profeta Isaia*, p. 573). Grotius refers it to Josiah, but his editor G. J. L. Vogel expresses his disagreement and refers it to faithful people more generally (Grotius, *Annotationes in Vetus Testamentum*, II, p. 114), though Calov agrees with Grotius (*Biblia Testamenti Veteris illustrata*, II, p. 298).

72 E.g. Fischer, *Buch Isaias*, II, pp. 153-54.

73 E.g. Duhm, *Jesaia*, p. 384.

74 E.g. Steck, *Studien zu Tritojesaja*, p. 192.

75 Cf. Ramis, *Isaías 40–66*, p. 257.

speaking anew in this different context but in a way that reaffirms and reapplies the earlier declarations.[76] The section as a whole thus encapsulates the message of Isaiah 1–55.

It has further concrete links with Jeremiah and Ezekiel, which works against the view that 56.9–57.13 comes from the preexilic period. The suggestion that it belongs in the exilic period is plausible if one assumes it refers to the life and worship of people left behind in Judah who were continuing the religious practices described by Jeremiah and Ezekiel. If it belongs in the late sixth century, one can imagine that people who had made the effort to 'return' to Judah might be unlikely to be involved in the kind of religious practices the passages attack, and might be driven to condemn people who had not gone into exile and were involved in them. If the material belongs to a later period, there would have been time for the descendants of people who had come from Babylon to assimilate to these customs. Its parallels with preexilic prophecy and its reworking of motifs from earlier prophets suggest that in living and worshipping as they are, people are behaving in the same way as their ancestors, and risk their fate. For 57.14-21, links with Isaiah 40–55 likewise suggest a date in the late sixth century or subsequently. Its taking up the words of these earlier chapters again suggests that the exilic prophet, too, and the Yhwh who speaks in those chapters, now address the situation of the Second Temple community. Isaiah 57.14-21 has the prophet and Yhwh doing so in more encouraging fashion than 56.9–57.13, as Isaiah 40–55 itself has a more encouraging overall tone than Isaiah 1–39. Indeed, 57.14-21 has striking overlaps with aspects of the attitudes Jeremiah ascribes to the prophets who falsely repeat the word *šālōm* (Jer 6.13-14). It thus 'reverses Jeremiah's message of woe and replaces it with a proclamation of restoration', yet does so without implying disagreement with Jeremiah and agreement with those other prophets. 'The prophets to whom Jeremiah objected had a valid message—but not one valid for their own time.' Furthermore, the present prophecy explicitly agrees with Jeremiah that there will be no *šālōm* for the faithless. It 'uses the rhetoric of reversal to underscore how apt Jeremiah's warnings were' while also indicating that they still apply in the present even though the possibility of *šālōm* is also open.[77]

Comment: 56.9–57.2

We have noted that at 56.9 nothing directly suggests a new section. It would be easy to assume that Yhwh continues to speak; indeed, this may be so, as will certainly be the case in 57.3-13. Yet the tone of the words is different, as are the addressees, and one might rather conclude that the prophet speaks through 56.9–57.2.

[76] Cf. Steck, 'Der sich selbst aktualisierende "Jesaja"'.
[77] Sommer, *A Prophet Reads Scripture*, p. 41.

56.9 All you animals of the wild,// come on and eat,// all you animals in the forest!

The line is a tricolon (3-2-2) comprising parallel noun phrases in the first and third cola with a double verbal expression at the centre. The verbal expression thus applies to the second noun phrase as well as to the first, and the two noun expressions form a merism for all possible dangerous beasts; 'wild' or 'open country' pairs in a similar way with 'forest' in Ezekiel 39.10.[78] But for the sake of the variation that parallelism likes, a prepositional expression in the third colon pairs with the construct in the first. The tricolon marks the beginning of a new section.

MT places its athnaḥ after 'animals of the wild' and then puts a conjunctive accent on 'eat', suggesting that 'all the animals in the forest' is the object of 'eat' rather than a second subject. This makes for a grammatically good sentence and one that coheres with MT's division marker, linking v. 9 with what precedes. It might then imply that v. 9 is a positive invitation to come and join in a festive meal on Mount Zion.[79] Tg, on the other hand, in a substantial expansion on this line promises that all the gentile kings that attacked Jerusalem will become food for the animals of the wild. The translator 'quite clearly longs for an end to Jerusalem's oppression, and for suitable treatment for those who have done the oppressing',[80] longings that fit in Isaiah 56–66 as a whole if not in this passage. In contrast Theodoret of Cyrrhus sees the verse as God's invitation to Jerusalem's enemies (he has the Romans in mind) to come and attack Jerusalem.[81] This in fact coheres well with the line's relationship with Jeremiah 12.8-9, which it seems to follow. There, Israel has been behaving toward Yhwh 'like a lion in the forest' and Yhwh commissions a summons to 'get all the animals of the wild to come on and eat'.[82]

One can see why interpreters might not link v. 9 with what follows. While it comes out of the blue and thus does not obviously link with what precedes, its links with what follows are also not immediately obvious. In the manner of a parable it requires its hearers to work out what it means and how it fits into its context. As they do so, they are drawn into the message and thus manoeuvred into allowing it to get home to them. Only as they work out the significance of vv. 10-11 does it become clearer

[78] Cf. Polan, *In the Ways of Justice toward Salvation*, p. 110.

[79] See the discussion in Raymond de Hoop, 'The Interpretation of Isaiah 56:1-9', *JBL* 127 (2008), pp. 671-95 (676-77). Cf. Cyril of Alexandria, Ἐξήγησις ὑπομνηματική εἰς τὸν προφήτην Ἡσαΐαν, columns 1250-56.

[80] Chilton, *The Glory of Israel*, p. 25.

[81] *Commentaire sur Isaïe* 171ab (III, pp. 192-95); cf. Jerome, *Commentariorum in Isaiam prophetam libri duodeviginti*, col. 543.

[82] Indeed, at Jer 12.9 some medieval mss have the qal 'come on' as here, instead of the hiphil 'get [them] to come on' (LXX and Vg also imply the qal). For the inf. abs., Jer 12.9 has *lᵉʾoklâ* instead of *leʾĕkōl*.

what v. 9 signifies. Following on 55.1-2, its invitation might be assumed to have positive connotations; in reality, it suggests an ironic contrast with the earlier invitation. It is when we see that v. 9 links with what follows that MT's punctuation of the line does not make very good sense. Rather the second noun expression stands in parallelism with the first and the double command addresses both.[83]

When the hearers have worked out that the image in v. 9 is a negative one, they might for a moment assume that the animals could be literally meant (see, e.g., 2 Kgs 17.25-26).[84] The object of their feasting might then be the produce of the land, which the lookouts are failing to protect. But the passage's links with Jeremiah 12.9-10 suggest that the prophet speaks metaphorically.[85] There, Yhwh has already commissioned the issuing of an invitation to 'all the wild animals' to come and 'eat', and also noted how shepherds have destroyed Yhwh's vineyard (cf. also Ezek 39.17). Further, Jeremiah 27.6 has observed that Yhwh has given 'the wild animals' to Nebuchadnezzar to serve him, and has implied that these animals are a figure for the nations that Nebuchadnezzar rules (cf. Jer 28.14; also Ezek 31.6, 13). Ezekiel has also already put together 'the animals of the wild' with the sheep whose shepherds have neglected them (Ezek 34.5, 8).[86] 'Animals in the forest' (such as lions and bears) come elsewhere as a metaphor only in Micah 5.7 [8], where they are an image for Israel itself prevailing over its enemies, but Jeremiah 5.6 speaks of a lion from the forest ravaging Israel. So the prophecy begins by inviting foreign nations to come and consume, and leaves the hearers to work out who are their victims. The image has a further background in the way animals did literally eat the bodies of people who died in battle. There is no need to hypothesize a context where Judah as actually threatened by invasion. Prophecy need not work like that, and a literalistic approach is inappropriate to an understanding of it. Its point lies in the sarcasm with which it castigates the incompetence of the leadership and warns where it will lead.[87] Likewise, it requires considerable reading into the line to take it as a description of the way the community's leaders have been in effect inviting the Persian authorities to impose taxation that is devouring the land's produce.[88]

[83] As David Qimchi already realizes (see 'ישעיה', on the passage).

[84] Cf. Duhm, *Jesaia*, p. 385.

[85] Cf. Beuken's comment that the context of Jer 12.7-17 clarifies the metaphor (*Jesaja IIIA*, p. 49).

[86] In Jeremiah and Ezekiel the phrase is *ḥayyat haśśādeh* or the like, not *ḥayᵉtô śāday*; see also the translation note on 56.9 above.

[87] Cf. Smith, *Rhetoric and Redaction in Trito-Isaiah*, p. 74.

[88] See Albertz, *Religionsgeschichte Israels in alttestamentlicher Zeit*, II, p. 551-52 (ET p. 504).

56.10 Its lookouts are blind, all of them;// they do not know.
All of them are dumb dogs,// they cannot bark.
They are snoozing, bedding down,// loving to doze.
11aα But the dogs are mighty in appetite;// they do not know 'enough'.

In Jeremiah or Ezekiel, the invitation in v. 9 would be a response to Israel's waywardness, and in due course 57.3-13 will either imply that connection here or add that connection. In the meantime the prophet makes a knight's move in turning to speak of lookouts.[89] When foreign nations attack a city, it is the responsibility of the city's lookouts to warn it (e.g. Ezek 33.1-6). Metaphorically, when trouble threatens a city, it is the responsibility of its leadership to warn it and turn it from its waywardness. In this connection, Israel's prophets in particular are its lookouts (Jer 6.17; Ezek 3.17; 33.7), though one might not need to confine this passage's reference to prophets; they might well include priests, given their teaching responsibility.[90] The problem is that the community's present lookouts are rather indulging themselves and issuing no warnings. The point is made in four lines (3-2, 3-3, 2-2, 2-3), in each of which the parallelism works by having the second colon make explicit an implication of the first. Insofar as the lookouts comprise or include prophets, this prophet's critique parallels those of prophets such as Jeremiah in relation to their fellow-prophets. As was the case in Jeremiah's estimate, once again these prophets are colluding with the people in their waywardness rather than confronting them.

They lack the basic qualifications to be lookouts. First, they are blind. While this is a deficiency of the people as a whole, which makes it hard for them to function as witnesses (e.g. Isa 42.18-19), the lookouts in particular have no knowledge of what is going on, of the danger their people are in. On this first occurrence, the phrase 'they do not know' is used absolutely, which is not odd; for instance, it is paralleled in the lines about people being rendered incapable of seeing or hearing in 6.9-10 (cf. 44.18).[91] But it nevertheless raises a question (what is it that they do not know?) which v. 11 answers with its two further uses of the phrase.

Second, they are dumb. While most Old Testament references to dogs are not complimentary, which in itself adds to the disrespectful, insulting nature of the prophet's words, the prophecy does recognize the theoretical possibility that the curs might be useful, as watchdogs. But these are watchdogs that cannot bark. There is a pathetic, almost laughable incongruity about the word 'dumb' following the word 'dogs' as there was about the word 'blind' following the word 'lookouts'; both phrases have 'all of them' attached, to underline the point.

[89] Lena-Sofia Tiemeyer ('The Watchman Metaphor in Isaiah lvi–lxvi', *VT* 55 [2005], pp. 378-400) sees this metaphor as running through 56.9–59.21.
[90] Cf. Tiemeyer, *Priestly Rites and Prophetic Rage*, pp. 113-26.
[91] Cf. Uhlig, *The Theme of Hardening in the Book of Isaiah*, p. 250.

Further (v. 10b), they are lazy. They are the kind of dogs that lie sleeping in the sun; they are also too lethargic to bark, or move. The word for 'snoozing' (*hāzâ*) comes only here and its meaning has to be guessed from the context; I follow Saadia,[92] and take it as onomatopoeic. 1QIs[a], LXX, Syr, Vg, Aq, Sym have or imply the familiar *ḥāzâ* 'see', taken to mean seeing dream visions.[93] While this makes good sense, restating the first line in v. 10, it is surely too easy a reading, though it does suggest a paronomasia. 'Seeing' is what they were supposed to be doing; they were actually doing something that sounds similar but is very different. While the verb *hāzâ* might be a familiar one that happens not otherwise to appear in the Old Testament, it might be a word the prophet invented in order to make the point about the difference between what the lookouts were doing and what they were supposed to do.

The dogs have a fourth characteristic, an insatiable hunger. They are mighty of *nepeš*, which here suggests desire or appetite. The second colon reexpresses the point in a way that also links back with the first of these four lines about the leaders *qua* dogs, and thus forms an *inclusio* with it. They lack knowledge of what is going on; they do not even know when to stop eating. 'Though they are lazy in all that relates to good government, yet they have a strong and ravenous appetite for food.'[94]

Chrysostom quotes v. 10 at the Jews who were members of his congregation[95] and Calov finds here the priests, Pharisees, and scribes of the Gospels.[96] On the other hand, Ignatius of Antioch applies its warnings to Christian teachers who teach falsehood,[97] and Cocceius applies them to self-indulgent bishops.[98] The Scottish satirist David Lyndesay (1490–1555) in his *Complaynt to the King's Grace* similarly applies them to the bishops of the Roman Catholic Church, seeing them as dogs who cannot bark—that is, preach, or teach Christ's law.[99]

56.11aβ Those people—they are shepherds// who do not know how to be discerning.
All of them have directed themselves to their own way,// each one to his own ill-gotten gain, every last part of him.

[92] Cf. Rosenberg, *Isaiah*, II, p. 445. Frederick E. Greenspahn (*Hapax Legomena in Biblical Hebrew* [Chico, CA: Scholars, 1983], pp. 85, 112) notes possible Arabic cognates meaning 'sleep' but also pertaining to confused speech. See further Paul, ישעיה פרקים מ-סו, II, p. 415 (ET p. 458).

[93] 1QIs[a] then reads *nw'm*, possibly from *n[e]'um*, the word for a prophetic declaration (cf. Pulikottil, *Transmission of Biblical Texts in Qumran*, p. 94), but perhaps simply an orthographic difference (cf. Qimron, *The Hebrew of the Dead Sea Scrolls*, p. 20).

[94] Calvin, *In Iesaiam prophetam*, p. 361 (ET vol. 4, pp. 189-90).

[95] Λόγοι κατὰ Ἰουδαιῶν 4.6

[96] *Biblia Testamenti Veteris illustrata*, II, p. 297.

[97] Ephesians 7.

[98] 'Synopsis Prophetiae Jesaiae', pp. 53, 54; cf. 'Curae majores in prophetiam Esaiae', p. 414.

[99] Lines 330-31, as quoted in Sawyer, *The Fifth Gospel*, p. 136.

12 'Come on, I'll get wine,// we'll quaff drink.
And tomorrow will be the same,// abundantly, exceedingly great!'

Four further lines (2-3, 3-3, 2-2, 4-3) give a parallel, more literal description of the problem with the community's leadership. Again it starts from questions about wisdom but moves on to questions about self-indulgence. Perhaps lack of insight leads to self-indulgence; perhaps self-indulgence takes away insight.

The opening demonstrative 'those [people]' might refer to the dogs but more likely takes up the first line's reference to lookouts. Metaphorically, the lookouts lack acquaintance with what is going on, because they are not paying attention. Literally, the shepherds similarly lack such acquaintance (strictly, 'shepherds' is also a metaphor, but it is a dead metaphor, like 'pastor' in English). They lack acquaintance with the kind of insight that makes leadership possible. They take no notice of what is going on in the community and/or of the action on Yhwh's part that these events in the community will lead to. So while one answer to the question, 'What do they not know?' is that they do not know when enough is enough (v. 11aα), this further answer is that they do not know how to give heed.

Indeed (the second line indicates), they lack the kind of insight that makes it possible to pay attention to Yhwh's way, which is a necessary even though not a sufficient qualification for the exercise of leadership, and they lack this insight through their own action. Insight is a moral quality, not merely an intellectual or pragmatic one. Instead of walking in Yhwh's way, they have turned to walk in their own way. It is as if they are repeating the waywardness of the people who give their testimony in 53.6, except that (unlike them) they have not seen the error of their ways. Over against 53.6, the difference is only rhetorical: the account in 53.6 is a visionary one, of insight that in actuality is not yet achieved, and towards which the vision is designed to push people; the aim of the present prophecy will be similar. Insofar as this prophecy takes up 52.13–53.12, then, in doing so it declares that nothing has moved on since the exile, which is an implication running through 56.9–57.21.

In the parallelism, the companion colon gives precision to how people have turned to their own way, in being concerned for their own 'ill-gotten gain'. The word (*beṣaʿ*) is another that recurs in critiques in Jeremiah (6.13; 8.10; 22.17; 51.13), Ezekiel (22.13, 27; 33.31), and elsewhere. It is a standard accusation in prophecy and a standard reality of human experience that people in positions of leadership make their position the means of doing well for themselves in ways that involve dubious honesty. EVV understand the last phrase then to emphasize that there are absolutely no exceptions to this rule (cf. Jer 5.1-6; Ps 12.2-3 [1-2]); grammatically, the phrase more likely indicates that the concern for ill-gotten gain dominates each person's entire life (no doubt a hyperbole either way). But the point about there being no exceptions is already made by the further 'all of them' (compare v. 10). All the wild animals and all the forest animals are invited to come to eat (v. 9) on the basis of the fact that the lookouts are blind, all of them, are like dumb dogs, all of them (v. 10), and have turned to their own way, all of them (v. 11).

As Tg makes explicit by adding 'They say', v. 12 gives us the shepherds' words in this connection. Their opening 'come' repeats the verb in v. 9 and hints that this 'come' is the reason for the earlier 'come'. The way v. 12 leads from 'come' to 'drink' and thus parallels the way v. 9 led from 'come' to 'eat' underlines the connection.

The verb 'get' makes the link with the reference to ill-gotten gain; the verb indicates that they take what does not belong to them.[100] So their words are not part of a drinking song or a proverb. Amos 4.1 further makes the link between wrongful gain and drinking, without using this verb, as may Amos 2.8; Isaiah 5.22-23. The reference to wine perhaps also connects with the description of the slumbering dogs, since alcohol is inclined to make one sleepy. The related implication that indulgence in alcohol and perceptiveness of insight are mutually exclusive parallels other prophets; this time the critique is one more characteristic of Isaiah 1–39 (e.g. 5.11-12; 28.1, 7; cf. also Amos 2.12; 6.6). The word for 'drink' (*šēkār*) also recurs from the Isaiah passages; it draws attention to the intoxicating nature of the drink in question (the related verb means 'be drunk'). The verb 'quaff' (*sābāʾ*) is a rare one, so that both verb and noun contribute to the second colon's heightening the affect of the first. And the line makes for another ironic contrast with 55.1. They have been invited to the feast of which that verse speaks, but they prefer the kind of feast that earlier prophets describe.

As the second line emphasized how waywardness characterized the shepherds' whole being, the fourth line emphasizes their far-reaching expectations.

57.1 The faithful person—he has perished,// and there is no one giving heed,
People of commitment—they are gathered up,// while there is no one discerning
That it is from the presence of calamity// that the faithful person has been gathered up;
2 He goes in peace as they rest on their beds,// the person who walks straight.

These closing four lines of 56.9–57.2 take up in two ways the leadership's failure of attention, its failure to heed.[101] Like 56.9-12, they begin with a line that is clear enough in itself but does not reveal where the following lines are going. It is plausible to infer that the account in v. 1a

[100] W. A. M. Beuken, 'Isa. 56:9–57:13', in J. W. van Henten *et al.* (eds.), *Tradition and Re-interpretation in Jewish and Early Christian Literature* (J. C. H. Lebram Festschrift; Leiden: Brill, 1986), pp. 48-64 (61).

[101] Cf. Hanson, *The Dawn of Apocalyptic*, p. 187.

of what is happening in the community describes a consequence of the shepherdly inaction that has just been depicted, and/or describes an aspect of the shepherds' action. At the very least, the leaders' focus on self-indulgence means they fail to fulfil their vocation to see that the community's life works out in a way that prevents ruthless people oppressing upright people. But the implication of the earlier reference to ill-gotten gain is likely that the leaders are themselves involved in this oppression, as is the case in the critique of leadership elsewhere in the prophets. This likelihood is increased by the reappearance of the verb 'discern' (*bîn* hiphil) in the second line (they are the only two occurrences of this root in Isa 56–66). After the link with Jeremiah 12.9-10 in 56.9, the link with Jeremiah 12.11 in 57.1a is noteworthy.

The first two lines in 57.1 (2-4, 3-2) are systematically parallel in form and content; they work aba′b′. Each begins with a noun describing the right-living. Each of the expressions precedes the verb and thus stands in emphatic position (in the first line, LXX achieves a similar effect by adding 'See how…', though this is also an instance of a homiletic use of this imperative in Isaiah).[102] Each of the expressions makes a contrast with the shepherds who were the subject of 56.10-12. The anarthrous plural construct expression in the second line complements the singular single noun with the article in the first. For the translation of *ṣaddîq* as 'faithful', see on 56.1. Applied to God, *ṣaddîq* 'is not a character trait' but rather points to 'his beneficent intervention';[103] the same is true when the word is applied to human beings. For *ʾanšê-ḥesed*, 'people of commitment', LXX has 'righteous people' (repeating the word from the previous line), while Vg and Aq have 'compassionate people' (Sym, Th have 'men of the people'). *Ḥesed* suggests the practice of love or grace or benevolence or mercy that either has no basis of obligation in a prior relationship, or goes beyond anything that could be expected on the basis of a relationship, especially where the other party has not been faithful. 'It is active, social, and enduring.'[104] It is not earned or conditional, yet it invites or looks for a responsive commitment from the other party; 'the one who demonstrates *ḥeseḏ* is justified in expecting an equivalent act in return'.[105] Evidently this expectation is not being fulfilled in the community. The analysis parallels Micah 7.2 and the wording overlaps with that verse.

In these opening two lines, the verbs then follow their subjects, a niphal plural participle complementing a qal singular qatal. The first has literal meaning; the second is a euphemism. Each second colon begins with an *ʾên* phrase, the first prefixed by *w*, the second by a preposition. In the first line, the predicate is then a phrase incorporating a qal participle, while in the second it simply comprises a hiphil participle.

[102] See Baer, *When We All Go Home*, pp. 42-51.
[103] B. Johnson, *TWAT*, VI, p. 917 (ET *TDOT*, XII, p. 257).
[104] H.-J. Zobel, *TWAT*, III, p. 56 (ET *TDOT*, V, p. 51).
[105] H.-J. Zobel, *TWAT*, III, p. 52 (ET *TDOT*, V, p. 47).

In the context, the reference to the faithful person, along with the reference to faithfulness in v. 12, makes a link with 56.1.[106] Its implication is that while there are people who are meeting the challenge in 56.1, their fate indicates that this is not true of the community as a whole, and in particular it is not true of its leadership. It also raises the question whether Yhwh's faithfulness, which Isaiah 56.1 went on to assert, is operative, if the faithful are allowed to perish. Behind 56.1 and 57.12, the reference to the faithful person makes a further link with 52.13–53.12 (see 53.11), the previous occurrence of this precise word, and vv. 1-2 parallel Isaiah 52.13–53.12 in more general terms.[107] Rabbi Aqiba sees it fulfilled in the deaths of Rabbi Simeon and Rabbi Ishmael.[108] Early church writers see a reference to Christ[109] and also a prophecy fulfilled in the suffering of the apostles;[110] it thus relates to the experience of subsequent Christian martyrs and to the need to be willing to face martyrdom.[111]

The parallel plural 'people of commitment' suggests that 'the faithful person' is collective,[112] so that if there is a link with Isaiah 52.13–53.12, the link implies that the earlier poem was understood collectively or was reinterpreted thus;[113] 'the faithful person' is used elsewhere for a whole class of people (e.g. Ezek 18.20).[114] Whether understood individually or collectively, it would be too much to infer that 'the faithful person' who has perished simply *is* the same person who is at least facing the possibility of death in 52.13–53.12.[115] But the sort of event the verses describe does repeat aspects of the pattern Isaiah 52.13–53.12 describes. That earlier vision expects to see the faithful person restored (before or after death) and to see him acknowledged, expects to see his tormenters recognize their error, and envisages the possibility that he can turn his accepting the cost of his obedience into an offering to Yhwh on their behalf. None of this appears in 57.1-2, though the link with that earlier vision might point the faithful back to these other aspects of that vision for their reflection when they do experience such oppression. Along with the assumption that 'the faithful' and 'the people of commitment' denote a

[106] Cf. Elliger, 'Der Prophet Tritojesaja', pp. 116-17.

[107] See Joseph Blenkinsopp, 'Who is the *Ṣaddiq* of Isaiah 57:1-2?', in P. W. Flint, E. Tov, and J. C. VanderKam (eds.), *Studies in the Hebrew Bible, Qumran, and the Septuagint Presented to Eugene Ulrich* (Leiden: Brill, 2006), pp. 109-20.

[108] Mekilta attributed to Rabbi Ishmael 75.1, as quoted in Neusner, *Isaiah in Talmud and Midrash*, p. 107.

[109] E.g. Justin, *First Apology* 48; Irenaeus, *Against Heresies* 4.34.

[110] E.g. Tertullian, *Against Marcion* 4.21.

[111] E.g. Justin, *Dialogue with Trypho* 16; Tertullian, *Scorpiace* 8.

[112] Cf. Koenen, *Ethik und Eschatologie im Tritojesajabuch*, p. 16.

[113] Cf. Hanson, *The Dawn of Apocalyptic*, p. 197.

[114] Alexander, *Prophecies of Isaiah* 2, p. 340.

[115] Luzzatto (*Animadversiones in Jesajae vaticinia*, pp. xxxiv-xxxv) takes it to refer to Isaiah himself; Calmet also mentions Josiah and Ezekiel as possible referents (*Le Prophéte Isaïe*, p. 594).

number of victims of oppression goes the assumption that the qatal verbs in the context ('has perished', 'has been gathered up') are gnomic.

On the other hand, it is explicit here that the faithful person, the people of commitment, have actually died, which in their case makes it too late for some of the vision in 52.13–53.12 to be realized. The good news for them takes a rather different form. The first two lines provide only the merest hint of that good news in the verb 'they are gathered up', a euphemism for dying in passages such as Genesis 25.8, 17 (P). Those passages make explicit that the person is gathered 'to his kin', which is what constitutes the implicit comfort in the expression; at death one joins one's family. The verb is used absolutely with this sense in passages such as Numbers 20.26. The modern secular equivalent expression would be the notion of dying 'a good death', which would be among other things a death with honour and integrity.

What is it that everyone among the leadership has failed to heed or discern? The second pair of lines in 57.1-2 (2-2, 4-2) goes on to explicate what it is that they take no account of. It is not merely the fact that the faithful and committed people have perished but that there is a sense in which they are fortunate in this respect, because by thus being at rest they escape the fate that is coming on the community. Aq, Sym, Th take v. 2 as jussive, 'May he come/may peace come' and 'may they rest'. But this fits less well in the context. Likewise the way the lines note the positive aspect to the passing of the faithful qualifies the impression one would otherwise form that vv. 1-2 are a lament.[116] Or rather, it points us to a different sense in which the lines are indeed a lament, continuing the protest that began in 56.10-12. Their actual point does not lie in noting that there is a rather Pickwickian sense in which the victims are fortunate. It lies in the fact that the leadership takes no notice of the consideration that generates this implausible claim. There is calamity coming which the victims will escape; the tragedy of the situation lies in the way the leaders take no account of this fact.

By its verse division, MT thus correctly links this *kî* clause with what precedes; it describes what the leaders did not pay heed to (it does not mean 'for', nor is it simply asseverative). The critique is not merely that they did not care about the fate of the committed faithful and therefore did not do anything to protect them. They did not care about their own fate. They did not note that the committed faithful were actually escaping something that the shepherds will experience. MT's verse division also neatly makes 'the faithful person' both open and close the verse. But it further implies that the *kî* clause comprises simply the one line, v. 1bβ, whereas rather it continues through v. 2. This understanding takes better account of the balanced two-line form of v. 1abα and also makes it possible to see vv. 1bβ-2 as comprising a further pair of parallel lines. They are not as neatly constructed as the earlier pair, but 'the person who walks straight' parallels 'the faithful person' and 'he goes in peace'

[116] So Elliger, *Die Einheit des Tritojesaja*, p. 9.

parallels 'has been gathered up'. In turn, 'they rest on their beds' makes an unhappy pairing with 'from the presence of calamity', in that their careless rest ignores the prospect of calamity. 'Peace' and 'calamity' also form a contrasting pair (see 45.7; also Jer 29.11).[117] At the same time, 'the faithful person has been gathered up' reprises v. 1abα by taking up the noun from the first line and the verb from the second, in chiastic order.

Translations usually assume that the people who rest on their beds are the faithful; 'their beds' are then their resting places in death (cf. LXX 'burial/burial place'). *Miškāb* can have this connotation (see Ezek 32.25; 2 Chr 16.14), while Job 3.17 speaks sardonically of death as involving 'resting'.[118] The implication will then be that singular and plural complement each other in v. 2 as in v. 1abα (cf. also 56.4-7). But this produces a jerky effect in v. 2. One might infer that the jerkiness issues in part from the line's having been subject to glossing (e.g. if 'they rest on their beds' or 'the person who walks straight' is an element later than the rest of the line).[119] Further, the people who were bedding down in 56.10 were the dogs, representing the community leaders who are in some sense responsible for the death of the faithful; the verb there was *šākab*, the noun here is *miškāb*. All this makes it more likely that the people resting on their beds are the leaders. The phrase at the centre of the line is then an asyndetic circumstantial clause, and by restating the point about the dogs from 56.10 the expression reformulates the point about their not taking any notice or giving heed to what is going on.

That the two lines comprising vv. 1bβ-2 take a positive view of the fate of the faithful is already suggested by their opening compound preposition 'from the presence of' (*mippᵉnê*), which often implies fleeing or escaping from something; it thus regularly points to causation.[120] In isolation, *rāʿâ* could be taken to denote the evil or wrong *by* which the faithful have been taken away, but in the context, it thus rather denotes the evil or trouble that is coming on the community from which the faithful escape (cf. Tg). This understanding fits the way v. 1bβ puts this phrase in emphatic position at the beginning of the line. In turn, the line as a whole (and the line that follows) confirms that the verb *ʾāsap* has a positive connotation. This faithful person is not merely 'taken away' (53.8, also followed by *min*) but gathered up. As well as suggesting a positive connotation in connection with death, the verb hints that the faithful person has been gathered up in the sense of cared for and protected (cf. Exod 9.19). Implicitly, Yhwh is the unspecified agent of the niphal verb (cf. Ps 27.10); Isaiah 58.8 will take up the verb in the qal in

[117] Cf. Polan, *In the Ways of Justice toward Salvation*, p. 122.

[118] See further Paul, ישעיה פרקים מ-סו, II, p. 418 (ET pp. 462-63).

[119] See, e.g., Thomas, 'ספר ישעיה', p. 89. Odeberg (*Trito-Isaiah*, p. 71) sees the whole of vv. 1bβ-2 as (*Die Tritojesajanische Sammlung*, p. 109) takes the last phrase as vocative, 'you who walk straight'; but there has been no other such addressing of a person.

[120] See BDB.

this connection. But there is no one (specifically, no one among the shepherds) paying heed to the fact.

The expression *yābô ʾ šālôm* is elliptical. Vg, Sym, and Th take *šālôm* as the subject, 'peace comes', but there are no other examples of *šālôm* as the subject of a verb.[121] Modern translations incline to take *šālôm* as the destiny of the verb, 'he goes to peace', but there are no other examples of this usage. LXX and Aq rather translate 'in peace', assuming that the absolute noun is used adverbially, and there are a number of instances of this absolute usage in connection with coming or going 'in peace' in various senses, not least the also elliptical 41.3 (also 1 Sam 16.4-5; 1 Kgs 2.13), and a number of descriptions of death as 'going in peace' (*bᵉšālôm*). A notable example is Genesis 15.15; the faithful see Abraham's experience repeated for them. Further, 2 Kings 22.20 has Huldah promising Josiah that he will be gathered up (the verb that recurs here in v. 1) into his tomb in peace so that he will not see the calamity (again, the word in v. 1) that is coming on the people (cf. also Jer 34.5).[122] The faithful person goes by means of violence but goes in peace in the sense of not experiencing its antithesis, calamity (cf. Isa 45.7), which is coming.[123] His experience thus contrasts with that envisaged for the faithless in 48.22, to be restated in 57.19-21.

The closing phrase repeats the adverbial construction, 'the one walking [in] his straightness' (cf. 33.15; 50.10).[124] Tg paraphrases 'who observe [*ʿăbad*] his teaching', apparently taking the suffix to refer to Yhwh, though that understanding draws attention to the fact that Yhwh has not been mentioned for a long time. Rather the suffix refers to the faithful person's insistence on walking straight or uprightly or truly. Given the word's rarity, we may note the appearance in 30.10 of *nᵉkōḥôt* set over against *ḥălāqôt* (cf. 57.6), where the two words indicate the kind of words people do not and do want to hear from prophets.[125]

None of the phrases used in vv. 1-2 thus suggest an afterlife more exciting than that of Sheol,[126] though in the context of the Wisdom of Solomon in a passage with a similar theme to that of vv. 1-2, similar phraseology (perhaps influenced by this passage) does carry that connotation (see Wisdom 3.3; 4.14, in the context especially of 4.7-19).[127]

[121] Words such as 'deliverance' can be the subject of 'come' (Isa 56.1; 58.8; 62.11; Koenen, *Ethik und Eschatologie im Tritojesajabuch*, p. 19); but these are things that 'come' in a sense that *šālôm* is not.

[122] Cf. David Qimchi, 'ישעיה', on the passage.

[123] It fits less well in the context to take the phrase as promising Yhwh's deliverance (Uhlig, *The Theme of Hardening in the Book of Isaiah*, p. 259).

[124] Cf. BDB.

[125] Sommer (*A Prophet Reads Scripture*, p. 88) sees 56.10–57.6 as a restatement of Jer 12.7-13 in light of Isa 30.9-14.

[126] Against B. Renaud, 'La morte du juste, entrée dans la paix', *Revue des sciences religieuses* 51 (1977), pp. 3-21.

[127] Croatto, *Imaginar el futuro*, pp. 58-62, where he also suggests that the figure of Enoch as described in Gen 5.22-24 (and that of Noah in Gen 6.9) lies behind not only the

Comment: 57.3-13

Confrontation resumes, but its basis, target, and technique are different from those in 56.9–57.2. It concerns the wrongdoing of people in general, not that of the leadership in particular; it concerns their religious practice rather than their oppression of one another; and it directly addresses the offenders rather than describing them in the third person. In this last respect it takes up the form of a speech in court. The bidding to 'draw near' is a bidding to come into the presence of the court (cf., e.g., 41.1); the accusation addressed to the defendants then follows in the body of vv. 3-13.

The subsection raises a number of difficult questions, at two related levels. It contains a number of rare or unique words and other expressions that are puzzling in the context, and this has led to many suggestions for emending the text or for understanding it in the light of expressions from related languages.[128] But we should be wary of toning down the poem's oddness. It 'has a manic quality, reflecting the picture of a people driven as by an inward demon, now here, now there', down into the canyon, up to the mountain.[129]

In addition, its attack on practices in which the community is involved uses a complex series of images and terms; what it is describing can be hard to identify. It talks in terms of sexual acts, and these have been understood to denote religious practices that constitute enacted prayers for the fertility of crops and flocks and people. It talks about the sacrifice of children, a practice known from elsewhere in the Old Testament and from other contemporary cultures, which among other possible significances could embody a recognition that God was the giver of life; this is the assumption behind the idea that firstborn offspring are owed to Yhwh, though human firstborn are to be redeemed (e.g. Exod 13.1-2 [P], 11-16 [D]). It talks about divination and Sheol in a way that implies offerings made in connection with seeking help from dead family members. And it talks about sending off envoys, which suggests embassies to foreign political powers. My conclusion regarding this portrait is as follows.

First, the notion of sending off political envoys makes sense in the context of Isaiah 1–39 (see 18.2) and on the theory that this passage belongs in the monarchic period, but it makes less sense in the Second

Wisdom passage but also Isa 57.1-2. Blenkinsopp (*Opening the Sealed Book*, pp. 264-65) notes that the Wisdom passage takes up Isa 52.13–53.12 as well as 57.1-2, which supports the idea that 57.1-2 itself takes up 52.13–53.12.

[128] Ginsberg calls vv. 6-11 an 'evidently very imperfect text' ('Some Emendations in Isaiah', p. 59). For further emendations and suggestions, see (e.g.) Scullion, 'Some Difficult Texts in Isaiah cc.56—66', pp. 111-14.

[129] Motyer, *Isaiah*, p. 472.

Temple period, and nothing in the context of this passage or of Isaiah 56–66 as a whole points in this direction. The word for 'envoys', *ṣîr*, is not an inherently political term but a rare alternative for *mal'āk* (cf. Prov 13.17).

Second, for the monarchic period both the Old Testament text and the discoveries of archaeology provide ample evidence of the practices of sacrificing children and of seeking contact with one's dead family members, and it is entirely plausible to assume that these continued during the exilic period and into the Second Temple period.[130] We have noted that in both these latter contexts, the devotees would include people who stayed in Judah (rather than being exiled) and their descendants, people who thus continued the practices of the monarchic period (cf. Jer 44, referring to people who later moved to Egypt). As time went on in the Second Temple period, it might be that the descendants of people who had been in exile were also involved.

The question of sexual acts that embody prayers for fertility is more complex. We have much less concrete information or evidence concerning the existence of such practices in Judah or Ephraim or among other peoples during any period, and the language about immoral acts in prophets such as Jeremiah and Ezekiel is at least sometimes a metaphorical way of passing a judgment on Judahite and Ephraimite attempts to combine the worship of other deities with worship of Yhwh, which involves metaphorical adultery and immorality (in Ezek 16, reference to child sacrifice is part of the tirade against this unfaithfulness). I have concluded that this language here in 57.3-13 functions in a similar way. It does not indicate that Judahites were involved in sexual acts in the context of their religious observance but that their religious practices constituted a religious equivalent to adultery and sexual immorality.[131]

If that is so, we are left with the practices of sacrificing children and of seeking contact with dead family members, for which sexual unfaithfulness is a metaphor (cf. Lev 20.6).[132] Whether it is so or not, we might then conclude that these are two aspects of the same religious devotion; people sacrificed children as one way of opening up the possibility of that communication with ghosts or spirits, a particularly sacrificial way of making a gift to people who have died or of making an offering to the

[130] See especially Susan Ackerman, *Under Every Green Tree* (Atlanta: Scholars, 1992), pp. 101-63. Middlemas (*The Troubles of Templeless Judah*, pp. 97-105) separates these two and argues that the passage refers only to the sacrifice of children.

[131] Cf., e.g., Brian H. Schmidt, *Israel's Beneficent Dead* (Winona Lake, IN: Eisenbrauns, 1995), p. 258. N. H. Snaith moves in the opposite direction, thinking that the passage refers to dedicating children to 'temple prostitution' ('The Cult of Molech', *VT* 16 [1966], pp. 123-24).

[132] Cf. Theodore J. Lewis, 'Death Cult Imagery in Isaiah 57', *HAR* 11 (1987), pp. 267-84 (282); *Cults of the Dead in Ancient Israel and Ugarit* (Atlanta: Scholars, 1989), pp. 157-58.

deity in charge of them in order to get guidance or help, instead of or as well as looking to Yhwh. Understood thus, the passage gains in coherence. Its vivid and unusual language and its variegated language all have one target.

The passage makes clear that there is division within the community over right forms of worship but it also indicates that the division does not concern different views of proper temple worship but different views of worship and other forms of devotion in other settings and/or different views about whether people could properly take part in temple worship and also in these other forms of worship and devotion (cf. 66.3). It seems over-inventive to take this polemic as a disguised 'lower-class' attack on the 'upper class' who were cooperating politically and economically with the Persian authorities.[133]

> 57.3 But you, draw near,// children of a diviner,
> Offspring of an adulterer and of one who acts immorally,// 4 in whom do you revel?

'But you' (*wᵉʾattem*, with the pronoun expressed) sets the 'you' over against the subject of the preceding verses, though it does so without making explicit who the 'you' are. In 56.1 the subject of the imperatives was surely the whole community; in 56.9 it was the animals invited to come and eat. In 56.10-12 the leaders were described rather than addressed; in 57.1-2 the faithful were described. The fact that the leaders were not previously addressed makes it neither necessary nor compelling to assume that they are addressed here, and the actions that will be critiqued are not ones that would especially characterize leaders as opposed to people in general. While there could be an implication that the leadership is subject to critique because of its complicity in the family practices the passage describes, rhetorically an opposite inference lies near to hand. The people in general might have enjoyed the attack on the leaders in 56.10-12 and might even have nodded at the comment on the destiny of the faithful in 57.1-2. But Amos 1.3–2.16 shows how it is famously unwise to agree with a prophet's attack on other people, and the ordinary people of Judah may have been caught out by their rapt attention to this prophet through 56.9–57.2. It is they who are now confronted.

These first two lines (2-2, 3-2) comprise two descriptions of the addressees, each with the short, two-stress second colon characteristic of a protest or lament. One is more literal and factual, one more metaphorical and indicating a value judgment. There is perhaps some irony about the opening verb, 'come [near]' (*qārab*), which can denote drawing near to Yhwh for worship, particularly on the part of priests (e.g. Ezek 44.15-16).

[133] See Albertz, *Religionsgeschichte Israels in alttestamentlicher Zeit*, II, p. 552 (ET p. 505).

But it is at least as significant that it can imply a challenge to an argument or to the giving of account (Isa 41.1; 48.16). The passage that follows cannot be analysed as following an actual form of speech such as a legal indictment and declaration of judgment but it does indeed constitute a charge of this kind, and the challenge to draw near would resonate with such a charge.

Describing people as 'children of a diviner' (the participle *ʿōnᵉnâ* is feminine) no doubt implies that they are so attached to divination that their attachment might seem to be innate; it is deep in their character. But in this connection the idiom 'children of x' usually involves not a personal noun but an abstract noun such as immorality, weakness, or transitoriness (e.g. Hos 4.6 [4], Prov 31.5. 8); compare the phrases in v. 4, 'children of rebellion' (there *yildê*) and 'offspring of deceit'. While the use of a personal noun in the idiom 'children of x' is also frequent, it carries the additional implication that the children were born of the person they resemble; they do not merely share a characteristic. There were three instances of this usage in the previous chapter (56.2, 3, 6), so that the 'children of a diviner' who turn their backs on Yhwh compare and contrast rather ironically with the 'children of a foreigner' who attach themselves to Yhwh. These are people who have adopted the diviner as their mother and learned her ways, or people whose own birth involved her ministrations, or people who are her children rather than children of Yhwh or children of Israel. In theory, they are the children of Abraham and Sarah (51.2);[134] but the prophet 'has expelled them from the progeny of Abraham'.[135]

Preexilic prophecy critiques recourse to diviners (e.g. Isa 2.6;[136] Jer 27.9; Mic 5.11 [12]); it is associated with the traditional religion of the land (Deut 18.10, 14). Involvement in divination implies seeking to discover the future by means of techniques associated with other deities, and then to take steps to avoid threats and ensure blessing. Subsequent verses will indicate other aspects of these practices and suggest that in particular it implies divination by making contact with dead people. It is odd that the word for diviner appears as *ʿōnᵉnâ* because the verb is usually poel; for the participle one would thus expect *mᵉʿōnᵉnâ* (see the forms in Deut 18.10, 14; Mic 5.11 [12]; and Judg 9.37 in a place name). The shorter form, corresponding to that of a qal participle, appears in the masculine plural in Isaiah 2.6 and Jeremiah 27.9, and v. 3 may follow that usage. Why might a prophet prefer that quasi-qal form? While Sym and Vg translate the word 'diviner', LXX 'lawless' and Tg 'evil' apparently link *ʿōnᵉnâ* with *ʿāwōn* (LXX anticipates its translation of *šeqer* at the end of v. 4), which points towards a possible answer: the quasi-qal form of

134 Cf. Oswalt, *Isaiah Chapters 40–66*, p. 476.

135 Theodoret of Cyrrhus, *Commentaire sur Isaïe* 171b (III, pp. 198-99).

136 Sommer (*A Prophet Reads Scripture*, p. 89) sees this as but the first of a series of links between Isa 57.3-15 and Isa 2.6-21.

the participle can point to the fact that divination involves waywardness. Such a paronomasia would fit within the rhetoric of 57.3-13.

Given the conviction that divination does indeed imply unfaithfulness to Yhwh, 'the children of a diviner' can also be described as the offspring of a couple who have behaved in an abhorrent way, an adulterous man and an immoral woman. The metaphor compares with Ezekiel's declaration that Jerusalem's father was an Amorite, its mother a Hittite (Ezek 16.3). For *zānâ*, translated 'act immorally', EVV have words such as 'prostitute', but the verb denotes any form of sexual activity that offends the social mores; it does not imply sex for money, though the English slur 'whore' is closer to the Hebrew usage.[137] In prophetic use of the metaphor from sexual activity, talk in terms of adultery and of immorality 'seems to have coalesced'; the distinction between unfaithfulness to a marriage and broader sexual immorality is lost.[138]

The prosody of vv. 3-4 works more neatly if we associate the first colon in v. 4 with v. 3.[139] Verse 3aα is then a summons and v. 4aα the question the summons raises, while inside this bracket, v. 3aβb is a double vocative. That understanding then makes it possible to give *ʿānag* hitpael its usual meaning 'revel' or 'delight', whereas linking it with what follows requires it here alone to mean 'mock'. The verb does have negative connotations, but these lie in the fact that people are revelling in other deities and resources rather than in Yhwh. The usage thus makes for a contrast with 55.3; 58.14. The verb and associated nouns are inclined to refer to 'sensual pleasure'[140] and can suggest sexual pleasure in particular (Cant 7.7), and this connotation fits here.

57.4aβb At whom do you open your mouth wide,// put out your tongue?
Are you not rebellious children,// deceitful offspring?—
5 You who inflame yourselves among the oaks,// under every verdant tree,
Who slaughter children among the canyons,// under the clefts in the crags.

On one hand, then, the addressees are turning to other resources; and on the other, they are thus despising their own resources. The opening *ʿal mî* makes for a contrast with the same expression in the second colon of the previous line. As they are misplacing their revelling, so they are misplacing their scorn. After the opening question marker, making this link with what precedes and here applying to both cola, the two cola (3-2) comprise parallel second plural hiphil yiqtol verbs and parallel objects

[137] The slur recurs in Wisdom 3.16, and Croatto (*Imaginar el futuro*, p. 63) sees vv. 3-4 as continuing the base for Wisdom 3–4's midrash.

[138] Freedman and Willoughby, *TWAT*, V, pp. 127-28 (ET *TDOT*, IX, p. 117). But their assumption that *zānâ* implies sex for pay and that the religious practices in question involved 'cultic prostitution' is questionable.

[139] Cf., e.g., Budde, 'Jesaia Kap. 40–66', p. 696.

[140] T. Kronholm, *TWAT*, VI, p. 231 (ET *TDOT*, XI, p. 214).

signifying parts of the face. Gaping in disbelief and sneering could be something the community is doing to people such as this prophet who confine themselves to Yhwh as their resource (cf. Ps 35.21). The same could be true of putting out the tongue, though this expression comes only here.

Yet the descriptions in the second line rather suggest an attitude to Yhwh. Again the line (2-2) has the short, two-stress second colon characteristic of a protest or lament, and again it comprises an opening question marker applying to both cola, 'Are you not', followed by parallel expressions. Here they are similar construct nouns (plural and collective singular) and similar abstract nouns for rebellion and deceit. It is against Yhwh that people rebel and it is Yhwh they think to deceive as they pretend to be Yhwh's people but covertly look to other resources. The rebellious children and the offspring compare and contrast with 53.10, 12. Like 57.1-2, this line suggests that nothing has changed since the situation that lies behind Isaiah 40–55 (or for that matter since 1.2). 'Rebellion' is a characteristic emphasis of Isaiah 40–66 (see also, e.g., 58.1 and the comment there; 59.12, 20), while deceit is a characteristic emphasis in Jeremiah (but cf. also Isa 59.3, 13). Retrospectively, then, the characterization in v. 4b does suggest that it was also Yhwh at whom people were sneering in v. 4aβ.[141] Perhaps they did not do this explicitly, which would have brought deceit out into the open. But it is the implication of their behaviour.

Verse 5 (2-3, 3-3) goes on to describe their acts more and more concretely. Each of the two parallel lines comprises a participial expression, a *b*- expression, and a *taḥat* expression. They are thus also internally parallel in a similar way to the previous two lines, with the participial expression applying to both cola and each leading into parallel prepositional expressions, one beginning *b*- and a compound expression following *taḥat*. 'Inflame yourselves' perhaps suggests arousing themselves into enthusiasm in worship and prayer in the manner of the Baal prophets in 1 Kings 18, though *ḥāmam* (like *yāḥam*) can also refer to animals in sexual heat and thus carry pejorative connotations like those in Jeremiah 2–3. The niphal of the verb comes only here; it generates a paronomasia with the form from *nāḥam* which closes v. 6.

The traditional worship of the land commonly takes place in open air sanctuaries where trees provide shade from the sun and shelter from the rain when needed, as well as symbolizing flourishing in nature; it is significant that the story told in 1 Kings 18 takes place on verdant Mount Carmel.[142] The phrase 'under every verdant tree' recurs in Deuteronomistic

[141] Cf. Joachim Becker, 'Zur Deutung von Jes 57,4a', *BN* 118 (2003), pp. 13-18.

[142] D. Winton Thomas, 'Some Observations on the Hebrew Word רַעֲנָן', in Benedict Hartmann *et al.* (eds.), *Hebräische Wortforschung* (W. Baumgartner Festschrift; Leiden: Brill, 1967), pp. 387-97, notes that the word *ra'anān* means luxuriant and flourishing rather than merely green.

and prophetic critique (e.g. Deut 12.2; 1 Kgs 14.23; Jer 2.20; Ezek 6.13).[143] The specific trees (*ʾēlîm*) may be oaks or terebinths;[144] while the two are similar, terebinths do not grow as tall and they generally grow in isolation, whereas oaks can grow in forests. The existence of an 'Oak of Weeping' (*ʾallôn*; Gen 35.8) and an 'Oak of Diviners' (*ʾēlôn me ʿônenîm*, from the same root as 'diviner' here; Judg 9.37) would support a link between such trees and rites related to mourning over lost family members and/or to seeking their guidance and help. Hosea 4.13 critiques rites under an oak or a terebinth (*ʾallôn, ʾēlâ*) that involve sexual unfaithfulness.[145] But it is a happy coincidence that *ʾēlîm* is also a homonym for a word meaning (false) gods; LXX, Vg, Syr, Tg, assume this meaning.[146] In this connection it might denote the spirits of those dead family members, given that *ʾĕlôhîm* can be used with this meaning (e.g. 1 Sam 28.13; Isa 8.19). This in turn makes one reflect further on the participle *nēḥāmîm*. It is not a form from *nāḥam*; the niphal participle would be *niḥāmîm* (the singular appears in, e.g., Jer 8.6). But it is very close to that form from the verb which will appear at the end of the next verse, which in this context would very appositely mean 'find consolation', part of what is involved in the rituals in question if people are seeking to find comfort in connection with bereavement. Indeed, LXX 'call on' (cf. Tg 'serve'?) and Vg 'console yourselves' take the participle as from *nāḥam* rather than as niphal from *ḥāmam/yāḥam*.[147]

Whereas that first form of worship (v. 5a) takes place in open-air sanctuaries in elevated places, the parallel line (v. 5b) describes worship that takes place in the depths and darkness of canyons.[148] 'Canyon' translates the word *naḥal*, which strictly denotes a wash or wadi, a valley where a stream flows, though in most cases does not do so all year round. Such valleys were commonly deep and steep-sided, more so than the word 'valley' necessarily suggests. This is especially so in the case of the *neḥālîm* around Jerusalem, which is significant for the comment the prophet makes in the parallel second colon. While one must be wary of the modern assumption that sacrificing children is manifestly much more terrible than worshipping false gods, the reference to canyons and clefts

[143] See P. Mommer, *TWAT*, VII, pp. 581-82 (ET *TDOT*, XIII, p. 559); more broadly on the history of the phrases here, William L. Holladay, '"On Every High Hill and under Every Green Tree"', *VT* 11 (1961), pp. 170-76.

[144] See the descriptions and discussion in Harold N. Moldenke and Alma L. Moldenke, *Plants of the Bible* (reprinted New York: Dover, 1986), pp. 178-79, 193-99.

[145] Cf. Blenkinsopp, *Isaiah 56–66*, p. 157.

[146] When referring to a tree it is more often spelled *ʾêlîm* (cf. Isa 1.29; 61.3), though see Ezek 31.14 and compare *ʾēlâ* (of which it is the *de facto* pl.) and *ʾēlôn*. Manfred Weise ('Jesaja 57 5f.', *ZAW* 72 [1960], pp. 25-32 [26]) suggests the word does double duty, with both meanings applying.

[147] Cf. Ottley, *Isaiah according to the Septuagint*, II, p. 355-56.

[148] Charles A. Kennedy ('Isaiah 57:5-6', *BASOR* 275 [1989], pp. 47-52) suggests that *naḥal* refers not to natural canyons but to rock-cut tombs.

points to the dark nature of this practice; even the verb *šāḥaṭ* draws attention to the act of slaughter rather than to the subsequent act of making an offering.

Jeremiah 7.31-32 associates the burning of children with Tophet in the Hinnom Valley, which runs to the west and south of Jerusalem and then joins the Kidron Valley, running east of the city. Jeremiah 19.11 also implies that Tophet was the location of a burial ground, while 2 Kings 23.6 locates a common burial ground in the Kidron Valley. Such a place would be a natural one for people to make offerings in connection with burials, with seeking to maintain relationships with dead family members, with leaving gifts of food or other offerings for them (cf. Deut 26.14), and with getting their guidance (Isa 8.19-20). But a rite designed to bring life is one that brings death.

57.6 Among the canyon's deceptions is your share;// they, they are your allocation.
Yes, to them you have poured a libation,// presented an offering;// in view of these things, should I relent?

Whereas vv. 3-5 addressed the worshippers in the plural, in v. 6 (2-3, 3-2-3) the prophecy uses the feminine singular. Perhaps it is significant that the change of addressee comes at the point where the prophet begins to speak of the sacrifice of children. It is their mother who is sacrificing them.[149]

The only feminine figure that has been mentioned in the near context is the diviner, the one who acts immorally (v. 3), and we should perhaps see her as the person directly addressed. While indirectly the pronouns will refer to the city of Jerusalem, it has not been explicitly addressed or referred to since Isaiah 52, though Isaiah 54 did address a woman who could be identified with the city. Both those earlier references stand in ironic contrast to the present passage, since they invited the woman-city to put on its splendour as its lookouts watch for its Lord returning, and they then promise it great fruitfulness. The present passage presupposes that the community's lookouts are failing to fulfil their task and that the community sees the key to fruitfulness as lying in other directions than relying on Yhwh. The eunuchs and the foreigners had been indirectly reassured in connection with the eunuchs' incapacity to share in making the city fruitful and the foreigners' inherent lack of rights there, but the city is itself feeling the need to take action to assure its fruitfulness and its future by means that sidestep Yhwh.[150] The passage suggests uncomfortable parallels with the portrait of Jerusalem before the exile and that

[149] Cf. Seitz, 'The Book of Isaiah 40–66', p. 491.

[150] See C. Nihan, 'Trois cultes en *Ésaïe* 57,3-13', *Transeuphratène* 22 (2001), pp. 143-67. He sees vv. 5-6 and 7-9 as a double critique of these.

of Babylon during the exile (e.g. 47.12-13; Jer 19.1-13) as well as contrasts with the destiny of Jerusalem as God has promised it. Both Jerusalem and Babylon were doomed to fall, and did so. Second Temple Jerusalem needs to find the fate of both cities a warning and not merely an encouragement. So the diviner, the one who acts immorally, stands for Jerusalem. She is Zion's alter ego, 'Zion, herself, in a troubling manifestation'.[151] Zion is supposed to be the antithesis of Babylon, but instead is its double.

She has chosen to have her 'share' or 'allocation' (*ḥēleq*, *gôrāl*) there in the canyons where her people make those offerings to or on behalf of their dead family members. The second colon parallels the first by means of the correspondence between 'share' and 'allocation' and also by the way 'they, they' takes up 'among the canyon's deceptions'. Indeed, the latter parallel raises the question whether the *b-* prefix on this phrase is a *b-* of identity: 'The very deceptions of the canyon are your share'.

Either way, v. 6a is itself a devastating statement, since both 'share' and 'allocation' are associated with the relationship between Yhwh, Israel, and the land: for instance, the people is Yhwh's share, Yhwh is the people's share, and each of the clans has a share or allocation in the land. For the city to choose shares or allocations in the canyons in connection with worshipping other deities is therefore to go back radically on its relationship with Yhwh. Jeremiah 13.25 thus turns upside down the connotations of such words: it is scattering that will be the city's allocation or destiny. The prophet here implies something similar in having Yhwh confirm the city's choice of share and allocation.

The point is underlined by means of another cunning paronomasia, as the word for 'deception' is a homonym of the word for 'share' (it otherwise comes only in Prov 7.21). The city has chosen as its share something that actually leads it astray. Vg, Th translate *ḥēleq* 'share' both times (LXX omits it the first time). MT's anomalous dagesh forte in the first word in some way draws attention to a question here.[152] Words from the root *ḥālaq* II are often translated smooth or slippery and thus flattering, the point about the comment then commonly being that they are therefore plausible and attractive but untrue. The adjective *ḥālāq* refers to flattering or deceptive divination in Ezekiel 12.24, and this connotation makes sense here. The deceptions are thus the deities the city has chosen to worship.[153] The city has chosen self-deception. And Yhwh will confirm its choice; its fate is to join that of the children slaughtered there. It is a very

[151] Cf. Mark E. Biddle, 'Lady Zion's Alter Egos', in Melugin and Sweeney (eds.), *New Visions of Isaiah*, pp. 124-39 (137).

[152] Cf. Ehrlich, *Randglossen*, IV, p. 202.

[153] Cf. Duhm, *Jesaia*, p. 388. W. H. Irwin ('The Smooth Stones of the Wadi', *CBQ* 29 [1967], pp. 31-40) achieves a similar result by translating 'the dead', hypothesizing another root *ḥlq* cognate with Ugaritic (cf. *HALOT*). Eitan ('Contribution to Isaiah Exegesis', p. 82) does something similar by hypothesizing on the basis of Aramaic the sense 'creatures', here referring to demons.

different 'share' from that in 53.12. The servant died for his people; they kill for themselves.

Tg understands the word to refer to the smooth rocks of the canyon (cf. BDB), but this involves some reading into the text, and it is not clear why the prophet should refer to smooth rocks. Perhaps Tg is based on 1 Samuel 17.40, where David gets his smooth stones from the canyon;[154] but there the word 'stones' is included, and the point of the stones is quite different from their point here. The theory that smooth stones are of some significance in worship involves considerable inference.[155]

Verse 6b adds another concrete reference to this worship; the pronoun 'them' confirms that the 'deceptions' are the deities the city worships in the canyons. It begins with parallel cola in which 'Yes, to them' applies to both and is followed by two second-person singular qatal verbs (one qal, one hiphil) of similar meaning, and two nouns of complementary meaning as the verbs' objects. Libations or drink-offerings are not mentioned in the regulations concerning offerings in Leviticus, but they are assumed elsewhere as a proper aspect of worship (e.g. Exod 29.40-41 [P]). The trouble is that the city has been pouring its drink offerings in a wrong direction. That reference is followed by an allusion to offerings in general, also made to these deceptive deities.

The line is then brought to an unexpected conclusion with a third colon taking the form of a rhetorical question. There are many occasions when Yhwh relents of an intention to chastise the people, sometimes before there is any change on their part (e.g. Amos 7.3, 6). But that relenting is an unpredictable, extraordinary sign of grace and mercy; one cannot expect it. Only when people themselves relent of their faithlessness can they actually expect Yhwh to relent (cf. Jer 18.1-10). This prophecy presupposes that at the moment there is no such relenting on their part. Indirectly, it is seeking to get them to relent, precisely by declaring that at the moment there is no divine relenting. With further paronomasia, this closing verb *ʾennāḥēm* recalls the opening verb in v. 5. The people are inflaming themselves and/or seeking to comfort themselves by their worship practices; Yhwh will not seek comfort by forgiving them.

57.7 On a high and lofty mountain// you have put your bed.
Yes, there you have gone up// to offer sacrifice,
8a And behind the door and the doorpost// you have put your memorial.

The prophecy resumes the confrontation concerning the diviner-city's unfaithful religious life, which makes Yhwh's relenting impossible. In other contexts, it would be natural to infer that the high and lofty

[154] Torrey makes the link with 1 Sam 17.40 (*The Second Isaiah*, p. 434).

[155] See especially the critique in Nihan, 'Trois cultes en *Ésaïe* 57,3-13' (see above), pp. 155-56.

mountain is Mount Zion: cf. 2.2; 40.9.[156] Indeed, the references to Yhwh's holy mountain in 56.7 and 57.13 underline the horrifying nature of what the prophet here describes in connection with an alternative mountain, which stands in contrast both with Isaiah 1–39 and with Isaiah 40–55.[157] The point is further underlined by the fact that elsewhere things that are high and lofty tend to get pulled down (e.g. 2.12-15; 5.15; 10.33). The real high and lofty mountain is what it is because of its association with the high and lofty God; indeed, for Mount Zion this description is rather an honorary one, because Mount Zion is not so high and lofty. Other things that do pretend to be high and lofty seek a stature that belongs only to Yhwh (e.g. 5.16; 6.1).

Further, the expressions more often make reference to elevated places where illegitimate worship is offered, sometimes alongside reference to canyons (e.g. Jer 2.20;[158] 3.6), and subsequent lines confirm this reference here. One might speculate that the line refers specifically to Bethel as a sanctuary near the centre of Babylonian provincial administration that could be fully functioning in the sixth century when the Jerusalem temple was not.[159] The allusion to making a bed and to sexual activity (see especially Ezek 23) also fits other such references, though the bed could be simply a mat to lie on while seeking to receive a message.[160] Once again the two lines in v. 7 (3-2, 2-2) are parallel. Each refers to a location, then includes a second-person singular feminine qatal verb, and closes with an object or objective. Given the parallelism, 'go up' (*ʿālâ*) would carry the resonances of climbing into bed (Gen 49.4; 2 Kgs 1.4). In the opening comments on vv. 7-13 we have concluded that the references to sexual activity are metaphorical and refer to the unfaithful nature of the worship offered at these elevated places, though this does not take much away from the comment that 'With child sacrifices in the valleys and the fertility cult on the top of every hill, the heights and depths of the land are polluted with idolatry'.[161]

Verse 8a (3-2) then comprises a further line with similar structure. It is especially closely parallel to v. 7a; again, reference to a location occupies the first colon, while the second comprises the verb *śamt* plus an object. Elsewhere a memorial is always associated with Yhwh (e.g. Exod 12.14

[156] So (e.g.) Susan Ackerman, 'Sacred Sex, Sacrifice and Death', *Bible Review* 6/1 (1990), pp. 38-44 (39). Hanson (*The Dawn of Apocalyptic*, p. 199) identifies the *miškāb* with the *miškān* that 'the priestly group' is building on Mount Zion (66.1-2).

[157] Cf. Childs, *Isaiah*, p. 467.

[158] William L. Holladay ('Was Trito-Isaiah Deutero-Isaiah After All?', in Broyles and Evans [eds.], *Writing and Reading the Scroll of Isaiah*, I, pp. 193-217 [197-98]) sees 57.5-7 as taking up and expanding on Jer 2.20, and sees further reminiscences of Jer 2 and 3 in 57.10, 16-19 (see pp. 199-201, 206); cf. Paul, ישעיה פרקים מ-סו, II, p. 421 (ET p. 463).

[159] So Middlemas, *The Troubles of Templeless Judah*, pp. 133-44.

[160] So Goulder, *Isaiah as Liturgy*, p. 135.

[161] Smart, *History and Theology in Second Isaiah*, p. 242.

[P]; 13.9 [D]; Zech 6.14; Neh 2.20), but Tg makes explicit that this memorial commemorates another deity. The line might point to the practice of traditional religious observances in the privacy of people's homes, which the prophets imply continued even when public worship met later Yahwistic standards. The reference to a memorial in connection with a doorpost would then be telling when contrasted with the Torah's expectations (Deut 6.9; 11.20). But the passage seems to concern public worship, and 'door' and 'doorpost' come together in connection with a city (Judg 16.3), a sanctuary (1 Kgs 6.31-34; Ezek 41.21-25), and Ms Wisdom's house (Prov 8.34).[162] The place is then a substitute for the temple, located on high with its alternative memorial on door and doorpost. If the memorial commemorates Yhwh, then the phrase might suggest that they have hidden their memorial behind the door. Or the line may refer to the horrible contrast between the profession people made in marking their home life as dedicated to Yhwh (one might then assume that *ʾaḥar* means 'with/beside' rather than 'behind'[163]) and the practices in the canyons and on the hills that the prophecy castigates. The references to sexual unfaithfulness elsewhere in the passage (whether literal or metaphorical) and its other instances of paronomasia would invite the addressees to see a link between 'memorial', *zikkārôn*, and the word for male, *zākār*; the word might even mean 'maleness' in the sense of a phallic symbol.[164] The woman-city has taken her man home, as the strange woman in Proverbs 9.13-18 wanted to do. Given the reference in the context to other concrete ancillaries to or forms of worship (bed, sacrifice), it is less likely that *zikkārôn* refers to 'remembering'.[165]

57.8b For from me you have gone away and gone up,// you have opened your bed wide.
You have sealed things for yourself from them, you have loved their bed;// you have beheld their love.
9 You have come to see the King in your oils,// you have multiplied your perfumes.
You have sent off your envoys far,// sent down as far as Sheol.

These four lines form the greatest concentration of uncertainty in the passage.[166] At the same time, their prosody works neatly. The four lines

[162] Elizabeth M. Bloch-Smith suggests the words denote the framed door of a rock-hewn tomb (*Judahite Burial Practices and Beliefs about the Dead* [JSOTSup 123; Sheffield: Sheffield Academic Press, 1991], pp. 119-21).

[163] Cf. *HALOT*'s definitions.

[164] So Paul, ישעיה פרקים מ-סו, II, p. 424 (ET p. 467).

[165] K. Koenen ('Sexuelle Zweideutigkeiten und Euphemismen in Jes 57,8', *BN* 44 [1988], pp. 46-53 [46-49]) argues that we should allow for both resonances, and makes the same point with regard to *gālâ* and other expressions in the verse.

[166] LXX's version of vv. 8b-9 as a whole is thus loose, as is Tg; it is partly followed by Vg (cf. van der Kooij, *Die alten Textzeugen des Jesajabuches*, p. 301). The same applies

are 4-2, 4-2, 3-2, 3-2, each comprising parallel cola, each colon beginning with a second-person *w*-consecutive verb beginning *wat*- and ending -*î*.[167] The opening reference to location in v. 8bα constitutes a more grievous and negative parallel to that in v. 8a, and this line later takes up both 'go up' and 'bed' from v. 7. For the verb translated 'gone away', most MT manuscripts have piel *gillît*, which is usually transitive with the meaning 'uncover' (cf. Vg). Its object will need to be inferred from the second colon; it then refers to uncovering the bed for a partner to get in, or perhaps to uncovering oneself. But two MT manuscripts have qal *gālît*[168] 'gone away [into exile]', and LXX, Aq, Sym, Th take the verb thus. This follows well on 'from me'.[169] The prophecy likely again trades on a word's plurivocity; in going up (to a high and lofty mountain) in order to go up (to bed), the city has gone into exile by uncovering itself or by uncovering its bed to those deceptive deities.[170]

In v. 8bβ, the reference to a bed continues the theme of the previous lines, but the opening allusion to 'sealing [things]' and thus covenanting nuances the point. Literally, the expression is 'you have cut'; the noun 'covenant' is omitted as in passages such as 1 Samuel 20.16. The prophet then expresses the nature of this covenant in rather snide fashion. It would have been natural to say that the city made the covenant 'with them', its lovers, the deceptive entities to which v. 6 referred, but the reference to 'them' is linked with the preposition *min*, and it is never used with this meaning. The only other references to covenant-making in Isaiah 40–66 use the preposition *l*- (see 55.3; 61.8), and this preposition does feature here, with ironic implications. Whereas Yhwh makes a covenant *with* or *for* them, when they make a covenant of the kind this line refers to, they are making a covenant with or for themselves. It is a solipsistic covenant. Of course 'they', the lovers, are parties to this covenant; its aim is to gain benefits from them. 'From them' thus contrasts with 'from me' in the preceding line. The city's commitment will (supposedly) guarantee that it receives from them the 'things', the prosperity and fertility that it needs. At 56.5 we noted several possible meanings for *yād*: the usual meaning is 'hand' (so Vg, Sym here), the usual metaphorical meaning is 'power' or 'strength',[171] while other possibilities are 'place' (Tg) and 'memorial' (JB), but the sexual theme in the context suggests 'penis' (cf. NRSV, TNIV's 'nakedness') or a quite different word *yad* meaning 'love' derived from *yādad* and similar to

to 1QIs[a] in vv. 7-9 (cf. Kutscher, הלשון והרקע הלשוני של מגילת ישעיהו השלמה, p. 449 [ET p. 561]).

[167] Cf. Polan, *In the Ways of Justice toward Salvation*, p. 141.

[168] See *HUB*.

[169] Thus there is no need for the 'excessively bold' hypothesis (McKenzie, *Second Isaiah*, p. 156) that *m'ty* represents a form of a denominative verb 'do a hundred times' (for which verb, see *DCH*).

[170] Cf. Shalom M. Paul, 'Polysensuous Polyvalency in Poetic Parallelism', in Fishbane and Tov (eds.), *'Sha'arei Talmon'*, pp. 147-63 (155).

[171] Cf. Barthélemy, *Critique Textuelle de l'Ancien Testament*, II, p. 412.

Ugaritic *yd*.[172] Perhaps there is another double entendre.[173] The prophet thus continues to work with an allegorical picture of Jerusalem and her many lovers (the other deities), like Ezekiel.

The implications of this covenant-making continue in v. 9, so that v. 8bβ connects forward as well as backward, and in a way v. 9a forms a pair with v. 8bβ. Identifying the opening verb *wattāšurî* is a complex question.[174] Sym and Vg 'you were put in order/adorned' might reflect the assumption that the form comes not from *šûr* but from *yāšar*[175] or might suggest *wattāsukî* from *sûk*, 'you were made up/beautified',[176] which produces good sense and good parallelism.[177] LXX has 'multiplied', which also produces good sense and good parallelism,[178] and 1QIs[a] *tšry* suggests that it took the verb as *šārâ*, which might have this meaning.[179] Tg has 'you performed the Torah'. But all the Versions may be paraphrasing a difficult text. Modern translations have 'journey' or the like, but the basis is thin for assuming the existence of such a verb (BDB's *šûr* I).[180] Ibn Ezra more plausibly links the verb with the noun *t*[e]*šûrâ* 'gift' (1 Sam 9.7) whose derivation is unknown.[181] It might then suggest 'you have endowed the king with oil', or given the existence of *šûr* II 'gaze, regard' it might presuppose that coming to see someone implies bringing a gift.[182] I take it as indeed an instance of the more common *šûr* II, suggesting 'come to see', in effect 'appeared', which also provides good

[172] See Aloysius Fitzgerald, 'Hebrew *yd* = "love" and "beloved"', *CBQ* 29 (1967) pp. 368-74 (371-72).

[173] Cf. Watson, *Classical Hebrew Poetry*, pp. 241-42.

[174] See *HALOT*.

[175] Cf. *HUB*.

[176] See, e.g., Klostermann, *Deuterojesaia*, p. 74.

[177] G. R. Driver suggested translating 'thou wast resplendent' ('Studies in the Vocabulary of the Old Testament vii', *JTS* 35 [1934], pp. 380-93 [389]) or 'thou wast drenched' ('Difficult Words in the Hebrew Prophets', in H. H. Rowley [ed.], *Studies in Old Testament Prophecy* [T. H. Robinson Festschrift; Edinburgh: T. & T. Clark, 1950], pp. 52-72 [58-59]), or repointing the phrase to an expression such as וַתְּשַׁרִי לְמֶלֶךְ 'you drenched your tresses [with oil]' ('Isaianic Problems', in Gernot Wiessner [ed.], *Festschrift für Wilhelm Eilers* [Wiesbaden: Harrassowitz, 1967], pp. 43-57 [54-55]; NEB reads וַתְּשָׁרִי לְמֶלֶךְ to give this meaning [so Brockington, *The Hebrew Text of the OT*, p. 196]). For further suggested emendations, see Joseph Reider, 'Contributions to the Hebrew Lexicon', *ZAW* 53 (1935), pp. 270-77 (276-77).

[178] On the basis of LXX, NEB adds וַתַּרְבִּי אֶת־תַּזְנוּתַיִךְ 'and multiplied your immorality' (cf. Brockington, *The Hebrew Text of the OT*, p. 196). But Ziegler (*Untersuchungen zur Septuaginta des Buches Isaias*, p. 129) notes that LXX's extra clause corresponds to Ezek 16.25; 23.19 LXX and was likely adopted from there to elucidate the difficult passage.

[179] P. Wernberg-Møller provides an Arabic verb that could have been equivalent to a verb *šārâ* or *šārar* with this meaning ('Two Notes', *VT* 8 [1958], pp. 305-8 [307-8]).

[180] Cf. Ackerman, *Under Every Green Tree* (see above), pp. 107-8. John Day, for instance, defends it (*Molech* [Cambridge: Cambridge University Press, 1989], p. 51).

[181] *The Commentary of Ibn Ezra on Isaiah*, p. 262. Cf. *HALOT*.

[182] So Yael Avrahami, *The Senses of Scripture* (London: T&T Clark International, 2012), p. 151.

parallelism with what precedes. As well as gazing at her lovers, Ms Jerusalem is displaying herself, made up in her unguent and her many perfumes.

The one to whom she is showing herself off is 'the King' (*melek*). Tg assumes that the line refers to a human king,[183] but the context suggests a deity, the king of Sheol, the deity whose name the Old Testament commonly vocalizes as Molek but was perhaps originally Malik.[184] Keeping in touch with dead family members to make offerings of what they need, and to gain their guidance and help, involves the city sending its representatives a very long way—all the way to Sheol. Sacrificing a child meant passing it over to Molek (Lev 18.21 [H]); the child would be killed as an animal was for a sacrifice, and then burned as happened with animal sacrifice so as to make the move from the visible world to the invisible world.

Once again the prophet pushes the allegory. Jerusalem literally sent envoys a long way in pursuing its political policies in relation to foreign kings, typically people more powerful than itself (cf. 18.2; 49.14); in this sense the background of the verse indeed includes a reference to a human king. In its allegory concerning the unfaithfulness of Jerusalem, with the references in the context to self-exposure, a bed for lovemaking, oil, immorality, and adultery, Ezekiel 23.16, 40 similarly speaks of the woman-city sending aides to Babylon. But the direct concern in v. 9 is that metaphorically this is what Jerusalem is doing in sending its representatives to the King in Sheol;[185] Sheol in the depths forms a pair with the high and lofty mountain of v. 7.[186] Possibly some people identified Yhwh with the King of Sheol, or would assume that the King of Sheol was Yhwh's underling. They would not see themselves as being disloyal to Yhwh in offering these acts of worship, but the prophet would not be able to accept their self-understanding.

57.10 Though you became weary with the length of your journey,// you have not said 'It's futile'.
You found life for your strength;// therefore you have not weakened.

[183] So also Tiemeyer, *Priestly Rites and Prophetic Rage*, pp. 199-206.

[184] See the entries under Malik and Molech in K. van der Toorn, B. Becking, and P. W. van der Horst (eds.), *Dictionary of Deities and Demons in the Bible* (Brill: Leiden; Grand Rapids: Eerdmans, 2nd edn, 1999). The word might also be revocalized so as to refer to a Molek sacrifice, the sacrificial offering of a child; but it is doubtful whether this word can have this meaning: see, e.g., John Day, *Yahweh and the Gods and Goddesses of Canaan* (Sheffield: Sheffield Academic Press, 2000), pp. 209-10. In association with one of the emendations of the preceding verb, Thomas ('ספר ישעיה', p. 90) revocalizes to produce a word meaning 'hair' from BDB's *mālal* III in its meaning 'hang down' (see *DCH*, V, p. 276).

[185] Ackerman (*Under Every Green Tree* [see above], p. 109) notes Ugaritic references to the far-away location of Sheol.

[186] Cf. Polan, *In the Ways of Justice toward Salvation*, p. 138.

11 For whom have you felt awe and reverence,// that you act deceptively?
Of me you have not taken thought;// you have not given heed to me.
Have I not been silent, yes from of old,// but to me you show no reverence?

Verse 10 (3-3) presupposes that it is indeed a long journey to Sheol, much longer than the literal journey to Egypt or Babylon. Which being interpreted means, there is huge effort (a huge sacrifice) involved in making the kind of offerings that these deceptive deities were believed to look for. The city would therefore get weary with the length of this journey, like Ms Babel wearied with the extent of her efforts to get guidance by means of divination (47.12). Yet the city would never give up. The reason is that it did find a form of life by these means. The same possibilities for understanding *yād* arise as arose for v. 8, and the passage might have the same meaning as there, but the section's liking for paronomasia makes it natural to think in terms of another meaning, and here it makes sense to see the word as an instance of the more familiar *yād* with its metaphorical meaning of power or strength. The city found new resources of strength and girded up its loins so as to continue with its sacrificial ventures. 'Journey' (*derek*), too, may carry the connotation of strength, including sexual vigour (cf. Jer 3.13; Prov 31.3).[187]

Verse 11 (3-2, 3-2, 4-3) speaks in a way that overlaps with v. 4.[188] For most of vv. 3-10, the focus has been on the priorities in the lives of the city and its people as they have given themselves to recourse to other deities. As vv. 3-13 draw towards their end, v. 11 speaks more explicitly about the other side of the coin, what all this implies for their attitude to Yhwh. In other contexts, the opening nouns could refer to a negative dread and fear, but there seems no need to hypothesize that the city was afraid of the deities it worshipped. More likely Yhwh's question takes up the mysterious fact that the city shows the positive attitude of awe and reverence to these other deities that it was supposed to show to Yhwh (cf. LXX, Aq). It is thus willing to be false and deceptive in its relationship with Yhwh. The city claims to be faithful to Yhwh, but its claim is a pretence.[189]

As the second line then puts it, the city has thus simply ignored Yhwh. 'Taken thought' (*zākar*), conventionally translated 'remember', is the verb from which comes the noun 'memorial' (v. 8); this link helps to underline the point. 'Given heed' in turn picks up from v. 1. They have not merely given no heed to the significance of the fate of the faithful. They have thereby failed to give heed to Yhwh, the one who is bringing the calamity that the faithful escape. In the way the line works, the opening 'me' stands in emphatic position and is the object of the verbs in both cola.

[187] See, e.g., Blenkinsopp, *Isaiah 56–66*, p. 161.
[188] See the discussion in Sekine, *Die Tritojesajanische Sammlung*, pp. 106-8.
[189] See R. Mosis's discussion of *kāzab* in *TWAT*.

Yhwh's silence (v. 11b) commonly suggests inaction. It is thus usually a negative feature of Israel's life (e.g. 42.14; 64.11 [12]), though insofar as it suggests slowness in acting against wrongdoing (cf. 65.6), it can have positive connotations when the wrongdoing is Israel's, and this seems to be the point here. Thus Tg speaks of Yhwh giving the people an extension of time (*ʾarkāʾ*, from the verb used to refer to Yhwh's being long-tempered). Before the exile Yhwh had long held back (*mēʿōlām*, almost 'forever') from chastising the city, and perhaps the implication is that Yhwh has been doing so again. The prophet speaks of God's impotence rather than God's omnipotence,[190] except that paradoxically it is a self-imposed impotence. But Yhwh's holding back from chastisement has not generated a response of reverence and submission from the city (Tg twice uses the verb *tûb*, the Aramaic equivalent to *šûb* 'return' or 'repent'); it has continued to give its reverence to those other deities. For the third time in v. 11b 'me' or 'I' appears in emphatic position before the verb (cf. vv. 8b, 11a).[191] 'I' will reappear thus in v. 12a.

57.12 I am the one who will declare your faithfulness;// your works—they will not avail you.
13a When you cry out, your abominable gatherings can rescue you;// a wind will carry all of them off, a breath of air will take them.

The divine long-temperedness will not continue forever. Instead of keeping silence, Yhwh will personally proclaim the city's *ṣᵉdāqâ*. JPSV has 'judgment', but it is doubtful whether *ṣᵉdāqâ* could be understood thus. Even though the two expressions are divided between the cola (3-2), 'your faithfulness' and 'your works' are a hendiadys denoting 'your deeds of faithfulness'. On the surface, Yhwh is 'acting for the moment in the guise of defence attorney'.[192] LXX (but not OL) and Syr have Yhwh declaring 'my faithfulness' and thus as referring to Yhwh's faithfulness to the city, and one might take MT's suffix as objective rather than subjective, with that implication, while Tg assumes that the colon refers to Yhwh's declaring what deeds count as faithfulness, but the end of the line is then difficult. More likely the colon is ironic. It might then refer to the faithfulness to Yhwh the city has not shown.[193] But the second colon suggests that rather it parallels the awe and reverence the people have shown, to other deities instead of Yhwh. They have undertaken faithful deeds, but the trouble is that they have been undertaken on behalf of other deities, which is why they will do the city no good; they will not give it the strength it seeks from them. It makes for an irony after 56.1 and for an ironic contrast with the psalmist's declaration of intent towards Yhwh, 'I will declare...your faithfulness' (Ps 71.18-19).

[190] Knight, *New Israel*, p. 15.
[191] Cf. Beuken, *Jesaja IIIA*, p. 47.
[192] Hanson, *The Dawn of Apocalyptic*, p. 201.
[193] Cf. Bentzen, *Jesaja II*, p. 126.

So *maʿăśayik* refers to the things the city has done (cf. 59.6), or perhaps to the things it has made (cf. 41.29), the images that will not avail (44.9-10).[194] Verse 13a (3-3)[195] will then be reexpressing the point even more sharply in its reference to the impossibility of finding rescue. The city is going to experience calamity and to cry out. The verb generates the paronomasia expressed more tightly in 5.7, though it works in a different way from that verse. The nature of the city's *ṣᵉdāqâ* means the city will *zāʿaq*. Whom will this cry address? Whether it addresses Yhwh or the other gods, it will get the city nowhere. Yhwh is preoccupied by exposing the nature of the city's life, which warrants chastisement. Yhwh *will* not rescue the city. And its other deities will prove they *cannot* rescue it; I take the verb as (ironic) jussive (so LXX, Vg).[196] 'Abominable gatherings' translates the plural of a word for a gathering or collection (*qibbûṣ*) that comes only here; it has the vowels of the word for something detestable (*šiqqûṣ*). It might refer to a collection of images or an assembly of the gods they represent or a gathering of dead family members.[197] The reappearance of this root here makes for an ironic contrast with its appearance at the close of 56.1-8.[198] Instead of rescuing the city, all these gods will simply be carried off by the wind. At the close of this warning, the point is expressed twice in different words.

57.13b But the person who takes refuge with me will own the land,// will possess my holy mountain.

The section closes with a promise (3-2). The prophecy turns out to present the hearers with a choice. The prophet seems not to expect that the city as a whole will change its ways. The choice therefore confronts individuals who are willing to dissociate themselves from the stance that the city as a whole takes. Instead of turning to other deities, such a person takes refuge with Yhwh. The verb (*ḥāsâ*) recurs in the Psalms, but comes in Isaiah 30.2 in a description of people who trust in the shade of Egypt,

194 So Bent Rosendal, '"Gerechtigkeit" und "Werke" in Jesaja 57,12', *SJOT* 8 (1994), pp. 152-54.

195 MT's analysis of the line is spectacularly implausible; it is hard to believe that the prophet would have seen 'a wind will carry' and 'a breath of air will take [them]' as each having one stress, and it seems much more likely that the prophet would understand the line as 3-3-2. But given that we have no real basis for determining the rhythm of lines, I seek to be rigorous in staying with MT's understanding.

196 M. Dahood, 'Hebrew–Ugaritic Lexicography ix' (*Biblica* 52 [1971], pp. 337-56 [343-44]) suggests that the negative in v. 12b carries over to this verb. GID suggests it might be an unmarked (rhetorical) question.

197 An Ugaritic word *qbṣm* seems to refer to the dead as people 'gathered' to their family, the root then being used as *ʾāsap* is used (cf. v. 2) (see Theodore J. Lewis, *Cults of the Dead in Ancient Israel and Ugarit* [HSM 39; Atlanta: Scholars, 1989], pp. 151-52).

198 Muilenburg, 'The Book of Isaiah: Chapters 40—66', p. 661.

and the promise also anticipates themes and phrases that will recur in Isaiah 56–66.[199]

The promise to people who do take refuge with Yhwh is that Yhwh's age-long promise to Israel will be fulfilled for them.[200] In the parallelism, the holy mountain may be another term for the land as a whole or may refer specifically to Mount Zion. Once again the phrase parallels a line near the close of 56.1-8. Perhaps people involved in the kind of offerings the section has critiqued thought they could thereby safeguard their inheritance. Actually, they were profaning it (Ps 106.38). The key to safeguarding it lay elsewhere. The people's practices in the *n*e*ḥālîm* imperil the *naḥălâ*.

Comment: 57.14-21

As the critique in 56.9–57.13 recalls preexilic prophecy, the divine commitment expressed in 57.14-21 recalls the commitments in Isaiah 40–55, and it has been suggested that this oracle comes from the same prophet as those chapters.[201] But its taking up words and themes from them parallels the way other parts of Isaiah 56–66 do so, and it more likely reflects a process whereby later prophets take up, reaffirm, and reapply earlier prophecies. Indeed, the passage reflects Isaiah 6 as well as Isaiah 40.[202] Later prophets may pick up earlier prophecies on the basis of their having been fulfilled (so that they can be fulfilled again) or on the basis of their not having been fulfilled (so surely they will be). A little of both would be true in this case, but the passage's presupposition is that the community's situation is the same as that presupposed by Isaiah 40–55. Here, too, the community seems to be abandoned by God and needs to be restored. Like prophecies in Isaiah 40–55, this prophecy sees Yhwh as not one who will be permanently angry (even though people have declined to turn back from their faithlessness) but as one who will bring comfort to people who are broken (even though they deserve to be in that state). The prophet overhears a voice commissioning the construction of a highway whereby Yhwh may return to the people. Yhwh does not insist that they turn from their faithlessness before there is any possibility of speaking of comfort, but does insist that they turn from their faithlessness if they wish to experience that comfort.

[199] Cf. W. A. M. Beuken, 'Isa. 56:9–57:13', in van Henten *et al.* (eds), *Tradition and Re-interpretation in Jewish and Early Christian Literature*, pp. 48-64 (53).

[200] Alonso Schökel (*A Manual of Hebrew Poetics*, p. 156) sees v. 13a as an aphorism.

[201] So W. W. Cannon, 'Isaiah c. 57 14-21 c.c. 60–62', *ZAW* 52 (1934), pp. 75-77.

[202] Cf. W. A. M. Beuken, 'Trito-Jesaja', pp. 74-78.

57.14 And someone says, 'Build up, build up, clear a road,// lift high the stumbling-block from my people's road'.

MT punctuates v. 14 as a single 3-4 line in which the opening verb applies to both cola and the rest of v. 14a is paralleled by the whole of v. 14b. This is implausible, like its understanding of v. 13a. If we did not have MT's punctuation, we might read it as two parallel lines, 3-2, 2-2:

> And someone says, 'Build up, build up,// clear a road,
> Lift high the stumbling-block// from my people's road'.

The opening verb would then apply to both lines. In v. 14a, the repeated verb in the first colon would be paralleled by the verb in the second, and the closing noun would apply to the first colon as well as to the second. In other respects the two first cola would be parallel and the two second cola would both manifest the noun *derek*, while in v. 14b as a whole the second colon would simply complete the first.

In isolation, the opening verb is enigmatic in its reference. LXX, Syr have 'they will say', suggesting that the form is impersonal third-person singular. MT links v. 14 with what precedes (we have noted that 1QIs[a] and 4QIs[d] locate a break after v. 13; 1QIs[a] also has a small space after v. 14). It thus provides a solution to the question of the verb's subject; it is the person who takes refuge in Yhwh, and who will own the land and possess Yhwh's holy mountain. But why does the verb not continue the *w*-yiqtol form of the preceding verb (as it does in 1QIs[a], *wyw'mr*), and why should the person in v. 13b be uttering the commission that follows? Rather, the clue to the verb's significance lies in its constituting the first of the links in vv. 14-21 with Isaiah 6 and 40. In Isaiah 6.3 one seraph would proclaim to another and say [*w^e'āmar*] 'Holy, holy, holy'. In 40.6, after a voice says 'Call out', someone says [*w^e'āmar*] 'Proclaim what?'[203] These links suggest that the voice speaking here is that of an unidentified heavenly being who speaks on Yhwh's behalf (compare 'my people' in 40.1b). The two link passages have different tense references, and here the verb might have yet another and denote a proclamation to be made in the future, but that would take something of the edge off the proclamation. More likely the tense reference follows that of 40.6.

The voice commissions the 'building up' of a 'road'. The recurrence of the noun *derek* makes for a link with 56.11; 57.10, and *derek* will recur again in v. 17 in association with 'ill-gotten gain' from 56.11, but otherwise the noun has different connotations each time ('way' in 56.11 and 57.17, 'journey' in 57.10), and its connotations here relate to its links with 40.1-11. The doubling of the verb corresponds to the doubling of the

[203] So MT; 1QIs[a] has *w'wmrh*, likely a first-person form corresponding to LXX and Vg (which also has a first-person form here in 57.14). Beuken (*Jesaja IIIA*, pp. 79-81) sees 'and someone says' as a gloss to make explicit that v. 14 refers back to 40.3.

first voice's verb in 40.1, 'Comfort, comfort', and the actual verb (*sālal*) is the one lying behind the word 'highway' (*m*ᵉ*sillâ*) in 40.3.[204] 'Clear a road' (*pannû dārek*) is the exact phrase in 40.3 except that here the noun is absolute and has a pointing that issues from its position before a pause. 'Lift high' (*hārîmû*) parallels 40.9 (*hārîmî*, because the addressee is the *m*ᵉ*baśśeret*), though the verb is used in a different way (there the command is to lift high the voice), and in substance the parallel lies rather with the declaration that every cleft will lift up and every mountain and hill fall down. The expressions will recur in an overlapping configuration and with overlapping meaning in 62.10.[205]

There is also some ambiguity about the addressees in v. 14. Continuity with what precedes might suggest that the prophecy addresses the community. The exhortation would then suggest the people's need to clear the way between themselves and Yhwh by abandoning the kind of wrongdoing described in 56.9–57.13. This bidding to clear the way (*pānâ* piel) would fit with the description of the shepherds as having turned to their own way (*pānâ* qal: 56.9). On the other hand, the actual addressee in vv. 6-13 was feminine singular, with v. 13a making a transition to speak of the individual who takes refuge with Yhwh. The masculine plural verbs would have to be taking up the masculine plurals in vv. 3-5. Further, in v. 14 'my people' are spoken of in the third person. Even if 'my people' are set over against 'the faithless',[206] this does not suggest that it is they who are expected to do the building up and clearing. It is other agents: hardly prophets (whose existence has not been mentioned),[207] more likely supernatural aides such as the ones addressed in 40.1-11.

There, in 40.3, the voice commissions a road for Yhwh to return to Jerusalem and/or to the people. Here, what will follow in 57.15-21 would fit with the idea of a road whereby Yhwh can return to the people. But the road in 40.3 is also a road for the people, who will return with Yhwh to Jerusalem (40.11). So another possibility here is that the road is one whereby both Yhwh and the people still in Babylon will return to Jerusalem (cf. 60.1–62.12). Either understanding (a road for Yhwh or for the people) would fit with the reference to the 'stumbling-block' (*mikšôl*) in 'my people's way', as this takes us back to 8.11-18. LXX and Vg translate with a plural (contrast Tg, Aq, Sym), but this obscures the link with 8.14, the one other occurrence of the word 'stumbling-block' in Isaiah. That this link with Isaiah 8 is more than coincidence is suggested by the fact that the stumbling-block stands in 'the way of this people' (8.11); in that passage, Yhwh will go on to speak of 'hiding my face' from Jacob (cf. v. 17 here).

[204] LXX omits both verbs; Vg avoids the repetition; 1QIsᵃ adds *hmslh*, augmenting the parallel with 40.3.

[205] Thus Ruszkowski (*Volk und Gemeinde*, p. 29), for instance, calls v. 14 'an adapted citation from Isa 62.10'.

[206] So, e.g., Schramm, *The Opponents of Third Isaiah*, p. 133.

[207] Against Blank, *Prophetic Faith in Isaiah*, p. 179.

In v. 14a LXX translates 'cleanse the ways before him'[208] and Tg has 'teach and exhort, turn the people's heart to the right way, lift high the obstacle of the faithless from the way of the congregation of my people'.[209] The reference to 40.3 in the Gospels (e.g. Mk 1.3) likewise applies 40.3 thus. It corresponds to Ezekiel's use of the word *mikšôl* in connection with waywardness (specifically unfaithfulness) that trips people up (e.g. Ezek 14.1-8).[210] But if the people are being urged to put away their own waywardness, it is odd that the prophet does not say 'remove *your* stumbling blocks'. The voice might, then, be commissioning the unnamed agents to remove the things that cause calamity, things such as the images Ezekiel speaks of. But a *mikšôl* is more than an obstacle, such as might stand between the people and Yhwh. It is something that makes people fall down. It can be something whereby God makes people fall over (e.g. Jer 6.21). Even in Ezekiel the point about the use of *mikšôl* is the calamity that follows the waywardness; Ezekiel's characteristic addition of the word 'waywardness' suggests that *mikšôl* in itself would not make the point that needed to be made. Waywardness issues in calamity. Here, what the unnamed voice commissions is the removing of the calamities that were caused by the wilfulness. Yhwh does not commission the people to remove the waywardness but commissions unnamed agents to remove the troubles this waywardness led to. This corresponds to the reference to 'my people' in 40.1, again not as the people who are addressed and commissioned to clear the way but as the objects of the double comfort. So the road is not a physical road for the people to tread, or a metaphorical road for Yhwh to tread, or an ethical road for the people to tread, but a way for the people to tread as they take up the life journey Yhwh wants them to be able to walk, which Yhwh is going to make possible for them. The talk of a road thus has a more down-to-earth meaning than was the case in 40.1-11, so as to 'reinterpret the concept of Yahweh's eschatological highway as a historical movement'[211]—the reversal of the transition from historical to eschatological that is usually associated with the movement from Isaiah 40–55 to Isaiah 56–66.

57.15 For the one who is high and towering has said this,// the one who dwells forever, whose name is 'Holy one':
'I dwell on high and holy,// and with the crushed and low in spirit,
In enlivening the spirit of the people who are low,// enlivening the heart of the people who have been crushed.

[208] 'Before him' implies a form from *pānîm* rather than the verb *pannû*.
[209] Cf. also Saadia, 'Version d'Isaïe de R. Saadia', pp. 50-53.
[210] So Lim, *The 'Way of the Lord' in the Book of Isaiah*, pp. 117-18, here.
[211] K. Koch, *TWAT*, II, p. 309 (ET *TDOT*, III, p. 290)—though he emphasizes the idea of Israel's walking the way of Yhwh's commandments.

Whereas v. 14 reported the speech of an unnamed speaker, vv. 15-21 report the declaration by Yhwh that lies behind that commission in v. 14. In v. 15aαβ (5-4) they are introduced by the form of words used by a messenger, which came in 56.1, 4. Here the one who sent the message is described not simply as Yhwh, as in other occurrences of the simple formula; the formula is elaborated in the manner of Isaiah 40–55 (e.g. 42.5; 43.1, 14, 16). Yhwh is '[the one who is] high and towering', further words from 6.1-3 (where they may apply to Yhwh or to Yhwh's throne); the related verbs came in 33.10. In the phrases in the parallel colon in turn, 'his name is "Holy one"' would be an appropriate summary of the seraph's words in 6.3. This God 'dwells forever'; in 8.18 the same participle describes Yhwh as one who 'dwells' on Mount Zion[212] and in 33.5 describes Yhwh as one who 'dwells' on high, while the noun translated 'forever' (*ʿad*) describes Yhwh as Father 'forever' in 9.5 [6].[213] In 8.18 the verb is intransitive, as is usually the case, and here Tg, Syr indicate that they take it in this way, by providing a preposition for their equivalent noun. The use of *ʿad* here without a preposition is not unique (e.g. Ps 104.5), and *mārôm* is used thus in association with a recurrence of *šākan* in the next line. But in these circumstances *ʿad* does usually have a preposition (as in Isa 45.17; 64.8; 65.18), and conversely *šākan* is occasionally transitive (e.g. Jer 17.6); LXX, Vg 'who inhabits eternity' take it so here (contrast OL).[214]

Yhwh's own words in the middle line (3-2) initially summarize the point once more; again the verb applies to both cola and the adverbial expressions are parallel. In form they, too, reflect the style of Isaiah 40–55, though in content they reflect formulations from earlier in the book. In 33.5, just noted, Yhwh 'dwells on high', as here. If we conclude that *šākan* is transitive in the previous line, so it could be here, suggesting 'I inhabit the height'; 'holy' would then qualify the noun.[215] But it is easier to infer that the noun *mārôm* is used adverbially and means 'on high'.

After all the emphasis on the exalted position of Yhwh, the parallel colon goes on to make a complementary point. The fact that Yhwh lives on high does not mean Yhwh stays away from the lowly. MT locates the athnaḥ at the midpoint of the verse and thus midway through this line, and perhaps suggests taking the *w* that opens v. 15b to imply 'but'.[216] It might also imply that the subsequent *ʾet* is the object-marker, anticipating

[212] S. W. Flynn find this meaning in the present verse ('Where is YHWH in Isaiah 57,14-15?', *Biblica* 87 [2006], pp. 358-70).

[213] I take the name of which this is part to refer to God not to the child who bears the name; see John Goldingay, 'The Compound Name in Isaiah 9:5 [6]', *CBQ* 61 (1999), pp. 239-44.

[214] But Croatto sees the phrase as involving an ellipse, so that it implies 'dwells on high/forever' (*Imaginar el futuro*, p. 89).

[215] So Delitzsch, *Jesaia*, p. 584 (ET II, p. 380).

[216] So, e.g., Pauritsch, *Die Neue Gemeinde*, p. 68.

the repeated verb ‘enlivening’ that follows (LXX makes that assumption).[217] Yet the prosody more likely works on the basis of the verse comprising three bicola rather than two tricola, with the verb ‘I dwell’ in v. 15aγ also applying to the second colon, v. 15bα, and *ʾet* being a preposition. ‘With the crushed and low in spirit’ then parallels, complements, and contrasts with ‘on high and holy’. A little like 56.1, the line thus combines emphases of Isaiah 1–39 (in the first colon) and of Isaiah 40–55 (in the second colon). Indeed, v. 15 has been called a one-sentence summation of biblical theology,[218] though the identical pair of attributes, grandeur and concern for the lowly, are also applied in Akkadian literature to Ishtar.[219]

For ‘crushed and low’, LXX has ‘faint-spirited’ and ‘broken in heart’ and Vg *contrito et humili spiritu*, which has similar meaning (cf. also Tg), but when this appears in English as ‘contrite and humble in spirit’ a quite different impression is conveyed. In Hebrew, the first adjective and the related verb *dākāʾ* regularly refer to breaking, wounding, or crushing something or someone; while some passages would allow the meaning ‘crushed and therefore contrite’, only Jeremiah 44.10 requires this meaning. In this context the double occurrence in Isaiah 53.5 is more significant; here *m*ᵉ*dukkāʾ* connotes objectively not subjectively humbled. Likewise the second adjective and the related verb *šāpal* regularly refer to an objective lowering or lowness (cf. 57.9). In 2 Samuel 6.22 David adds ‘in my eyes’ to make the subjective point. The verb appears with this significance in threats in Isaiah 2.9, 11, 12, 17; 5.15; 10.33; 29.4; here in 57.15 the prophecy starts from the fact that Yhwh has fulfilled these threats. Indeed, it adds, the people are not only physically low but low in spirit. There is some oxymoron involved in that phrase. Spirit stands for dynamism and energy; but this people’s dynamism and energy has become tiredness and lethargy (which is very different from lowliness and contrition). That the expression refers to lowness of spirit rather than lowliness of spirit will be confirmed by v. 16b. It follows that the line is not referring to a group of meek and lowly people within the community, but as usual to the state of the entire community.[220] While passages such as the Mekilta attributed to Rabbi Ishmael take the verse to refer to meekness, a saying attributed to Rabbi Alexandri says, ‘If an ordinary person should make use of a broken vessel, it is demeaning to him, but as to the Holy One, blessed be he, all the vessels that he uses are broken’.[221]

[217] See Bentzen, *Jesaja II*, p. 127.
[218] Oswalt, *Isaiah Chapters 40–66*, p. 487.
[219] Cf. Paul, ישעיה פרקים מ-סו, II, p. 431 (ET p. 474).
[220] Cf. Beuken, *Jesaja IIIA*, p. 85.
[221] Mekilta attributed to Rabbi Ishmael 55.1 and Lev. R. 7.2, as quoted in Neusner, *Isaiah in Talmud and Midrash*, pp. 105, 282.

How, then, do the fact that Yhwh is on high and holy and the fact that the people are crushed and low in spirit relate to each other? A third line (3-3) answers that question in two parallel cola, each beginning (unusually) with the same verb form, an infinitive, following it with a construct term for the inner nature of the person, and then adding a plural absolute that takes up the root of a singular word from the previous line (in the case of the second word, now using a participle rather than an adjective, for variety, and reversing the order of the words). The high and holy God acts to renew the low and crushed. Yhwh does not wait until people become contrite and lowly; this would involve waiting for a long time. Yhwh acts on the assumption that it is the act of renewal that will generate the response of lowliness and contrition; at least, this is the only hope. The spirit and heart of people is not only low and crushed but dead and needing to be brought back to life.

57.16 For I do not always contend,// I am not irate forever.
For before me the spirit would faint,// the breathing beings I myself made.

The yiqtol verbs in vv. 15 and 16b refer to Yhwh's characteristic action, and it makes sense to understand the opening yiqtol in v. 16 in the same way rather than as referring to the future, with EVV. The yiqtols in the almost-identical Psalm 103.9 have the same significance.[222] It is the facts in v. 16 that lie behind the commissions and encouragements in vv. 14-15. The two cola in v. 16a (4-3) stand in neat parallelism: the 'for' applies to both but is picked up by the *w* in the second colon, the negative is then repeated, the parallel temporal expressions follow, and each colon closes with a first-person yiqtol verb. There is no doubt that Yhwh has been contending with the people about their behaviour (3.13, and more frequently elsewhere in the Prophets: e.g., Jer 2.9; Hos 4.1; Mic 6.1-2). It is as if Yhwh has been bringing a case against a neighbour before the court at the city gate. Like such a person, Yhwh has been furious with this neighbour who has done wrong. The word for being irate or furious (*qāṣap*) is one that has recurred in Isaiah, especially in Isaiah 40–55 (47.6; 54.8), but Yhwh has promised to give up this fury (54.9). It has also come in Lamentations, in its last agonized verse; but Lamentations Rabbah declares that Isaiah 57.16 answers Lamentations.[223] Yhwh is not like someone who always holds a grudge against a neighbour even after being vindicated and the neighbour has made compensation. Verse 16 announces a new divine strategy.[224]

222 Nurmela (*The Mouth of the Lord Has Spoken*, pp. 96-97) notes that Isa 40–55 alludes to Ps 103 and suggests that this supports the idea that this verse alludes to the psalm.

223 Lam. R., on Lam 5.20.

224 Obara, *Le strategie di Dio*, p. 326.

The second line (3-3) comprises parallel cola that provide further background and rationale for Yhwh's stance. Once again the line begins with a 'for' applying to both cola and picked up by a *w*. In each colon there then come nouns of related meaning (one singular, one plural), followed by terms referring to the speaker, 'before me' and 'I' (the pronoun that is unnecessary from a purely semantic angle). Finally the verbs close the cola, as they did in v. 16a, but they contrast sharply, a third-person yiqtol and a first-person qatal, one that refers to fainting and applies to both cola, the other to making and applying only to the second. The reference to the spirit (*rûaḥ*) fainting generalizes in new terms the realities of which v. 15 spoke. It is before Yhwh that the spirit faints (more literally, 'from before me'), if Yhwh assails it as Yhwh has. The comment makes a similar point to 40.27-31, though it uses different words. But Yhwh is one who gives breath and spirit (*nᵉšâmâ* and *rûaḥ*; 42.5), who was the one who put *nišmat-rûaḥ* into the world's creatures (Gen 7.22 [P]), who thus made breathing creatures (*nᵉšâmôt*); the word for breath can be used with a similar meaning to *nepeš* and this is presumably the significance of the plural *nᵉšâmôt*. The fact that Yhwh made human beings makes it impossible to be satisfied with their having been put down. It also makes it possible to do something about it.

A number of the divine words in Isaiah 40–55 can be seen as responses to Israel's accusations against Yhwh, and this understanding also make sense here. One could imagine the people protesting, 'We are crushed and low in spirit, and Yhwh is too high and lofty to be involved with us. Yhwh has withdrawn from us and hit us and evidently plans to contend angrily with us forever'. 'On the contrary', Yhwh says, 'I do not contend or stay angry. How could that be true? I am the one who created these people.' As can happen in Isaiah 40–55, then, Yhwh is quite willing to admit the charge of having acted thus, but responds by saying 'Yes, but this does not go on forever'.

57.17 At the waywardness of its ill-gotten gain I was irate;// I would hit it, hiding—I would be irate.
It lived turning to the way of its own heart;// 18 I have seen its ways, but I will heal it.

How do these declarations in vv. 17-18a (3-3, 4-3) relate to what precedes? They give an answer to a question raised by vv. 15-16. If Yhwh is the loving and committed creator, what explains the crushing and hitting and anger? In Isaiah 40–55 there is a second element to Yhwh's response when accused of abandoning the people and afflicting them. 'Yes I did', Yhwh says, 'and I had good reason'. So it is here. The word order is thus significant, as the opening phrase provides the justification for why Yhwh was irate, struck out, and hid. In terms of prosody, the opening phrase applies to the second colon as well as the first; the first

'I was irate' is then expanded in 'I would hit it, hiding—I would be irate (the Hebrew does not quite repeat the verb denoting 'I was irate', as the first time the verb is qatal, the second time simple *w* plus yiqtol). The anger, striking, and hiding are those of the fall of Jerusalem, the destruction of the temple, and the exile. Yet we have noted that waywardness (*ʿāwôn*)[225] was already hinted at in the reference to the diviner (*ʿōnᵉnâ*) in 57.3, while the leaders were attacked for their concern with ill-gotten gain in 56.9. So while here the prophecy looks behind the people's present waywardness and the dishonesty of its leadership to the more general dishonesty and waywardness of the time that preceded and issued in the exile, it also implies that these have continued in the Second Temple community, which would justify a continuing anger, striking, and hiding.[226] These declarations may also hint that the practices condemned in 56.9–57.13 are at least in part reactions to a sense that Yhwh has abandoned the community. This in turn would imply that the relationship between Yhwh and the people has got into a vicious circle. They are wayward; Yhwh abandons; so the people are wayward some more; so Yhwh abandons some more; and so on forever. (If one is to look for a grammatical antecedent to the 'its' in v. 17a, this is more likely 'my people' in v. 14[227] than the crushed and low person in v. 15, since this person has already been pluralized later in that verse.) The background of the new strategy is thus 'the failure of the previous strategy'.[228]

MT's verse division suggests that v. 17b then restates v. 17a. This fits with the link between 'ill-gotten gain' and people directing themselves to their own way in 56.11. But it is as plausible to understand v. 17b as a declaration that after 587 nothing changed; v. 17b then begins a line making a new point, which in due course opens up the possibility of taking vv. 17-19 as a sequence of bicola, a more probable arrangement than that implied by MT's verse division. Verses 17b-18a are then the first of these bicola, with the relationship between the two cola being one of contrast. This understanding fits the pattern suggested by Isaiah 40–55, which already affirmed that in the exile the people continued declining to learn any lessons or change their ways (e.g. 42.18-25). They continued to walk their own way rather than forsaking it (53.6; 55.7). There has indeed been only crushing and lowness of spirit, not contrition and lowliness of spirit. It is still the case that they turn to their own way (see 56.11). The adjective 'turning' (*šôbāb*) comes only here and in Jeremiah 3.14, 22 and the existence of other verbal links between 57.14-21 and Jeremiah 3 (notably the reference to 'healing' in 57.19) suggests that 57.14-21 may be alluding to Jeremiah 3.[229] In v. 18a, the illogic of Isaiah 40–55 once

[225] On this translation of *ʿāwôn*, see the comment on 59.2.
[226] Concerning this verb, too, see on 59.2.
[227] Cf. Kessler, *Gott geht es um das Ganze*, p. 33.
[228] Obara, *Le strategie di Dio*, p. 329 (see the comment above on v. 16).
[229] So Sommer, *A Prophet Reads Scripture*, p. 53.

more continues; one might compare specifically the transition from 42.18-25 to 43.1-8. (Ibn Ezra comments that the way Yhwh speaks in the past tense supports his view that the prophet lived in the late sixth century and not in the eighth.[230]) Yhwh speaks of having seen their ways not in the sense of seeing what has been happening to them (though that is true) but of having seen the ways in which they behave (cf. 58.13; 66.3); the plural 'ways' complements the singular 'way' of v. 17b. 'Way' is a key word in the section (see 57.10, 14a, 14b as well as 56.11; 57.17, 18). Notwithstanding the persistence of their waywardness (rather than because I have seen their repentance: so Tg[231]), Yhwh declares 'I will heal them'. Yhwh hit and wounded; Yhwh binds and heals (cf. Hos 6.1). Here there is another triangular link between chapters 1–39, 40–55, and 56–66. Isaiah 6 declared that the people were to be blinded and not healed; 42.18–43.13 declared that they were indeed blind, but followed this with promises that the blind are to become witnesses; 57.18 affirms that they are to be healed. The talk of healing thus links with the talk of hitting, though it is noteworthy that Tg (*šᵉbaq*) and Vg (*dimitto*) have 'let go'. This suggests they understood the verb as *rāpâ* rather than *rāpāʾ*, implying 'forgive'.[232] Both healing and forgiving is the way Yhwh will go about removing the things that make people stumble.

57.18b I will lead it and restore all comfort to it;// for its mourners, 19 as the fruit of lips I am creating well-being,
Well-being for the far and for the near,// Yhwh has said, I will heal it.

Verses 18b-19a (4-4) spell out that point. The talk of Yhwh's leading perhaps takes up the reference to a way for the people to get back to their land or to get to their destiny (v. 14); Yhwh will lead the people on that one-time journey (cf. also 58.11). Nearer to hand is the reference to the people's way in v. 17b. Yhwh's leading will ensure that the people walk Yhwh's way (cf. 48.17). As healing reverses hitting, leading reverses the people's walking in its own way.[233] This is part of the comfort Yhwh will bring. We have noted that the double 'comfort' of 40.1 was hinted at in v. 14; here the prophecy introduces the plural noun *nᵉḥummîm*. In Isaiah 40–55, the root can suggest both words of comfort and action bringing comfort, and both connotations are appropriate here. Yhwh promises to 'restore' comfort. Elsewhere in Isaiah 56–66 this verb (*šālēm* piel) is a frightening one, signifying recompense for wrongdoers (59.18; 65.6; 66.6), though the qal does refer to the completion of mourning (60.20).

230 *The Commentary of Ibn Ezra on Isaiah*, p. 264.

231 On the stress on repentance in such passages in Tg Isaiah, see Chilton, *The Glory of Israel*, pp. 37-46.

232 Final *h* verbs can replace their *h* by ʾ, and Jer 38.4 is an example for this verb; see GK 75rr. For *wrpʾtyw* 1QIs[a] has *wrptyhw*, 4QIs[d] *wrptyw*.

233 Cf. John S. Kselman. 'A Note on *wʾnḥhw* in Isa 57:18', *CBQ* 43 (1981), pp. 538-42.

Here it denotes a positive kind of compensation, carrying the overtones of *šālôm*. The point will become explicit in the parallel colon, v. 19a; we could translate 'restore great comfort...I am creating restoration...' to make the point.

First, indeed, in the second colon reference to the people as mourners also follows. MT links it with the words that precede, as part of v. 18b, but the balance of the cola suggests that '[and] for its mourners' begins the second colon. 'Mourning' is another word that recurs in Isaiah 56–66 (60.20; 61.2-3; 66.10). The references do not suggest that only some people are mourning over the state of the city and people. Everyone is affected by its sorry state; its mourners are the people as a whole, grieving over the crushing and humiliation that city and people have experienced. They are the same people as the crushed and low in spirit of v. 15.[234] For the mourners God is 'creating' something new. The verb is another favourite one in Isaiah 40–55, the most substantial repository of occurrences of the word in the Old Testament. The participle comes seven times there, and will come three further times in 65.17-18. Indeed, Yhwh's self-description in 45.7 is as one who 'creates darkness' and 'makes *šālôm*'; it is almost a description as one who creates *šālôm*, the phrase that comes here.

Whereas for the most part vv. 14-21 do not present us with exegetical enigmas in the manner of vv. 3-13, vv. 18b-19a does offer one difficulty in the phrase 'the fruit of lips', which MT takes as the close of the colon. The phrase appears only here (LXX omits 'I am creating...as the fruit of lips'; Vg again has a past verb). Hebrews 13.15 uses the expression to denote a metaphorical sacrifice consisting in praise. Hebrews thus combines the wording of v. 19a with an image recalling the more difficult expression in Hosea 14.3 [2], where MT has 'we will render [as?] bulls our lips'. The verse in Hosea might imply that praise is equivalent to sacrifice; but if so, it does so very elliptically. Strikingly, it uses the verb *šālēm* (piel), which appeared here in the previous line, translated 'restore'. But more likely the clue to understanding v. 19a lies in passages such as Proverbs 12.14, 'from the fruit of a person's mouth he gets his fill of good', and 18.20, 'from the fruit of a person's mouth his stomach gets its fill'. Here, then, the fruit of the lips is *šālôm*.

By taking 'the fruit of lips' as the close of the colon, MT links the occurrence of *šālôm* which follows with the second occurrence of that word (cf. LXX, Vg; 1QIs[a] omits the repetition). Further, its verse division implies the translation 'As one who creates the fruit of lips, "Well-being, well-being, for the far and for the near", Yhwh has said'.[235] The repeated noun would then imply 'true well-being', 'complete well-being', 'nothing but well-being'. Yet the paseq or separator, a vertical line placed between

234 Cf. Marti, *Jesaja*, p. 372 (though he assumes that all the terms refer to a group within the community).

235 Cf. *TTH* 161.2; and Tg.

the words, also suggests that MT did not treat them as a compound expression (compare 26.3; Jer 6.14; 8.11; 1 Chr 12.19; contrast Isa 58.1 below; Gen 14.10; Deut 16.20). One occurrence of 'well-being' might then apply to the far, one to the near.[236] But more likely, the first *šālôm* stands in apposition to 'the fruit of lips' and explains what this fruit is. Taking this first *šālôm* as the object of 'create' fits the precedent in 45.7, and further associates this first *šālôm* with the verb *šālēm* and also gives the second line a more plausible length.

The first line, then, promises that well-being will be the fruit of lips. Whose lips are these? The phrase might still mean that Yhwh will open the mouths of the mourning community, an idea paralleling Isaiah 40–55 even if the expression does not, in such a way that its praise and testimony will issue in Yhwh's showing well-being to it. It might more directly take up the fact that the people's lips have been unclean (6.5); perhaps the lips have been purified so that they can produce fruit, the faithfulness that was absent from lips that spoke deceit and will now issue in well-being. It might take up the fact that Isaiah's own lips were unclean, but were purified (6.5, 7), so that they can serve Yhwh by speaking of well-being; the lips could then be the prophet's. As in v. 18, Tg introduces an explicit reference to people turning to Yhwh in repentance. Any of these understandings might cohere with the idea that praise is the fruit of lips. But the link with 45.7 makes it more likely that the lips are Yhwh's, the lips that speak throughout vv. 15-21. These lips speaking words that comfort and commissioning acts that comfort will generate the people's well-being.

The second line (3-3) then explicates the extent of God's gift of well-being: it belongs to people far away as well as people near. We have noted parallels between v. 15a and 33.5, 10; reference to the far away and the near parallels 33.13, where it likely denotes foreign nations and people in Judah. Ephesians 2.17 thus uses the wording of this verse to make the same point as 56.8, in whose light v. 19bα would be referring to Judahites and foreigners. But the line goes on to nuance the nature of this well-being and in doing so returns to the image of healing, so that the second line summarizes and closes off the first line. Here MT has *w*-consecutive plus perfect, matching its earlier simple *w* plus yiqtol verbs, while LXX has future, but once again Vg has a past tense verb. Tg again has 'let go', but Vg (which had 'let go' before) has 'heal'. The fact that it does explicate the nature of God's gift of well-being as involving healing suggests a specific link with Judah, the entity that Yhwh has hit; the phrase thus likely denotes the dispersion community and the Jerusalem community, or functions as a merism for the whole people[237] (Tg understands it to refer to people who are faithful to the Torah and people who are penitent and have returned to such faithfulness; it thus implies that

[236] So Saadya, 'Version d'Isaïe de R. Saadia', p. 51.
[237] So e.g., Berges, *Das Buch Jesaja*, p. 472.

faithfulness and penitence are the responsibility of individuals within the community).[238] The section has focused on the situation of the Jerusalem community, but it has not lost sight of the fact that the Judahite community lives divided between people in Judah and people in Babylon and elsewhere. It has not written them off. There is no pointer towards taking the promise eschatologically[239] if this implies it denotes something necessarily far off in time.

The intercalated, resumptive 'Yhwh has said' is a brief but important reaffirmation. This is a promise of God, so it can be relied on.

57.20 But the faithless: they are like the sea tossing,// because to be still: it cannot.
Its waters toss muck and mud;// 21 'there is no well-being' (my God has said) 'for the faithless'.

The subsection and the section close with a balanced pair of long bicola (3-4, 4-5). The faithless (*rāšaʿ*) bookend the two lines, appearing for the only time in Isaiah 56–66. The term is the antonym of faithful (*ṣaddîq*). The faithful are people who do right by those with whom they are in relationship (by God, and by the other members of their community); the faithless are people who do wrong (by both). The two sides to such faithlessness have thus been illustrated in 56.9–57.2 and 57.3-13. The prophecy presupposes that the community as a whole comprises both the faithless and the faithful, though there is nothing very distinctive about the Second Temple community in that respect.[240] In terms of content, it would be easy to take v. 20 as the prophet's words, but there was no indication at the end of v. 19 that Yhwh had stopped speaking, Yhwh is speaking in v. 21, and the references to 'the faithless' do bookend the two lines; all this suggests that Yhwh speaks through vv. 20-21.

The second reference makes clear that the lines are taking up another motif from Isaiah 40–55. Whereas 45.7 presented Yhwh's self-description as creator of darkness and shaper of *šālôm*, 48.17-18 recognized that Israel had declined to walk in the ways Yhwh had pointed to (cf. v. 18 here) and consequently had not experienced *šālôm* and *ṣᵉdāqâ* that were like a river or like the waves of the sea. After a double affirmation of Yhwh's provision of water for people being led through parched places, the final comment in 48.21, closing off Isaiah 40–48 as a whole, was then that 'there is no *šālôm* (Yhwh has said) for the faithless'. Here, the two lines begin and close with reference to the faithless, then sea and waters reappear with negative connotations rather than the positive ones that attach to them in 48.18 and 20, and finally the last comment in 48.21 reappears in exactly the same form here except for the replacing of the name 'Yhwh' by the description 'my God'.

[238] Cf. Chilton, *A Galilean Rabbi and his Bible*, p. 54.
[239] So Volz, *Jesaja II*, p. 220.
[240] As Whybray (*Isaiah 40–66*, pp. 208-9) implies.

The simile of the sea tossing (*gāraš* niphal; intransitive as in Vg rather than passive as in LXX) and its waters tossing (*gāraš* qal) muck and mud is innovative, even though the verb is a familiar one (mostly in the piel) for God or the Israelites tossing the Canaanites out of the land. An advantage of the innovation is that it generates a paronomasia such as interprets the nature of faithlessness. The faithless are the *rᵉšāʿîm*; 'the sea tossing' is *yām nigrāš*. Thus five of the six consonants (including the vowel letter *y*) in 'faithless' recur in 'the sea tossing'. Further, the line has rather the nature of a riddle: 'How are faithless like the sea tossing? In that they cannot rest and they toss up muck and mud.'[241]

On the other hand, the description of the faithless unable to be still exactly corresponds to Jeremiah 49.23 and also contrasts with promises in Isaiah 30.15; 32.17, while the imagery additionally recalls that of the Ugaritic story of the conflict of Baal and the Waters.[242] The point made by this vivid image is then made more prosaically by the closing comment about *šālôm*.[243] The sea and its waters are not at peace and they do not produce anything worth producing; this will be the ongoing experience of the faithless.

The placing of the closing comment at 48.22 and at 57.21 divides Isaiah 40–66 into three very roughly equal parts,[244] though exegetically this does not seem very significant (it would be entirely apposite if also repeated at the end of Isaiah 66, and it would then seem more significant as a marker).[245] If it is more original here than at 48.22,[246] it is also firmly embedded and indispensable as the conclusion of the argument there.[247] Thus for people reading the book sequentially, vv. 20-21 provide another solemn reminder that while the promises in vv. 14-19 do not presuppose that their audience has become contrite and lowly and has changed its ways, they do require a response of that kind if they are to be effective.

241 Cf. Koenen, *Ethik und Eschatologie im Tritojesajabuch*, p. 20.

242 Cf. James A. Montgomery, 'Ras Shamra Notes IV', *Journal of the American Oriental Society* 55 (1935), pp. 268-77 (270); also Scullion, 'Some Difficult Texts in Isaiah cc.56—66', pp. 114-15.

243 LXX has χαίρειν, as at 48.22, the Greek form of greeting that is equivalent to *šālôm* (Ottley, *Isaiah according to the Septuagint*, 2, p. 332).

244 Cf. Friedrich Rückert, *Hebräische Propheten: Erste Lieferung* (Leipzig: Weidmann, 1831), pp. 18, 30. Joachim Becker ('Zur Beurteilung von Jes 48,22 und 57,21', *BN* 119-20 [2003], pp. 5-7) takes it as evidence that Isa 40–66 is one entity, not two entities comprising chapters 40–55 and 56–66. Banwell ('A Suggested Analysis of Isaiah xl–lxvi') similarly takes it as a clue to analysing chapters 40–66. See further John W. Olley, '"No Peace" in a Book of Consolation', *VT* 49 (1999), pp. 351-70.

245 'It is relatively easy to affirm that these colophons are the work of a later editor; less easy to discover what particular purpose was being served by them' (Peter R. Ackroyd, 'Isaiah I–XII: Presentation of a Prophet', in *Congress Volume: Göttingen 1977* [Leiden: Brill, 1978], pp. 16-47 [30], reprinted in Ackroyd, *Studies in the Religious Tradition of the OT*, pp. 79-104, 266-74 [91]).

246 So, e.g., Duhm, *Jesaia*, p. 395.

247 Cf. Goldingay and Payne, *Isaiah 40–55*, II, p. 150. Lim (*The 'Way of the Lord' in the Book of Isaiah*, p. 120) describes the occurrence here as a 'quotation' from 48.22.

Conclusion

While it would make sense to begin a new chapter at 56.9, the English chapter division highlights the contrast between the faithful foreigner in 56.1-8 and the faithless Israelite leadership in 56.9–57.21.[248] As the introduction to Isaiah 56–66, Isaiah 56.1-8 set forward 'an inclusive view of the ideal community of Israel', but what now follows presents the other side of the coin; the dream is followed by the nightmare.[249] Whereas 56.1-8 asserted that outsiders could become insiders on the basis of their observing the fundamental covenant commitment, this subsequent section asserts that insiders can become outsiders on the basis of their failing to keep such commitments.

For the people it addressed, 56.1-8 was confrontational and not merely comforting; it challenged them regarding the new stance they needed to take to people they were inclined to exclude. For the people of whom it spoke, the eunuchs and the foreigners, it also implied a challenge. The transition from 56.1-8 to 56.9–57.21 is thus not 'totally abrupt'.[250] The expectation that both the community as a whole and foreigners and eunuchs in particular should act in faithfulness is here supplemented by an exposition of this expectation regarding leaders and people in general.

Conversely, 56.9–57.21 is not wholly confrontational but also encouraging. On one hand, it upbraids the community's leadership for the self-indulgence that a position of leadership makes possible and that is commonly characteristic of leaders, and for its deliberate blindness to what is wrong with the community. It upbraids the community as a whole for religious observances designed to seek guidance or help through making offerings to the gods who look after its dead family members or to these family members themselves, even the sacrifice of its children. The sacrifice of children is horrific, yet to judge from the attention given to different aspects of the people's religious observances, its horror is but one aspect of a broader dreadfulness that focuses more on what people's actions indicate about their attitude to Yhwh. How far they will go in observances that actually lead nowhere!

The prophecy warns faithless people that the distance they are prepared to travel does not mean that they can then expect to experience things going well for them; rather the opposite. Indeed, it ironically suggests that faithful people who have lost their lives are strangely blessed because they will escape the calamity that is coming on the community. It promises that the person who stays faithful to Yhwh will keep a share in

[248] Cf. Zapff, *Jesaja 56–66*, p. 355.

[249] Cf. Miscall, *Isaiah*, pp. 131-32.

[250] So Marti, *Jesaja*, p. 365. See Raymond de Hoop, 'The Interpretation of Isaiah 56:1-9', *JBL* 127 (2008), pp. 671-95; also 'Unit Delimitation and Exegesis', in R. de Hoop, M. C. A. Korpel, and S. E. Porter (eds.), *The Impact of Unit Delimitation on Exegesis* (Leiden: Brill, 2009), pp. 1-28.

the land. And it promises that Yhwh reaches out to people who are crushed and low in spirit; things will go well for them. Indeed, the promises in 57.14-21 express a 'remarkably similar' outlook to that of the 'false prophets' whom Jeremiah opposed (see Jer 6.13-14). In other words, the prophet 'reverses Jeremiah's message of woe and replaces it with a proclamation of restoration'.[251] The similarity illustrates how a true prophet is someone who knows what time it is—what time it is now and what time it was when a text was written.[252]

God's promises in 57.18-19 'might appear to resolve the ongoing problem of Israel's disobedience. But the text does not end there…. Wickedness can persist despite every divine offer and act of reconciliation.'[253]

[251] Sommer, *A Prophet Reads Scripture*, pp. 40, 41.

[252] See Eva Osswald, *Falsche Prophetie im Alten Testament* (Tübingen: Mohr, 1962); cf. J. A. Sanders, 'Hermeneutics', in *The Interpreter's Dictionary of the Bible Supplementary Volume* (Abingdon: Nashville, 1976), pp. 402-7 (404-5).

[253] Darr, *Isaiah's Vision and the Family of God*, p. 71.

III

ISAIAH 58.1–59.8

Translation and Notes

1 Call with full throat,[1] do not hold back,// like the horn lift up your voice.
Tell my people about their rebellion,// the household of Jacob about their offences.
2 And[2] day by day they have recourse to me,// they delight in acknowledging my ways,
Like a nation that has done what is faithful// and not abandoned its God's exercise of judgment.
They ask me for faithful acts of judgment[3],// they delight in drawing near God.[4]
3 'Why have we fasted and you have not looked,// afflicted ourselves[5] and you do not acknowledge it?'
Now: in your fast day you find your[6] delight,// but all the people who toil for you[7]—you oppress.[8]

[1] LXX's 'with strength' might imply בגבורה for בגרון (Budde, 'Das Buch Jesaia Kap. 40–66', p. 699).

[2] I understand the difficult ו (missing in 1QIs[a, b]) to introduce a circumstantial clause (on which see *TTH* 156-60, summarized in BDB, p. 253, without commenting on this verse); the object 'me' and the adverbial expression precede the verb. The clause is difficult because it involves an ellipse; the explication of the nature of the rebellion and the offences indeed begins here but becomes more distinct only in vv. 3b-5. One might more specifically take the clause as concessive (e.g. Duhm, *Jesaia*, p. 395). Kosmala ('Form and Structure of Isaiah 58', *ASTI* 5 [1966–67], pp. 69-81 [72]) implies that the ו suggests 'so that', but this leaves the transition to v. 3 even harder. M. Dahood ('*Ṣîr* "emissary" in Psalm 78,49', *Biblica* 59 [1978], p. 264) sees it as emphatic ו, referring to JM 177n, *HALOT* (though they do not give this example).

[3] Tg, LXX have sg.; Syr implies משפט וצדק.

[4] The verb closes with an additional (paragogic) nun (as did the verse's opening verb).

[5] נפשנו, literally 'ourself'; 1QIs[a, b] have the more expected pl. נפשותינו/נפשתינו (cf. LXX, Tg; Vg has sg.).

[6] The suffix can be understood from the suffixed words elsewhere in the line.

[7] KJV 'labours' takes impersonally, which generates good parallelism, but it is harder to make sense of this as object of נגש hiphil, and MT's distinctive pointing of עַצְּבֵיכֶם suggests a desire to distinguish this noun from similar ones that do have impersonal meaning. The personal meaning leads well into what follows. Syr 'your idols' (cf. Tg 'your stumbling blocks/offences') links the noun with עצב II rather than עצב I (and see next note). LXX 'your underlings' translates loosely. Vg 'your debtors' might suggest עַבְטֵיכֶם (e.g. Köhler, *Der Prophet der Heimkehr*, p. 201), but more likely derives from the context (see comment).

[8] The verb תנגשו closes the line, with the נ unassimilated. Tg 'bring near' (cf. Syr) presupposes שׁ for שׂ.

4 Now: it is so as to engage in strife and contention[9] that you fast,// and so as to hit with faithless fist[10].
You do not fast today[11]// so as to make your voice heard on high.
5 Will this be the kind of fast[12] that I would choose,// a day for someone to afflict himself?
Will it be for bowing his head like a bulrush// and spreading sackcloth and ash?
Will this be what you would call[13] a fast,[14]// a day acceptable to Yhwh?

6 Will not this be the fast[15] I would choose:// loosing faithless chains,// untying the cords of the yoke,
Sending off the broken, free,// and that you would tear apart[16] every yoke?
7 Will it not it be dividing[17] your food with the hungry person,// and that you will take the afflicted, downtrodden,[18] to your house?[19]

[9] 1QIs[a] has ולמצא; in MT the ל on ריב does double duty (Scullion, 'Some Difficult Texts in Isaiah cc.56—66', p. 115).

[10] LXX 'hitting the lowly with fists' might imply רש for רשע (cf. Lowth, *Isaiah*, p. 376), but *HUB* suggests LXX is following its understanding of עצביכם as 'your underlings'. Watts (*Isaiah 34–66*, p. 837) 'an adversary' takes רשע as the object of the verb, against MT accents, but this requires one to interpret רשע personally (or to repoint) and in an odd way. For the adjectival construct usage, cf. v. 6 (also Mic 6.10-11; Pss 125.3; 141.4; Prov 10.2).

[11] Not 'daily' (Hanson, *The Dawn of Apocalyptic*, 100-1) nor 'as (you have) today' (Watts, *Isaiah 34–66*, p. 837): the כ indicates exact point of time (see John Goldingay, '*Kayyôm hazzeh* "On This Very Day"', *VT* 43 [1993], pp. 112-15).

[12] More literally, 'Will be like this the fast'.

[13] For MT תקרא 1QIs[a] has pl. תקראו, assimilating to v. 4 (cf. Kutscher, הלשון והרקע הלשוני של מגילת ישעיהו השלמה, p. 299 [ET p. 395]).

[14] Literally 'Is it for this that you call a fast' (cf. Watts, *Isaiah 34–66*, p. 837), but it is quite common for the object of קרא to be governed by ל (see BDB, p. 896).

[15] 1QIs[a] adds אשר, making explicit that a relative clause follows.

[16] Both verbs in the line are resultative piel (see Jenni, *Das hebräische Pi'el*, pp. 183, 193-96), suggesting the effect of the action. For תנתקו LXX, Th, Vg have sg. for MT's pl., but sg. and pl. interweave through the passage and they are likely tidying the passage. M. Dahood, 'Hebrew–Ugaritic Lexicography vii', *Biblica* 50 (1969), pp. 337-56 (340-41) takes MT's verb form as an Ugaritic-style sg.

[17] For פרס, many mss have פרש (see *HUB*; and cf. BDB).

[18] מרודים looks as if it should be a qal passive participle from מרד 'rebel' (cf. Vg), but this makes poor sense. LXX 'roofless' and Vg 'wandering' in the sense of 'homeless' give good sense in the context but are hard to justify, as can be seen from BDB's entry under רוד and *HALOT*'s entry under both רוד and מרוד. Further, 'homeless' does not fit very well in the other occurrences, in Lam 1.7; 3.19. There, LXX seems more plausibly to link it with רדד or רדה or a byform מרד (cf. *DTT*). This fits here (cf. Gesenius, *Philologisch-kritischer und historischer Commentar über den Jesaia* 2, p. 227). G. R Driver ('Literary and Linguistic Problems', *JTS* 38 [1937], pp. 36-50 [49]) repoints מוּרַדִּים and derives from רדד itself. A number of emendations have been proposed (see BDB, Thomas, 'ספר ישעיה', p. 92): for example, assuming it comes from רוד, Duhm (*Jesaia*, p. 398) suggests מורדים 'homelessness'. Frants Buhl (in his 1915 revision of Wilhelm Gesenius's *Hebräisches und aramäisches Handwörterbuch über das Alte Testament* [repr., Berlin: Springer, 1949], p. 460) suggests the inwardly transitive hiphil participle מְרִדִים, which could denote wandering or restlessness.

[19] Ehrlich (*Randglossen*, IV, p. 208) suggests that Vrs 'to your house' implies ביתך (haplog.), but 1QIs[a, b] correspond to MT and the suffix can be understood from 'your food' in the first colon.

When you see someone naked, cover him,[20]// and not hide[21] from your own flesh and blood?[22]

8 Then your light will break out like the dawn,// your restoration flourish quickly.

Your faithfulness will go before you,// Yhwh's splendour will gather you.[23]

9 Then you will call and Yhwh—he will respond;// when you cry for help, he will say 'Here I am!'[24]

If you do away with the yoke from your midst,// pointing the finger, speaking[25] harmfulness,

10 And offer[26] yourself[27] to the hungry,// satisfy the needs of the afflicted person,

[20] 1QIs[a] makes explicit that this is בגד '[with] a garment' as in Ezek 18.7, 16 (Kutscher, הלשון והרקע הלשוני של מגילת ישעיהו השלמה, p. 434 [ET p. 543]).

[21] 1QIs[a] lacks the verb's final ם, presumably just a slip (Kutscher, הלשון והרקע הלשוני של מגילת ישעיהו השלמה, p. 205 [ET p. 273]).

[22] Verses 6-7 include four infinitives standing in apposition to the subject of the sequence of clauses ('this'; but *IBHS* 35.3.3b sees them as objects of 'choose'). Such infinitives are usually construct, but here three are absolute; only שלח is construct (see JM 123b; 124b). As commonly happens, finite verbs continue the infinitival construction in vv. 6bβ; 7aβb, though it is also unusual for a finite verb to follow an infinitive absolute (see JM 123b, 124b, 124q).

[23] In 52.12 אסף is used in the piel with the meaning 'come behind you'. Oort ('Kritische Aanteekeningen', p. 474) repoints as piel here; but see Jenni, *Das hebräische Pi'el*, pp. 159-60. While Vg, Tg assume that as usual the qal verb means 'gather', LXX περιστελεῖ suggests 'clothe, cover, protect' (see further Ziegler, *Untersuchungen zur Septuaginta des Buches Isaias*, p. 130).

[24] The simple *w*-yiqtol suggests that the first clause is subordinate to the second.

[25] Following on from שלח ('pointing'), an imperatival form, one would parse דבר as an imperative, but this does not make sense in the context, and it is necessary to take שלח as an anomalous infinitive (cf. GK 65a) and דבר as a regular one. 1QIs[a] ושלוח makes this explicit. Aq, Sym, Th have participles.

[26] ותפק is a shortened yiqtol form, continuing the 'if' construction, with simple ו because the verbs are parallel in time reference. Duhm (*Jesaia*, p. 399) suggests repointing to וְתָפִיק, the regular yiqtol form. But Motyer (*Isaiah*, p. 482) compares GK 109h. On the basis of a similar Arabic word, Alfred Guillaume suggests the verb means 'give repeatedly' ('Hebrew and Arabic Lexicography', *Abr-Nahrain* 1 [1959–60], pp. 3-35 [31]).

[27] For נפשך, LXX has 'the bread from your self/life/spirit/heart', Syr simply 'your bread/food', as do some post-MT Hebrew mss. They thus assimilate to v. 7. In MT נפשך takes up the other occurrences of נפש in the context, and it is thus unlikely that לחמך is the original reading (so Lowth, *Isaiah*, p. 377) or that LXX has combined two readings (see *HUB*; Armstrong, 'A Study of Alternative Readings in the Hebrew Text of the Book of Isaiah', pp. 118, 153). Aq, Sym, Th correspond to MT. G. R. Driver ('Hebrew Notes', *ZAW* 52 [1934], pp. 51-56 [53-54]) translates נפש 'abundance' on the basis of an aspect of the meaning of Akkadian *napšu*, though this led to some argument over the parallel: see W. von Soden, 'Zu *ZAW* 52, 53f', *ZAW* 53 (1935), pp. 291-92; G. R. Driver, 'Suggestions and Objections', *ZAW* 55 (1937), pp. 68-71; W. von Soden, 'Nachwort zu G. R. Drivers Objections', *ZAW* 55 (1937), pp. 71-72. Victor Avigdor Hurowitz ('A Forgotten Meaning of *nepeš* in Isaiah lviii 10', *VT* 47 [1987], pp. 43-52) has provided new support for Driver, translating נפש 'sustenance'. But Thomas Staubli urges the

Your light will shine forth in the darkness, your gloom like midday.
11 Yhwh will lead you continually// and satisfy your needs in scorched places.
He will equip[28] your frame[29];// you will be like a watered garden,
Like a spring of water,[30]// whose water does not fail.[31]
12 People from among you will build up[32] lasting ruins;// you will raise up foundations from generations ago.
You will be called 'Repairer of breaches,// restorer[33] of streets[34] for living on[35]'.

13 If you turn back your foot from the Sabbath,// doing[36] what you delight in[37] on my holy day,
But call the Sabbath 'Revelling',// Yhwh's holy [day][38] 'Honourable',
And honour it instead of going your own ways,// instead of finding your delight and speaking your word,

meaning 'throat' ('Die Darbringung der *näfäsch* in Jes 58,3-12', in D. Böhler, I. Himbaza, and P. Hugo [eds.], *L'Ecrit et l'Esprit* [Göttingen: Vandenhoeck & Ruprecht, 2005], pp. 310-24), implying 'offer the food that passes through the throat' (cf. also Thomas Staubli, 'Maat-Imagery in Trito-Isaiah', in Marti Nissinen and Charles E. Carter [eds.], *Images and Prophecy in the Ancient Eastern Mediterranean* [Göttingen: Vandenhoeck & Ruprecht, 2009], pp. 41-50).

28 1QIs^{a} has יחליצו, hiphil pl., 1QIs^{b} יחלצו, niphal pl., both implying '[your frame, lit. bones] will be strong' (see *DCH*; cf. Kutscher, הלשון והרקע הלשוני של מגילת ישעיהו השלמה, p. 299 [ET p. 394]). Secker ('Annotations') emends יחליץ to יחליף 'renew' (cf. 40.29, 31).

29 Some medieval mss have ועצמתך 'your strength' (see Thomas, 'ספר ישעיה', p. 92; cf. 40.29; 47.9).

30 Ludwig Köhler ('Emendationen', in Karl Budde [ed.] *Vom Alten Testament* [Karl Marti Festschrift; Berlin: Töpelmann, 1925], pp. 173-80 [177]) moves ממך from v. 12, reads it as מעיך 'your inward parts/love [like a spring of water]', and then suggests that this form of the text lies behind John 7.38.

31 LXX has a reduplicated text in Rahlfs, *Septuaginta*, II, p. 645; contrast Ziegler, *Buch Isaias*, pp. 338-39.

32 LXX and Vg have a passive verb (cf. 44.26), though in LXX this is part of a broader recasting of the line, and a passive verb followed by מן denoting the agent is almost as rare a usage as MT's own (cf. Delitzsch, *Jesaia*, p. 594 [ET II, p. 392]). MT might have been assimilated to 61.4, where the variant is not repeated.

33 For MT's poel משבב, 1QIs^{b} has hiphil משיב.

34 De Lagarde (*Prophetae chaldaice*, p. l) reads נתיצות ('things that are demolished') for נתיבות. On the basis of cognates in Akkadian and Arabic, G. R. Driver takes the word to mean 'what is hacked down' ('Notes on Isaiah', p. 48). NEB repoints to נְתַבּוֹת (so Brockington, *The Hebrew Text of the OT*, p. 196), with a similar sense.

35 G. R. Driver repoints לָשֶׁבֶת to לְשַׁבֵּת 'by clearing [them]' ('Linguistic and Textual Problems', p. 405) by analogy with an Akkadian expression.

36 1QIs^{a}, 4QIs^{n} provide מ'from' prefixed to the verb, which Morrow ('The Text of Isaiah at Qumran', p. 155) calls the 'preferred' reading; in MT the force of the preposition carries over from the first colon.

37 Mss and Vrs vary over whether they read sg. or pl. The pl. is unusual.

38 LXX has 'things that are holy to your God'. 1QIs^{a} has ולקדש, but 1QIs^{b} and other Hebrew witnesses (see *HUB*) have ולקדוש and 1QIs^{a} is emended thus.

14 Then you will revel over Yhwh,// and I will make you ride[39] over the heights[40] of the land// and eat[41] the possession of your ancestor Jacob.
For Yhwh's mouth has spoken.

1 Now. Yhwh's hand is not too short to deliver,[42]// his ear is not too heavy to listen.[43]
2 Because rather, your wayward acts—they have been things that separate[44]// you and your God.[45]
Your offences—they have hidden his face[46]// from you,[47] from listening.
3 Because your hands—they have become polluted/have been polluted[48] with blood,// your fingers with waywardness.
Your lips—they have spoken deceit,[49]// your tongue—it talks oppression.
4 There is no one summoning with faithfulness,// there is no one entering into judgment[50] with truthfulness.

[39] 1QIs$^{a, b}$ have והרכיבכה/והרכיבך ('and he will…; cf. LXX, Tg), an easier reading.

[40] The form is pleonastic; K implies בָּמוֹתֵי but Q regularly shortens it thus (see GK 87s, 95o; JM 97Eb). 1QIs^{a} has בומתי, but 1QIs^{b} במתי. LXX 'good things' paraphrases in light of v. 14b; contrast Aq, Sym, Th.

[41] 1QIs^{a} has והאכילך ('and he will…'; cf. LXX, Tg, but here 1QIs^{b} corresponds to MT), an easier reading.

[42] LXX's 'Is the Lord's hand not strong to deliver?' perhaps safeguards against the merest suggestion that Yhwh's hand might be too short (so Charles T. Fritsch, 'The Concept of God in the Greek Translation of Isaiah', p. 167).

[43] The pl. in 1QIs^{a} is perhaps assimilation to the more common pl. which appears in particular in 6.10; 42.20; 43.8; see the comment, on the link with these passages.

[44] Or 'they have become things that separate' or simply (in accordance with later usage) 'they have separated' (see *DG* 113 remark 2; *TTH* 135.5; and the comment below).

[45] 1QIs^{b} has the more usual בין…ובין for בין…לבין, which appears only here (BDB, p. 107).

[46] פנים appears without suffix in MT and 1QIs$^{a, b}$. Elsewhere this expression involves a suffix on the noun (e.g. 64.6 [7]). Vrs provide a suffix; if the original did have פניו, the ם would be dittog. or enclitic ם (Scullion, 'Some Difficult Texts in Isaiah cc.56—66 ', pp. 115-16). While 53.3; Job 34.29 have no suffix (and cf. Job 30.9), in this construction 'פנים is virtually reflexive' (Odeberg, *Trito-Isaiah*, p. 177), like other words for parts of the body whose suffix can be understood from the subject of the verb. Oswalt (*Isaiah 40–66*, p. 514) compares the idiom 'pay regard to a face', that is, show partiality (Deut 1.17; 16.19), but there the noun does not refer to a particular face. Tg has 'caused the withdrawing of the face of my presence [שכינה] from you' and may thus take פנים to refer to the Shekinah; but we have no other evidence of this idea in OT times. Tg also suggests taking the expression to mean 'they made him hide [his] face from you'. This would be not so much the grammatical meaning as inferring a construction that involves an ellipse.

[47] MT's accents link 'from you' with what precedes (cf. LXX, Vg), but this makes for a rhythmically odd line, and it makes sense to think that 'from you, from listening' means 'from listening to you'.

[48] The anomalous form נְגֹאֲלוּ looks like a composite reading, a cross between niphal נִגְאֲלוּ and pual גֹּאֲלוּ (Ibn Ezra, *The Commentary of Ibn Ezra on Isaiah*, p. 271; cf. GK 51h).

[49] 1QIs^{a} lacks this colon.

[50] LXX κρίσις perhaps suggests משפט for נשפט, but it may just be translating the unusual expression loosely.

Relying on nothingness, speaking emptiness,// conceiving trouble and giving birth to harmfulness![51]

5 It is a serpent's eggs they have broken up,[52]// a spider's webs[53] they spin.

One who eats of their eggs—he will die,// and one who tramples/one that is trampled,[54] an adder breaks out.[55]

6 Their webs[56]—they will not do for clothing;// they will not cover themselves[57] with the things they make.

The things they make are things of harm;// the doing of violence is in their hands.[58]

7 Their feet—they run to evil;// they hurry to shed innocent blood.[59]

Their plans are plans of harm;// destroying and smashing[60] are on their highways.

8 The way of well-being they have not acknowledged;// there is no exercise of judgment on their tracks.

Their paths they have made crooked for themselves;// no one walking that way[61] has acknowledged well-being.

[51] 1QIs[a, b] have the expected finite verbs בטחו and הולידו for MT בטוח and הולד, and 1QIs[b] has דברו for MT ודבר (1QIs[a] also has the spelling variant הרוה for MT הרו). The idiomatic use of the infinitive would no longer be current in their day.

[52] Resultative piel (Jenni, *Das hebräische Piʿel*, pp. 179-80). For MT's qatal בקעו 1QIs[a] has yiqtol יבקעו, assimilating to the next colon.

[53] For קורי Tg קוין might suggest קוי 'lines', with the same implication.

[54] On the seghol, see GK 27u; 73d; but GK 80i suggests this may be another composite form, a cross between m. active הַזֹּרֶה 'one [person] who tramples' (cf. LXX?—but on LXX in this line, see David Weissert, 'Der Basilisk und das Windei in LXX—Jes 59 5', *ZAW* 79 [1967], pp. 315-22) and f. passive הַזּוּרָה 'one [egg] that is trampled' (cf. Tg 'warm' and thus hatch). Preben Wernberg-Møller ('A Note on זור "To Stink"', *VT* 4 [1954], pp. 322-25) suggests the verb is actually זור II, which he takes to mean 'stink'; hence 'the stinking thing [the egg] breaks out as an adder'. But this seems to require considerable inference.

[55] Vg implies 'breaks forth [hatches] into an adder', accusative of result (cf. JM125o). But it is more straightforward to take 'adder' as the subject. LXX has 'basilisk', a legendarily dangerous serpent, but perhaps also a word for a snake that would be familiar in the translator's Egyptian context (cf. Stanley E. Porter and Brook W. R. Pearson, 'Isaiah through Greek Eyes', in Broyles and Evans [eds.], *Writing and Reading the Scroll of Isaiah*, II, pp. 531-46 [536]). NEB's rendering of אפעה as 'rottenness' seems to derive from the philological suggestion by G. R. Driver noted by Wernberg-Møller ('A Note on זור' [see above], p. 315). For אפעה, 1QIs[a] has אפע (cf. 41.24), but 1QH 2.27-28 corresponds to MT (cf. Wernberg-Moller, 'The Contribution of the *Hodayot* to Biblical Text Criticism', pp. 149-50).

[56] For קוריהם, Tg perhaps suggests קויהם (cf. translation note on v. 5a).

[57] For MT יתכסו (hitpael), 1QIs[a] has יכסו (presumably piel).

[58] LXX lacks the last colon.

[59] As opposed to 'the blood of the innocent'; MT has דָּם not דַּם, which appears in the expression דם הני. But the two expressions have the same meaning; 'innocent blood' is metonymy for 'the blood of the innocent'.

[60] 1QIs[a] adds חמס 'violence', which came in v. 6 and will accompany שד ושבר in parallelism in 60.18 (Kutscher, הלשון והרקע הלשוני של מגילת ישעיהו השלמה, p. 434 [ET p. 543]), though it may also reflect a concern of the Qumran community (cf. Pulikottil, *Transmission of Biblical Texts in Qumran*, pp. 70-71, 184).

[61] Instead of בה one would expect בם, which Vrs supply.

Introduction

Most MT manuscripts and 1QIs[a] mark 58.1-14 as a chapter. Questions do arise in connection with the relationship of vv. 13-14 to vv. 1-12, as vv. 13-14 bring a change in moving to talk about the Sabbath, and 1QIs[a] has a further chapter break before vv. 13-14. But there are structural and linguistic links between these closing verses and what precedes, and if vv. 13-14 are a later addition, they are devised to follow on vv. 1-12.[62] Yet further, Isaiah 58 has links with Isaiah 59, and the two chapters have been seen as one unit.[63] Both are concerned with *mišpāṭ*, *ṣ*ᵉ*dāqâ* and *ṣedeq*, with what the people 'acknowledge' (*yāda*ʿ), and with their 'rebellions' and 'offences'. More distinctively over against other passages, light, darkness, gloom, and midday in 58.10 recur in 59.9-10. In form and function, the confrontation in Isaiah 58 continues into Isaiah 59.

When the English Bible then makes 59.1-21 itself a chapter, this also compares somewhat with the MT manuscripts and 1QIs[a], which mark the beginning of Isaiah 59 and then the beginning of Isaiah 60 as either a new paragraph or a new chapter, and have no clear trend in divisions within Isaiah 59. John L. McKenzie declares that Isaiah 59.1-20 'forms an obvious unity',[64] but does not say what it is that makes this unity obvious, and its unity has not been obvious to everyone.[65] Westermann calls it 'a most curious and odd creation' then curiously and oddly adds that 'it is plainly a unity'.[66] The tensions between these two observations themselves suggest that the questions about Isaiah 59 as a unit are more complex than those concerning Isaiah 58.

In form, 59.1-8 represents a prophetic indictment that initially addresses 'you' but goes on to describe 'them'; it is this section that thus continues the confrontational address characterizing 56.9–58.14. Verses 9-15a are a congregational lament and acknowledgment of waywardness and rebellion in which 'we' address Yhwh. Verses 15b-20 [21] is a prophetic vision and promise of Yhwh acting in deliverance, with a prose promise as an endnote. This analysis of the sections in the chapter coheres

62 Cf. Bernd Jørg Diebner, 'Mehrere Hände—Ein Text: Jes 58 und die Grenzen der Literarkritik', *Dielheimer Blätter zur Archäologie und Textüberlieferung der Antike und Spätantike* 29 (1998), pp. 139-56; see also Park, *Die Gerechtigkeit Israels und das Heil der Völker*, pp. 199-286; Bohdan Hrobon, *Ethical Dimension of Cult in the Book of Isaiah* (Berlin: de Gruyter, 2010), pp. 197-205. Polan (*In the Ways of Justice toward Salvation*, p. 233) sees Isa 58 as a chiasm; while this involves ignoring vv. 7-9 and 11-12, the parallels between vv. 2 and 13 are noteworthy.

63 See, e.g., König, *Jesaja*, pp. 498-505.

64 *Second Isaiah*, p. 171. Fitzgerald ('A Rhetorical Analysis of Isaiah 56–66', pp. 169-73) formulates a case for taking the chapter as a unity, mostly on the basis of word repetitions.

65 Cf. Ruszkowski's comment, *Volk und Gemeinde*, p. 60.

66 *Jesaja Kapitel 40–66*, p. 274 (ET p. 344).

with the section marker in 1QIs[a] after v. 8 and the chapter marker after v. 15a. (Some MT mss have a section divider before v. 15a.) Some words recur within the different sections as happens between Isaiah 58 and Isaiah 59; these include rather common words such as 'offences', 'wayward acts', 'acknowledge', and 'deceit', but also the less common *hāgâ* (talk/murmur) and the infinitival pair 'speaking' and 'conceiving'. The word *mišpāṭ* comes in all three parts of Isaiah 59 (v. 8, then vv. 9, 11, 14, then v. 15b), and thus constitutes at least a redactional link between the sections[67] (it came earlier in 56.1 and 58.2 and it will reappear in 61.8; the verb *šāpaṭ* occurs in v. 4, also in 66.16).

Such links show that Isaiah 59 can indeed be interpreted as one unit,[68] though they do not show that it should be read that way, and the differences between the three elements in the chapter are at least as obvious as the links.[69] Further, if it is a unit and is properly seen as a chapter, what kind of unit is it? While it has been described as a sermon,[70] it is more often seen as a liturgy in which different persons speak.[71] This might imply that it is a combination of elements of separate origin that have been brought together to form an organic whole.[72] It might better be called a narrative.[73] Following on the indictment in vv. 1-8, then, vv. 9-15a are a confession that reacts to the indictment, and vv. 15b-20 [21] are a prophetic response to the people's penitence; only here is there an answer to the question lying behind 59.1.[74] But the notion that an existent liturgy of this kind was simply incorporated into a collection of prophetic material seems questionable, and if the chapter were a liturgical unity (even one composed by the prophet for actual use), one would expect the transitions between its different elements to be smoother. The idea that it comprises a kind of quasi-liturgy composed by a prophet is more plausible. But then the arrangement is in effect a purely literary one, like other aspects of the arrangement of the chapters, and it needs to be seen in that broader context.

Further, the verbal links between chapters 58 and 59 are largely confined to 59.1-15a and the links internal to Isaiah 59 are largely confined to vv. 1-8 in relation to vv. 9-15a.[75] The suggestion that *hôšîaʿ* and *gōʾēl*

[67] See Daniel Kendall, 'The Use of Mišpaṭ in Isaiah 59', *ZAW* 96 (1984), pp. 391-405.

[68] Koenen offers a detailed account in *Ethik und Eschatologie im Tritojesajabuch*, pp. 59-61.

[69] Cf. Volz, *Jesaia II*, pp. 230-31; Sekine, *Die Tritojesajanische Sammlung*, pp. 137-38.

[70] E.g. Herbert, *Isaiah 40–66*, p. 150.

[71] So Hermann Gunkel in his introduction to Hans Schmidt, *Die Grossen Propheten* (Göttingen: Vandenhoeck & Ruprecht, 2nd edn, 1923), p. lx; cf. e.g., Elliger, *Die Einheit des Tritojesaja*, pp. 15-20; Fohrer, *Jesaja*, III, p. 214; Alonso Schökel and Sicre Diaz, *Profetas*, I, pp. 359-61.

[72] See Volz's critique, *Jesaja II*, pp. 230-31.

[73] So Croatto, *Imaginar el futuro*, p. 145 (but he puts the word in quotation marks).

[74] Muilenburg, 'The Book of Isaiah: Chapters 40—66', p. 686.

[75] Judith Gärtner ('Erlebte Gottesferne: Drei schriftexegetische Antworten [Jes 58,1-12; 59,1-15a; 57,14-21], in F. Hartenstein u. M. Pietsch [eds.], *'Sieben Augen auf einem*

(deliver, restorer) form an *inclusio* in 59.1 and 20 seems lame. It would thus be more plausible to treat 59.1-15a as a unit than so to treat 59.1-20 [21].[76] Yet the formal links between 58.1-14 and 59.1-8 need also to be taken into account, along with the formal contrast between 59.9-15a and the confrontation in the whole of 56.9–59.8. In other words, 59.9-15a constitutes a possible response to the whole of 56.9–59.8, not just to 59.1-8 or to 58.1–59.8. This in turn fits with another consideration that will emerge from subsequent chapters. In the chiastic structure of Isaiah 56–66 as a whole, 59.1-8 closes off the indictments in 56.9–59.8, which then find a parallel in 65.1–66.16. Isaiah 56.9-15a finds a parallel in the further lament and confession in 63.7–64.11. Isaiah 59.15b-21 finds a parallel in the further vision of Yhwh in judgment in 63.1-6. The three sections of Isaiah 59 do relate to one another in the way suggested by the liturgy hypothesis, but they do so within the context of the literary arrangement of Isaiah 56–66, not as parts of an actual liturgy.

There is little indication that 59.1-8 was in origin a continuation of the oracle in 58.1-14; rather a separate confrontational oracle has been added to those in 56.9–58.14, bringing to a close the collection of confrontational prophecies that occupy 56.9–59.8. In light of its closing with a similar warning to that in 57.21, I treat 56.9–57.21 and 58.1–59.8 as slightly separate, parallel parts of this collection.[77] I then treat 59.9-15a and 59.15b-20 [21] as separate sections.

Like 56.9–57.21, Isaiah 58 opens in a way that could suggest the words of a preexilic prophet confronting Ephraim or Judah about the mismatch between its religious profession and its ignoring of Yhwh in the rest of its life; see especially 1.10-20.[78] But here the confrontation concerns fasting not praise and it overtly seeks to open up the way to restoration instead of closing with judgment.[79] Its focus on fasting is distinctive. Old Testament references to communal fasting include Jeremiah 14.12; 36.6, 9; Joel 1–2; Zechariah 7–8; also Ezra 8.21-23; Nehemiah 9.1. These may suggest that fasting is mainly an exilic and post-exilic practice, related to

Stein' [Sach 3,9]: Studien zur Literatur des Zweiten Tempels [I. Willi-Plein Festschrift; Neukirchen: Neukirchener, 2007], pp. 81-100) sees 59.1-15a as a response to 58.1-12 (57.14-21 being a later response).

[76] Cf., e.g., Fischer, *Buch Isaias*, II, p. 161-69 (he links it with Isa 58); Vermeylen, *Du Prophète Isaïe à l'Apocalyptique*, II, pp. 467-68 (he treats vv. 5-8 as secondary).

[77] Cf. Steck, *Studien zu Tritojesaja*, pp. 169-86 (he compares 56.9–57.21 with 58.1–59.21 as a whole).

[78] Vermeylen traces a detailed parallelism with 1.10-20 in *Du Prophète Isaïe à l'Apocalyptique*, II, pp. 464-65, while Gray examines the 'trajectory' extending from chapters 1 to 58 (esp. 1.16-17 to 58.6-10) in his *Rhetoric and Social Justice in Isaiah*. Diebner ('Mehrere Hände' [see above], p. 156) compares the relationship of vv. 1-12 and 13-14 with that between Isa 1–55 and 56–66, which Rendtorff (see the comment on 56.1) sees embodied in 56.1. Sommer (*A Prophet Reads Scripture*, pp. 76-78) sees a link with Micah 3.5-12, but the points of connection are not very distinctive.

[79] Cf. Pauritsch, *Die neue Gemeinde*, pp. 86-87.

the circumstances of the fall of Judah and of Judah's ongoing difficulties.[80] Reference to people not having enough to eat is also distinctive. While shortage of food and other such lacks are a threat in preexilic prophecy, they are an actuality only in Lamentations, and subsequently by implication in accounts of life after the exile in passages such as Nehemiah 5. In turn the promises of light, restoration, and God's acting in faithfulness fit the themes of exilic prophecy and of Isaiah 60–62, and towards the end of the chapter the promise of rebuilding matches the context of the late-sixth to mid-fifth centuries in Jerusalem. The chapter's closing exhortation concerning the Sabbath fits 56.1-8 and the context of Nehemiah. While its reference to building up the city may presuppose that the temple has been restored whereas the city has not, we cannot be more specific about whether the chapter comes from the end of the sixth century or from the fifth. The 'today' of v. 4 may indicate that the prophecy was declaimed on the occasion of a corporate fast, presumably in the temple courts, perhaps the kind of fasting occasion referred to in Zechariah 7–8.[81]

The chapter alternates between second singular (58.1, 5, 7-14) and second plural (58.3-4, 6; LXX, Vg, Tg, Syr also have plural in v. 5, and as is commonly the case there are variants over number at other points in the chapter).[82] Initially this alternating issues from the fact that the chapter has the rhetorical form of a commission to a prophet, though it does not maintain this rhetoric throughout. It begins in vv. 1-3a by relating words spoken to the prophet by Yhwh, who commissions the prophet to address the people and talks about them in the third person. The form of the chapter as a prophet's report of a commission thus means the people listen to Yhwh talking about them rather than to them, and in vv. 2-3a Yhwh reports to the prophet what they are doing and saying. But v. 3b then abandons the rhetorical form of address to the prophet and in three lines through vv. 3b-4 speaks to the people directly instead of speaking about them, responding to the words reported in v. 3a. Verses 3b-4a open this response with two lines beginning with an aggressive 'Now' (*hinnēh*), and v. 4b draws a conclusion from these confrontations. Then, for the succeeding three lines that comprise v. 5, Yhwh reverts to second singular, which suggests a return to addressing the prophet, effectively taking up again the process whereby the people overhear what Yhwh says to the prophet. Its three rhetorical questions, all beginning *hă*, close off vv. 1-5.

[80] Cf. H. D. Preuss, *TWAT*, VI, p. 962 (ET *TDOT*, XII, p. 300), following Hans-Jürgen Hermisson, *Sprache und Ritus im alttestamentlichen Kult* (Neukirchen: Neukirchener, 1965), pp. 76-84.

[81] Volz (*Jesaja II*, p. 224) thinks rather of the synagogue; Julius Morgenstern saw it as a synagogue address on the Day of Atonement ('Two Prophecies from the Fourth Century B.C. and the Evolution of Yom Kippur', *HUCA* 24 [1952–53], pp. 1-74 [22]).

[82] Mitchell Dahood ('Hebrew–Ugaritic Lexicography vii', *Biblica* 50 [1969], pp. 337-56 [340-41]) suggests that the pl. is actually an unusual sg. form.

Through vv. 6-14 Yhwh goes on to address the people, alternating between challenges about the kind of action Yhwh looks for that contrasts with what vv. 1-5 have described (vv. 6-7, 9b-10a, 13) and promises about the consequences that will follow if they take this action (vv. 8-9a, 10b-12, 14).[83] There is no need to assume that originally vv. 6-7 must have had the same 'if'-form as vv. 9b-10a and 13.[84] In the opening challenge, Yhwh continues to use a plural form of address (v. 6) but then moves to the singular form. Such address to 'my people' in the second person singular compares with 3.12; 10.24; 26.20; whereas the plural address compares with 6.9; 51.4, 7. While the singular could have been used to make clear that Yhwh's expectation makes demands of each individual, when we get to '[people] from [among] you' in v. 12 the singular must be referring to the people as a whole (that is, to 'my people', 'the household of Jacob', the entity the prophet is commissioned to address in v. 1). It is then more likely that this is so through vv. 7-14, in a way that is more natural in Hebrew than in English, where our not distinguishing between second-person singular and plural makes us less familiar with thinking of a corporate entity in the singular, and where clauses beginning 'the people is…' seem wrong. Related to the changing way in which people are addressed is the way the passage moves between Yhwh being the speaker and Yhwh being spoken of in the third person, sometimes within a verse and thus with harshness to our ears: see vv. 5, 13, and especially v. 14, where variation among manuscripts and the Versions shows that it is not only modern Western ears that sense this harshness.

Whereas 58.1-14 begins by talking about the community and then makes a transition to direct address, 59.1-8 follows the opposite sequence, though Isaiah 58 uses the second-person singular, Isaiah 59 the plural (after v. 1, the lines come in pairs). Whereas vv. 1-3 address people in the second person, vv. 5-8 describe them in the third person; v. 4 is a transitional verse. Verses 5-8 might then be referring to a group of people rather than to the community as a whole, though there is no concrete pointer to that. The further difference that vv. 4-8 have parallels with Proverbs and Job has encouraged the view that vv. 4-8 or 5-8 are later expansions of vv. 1-3 or 1-4.[85] But the move between third-person description and second-person address already featured in Isaiah 58 without suggesting that the material was of separate origin.

The section as a whole works in poetic bicola with much use of parallelism, though it includes two prosaic occurrences of *ʾăšer* (58.2, 11). It makes use of rhetorical questions, on the people's part but then in response on Yhwh's (58.3, 5-6). A forceful feature of 59.1-8 is the

[83] In substance it might then be true that v. 9 sums up the dynamic of the passage (e.g. Gray, *Rhetoric and Social Justice in Isaiah*, pp. 72-74), but structurally or rhetorically its two halves do not belong together.

[84] Against Westermann, *Jesaja Kapitel 40–66*, p. 265 (ET p. 333).

[85] So, e.g., Duhm *Jesaia*, p. 401.

frequent placing of the subject or the object before the verb and the employing of various forms of the verb (qatals, yiqtols, infinitives) with essentially the same significance. It makes use of repetition: *mišpāṭ*, *ṣᵉdāqâ*, and *mišpᵉṭê ṣedeq* in 58.2, 8, then *šapaṭ* and *ṣedeq* in 59.4; 'delight' in 58.2a, 2b, 3, 13a, 13b; 'acknowledge' in 58.2, 3; 59.8a, 8b; 'fast' in 58.3a, 3b, 4a, 4b, 5a, 5b, 6; 'now' in 58.3, 4; 'will…not be' opening 58.6 and 7 and 'then' opening 58.8 and 9; the 'yoke' in 58.6a, 6b, 9; 'afflict' in 58.3 and 5 and 'afflicted' in 58.7 and 10; 'the fast I would choose' in 58.5, 6; 'faithless' (the noun used adjectivally, the antithesis of *ṣᵉdāqâ*) in 58.4, 6; *nepeš* in 58.3, 5, 10 (twice), 11; *šābet* and *šabbāt* in 58.12, 13a, 13b; 'revel' in 58.13, 14; 'break' in 59.5; *maʿăśeh* in 59.6; 'harm' in 59.6-7; 'plans' in 56.7; 'well-being' in 59.8. The repetition of *mišpāṭ*, *ṣᵉdāqâ*, and *mišpᵉṭê ṣedeq* makes a point about the necessary link between the people's actions, their prayers, and Yhwh's actions. The repetition of 'delight' makes a related point about right and wrong delight. The repetition of 'acknowledge' makes another related point about (alleged) acknowledgment of Yhwh and Yhwh's acknowledgment of people. The repetition of 'fast' underlines the fact that this is the chapter's theme and helps to make a contrast between fasting as the people see it ('we fast', 'your fast', 'you fast') and 'the fast that I would choose'. It is one of a number of instances of Yhwh's taking up the people's words and giving them a new twist. The repetition of 'yoke' suggests a paronomasia involving the very similar word for 'injustice' (see comment). Taking up the references to self-affliction by using the adjective 'afflicted' and then the participle 'afflicted' underlines the disjunction in people's behaviour. 'Loosing faithless chains' contrasts with 'hitting with faithless fist'. The focus on one's own *nepeš* (58.3, 5) contrasts with giving one's *nepeš* and being concerned for the *nepeš* of the other (58.10), though that will find its reward (58.10). The repetitions at the beginning of lines in 58.5, 6-7, and 8-9 serve to bind and reinforce the sequences of parallel clauses they introduce. The collocation of *šābet* and *šabbāt* suggests the link between making it possible for people to live in the city and observing the Sabbath. The repetition of 'revel' underlines the link between keeping Sabbath and enjoying Yhwh's blessing. The use of *bāqaʿ* (break) in the qal and then the niphal underlines the irony of what the verbs refer to. The repetition of *maʿăśeh* perhaps suggests another irony (see the comment). The repetition of 'well-being' in the abb'a' arrangement of 59.8 brings the subsection to a close and makes a parallel with 57.19-21.

Isaiah 58 does not correspond to any of the regular forms of prophetic speech.[86] There are various views of its redactional history. Kosmala sees vv. 3-11a as the main poem, with vv. 1-2 a separate poem that has been

[86] K. Arvid Tångberg (*Die prophetische Mahnrede: Form- und traditionsgeschichtliche Studien zum prophetischen Umkehrruf* [Göttingen: Vandenhoeck & Ruprecht, 1987], pp. 125-27) sees it as an example of a warning speech or call to conversion.

turned into an introduction to it, v. 11b and v. 12 as supplements, and vv. 13-14 as a later addition.[87] Diethelm Michel sees vv. 1-3a, 5-9a as the passage's original core; vv. 9b-12, and 3b-4, 13-14 are a series of additions.[88] Koenen sees vv. 3-12 as the passage's original core; vv. 1-2 and 13-14 are later additions.[89] Sekine sees vv. 3-14 as the passage's original form; vv. 1-2 are redactional additions.[90] Theodor Lescow sees vv. 1-8 as an example of a three-stage prophetic instruction; vv. 9-12 (and vv. 13-14) are therefore later additions.[91] Klaus Seybold takes a series of alliterations and repetitions (*q/k*, *hēn*, *hă*, *hălô*ʾ, ʾ*āz*) as one key to identifying the chapter's original form.[92] I have treated it as a single composition, which indeed utilizes a variety of traditional forms. I do not see reason to believe that the individual elements had any earlier independent existence, though it may be that vv. 13-14 are an addition designed to follow vv. 1-12. Yet the conviction that vv. 13-14 is secondary[93] depends in part on the assumption that a prophet who attacked fasting and advocated concern for the needy in the manner of vv. 1-12 would hardly then be concerned for a practice such as Sabbath observance.[94] This may be reading modern convictions into the text.

Comment: 58.1-14

58.1 Call with full throat, do not hold back,// like the horn lift up your voice.
Tell my people about their rebellion,// the household of Jacob about their offences.

Tg begins 'Prophet!' (repeated in v. 3b), correctly identifying the addressee of the commands that open the chapter. Indeed, one might see this summons as continuing the 'my God has said' in 57.21.[95] But it may relate to what precedes in a way that contrasts with that declaration. We have noted that the closing comment at 48.21 and at 57.21 divides Isaiah 40–66 into three very roughly equal parts. It is then also the case that Isaiah 40 itself begins with a summons to proclaim, that Isaiah 49 begins with a testimony regarding a prophet's mouth, and now Isaiah 58 begins with a summons to proclaim. Thus each of these major parts of Isaiah 40–66 begins with some allusion to Yhwh's commission to speak.

[87] 'Form and Structure of Isaiah 58' (see above).

[88] 'Zur Eigenart Tritojesajas', pp. 193-96.

[89] *Ethik und Eschatologie im Tritojesajabuch*, p. 103.

[90] *Die Tritojesanische Sammlung*, pp. 121-31.

[91] 'Die dreistufige Tora', *ZAW* 82 (1970), pp. 362-79 (369-70); cf. the introduction to 56.1-8 above.

[92] 'Jes 58,1-12', in *'Sieben Augen auf einem Stein' (Sach 3,9): Studien zur Literatur des Zweiten Tempels* (I. Willi-Plein Festschrift; Neukirchen: Neukirchener 2007), pp. 345-58.

[93] So Koppe, *D. Robert Lowth's Jesaias*, IV, p. 104-5.

[94] Cf. Beuken, *Jesaja IIIA*, p. 122.

[95] Cf. Steck, 'Der sich selbst aktualisierende "Jesaja"', p. 217.

The initial and final expressions in the line, 'call' and 'lift up your voice', would themselves suggest commissioning the proclamation of a prophet and would point to a setting such as that of the temple courts. Whether or not the temple has been restored and whether or not the prophecy is delivered on a set fasting occasion there, it would be the community's natural meeting point and a prophet's natural preaching location, in the way described in Jeremiah.

The intervening expressions, 'with [full] throat, do not hold back, like the horn' are more novel, so that the relationship between the familiar and the innovative in the two cola is itself distinctive. In substance, the expressions together indicate that there is need for the prophet's proclamation to be unrestrained and loud. The reason may be that its substance is very important and/or that the audience will not be inclined to take any notice and/or that other, rival proclamations will compete for attention.

Following on 57.14-21 with its recollecting of 40.1-11, an exhortation to 'call' and to 'lift up your voice' might seem to point to good news (cf. 40.2, 6, 9, the only other verse where the precise bidding 'lift up your voice' comes; also Zech 1.14, 17). But other precedents for the commission to 'call' are less happy (e.g. Jer 4.5; 11.6; cf. also Jonah 1.2; 3.2). The less familiar expressions also point in the unhappier direction. Perhaps Yhwh assumes that the prophet could be tempted to give up this proclamation, and issues a bidding not to do so; that possibility suggests bad news rather than good news, but it may also indicate that the prophet is not to give up hope of people's heeding the warnings.[96] And the horn (not a metal musical instrument like a trumpet, *ḥăṣōṣᵉrâ*, but a literal animal horn, *šôpār*), whether literal or figurative, is commonly a means of announcing something threatening and dangerous, which it is urgent that people heed (e.g. Jer 4.5 again; also Ezek 33.1-9;[97] Hos 8.1;[98] Zeph 1.16). But if rhetorically the point about the commands in v. 1a is to make a point to the indirect addressees, the people themselves, then its function is to underline how seriously they must take what follows.

'Tell my people' again leaves open the question whether the prophet is to bring good news or bad. The verb had positive implications in 48.20, though sardonic ones just now in 57.12 (and in Jer 4.5 once more). The appellative 'my people' is in theory a term of endearment (again, see 40.1, taken up in 57.14; also 63.8; 65.19, 22), but it can have its significance turned upside down. The fact that this is 'my people' can heighten the scandal of its wrongdoing. It is where Isaiah began (1.2-4), where Yhwh spoke about 'my people' having 'rebelled against me' and about its being characterized by 'offences', and it is now 'rebellion' that Yhwh speaks of here (cf. 57.4), then of 'offences'. The wording is even closer

[96] Cf. Saadia, 'Version d'Isaïe de R. Saadia', p. 55.

[97] On which Odeberg (*Trito-Isaiah*, pp. 120-21) sees this passage as dependent.

[98] Paul (ישעיה פרקים מ-סו, II, p. 439 (ET p. 482) sees possible influence from Hos 8.1-2 on vv. 1-2.

to Micah 3.8, 'to tell Jacob about its rebellion, Israel about its offences'.[99] 'Household of Jacob' is another term of endearment and reassurance that can also become the basis for a confrontation (e.g. 46.3; 48.1; the expression follows on in Mic 3.9). In the abcb′c′ parallelism in this line, the verb applies to both cola, 'to the household of Jacob' corresponds to 'to my people', and '[about] their offences' (plural) corresponds to '[about] their rebellion' (singular). 'Offences' was another expression in 40.1-2, but the presupposition of 58.1 is that the problem of the people's offences has been solved neither by its having paid the penalty for them (because since then, it has committed some more) nor by Yhwh's having forgiven them (44.22, the previous occurrence of the word in this book), as 59.2, 12 will confirm. I translate *ḥaṭṭ'â*, traditionally rendered 'sin', by the word 'offence'; etymology and occasionally usage suggests it denotes a falling short of Yhwh's expectations, a failure to reach them or even to aim at them. It implies 'the religious disqualification of specific modes of human behavior'.[100] But one offends against a person; the result is to injure a relationship.[101] In contrast *peša'* (traditionally 'transgression') denotes deliberate rebellion, the conscious flouting of someone's authority, though with far-reaching implications: 'whoever commits *peša'* does not merely rebel or protest against Yahweh but breaks with him, takes away what is his, robs, embezzles, misappropriates it.'[102] Both verbs thus designate wrongdoing that impacts a relationship.

So the prophet begins by establishing the continuity of what will follow with Yhwh's words to the community in earlier centuries and establishing the impossibility of its avoiding the declaration that it has to face the same confrontation as its ancestors before the exile. The prophecy has all the 'edge' of the old prophetic utterances.[103]

58.2 And day by day they have recourse to me,// they delight in acknowledging my ways,
Like a nation that has done what is faithful// and has not abandoned its God's exercise of judgment.
They ask me for faithful acts of judgment,// they delight in drawing near God.

In the parallelism of the line, in substance 'they delight' corresponds to 'day by day': they come before Yhwh day by day because they delight to do so. And in substance, 'in acknowledging my ways' corresponds

[99] Cf. Park, *Die Gerechtigkeit Israels und das Heil der Völker*, pp. 217-18.
[100] K. Koch, *TWAT*, II, p. 858 (ET *TDOT*, IV, p. 309).
[101] R. Knierim, *THAT*, I, p. 545 (ET *TLOT*, I, p. 409).
[102] R. Knierim, *THAT*, II, p. 493 (ET *TLOT*, II, p. 1036); cf. H. Seebass, *TWAT*, VI, p. 803 (ET *TDOT*, XII, pp. 144-45).
[103] Westermann, *Jesaja Kapitel 40–66*, p. 267 (ET p. 335) (his comment on vv. 3b-4). Tertullian interprets Jesus' ministry in light of it (*Adversus Judaeos* 9.29-30).

to 'they have recourse to me'. Tg plausibly paraphrases *dāraš* ('have recourse') to mean 'they seek teaching',[104] though beyond that it may suggest seeking Yhwh's help and intervention, as in 55.6; 65.10. The more literal translation 'seek me' has misleading connotations in English; they are not seeking a sense of being in God's presence. The elders seeking a word from Yhwh via Ezekiel (Ezek 20.1; cf. 33.20)[105] points to the link between seeking a message and seeking help: people seek a word that declares that Yhwh intends to act.[106] In turn, acknowledging Yhwh's ways could imply recognizing the ways Yhwh expects of them or recognizing the ways Yhwh has acted on the people's behalf in the past (on either understanding, in a context such as this, *yāda*ʿ means more than merely 'knowing')[107]. In the former case Yhwh speaks ironically both of their delighting and of their recognition, because they do not really enthuse over Yhwh's expectations nor acknowledge them by the way they live. This understanding would correspond to the significance of 'your ways' when the word recurs towards the close of the chapter, in v. 13 (cf. 66.3). On the other hand, the latter understanding makes for a further link with 55.6-9, with its references to 'my ways' and 'your ways', Yhwh's ways of acting (through Cyrus) and the people's ways of acting in the sense of the way they would go about restoring Jerusalem (which would be very different from Yhwh's way). The people Yhwh is talking about are people who have responded to the invitation in 55.6-9 and have come to look at Yhwh's acts in Yhwh's way. The kind of prayers they are praying would be illustrated by 63.7–64.11 [12] and also by Ezra 9 and Nehemiah 9.

On either understanding of the first line, the second line indirectly indicates why there is a problem about this having recourse and delighting. It requires that *mišpāṭ ûṣᵉdāqâ* characterize the community's life. Their exercise of authority needs to be undertaken with faithfulness. But either people go through the motions of enthusing over Yhwh's expectations of them but actually do not implement them, or they look for Yhwh to behave toward them with *mišpāṭ ûṣᵉdāqâ* but do not embody these characteristics in their own life. 'Like a nation' applies to both cola; the move from 'people' and 'household' (v. 1) to 'nation' (*gôy*) perhaps underlines the slur in this line, though the second colon does refer to 'its God'. The negative 'has not abandoned' parallels the positive 'has done', and as commonly happens the compound expression *mišpāṭ ûṣᵉdāqâ* is divided between the cola.

[104] Cf. Odeberg, *Trito-Isaiah*, pp. 127-31; he stresses seeking a word from a prophet.

[105] Cf. Delitzsch, *Jesaia*, p. 588 (ET II, p. 385).

[106] Tiemeyer (*Priestly Rites and Prophetic Rage*, pp. 90-92) suggests that the people critiqued in v. 2 are the priests who should have been challenging the people (v. 1); but this requires considerable inference.

[107] Lambert questions whether 'acknowledge' is an appropriate translation of ידע but he does see the verb as suggesting 'responding intelligently (or appropriately) to some state-of-affairs' ('A Contextual Study of *yd*ʿ in the Book of Isaiah', p. 270).

The third line rephrases the first and second. Once again, in other contexts, the 'faithful acts of judgment' could be the decisions Yhwh makes about what constitute faithful acts on the people's part, so that the request concerns guidance concerning what is right, but the context rather suggests reference to faithful acts on Yhwh's part. 'They ask' corresponds to 'they have recourse to me' (compare the association of these two verbs in 65.1; also Jer 37.7, 17). The precise phrase 'faithful acts of judgment' (*mišpᵉṭê ṣedeq*) comes only here (Ps 119.7, 62, 106, 164 does speak of 'your faithful acts of judgment') but it corresponds to *ṣᵉdāqâ* and *mišpāṭ*. 'Delight in' exactly repeats the earlier verb. Further, *mišpāṭ ûṣᵉdāqâ* along with the question of what one delights in were concerns in 56.1-8, which this chapter is now taking up, with some irony. There, eunuchs were choosing what Yhwh delights in; here, Israelites are involved in some delighting that contrasts with Yhwh's commitment to and expectation of *mišpāṭ ûṣᵉdāqâ*. 'Drawing near God' constitutes another reexpression of what is involved in having recourse to God. It, too, suggests coming to the temple to discover what God expects or to seek for God to act (see Ps 73.28, the only other occurrence of the actual noun). One might alternatively see the construct as a subjective genitive, 'God's drawing near', which would then directly denote God's coming to act (cf. the related verb *qārēb* in Ps 69.19 [18]; Lam 3.57; also Mal 3.5, in a threatening sense).[108] In Isaiah 46.13, Yhwh causes his *ṣᵉdāqâ* to draw near; the implication would be similar. The last clause is inverted so that the line works abb′a′ and thus suggests the close of a subsection, and this effect is heightened by the lengthened form of the verb.[109]

Verse 2 has set up a disjunction with v. 1. The people are rebels, given that they are consistently seeking instruction and help from Yhwh. How can this be?

58.3 'Why have we fasted and you have not looked,// afflicted ourselves and you do not acknowledge it?'
Now: in your fast day you find your delight,// but all the people who toil for you—you oppress.

Tg, LXX preface the verse with 'They say', correctly indicating that the prophecy makes a transition from being implicitly words of Yhwh concerning the community but addressed to a prophet, to being implicitly words of the community addressed to Yhwh. They do not constitute a response to Yhwh's words but rather an account what people were saying when they approached Yhwh in the way described in v. 2 or what they were saying in light of the fact that approaching Yhwh got them

[108] See Theodoret of Cyrrhus, *Commentaire sur Isaïe* 173a (3.212-13), with his comments on Sym and Aq.

[109] See the translation note.

nowhere. The line resolves the ambiguity about v. 2. They approached Yhwh seeking for Yhwh to act with *mišpāṭ ûṣᵉdāqâ* but Yhwh did not do so. The 'Why' applies to both cola, each time strictly qualifying only the second of the pair of verbs. The question is, 'When we fasted, why have you not looked? When we afflicted ourselves, why have you not acknowledged it?' Tg omits the negatives, in the conviction that of course God must see and know, but once more the point is that *yādaʿ* has the connotation of 'recognize' or 'acknowledge'. While the questions look for a response, they compare with the 'Why' of a protest psalm such as Psalm 44.24-25 [23-24]; the people are not exactly looking for information in the form of an explanation but looking for a change in Yhwh's stance. They also imply that Yhwh's failure to look or acknowledge will soon raise the question 'Why do we bother? Why have we fasted or afflicted ourselves, if we get no response?' There is some irony about the people asking pointedly why Yhwh has not looked or acknowledged, given that this is elsewhere Yhwh's accusation concerning them.

In the parallelism of the two cola, 'afflicted ourselves' balances 'fasted' (the first consonant in 'fast' is strengthened for emphasis), 'and not' is simply repeated, and finally the yiqtol 'acknowledge [it]' balances the qatal 'have looked'. There is some controversy about whether 'afflict oneself' (*ʿānâ* piel followed by *nepeš*) intrinsically denotes fasting[110] but here the parallelism makes explicit that this is its implication. This self-affliction involves the *nepeš*, the person as a whole. It obviously affects the body; it also affects the 'soul', the word that traditionally translates *nepeš*. Isaiah 58 is part of the haftarah for Yom Kippur (the haftarah begins at 57.14) but the chapter itself is not specific enough to imply that the fasting to which it refers is that associated with this occasion in particular.[111] Nor is it the kind of fasting whereby a person might seek to develop self-discipline or the kind that gives bodily expression to one's repentance, but the kind that takes place in a time of need or crisis and accompanies prayer for God to respond and deliver. Zechariah 7–8 refers to a sequence of such fasts related to the destruction of Jerusalem, and it may be these fasts that the prophecy refers to; the stance those chapters take in relation to fasts overlaps with the one this prophecy will take, but the fasting Zechariah refers to would be likely to imply the contrition expressed in Lamentations (and Isa 63.7–64.11 [12], Ezra 9, and Neh 9, noted above), which v. 2 does not imply here. Further, the question the people are asking is different from the one addressed to priests and prophets in Zechariah 7.3. On the surface, at least, that is a serious and open question looking for a straightforward answer. This is a more rhetorical one, the kind of question people ask in a psalm. It presupposes that there is no reasonable explanation for Yhwh's failure to take notice.

110 See Jacob Milgrom, *Leviticus 1–16* (New York: Doubleday, 1991), p. 1054.

111 Against Morgenstern, 'Two Prophecies of the Fourth Century B.C.'; Paul, ישעיה פרקים מ-סו, II, p. 438 (ET pp. 480-81).

It does look for a response, yet not in the form of an explanation but in the form of a promise to take action.[112]

Yhwh's actual response in effect presupposes a questioning of their assumption that Yhwh neither looked nor knew. Actually Yhwh had looked carefully and knew very well. Once again Tg helps the audience along by beginning the second line, 'Prophet, say to them'. What is Yhwh's accusation? If the critique concerned the Sabbath, saying that they were finding delight could imply that they are doing business instead of observing the day.[113] But the context does not suggest that their failure to observe the day lies here. Generally, there is nothing wrong with working on a fast day (the Day of Atonement is an exception, because of its particular solemnity and importance; see Lev 16.29 [P]). It is common for fasting to mean simply refraining from food, at least during the day (it may be fine to eat after dusk), but in other respects to let life go on. Further, the prophet's critique is not that religion is its own reward, that all worship must be offered for the sake of Yhwh alone, that people should be fasting for the sake of devotion not for what they got out of it. There is doubtless a truth in that declaration, but the Old Testament also recognizes that there is a place for pleading with God for things and backing up such pleas with a demonstration of seriousness such as fasting. The prophet does not seek to replace a 'non-manipulative' form of religion by one that is not seeking to get God to do what we want, but to show people what they need to do if they are to get God to do what they want.[114]

Rather the problem is what accompanies the fasting. People have the same positive attitude to fasting that they have to acknowledging Yhwh's ways and approaching God: the noun 'delight' takes up the related verb that recurs in v. 2. They are glad to commit themselves to the fasting that accompanies their prayer for Yhwh to act with *mišpāṭ ûṣᵉdāqâ*, as they are glad to commit themselves to worship. Their fasting is an indication of how serious they are, how they truly mean their prayers. The problem the prophecy raises is that they are also involved in oppressing their workers. If this is a critique of the community as a whole, then the victims of this treatment are the individuals that many families would have as servants, the people whom the Sabbath regulation (for instance) seeks to protect (Deut 5.14). Possibly the idea is that the rest of the family are indeed giving up work in order to fast but they are not letting their workers also do so. They might thus be requiring hard work of them when fasting makes them weak, or be involved in oppressive employment

[112] On the comparison of the two passages, see further Park, *Die Gerechtigkeit Israels und das Heil der Völker*, pp. 241-49.

[113] See 56.4-5 and the comments above. On the basis of an Akkadian analogy, Paul (ישעיה פרקים מ-סו, II, p. 440 [ET p. 484]) sees the unique expression 'find delight' as a technical term for doing business (cf. JPSV).

[114] Cf. Schramm, *The Opponents of Third Isaiah*, pp. 135-36; Michael L. Barré, 'Fasting in Israel', *BTB* 15 (1985), pp. 94-97; against Hanson, *The Dawn of Apocalyptic*, p. 110; Leslie J. Hoppe, 'Isaiah 58:1-12', *BTB* 13 (1983), pp. 44-47.

practices on the very day when they are also fasting, or be joining in a community fast one day and involved in these practices the day before and the day after. The point is underlined by a kind of tautology in the second colon. These workers are not merely employees or servants but 'toilers' (*ʿāṣab*), people whose work involves pain. So to say that their bosses are 'oppressing' them (the word used to describe the Israelites' oppressive bosses in Egypt in Exod 3.7; 5.6, 10, 13, 14) is to make the same point in a different way. The scandal of their action is expressed by the contrast between the two cola that ought to be parallel but stand in tension, particularly in the verbal expressions that close the two cola, 'you find [your] delight' and 'you oppress'. The prophecy makes no comment on the link or tension between fasting and oppressive behaviour. The prophet likely assumes that the problem is self-evident. But the earlier stress on *mišpāt ûṣᵉdāqâ* points towards the way one could explicate the issue. It is not possible to fast and pray for Yhwh to show *mišpāṭ ûṣᵉdāqâ* if one is not practising *mišpāṭ ûṣᵉdāqâ* oneself. There is an incoherence about people's religious life.[115] As a result, they *seek* Yhwh day by day and delight in acknowledging Yhwh (v. 2), but on the day of their fast they *find* only their own delight and no acknowledging of them by Yhwh (v. 3).[116] But to fast by attending to the needs of others involves faith in God alone not in goals you can attain.[117]

The prayer and the response, then, might suggest that 'the efforts of the reform coalition at a religious and cultic renewal of society were really bearing fruit and meeting with widespread consent. Nevertheless in the economic and social sphere society looked quite different.... A harsh, heedless business practice stood in blatant contradiction to the widely accepted desire for religious renewal.'[118] It will give sharpness to this point if *nāgaś* signifies more specifically 'the assertion of a right to seize property...by virtue of the personal liability of debtors'.[119]

58.4 Now: it is so as to engage in strife and contention that you fast,// and so as to hit with faithless fist.
You do not fast today// so as to make your voice heard on high.

LXX takes the opening *hēn* as the particle 'if' rather than a demonstrative, which gives a good sense to the verse: if that is the way you fast, your prayer does not reach God. But this usage of *hēn* is strictly an

[115] Cf. J. Severino Croatto, 'Del aňo jubilar levitico al *tiempo* de liberación profetico (Reflexiones exegéticas sobre Isaías 61 y 58, en relación con el Jubileo), *Revista de Interpretación Bíblica Latinoamericana* 33 (1999) (http://www.claiweb.org/ribla/ribla33/del%20ano%20jubilar%20levitico.html), §2.2.1.

[116] Koenen, *Ethik und Eschatologie im Tritojesajabuch*, pp. 94-95.

[117] Patricia K. Willey, 'Repairing the Breach', *Church and Society* 83/2 (1992), pp. 10-21 (21).

[118] Albertz, *Religionsgeschichte Israels in alttestamentlicher Zeit*, II, p. 537 (ET p. 494).

[119] E. Lipiński, *TWAT*, V, p. 231 (ET *TDOT*, IX, p. 214).

Aramaism and a late usage (1QIs[a] disambiguates the expression by reading *hnh* [*hinnēh*]). More likely this *hēn* forms a pair with the one that opened v. 3b, as happens in 40.15; 50.9; 54.15-16; 55.4-5.[120] Verse 4a therefore takes further the charge in v. 3bβ. In itself, it comprises parallel cola, with 'Now…you fast' applying to both halves and with *l*[e] expressions occupying the rest of the first colon and the whole of the second. People's fasting takes place alongside strife, contention, and violence; the violence issues from the strife and contention. It is almost as if they are involved in fasting in order to engage in such activities (*l*[e]). The point is hardly a psychological one, that hunger makes them grumpy. Strife (*rîb*) and contention (*maṣṣâ*) can refer to physical violence of the kind v. 3b presupposes, but 'strife' in particular usually refers to arguments, and specifically to legal battles. More likely, then, v. 4a adds a further, distinct charge to the one in v. 3b. As well as ill-treating their workers, people are involved in legal procedures that enable them to punish people physically (for instance, for alleged wrongdoing or for debt) in the way Ahaz did Naboth, perhaps in order to be able to dispossess people of their land by force.[121] They thus again behave with *reša*ʿ (faithlessness), the opposite of the *ṣ*[e]*dāqâ* that the prophet has been emphasizing, and thereby risk becoming subject to the threats in 57.20-21. The lack of fit in their action is underlined by the paronomasia between 'contention' and 'fast' (*maṣṣâ* and *ṣôm*).[122] The two words look or sound related and they come together in people's lives, but they really should be antithetical.

The second line forms the negative equivalent to v. 4a; it is not internally parallel (the second colon simply completes the first) but it is parallel to that preceding line. The aim of their fasting was indeed to make their voice heard on high. It was to commend themselves to Yhwh as people seriously seeking to get Yhwh to hear their prayer for *mišpāṭ ûṣ*[e]*dāqâ*. But they are not fasting in such a way as to achieve this end.

58.5 Will this be the kind of fast that I would choose,// a day for someone to afflict himself?
Will it be for bowing his head like a bulrush// and spreading sackcloth and ash?
Will this be what you would call a fast,// a day acceptable to Yhwh?

In case the point is not clear, Yhwh explicates the nature of the fast that people are indulging in, which is not the kind that helps make their voice heard on high. MT's verse division appositely holds together the three lines with their parallel openings and thus makes the first and last cola

[120] See Goldingay and Payne, *Isaiah 40–55*, II, p. 358-59. Torrey (*Second Isaiah*, p. 438) takes both instances of *hēn* to mean 'if'.

[121] See Albertz, *Religionsgeschichte Israels in alttestamentlicher Zeit*, II, p. 540 (ET p. 496).

[122] Cf. Duhm, *Jesaia*, p. 397.

form a bracket around the whole in spelling out the point. The verse concerns the kind of fast that Yhwh does not 'choose'. The verb is a unique one in this connection. The Old Testament speaks of Yhwh choosing Zion and choosing a place for worship (and of course of choosing Israel and choosing David), but not elsewhere of choosing observances or rites. Indeed, it often critiques Israel for choices it makes in this connection (e.g. 1.29; 40.20; 41.24; and especially 65.12; 66.3-4). So here there is an irony. Their fasts are as bad as the abominable rites that they sometimes choose, and there is no way Yhwh would choose them in the way the Israelites do. In other words (the closing colon declares), the kind of fast they choose is not one that would ever be acceptable to Yhwh. Both the verb 'choose' and the question of what is 'acceptable' make further links with 56.1-8, which speaks of eunuchs 'choosing' what Yhwh 'delights in' and of foreigners' sacrifices being 'acceptable' on Yhwh's altar. So this term doubles up the prophecy's irony. Over against the prospect of foreigners' observances finding acceptance (cf. also 60.7) is the prospect of Israelites' observances finding none (cf. Jer 6.20). The prophecy's reference to a day acceptable to Yhwh comes suggestively sandwiched between Yhwh's allusion to 'a time acceptable to me' (49.8) and the subsequent allusion to 'a year acceptable to Yhwh' (61.2). Two implications might be drawn from this collocation of phrases. One is that the people's unintended designation of a fast Yhwh would not choose and a day Yhwh would not accept is not the first or last word on the subject. The phrase 'a day acceptable to Yhwh' resembles expressions for the day when Yhwh acts to deliver the people (49.8; 61.2).[123] The other is that the day acceptable to Yhwh becomes a promise they have some responsibility to implement. The prophecy has 'actualized' the promise in Isaiah 40–55 in such a way as to give it a significance in terms of social ethics.[124]

The description of the fast that Yhwh would not choose, the day that does not win Yhwh's acceptance, comes between these framing cola. The first description (v. 5aβ) restates the people's own words in v. 3aβ. The second and third descriptions (v. 3bαβ) amplify what is involved in such observances. One prostrates oneself like a reed that has been broken and bent over, and one lays down sacking covered with ash and lies prostrate on that. Is this the right way to define a fast? At one level the answer is, 'Yes, Yhwh does choose such acts' (e.g. 20.2; 22.12; 37.1-2). Ahab undertakes them and Yhwh accepts them as a self-lowering that warrants the suspension of his punishment for having Naboth killed (1 Kgs 21.27-29; cf. Neh 9.1; Est 4.1-3). Jesus expects that people will fast, and Acts refers to fasting in the early church. Perhaps, then, this prophet does not question the practice of people afflicting themselves in such ways and of

[123] It is partly on the basis of it that Lau calls Isa 58 'an eschatological text' (*Schriftgelehrte Prophetie in Jes 56–66*, p. 240), though by this I think he means it concerns the consummation of Yhwh's ultimate purpose.

[124] Lau, *Schriftgelehrte Prophetie in Jes 56–66*, p. 260.

individuals committing themselves to such observances (each person is afflicting his or her *nepeš*). The problem is that self-affliction becomes empty ritual when fasting is accompanied by the action described in vv. 3b-4 (the problem is not that people are afflicting their body and not their heart or spirit). Yet the sharp antithesis indicated by the questions that follow in vv. 6-7 implies that the prophet is not concerned to make a balanced and nuanced theoretical statement about when fasting is acceptable and when it is not. Whatever might in theory be said in other contexts, this prophet is simply dismissing fasting in favour of the actions that will be described in the following verses.

It is surprising to discover that the verb 'you would call' is singular. The implication is that Yhwh's rhetorical questions through v. 5 have been directly addressing the prophet, like v. 1. They are thus closing off vv. 1-5. Of course the community remains the audience that is indirectly addressed; it is intended to overhear the questions and it is compelled to provide them with an answer, so that the plural verb *tqr'w* in 4QIs[d] is not inappropriate.

58.6 Will not this be the fast that I would choose:// loosing faithless chains,// untying the cords of the yoke,
Sending off the broken, free,// and that you would smash every yoke?
7 Will it not be dividing your food with the hungry person,// and that you will take the afflicted, downtrodden, to your house;
When you see someone naked, cover him,// and not hide from your own flesh and blood?

Reversing the movement in the preceding verse, v. 6 eventually reveals that Yhwh is now addressing the community, as the final colon moves from infinitives to a finite verb whose subject is plural. It is a common idiom to transition from infinitives to finite verbs in this way, but rhetorically the change functions to signal the change of addressee. In a converse move to that in 4QIs[d] at the end of v. 5, LXX and Vg have a singular verb here. But the transition to plural links to a transition to a series of new parallel subsections that describe positively what Yhwh does look for from the community, and what fruits (what acts of *mišpāṭ ûṣᵉdāqâ*, we could say) will follow.

In MT, the transition to a new subsection is marked by a tricolon comprising v. 6a. LXX adds after the first colon λέγει κύριος, which could represent a phrase such as *nᵉ'um yhwh*, and could turn v. 6a into two regular bicola instead of a tricolon. That, too, would point to something of a new beginning at v. 6. In speaking of the fast that Yhwh would in fact choose (taking up the phrase from v. 5a), Yhwh either redefines fasting so that it becomes a metaphor, or implies that acceptable fasting needs to be accompanied by other actions that are the opposite of the actions described in vv. 3b-4.

The subsequent four cola in v. 6aβγb constitute four descriptions of one kind of action; the second pair of descriptions (v. 6b) parallel the first pair (v. 6aβγ) and take their point further. The most literal description in the third of these four cola (v. 6bα) refers to freeing people who are broken. To break people need not be wrong; Yhwh does it in judgment (Hos 5.11; cf. Ps 74.14). But the verb usually denotes driving people down into the ground one way or another when there is no basis for doing so. The reference to letting the broken go 'free' suggests that the breaking involves something like enforced servitude of the kind Nehemiah 5 describes; indeed, the verses as a whole would make entire sense in the context of the situation described in Nehemiah 5.

'Free' usually refers to the liberty of a free citizen after servitude (nearly all the occurrences come in Exod 21 in the Covenant Code; Deut 15; and Jer 34). This will fit with the reference in the first of the four cola (v. 6aβ) to 'loosing faithless chains'. The chains will be metaphorical; we have no reason to think that Israelite servants worked in chain gangs. But though they are metaphorical, they are absolutely real. And they are faithless. They ignore the obligation of faithfulness that members of the community owe one another (cf. v. 4), and they do so to their peril (57.20-21). Fasting requires the loosing of such metaphorical chains so that their prisoners can go free. This notion of freeing prisoners will be taken further in 61.1-3, though in that testimony the imagery relates to the bondage of the community as a whole, as it does in Isaiah 40–55. In those chapters it was the vocation of the one addressed in 42.6-7, which in that context was Israel as God's servant, but it is then a role Yhwh has to see fulfilled for Israel itself. And Yhwh has done so. But what is Israel doing? Instead of modelling or facilitating it in relation to other peoples, it is failing even to embody it in its own life (which would perhaps be the way it brought freedom to other peoples). The prophet implies that people fail to recognize how their behaviour contrasts with the way Yhwh had treated the community in releasing it from bondage to Babylon. There needs to be a connection between such acts of deliverance by God and the lives of the beneficiaries of God's acts.[125] The prophecy's logic is similar to that in the Torah's exhortations to treat people who become impoverished and become servants in a way that that reflects an awareness of how Yhwh delivered Israel from servitude in Egypt.[126] 'As people who had an experience and a memory of "the yoke" of exile themselves and who, further, had felt that yoke broken by God in their release from captivity, they should have been the people committed to maintaining and extending the freedom of others, especially the freedom of their neighbors.'[127]

[125] Cf. Kessler, *Gott geht es um das Ganze*, p. 41.

[126] Cf. Westermann, *Jesaja Kapitel 40–66*, p. 268 (ET p. 337).

[127] Gray, *Rhetoric and Social Justice in Isaiah*, p. 77.

Interpreting the other two cola, vv. 6aγ and 6bβ, is slightly more complex. In MT these are further parallel metaphorical descriptions of the freeing of servants. A yoke is a bar of wood that rests on an animal's neck and is fastened to the bar of the plough itself with ropes that also go under the animal's neck. The servants are like animals so bound by ropes and a yoke; freeing them means untying the cords. But 'untie' may be an under-translation of *natar* (hiphil); 'tear off' might be justified.[128] Either way, freeing the bound means (more radically) smashing the yoke the cords bind. But for the 'yoke' (*môṭâ*) Tg implies *muṭṭeh*, 'injustice' in the sense of illicit legal decisions; so also Syr in v. 6a, though in v. 6b it has 'bond'. 1QIs[b] has *mṭh* each time, but 1QIs[a] has *mṭh* then *mwṭh*. In v. 6a LXX has 'forced agreements', Vg 'oppressive ties; in v. 6b LXX has 'unjust contract', Vg 'burden' (see further v. 9b). Reference to perversion of justice would fit v. 4a; reference to a yoke would fit the allusion in this verse to chains and cords. In terms of the verse as a whole, it makes little difference which way we point the noun. Perhaps the prophet wanted people to think of both words, or perhaps wanted us to read one word in the first line and the other word in the second, or perhaps to read *môṭâ* both times in v. 6 but *muṭṭeh* in v. 9.

In v. 7 two further parallel lines then put the point in proactive terms. They revert to singular address but hardly refer to the prophet and while they might imply that the obligations they describe apply to each individual, in the context especially of v. 12 they more likely address the community as a whole as one unit (they also combine singular and plural in the references to the needy). Suppose I have no one in debt to me? Verse 7 gives an answer that indeed can apply to ordinary people and not just to leaders or wealthy landowners.[129] 'A crowd of socially disadvantaged people passes before the eyes of the audience: people deprived of their rights, broken, servants, prisoners, hungry, homeless, freezing.'[130] Instead of taking advantage of people who get into difficulties and turning them into servants who can never escape, fasting means or needs to be accompanied by action that helps them keep their freedom. Here there are three specific, complementary, but different actions. First, there is the sharing of food with the person who has not been able to grow enough or has had to pay too much in imperial taxes to be able to last the year out. The verb is suggestive (it occurs in this connection only here, and perhaps in Jer 16.7). It carries the connotations of 'breaking' bread. The action involves not merely sending one's surplus or a small portion to the needy, but dividing it with them. One does not even write a large cheque, but physically join with them.[131] And one serves them in sharing with them:

[128] See P. Maiberger's discussion in *TWAT*.

[129] Cf. Jerome, *Commentariorum in Isaiam prophetam libri duodeviginti*, col. 566.

[130] Volz, *Jesaja II*, 226; cf. Westermann, *Jesaja Kapitel 40–66*, p. 269 (ET p. 337).

[131] Cf Kwesi A. Dickson, 'He Is God Because He Cares', *International Review of Mission* 77 (1988), pp. 229-37 (233).

'Break your bread *for* the hungry'. This then links with the second colon. One does not send food to the needy but invites them into one's home to eat with the family. The asyndetic compound expression 'afflicted, downtrodden' is odd. The two words come together without asyndesis in Lamentations 1.7; 3.19 in referring to Jerusalem's 'days of affliction and downtrodden-ness' and to the lamenter's 'affliction and downtrodden-ness'. Perhaps 'afflicted' is a gloss from there to explain the very rare word translated 'downtrodden' (it is missing from Syr), but if so, it generates a suggestive link with the verb 'afflict' in vv. 3, 5. Unfortunately English translations' 'homeless' for 'downtrodden' (and LXX's vivid 'people without a roof') is only an inspired guess from the context and is unlikely to be the word's meaning.[132]

Taking in downtrodden people would also involve giving them something decent to wear (v. 7bα). In the Old Testament, 'nakedness is a sign of poverty, need, vulnerability, grief, captivity.'[133] It need not imply that they are wearing nothing at all, any more than is the case in 20.1-4. It does mean that they have only the tattiest clothes, of the kind that make it impossible to join without shame in the company of ordinary people. The final colon (v. 7bβ) backs up all three that precede it. Ignoring people's needs and downtrodden-ness involves hiding from them. How can you do so when they are (literally) 'your flesh'? LXX and Tg make explicit that the expression suggests not merely that they are human beings like you; there are no instances of 'your flesh' having this meaning. Rather it means they belong to your people (cf. Gen 2.24; also 37.27); compare the English phrase 'your own flesh and blood' (and Hebrew 'your bone and flesh', e.g., 2 Sam 5.1).[134] Deuteronomy 22.1-4 issues a series of similar exhortations using the same rare verb for 'hide' (*ʿālam* hitpael) grounded in Deuteronomy's typical but equivalent fashion in the fact that the other person is your brother. In turn, one can see the prophet's emphasis taken up in Jesus' expectations concerning the way disciples are to treat their brothers (Matt 25.31-46). The move to finite verbs after v. 7aα, while idiomatic, makes for a further link with the exhortatory form of Deuteronomy.[135] The correlation of feeding the hungry and clothing the naked also appears in Ezekiel 18.7, whose context has other links with that of this chapter (including a stress on *mišpāṭ ûṣᵉdāqâ*).

Jewish exposition extends the application of the colon to an obligation to care for a wife whom one has divorced; she is still one's flesh and blood.[136] Expressions from the two verses reappear in CD 13.10 and CD 7.1; 8.6. Phrases from v. 6 are similarly combined with lines from Isaiah

[132] See the translation note.

[133] H. Niehr, *TWAT*, VI, p. 380 (ET *TDOT*, XI, p. 354); he notes that it is also a sign of adultery, which is less significant in this context.

[134] Mitchell Dahood ('The Chiastic Breakup in Isaiah 58,7', *Biblica* 57 [1976], p. 108) rather pairs this 'flesh' (i.e., meat) with the bread in v. 7a.

[135] Westermann, *Jesaja Kapitel 40–66*, p. 269 (ET p. 337).

[136] E.g. Lev. R. 34.13.

61 in Luke 4.16-22, while v. 7 is the inspiration of Matthew 25.31-46, which makes the same appeal to family or quasi-family solidarity.[137] Rabbi Abin comments that bringing the poor into your own home is equivalent to offering first fruits in the temple (which was no longer possible)—he notes that the wording concerning the former is the same as that of the regulation concerning the latter, 'you bring into the house' (cf. Exod 23.19, where the reference is to Yhwh's house).[138]

58.8 Then your light will break out like the dawn,// your restoration flourish quickly.
Your faithfulness will go before you,// Yhwh's splendour will gather you.
9a Then you will call and Yhwh—he will respond;// when you cry for help, he will say 'Here I am!'

Three lines of promise describe what will follow a positive response to the implicit exhortation in vv. 6-7. It transpires that the link between the bidding to 'call' (v. 1) and that in Isaiah 40.1-11 is not merely ironic. The three lines utilize a nature metaphor, a military metaphor, and a relational metaphor, though all have a background in familiar ways of describing Yhwh's relationship with the people and Yhwh's manner of acting towards it. In general terms all three lines are thus parallel; they are also more closely internally parallel. The prophecy continues to speak in the second person singular, and this might invite individuals to see how each person can share in the promises' fulfilment, but the fact that more directly the second singular entity continues to be the community as a whole is suggested by the verses' imagery, which relates to the community's destiny. This is so for v. 8a (e.g. 45.8; 60.1-3; 62.1-2; Jer 30.17) and v. 9a (see 65.1-2, 24), and even more explicitly for v. 8b.

The nature metaphor is itself a double one.[139] After the 'then' applying to both cola, 'your restoration' parallels 'your light', 'quickly' parallels 'like the dawn', and 'will flourish' parallels 'will break out'. Light is a prominent image for blessing and new life replacing darkness, gloom, trouble, and death, not least in Isaiah (e.g. 9.1 [2]; 45.7; 59.9). Here the prophet appeals to the miraculous speedy way in which morning can dawn in the Middle East. In turn, 'restoration' (*ʾărukâ*) suggests the growth of new flesh in the healing of a wound (cf. Jer 8.22; 30.17), while 'flourish' (*ṣāmaḥ*) suggests plants shooting up to full height (cf. 42.9; 43.19; 44.4; 45.8; 55.10; 61.11). Both images point to something transcending what one usually sees. This will be no gradual healing and gradual growth but a miraculous transformation.

[137] Cf. Croatto, *Imaginar el futuro*, pp. 123-24.
[138] Jerusalem Talmud, Peah 5.5.
[139] See Daniel Grossberg, 'The Dual Glow/Grow Motif', *Biblica* 67 (1986), pp. 547-54, on this double motif here and elsewhere.

Verse 8b answers the question how this will come about. Whereas the nature metaphor implies that it issues from links built into the nature of created reality, the military metaphor complements it by invoking the direct personal activity of God. The line takes up the language of 52.12, though it tweaks it in several ways.[140] There the prophet promises that as people leave (presumably from Babylon), 'Yhwh is going before you, Israel's God is bringing up your rear'. An army or a people on the march expects to have its king at its head, knowing where he is going and able to take it there. It will also have people bringing up its rear, and the travellers at the back may be especially tired and/or vulnerable. Someone has to come at the back (cf. Num 10.25), and this allusion may have no special significance, and/or may be present only for the sake of parallelism. Here, first it is 'your faithfulness' that will go before you. The parallelism makes explicit that this expression denotes Yhwh's act of faithfulness or deliverance (*ṣedeq*) to the people, not its own faithfulness. The promise anticipates and is taken up in 62.1, which refers to Jerusalem's faithfulness or deliverance. To put it another way, it is Yhwh's splendour or glory or honour (cf. especially 40.5), manifest in the act of restoration, that goes before the people. While it may be that *ṣedeq* can elsewhere be distinguished from *ṣᵉdāqâ* as the less concrete term, it is thus doubtful whether this distinction can be observed in Isaiah 56—66, which may reflect the way in which the two words become more synonymous in later Old Testament times.[141] In this second colon, the parallel verb *ʾāsap* comes in the qal rather than the usual piel, which at least allows for the connotation 'gather' (see, e.g., 11.12) as well as that of 'travel behind'.

The relational metaphor (v. 9a) takes up the assumption about prayer that underlies the questions in v. 3 and confirms that assumption. The pairing of 'call' and 'respond' has a background in the Psalms (e.g. 4.2, 4 [1, 3]; 17.6; 22.3 [2]; 27.7; 91.15; 102.3; 118.5; 120.1). Such passages make clear that 'responding' or 'reacting' is not merely a matter of a verbal 'answer'. It implies action.[142] The pairing will recur in these chapters (65.12, 24; 66.4; cf. also the different formulation in 65.1). It expresses 'the profoundly dialogical nature of the relationship between God and human beings in the OT'.[143] Here, indeed, this metaphor is also reworked, and in an astonishing way. The metaphor presupposes the relationship of servant and master. A master calls, and his servant responds, saying 'Here I am!' Verse 1 had begun with this assumption, which implies it underlies at least the whole of vv. 1-5. But here the

[140] Cf. Zimmerli, 'Zur Sprache Tritojesajas', pp. 219-21; Klaus Koenen, 'Zur Aktualisierung eines Deuterojesajawortes in Jes 58,8', *BZ* 33 (1989), pp. 255-58.

[141] Cf. B. Johnson, *TWAT*, VI, p. 916 (ET *TDOT*, XII, p. 256).

[142] Cf. F. L. Hossfeld and E.-M. Kindl, *TWAT*, VII, p. 124 (ET *TDOT*, XIII, p. 115), referring to C. J. Labuschagne, *THAT*, II, pp. 337-38 (ET *TLOT*, II, pp. 928-29).

[143] F. J. Stendebach, *TWAT*, VI, p. 242 (ET *TDOT*, XI, p. 224).

relationship is reversed as the servant calls and the master responds, saying 'Here I am!' The promise repeats one in 52.6; Yhwh will recall relating to the people that way in 65.1. The Psalms also presuppose that when the servant is in need, the master has a commitment to the servant that is the obverse of the servant's commitment to the master, and that this also applies to the relationship of Yhwh and servant. Thus this call is not a summons to fulfil a duty but a cry of pain and a cry for help. It is the only occurrence in Isaiah of the verb *šāwa*ʿ with its neat similarity to the verb denoting the act the plea looks for, *yāšaʿ*.[144] The use of *ʿānâ* I ('respond') in the midst of occurrences of words from *ʿānâ* III (ill treat) suggests another paronomasia;[145] when the community experiences *ʿānâ* III, from Yhwh it then experiences *ʿānâ* I. The master promises to be available in such circumstances. Tg paraphrases 'he will say "Here I am!"' as 'he will do what you ask', and may seem to water down the promise (though it keeps the 'Here I am' at 65.1), but it does spell out its implications. In the parallelism, 'then' again applies to both cola. There are two second-person singular verbs of comparable meaning, with the second intensifying the first in meaning and in form (piel following qal). There are then two third-singular verbs of comparable meaning, though this time the second verb has less character than the first, slowing down the line before it comes to its climax with its last word, that extraordinary 'Here I am!' In terms of words that declaration parallels 'Yhwh' in the first colon, which underlines the declaration's extra-ordinary nature.

The Talmud comments that the person to whom this line applies is the one who loves his neighbour, shows friendship towards his relatives, marries his sister's daughter, and lends a sela to a person in need.[146]

58.9b If you do away with the yoke from your midst,// pointing the finger, speaking harmfulness,
10 And offer yourself to the hungry,// satisfy the needs of the afflicted person,
Your light will shine forth in the darkness, your gloom like midday.

MT's verse division suggests it takes v. 9b as dependent on what precedes, but it is difficult to construe the interrelationship of the clauses that follow on that basis. Rather, the 'if' clauses in vv. 9b-10a lead into the promises in vv. 10b-12. As in v. 6, for the 'yoke (*môṭâ*), Tg, Syr imply *muṭṭeh* 'injustice, perjury, fraud'. 1QIs[b] again has *mṭh*, but 1QIs[a] *mwṭh*; LXX, Vg have 'bond'. In the parallelism, the opening phrase 'if you do away with from your midst' applies to both cola, and the parallel

[144] Cf. Saadia's comment, 'Version d'Isaïe de R. Saadia', p. 57. Gray (*Rhetoric and Social Justice in Isaiah*, pp. 95-97) emphasizes the forcefulness of this verb.
[145] Berges, *Das Buch Jesaja*, p. 475.
[146] B. Sanhedrin 76b. A sela is a unit of money, perhaps half a shekel.

colon then comprises two further objects for the verb. Pointing the finger[147] and speaking harmfulness suggest false accusation and perjury, so that contextually 'injustice' fits best here of all three occurrences of *mṭh*.

As v. 9b thus reexpresses v. 6, v. 10 then reexpresses v. 7. LXX's 'give bread from your self/heart' (OL thus nicely has *ex animo*) works out the implications of its exhortation in light of v. 7; offering oneself will need to find expression in offering one's bread (cf. James 2.16). But the sequence whereby v. 10 follows v. 7 implies the correlative point, that offering food needs to be an expression of offering oneself. MT takes up the chapter's repeated occurrences of *nepeš* (vv. 3, 5, 11). Instead of afflicting themselves, they need to be giving themselves (Tg thus suggestively has 'your soul languishes', taking the verb as *pûq* I rather than *pûq* II). The second colon perhaps hints at the same point in again speaking not merely of giving some bread but of satisfying the person; *nepeš* comes in both cola. The two occurrences actually come next to each other at the centre of the line, which more literally reads 'and [if you] offer to the hungry yourself and [thus] the self of the afflicted you satisfy'. This links with the fact that 'satisfying' (*śāba*ʿ hiphil) implies satiating or filling. 'Afflicted' also takes up the earlier use of *ʿānâ* (vv. 3, 5) and of *ʿăniyyîm* (v. 7) and continues the exhortation regarding self-affliction and concern for the afflicted. Here the word represents a niphal participle (as in 53.7) rather than the usual adjective and suggests a person who was a regular member of the community but has now lost their position and has no social power as well as no food. Juxtaposing reference to affliction and reference to hunger supports the inference that afflicting oneself by making oneself hungry is useless without offering oneself to the hungry and afflicted.

As the if-clauses reexpress vv. 6-7, v. 10b reexpresses v. 8a. So 'your light' recurs, while 'will shine forth in the darkness' reformulates 'will break out like the dawn'; this reformulation happens again in 'your gloom like noonday'. Either the verb in the first colon applies also to the second, by metonymy (cf. LXX), or we should assume 'will be' (cf. OL, Vg, Tg).[148] Here the comparison is not merely between the dark of night and the sudden brightness of dawn, but the deep darkness of night and the dazzling brightness of noon. While there is a general similarity between the earlier promises in v. 8 and those to come in Isaiah 60, here the relationship is much closer. All the words in the first colon will recur in 60.1-3, while both words in the second colon will recur in Isaiah 59. Before we reach 60.1-3, then, this chapter has already made it impossible for us to read that chapter as if its promise presupposed no expectations

[147] See Charles Hauret, 'Note d'exégèse: Isaïe, lviii, 9', *Revue des sciences religieuses* 35 (1961), pp. 369-77.

[148] There is no need to add a verb to the second colon, with Thomas, 'ספר ישעיה', p. 92.

of the community. If Isaiah 60–62 is older than Isaiah 58, as is commonly thought, then Isaiah 58 'responds to' Isaiah 60;[149] but within the book of Isaiah, Isaiah 60 responds to Isaiah 58.

58.11 Yhwh will lead you continually// and satisfy your needs in scorched places.
He will equip your frame;// you will be like a watered garden,
Like a spring of water,// whose water does not deceive.
12 People from among you will build up lasting ruins;// you will raise up foundations from generations ago.
You will be called 'Repairer of breaches,// restorer of streets for living on'.

Whereas the challenges and the promises in vv. 6-9a divided syntactically, in vv. 9b-12 they are syntactically linked because the challenges comprise an extended if-clause; vv. 11-12 thus continue the extended main clauses begun in v. 10b. MT implies that v. 11 comprises two tricola; three bicola would be more usual. In the immediate context, the promise of leading might suggest accompanying and guiding on a journey, but the line takes up the metaphor from v. 8b, where the people is on a journey to its destiny; Yhwh promises to make sure it gets there without getting lost (cf. Exod 13.17, 21; 32.34). LXX ('be with you'), like Tg, assumes that the opening verb is *nāḥâ* 'lead, guide'. In contrast, Vg implies it is *nûaḥ* hiphil 'give rest' (cf. Exod 33.14; Deut 25.19; Josh 1.13), which would also fit in the context, but the actual verb form cannot be read as a hiphil and would have to be emended.[150] With the subject 'Yhwh' applying to both cola, the second parallels the first, using a different image but also one that fits with the notion of a journey if that journey passes through 'scorched places'. The journey to the land was one where Yhwh 'satisfied' the people's needs (Pss 81.17 [16]; 105.40; Exod 16.3, 8, 12, though mostly with irony). But more often the language of 'satisfying' or 'satiating' (it is a generous, extravagant word) applies to Yhwh's munificent provision in the land (e.g. Deut 6.11; 11.15; 26.12). That connotation would lead well into the lines that follow, which in turn points to another possible way of understanding the word translated 'scorched places'. It comes from the root *ṣḥḥ*, which can refer to the effect of the sun as dazzling bright (Cant 5.10) as well as scorching and parching (Isa 5.13), and Vg takes the noun here to mean 'splendours' (cf. Sym, Aq, Th, and the paraphrase in LXX and Syr).[151] That understanding would fit well with the references to bright light in v. 10. Either way, Yhwh's satisfying of needs (*nepeš* again) will correspond to the people's satisfying of the needs of the afflicted person (v. 10).

149 H. G. M. Williamson, 'Promises, Promises!', *WW* 19 (1999), pp. 153-60 (155).
150 Cf. Ehrlich, *Randglossen*, IV, p. 209.
151 Cf. Koenen, 'Textkritische Anmerkungen', pp. 564-65. Torrey (*Second Isaiah*, p. 439) links the word with an Arabic root *ṣaḥ* meaning 'good, sound, healthy'.

In the middle line, the first colon takes another expression from earlier in the book and doubly tweaks it. Isaiah 40.29-31 speaks of God giving the weak great 'strength' (*ʿoṣmâ*) so that they 'renew' their might (*ḥālap* hiphil). Here the prophet speaks of the people's 'frame', literally bones (*ʿăṣāmôt*), a common way to speak concretely of human strength (cf. 66.14), and of its being 'equipped' as if for war (*ḥālaṣ* hiphil, the only occurrence of the hiphil). 1QIs[a, b] have a plural verb, implying 'your bones will strengthen' (Tg refers the strengthening of the bones to eternal life). This promise will contrast with the way one's bones can shake (Jer 23.9), loosen (Ps 22.14 [13]), rot (Hab 3.16), or break (Isa 38.13; Lam 3.4). In turn, the parallel colon also recalls imagery from earlier in Isaiah (e.g. 43.20), but works with it in a different way, applying it to the people itself, not to the environment, in the manner of Jeremiah rather than Isaiah 40–55. The wording in fact almost exactly corresponds to a colon in Jeremiah 31.12, part of an extended promise of Yhwh's restoration of the people the other side of the exile and of Yhwh's bountiful provision. That passage also speaks of Yhwh 'satisfying' the people and of the *nepeš* of the priests being filled, so perhaps Jeremiah 31.7-14 is a broader inspiration for this prophecy.[152]

The third line elaborates the simile from the second. The 'spring of water' again takes us back to earlier promises in this book; 41.18 is the only other occurrence of this phrase in the Old Testament. In its imagery, its context elaborates on that promise. Here the prophet underlines it by the key undertaking that it will not fail and thus deceive. Israelites were used to springs and brooks that ran well in the winter but failed in the summer when they were most needed (cf. Jer 15.18). Yhwh's provision for the community will not be of this kind. Actually, a spring that fails in the summer could not really be accused of deceiving; the line may rather allude to a spring that fails before summer, when one would have a right to expect it to flow.

Verse 12 portrays the restoration in other, more literal terms. It makes more explicit that vv. 7-11 have been addressing the community. It is people 'from you' (masculine singular)[153] who will do the work, and the work they will do is the building up of the city. Jeremiah 25.9 warns that the land is to be turned into 'lasting ruins'; v. 12 reverses that warning. While in a superficial sense the words are more literal, they are hyperbolic and may not be designed to imply a literal 'myth of the empty land':[154] 'the emptiness and desolation of the land...functions not as a

[152] See further Cassuto, 'On the Formal and Stylistic Relationship between Deutero-Isaiah and Other Biblical Writers', pp. 149-52.

[153] M. Dahood (in his review of Kutscher, *The Language and Literary Background of the Isaiah-Scroll*, *Biblica* 56 [1975], pp. 260-64 [263]) suggests that the odd expression *mmk* functions as a substantive meaning 'your offspring'.

[154] See, e.g., Hans M. Barstad, *The Myth of the Empty Land* (Oslo: Scandinavian University Press, 1996).

polemical exclusionary tactic against dissident Yahwistic communities, but as part of a grander sweeping portrait of Yahweh's activity in history'.[155] The colon's wording will reappear in 61.4 without 'from you' (diachronically, again it may be that Isaiah 61 is older and that this line is dependent on 61.4).[156] But the effect of the 'from you' and the second-person verb in the second colon is to emphasize the agency of the restoration work. In 61.4 the identity of the builders is left vaguer (in 45.13 it was Cyrus; in practice, both Persian emperors and Judahite leaders and labourers were involved). The stress on 'you' is not a challenge; it remains part of the promise expressed through vv. 10b-12. It is a promise about what the people will be able to achieve. Restoring 'genuine communal solidarity' will have 'community-building effects'.[157] The parallel colon then approximately reverses the word order from the first, so that the two cola work approximately abb′a′, 'people from among you will build up lasting ruins, foundations from generations ago you will raise up'. The second noun phrase nuances the meaning of the first. In Jeremiah, 'lasting' (*ʿôlām*) looked forward. Here, 'foundations from generations ago' looks backward, and given that 'lasting' can also do so (e.g. 44.7; 51.9; 63.9, 11), retrospectively 'lasting ruins' are ruins that threatened to last forever and have indeed seemed to last forever (EVV have translations such as 'age-old').

The stress on the builders' identity is taken up in v. 12b. Because *they* will do the building work, they will make a name for themselves. 'You will be called' applies to both cola, which are then completed by parallel and complementary epithets. On one hand, the people will gain a name as people who filled the gaps in the city's walls that had stood there since the destruction of the city in 587. On the other, they will also gain a name as people who rebuilt the city within these walls in such a way that its thoroughfares could become habitable again. Once more, the background is the city's devastation in 587, which would be one of the factors that meant it remained under-populated even after exiles were free to return and even after the rebuilding of the temple (see Neh 11.1-2 as well as the detailed account of the rebuilding of the walls in Nehemiah). The prophecy is concerned equally for the people's inner needs and their outward needs. The prophet has not given up looking for Yhwh's imminent concrete activity in connection with the community's destiny, in relation to the particularities of its historical context.[158]

[155] John Kessler, 'Images of Exile', in E. Ben Zvi and Christoph Levin (eds.), *The Concept of Exile in Ancient Israel and its Historical Contexts* (Berlin: de Gruyter, 2010), pp. 309-51 (344).

[156] See, e.g., Ruszkowski's comments, *Volk und Gemeinde*, pp. 43-44

[157] Hanson, *Isaiah 40–66*, p. 206 (it is actually his comment on v. 8).

[158] Cf. Childs, *Isaiah*, p. 480

58.13 If you turn back your foot from the Sabbath,// doing what you delight in on my holy day,
But call the Sabbath 'Revelling',// Yhwh's holy [day] 'Honourable',
And honour it instead of going your own ways,// instead of finding your delight and speaking your word,
14 Then you will revel over Yhwh,// and I will make you ride over the heights of the land// and eat the possession of your ancestor Jacob.
For Yhwh's mouth has spoken.

The pattern of challenge and promise repeats for the third time; and as in vv. 9b-12, challenge and promise are syntactically linked by the use of conditional clauses. The move to speaking of the Sabbath is surprising. 1QIsª perhaps recognizes this fact by the way it separates vv. 13-14 from what precedes.[159] Yet it links with the observations about the Sabbath in 56.1-8 (see the comments on 56.2, with which v. 13 has a number of verbal links). Sabbath is designed to be an expression of *mišpāṭ ûṣᵉdāqâ*, in relation to Yhwh and in relation to other people (Amos 8.4-6 is concerned about the Sabbath as part of being concerned about honesty in relation to poor people). One reason for the command concerning its observance is that the heads of households thereby give their workers opportunity to rest (Deut 5.12-15). If people were keeping Sabbath by not working but requiring their workers to work, this would make for a link with the chapter's earlier critique concerning fasting. It has also been argued that the chapter as a whole has links with the instructions for the Day of Atonement, the Sabbath Year, and the Year of Jubilee in Leviticus 16 [P]; 23; 25 [H].[160] Further, there is a nice paronomasia about the move from the last word in v. 12, 'living in' (*šābet*), to 'Sabbath' in v. 13 (*šabbāt*). And the occurrence of the word 'streets' (*nᵉtîbâ*), the penultimate word in v. 12, makes one expect an occurrence of 'way' (*derek*) with which it regularly occurs in parallelism (e.g. 42.16; 43.16; 59.8).[161] There might be another link with what precedes lying in the possibility that the Sabbath was itself assumed to be a fast, as was the case in some later contexts.[162] In substance, whereas the modern reading of vv. 1-12 sees the verses as concerned with social justice, vv. 1-5 were concerned with people's attitude to God, not just with their attitude to other people. If the concern with Sabbath has in the background not only the oppression of workers but also a concern with the people's relationship with

[159] So Oesch, *Petucha und Setuma*, p. 222; cf. Berges, *Das Buch Jesaja*, p. 477.
[160] Cf. Tomás Hanks, *Opresión, pobreza y liberación* (San José, Costa Rica: Caribe, 1982), pp. 141-58 (ET Thomas D. Hanks, *God So Loved the Third World* [Maryknoll, NY: Orbis, 1983], pp. 97-105, 141-44); Park, *Die Gerechtigkeit Israels und das Heil der Völker*, pp. 235-40; Hrobon, *Ethical Dimension of Cult in the Book of Isaiah* (Berlin: de Gruyter, 2010), pp. 201-5; Fishbane, *Biblical Interpretation in Ancient Israel*, p. 305.
[161] Cf. Ron du Preez, 'Linguistic Links between Verses 12 and 13 of Isaiah 58', *AUSS* 30 (1992), pp. 115-21.
[162] See Ruszkowski, 'Der Sabbat bei Tritojesaja', pp. 65-69.

God, the move to talk about the Sabbath would not be so abrupt. Verses 13-14 then provide another aspect of the answer to the question in v. 3a.[163]

The community's relationship with God involves turning its foot back from the Sabbath. The prophet does not speak of turning its foot *on* the Sabbath (so OL);[164] it is not referring to avoiding travel. Rather people must turn their foot back *from* the Sabbath in the sense of treating it as Yhwh's territory. It belongs to Yhwh in the way the temple area and the sacrifices belong to Yhwh; none are to be encroached on. As usual, neither does the point about the Sabbath lie in worship; the main point about the Sabbath is not worship. The parallel colon then does point to an analogous issue with the Sabbath to the one raised by fasting. The line's parallelism is neatly worked. The omission of the expected 'from' on 'doing' points to the way the line works. 'If you turn back your foot from' in the first colon applies also to the second; 'doing what you delight in' applies also from the second colon to the first; and 'the Sabbath' is paralleled by 'my holy day'. As fasting can be a means of indulging in their own delight, or at least can accompany it, if they oppress their workers (vv. 1-4), so can the Sabbath, either because they do not let their workers have their rest day or because they simply indulge in their desire to do business (cf. Neh 13). The reference to keeping off and to the Sabbath's being Yhwh's holy day does suggest that the focus lies on what people's activity says about their attitude to Yhwh.[165]

The contrasting positive requirement in v. 13bα fits with this emphasis. Here, 'but call' applies to both cola. 'The Sabbath' is paralleled by 'Yhwh's holy [day]', an elliptical expression that is nevertheless easy enough to understand and provides some variety over against the previous line. The positive requirement is expressed in the parallel expressions 'revelling' and 'honourable'. They are indeed complementary. 'Revelling' suggests a discrete or quiet enthusiasm; the expression (*ʿōneg*) generates the name of the Jewish Friday evening or Saturday celebration, Oneg Shabbat. There is nothing wrong with the Sabbath being something you revel in, something that gives you pleasure. But 'honourable' reminds its observers to maintain their discipline.

Verse 13bβ again reminds the community that this honouring involves both a ceremonial aspect and a substantial aspect. Once more, 'honouring it' applies to both cola. 'Going [literally, doing] your own ways' forms an *inclusio* with v. 2. The point is explicated in the parallel colon; it implies doing what you like, which is in turn elliptically explained as 'speaking

[163] Sekine, *Die Tritojesajanische Sammlung*, pp. 128-30.

[164] Also cf. M. Dahood, 'Hebrew–Ugaritic Lexicography v', *Biblica* 48 (1967), pp. 421-38 (427), who gives *min* the meaning *b*- that it might have in Ugaritic.

[165] CD10.19-20 takes up phrases from v. 13 in connection with extending the Sabbath rules: see George J. Brooke, 'Isaiah in the Pesharim and Other Qumran Texts', in Broyles and Evans (eds.), *Writing and Reading the Scroll of Isaiah*, II, pp. 609-31 (612-13).

your word'. We might use the expression 'saying what you like'. The nature of this speaking might be inferred from vv. 3-4 (cf. also Hos 10.4, where the phrase also comes). But an analogous Akkadian expression means 'conclude an agreement' over a business matter (cf. Gen 24.33 [J]), and this understanding makes good sense.[166] In this verse, the chapter's last two references to delighting (*ḥpṣ*) draw attention to the way 'the emotional element' in the verb and the noun often 'takes a back seat to the element of will'.[167] LXX explicates the line in terms of not lifting up your foot for work, nor speaking a word in anger from your mouth.

Verse 14 goes on to declare that proper revelling in the Sabbath will make it possible to revel over Yhwh; the unusual preposition *ʿal* makes possible a nice paronomasia with the parallel colon. LXX and Syr have 'trust', a more familiar expression, but the substitution loses the link with v. 13 and with 55.2; 57.4, where LXX translates more literally.[168] The Mekilta attributed to Rabbi Ishmael infers that one needs to take a Sabbath rest from even the thought of work, if one is to revel in Yhwh.[169]

The affirmation links and contrasts with 57.4, where the prophet asked who people were revelling in when they should have been revelling in Yhwh. While MT suggests seeing v. 14 as two bicola, it is common to close a section with a tricolon, and the parallelism between the middle two cola, vv. 14aβ and 14bα, suggests that more likely this is the arrangement here, with v. 14bβ standing outside the metre. Verse 14aβ is a reworking of Deuteronomy 32.13a, with the same variation between Q and K. While *bāmôt* usually denotes 'high places' in the sense of local sanctuaries, it can also refer to the literal heights of an area such as the Judahite mountains. Yhwh's walking on such heights (Amos 4.13; Mic 1.3; Job 9.8) is a mark of sovereign power, and Deuteronomy 32.13 may have the same implication in connection with Israel's riding on the heights.[170]

The verb 'eat' continues the reworking of Deuteronomy 32.13, but v. 14bα then goes its own way. It does so in a fashion that confirms the above possibility about the significance of the 'riding', because it will

[166] Cf. Paul, ישעיה פרקים מ-סו, II, p. 449 (ET pp. 494-95), and JPSV; also Koenen, *Ethik und Eschatologie im Tritojesajabuch*, p. 90.

[167] G. J. Botterweck, *TWAT*, III, p. 114 (ET *TDOT*, V, p. 105), taking up Karl Elliger's comments on Yahweh's *ḥpṣ* in Isaiah 40–55 (*Deuterojesaja: 1. Teilband: Jesaja 40,1–45,7* [Neukirchen: Neukirchener, 1978], p. 286).

[168] Driver links the word with an Arabic verb meaning 'be dependent on' ('Notes on Isaiah', p. 48).

[169] Mekilta attributed to Rabbi Ishmael 53.2, as quoted in Neusner, *Isaiah in Talmud and Midrash*, p. 103.

[170] Cf. A. D. H. Mayes, *Deuteronomy* (London: Oliphants, 1979), p. 386. On the expression in the Old Testament, see James L. Crenshaw, '"Wᵉdōrēk ʿal bāmŏtê ʾāreṣ"', *CBQ* 34 (1972), pp. 39-53. On broader links between 58.11-14 and Deut 32, see Fishbane, *Biblical Interpretation in Ancient Israel*, pp. 478-79; Sommer, *A Prophet Reads Scripture*, pp. 134-36.

mean the people can eat the possession of Jacob. LXX and Vg translate *naḥălâ* 'heritage', but the word's emphasis lies on the secure possession of a piece of property rather than on the way it is acquired, as is reflected in the frequency with which the Old Testament speaks of Yhwh's *naḥălâ*. The word comes only a few times in Isaiah, and its occurrence here again reflects Deuteronomy 32, where it refers to Jacob as Yhwh's possession (Deut 32.9). Here it is Jacob that does the possessing (Ps 47.5 [4] is a related formulation). The addition of 'your ancestor' is unique; only here in the Old Testament is Jacob so described. The promise referring to Jacob makes for a nice *inclusio* with the confrontation of Jacob's household in v. 1. And whereas there Yhwh was not speaking to that household, here it is directly addressed. The kind of activity on the Sabbath that v. 13 has attempted to proscribe would at least include business activity; v. 14 promises that keeping Sabbath will achieve what ignoring Sabbath seeks to achieve.[171]

The closing single colon closes off the chapter with an affirmation that underlines its challenges, its demands, and its promises, and does so in a particularly vivid way in suggesting that the origin of the words in Yhwh is so real it is as if Yhwh's own mouth uttered them. Perhaps the prophet implies a sense of hearing these words as from Yhwh.

Comment: 59.1-8

59.1 Now. Yhwh's hand is not too short to deliver,// his ear is not too heavy to listen.

The subsection begins by taking up a question of Yhwh's from 50.2, 'Is my hand really too short to redeem?'[172] (LXX assimilates to 50.2 by turning the statement here into a question); *hēn* (now) also occurs twice in 50.1-2. It is not so much a deictic like 'there' or 'behold' as 'an exclamation that serves to ground and define the material that follows and 'to introduce a fact upon which a following statement or command is based'.[173] In 50.1-2 the question came within the last of a series of responses to a protest by Ms Zion concerning Yhwh's abandonment of her. (Formally, there is thus another correspondence, as 49.14–50.3 is a construction built out of materials of varying origin, with 50.1-3 coming at the end, and 59.1-8 has a similar relationship with and place in 56.9–59.8.) Here, too, one may imagine v. 1 as a response to such a question, though it may rather have a purely textual relationship with that earlier prophecy and issue from the prophet's reflection on the prophecy without

[171] Cf. H. A. Brongers, 'Einige Bemerkungen zu Jes 58 13-14', *ZAW* 87 (1975), pp. 212-16.

[172] Cf. Ruszkowski's comments, *Volk und Gemeinde*, pp. 63-64.

[173] Thomas O. Lambdin, *Introduction to Biblical Hebrew* (New York: Scribner's, 1971), p. 169; cf. *IBHS* 40.2.1c. They are referring to *hinnēh* but the same applies to *hēn*.

indicating that the people were again actually making the comment about Yhwh's hand. In relation to 58.3, it excludes one possible unstated answer to the question articulated there.

When people act violently against others, they stretch out their hand or their arm with their weapon. The image is applied to Yhwh in a series of telling connections. It appears in relation to Egypt at the exodus (e.g. Exod 6.6; 7.5; 15.12; Deut 4.34; 5.15). Earlier in Isaiah it appears in relation to Yhwh's punishing Israel (Isa 5.25; 9.11, 16, 20 [12, 17, 21]; 10.4; also e.g., Ezek 6.14; 14.13; 16.27; Zeph 1.4). It also appears in promises that Yhwh will put down Israel's enemies in order to restore Israel (Isa 14.26-27; Jer 51.25; Ezek 35.3; Zeph 2.13). That is the implication here. Israel still needs deliverance: Ezra–Nehemiah would imply both from Persia and from neighbouring peoples, to whom those other promises also allude. But the one other specific reference to the possibility of Yhwh's hand being too short (Num 11.23 [JE]) affirms that Yhwh can indeed act to bring trouble. It is not too short to punish. In the context this applies to punishing Israel; the length of Yhwh's arm is not an unqualified reassurance. Thus the addition of 'deliver' is vital.

The two cola are neatly parallel, abcda'b'c'd'. The opening *hēn* applies to both; it is picked up by the opening *w* in the second. There are then two third-person singular feminine qal stative verbs, each preceded by *lōʾ*. Two expressions referring to parts of Yhwh's 'body' follow. The cola then close with infinitives absolute, prefixed by *min*. There is some alliteration within each pair of verbs: the first two each begin with a *k* sound and have rhyming vowels. The last two both include a *šin* and close with *ʿayin*.

The image in the second colon links with the one in the first in that both presuppose the converse of the verb 'extend'. As one extends one's hand to act, one extends one's ear to listen. The Psalms urge Yhwh to do so (e.g. Pss 17.6; 71.2), and prophets complain that Israel has failed to do so (Jer 7.24, 26; 11.8). Yhwh's ear should be extended to listen and Yhwh's hand should be extended to act, but as far as Israel can see, Yhwh's hand is short and Yhwh's ear heavy, as if Yhwh can lift neither (the image in EVV of a 'dull ear' does not convey the metaphor). Between them the two cola take up the two basic elements in a typical prayer, for God to *listen* and to *deliver*.[174]

That the statement in v. 1 issued from the prophet's reflection on an earlier prophecy gains support from the way the parallel statement also takes up an earlier prophecy. While the idea of ears being extended is common, only two other passages utilize the negative correlate of ears being heavy. The origin of the idea seems to be Isaiah 6.10, where Yhwh bids Isaiah 'make [this people's] ears heavy' so that they may not listen with their ears, turn and be healed. Passages in Isaiah 40–55 presuppose that this has happened, though they also bid the people now to extend

[174] Westermann, *Jesaja Kapitel 40–66*, p. 275 (ET p. 345).

their ear in order to listen to Yhwh (42.20; 43.8; 48.8; 55.3). Zechariah 7.11 is the other passage that uses the image of heavy ears, speaking of people themselves having made their ears heavy. In light of the earlier usage, there is some irony about the prophet's comment here, as is often the case in Yhwh's response to a protest. They are accusing Yhwh of having heavy ears—but they are the people with this shortcoming. *Israel's* ears are too heavy to listen to Yhwh (6.10) and *Israel* cannot deliver. In addition, the reference to Yhwh's listening has an unhappy link with 58.4, where the people asked why Yhwh did not pay attention to their fasting and Yhwh snorts that the rest of their lives indicates why Yhwh did not listen to them.

Aq, Sym, Th translate the first verb with an aorist, while LXX translates the second verb the same way, and they more dynamically imply that Yhwh's hand has *become* short and his ear has *become* heavy. The interpretation may reflect the way stative verbs often came to be understood in an inchoative way in PBH.[175]

59.2 Because rather, your wayward acts—they have been things that separate// you and your God.
Your offences—they have hidden his face// from you, from listening.

Verse 1 presupposed that Israel needs deliverance and asserted that the lack of it is not to be attributed to Yhwh's shortcomings. Verse 2 begins to explain the real reason for the lack; this explanation will occupy the whole of the rest of vv. 2-8. Thus the line begins with *kî ʾim*, *kî* strengthened by the pleonastic *ʾim*.[176] Then an extensive sequence of cola and lines bring the subject up to the front of the clause into emphatic position and thus keep underlining the contrast with v. 1. The problem lies not in Yhwh but in 'you': your wayward acts, offences, hands, fingers, lips, tongue. There is no parallelism within the two lines that comprise v. 2; each second colon simply completes the first. But the two lines themselves are broadly parallel. After the opening *kî ʾim*, picked up in v. 2b by *w*, both lines begin with a feminine plural word for wrongdoings with a second-plural suffix, which constitutes the subject. The rest of the lines are then essentially parallel in content, though not formally so.

'Wayward acts' (*ʿāwōn*) and 'offences' (*ḥaṭṭāʾt*) are two of the Old Testament's common words for wrongdoing. As Israelite readers might be aware of the link between the second noun and the verb to which it is related etymologically,[177] so they might link the first noun and the verb *ʿāwâ*; 'waywardness' then points to the noun's resonances better than less

[175] See Aaron Koller, 'Diachronic Change and Synchronic Readings', *JSS* 57 (2012), pp. 265-94 (278-90).
[176] EVV's 'But' rather understates the significance of the expression.
[177] See the comment on 58.1.

colourful terms such as 'iniquity' and 'sin'. It suggests twisting one's path, perversity.[178] Given the link between v. 1 and 50.2, it is likely no coincidence that 'your wayward acts' featured in 50.1; the reference to separating and hiding the face are then equivalent to the language of divorce and sending away in 50.1.

The notion of separation is usually a positive one; v. 2a thus picks up the ironically negative connotation of the idea from 56.3, though it takes it in a different direction, and only here in the Old Testament is the verb used in a figurative sense.[179] It positively suggests Yhwh's separating Israel from other peoples with their objectionable ways (Lev 20.24-26 [H]; 1 Kgs 8.53), separating Levi from the other clans for their ministry (Num 16.9 [P]; Deut 10.8), and separating Aaron's line from the rest of the clan for the priesthood (1 Chr 23.13), and also Israel's separating itself from other peoples and their ways in order thus to belong distinctively to Yhwh (e.g. Ezra 6.21; 9.1; 10.11; Neh 9.2). The community's waywardness has turned the idea of separation upside down. It has become a notion that distinguishes the people from Yhwh rather than associating them with Yhwh. The recurrence of the notion in Ezra–Nehemiah suggests a particular link and connotation. Ezra and Nehemiah deal with a situation in which people have not separated themselves in the required sense from other local peoples. The prophecy suggests that this has resulted in another kind of separation. While *hāyû mabdîlîm* might simply be a periphrastic equivalent for *hibdîlû*, it is then odd that the prophet did not use that straightforward verb (as 56.3 did). It draws attention to a contrast over against another kind of positive separation. The only other occurrence of the verb *hāyâ* followed by *mabdîl* is Genesis 1.6 [P], where the sky dome forms a positive barrier holding back the waters in the heavens from the world below. The separation here in v. 2 is again a contrastingly negative one.

The second line explains the nature of the separation by means of a frightening image, though it is again one familiar from earlier prophecy, and from psalmody and elsewhere. We look to someone's face in order to relate to them in some way; servants look to their masters or mistresses for their support and provision, and Israel looks to Yhwh like that (Ps 123.1-2). But if servants have fallen short of their responsibilities, they cannot expect this logic to work, and so it is with Yhwh's servants. Yhwh's face is hidden. Conversely masters and mistresses look to their servants and act on their behalf. The idea is then that if Yhwh looks, Yhwh will not be able to resist the temptation to act in deliverance. Looking suggests providing, delivering, and blessing. It is a common image when psalms speak of God failing to act on behalf of a person

[178] BDB (p. 730) distinguishes two roots *ʿāwâ* but their meaning overlaps and an Israelite might not distinguish too sharply between them.

[179] Cf. Benedikt Otzen, *TWAT*, I, p. 520 (ET *TDOT*, II, p. 3).

under attack, often accompanied by the question 'Why?' (e.g. Pss 44.25 [24]; 88.15 [14]). Yhwh had warned the people that their following other masters would mean 'I will hide my face from them' (e.g. Deut 31.17-18), and had declared on the eve of the fall of Jerusalem that 'I have hidden my face from this city' because of its people's wickedness (Jer 33.5). In Isaiah 54.8 Yhwh granted that in the exile, 'I hid my face from you' (cf. Ezek 39.23-24), but added that it was only 'for a moment'. Isaiah 57.17 has referred to Yhwh's simply 'hiding', and 64.7 [6] will declare that 'you have hidden your face from us' but will acknowledge that this is because of our wayward acts. It is that declaration that this prophecy makes once more. The end of the exile does not mean the ending of that hiding of the face because it has not meant the end of waywardness and offences. Here the effect of the image is augmented by the addition of 'from listening', which also implies that the emphasis earlier in the line lay on Yhwh's looking rather than on the servants' looking. Both looking and listening are important to making Yhwh act to deliver. LXX has 'from having mercy', which is the implication of listening and broadly corresponds with 50.2.

59.3 Because your hands—they have become polluted/have been polluted with blood,// your fingers with waywardness.
Your lips—they have spoken deceit,// your tongue—it talks oppression

The two lines are internally parallel and also parallel to each other. The first refers to actions, the second to words. Both will take up the uses of hands and lips in worship. People hold out their hands in appeal to God and make that appeal with their lips, but when looking, what God sees is the blood on the hands, and when listening, what God hears is the people's scheming words. The opening 'because' resumes from v. 2 and indicates that v. 3 will give more specificity to the charge issued there, while putting the subjects of the verbs at the beginning of the clauses continues the assertion that the problem lies with *you* not with *Yhwh*.

After the 'because', the first line works abca′c′, incorporating two plural nouns with second-plural suffixes and two singular nouns prefixed by *b*. The plural nouns extend 'the pulsating sound of the pronominal suffix' *-kem* that runs through vv. 2-3.[180] Here, 'fingers' gives precision to 'hands', and 'waywardness' (picked up from v. 2a) gives precision to 'blood'. The verb for 'be/become polluted'[181] is *gāʾal* II, which is much rarer than the usual *ṭāmēʾ*; it comes mainly in Ezra–Nehemiah and Malachi. Blood is a classic source of pollution (cf. Lam 4.14).[182] One cannot go into the presence of the living God when one has been in such

[180] Polan, *In the Ways of Justice toward Salvation*, p. 253.
[181] See the translation note.
[182] Lau (*Schriftgelehrte Prophetie in Jes 56–66*, p. 207) describes 'they have become polluted/have been polluted with blood' as 'cited from Lam 4.14'.

close contact with death (thus the verb comes with some irony in Isa 63.3). But here the second colon with its further reference to 'waywardness' makes explicit that the prophecy refers not to the pollution that issues from regular contact with death, which carries no moral guilt, but from involvement in causing death, which is doubly polluting, for both theological and ethical reasons. The colon's point is thus the same as that in 1.15-16, though those verses do not use a technical term for defilement. Here the use of *gāʾal* II makes for an ironic contrast with 44.22. There the basis for confidence that Yhwh wipes away sin lies in the verb *gāʾal* I, in the fact that Yhwh has 'restored' the people. This chapter will shortly picture Yhwh coming to Zion as *gōʾēl* (59.20; cf. also 63.9). Both these homonyms can be significant for Israel. They have to choose which will apply.

The second line explains how the people's hands came to be thus polluted. You do not have to be a thug or a hit man for it to happen. Behind the effect on hands and fingers is the use of lips and tongue. Metaphorically, people's hands are covered in blood even if they are one or two stages distanced from directly killing someone, like the people who gave false testimony in the Naboth story (1 Kgs 21). The line works abca′c′b′. The cola begin with two more nouns having second-plural suffixes (though one is masculine plural, one feminine singular). Its two verbs have similar meaning, though one is third masculine plural qatal, the other third feminine singular yiqtol; further, the second is the rarer and altogether more interesting verb *hāgâ* which suggests murmuring, muttering, or talking quietly, the way one does when involved in deceit. In contrast, within the third pair, the first noun is the more specific, the second the more general. Isaiah's declaration about his and his people's lips being polluted (*ṭāmēʾ*) as a result of waywardness and offences (6.5-7) suggests that the prophecy is taking up that chapter's language, as in v. 1, and once again declaring that nothing has changed.

Rabbi Eleazar comments that 'hands' refers to the judges, 'fingers' to their scribes, 'lips' to their clerks, and 'tongue' to the litigants.[183]

59.4 There is no one summoning with faithfulness,// there is no one entering into judgment with truthfulness.
Relying on nothingness, speaking emptiness,// conceiving trouble, giving birth to harmfulness!

Two more lines restate the point further; they are parallel to each other and also to v. 3b, and also internally parallel. The first works abca′b′c′. 'There is no one' recurs. Two participles follow, one qal, one niphal. The cola close with two *b*- expressions. The lament 'there is no one summoning' recurs from Hosea 7.7 and will recur again in Isaiah 64.6 [7],

[183] B. Shabbat 139a.

while the broader lament 'there is no one…' recurs from passages such as Psalm 14.1-3; Jeremiah 12.11; Micah 7.2. No doubt there is hyperbole in those other passages, and here.[184] In Hosea 7.7 and Isaiah 64.6 [7] 'summoning' refers to calling on God, and Tg takes it thus to denote prayer here. This would follow well on vv. 2-3, but what it leads into implies that 'summons' rather suggests an appearance before the community court (cf. Job 5.1; 9.16; 13.22).[185] The summons might be uttered by the party who claims to be in the wrong, or uttered to the court itself before which this person has made a charge. The prophecy implies that each member of the community or each member of the body of elders that comprises the court is corrupt. The second colon disambiguates the verb, since the niphal of *šāpaṭ* suggests the action of people bringing a charge rather than that of the court deciding it, for which the qal would be appropriate. The sharpness in the line then comes in the *b*- expressions. The combination of *mišpāṭ* with *ṣedeq* or (more often) *ṣᵉdāqâ* is a fundamental prophetic expectation, as is the exercise of *ʾĕmûnâ*. The Prophets expect relationships in the community to be characterized by people doing the right thing by one another and living in truthfulness. This expectation is frequently disappointed. In this community the prophet sees it as invariably disappointed.

Verse 4b directly expresses the point. Each colon incorporates two infinitive absolute verbs, such as can express an action forcefully and vividly,[186] and two nouns. In each colon there is a disjunction between the verb and the noun. 'Rely' does not go with 'nothingness' and 'speaking' should have as object something possessing substance rather than lacking it. Even more forcefully in the second colon, one expects 'conceiving' and 'giving birth' to have more positive objects than 'trouble' and 'harmfulness'. Relying on or trusting (it is the only occurrence of *bāṭaḥ* in Isaiah 56–66) nothingness or emptiness (*tōhû*, *šāwʾ*) would elsewhere suggest relying on other gods or on political alliances, and the former would fit with 57.3-13 (and with Tg's understanding of 'summoning'), but the narrower context here rather suggests people thinking they can safely utilize accusations that are empty, that have no link with reality, and can safely base their hopes for the future on profiting by means of such accusations. The second colon expresses the point in a metaphor. It corresponds almost exactly to Job 15.35a; the image also occurs in Psalm 7.15 [14] and is perhaps a proverbial expression.[187] Such an origin might be another factor lying behind the use of the infinitives (extended backwards into v. 4a), which can be a feature of proverbs. People's scheming is what conceives trouble, and their implementing their plans brings

[184] Cf. Beuken, *Jesaja IIIA*, p. 130.

[185] Vg makes *iustitia* the direct object and Ibn Ezra (*The Commentary of Ibn Ezra on Isaiah*, p. 271) 'calls for' (but this would require *l*), while Ehrlich translates 'cries out' (*Randglossen*, IV, p. 210), but none of these fits well into the context.

[186] *DG* 103b.

[187] See, e.g., Luther, *In Esaiam prophetam enarraciones*, p. 489 (ET p. 296).

harmfulness to birth. Most of what precedes would have made one assume that they are generating trouble for other people, but LXX and Th assume they have conceived trouble for themselves. This fits with the parallels in Job and the psalm (cf. also Ps 17.17 [16]; Job 4.8), and it is one possible implication of their having relied on emptiness. They are self-deceived as well as deceiving others. The possible double significance of their actions will continue in the verses that follow.

59.5 It is a serpent's eggs they have broken up,// a spider's webs they spin.
One who eats of their eggs—he will die,// and one who tramples/one that is trampled, an adder breaks out.

By using noun clauses and infinitives, v. 4 formally abandoned the direct address that characterized vv. 2-3 (and by implication v. 1). Although it would have been easy to resume direct address, instead the rest of the section speaks of the wrongdoers in the third person. Rhetorically the effect is to make the audience (who in reality are still addressed) look at themselves as a third party, as if they are someone else, even though they know that they are not.

Verse 5a adds two more concrete metaphors to the one in v. 4bβ. The point of the first is then expounded in v. 5b, the point of the second in v. 6. Once again the word order is unusual, with the objects of the verbs coming first in v. 5a, the subject in v 5bα (again in v. 6aα). Verse 5a is neatly parallel, abca′b′c′ (a construct plural, an absolute noun, and a third-person plural verb—one piel qatal, one qal yiqtol). The word for 'serpent' indicates some sort of venomous snake, though we do not know what sort. Tg apparently links the 'breaking' of v. 5a with the process of hatching, but v. 5b rather suggests it is a breaking that is preliminary to eating.[188]

Verse 5b is less neatly parallel, abca′c′b. Each colon begins with a participle; the first is active, but the nature of the second is less clear.[189] The first portrays a person eating a serpent's egg and getting poisoned. This first establishes the reason for breaking the egg (v. 5a): it was preliminary to eating it. But what the person eats turns out to be poisonous (cf. Job 20.12-16).[190] One reading of the second participle then makes it closely parallel as it portrays a person smashing the shell of an egg, presumably to eat it, but finding that an adder breaks out of the shell when doing so, and again threatens the person's life. On the other reading, the participle refers to the egg that is trampled. But is the victim the person who did the trampling or is it someone else?

[188] Cf. Penna, *Isaia*, p. 574.
[189] See the translation note.
[190] Cf. Kissane, *Isaiah*, II, p. 247.

> 59.6 Their webs—they will not do for clothing;// people will not cover themselves with the things they make.
> The things they make are things of harm;// the doing of violence is in their hands.

Each of the two lines comprises cola that are parallel in content but diverse in expression. The prophet could have made each of them parallel by saying, 'and the work of their hands is violence' and 'the things they make—they will not cover them'. Evidently the prophet had no fixed view about how lines had to turn out and could keep the hearers on their toes by working in varying ways.

The first line explains the image of the spider web in a different direction from the one we might have expected. A spider's web is designed to catch insects, and this fits the context of v. 5; the wayward are the spiders, their victims are the insects. But v. 6 begins by making the point that there is nothing substantial about a spider's web, and there is nothing substantial about what these faithless, truthless people construct. It is weaving, all right, but it is not the kind of weaving that generates clothing. Once more the victim of the deceit might be the deceiver or the deceiver's quarry.

The second line returns to generalization, and it is again open to suggesting the harm and violence they did to other people or to themselves. Eitan notes that the Arabic word *ġašiya* meaning 'cover' could have a Hebrew cognate *ʿāśâ* with a related noun *maʿaśeh* 'covering', and thus would make for a good paronomasia here.[191] But even on the basis of the usual meaning of *ʿāśâ*, the context perhaps indicates that the violence is exercised through judicial procedures rather than by people directly getting blood on their hands.[192]

> 59.7 Their feet—they run to evil;// they hurry to shed innocent blood.
> Their plans are plans of harm;// destroying and smashing are on their highways.

Again the subject in v. 7a is brought up ahead of its verb, and the two cola in v. 7a are parallel in content; so are those in v. 7b. 'Hurry' corresponds to 'their feet—they run'; they are so eager to engage in wrongdoing, they cannot wait. Then 'to shed innocent blood' gives specificity to the meaning of 'to evil'. In the second line, in two noun clauses in abb'a' order, 'destroying and smashing' gives colour to 'plans to do harm', while 'on their highways' moves on to the implementation of 'their plans'. In addition, reinforcing the repetition of the long word for plans, *maḥšābōt*, is the alliteration of destroying and smashing, *šōd*

[191] 'A Contribution to Isaiah Exegesis', p. 83.
[192] Cf. H. Haag, *TWAT*, II, pp. 1057-58 (ET *TDOT*, IV, p. 484).

wāšeber. At the same time, there is an abb'a' aspect to the lines as a whole, as the opening reference to running feet pairs with the closing reference to highways; and planning to do harm pairs with shedding innocent blood.

The ambiguity continues. People's urgency seeks to bring trouble to others by shedding innocent blood, but they may bring trouble to themselves. The first line corresponds to Proverbs 1.16, except that it adds the word 'innocent' (cf. Prov 1.11; LXX omits it here). The expression 'innocent blood' is a common one (e.g. Jer 7.6, a chapter with which this prophecy has a number of links). The context in Proverbs emphasizes the way people who act thus end up shedding their own blood. As is the case with the reference to violence, when literally understood the line no longer refers to scheming to rob people of their livelihood and their lives by legal means but to more active wrongdoing, though this may be a metaphor. The two passages feature among a number in the Old Testament that describe the speed with which humanity turns to wrongdoing (e.g. Prov 6.18).[193]

Initially, the second line pulls back again from the concrete image to resume talk of their scheming (cf. vv. 3-4). LXX and Vg take *maḥšābōt* to mean 'thoughts', but *ḥāšāb* and related words rather suggest planning, as in 55.8-9. Indeed, the repetition of 'plans' and the fact that v. 9 goes on to work with the image of 'ways' suggests a direct link with 55.8-9, though the link is verbal rather than substantial.

> 59.8 The way of well-being they have not acknowledged;// there is no exercise of judgment on their tracks.
> Their paths they have made crooked for themselves;// no one walking that way has acknowledged well-being.

The last pair of lines take abb'a' form, with each word in the first colon recurring in the last; this contributes to closure at the end of the section. The middle two cola are also parallel to each other in substance. Every colon works with the image of a road that people walk, which is continued and developed from v. 7. It suggests further links with Proverbs, which makes much use of the image of the way.[194] Proverbs contains most of the Old Testament references to crookedness (*ʿāqaš*, *ʿiqqēš*), many in this connection (e.g. 2.15; 10.9), and most of its references to tracks (*maʿgālâ*; e.g. 2.15), as well as references to paths (*nᵉtîbâ*; e.g. 1.15). But the book of Isaiah is also fond of the various words for 'way' that come in vv. 7-8, used literally or metaphorically. Indeed, the notion of the way recurs in the Old Testament. Its assumption is that humanity is on a

[193] Cf. H. Ringgren, *TWAT*, IV, p. 714 (ET *TDOT*, VIII, p. 139).

[194] See, e.g., Stuart Weeks, *Instruction and Imagery in Proverbs 1—9* (Oxford: Oxford University Press, 2007), pp. 73-79.

journey, but it is not a journey distinctive to each individual or even to each community in which individuals find their way to their distinctive destiny. It is rather a journey that individuals and communities walk whose point lies as much in the travelling as in the arriving, because it is a journey that follows a moral route laid out by God. 'The figure of the way is the central symbol of biblical ethics.'[195]

> It was a good word because it was drawn from the vicissitudes of daily life, from a land of many roads and paths in which walking was the usual manner of going from one place to another. It was a good symbol because it involved beginning and end and the intention which prompted the journey. There were different ways a man might take, and his journey involved decision or choice on the right or the wrong road.[196]

Paradoxically, the route in question generates well-being even as one travels along it, but if one deviates from the moral path that Yhwh has laid out and makes one's way crooked, one sacrifices that well-being.

Following on the reference to plans, the reference to ways reinforces the impression of a reminiscence of Isaiah 55.8-9, but also of the expressions being used in quite a different connection. They thus create something of an irony. The point in 55.8-9 is that Yhwh has a plan for a way of bringing about the exiles' restoration, but it does not correspond to the kind of way the exiles would plan. The plural nouns suggest that this is not just a one-off occurrence; there is commonly a difference between the ways Yhwh plans and the ways people would plan. But in 55.8-9, at least Yhwh and people have the same end in mind, to get the Judahites back home and get the nation reestablished. One could say that both are aiming at the way of well-being (cf. 55.12).

Here the plans avoid the way of *šālôm.* When the Old Testament refers to inner peace, it does so by using expressions such as 'do not be afraid'; it does not use *šālôm* in this connection. By *šālôm* it can mean harmony in the community, which the action of the faithless would imperil, but it would be an allusive way of introducing a new idea at the end of the section. More likely the *šālôm* is that of the faithless and/or their victims; again there is some ambiguity, which adds to the irony of the link with Isaiah 55. Directly, people are refusing to acknowledge the way that leads to the *šālôm* or well-being of those they are scheming against, in order (for instance) to deprive them of their land by making sure that there is no exercise of judgment or authority (*mišpāṭ*) in the community of the kind that would stop them implementing their will.[197] This is the way people are making crooked paths for themselves to tread. But indirectly, it is

[195] Muilenburg, 'The Book of Isaiah: Chapters 40—66', p. 690.

[196] James Muilenburg, *The Way of Israel* (New York: Harper, 1961), p. 33; cf. Jones, *Isaiah 56–66 and Joel*, p. 60.

[197] On *mišpāṭ*, see the comment on 56.1.

their own well-being they are failing to recognize, they will find that the community's failure to exercise judgment works against them, and they are carving out paths that will turn out to be crooked in their effect on themselves. This negative understanding of the effect of their action fits with the further warnings about well-being in 57.19-21 and earlier in 48.22. As in 58.3, *yāda'* signifies not merely that they do not know what well-being is or know the way to it. Nor does it signify that they do not experience well-being, though that will also be true. It refers to an act of the will whereby one recognizes the nature of well-being and the way to it, and takes that road.

If once again it seems unlikely that the whole community was guilty of the wrongdoing that is attacked, this may indicate that the prophet is using the rhetoric of the hell-fire sermon.[198] In Romans 3.15-17 Paul uses vv. 7-8 to describe humanity in general, following on a quotation from Psalm 14. The collection of quotations that appears in Romans 3.13-18, including Isaiah 59.7-8, was then included in Psalm 14 in some manuscripts of LXX.

Conclusion

Whereas preexilic prophecy speaks about a mismatch between enthusiastic worship and generous sacrifice on one hand, and a failure of *mišpāṭ ûṣᵉdāqâ* on the other, the mismatch this prophecy critiques is a contrast between fasting and a failure of such *mišpāṭ ûṣᵉdāqâ*. Here, at least, fasting is not a spiritual discipline designed (for instance) to wean people from excessive attachment to earthly things. It is an act of self-denial intended to add force to people's pleas, a way of showing God that they are serious in their praying, designed to add to the pressure on God to respond to their prayers. Evidently it is not working. People are fasting and praying, but Yhwh is not responding. As happens elsewhere, the prophecy takes up the protests that characterize people's laments, agrees that the facts on which the laments are based are true, but declares that there is entirely good reason for Yhwh's not responding to the prayers and fasting. The people's prayer involves the typical rhetorical questions of a protest psalm (58.3a), but the risk with rhetorical questions is that they may get treated as real questions, and this is what happens in 58.3-5. There is an answer to the people's 'Why?' Prayer and fasting imply a submission of oneself to God, but the community's life is not characterized by such submission. They need to recognize 'that they cannot force divine favour by fasting, but that they can elicit it by feeding the hungry'.[199] The chapter attacks 'false conversion' and goes on to describe

[198] Cf. Whybray, *Isaiah 40–66*, p. 221.
[199] Fishbane, *Biblical Interpretation in Ancient Israel*, p. 304.

the nature of 'real conversion'[200] (conversion in the sense of the Godward turning that is the ongoing obligation of the people of God).

> Fasting bears no fruit unless it is watered by mercy. Fasting dries up when mercy dries up. Mercy is to fasting as rain is to earth. However much you may cultivate your heart, clear the soil of your nature, root out vices, sow virtues, if you do not release the springs of mercy, your fasting will bear no fruit.... When you fast, if your mercy is thin your harvest will be thin; when you fast, what you pour out in mercy overflows into your barn. Therefore, do not lose by saving, but gather in by scattering. Give to the poor, and you give to yourself. You will not be allowed to keep what you have refused to give to others.[201]

There is 'an indissolubility between attitudes to God and attention to the neighbour'.[202] Specifically, the prayers that people's fasting undergirds are prayers for Yhwh to act with *mišpᵉṭê ṣedeq*, but *mišpāṭ* and *ṣᵉdāqâ* do not characterize the people's own life. The use of these related expressions in connection with God's action and the community's action (cf. also 58.8) takes up the use of *mišpāṭ* and *ṣᵉdāqâ* at the beginning of these chapters, in 56.1. Mark Gray thus suggests that Isaiah 58 sponsors a justice approach rather than a charity approach to social problems, a radical stance though not one that implies rebellion against the imperial authorities.[203]

The nature of the promises in 58.6-14 has led to the chapter being called 'eschatological', though if the word applies to them, it will be in the sense that they promise the ultimate fulfilment of Yhwh's purpose by a spectacular supernatural action, rather than (for instance) that they belong to a future that has little link with the present.[204] They make promises to the prophet's community, and their challenges may not be put off until the eschaton; indeed, whereas the sabbatical and jubilee visions look for the community to give practical expression to its concern for the needy once every seven or forty-nine years, Isaiah 58 looks for it to characterize the people's regular life.[205] On the basis of this chapter Leviticus Rabbah associates twenty-four blessings with one's caring for the poor.[206] In effect, the promises in the three subsections of 58.6-14

[200] Albert the Great, 'Postilla super Isaiam', pp. 549, 551. Earlier Christian expositors routinely use the passage to support the idea that God is not interested in Jewish observances (e.g. *Epistle of Barnabas* 3; Justin, *Dialogue with Trypho* 15). On the other hand, the passage embarrasses Tertullian because it is quoted by people who oppose fasting (see *On Fasting*, esp. 2, 15).

[201] Peter Chrysologus, Sermon 43 (PL 52, cols. 320, 322).

[202] Obara, *Le strategie di Dio*, p. 237.

[203] *Rhetoric and Social Justice in Isaiah*, pp. 89, 91.

[204] See, e.g., Lau, *SchriftgelehrteProphetie in Jes 56–66*, p. 240.

[205] Cf. J. Severino Croatto, 'Del año jubilar levitico al tiempo de liberación profético', *Revista de Interpretación Bíblica latinoamericana* 33/2 (1999), pp. 76-96.

[206] Lev. R. 34.11-16.

begin where 58.1-5 began, with the people's prayer for Yhwh's *mišpāṭ ûṣᵉdāqâ*; they indeed use the second of those words (58.8-9a). They go on to make the promises more specific (58.10b-12, 14), with imagery that suggests the paradoxical principle that self-denial in generosity actually generates bodily flourishing.

Interpreters of the preexilic prophets' dismissal of Israel's worship have argued over whether the prophets totally dismiss all such worship and believe that right conduct in society is the only action Yhwh is interested in, or whether they are simply dismissing worship that is unaccompanied by right conduct in society or right attitude of heart. The prophets themselves might regard this argument as a way of avoiding their point. They are not concerned with a question of principle. They are concerned with what this community does *now*. Yet they include prayer as well as sacrifice in their polemic (see 1.10-20) and they do themselves pray, which suggests that if they were concerned with the question of principle, they would affirm the place of worship, prayer, and fasting in the people's relationship with Yhwh. The incorporation of their words in the Torah, the Prophets, and the Writings, which often emphasize worship, prayer, and fasting, implies at least that they can reasonably be understood that way.

This prophecy, specifically, is not concerned with the theoretical question whether fasting is a proper practice, but with Yhwh's total abhorrence for fasting as practised. Its rhetorical strategy then differs from that of passages such as 1.10-20. Those passages do not say that worship is to be redefined as something practised in community relationships rather than in religious acts in the temple, which the potential of the verb *ʿābad* 'serve' would make it easy to do. Rather, they simply declare that Yhwh loathes people's worship, their 'service'. This prophecy's strategy is to redefine fasting, so radically that it does become a metaphor for something else. The fasting that will be acceptable to Yhwh is the kind that embodies a submission to Yhwh characterizing the whole of life. Fasting is an act of self-denial. Such self-denial needs to be embodied in relationships with one's underlings. If people are to eat less than usual, there would be some obvious logic in making this practice an occasion for sharing one's food with other people who need it.

Like the prophetic polemic about sacrifice, the prophecy's point is thus not that people are outwardly fasting but that they lack the right inner attitude. Indeed, it makes clear that they are totally sincere in their self-affliction. They delight in acknowledging Yhwh's ways and in coming before Yhwh, and they do afflict themselves (their *nepeš*). They are not just outwardly pretending. The problem is that their sincere seeking is not matched by the rest of their life.[207] The prophecy does not challenge them

[207] Cf. Mark Gray, 'Justice with Reconciliation', in J. Middlemas, D. J. A. Clines, and E. Holt (eds.), *The Centre and the Periphery* (W. Brueggemann Festschrift; Sheffield: Phoenix, 2010), pp. 159-77 (163-64).

to a new inner attitude but to a new outward practice. In effect, their manner of life constitutes a massive denial of the oneness of the people, like that implied by Nehemiah 5, which illustrates the kind of social practice the prophecy attacks.[208] Fasting is a matter of 'moral passion under discipline for the things of God'.[209]

The subsections in 58.6-14 make God's restoration contingent on human action in a way that 56.1-2 and 57.7-14 do not, though this need not imply that it thinks in legalistic fashion.[210] It is not seeking the mere formal observance that would be characteristic of legalistic assumptions; indeed, such observance is its target. Rather, it knows that there must be a harmony between human acts and divine acts, but this 'must' is more logical and theological than legal, as was the case in 56.1-2. It is again a covenantal 'must' rather than a contractual one. The principle is expressed in the correlation between divine and human *mišpāṭ ûṣᵉdāqâ*. Isaiah 56.1 juxtaposed the divine and the human *mišpāṭ ûṣᵉdāqâ* in systematically ambiguous fashion. These can relate in either way: divine initiative can stimulate human response, or human initiative can stimulate divine response. Whereas 57.7-14 specified the relationship between these in one way, 58.6-14 does so the other way.

Isaiah 59.1-8 continues the same understanding though it reverses the rhetoric. It begins as a response to a protest on the part of the community that Yhwh is not acting to deliver it. In the Psalter most such protests implicitly or explicitly claim that the community is in trouble but has done nothing to deserve it. Yet some such protests (and more of the prayers outside the Psalter, especially in Lamentations and Ezra–Nehemiah) acknowledge that it is the community's waywardness that has brought down trouble on it. There were doubtless occasions when people assumed they had done wrong when in fact they had not (at least, this is true of Christian spirituality). There were certainly occasions when they assumed they did not deserve the trouble they were in, when in fact they had deserved it. The prophet's message in 59.1-8 presupposes the second kind of context.[211] The declarations in 59.2-3 might seem to stand in tension with declarations that Yhwh wipes away sins in 44.22.[212] Actually, Yhwh's restoring the people does promise forgiveness, but it is designed to make repentance possible not unnecessary. Once again, 'Third Isaiah is not a legalist',[213] though neither do Isaiah 40–55 or Isaiah 56–66 point to antinomianism.

Hans-Joachim Kraus entitles a study of Isaiah 56–66 'Die ausgebliebene Endtheophanie', the final appearance of God that has not

[208] See Willy Schottroff, '"Unrechtmäßige Fesseln auftun, Jochstricke lösen"', *Biblical Interpretation* 5 (1997), pp. 263-78 (275).

[209] Brueggemann, *Using God's Resources Wisely*, p. 65.

[210] Cf. Elliger, 'Der Prophet Tritojesaja', p. 119.

[211] Cf. Hanson, *Isaiah 40–66*, pp. 207-9.

[212] Cf. Marti, *Jesaja*, p. 377.

[213] Elliger, 'Der Prophet Tritojesaja', p. 121.

arrived.[214] Brooks Schramm follows him, commenting that 'the real interest of these chapters is to explain why the delay in the arrival of God's salvation has occurred'; he sees 59.1-2 as illustrating the point.[215] There is more than one problem with this view.[216] One is that even 59.1-2 does not refer to delay and need not imply it. The lines may indeed respond to a protest by the people that Yhwh is neither listening to them nor delivering them, but such protest s occur or are implied elsewhere in the Old Testament without any suggestion that a promised deliverance has failed to arrive. The distinctiveness about 59.1-2 over against protest psalms is that it blames the community rather than Yhwh; the community needs to put its life right if God is to act on its behalf. But there is no specific indication that the shortcomings in its life explain why promises have not been fulfilled for it.

The jumping off point for 59.1-8 lies in 50.2 and behind that 6.10, and 59.1 opens up the question to which 59.2-8 provide the snorting response. But this precise textual or contextual link with earlier chapters in Isaiah does not exactly set the agenda or provide the seed thought for all that follows; it 'addresses the question of Israel's sinfulness in a very different way from chapter 50, probing deeply into the theological nature of sin and evil' rather than being merely concerned with one particular demonstration of waywardness.[217] Paul's utilization in Romans 3 of verses from this section, to make a point about the sinfulness characteristic of Israel as a whole and humanity as a whole, is thus not so far from the chapter's own spirit. One pointer to this fact is the variety of terms to describe human wrongdoing that recur (waywardness, offences, malice, nothingness, emptiness, trouble, harmfulness, violence, evil, crookedness). Another is the variety of verbal forms the passage uses, which individually and together suggest the ongoing characteristics of the community's life. So the qatals suggest what has been and still is; the yiqtols suggest what is regularly the case; the infinitives suggest something timeless. Yet another pointer is the way 59.1-8 parallels the charges in 1.10-20, as 58.1-14 had done, though it is more explicit in taking up its charges. It also reverses its rhetoric, as it does that of 57.7-14: whereas 1.10-20 warns the community that Yhwh will not listen to its prayers because it has blood on its hands, 58.1-8 explains to the community that the reason Yhwh has not listened to its prayers is that it has blood on its hands. Its links with 50.2, 6.10, and 1.1-20 are not its only links with other scriptural material. It also implies links with other passages in Isaiah 40–55, as well as with passages such as 6.5-7; Lamentations 4.14; Job 15.35; and Proverbs 1.16.

214 *ZAW* 78 (1966), pp. 317-32.

215 Schramm, *The Opponents of Third Isaiah*, p. 81.

216 See further the 'Conclusion' section on 56.1-8, above.

217 Childs, *Isaiah*, pp. 485, 486 (commenting on Isa 59 as a whole).

The rhetoric and content of the material in 58.1–59.8 as a whole raises a further question. When Yhwh speaks about 'my people', 'the household of Jacob', in 58.1-3a, it gives the impression that the confrontation will concern the people as a whole. But Yhwh's comments in response to the complaint reported in 58.3a indicate that the confrontation actually concerns the way some people within the community are treating other people within the community and declining to share resources with the resourceless. They are challenged to change their ways. The consequences of their doing so will then constitute good news for the people as a whole as it will open up the possibility of Yhwh's blessing the community as a whole. At present, however, their action means that the people as a whole suffer, and will continue to do so. The oppressed will thus pay a further price beyond their oppression at the hands of their oppressors. They also already share in the delay of Yhwh's work of restoration as a result of that wrongdoing, even if delay in the fulfilment of promises is not the background of the protests. The corporate nature of a community means that the relatively innocent pay a price in more than one way for the wrongdoing of the guilty. The prophecy's rhetoric corresponds to that of preexilic prophecy; it does not divide the community into the faithful and the faithless, or does so no more than earlier prophecy did, at least in terms of whether the faithless suffer more than the faithful.

As Isaiah 58 addressed 'my people', 'the household of Jacob', so 59.1-8 contains no suggestion of addressing only a group within the community. Once again, while the prophecy discusses the fate of the whole community, it refers only to the wrongdoing of people with resources and power.[218] The logic or the problem in 58.1–59.8 indeed parallels that in preexilic prophecy. There, too, prophets commonly attack the oppression of the have-nots by the haves, yet declare a consequent judgment and a deliverance to follow that will affect the whole people. There is no suggestion here that the people who are to be restored are only the oppressed. People who give up oppression are to be restored. The understanding of community and individual or of powerful and needy within the community is again the same as that in earlier prophecy. The implicit problem in speaking about judgment and deliverance is the same. It is not the case that the powerful will be judged and their victims delivered.[219] It is 'my people' who are confronted (v. 1).

One significant consideration here is that we should not assume the prophet's critique to apply to a relatively small segment of the community, who are well off, who hold power, and who are oppressing people without power or resources—a group such as the priests.[220] There is no indication that the priests are the prophecy's target, and they could hardly

[218] See the discussion in Park, *Die Gerechtigkeit Israels und das Heil der Völker*, pp. 213-14, 230-32.

[219] Against Hanson, *The Dawn of Apocalyptic*, p. 107.

[220] E.g. Hanson, *The Dawn of Apocalyptic*, p. 109

be seen as 'my people' 'or 'the household of Jacob'.[221] Nor does the passage refer to the objects of its polemic as 'wealthy'. Given that 56.9-12 shows that it is quite possible to critique the community's leaders directly, it is not obvious why this prophecy should speak as if confronting the whole people if the wrongdoers are a relatively small group of leaders.

More likely the critique indeed applies to the community as a whole. The prophecy's model may then be the one presupposed by the Torah and by the portrait in Ruth, which assumes that there will be some individuals and some families that get into economic trouble, and that it is then the responsibility of other families and of the community in general to help them through. The prophecy presupposes that the community as a whole is ignoring this responsibility. The problem is not that there are a small number of rich and powerful people and a large number of poor and powerless, but that the community as a whole is involved in neglect of a minority of people who lack food, homes, and clothing, as would be the case in a country such as the U.K. or the U.S.A. It is still the case that the people who are neglected and downtrodden experience this further injustice, that they suffer a further undeserved loss beyond their hunger and neglect at the hands of the community as a whole. And presumably the prophet does not expect to be included in the 'no one', like a preexilic prophet (and that prophet's disciples).

Karl Barth finds suggestive the correlation of the idea of the Old Testament 'day of Yhwh' and the New Testament 'Lord's day'; the Lord's day is the embodiment of Yhwh's day. This correlation is then also implicit in the significance of the Sabbath as 58.13-14 describes it; the Sabbath is to be an embodiment of the concerns of Yhwh's day.[222] Jürgen Moltmann adds that 58.13-14 reflects the conviction that 'recovery of health of the body belongs to the laws about the Sabbath…. The weekly Sabbath and the recurring sabbath years are the biblical foundations for the spirituality of the body and the spirituality of the earth… The constant disciplining and repression of the body which modern industrial society requires of is members, and the constant subjection and exploitation of the earth which that society pursues, make human beings numb and the earth infertile'.[223]

221 Cf. Koenen, *Ethik und Eschatologie im Tritojesajabuch*, p. 92.

222 See Barth, *Die Kirchliche Dogmatik*, III/4, p. 61 (ET p. 56).

223 *Der Geist des Lebens* (Munich: Kaiser, 1991), p. 108; ET *The Spirit of Life* (Minneapolis: Fortress, 1992), pp. 96-97.

IV

ISAIAH 59.9-15a

Translation and Notes

9 Therefore the exercise of judgment is far from us// and faithfulness does not overtake us.
We look for light, but there—darkness;// for shining brightness—in deep gloom[1] we walk about.
10 We grope[2] like blind people along a wall;// like people with no eyes we grope.[3]
We have stumbled at midday as if it was dusk,[4]// among the sturdy[5] like people dying.[6]

[1] 'Shining' and 'deep' represent the fact that the words are (intensive) pl. (1QIs[a] has s. באפלה for the second, as in 58.10). Syr and Vg provide a copula to smooth the line.

[2] The verb נגש comes only here in the OT (though see Henoch Yalon, 'נגש–גשש', *ZAW* 44 [1926], pp. 322-23) but it is known in PBH (see *DTT*), where it can also mean 'hit', and it would make sense to think of the blind person accidentally striking against a wall (cf. Torrey, *Second Isaiah*, p. 441). But Vrs take it as a synonym of משש and thus to mean 'grope for, feel'. The cohortative form is unexpected. It is one of the 'pseudo-cohortatives' listed in *IBHS* 34.5.3, but *TTH* 52 sees it as suggesting the efforts made to find the way. Klostermann (*Deuterojesaia*, p. 82) sees the ה as object suffix, referring to the darkness (cf. Exod 10.21). 1QIs[a] has yiqtol נגשש (though נגששה at the end of the line).

[3] While LXX and Tg follow MT in repeating the verb in this line, Vg has two different words, and one might emend either to the more familiar נמששה (Tg's verb; cf. Deut 28.29), with similar meaning (e.g. Graetz, *Emendationes*, p. 34). But Isa 59.10 corresponds to Deut 28.29 in repeating the verb, even though it is a different verb.

[4] LXX, Sym, Vg, Tg assume that the כ applies to the second noun as well as the first, 'as at dusk' (so also Ehrlich, *Randglossen*, IV, p. 211).

[5] LXX omits the hapax אשמנים, whose meaning Odeberg describes as 'beyond finding out' (*Trito-Isaiah*, p. 184). Vg has another word for 'dark', and Tg perhaps takes it to mean 'graves'. These understandings might assume that it comes from a root אשם II, possibly a byform of שמם. See, e.g., G. R. Driver, 'Confused Hebrew Roots', in B. Schindler (ed.), *Occident and Orient* (M. Gaster Festschrift; London: Taylor's, 1936), pp. 73-83 (77-78). But this involves more inference than the assumption that it is linked to שמן and indicates something that contrasts with 'the dying/dead' as 'midday' contrasts with 'dusk'. The word might be an abstract noun suggesting 'good health' (e.g. Klostermann, *Deuterojesaia*, p. 82; Fischer, *Buch Isaias*, II, p. 168). But in the context 'among the healthy' fits better in making a contrast with the dead/dying, like the contrasts between groups of people in v. 10a: e.g. Koenen, 'Textkritische Anmerkungen', pp. 565-67, after a review of many possibilities; Massimo Baldacci, 'Due misconoscuiti parallelismi ad Isaia 59,10', *Bibbia e Oriente* 22 [1980], pp. 237-42. Baldacci follows

11 We growl[7] like bears, all of us;// like doves we murmur away.[8]
We look for the exercise of judgment and there is none;// for deliverance—it is far from us.[9]
12 Because our rebellions before you are many;// our offences—they have testified against us.[10]
Because our rebellions are with us;// our wayward acts—we acknowledge them:
13 Rebelling and acting false against Yhwh,// turning away from following our God,
Speaking falsehood[11] and conceiving[12] lies,[13]// talking[14] from the inner person[15] words of deceit.

1QIs[a] באשמונים implying בְּאֶשְׁמוֹנִים; cf. Beegle (‘Proper Names in the New Isaiah Scroll’, p. 29), who links it with the name of the Canaanite god of healing, Eshmun and translates ‘in good health’. For possible emendations, see (e.g.) T. K. Cheyne, ‘A Dark Passage in Isaiah’, *ZAW* 25 (1905), p. 172; Johannes Meinhold, ‘Jes 5910’, *ZAW* 40 (1922), pp. 156-57; Perles, *Analekten zur Textkritik des AT: Neue Folge*, p. 13.

[6] Tg (though apparently not LXX or Vg) implies that the ב again applies to the second noun as well as the first. So also Ehrlich, *Randglossen*, IV, p. 211, who translates ‘stumble over the sturdy as over the dead’: that is, people who should be flourishing have hit bad times and are lying there as if they are dead. But this understanding assumes a considerable change in the way the simile works as well as in the meaning of the preposition.

[7] LXX associates this verb with the previous colon.

[8] LXX ‘they will walk together’ is perhaps influenced by 11.7 (*HUB*).

[9] Vg and Syr again provide a copula after ‘for deliverance’, to smooth the line.

[10] Sg. verb follows pl. noun, perhaps because it is treated as collective (GK 145k; JM 150g; *DG* 26). 1QIs[a], LXX, Vg have a pl. verb.

[11] עשק commonly denotes oppression or concretely extortion, but in Syriac the equivalent verb can carry this more specific connotation, which Vrs assume here and which fits well; cf. J. van der Ploeg, ‘Notes lexicographiques’, *OTS* 5 (1948), pp. 142-50 (142-44). Marti (*Jesaja*, p. 378) suggests עִקֵּשׁ ‘[something] crooked’ (cf. Prov 8.8).

[12] In the expression וְסָרָה הֹרוֹ MT links the verb with the second colon, implying ‘speaking of fraud and treachery, conceiving and talking from the heart words of deceit’. But this makes for an oddly uneven line (2-4 given MT’s maqqephs, 3-5 in terms of words). Perhaps the redivision came about through the inversion in this clause and the familiarity of the expression ‘speaking of סָרָה’ (Deut 13.6 [5]; Jer 28.16; 29.32; cf. Lau’s comments, *Schriftgelehrte Prophetie in Jes 56–66*, pp. 216-17). I take the infinitive as poel of הרה rather than hiphil of ירה or qal passive (so J. Barth, *Die Nominalbildung in den semitischen Sprachen* [Leipzig: Hinrichs, 1894], p. 77), which is harder to make sense of in the context. 1QIs[a] lacks this verb and Duhm (*Jesaia*, p. 406) deletes it.

[13] סרה has usually been taken as a rare noun from the verb סור, which suggests the meaning ‘apostasy’ (cf. LXX), but most OT occurrences make better sense taken on the basis of Akkadian usage to come from a root סרר and to refer to dishonesty and specifically to false testimony. This makes good sense here. See van der Ploeg, ‘Notes lexicographiques’ (see above); Ernst Jenni, ‘Dtn 19,16: *sarā* “Falschheit”’, in A. Caquot and M. Delcor (eds.), *Mélanges bibliques et orientaux* (H. Cazelles Festschrift; Neukirchen: Neukirchener, 1981), pp. 201-11; *HALOT*.

[14] On the form of הֹגוֹ, see the translation note on הֹרוֹ. Duhm (*Jesaia*, p. 403) repoints to qal הָגוֹ.

[15] Budde (‘Jesaia Kap. 40–66’, p. 702) takes מִן to mean not ‘out of’ but ‘away from’ in the sense of ‘without’ (cf. *DCH*, V, p. 341b), thus ‘senseless’. JPSV understands לב to mean ‘throat’ as the upper part of the chest, for which לב has an Arabic cognate; see

14 So the exercise of judgment has turned away;[16]// faithfulness—it stands afar.
Because truthfulness has stumbled in the square;// straightness—it cannot enter.
15 Truthfulness has gone missing;// the one who turns from evil is one despoiled.[17]

Introduction

On the semi-independence of 59.9-15a in relation to 59.1-8 and 15b-20 [21], see the Introduction to 58.1–59.8. As a lament and confession, vv. 9-15a is different in form from what precedes and constitutes one kind of response that is appropriate to 56.9–59.8 as a whole (the other kind is action). It takes up words from 59.1-8 in particular in a way that suggests it must have been composed on the basis of and to follow 59.1-8. Light, darkness, gloom, and midday in vv. 9-10 recur from 58.10.

Elsewhere, 'therefore' (*ʿal-kēn*) is almost invariably a particle linking two parts of a statement; 57.10 is the only other occurrence in Isaiah 56–66. After an indictment like the one in 59.1-8 one would not be surprised to find a 'therefore' announcing what will follow. This would be a formal basis for inferring that these verses form part of a longer section that directly continues 59.1-8. But what would be the nature of the link between them? When 'therefore' connects two parts of a statement, it characteristically does so through the second statement's describing a response to or a consequence of some wrongdoing or calamity (e.g. 9.16 [17]; 13.7; 17.10; 24.6, 15; 25.3; 30.16). That would be a plausible dynamic to incorporate here. But neither the indictment nor the declaration about consequences correspond to those in such passages. And if this were the community's actual response to the prophet's word, a simple 'therefore' would be an implausible transition and beginning. The same

H.-J. Fabry, *TWAT*, IV, p. 415 (ET *TDOT*, VII, p. 400); and H. L. Ginsberg, 'Lexicographical Notes', in *Hebräische Wortforschung* (W. Baumgartner Festschrift; Leiden: Brill, 1967), pp. 71-82 (80).

[16] With LXX and Vg, I take והסג as simple ו with the verb keeping its past meaning, like that in v. 9 where also it is paralleled by a yiqtol. Koenen (*Ethik und Eschatologie im Tritojesajabuch*, pp. 59-60) rather takes it as *w*-consecutive and as meaning 'turns away'. On either understanding it refers to God's not having acted in משפט rather than to a human failure to act in משפט. 1QIs[a] has first-person ואסיג.

[17] LXX takes רע as from רעה III and to refer to 'understanding', or implies מדע (cf. Ulrich 'Light from 1QIsa[a] on the Translation Technique of the Old Greek Translator of Isaiah', p. 201), and implies a form of שׂכל instead of שׁלל (Klostermann, *Deuterojesaia*, p. 83). Rashi ('ישעיה', on the passage) takes שׁלל to mean 'be mad', and G. R. Driver supports this on the basis of a possible Arabic cognate ('Problems in Job', *American Journal of Semitic Languages and Literature* 52 [1935–36], pp. 160-70 [160]). For possible emendations, see (e.g.) Marti, *Jesaja*, pp. 378-79.

applies to the suggestion that the prophecy is quoting a prayer they have been praying.[18] Nor is there any indication that vv. 9-15a are the response of a faithful remnant, identifying with the nation's waywardness.[19]

Yet one can see how the move from vv. 1-8 to the 'therefore' of vv. 9-15a is a rhetorical variant on the one in those other passages. Verses 9-15a continue to be the prophet's words. The move from addressing the people confrontationally as 'you', or speaking of them dismissively as 'they', to identifying with them in speaking as 'we' is indeed abrupt. LXX testifies to the point by turning the first-person forms into third-person forms in vv. 9-11a,[20] though it then reverts to following MT. But we should not use criteria derived from the nature of oral forms to decide whether a complex unit was created this way.[21] In fact the best occurrence of *ʿal-kēn* with which to compare 59.9 is 5.25, not least because it is also something of a puzzle. It, too, follows on another 'therefore' (*lākēn*) and it is usually taken to belong to a different subsection from what precedes. The verse's presence at that point is usually taken to issue from some redactional activity. The *ʿal-kēn* therefore has a rather vague relationship with its context. Perhaps it originally followed on from some other material, such as a first-person statement in which people acknowledged their waywardness. Or perhaps the 'therefore' is anticipatory and is explained by the 'because' clauses in vv. 12-15a and we should render it 'this is why…' rather than 'that is why…'[22] There is a similar anticipatory 'therefore' in Jonah 4.2, though there the beginning of the verse does imply the reason for the 'therefore'.[23] The expression makes v. 9a the only four-stress colon in the section, which might mark it as extra-metrical but is hardly a basis for inferring that it is secondary; and it would seem unlikely that an expression whose linking significance is slightly unclear was actually an addition.[24]

There are two other features of vv. 9-15a that we need to consider in this connection. One is the recurrence of *mišpāṭ*, *ṣᵉdāqâ* and *yᵉšûʿâ* in vv. 9, 11, and 14. Verse 9 follows directly on v. 8 with its references to *mišpāṭ* and *ṣᵉdāqâ*, which take up the dual reference of this hendiadys in 56.1. It is the absence of these in the community (59.8; cf. 58.2) that

[18] So Koenen, *Ethik und Eschatologie im Tritojesajabuch*, p. 60.

[19] So Childs, *Isaiah*, p. 486; Conrad (*Reading Isaiah*, p. 103) similarly sees the 'we' of vv. 9-15a as taking responsibility for the consequences of the actions of the larger group to which the 'they' of vv. 1-8 refers.

[20] Thomas R. Yoder Neufeld (*'Put on the Armour of God'* [Sheffield: Sheffield Academic Press, 1997], pp. 42-43) sees here an aspect of heightening the negative characterization of the people in LXX.

[21] See Hanson, *The Dawn of Apocalyptic*, p. 119.

[22] Cf. Kissane, *Isaiah*, II, p. 248.

[23] The same is true of the examples cited by R. Frankena, 'Einige Bemerkungen zum Gebrauch des Adverbs *ʿal-ken* im Hebräischen', in *Studia biblica et semitica* (T. C. Vriezen Festschrift; Wageningen: Veenman, 1966), pp. 94-99. Beuken (*Jesaja IIIA*, p. 135) also notes the distance between the 'therefore' and the 'because'.

[24] Against (e.g.) Volz, *Jesaja II*, p. 235.

explains their absence in Yhwh's action (59.9). While *mišpāṭ*, *ṣedeq* and *yāša'* did come in vv. 1-8, their meaning there thus only overlapped with the meaning of the words in vv. 9-15a. The latter were closer to picking up the meaning in 56.1-2. They also overlap more significantly with 58.1-2, which refers to rebellion/offences as well as to *mišpāṭ* and *ṣᵉdāqâ*. What these various features suggest is that 59.9-15a relates to 56.1–59.8 rather broadly, and not simply or very directly to 59.1-8. It comprises an appropriate response to where the chapters have been so far, with the 'therefore' suggesting 'so all that is why…'.

This understanding of 59.9-15a will be confirmed when we come to the second half of Isaiah 56–66 and discover that 63.7–64.11 is a confession and prayer that balances the present one in the chiastic structure of Isaiah 56–66. The section's place in this structure further coheres with the looseness of its relationship with what immediately precedes it.

The prayer contains no actual petition. The lines are a series of parallel bicola. It begins by acknowledging unfulfilled hopes in vv. 9-11, in the manner of a protest psalm, and it acknowledges the reasons in vv. 12-13, also in the manner of a small number of protest psalms. It then goes through this sequence again more briefly in vv. 14a and 14b-15a.[25] Whereas the rhetoric of 59.1-8 first invited the community to hear itself addressed ('you') and then invited it to stand at a distance from itself and look at itself ('they'), the prayer form of 59.9-15a ('we') invites the community to take this confession on its lips and thus relate to the prophecy's words in yet another way, and a more self-involving one. The composition is literary rather than liturgical. We are not to imagine a prophet addressing the community and going on from an oral critique to an oral confession in which they are invited to join.[26] If it is a liturgy, it is an imaginary one.

For the prophet, vv. 1-8 involved some distancing from the people, which could encourage self-righteousness on a prophet's part. In contrast, vv. 9-15a express the prophet's identification with the people.[27] A formal indication of this identification is that the repeated *-kem* suffixes of vv. 2-3 give way to *-nû* suffixes and *nᵉ*- and *ne*- preformatives in vv. 9-13.[28] The abruptness of the transition is reduced if we assume that the prophet is not formulating a prayer they need to pray, in order to draw them into it (though that may be an implication)[29] but praying on their behalf the

[25] Volz (*Jesaja II*, pp. 230, 234) sees vv. 13-15a as a later addition.

[26] So, e.g., Elliger, *Einheit des Tritojesaia*, pp. 16-17.

[27] Cf. Hanson, *Isaiah 40–66*, p. 211.

[28] Polan, *In the Ways of Justice toward Salvation*, p. 255.

[29] Cf. Theodoret of Cyrrhus, *Commentaire sur Isaïe* 174b (3.230-31); cf. Jerome, *Commentariorum in Isaiam prophetam libri duodeviginti*, col. 579; Eusebius of Caesarea, *Der Jesajakommentar*, p. 366. Such Christian interpreters then see the passage as describing the guilt of Jews who did not recognize Jesus (cf. Haymon of Halberstadt, *Commentariorum in Isaiam libri tres*, cols. 1026-28). Cf. also Bonnard, *Le Second Isaïe*, p. 326.

prayer they need to pray.[30] It is common to quote Elliger's description of the verses as a penitential prayer that the people are praying in the prophet's imagination (*Phantasie*).[31] Verses 9 and 12 recall the prayer of this kind in Jeremiah 14.19-20.[32] While the move between confrontation and vicarious confession parallels that in Jeremiah 14.1–15.4, the move here is the reverse of the one there.

Comment

59.9 Therefore the exercise of judgment is far from us// and faithfulness does not overtake us.
We look for light, but there—darkness;// for shining brightness—in deep gloom we walk about.

On 'therefore' and the passage's relationship with its context, see the introduction to 59.9-15a. All that has preceded in 56.1–59.8 or 56.9–59.8 or 58.1–59.8 or simply in 59.1-8 explains the ongoing facts about the community's situation that v. 9 begins to describe, with the prophet acknowledging reality on behalf of the community. The promise in 56.1 has not been fulfilled. Yhwh said deliverance was 'near' but actually it is 'far'; Yhwh said it was 'coming' but actually it has not 'reached us'. The reason is that the challenge has not been met.

The two lines are both internally and mutually parallel. Verse 9a works abcdb′c′. The 'therefore' is picked up by the opening *w* in the second colon and the 'from us' is substantially paralleled by the suffix on the second verb. 'Does not reach' (yiqtol) as a less common and more concrete verb then parallels 'is far' (qatal of a stative verb). 'Faithfulness' pairs with 'the exercise of judgment' (*mišpāṭ* and *ṣᵉdāqâ*), the two elements in that hendiadys suggesting an exercise of authority that expresses faithfulness.[33] Isaiah 46.13 promised that faithfulness would not be far from the people; contrast the use of the verb in 49.19; 54.14. Actually it is.

The second line puts the same point in vivid metaphors that are familiar but newly minted. In addition, the syntax is compressed, even more than that in Jeremiah 8.15; 14.9 which make a a similar pair of contrasts.[34] The 3-3 line comprises four clauses. In the first colon, MT hyphenates 'but there—darkness' as a compound expression with one stress. In the second, we have to understand the verb from the first colon as also governing 'for shining brightness'. Then the prepositional expression comes before rather than after the verb, so that the two verbs form a

[30] So Smith, *Rhetoric and Redaction in Trito-Isaiah*, p. 120.

[31] Elliger, *Die Einheit des Tritojesaia*, p. 17; see, e.g. Pauritsch, *Die Neue Gemeinde*, p. 90.

[32] See Ruszkowski, *Volk und Gemeinde*, pp. 64-67.

[33] See the comment on 56.1.

[34] Cf. Lau, *Schriftgelehrte Prophetie in Jes 56–66*, p. 213.

bracket around the line, which we could see as working abcb′c′a′. Further, both nouns in this second colon are plural, are the only instances of the plural noun in the Old Testament, and do not make sense as regular numerical plurals. So the listener has to work hard to stay up with the prophet through the line. In the parallelism, two very familiar nouns give way to two much rarer ones, two masculine nouns give way to two feminine ones, and two singular nouns give way to two plural ones.

Light and dark are standard images for blessing and calamity and at least this imagery would be quite familiar. It is prominent in Job, who speaks of looking for and hoping for light in 3.9; 30.26,[35] and helps us see the background in the literal experience of longing for morning to come (perhaps because some danger will then be over) which is the stronger when one cannot simply turn on the light and read a book. But the imagery is also prominent in Isaiah. In 8.19–9.1 [2] the prophecy first uses dark and deep darkness as an image for the calamity God intends to bring, and comments that it will involve 'walking in darkness'. Then it speaks of seeing light and of that light shining brightly on the people (the verb is *nāgah* from which the noun 'brightness' comes). Isaiah 42.16 takes up the imagery in restating that promise and 58.8, 10 does so again, while 45.7 affirms in this connection that Yhwh is the shaper of both light and dark—that is, of well-being and trouble. The people's point is then that they have been 'looking' for the fulfilment of such promises but have seen none. This verb, too, is one that has appeared earlier in promises that people who looked to Yhwh for deliverance would find it (e.g. 40.31; 49.23). But it is also the language of lament (e.g. Pss 25.5, 21; 69.21 [20]).[36] The community still looks and does not find, so that here the talk of looking suggests not hope but 'a tone of despair and desperation'.[37]

In v. 9bβ, brightness (*n*e*gōhâ*) is a much rarer and sharper equivalent to light, especially in the unique plural. As an image for restoration or blessing it is almost confined to Isaiah (4.5; 50.10; 60.3, 19; 62.1), but its key original appearance comes in Amos 5.20, where the prophet warns that Yhwh's ray will be dark not light and deep darkness not brightness. There are the differences from Amos that 'dark' is there an adjective and here both 'brightness' and 'deep darkness' are plural, changes which also mean that a pair of masculine singular nouns is paralleled by a pair of feminine plural nouns. Yet it is significant that all four nouns in the line recur from Amos 5.20. There is some irony in the link. Amos's point was that people thought Yhwh's day would bring light and brightness but actually it will bring dark and deep darkness. Here in v. 1 'we' are again looking for light and brightness but actually experiencing dark and deep darkness, as Amos warned, and for the same reasons. Once more it transpires that the moral and social issues raised by the preexilic prophets

[35] Cf. Calov, *Biblia Testamenti Veteris illustrate*, II, p. 309.
[36] G. Waschke, *TWAT*, VI, p. 1233 (ET *TDOT*, XII, p. 572).
[37] Oswalt, *Isaiah Chapters 40–66*, p. 522.

are not ones confined to their time, and therefore neither are the consequences that follow. The exile did not change anything much about the people and neither therefore did it change much about their experience. Indeed, 'total, deep darkness' suggests things are worse than ever; the prayers in Ezra–Nehemiah could be assumed to take a similar gloomy view.

59.10 We grope like blind people along a wall;// like people with no eyes we grope.
We have stumbled at midday as if it was dusk,// among the sturdy like people dying.

Again the two lines are both internally and mutually parallel. In the first, the repeated verb brackets the line; it is unusual though not unique for the same verb to be repeated in a line. The parallel with the wording of Deuteronomy 28.29 (though there the repeated verb is *māšaš* not *gāšaš*) suggests that this is a fulfilment of that warning concerning the consequences of ignoring Yhwh's requirements. Inside the two verbs are the two expressions for blindness, the second more concrete and vivid. At the end of the first colon is the word '[along a] wall', which applies to both cola. While the verb for 'grope' comes only here, the descriptions of the people again recall Isaiah 40–55 while the reference to the wall recalls Amos 5.19-20. The latter would hardly count for anything on its own, but in combination with the four nouns in v. 9b and the shared reference to a bear in 59.11, the link suggests that this prophecy was in part inspired by Amos's imagery.[38] There, someone has leant on a wall thinking it is safe to do so and has been bitten by a snake, which might especially happen to a blind person. And perhaps that is the prophet's point; the blind person who gropes along a wall will probably end up in trouble in some way. The parallel line may indicate how.

The notion of moral or religious blindness as a punishment again goes back to Isaiah 6.10, but the line's more precise links are with the references in Isaiah 40–55 to the blindness of people who (allegedly) have eyes and to Yhwh's promise to open these eyes (42.7, 16, 18, 19; 43.8). But in 59.10 there is not much hint of the idea of moral or religious blindness. The earlier references show that actually darkness and blindness are related images (see, e.g., 42.7, 16), presumably because blindness is like being in the dark and being in the darkness of a dungeon is like being blind. So the lament in v. 10a continues that in v. 9b, describing the deprived state of the community.

[38] Bernard Gosse sees Amos 5.18-20 as influential on the redaction of Isa 56–59 (see 'La rédaction du livre d'Isaïe en rapport au livre d'Amos et au Psautier', *Henoch* 20 [1998], pp. 259-70 [265-66]).

Verse 10b adapts the metaphor once more. Instead of light as bright as dawn breaking into darkness, even noon is like dusk.[39] Here the 3-2 line works abcb′c′ with the verb applying to both cola. Then two *b*- expressions (one dual, one plural) and two *k*- expressions (one singular, one plural) balance each other. The line continues to work with the image of blindness. That affliction may mean people merely grope, but it may mean they fall over. It can happen to anyone at dusk when it becomes harder to see (*nešep* etymologically denotes a breeze, but in usage it denotes the time the breeze often comes, at twilight). But it can happen to blind people at midday. Thus blind people make their way along the street looking just as well-fed, well-built and full of life as anyone else (etymologically, they are 'fat', but that would be pejorative in English). But they fall over as if they are falling down dead or as if they are already lifeless (contrast the promise in 40.30). It is as if they are in Sheol (cf. Ps 88.6-7 [5-6]).[40]

Psalm 22.30 [29] makes the contrast between people who are *dāšēn* (sturdy or well-to-do) and people who are near death, though not in a comparable connection; but perhaps it is a familiar antithesis. It is more pointed that '"stumbling"...is also a way of describing the effect of sin in prophetic preaching (e.g. Hos 5:5; 14:2 [1], 10 [9]; Isa 3:8; Jer 6:15, 21)'.[41]

59.11 We growl like bears, all of us;// like doves we murmur away.
We look for the exercise of judgment and there is none;// for deliverance—
it is far from us.

Once more the two lines are both internally and mutually parallel. In the first, the verbs come at either end of the line and are nicely alliterative, *hāmâ* and *hāgâ*; the forms in fact rhyme. In Psalms 42–43 *hāmâ* refers to the inner disquiet of a person whom God seems to have abandoned and who is prevented from getting to the temple (cf. 55.18 [17]; 77.4 [3]). Even more tellingly, it refers to the lament of people who survive the fall of Jerusalem and take refuge in the mountains 'like doves' and whimper or moan 'all of them', because of their waywardness (Ezek 7.16; cf. also Jer 4.19; 48.36; Isa 16.11). The second verb is also used in connection with Moab's suffering and of Hezekiah's (Isa 16.7; 38.14; Jer 48.31). It is the one used in a different connection in 59.3 and it will recur in that earlier connection in v. 13. The two *k*- clauses likewise correspond but come in different positions. In isolation we would assume that the verb *hāmâ* applied to bears meant they were growling aggressively or roaring, and the parallelism of bears and doves is unexpected; bear and lion in

[39] Oswalt, *Isaiah Chapters 40–66*, p. 521.
[40] Cf. Zapff, *Jesaja 56–66*, p. 377.
[41] Blenkinsopp, *Isaiah 56–66*, p. 193.

Amos 5.19 is more predictable. Perhaps the image presupposes a bear robbed of her cubs (2 Sam 17.8; Prov 17.12), who is indeed a threat, because she cannot find them. The parallel image is easier, since the dove's cooing is often (though without reason) thought to be a sad sound; not for nothing is it called a 'mourning dove'. A Babylonian prayer of lament and confession to Ishtar uses the same image, 'I mourn like a dove night and day'.[42] In the first colon 'all of us' underlines the point, as it does in Ezekiel 7.16. In the second, the repetition of the verb does so: literally, 'in murmuring we murmur'.

In v. 11b the initial protest or lament element in the confession comes to an end with a return to the more general theological language of v. 9a, which thus forms an *inclusio* around vv. 9-11. But first the opening verb is picked up from the opening of v. 9a, and the rhetoric of the line corresponds more to that of v. 9b. After the verb, the two cola are parallel. 'For deliverance' complements 'for the exercise of judgment'. It is thus also equivalent to 'faithfulness' (which implies faithful action of this kind) in v. 9a. 'Deliverance' accompanied 'the exercise of judgment' and 'faithfulness' in 56.1. JPSV now translates *yᵉšû ʿâ* 'victory', but in general this is a misleading translation, and a shift in the word's implications from those in 56.1 (and 59.1) is unlikely. 'It is far from us' (the phrase from v. 9a, except for the necessary gender change) complements 'and there is none' (a new expression here, but one whose gloomy implications are illustrated in 41.17; 45.21).

It is now clear that vv. 9-11 work as a chiasm:[43]

9a The exercise of judgment is *far from us*
 9b *We look for* light
  10a We grope like [*nᵉgašᵉšâ k*...]...we grope like [*k*...*nᵉgašēšâ*]
   10b We stumble at midday
  11a We growl like [*nehᵉmeh k*...]...we murmur like [*k*...*nehgeh*]
 11bα *We look for* the exercise of judgment
11b Deliverance *is far from us.*

59.12 Because our rebellions are many before you;// our offences—they have testified against us.
Because our rebellions are with us;// our wayward acts—we acknowledge them.

Most descriptions of Israel's affliction such as the one in vv. 9-11 are followed by a declaration along the lines of 'all this has come upon us when we have not put you out of mind' (Ps 44.18 [17]). But occasionally people who summon Yhwh 'from the depths' and are looking to Yhwh to take action know that it is acts of waywardness that explain why they are

[42] *ANET*, p. 384; cf. Stummer, 'Einige keilschriftliche Parallelen zu Jes. 40–66', p. 186.
[43] Cf. Polan, *In the Ways of Justice toward Salvation*, p. 276.

in the depths (see, e.g., Ps 130). This is so in Lamentations and in other post-exilic prayers in Ezra–Nehemiah, and it is so here, in light of the attacks in 56.9–59.8. The prophet thus goes on from acknowledging the reality of the community's circumstances in vv. 9-11 (with which it might agree) to acknowledging the reasons (over which it might be more hesitant).

Yet again the lines are internally and mutually parallel. Both lines begin with a 'because' that applies to both cola, with a *w* to pick it up in each second colon. The two nouns are parallel, as in 58.1 (rebellion already also in 57.4, offences in 59.2), though here both are plural, and in the second the noun is put in emphatic position before the verb. At the same time, this effect is countered by the fact that the second verb is a much more vivid one than the first. The two closing expressions also complement each other, with the second heightening the point. The people's wrongdoings are not only 'before us' (as in Ps 51.5 [3]) but 'before you' (Ps 90.8; also Isa 1.16). And 'before' is *neged*, 'rather stronger and distincter' than *lipnê*.[44] 'There is…much weight in the phrase "before thee".'[45] Yet maybe they are just sitting there and Yhwh might not notice them? Not so. They are there testifying 'against us'. They function a little like Abel's blood 'crying out' from the ground. They keep making a noise, demanding that the president of the heavenly court listen to the charges they bring.

Verse 12b is a succinct and perhaps grieving 2-2 line (MT hyphenates the *kî* with the noun that follows). Here rebellions pair with wayward acts (as in 59.2, where see the comment; the singular came in 57.17). The multiplicity of the rebellions (v. 12a) is thus also suggested by the repetition of the noun in the second line, by the multiplying of words to describe them, as offences and wayward acts as well as rebellions, and by the fact that all four words are plural. In turn, 'we acknowledge them' complements '[are] with us'. Notwithstanding the fact that the first colon is a noun clause (or might the parallelism of the lines invite us to understand it as 'because our rebellions are many with us'?), the rhetoric of the line works in a similar way to that of v. 12a, with the second noun preceding its verb but the verb itself then one that heightens the point made by the equivalent expression in the first. Not only are the wrongdoings 'with us', again in such a way that they might be just sitting there and we might be ignoring them. No, 'we acknowledge them'. In 58.1 Yhwh protested at the manner of people's acknowledgment of Yhwh's ways; they do so with enthusiasm but in a fashion that does not carry over into their everyday lives. In 58.3 Yhwh thus notes their consequent puzzlement at Yhwh's not acknowledging their acts of spiritual commitment. The problem, 59.8 adds, is that in reality they have not acknowledged the way of well-being. Acknowledging their wayward acts would

[44] BDB.

[45] Calvin, *In Iesaiam prophetam*, p. 377 (ET IV, p. 257).

open up the possibility of reworking this dynamic: compare Psalm 51.5 [3], where rebellions, acknowledgment, and offence, as well as 'before me' all occur. But whereas Psalm 51 goes on to plead for forgiveness and restoration, Isaiah 59 confines itself to confession and only by implication casts itself on God's mercy as a kind of *Gerichtsdoxologie*, an acknowledgment of God's justice. Yet the similarity with Psalms 51 and 90 may indicate that the prophet takes up the way the congregation would have made its confession in the context of exilic worship (compare the closing verses of Ps 51).

59.13 Rebelling and acting false against Yhwh,// turning away from following our God,
Speaking of extortion and conceiving lies,// talking from the inner person words of deceit.

A further pair of mutually and internally parallel lines offer the neatest formal parallel with 59.1-8 as they comprise a series of infinitives absolute (cf. 59.4b), though that earlier series was syndetically unrelated to its context, whereas here they may stand in apposition to the nouns in v. 12 and be the further objects of 'acknowledge'.[46] But the usage recurs in Jeremiah 7.9 and Hosea 4.2. Each line comprises a double infinitival expression in the first colon and a single infinitival expression in the second colon. All four clauses have approximately the same meaning, though v. 13a refers to action in relation to God whereas v. 13b refers to action in relation to other people.

In v. 13a, within the parallelism internal to the first colon the frequent pattern applies whereby the opening verb is a common one and the second a less usual expression that also nuances the first. 'Rebelling' picks up from the twofold appearance of the related noun in v. 12; it was the third word in v. 12a, the second in v. 12b, and it now comes first. The word thus moves inexorably towards the beginning of the line, and suggests despondency and hopelessness as in Ezekiel 33.10 rather than a hope that is aware of the possibility of restoration as in Isaiah 53.5.[47] 'Acting false' (*kāḥaš* piel) against Yhwh indicates that the rebellion is covert rather than open. The prophet has people acknowledging that whereas they professed continuing commitment to Yhwh, reality was different. The second colon makes that point explicit. The speakers acknowledge that they have 'turned back from after Yhwh', by implication to follow after other deities, in the way the prophecy has alleged (see especially 57.3-13). The description of Yhwh as 'our God' heightens the enormity of these acts.

[46] Cf. GK 113d; *IBHS* 35.3.3b. But *DG* 103b takes them as similar to those in v. 4. 1QIs[a] has פשועו for MT פשע, ודברו for MT דבר, הגוא for MT הגו, all likely emerging from unease with the infinitives.

[47] Cf. Koole, *Jesaja III*, p. 198 (ET p. 190).

The first colon in v. 13b follows a similar pattern. While the combination 'speaking of extortion' otherwise occurs only in Psalm 73.28, the verb and the idea are common ones. The noun (*ʿōšeq*) can be rendered 'oppression', but it carries the particular connotation of extracting money or resources from people on an illegitimate scale or by illegitimate means, or otherwise depriving needy people of their rights (e.g. Lev 5.21, 23 [6.2, 4]; Ps 10.11 [10]). Thus the phrase makes clear that v. 13b moves from a confession of wrongdoing in relation to God to a confession of wrongdoing in relation to other people in the community; here again it is thus acknowledging the truth of the prophecies' allegations (see 56.9–57.2, also 58.1–59.8). 'Speaking of' is then expressed more vividly as 'conceiving'; the two verbs came close together in 59.4 (though there 'conceive' was the regular qal). There, people were accused of conceiving 'trouble'; here, they acknowledge conceiving 'lies'. Speaking lies means claiming that someone said or did something that they did not say or do. The colon as a whole then comprises a hendiadys: they conceive extortion and speak lies in order to make it happen;[48] to 'speak of extortion' does not mean merely having an exploitative attitude.[49] The parallel colon in v. 13b restates the phrase. 'Talking' (*hāgâ*) takes up the verb from v. 3, used in a similar context to denote the kind of talk that is done rather quietly, in this case so that other people cannot hear its plotting (the verb was used in a different sense in v. 11). But the talk comes 'from the inner person', 'from [their own] heart';[50] it is the result of the process of inner conceiving just referred to. 'Deceit', too, takes up an expression from v. 3 (earlier from 57.4).

59.14 So the exercise of judgment has turned away;// faithfulness—it stands afar.// Because truthfulness has stumbled in the square;// straightness—it cannot enter.
15a Truthfulness has gone missing; the one who turns from evil is one despoiled.

LXX's 'we turned away…' raises the question whether the whole of vv. 14-15a might continue to describe the community's wrongdoing.[51] On this understanding *mišpāṭ ûṣᵉdāqâ* refer to human obligations and the move between vv. 9 and 14 parallels that within 56.1. But the reference to *mišpāṭ ûṣᵉdāqâ* being far away is very close to the language of v. 9 and more likely the phrase again refers to God's action. The last three lines of the section then form a reprise and summary of vv. 9-13 with their two parts, further underlining the link between the community's experience and the causes of it. The first line summarizes the lament in parallel cola,

[48] Beuken (*Jesaja IIIA*, p. 140) sees 'extortion' and 'lies' as a hendiadys.
[49] Contrast E. Gerstenberger, *TWAT*, VI, p. 445 (ET *TDOT*, XI, p. 415).
[50] König, *Jesaja*, p. 503.
[51] Perhaps LXX read הסג as another infinitive absolute, following on those in v. 13, which it translates as 'we' (GID).

arranged abcc′b′a′, which helps to signal that this line stands alone; it is the only line in the section that does so. In contrast, it gives no signal at its opening that it is about to return to a protest at the community's experience, because it again uses the verb *sûg*, which came in the previous verse. There it denoted the people's turning away from following Yhwh. Here it refers to a responsive turning away (*mēʾaḥar* in v. 13, *ʾāḥôr* here) by Yhwh. The usage already points in another way to the link between the two actions. More precisely, however, v. 14a refers to a turning away by *mišpāṭ*, and suggests a more intrinsic link in the ordering of reality between the two events whereby *mišpāṭ* 'naturally' issues from the following of God and 'naturally' does not issue from turning from God's ways. In the structure of the line, the two adverbial expressions of place, 'away' and 'afar', stand at the middle of the cola. At the centre of the line comes the familiar *mišpāṭ ûṣᵉdāqâ*. At its close, the verb 'stands' adds to the weight of 'has turned away'. It was not just a momentary turning that might lead to a quick returning. The situation is at a standstill. The turning away of these two personified qualities contrasts with the accompanying of the 'illustrious escorts' in 58.8.[52]

The closing two lines then summarize the reasons for this turning and standing, again beginning with a 'because'. Whereas in vv. 9-12 the protest thus occupied more lines than the confession, here the confession occupies more lines than the protest. As has been the case throughout the section, the two lines are both mutually and internally parallel. In v. 14b, as in the previous line, the two subjects stand together at the centre of the line, with the effect each time of locating the second of them in front of its verb. So 'truthfulness and uprightness' come together. 'Truthfulness' (*ʾĕmet*) occurs in Isaiah 56–66 only here and in the next line, though *ʾĕmûnâ* occurred in v. 4. The rare 'straightness' (*nᵉkōḥâ*) came in 57.2. Again the prayer is acknowledging the truth in the prophecy's accusations. The remainder of the two cola in v. 14b suggests a vivid picture. On one hand, the fate of truthfulness is that it has fallen over in the public square. This is the place where trade is carried out and therefore dishonesty is practised. Even more significantly it is where the elders meet to deal with disputes and accusations in the community. Truthfulness has collapsed there. This time the verb recurs from v. 10, with similar implications to those attaching to the repetition of *sûg*. Why do we go around stumbling? Because we have let truthfulness stumble. There is an inner link between the two. The remainder of the second colon puts the consequences even more sombrely. As *mišpāṭ ûṣᵉdāqâ* have not only turned away but stand firm there at a distance, so truthfulness and straightness have not only stumbled, and not merely stumbled so that they cannot get up again. They have disappeared; it is as if they have been thrown out of the public square, and they are now denied access. There are security guards on duty at the entrance of the square, and their task is to make sure that truthfulness and straightness do not get in.

[52] Cf. Alonso Schökel, *A Manual of Hebrew Poetics*, pp. 123, 124-25.

Verse 15a reformulates the point and takes it even further. The first colon directly restates the implication of v. 14bβ. In the parallelism the concrete complements the abstract and the verb makes the description even more horrifying. The community's responsibility is to put down evil and encourage good. Instead, it not only overlooks evil or even encourages it. It actively discourages good. If people do see the error of their ways and turn from evil, its reaction is to take advantage of their new-found naivety and plunder them. The hitpoel form of the verb implies that they are opening themselves up to such plundering.[53]

'These people are living in a moral wilderness'.[54] The section puts on the lips of the community an acknowledgment that all this is true. It is not clear how far the community actually took this confession onto its lips.

Conclusion

The prayer is a protest at the community's situation, which nevertheless acknowledges that people's waywardness is the explanation for it. The combination is striking, but psalms from time to time combine these two notes. Like such psalms, when this prayer speaks '*de profundis*',[55] it is both out of suffering and out of an awareness of sin. It takes up the exhortation and promise in 56.1 and acknowledges with grief that the promise has not been fulfilled but that this is because the exhortation has not been heeded. If the people hope to move Yhwh to bring about a change in their situation, both parts of this acknowledgment are vital.

[53] Oswalt, *Isaiah Chapters 40–66*, p. 524

[54] Blenkinsopp, *Isaiah 56–66*, p. 194.

[55] Penna, *Isaia*, p. 575.

V

ISAIAH 59.15b-21

Translation and Notes

15b Yhwh has seen, and it was evil in his eyes[1]// that there was no[2] exercise of judgment.

16 He has seen that there was nobody,// and he was devastated[3] that there was no one intervening.

So his arm has effected deliverance for him;// his faithfulness[4] – it has supported him.

17 He has clothed himself with faithfulness as a coat of mail// and with a deliverance helmet on his head.//

He has clothed himself with redress garments as clothing,// wrapped on passion as a coat.[5]

18 In accordance with[6] due recompense, in the manner of the one on high[7]// he will pay back fury to his foes.

[1] For וירע בעיניו, Hermann Gunkel suggested בעיניו וַיֵּדַע 'has seen with his eyes and come to know', which makes the line 3-3 (*Schöpfung und Chaos in Urzeit und Endzeit* [repr., Göttingen: Vandenhoeck & Ruprecht, 1921], p. 108 [ET *Creation and Chaos in the Primeval Era and the Eschaton* (Grand Rapids: Eerdmans, 2006), p. 73]).

[2] For כי־אין 4QIs^e has כאין; a slip.

[3] LXX 'he observed' (cf. Tg), perhaps to avoid the strong anthropomorphism; contrast Vg.

[4] Arie Rubinstein ('Word-Substitution in Isaiah lxiii.5 and lix.16', *JSS* 8 [1963], pp. 52-55) suggests that the text originally read אמתו 'his forearm' (for which see *DCH*).

[5] LXX, Syr omit v. 17bβ. In v. 17bα LXX also omits 'as clothing', as does Vg, and Lowth (*Isaiah*, p. 379) notes that George Jubb (Professor of Hebrew at Oxford in Lowth's day) suggested deleting it. Syr, too, omits one of the 'redundant' words in v. 17bα, but it seems to be the first (that is, Syr reads 'with redress clothing'); so also Th. But Volz (*Jesaja II*, p. 235) is surely right that if there is a gloss in the line, it is the more familiar בגדי 'garments'. Tg is so paraphrastic it is hard to guess its text. Aq, Sym, follow MT.

[6] On the very rare pleonastic compound preposition כעל (cf. 63.7) see BDB, p. 455a. Tg 'the Lord [of recompense]' suggests בעל for כעל, a reading in the (perhaps thirteenth-century) haggadic compilation Yalkut Shimoni (*HUB*).

[7] For the second כעל Tg גמלא could imply גְּמוּל; this avoids the tricky repetition of כעל from the beginning of the line which could be taken as dittog. (cf. Dillmann, *Jesaia* [1890 edn], p. 502), but it does issue in four occurrences of the same noun in the verse (Duhm calls it an instance of emendation as a sport [*Jesaia*, p. 405]). Verse 18a as a whole is problematic but 'reconstruction of the original text would be mere guess-work' (Odeberg, *Trito-Isaiah*, p. 194; cf. Sekine, *Die Tritojesajanische Sammlung*, p 133). For further examples of attempts, see (e.g.) Koenen, *Ethik und Eschatologie im Tritojesajabuch*, pp. 72-73. Jer 51.56 perhaps represents the first attempt to turn v. 18a into

Recompense to his enemies,// recompense to distant shores he will pay back.
19 So they will revere[8] Yhwh's name from the setting sun,// from the rising of the sun his splendour.
When an adversary[9] comes like a river, // Yhwh's wind raises a banner against him.
20 He will come to Zion[10] as restorer,// to those in Jacob who turn from rebellion[11]// (Yhwh's declaration).[12]
21 'So I: this is my covenant with them',[13] Yhwh has said. 'My breath which is on you and my words which I have put in your mouth will not be missing from your mouth and from the mouth of your offspring and from the mouth of your offspring's offspring[14] (Yhwh has said)[15] from now and forever'.

Introduction

On the relationship of 59.15b-21 to what precedes, see the introduction to 58.1–59.8. That section constituted a confrontation concerning wrong-doing in the community, which was broadly the burden of 56.9–59.8 as a whole. In 59.9-15a the prophecy has then gone on to voice the kind of protest and confession to Yhwh that needs to issue from recognition of those facts about life in the community. Now comes a prophetic response to this protest and confession. The MT versification holding together the two lines that comprise v. 15 testifies to the close relationship of vv. 15b-21 to vv. 9-15a. In itself it would indeed be entirely plausible to see v. 15b as simply continuing the description in vv. 14-15a, and the *w*-consecutive

something more straightforward. LXX rather shortens v. 18 as a whole, perhaps simply omitting v. 18b, but whereas other omissions and variations in LXX in vv. 15b-20 likely reflect unease with the substance of MT, this abbreviation likely reflects the repetitive nature of MT. Its incorporation of 'shame' likewise avoids the repetition of 'recompense'.

8 The MT mss are divided over whether to read וייראו from ירא or וְיִרְאוּ from ראה (see *HUB*).

9 For צר 1QIs[a] has צור, from which Alexander Rofé ('Isaiah 59:19 and Trito-Isaiah's Vision of Redemption', in Vermeylen [ed.], *The Book of Isaiah: Le Livre d'Isaïe*, pp. 407-10) infers ציר 'envoy'.

10 1QIs[a] has אל for ל, more likely by dittog. than to signify movement rather than benefit (the meaning of the subsequent ל), or for some other theological reason (against Pulikottil, *Transmission of Biblical Texts in Qumran*, p. 78).

11 LXX has 'he will turn impiety from Jacob' (cf. Tg). This might reflect the unusual nature of the Hebrew expression, literally 'the turners of rebellion', or might suggest a messianic interpretation (so Volz, *Jesaja II*, p. 235), or might suggest that it read לשוב not לשבי (GID).

12 LXX omits this last phrase.

13 1QIs[a] אתם implies the expected אִתָּם 'with them' for אוֹתָם 'them'; the Reuchlin ms of MT reads this, and Vg, Tg may also imply it.

14 LXX omits 'from the mouth of your offspring's offspring', perhaps by homoioteleuton (GID).

15 1QIs[a] omits this second אמר יהוה in the verse.

with which it begins would encourage that assumption. But each line through vv. 15-17 begins with *w*-consecutive and these three verses as a whole cannot be understood as simply continuing vv. 9-14. In retrospect v. 15b is in fact the plausible point to see the move from the protest and confession uttered by the prophet on the people's behalf, to an account of Yhwh's response.

More precisely it is a prophetic response, because the section does not take the form of divine words but of a prophet's words concerning Yhwh. The antithesis should not been drawn too sharply; v. 20b does eventually identify the verses as 'Yhwh's declaration'. Yet it is note-worthy that this *prophetic* word follows on the prophetic prayer in vv. 9-15a. The prophet's vision of what the community needs Yhwh to say follows on the prophet's expression of what the community needs to say to Yhwh.

Verses 15b-20 are commonly described as a Divine Warrior Hymn.[16] The term suggests an act of praise that celebrates a victory Yhwh won at creation or at the Reed Sea or in a subsequent historical event, or a victory Yhwh will win at the End. Outside the Old Testament, a classic instance of such a celebration is the Babylonian creation story Enuma Elish.[17] Characteristically, the deity takes on combat with opposing forces that imperil order in the world and the community, wins a victory that establishes permanent order there, thereby ensures the community's deliverance and safety, and opens up the possibility of peace and blessing for it; the community then proclaims the deity's victory. Here, vv. 15b-20 indeed celebrate the way Yhwh undertook such a battle, because no one else would do so. It at first speaks as if Yhwh has already undertaken the battle, but it then becomes clear that this is so only in the prophet's vision (as is commonly the case in the Prophets). In this celebration the emphasis lies on the armour Yhwh is wearing, with its significance for the community: for example, faithfulness, deliverance, redress, restoration. While the talk of deliverance thus has associations with the law court and with 'concepts of legal protection', Yhwh is presented 'less as a judge than as a warrior' who is 'taking the law into his own hands'.[18] Further, the motivation for Yhwh's action is not merely legal (as if Yhwh were the agent in a Western law court) but relational. Redress, faithfulness, restoration, and deliverance are closely associated in the mutual commitment of a community.

There is another sense in which the term 'vision' may apply to the section, if it constitutes the report of a vision the prophet has seen. It is then not only Yhwh who has 'seen' (vv. 15, 16); the prophet has done so. The implicit claim to have seen and not merely heard enhances the sense

[16] So, e.g., Hanson, *The Dawn of Apocalyptic*, p. 118; see further pp. 300-15.

[17] For which see, e.g., *ANET*, pp. 60-72, 501-3.

[18] J. Sawyer, *TWAT*, III, p. 1052 (ET *TDOT*, VI, pp. 456-57); see further Sawyer, *Semantics in Biblical Research* (London: SCM; Naperville, IL: Allenson, 1972).

of reality conveyed by the words that follow. 'I have not merely heard (but maybe my hearing deceived me); I have seen with my own eyes'. And although the community itself continues to be in the position of people who merely hear, they are invited to share in the prophet's vicarious seeing, to respond like people who have seen and not just heard, and thus to respond with a greater certainty that accepts the greater certainty of what is portrayed.

The prophetic account of Yhwh's action begins in the qatal (to be more accurate, mostly the verbs are *w*-consecutive plus yiqtol; vv. 15b-17) then moves to yiqtol. In themselves vv. 15b-17 could thus describe ways God had actually acted in the past. Yhwh acted in bringing Israel out of Egypt and defeating Pharaoh at the Reed Sea,[19] and the portrait of Yhwh as a warrior recalls Exodus 15.3.[20] Or they could describe Yhwh's action in taking the Judahites into exile, with Yhwh the warrior fighting against the people rather than for them.[21] The language also recalls Isaiah 42.13, which refers to Yhwh's action in putting down Babylon to make it possible for the Judahites to come home. But the way vv. 15b-21 follow on vv. 9-15a suggests rather that this new subsection relates to the same absence of *mišpāṭ* that the preceding verses referred to. A supporting consideration is the passage's many links with 63.1-6,[22] which (indeed) is often taken to be older and/or to provide keys for understanding 59.15b-20[23] (though the relationship has been seen as the reverse).[24] While we will consider these links when we come to 63.1-6, we may note that the latter is universally taken to describe an act of judgment to come in the future rather than one that took place in the past.

The vision report also recalls 52.13–53.12 (though that was an auditory rather than a visionary experience), which described a series of events that had begun but not finished. There, the servant's humiliation and recognition by his fellows were past but his restoration was still future. Of course this says nothing about where things are in the world outside the vision; there, for instance, the humiliation may be past but both the recognition and the restoration future, or the whole scene may relate to the future, or the whole scene may relate to the past. It makes sense to understand 59.15b-20 in a parallel way: in vision, the prophet has witnessed the initiation of the process whereby Zion's restoration and the nations' recognition of Yhwh will be effected, but the concrete events

[19] Cf. Pauritsch, *Die Neue Gemeinde*, p. 92.

[20] On the broader Old Testament background, see Thomas R. Yoder Neufeld (*'Put on the Armour of God'* [Sheffield: Sheffield Academic Press, 1997], pp. 23-24) and his references.

[21] So Kissane, *Isaiah*, p. 250.

[22] Kissane (*Isaiah*, p. 250) himself notes the particular link between 59.15b-16a and 63.5.

[23] See, e.g., Fischer, *Buch Isaias*, II, p. 169; and the lengthy argument in Stromberg, *Isaiah after Exile*, pp. 34-38.

[24] Cf. Vermeylen, *Du prophète Isaïe à l'apocalyptique*, II, p. 469.

that will achieve this are still to come. It is in the light of this fact that in English perfect verbs are appropriate in vv. 15b-17. The account in the vision does correspond to the objective situation. The prophet knows that Yhwh has determined to bring about the process of restoration and recognition, but of course also knows that Yhwh has not yet acted. The rhetorical purpose of the section is to get the community to see the situation in this way and to look at themselves in light of that reality. At the moment what they can see is waywardness (their own and/or that of which they are victims). They are invited to live in the conviction that Yhwh has actually determined, and in this sense has initiated, the process whereby restoration will come. The section's rhetorical technique is thus the same as that when a prophet says 'Yhwh has said this', indicating that the divine word has been spoken, that events will therefore follow, and that the community therefore needs to live in light of that fact.

Comment

59.15b Yhwh has seen,// and it was evil in his eyes// that there was no exercise of judgment.

16a He has seen that there was nobody,// and he was devastated that there was no one intervening.

The report begins with a 2-2-2 tricolon, which as such hints at the transition to a new section and to a move from the protest in vv. 9-15a to the words of Yhwh.[25] The pair of lines comprising vv. 15b-16a manifest mutual parallelism as well as some internal parallelism. In v. 15b the first colon raises the question 'What did Yhwh see?' and the second answers it, but does so in a way that raises the further question 'and why did it displease him?', which the third colon then begins to answer. So the line comprises three clauses that develop. Yhwh saw something. What was it? Something displeasing. Why was it displeasing? Because there was no *mišpāṭ*. There is some paronomasia between the first two verbs, *wayyar'* and *wayyēra'*. Seeing and being displeased are close together. In 58.3 people had protested that Yhwh had not looked at their fasting (*rā'â*); the prophet had given one response there, but here gives another. In v. 15a Yhwh had uttered a remonstration concerning the fate of people who turn from evil; the recurrence of reference to 'evil' in v. 15b indicates Yhwh's willingness to identify with such people.

That in turn poses another question. What kind of *mišpāṭ* is the prophet speaking of?[26] The close of 58.1–59.8 lamented the absence of any exercise of *mišpāṭ* within the community's own life; it had failed the challenge set by 56.1. In contrast, the protest in 59.9-15a went on to

[25] Cf. Koenen, *Ethik und Eschatologie im Tritojesajabuch*, p. 65.
[26] On *mišpāṭ*, see the comment on 56.1.

lament the other sense in which *mišpāṭ* was far from the community as a whole in its distress, when there was no exercise of *mišpāṭ* to bring deliverance to it, and it would be odd if Yhwh, too, were not also distressed at this absence of *mišpāṭ*. The account of the Second Temple community in Ezra, Nehemiah, Haggai, and Zechariah would make it possible for a prophet to be looking for the action of warrior Yhwh either against wrongdoers within Judah or against imperial overlords outside it. Which sort of *mišpāṭ* is Yhwh concerned about in vv. 15b-20? Through vv. 15b-17 either could be mind, but by the end of v. 18 only the second is possible. In the meantime, vv. 15b-17 raise the possibility that these are not merely two separate references of the one word but facets of the same reality. There is neither form of *mišpāṭ* in the community, and both aspects of this displease Yhwh.

Verse 16a begins the second of this pair of lines with the same verb as the first, and then goes on substantially to parallel it. In doing so, it first jumps to a noun clause introduced by *kî-'ên*, 'that there is no'. It thus parallels the last clause in v. 15b. In 50.2 there was nobody in Judah responding to Yhwh and in Jeremiah 5.1 there was no one acting with *mišpāṭ* or being faithful; here, either idea would follow well on vv. 1-15a. But it turns out that the poetic line works like the previous one; in typical fashion the second colon clarifies the first. The first colon raises the question 'there was nobody doing what?', and the second answers that 'there was no one intervening'. The effect of the triple repetition of *ʾên*, 'there is no', is to 'heighten the dramatic effect and add a note of the superlative', as in 6.3; Jeremiah 7.4; 22.29; Ezekiel 21.27; this is also the chapter's third occurrence of *ʾên* in association with a form from the root *šāpaṭ* (see vv. 4, 8).[27]

'He was devastated' in turn takes further 'he saw'. Tg understands this last clause then to declare that 'there was no intercessor', which fits the probable meaning of *pāgaʿ* (hiphil) in passages such as Jeremiah 36.25 and Isaiah 53.12.[28] But intertextual relationships within Isaiah or in relation to other books do not imply that an expression has the same meaning when it recurs in another passage. Indeed, 'the anxiety of influence' often has the opposite implication.[29] Both in the qal and the hiphil, *pāgaʿ* has broader meaning, and here, following on vv. 9-15a, it would be odd to regret the absence of an intercessor; rather, the colon regrets the absence of someone intervening. If the verb does refer to intercession in 53.12 and if the present passage is taking up that verse, here the prophet may take the verb to mean 'intervene' in 53.12. Following on that verse, the

[27] Polan, *In the Ways of Justice toward Salvation*, p. 294.

[28] So Ibn Ezra, *The Commentary of Ibn Ezra on Isaiah*, p. 274; and on 53.12, Goldingay and Payne, *Isaiah 40–55* 2, pp. 330-31.

[29] See Harold Bloom, *The Anxiety of Influence* (Oxford: Oxford University Press, 2nd edn, 1997).

comment will then be expressing dissatisfaction with the non-fulfilment of the vision in 53.12; at this point within 59.15b-20, the missing intervention might indeed be one relating to the community's internal life or to its external life, to bring *mišpāṭ*. The prophecy attributes this dissatisfaction not merely to the readers of the earlier vision or to the prophet but to Yhwh. 'By the word "wonder"' (the word rendered 'devastated' in the translation above), Calvin comments, 'the prophet describes also God's fatherly care'; and even if the community does not share this wonder, 'our indifference does not prevent the Lord from rendering assistance to his Church'. The prophet of course does not mean that God is 'liable to those passions, so as to wonder at anything new or uncommon'; in speaking thus, 'God is accommodating himself to us.... When he says that the Lord "wonders", he means that we are excessively dull and stupid.'[30] Zwingli, too, sees the prophet as speaking anthropopathically.[31] The temptation to sidestep what the prophet says is heightened if we see the use of this verb as belonging to the speech of lament (cf. Ps 143.4).[32]

Who would Yhwh have expected to see acting? The 'nobody' of v. 16a was 'no *ʾîš*', though this would not exclude its being a supernatural aide; Yhwh would then be referring to an aide who had the task of implementing *mišpāṭ*, along the lines of the expectation in Psalm 82 (*ʾîš* applies to a god in Isa 36.18; 41.28). That might relate to wrongdoing within the community or to the wrongdoing of imperial oppressors. It is more obvious, however, to take the *ʾîš* as a human figure. Within the unfolding of the book of Isaiah, the man might then be a shoot from Jesse's stump such as the one described in 11.1-5, who is described as clothed in garments like the ones that will shortly appear here, though there is some uncertainty about whether 11.1-5 antedates this passage.[33] The word might denote someone else within the community acting on behalf of people who are being wrongly treated, fulfilling the role Nehemiah fulfilled. But we have also noted that the picture of Yhwh as warrior recalls 42.13, and the book of Isaiah speaks of the Babylonian or Persian king as the 'man' taking action in history (14.16; 40.13; 46.11). Cyrus did make it possible for the Judahites to go home and rebuild the temple, but did not fulfil the full prescription in Isaiah 40–55. Yhwh's point would then be that there is no one like a messianic king or a governor or an emperor taking action.[34]

[30] Calvin, *In Iesaiam prophetam*, p. 378 (ET IV, p. 264).

[31] Zwingli, *Complanationis Isaiae Prophetae*, p. 390.

[32] So Beuken, *Jesaja IIIA*, p. 143.

[33] Cf. Neufeld, *'Put on the Armour of God'* (see above), p. 27.

[34] Matthew J. Lynch sees the implication that the nations had a responsibility for seeing that there was *mišpāṭ* in Israel, and they have failed ('Zion's Warrior and the Nations: Isaiah 59:15b–63:6 in Isaiah's Zion Traditions', *CBQ* 70 [2008], pp. 244-63 [250-51]).

59.16b So his arm has effected deliverance for him;// his faithfulness – it has supported him.
17 He has clothed himself with faithfulness as a coat of mail// and with a deliverance helmet on his head.//
He has clothed himself with redress garments as clothing,// wrapped on passion like a coat.

Fortunately for Israel, when Yhwh sees, action is bound to follow; hence the plea to 'look' reappears in protest psalms. Here three lines describe how Yhwh has not only seen but set about acting in connection with the kind of need described in vv. 9-15a. Does this presuppose that the people have indeed prayed the way the prophet modelled or that the prophet's prayer can be effective whether or not the people join in? But the action described in vv. 16b-17 has happened only in the prophet's vision and the rhetorical function of the prophecy is to drive people to respond to God. In whatever sense the prophet's prayer is enough, the prayer will open up the possibility of fulfilment. Or perhaps the prophecy is designed to stimulate people to pray along the lines of vv. 9-15a in the confidence that the action described in vv. 15b-20 could then follow. Each of the lines is internally parallel. They are also broadly parallel in relation to one another, forming a stepped sequence in which v. 16b talks of action and specifically of deliverance and faithfulness, v. 17a talks of faithfulness and deliverance and also of clothing, and v. 17b talks of clothing and also of redress and passion.

Talk of Yhwh 'delivering' is not surprising in this context; *yāšaʿ* hiphil came in v. 1, 'deliverance' in v. 11 and in 56.1, and words from this root are frequent elsewhere in the book. JPSV's 'won triumph', like 'victory' in 59.11, is misleading. While the action indeed involves a victorious triumph, it is one achieved as an act of deliverance, and it is to this that the expression points. 'Yhwh's arm' has not otherwise appeared in Isaiah 56–59, though it came often enough earlier in Isaiah, and in association with 'deliverance' in 51.5; 52.10. The association of these two also appears in the Reed Sea story (Exod 14.13; 30; 15.2, 16). The emphasis in references to Yhwh's arm lies on the idea of Yhwh as a warrior.[35] The opening colon could thus make people think of Yhwh's action at the Reed Sea and of Yhwh's earlier promises of a repetition of that action. 'Faithfulness' is another word at home in Isaiah 56–59 (56.1; 57.12; 58.2; 59.9, 14), not least because of its useful ambiguity, its capacity to refer to God's action or ours. It is not an Exodus word (though Judg 5.11 and 1 Sam 12.7 might well include the Reed Sea event in their lists of Yhwh's faithful acts). So if the first colon pictures the act of deliverance that Yhwh has initiated (in the prophet's vision) as one analogous to that victory, the second colon goes on to picture it in the terms of Isaiah 56–66. In addition, it thereby introduces a novel note into the divine warrior image, especially over against its Middle Eastern background.

[35] Cf. F. J. Helfmeyer, *TWAT*, II, p. 653 (ET *TDOT*, IV, pp. 133-34).

Marduk equips himself with weapons such as bow and arrow that are then further identified as lightning and wind but not as qualities such as faithfulness.[36] The verse is also distinctive in speaking of Yhwh's faithfulness supporting Yhwh; 63.5 will interestingly complement the expression by speaking of Yhwh's rage supporting him. Yhwh can act in deliverance because the *ṣ*^{e}*dāqâ* that is inherent in Yhwh sustains such action.[37] Here JPSV has 'victorious right hand' (expanding the translation in light of Ps 98.1-2, which also speaks of Yhwh achieving deliverance 'for himself'), losing the theological connotations of *ṣ*^{e}*dāqâ*. The second colon thus gives the background to or explanation of the first. Further, it helps to interpret the sense in which Yhwh's arm effected deliverance 'for him'. It is the necessary realization of Yhwh's own character, an act that emerges from Yhwh's character and aims at the fulfilment of Yhwh's purpose. LXX has 'he defended them with his own arm and in his mercy upheld them' (cf. Tg); MT could seem to imply that Yhwh is the one who needs delivering, and LXX safeguards against that idea (Aq, Th, Sym follow MT). In general, LXX tends to be more abstract than MT in this section.[38] Syntactical parallels to the 'for him', such as Judges 7.2, are not very helpful in this connection, because there Israel is achieving deliverance for itself as well as by itself. But they do point to another sense in which Yhwh acts in deliverance 'for himself'. Yhwh does not need to depend on anyone's help (cf. the reference in 40.13 to Yhwh's needing no *ʾîš* to offer advice on how to run the world). Yhwh's arm is Yhwh's own means of acting.

In v. 17a the move to talk of putting on faithfulness as one clothes oneself with a garment involves a common Old Testament image. Yhwh puts on majesty, strength, honour, and glory (Pss 93.1; 104.1).[39] Only here does someone put on faithfulness, and this hints that the image is a more aggressive one than it might sound even if one translates *ṣ*^{e}*dāqâ* 'justice'. JPSV makes the point as it continues the translation 'victory' (and 'triumph' in the parallel colon), though this translation again loses the theological connotations of *ṣ*^{e}*dāqâ*. The word refers to the kind of commitment that makes one do right by one's people in active ways. It is the simile that makes explicit the warlike way in which Yhwh will be pursuing *y*^{e}*šûʿâ* and *ṣ*^{e}*dāqâ*. Yhwh is described as a war hero in a way analogous to descriptions of Marduk in *Enuma Elish*.[40] The precise term for a coat of mail, the ancient equivalent to a bullet-proof vest, otherwise

[36] Cf. Neufeld, *'Put on the Armour of God'* (see above), p. 28.

[37] On the role of the pronoun *hîʾ* emphasizing *ṣ*^{e}*dāqâ*, see Stephen A. Geller, 'Cleft Sentences with Pleonastic Pronoun', *Journal of the Ancient Near Eastern Society of Columbia University* 20 (1991), pp. 15-33 (31).

[38] See Neufeld, *'Put on the Armour of God'* (see above), pp. 44-46.

[39] Bernard Gosse ('Les introductions des Psaumes 93-94 et Isaïe 59,15b-20', *ZAW* 106 [1994], pp. 303-306) sees the introductions to Pss 93 and 94 as relating to this passage's promises.

[40] See Paul, ישעיה פרקים מ-סו, II, p. 463 (ET p. 509).

appears only in the story of the Ephraimite king in 1 Kings 22.34 and 2 Chronicles 18.33. It involves the fastening of overlapping metal plates on leather.[41] It might seem the kind of armour a commander-in-chief wears and one might assume that ordinary footsoldiers would be less well-protected; Yhwh dresses like a commander-in-chief. But the variant form of the word in 2 Chronicles 26.14; Nehemiah 4.10 [16] gives a more democratic impression; see also 1 Samuel 17.5, 38. The parallel colon extends the point; the verb applies to both cola, so that the second colon has more room to describe the commander's head-gear. The helmet accompanies the coat of mail in references to pieces of armour in 1 Samuel 17.5; 2 Chronicles 26.14. It contributes to the warrior's capacity to effect deliverance. Both items are defensive, protective attire.

Verse 17b adds to the warrior's apparel. It first repeats the verb from v. 17aα but then in the parallel colon provides another verb instead of letting the first verb carry over. It also strengthens that first verb by adding its cognate noun, and strengthens both verbs by a strictly unnecessary further noun for clothing. These noun expressions also parallel the pair in v. 17a, though metaphor and simile come in reverse order. More significant are the further nouns associated with each of these. NRSV and TNIV render the first, *nāqām*, 'vengeance', but this gives a partly misleading impression. While 'vengeance' correctly suggests the strong feelings attached to *nāqām*, it also implies that these strong feelings are attached to getting one's own back for wrong that has been done to oneself, whereas *nāqām* can equally imply exacting cooler 'retribution' (JPSV), or imposing proper punishment, or requiring 'redress' for deeds done to someone else. It is the last that Yhwh is doing here, but with the emotional aspect suggested by 'vengeance'. This emotional aspect to *nāqām* is then affirmed by the parallel reference to the warrior's *qinʾâ*. This word can imply 'fury' (NRSV), but also in other contexts jealousy. Its specific connotation is the strong emotions felt by the warrior, which are part of what provides the energy to go into battle with all guns blazing. Being dressed not only in faithfulness and deliverance but also in redress and passion means there is no doubt Yhwh will successfully take the action the people need. To put it another way, being dressed in faithfulness and deliverance without redress and passion might not be enough, while being dressed in redress and passion might be dangerous because these would then lack the proper direction. At the same time, the line adds no reference to a concrete offensive weapon; the abstract nouns take the place that might be occupied by defensive weapons.

The picture of Yhwh putting on armour is taken up in Wisdom of Solomon 5.15-23 and becomes the dress of human warriors in Ephesians 6.14-17; 1 Thessalonians 5.8.[42]

[41] Koole, *Jesaja III*, p. 208 (ET p. 201).

[42] See further Skehan, 'Isaias and the Teaching of the Book of Wisdom', p. 294; Ernst Haag, 'Die Waffenrüstung Gottes nach Jesaja 59', *Trierer Theologische Zeitung* 115 (2006), pp. 26-49 (44-49).

59.18 In accordance with due recompense,// in the manner of the one on high he will repay// fury to his adversaries.
Recompense to his enemies,// recompense to distant shores he will repay.
19a So people will revere Yhwh's name from the setting sun,// from the rising of the sun his splendour.

In this further three-line sequence, the first two lines again parallel and nuance vv. 16b-17 while the third states the consequences, but all three have yiqtol rather than qatal verbs.[43] The prophet thus speaks of events not as already actual because they have been determined by Yhwh, but as future because that is what they are from the perspective of the people. Yhwh has put on the armour for action; here is the action that will now follow. The move is marked by another 2-2-2 tricolon like that in v. 15b.

Once again the first two lines are also mutually parallel in content, and partially so in form. Both first cola comprise a phrase referring to 'recompense' that cannot stand alone; it needs what follows to complete a clause. Conversely, each first colon anticipatorily qualifies what follows even though the latter could stand alone. The second cola in the first and second line have their verb form in common and work abcd then d′c′b′. MT's accents divide the verse after 'recompense to his enemies'; one might read the resultant v. 18a as 2-2-2-2 with a division after 'he will repay':

> In accordance with due recompense, in the manner of the one on high he will repay
> Fury to his adversaries, recompense to his enemies.

This understanding works well with the parallelism between 'fury to his adversaries' and 'recompense to his enemies'. But the parallelism between the two clauses about repaying rather suggests the line division above, which understands the verse to work 2-2-2 and 2-3. By its repetitions the whole verse emphasizes 'recompense' and 'repay' and thus underlines the redress that v. 17b referred to.

The opening prepositional expression *k*ᵉ *'al* comes only five times (another is 63.7), with varying meanings, though here the sense is clear enough. The same expression recurs later in the line, without a noun to follow. There, while the construction could involve an ellipse, 'as the like of due recompense so [is] the like [of the way] he will pay back…',[44] the construction is very elliptical and unparalleled.[45] But there are a number of passages where *'al* might be understood as a noun for God as 'one who

[43] This is Frederick C. Harding's starting point for arguing that vv. 16-17 belong with 63.1-6 rather than here, see 'The Oracle against Edom (Isa. 63 1-6 and 59 16-17)', *JBL* 33 (1914), pp. 213-17. Neufeld (*'Put on the Armour of God'* [see above], p. 21) suggests translating as present and interprets as describing Yhwh's habitual action, but this is hard to maintain through vv. 18-20.

[44] Cf. BDB, p. 455.

[45] GK 118s defends only the first occurrence.

is on high' (e.g. Pss 7.11 [10]; 68.35 [34]),[46] and the line makes better sense on the understanding that this is the significance of the word's second occurrence.[47] Since KJV, translations have then taken the feminine plural *gᵉmulôt* to mean 'deeds', which fits the meaning of the verb *gāmal*. But on its other two occurrences the noun means 'recompense', like masculine *gᵉmûl*, which comes twice in the next line. While the plural might be spelled out in these two singulars, the translation 'due recompense' rather takes it as intensive; certainly the masculine singular complements the feminine plural. Given that 'recompense' need not be a threatening notion (see 2 Sam 19.36 [37] for the feminine word),[48] and the same is true of 'repaying' (see 1 Sam 24.19 [20]), the last two words of the second colon, 'fury to his adversaries', remove any ambiguity in the first. In substance, 'fury' takes up and gives precision to the 'passion' of v. 17b. It is another emotion that gives a person the energy and drive to do what needs to be done; in the New Testament, compare 1 Thessalonians 1.10, and with regard to human beings, compare the way rage is a fruit of the coming of God's breath on Saul (1 Sam 11.6-11).

'Recompense to his enemies' restates the point. In Isaiah, and in the Old Testament in general, deliverance and punishment are related. An aspect of the good news in these references to 'his adversaries' and 'his enemies' is that Yhwh does make oppressors 'his' adversaries and enemies, and will therefore treat them as such. The only other place in Isaiah where reference to Yhwh's 'adversaries' and 'enemies' occurs in parallelism is 1.24, and there these people from whom Yhwh 'exacts redress' are Judahites, not foreign oppressors. But this does not provide evidence that the terms have this reference here.[49] And in any case, in 1.24 they are not a group within the community, but the community as a whole. In Nahum 1.2 the two terms refer to foreign oppressors, specifically Assyria, in a passage that also refers to Yhwh's passion, fury, and redress. This suggests that the opening of Nahum is a significant intertext for 59.15b-20. That link begins to weight the significance of Yhwh's action as relating to outside oppressors rather than to people within the community. 'He will thrash their hides as He did in the case of Sennacherib.'[50] By dealing with Judah in the manner of an imperial power, they are treating Judah as if it belonged to them, which is the mistake Pharaoh made in treating Yhwh's firstborn son as if it was his servant. This understanding is confirmed by the final colon in v. 18. If previous lines

[46] Cf. *DCH*, VI, pp. 398-99; see further the translation note on 63.7.

[47] I follow Torrey (*Second Isaiah*, p. 442) in thinking that the two occurrences of *kĕ ʿal* have different meanings, but he takes the second as a hypothesized temporal adverb (see Payne's comment, 'Characteristic Word-Play in "Second Isaiah"', p. 225). I follow Klostermann (*Deuterojesaja*, p. 84) in seeing the second as an occurrence of this divine title, though he understands both occurrences in this way.

[48] See K. Seybold on *gāmal* in *TWAT*.

[49] Against Steck, *Studien zu Tritojesaja*, p. 189.

[50] Luther, *In Esaiam prophetam enarraciones*, p. 496 (ET p. 306).

had pointed to the idea that the adversaries and enemies are people within the Jerusalem community, we might have inferred that the complementary nature of the cola in the second line of v. 18 consisted in their referring to foes within Judah and foes among foreign peoples.[51] But when there has been no such indication, it is more natural to take the people on distant shores to be the foes. To put it another way, 'distant shores', the only new word in the second colon, removes any ambiguity about the identity of the adversaries and enemies. The word (*ʾiyyîm*) is an especially common one in Isaiah 40–55, but there (and usually elsewhere) it refers to helpless far-off peoples who will benefit from Yhwh's political action in putting the empire down and will acknowledge Yhwh's action on Israel's behalf (cf. 60.9). 'Islands' (Vg) is misleading (LXX also elsewhere renders 'islands'; here it does not include the word in considerably shortening v. 18 to avoid its repetitiveness). The expression denotes foreign countries as places that one would usually reach by sea. But the point is these places' far-off-ness and/or foreignness, so the word could apply to far-off foreign peoples who make themselves enemies of Yhwh. You do not evade Yhwh's retribution by being a long way away. Reference to the ends of the earth also comes in 52.10, noted in connection with vv. 16b-17.

MT's verse division makes v. 19a a new start, but a statement about people coming to recognize Yhwh commonly links back to a declaration such as has appeared in v. 18. Indeed, 41.5 spoke of the distant shores seeing Yhwh's action and fearing/revering, though 42.4 and 61.5 also spoke of them waiting for Yhwh and for Yhwh's teaching (cf. 60.9). That adds some poignancy or irony to the fact that MT manuscripts vary over whether they spell the verb in v. 19a as 'fear/revere' or 'see'. In 45.6 the aim of Yhwh's action is that people may 'acknowledge from the rising of the sun and from its setting that there is none but me', while the parallelism of Yhwh's name and Yhwh's splendour comes in 42.6; 43.7. The context there leaves open whether this is a positive, creative acknowledgment or a sad fruitless one, and the same is true here. The line is neatly parallel, with the opening verb governing both cola and the expressions 'from the setting' and 'from the rising of the sun' and then 'Yhwh's name' and 'his splendour' being parallel. The former pair is litotes for the whole world, while the latter suggests 'his glorious name'.

59.19b When an adversary comes like a river,// Yhwh's wind raises a banner against him.
20 He will come to Zion as restorer,// to those in Jacob who turn from rebellion// (Yhwh's declaration).

[51] So K. Seybold, *TWAT*, II, p. 31 (ET *TDOT*, III, p. 29); cf. Steck, *Studien zu Tritojesaja*, p. 187.

The two lines comprising vv. 19b-20a go together with the two lines comprising vv. 15b-16a to form a bracket around the intervening three-line units in vv. 16b-17 and 18-19a. Verses 19b-20a is then supplemented by the declaration formula closing off vv. 15b-20. Verses 19b-20a are mutually parallel bicola, with the two occurrences of the verb 'come' standing in particular parallel. Yhwh's coming (v. 20a) contrasts with the adversary's coming (v. 19b). In v. 19b, the second colon completes the first; in v. 20a, the second parallels the first.

In v. 19b, MT and the versions have different understandings of each colon. The meaning of *ṣar* is crucial to the sense of the first colon. I have followed Syr, Tg, Sym, Th, which imply it is the common noun from *ṣārar* II and means 'adversary'. The adversary might be Yhwh; the second colon would then restate the first. But in v. 18 'adversaries' were set over against Yhwh, and more likely this adversary, too, is someone opposed to Yhwh's purpose; the second colon then reports Yhwh's response. The link with v. 18 also undermines the alternative possibility that *ṣar* is the common noun deriving from *ṣārar* I meaning 'distress' (as in 63.9), unless we think that the prophet is working here with paronomasia. The assumption that it is one or other of these nouns is also suggested by MT's disjunctive accent on *kannāhār* and by its thus pointing that word's first syllable as incorporating the article, whereas *ṣar* is anarthrous. Tg takes *kannāhār* to signify 'like *the* river' and makes explicit that the river is the Euphrates, but in a comparison the definite article need not have this implication.[52] In contrast, LXX, paraphrasing the line as a whole 'Because anger will come from the Lord like a violent river; it will come with fury', seems to take *ṣar* as the less common adjective from *ṣārar* I meaning 'narrow'; more literally, 'he will come like a narrow stream' (cf. Aq, Vg; the relationship with v. 18a would again imply paronomasia). But this involves considerable reading into *ṣar* in inferring from 'narrow' to 'confined' to 'powerful'.

The meaning of *nōsᵉsâ* is then crucial to the meaning of v. 19bβ. Vg 'drives' implies the word is polel participle from *nûs*. This raises several difficulties. The participle lacks its preformative; the form is actually that of the qatal, as Th recognizes. But the qatal hardly fits. Further, the word should mean 'causes to escape' or 'puts to flight' (cf. Tg, Syr?). Aq, Th rather link it with *nēs* 'banner'. It would then be part of a denominative verb *nāsas* (cf. Ibn Ezra)[53] and a qal participle rather than a qatal. It signifies a commander-in-chief initiating military action.

A river can be a positive image (e.g. 48.18) or a negative one (e.g. 8.7-8); here the latter fits. As in 8.7-8 powerful forces embodied in the people's enemies may assail it (cf. Ps 93.3). But like Baal storming against Sea or River, in Genesis 8.1; Exodus 14.21; 15.8, 10 (and perhaps

[52] Cf. GK 126o; JM 137i; *DG* 31c. LXX, Aq, Sym Th, lack the article, though this is an aspect of their broader different understanding of the line.

[53] *The Commentary of Ibn Ezra on Isaiah*, p. 275.

Gen 1.2) God's *rûaḥ* storms against destructive or tumultuous waters;[54] the image will reappear in Isaiah 63.11-14.[55] Verse 19b thus recalls creation and exodus and brings something of a climax. God also storms against such forces embodied in enemies of Israel.[56]

Verse 20a reexpresses the point in its parallel cola. The verbal phrase 'he will come as restorer' applies to both. The two *l* expressions are then parallel, the single word 'Zion' in the first and the entire contents of the second colon. The reference to Zion is the first since Isaiah 51–52 and thus the first in Isaiah 56–66; it announces a theme that will be central to Isaiah 60–62.[57] Given that reference to Zion was common through Isaiah 1–55, Zion is a focus of the whole book of Isaiah.[58] Reference to Zion and Jacob in parallel cola comes elsewhere only in Lamentations 1.17, but in a more general sense Jacob and Zion did appear in a kind of parallelism in Isaiah 40–55, where Jacob has the prominence in Isaiah 40–48 and Zion in Isaiah 49–55. And for the people in the Persian period, Zion is the home of the people of Jacob.

Grammatically, the translation 'a restorer (*gô'ēl*) will come to Zion' is possible' and one could then discuss whether this restorer is someone such as Cyrus or the Messiah.[59] But elsewhere in Isaiah 'restorer' (*gô'ēl*) is always a term to describe God, nor are there parallels elsewhere in the Old Testament for the use of the term to refer to a messianic figure or to a person such as Cyrus; though again 'restorer' and 'Zion' come together only here. The word 'denotes that He will be the kind of Redeemer who will exact blood vengeance from the hands of the enemies, as the nearest relative of a victim wreaked vengeance on the murderer' (Num 35.19-21 [P]).[60]

'Turning from rebellion' is not a phrase that occurs elsewhere, but the idea is one that resonates with Isaiah 1–39 and 40–55 (see especially 1.2, 26-28, where Zion also appears); we have already noted parallels in v. 18 with 1.24. We have concluded that Yhwh's taking action on behalf of *mišpāṭ* meant attacking the people's external oppressors or attackers rather than acting against injustice within the community. But this is not to say that the entire community in its oppressiveness can expect to

54 But Ma (*Until the Spirit Comes*, pp. 113-17) argues for giving *rûaḥ* a positive sense.

55 P. A. H. de Boer, in 'יהוה as Epithet Expressing the Superlative' (*VT* 54 [1974], pp. 233-35 [235]), sees this as an example of the superlative usage.

56 See H. A. J. Kruger, 'Who Comes: Yahweh or Nahar?', *OTE* 10 (1997), pp. 84-91, 268-78 (271-76).

57 Abramowski ('Zum literarischen Problem des Tritojesaja', p. 123) thus sees this as an indication that 57.14–62.12 forms a unit.

58 See the Introduction above, section 6.

59 See, e.g., Calmet, *Le Prophéte Isaïe*, p. 631.

60 Luther, *In Esaiam prophetam enarraciones*, p. 498 (ET, p. 308). Cf. Jeremiah Unterman, 'The Social-Legal Origin for the Image of God as Redeemer גואל of Israel', in D. P. Wright, D. N. Freedman, and A. Hurvitz (eds.), *Pomegranates and Golden Bells* (J. Milgrom Festschrift; Winona Lake, IN: Eisenbrauns, 1995), pp. 399-405.

benefit from Yhwh's action. In order to be its beneficiaries, people have to turn from rebellion. They cannot trust in the idea that God is committed to them just because they are Israel and that God is against the nations just because they are the nations.[61]

Polan sees v. 20aα as an *inclusio* with 56.1bα.[62] While there is a broad parallel between the two cola, the parallel is not very specific and it is difficult to imagine that someone either reading a scroll or listening to it being read would spot it. But in a broader sense v. 20 as a whole has a similar role at the close of Isaiah 56–59 to that of 56.1 at the beginning. As 56.1 at the beginning of the chapters summarized the drift of Isaiah 1–39 and 40–55, so 59.20 near their close summarizes it again. It sums up on one side Yhwh's commitment to restoring Zion and on the other side the necessity for the community to respond to Yhwh. At the close of Isaiah 56–59, the section thus repeats the theme of 56.1: it is certain that Yhwh will act in *mišpāṭ*, but people who do not themselves take up a commitment to *mišpāṭ* and *ṣ*ᵉ*dāqâ* will not benefit from this.

The closing declaration formula underlines the possibility and the necessity of believing what the prophet said. It characteristically adds force to Yhwh's commitment. It, too, is a common feature of Isaiah 40–55;[63] it came in an extended form in 56.8, but this is the first occurrence of the regular short form. Once again, then, this closing colon underlines the prophecy's links with Isaiah 40–55 as well as serving to close off the section.

Paul quotes v. 20a and the opening words of v. 21 in Romans 11.26-27 (he completes his quotation with words from 27.9). In the first colon he has 'from Zion' (as then does OL), but accounts of Yhwh's acting or appearing often refer to where Yhwh came 'from' as (Zion, in Pss 14.7; 50.2), and Paul is likely influenced by such familiar parallels,[64] though MT would work just as well for his argument.[65] LXX's translation 'for the sake of Zion' may reflect a desire to encourage the Jewish community itself.[66] In the second colon Paul's version corresponds to LXX,[67] and Barth seems to follow in commenting that God 'comes in and with

[61] Cf. Lynch, 'Zion's Warrior and the Nations' (see above), pp. 253-54.

[62] *In the Ways of Justice toward Salvation*, pp. 19-22.

[63] See further Goldingay and Payne, *Isaiah 40–55*, II, pp. 172-73.

[64] Cf. Westermann, *Jesaja Kapitel 40–66*, p. 279 (ET p. 351). Thus it is less likely that Paul's text points to the original reading (so Duhm, *Jesaia*, pp. 405-6) or that Paul's understanding links with the possibility that *l*- can mean 'from' (so Mitchell Dahood, 'Ugaritic and the Old Testament', *ETL* 44 [1968], pp. 35-54 [47]).

[65] On issues raised by Paul's citation see further, e.g., Christopher D. Stanley, *Paul and the Language of Scripture* (Cambridge: Cambridge University Press, 1992), pp. 166-74; Wagner, *Heralds of the Good News*, pp. 276-94; Shum, *Paul's Use of Isaiah in Romans*, pp. 235-45; Wilk, *Die Bedeutung des Jesajabuches für Paulus*, pp. 38-40, 56-58, 64-73, 199-203, 242-46.

[66] Cf. Baer, *When We All Go Home*, pp. 226-28.

[67] See the translation note.

conversion from transgression in Jacob'; repentance is God's gift.[68] It is a profound theological point, though not one made by MT here. Jerome[69] and Ibn Ezra[70] also assume that the redeemer is the Messiah (cf. KJV 'and the Redeemer shall come to Zion'),[71] but the context offers no clue to such a change of subject, and the Messiah does not otherwise feature in Isaiah 40–66. The expression 'those who turn from rebellion' recurs a number of times in the Qumran scrolls (e.g. 1QS 10.20; 1QH 2.8-9; 6.6; 14.24; CD 2.5; 20.17) as a term for the community.[72]

59.21 'So I: this is my covenant with them', Yhwh has said. 'My breath which is on you and my words which I have put in your mouth will not be missing from your mouth and from the mouth of your offspring and from the mouth of your offspring's offspring (Yhwh has said) from now and forever'.

At its close the section moves from poetry to prose and addresses a masculine singular 'you'. Who is this 'you'? In 56.1–59.3 Yhwh from time to time addressed the community in the masculine plural or the feminine singular, and in 60.1-22 will pick up that usage. In 58.1 Yhwh addressed the prophet in the masculine singular and in 58.7-14 so addressed the community. Here, the usage would thus allow 'you' to be either the people or the prophet,[73] and the same is true about the content of the promise that will follow. But the verse begins by speaking of the people as 'them', and while it is not impossible for there to be a move within the verse from speaking of the people as 'them' to addressing them as 'you' singular, it would be odd, and more likely 'you' is set over against 'them' and refers to the prophet. Yhwh addresses the prophet as an individual, then, as in 58.1.[74] The link with 58.1 supports MT's taking the verse to close off what precedes rather than introducing Isaiah 60–62. The words recall those in earlier and later passages in which the prophet speaks (48.16b; 50.4; 61.1) and passages that speak about Yhwh's servant and could plausibly be applied to the position of a prophet (42.1; 53.10).[75]

[68] *Die kirchliche Dogmatik* IV/2, p. 655 (ET p. 579).

[69] *Commentariorum in Isaiam prophetam libri duodeviginti*, col. 584.

[70] *The Commentary of Ibn Ezra on Isaiah*, p. 276.

[71] Cf. also Heinrich Gross's paper on messianism in the Old Testament, which takes its title from this verse, 'Zion's Redeemer', *Concilium* 10/3 (1967), pp. 44-49.

[72] Cf. Morrow, 'The Text of Isaiah at Qumran', p. 190.

[73] Bernard Gosse suggests is is the high priest ('Isa 59, 21 et 2 Sam 23,1-7', *BN* 68 [1993], pp. 10-12; cf. 'L'universalisme de la Sagesse face au Sacerdoce de Jérusalem au retour de l'exil', *Transeuphratène* 13 [1997], pp. 39-45), but the context gives no indication of this.

[74] Cf. Steck, *Studien zu Tritojesaja*, p. 182.

[75] See Kellermann, 'Tritojesaja und das Geheimnis des Gottesknechts', though he sees the passages in Isa 56–66 as specifically relating to the so-called Servant Songs in Isa 40–55; also Steck, 'Der sich selbst aktualisierende "Jesaja"', on broader links with 'the Isaiah of the book'.

The fact that the first-person testimony or claim in 61.1-3 comes at the centre of the chiasm formed by Isaiah 56–66 as a whole underlines the importance of the prophet to the prophecy, paralleling the dynamic of Isaiah 40–55. Other comparable first-person notes come at the end of Isaiah 57 and at the end of Isaiah 61. Commentators such as Jerome once more take the 'you' as the Messiah,[76] but again there is no indication of such a change of reference. In contrast, the ninth-century commentator Hayman of Halberstadt takes it as a reference to the succession of prophets who will follow Isaiah ben Amoz.[77]

The verse is commonly seen as a later addition to the material[78] but both transitions (to prose and to reference to the prophet) are common enough in the book as a whole and in Isaiah 56–66 in particular, so there is no particular reason to infer this. If it is an addition, then it has become part of the material as a whole and an element in the prophet's self-presentation as the chapters offer it.

Yhwh's opening words, with the extraposed 'So I' conveying 'a ring of self-assertion',[79] recall the divine announcement about the covenant in Genesis 9.9 [P]. They are even closer to Yhwh's words to Abraham in Genesis 17.4 [also P], significantly because here, too, Yhwh speaks of a one-sided commitment to the people. Isaiah 56.1-8 twice referred to 'covenant' in a rather different connection. In speaking of Yhwh's commitment to the people, the covenant idea here slightly more resembles that in 61.8 (cf. 42.6; 49.8; 54.10; 55.3),[80] but it is distinctive for being brought into association with the prophet's ministry. Yhwh's breath is on the prophet and Yhwh's words are in the prophet's mouth. The language will be taken up in the prophet's testimony in 61.1. The image of the prophet's ministry is quite supranatural. When Yhwh's breath is on a person, something extraordinary happens, something that would not issue from people being 'themselves'. Yhwh's *rûaḥ* suggests the power, unpredictability, and invisibility of the wind; people see its result but not the thing itself. The link between breath and wind suggests that the wind is Yhwh breathing. The image occurred in a connection a little like this one in v. 19, and even raises the question whether the lifting of a banner against the adversary happens through Yhwh's breath/wind/spirit being put on the prophet.[81] Isaiah 61.1 would then make for a telling contrast as well as comparison with this section. In 42.1 it is Yhwh's servant upon whom Yhwh's breath comes, and I take the reference there implicitly to

[76] *Commentariorum in Isaiam prophetam libri duodeviginti*, col. 584.

[77] *Commentariorum in Isaiam libri tres*, col. 1030.

[78] So, e.g., Duhm, *Jesaia*, p. 406. Volz (*Jesaja II*, p. 235) calls it a 'fragment'.

[79] T. Muraoka, *Emphatic Words and Structures in Biblical Hebrew* (Jerusalem: Magnes, 1985), p. 95.

[80] Cf. Bernard Gosse, 'L'alliance d'Isaïe 59,21', *ZAW* 101 (1989), pp. 116-18.

[81] Emmerson (*Isaiah 56–66*, p. 16) suggests that it was the recurrence of the word *rûaḥ* that led to the placing of v. 21 here, following on v. 19.

be to God's involvement with the people as a whole. But the more spectacular manifestations of Yhwh's breath coming on people occur in connection with prophets such as Elijah and Ezekiel.

Talk of Yhwh's breath leads into talk of Yhwh's words, suggesting that it points not to extraordinary bodily experiences such as ones that came to Elijah and Ezekiel but to its issuing in the prophet's having words of supernatural origin, as also happened in their case. This understanding is implicit in Tg's 'my holy spirit which is on you and my words of prophecy which I have put in your mouth…'. The expression 'I have put in your mouth' indicates that the prophet does not devise the words of the prophetic message, or even consciously receive them from the sovereign master and then repeat them. The prophet's mouth opens and words come out that the prophet's conscious mind was not involved in forming. The prophet discovers what those words are in the same way and at the same moment as the people listening to them.

Yhwh's covenant commitment is to ensure the gift of such an endowment always and thus also to ensure that such prophetic words address Israel, or more specifically 'Zion' and 'those in Jacob who turn from rebellion' who are the antecedents of 'them'. Old Testament thinking rather excludes the idea that the capacity to be a prophet can be inherited, as priesthood and kingship can be.[82] So the offspring to whom Yhwh refers are not the prophet's biological children and grandchildren but the 'sons of the prophet' and the grandsons who respond to Yhwh in the same way as the prophet and take up such a ministry. They are moral and religious offspring, like those promised to the servant in 53.10. In Joshua 1.8 the expression 'shall not be missing from your mouth' relates to the book containing Moses' teaching and the clause is a command. Rashi,[83] too, assumes the prophecy refers to the Torah, though he takes it as a promise that it will not be forgotten by them. The promise is analogous to that in Jeremiah 31.31-34, though the similarity between the passages is not at all close enough to say that this verse 'alludes explicitly' to the Jeremiah passage.[84] Here the words in Joshua have come to be a promise referring to the prophetic word.[85]

What is the significance of the promise at this point? Verses 15b-20 have been speaking of what is to happen, and one might have thought they denoted something that was imminent and final. But vv. 19b-20 in

[82] Cf. Dillmann, *Jesaia* [1890 ed.], p. 503.

[83] 'ישעיה', on the passage.

[84] Against S. Tengström, *TWAT*, VII, p. 417 (ET *TDOT*, XIII, p. 395).

[85] Alexander Rofé ('The Piety of the Torah-Disciples at the Winding-up of the Hebrew Bible', in H. Merklein, K. Müller, and G. Stemberger [eds.], *Bibel in jüdischer und christlicher Tradition* [J. Maier Festschrift; Frankfurt: Hain, 1993], pp. 78-85 [82-85]) sees the meaning as the same as in Josh 1.8. But the word being in someone's mouth (cf. Jer 1.9) supports the idea that the promise refers to the prophet. Cf. Ma's arguments, *When the Spirit Comes*, pp. 133-34.

particular may have implied a recognition that adversaries coming like a flood, but Yhwh putting them down, will be an ongoing experience. Alongside that acknowledgment, v. 21 promises the community a repeated and ongoing prophetic ministry.[86]

Conclusion

Hermann Gunkel suggested that the prophecy's perspective is 'apocalyptic' or 'eschatological' in the sense that it does not refer to a concrete historical event involving the peoples of the prophet's day but to an event involving an enemy of the final days to come in an undateable future that will bring history to an end, rather like the prophecies of Gog and Magog in Ezekiel 38–39.[87] Hanson similarly comments that prophecy of this kind has stopped associating God's activity with real history (for Isa 40–55, it was the rise of Cyrus, the fall of Babylon, and a return to Jerusalem) and has also stopped expecting the community to take responsibility for its destiny and for the political order (for instance, by witnessing to Yhwh's activity or arguing for Yhwh's lordship in the community).[88] The vision in this section is unrelated to such down-to-earth realities. Mercedes García Bachmann wonders about the possibility of another kind of intervention: 'Were there human mediations, the Divine Warrior would not need to act; were there mediations, conflict, violence, suffering, and injustice would have been kept at bail [*sic*] before so many people suffer them and die from them.'[89]

There does not seem reason to think that the passage refers to the End in a way that does not carry implications for the community's own future, though like other prophecies its promises are larger than life. Prophet and community will be familiar with the way prophets have often spoken in a fashion that is larger than life but that sees some fulfilment in their own experience, whether in bringing the day of Yhwh as a day of judgment or bringing a day of restoration. It would be natural for the community to take this prophecy in that way. Calvin puts a more positive spin on the phenomena Hanson notes by commenting that the prophecy's significance lies in the fact that when we indeed have no way of delivering ourselves, 'the Lord will find sufficient assistance in his own arm'.[90] On the basis of vv. 19b-20, Rabbi Jonathan comments, 'When you see a

[86] Gosse (e.g. *Structuration des grands ensembles bibliques et intertextualité à l'époque perse*, pp. 8-11) sees the promise as a justification of the redactional work that brought the book of Isaiah into existence.

[87] For Gunkel, see the translation note on v. 15b.

[88] Hanson, *The Dawn of Apocalyptic*, pp. 126-34.

[89] '"And YHWH Saw and Was Displeased": Mediation as Human Responsibility (Isaiah 59)', *Lectio difficilior* 2005/1, pp. 1-11 (8). I suspect that 'bail' should read 'bay'.

[90] Calvin, *In Iesaiam prophetam*, p. 378 (ET IV, p. 265).

generation overwhelmed by many troubles like a river, hope for him [the Messiah]',[91] while Lamentations Rabbah sees v. 20 as an answer to Lamentations 1.6.[92]

Postcolonial insights cohere with such attitudes. While a prophet might challenge imperial authorities to take responsibility for their policies, this prophet addresses not the leadership or the citizens of a superpower but its colonial victims. Politically speaking, the prophet's challenge is to conscientize the community into believing that there is hope in the situation, not because they have unrecognized scope to take responsibility for their destiny, but because their lack of such scope need not matter, since Yhwh is committed to them. And paradoxically, coming to realize this fact may make it possible to take a proper form of responsibility for their destiny.

[91] B. Sanhedrin 98a.

[92] Lam. R. 33, on Lam 1.6.

VI

ISAIAH 60.1-22

Translation and Notes

1 Get up, be alight,[1] because your light has come;// Yhwh's splendour has shone forth upon you.
2 Because there:[2] the darkness[3] will cover the earth,// pitch dark[4] the peoples.
But upon you Yhwh will shine forth,// his splendour will appear upon you.
3 Nations will walk to your light,// kings[5] to your shining brightness.[6]

4 Lift your eyes around and look:// all of them have gathered, they have come to you.
Your sons will come[7] from afar,// your daughters will support themselves[8] on the hip[9].
5 Then you will revere[10] and glow,// your heart will be in awe[11] and swell.[12]

[1] LXX repeats φωτίζου, assimilating to the repetition in 51.9, 17; 52.1, 2, and adds the vocative 'Jerusalem'.

[2] But C. J. Labuschagne ('The Particles הן and הנה', *OTS* 18 [1973], pp. 1-14 [13]) sees this as a possible example of concessive הנה.

[3] LXX lacks the article on החשך, which might be dittog.; there are no other instances of the article in the chapter's consonantal text in vv. 1-11.

[4] 1QIs[b] provides the article, assimilating to the previous colon.

[5] On the basis of Ugaritic parallels, M. J. Dahood ('Ugaritic *drkt* and Biblical *derek*', *Theological Studies* 15 [1954], pp. 627-31 [630]) argues from the parallelism that מלכי here (and in 60.16; 62.2) means kingdoms rather than kings.

[6] For לנגה 1QIs[a] has לנגד, perhaps simply a slip; the ms seems to have been corrected (cf. Kutscher, הלשון והרקע הלשוני של מגילת ישעיהו השלמה, p. 198 [ET p. 263]). But cf. Tg 'toward [your shining]'.

[7] Klostermann (*Deuterojesaia*, p. 86) amends יָבֹאוּ to hiphil יָבִיאוּ 'they [the nations and kings] will bring your sons'; another possibility is hophal יֻבָאוּ '[your sons] will be brought' (cf. Paul, ישעיה פרקים מ-סו, II, p. 474 [ET p. 520], referring to N. H. Tur-Sinai, פשוטו של מקרא III/1 [Jerusalem: Kiriat Sepher, 1967], p. 142).

[8] 1QIs[b] has תנשינה, two medieval mss that might contain extra-masoretic readings (K30 and 96) add תנשאנה (*HUB*), while LXX and Tg have 'will be carried', all assimilating to 49.22. Eitan ('A Contribution to Isaiah Exegesis', pp. 83-84) suggests תְּאֻמֶּנָה (cf. NEB's תְּאַמֶּינָה; see Brockington, *The Hebrew Text of the Old Testament*, p. 196) from a hypothesized verb אמם cognate with Arabic *'mm* meaning 'walk ahead' (cf. *imam* 'leader').

[9] For צד Syr suggests צָב 'palanquin' (cf. 66.20); cf. Felix Perles, 'A Miscellany of Lexical and Textual Notes on the Bible', *JQR* n.s. 2 (1911–12), pp. 97-132 (116).

[10] Most MT mss read תראי from ראה; so also Vrs. Two MT mss, the Mekilta, Tanḥuma, and some other medieval and late mss read תיראי from ירא (*HUB*). See the comment.

[11] 1QIs[a] lacks ופחד.

Because the sea's multitude will turn over to you,// the might of the nations will come[13] to you.

6 A stream[14] of camels will cover you,// dromedaries[15] of Midian and Ephah;// all of them[16] will come from Sheba.

They will carry gold and frankincense// and bring news of[17] the great praise[18] of Yhwh.

7 All the flocks of Qedar will gather to you;// the rams of Nebaiot will minister to you.[19]

They will come up for acceptance[20] on my altar// and I will glorify[21] my glorious house.[22]

8 Who are these that fly[23] like a cloud,[24]// like doves to their holes?[25]

[12] For MT ורחב Graetz (*Emendationes*, p. 34) reads ורהב 'be proud', with two medieval mss that might contain extra-masoretic readings (K30 and 150) (*HUB*); Ehrlich (*Randglossen*, IV, p. 214) suggests וחרד 'tremble'.

[13] 1QIs^{b} has יבוא (sg. verb to match the subject) for MT יבאו; Tg implies hiphil יביאו. MT's pl. may be attracted to the pl. 'nations' which immediately precedes.

[14] שפעת is traditionally rendered 'multitude', but this seems a bland understanding of a rare word usually governing a word meaning 'cover'; Paul (ישעיה פרקים מ-סו, II, p. 476 [ET p. 522]) argues for 'dust cloud' (cf. JPSV). See further *DCH*.

[15] More literally, 'young camels'.

[16] Scullion ('Some Difficult Texts in Isaiah cc.56–66', p. 116) repoints כֻּלָּם to כֵּלִים, pl. of כְּלִי, and translates 'cargoes'.

[17] Ehrlich (*Randglossen*, IV, p. 214) emends to the more usual יספרו 'announce'.

[18] I take the pl. as intensive, as in Ps 22.4 [3]. Blenkinsopp (*Isaiah 56–66*, p. 206) notes that תהלת is written thus defectively and suggests MT mis-punctuates the sg. noun; Vg has sg. LXX's τὸ σωτήριον reflects its liking for this and related words (cf. Brockington, 'The Greek Translator of Isaiah and his Interest in δοξα', pp. 25-26, 30-32).

[19] ישרתונך incorporates energic נ (see GK58i). LXX perhaps sees the expression as odd and to make it less specific repeats 'will come to you' from the same position in v. 5, but Aq, Sym, Th, Tg have 'minister'. Klostermann (*Deuterojesaia*, p. 86) calls the verb 'impossible' here and sees it as imported from v. 10a; he suggests ישחרונך 'seek you earnestly [getting up early to do so]'; cf. Hos 5.15. Thomas ('ספר ישעיה', p. 95) simply deletes the verb.

[20] For על־רצון 1QIs^{a} has the expected לרצון על; cf. LXX, Tg, assimilating to the more usual expression in 56.7. Klostermann (*Deuterojesaia*, p. 87) suggests 'with willingness', but there is no parallel for this meaning with על and the context suggests 'acceptance'. For עלה meaning 'go up onto' and thus not needing a preposition, see Gen 49.4.

[21] LXX implies third sg. יְפָאֵר 'will be glorified' for MT אפאר, assimilating to the other verbs in vv. 1-9.

[22] LXX avoids the repetition by calling it 'my prayer house', repeated from 56.7.

[23] 1QIs^{a} תעופפנה for MT's תעופינה replaces the more common qal by the polel, used distinctively elsewhere in Isaiah (Pulikottil, *Transmission of Biblical Texts in Qumran*, p. 56).

[24] In the midst of the line Tg provides an answer to the question: it is the returning exiles. Walter C. Bouzard ('Doves in the Windows', in B. F. Batto and K. L. Roberts [eds.], *David and Zion* [J. J. M. Roberts Festschrift; Winona Lake, IN: Eisenbrauns, 2004], pp. 307-17 [315]) suggests that עב is not the noun from עוב 'cloud' but עב from עבב, which means something like 'canopy'; but this requires us to assume that the preposition כ has the same meaning as ב, which is hard in the context where כיונים 'like doves' looks like an expression in parallelism with כעב.

9 Because for me[26] distant shores[27] wait[28],// Tarshish ships at the first,[29]
To bring your children[30] from afar,// their silver and gold with them,
For the name of Yhwh your God,// for Israel's holy one, because he has glorified you.

10 Foreigners will build your walls,// their kings will minister to you,
Because in my fury I struck you down,// but in acceptance I have had compassion on you.
11 Your gates will open[31] continuously;// day and night they will not shut[32],
For bringing to you the might of the nations,// with their kings also being led along.[33]
12 Because the nation and the kingdom that will not serve you:// they will perish, and the nations[34] will become a total[35] waste.

[25] LXX 'their young' might imply אפרחיהם for MT ארבתיהם (Ottley, *Isaiah according to the Septuagint*, II, p. 367), but may also reflect uncertainty about MT's meaning. Oort ('Kritische Aanteekeningen', p. 474) suggests על אבריהם 'on pinions' (cf. 40.31; of doves in Ps 55.7 [6]).

[26] Oort ('Kritische Aanteekeningen', p. 474) suggests כְּלֵי 'vessels of' (the distant shores) for כִּי־לִי, but this implausibly reduces the colon's link with 51.5.

[27] For איים Duhm (*Jesaia*, p. 409) reads ציים 'ships', improving the parallelism; see also the next note.

[28] Luzzatto (*Animadversiones in Jesajae vaticinia*, p. xxxviii) suggests יִקָּווּ 'gather' for יְקַוּוּ, Oort ('Kritische Aanteekeningen', p. 474) יקלו 'hasten'; Ehrlich (*Randglossen*, IV, p. 215) יקנאו = יקנו 'be jealous'; these again implausibly reduce the colon's link with 51.5, though Torrey makes a virtue out of this point in translating MT as 'gather' and seeing it as an example of the prophet's fondness for using words with altered meaning (*Second Isaiah*, p. 449).

[29] For בראשנה Elliger (*Die Einheit des Tritojesaja*, p. 20) suggests בְּרֹאשָׁם 'at their head'.

[30] For בניך 1QIs[a] has בני 'my children', assimilating to 43.6; Koenig also suggests a link with 42.4 in 1QIs[a] (*L'herméneutique analogique du Judaïsme antique d'après les témoins textuels d'Isaïe*, pp. 366-69).

[31] On the regular understanding of the piel, the subject would be the foreigners and kings and the piel would be resultative. Some medieval mss have pual וּפֻתְּחוּ (*HUB*), while GK 52k suggests niphal ונפתחו and Scullion ('Some Difficult Texts in Isaiah cc.56—66', pp. 116-17) qal passive פֻּתְחוּ; cf. LXX, Tg, Vg, though Vrs may simply be assuming that the verb is impersonal third pl. M. Dahood (*Proverbs and Northwest Semitic Philology* [Rome: Pontifical Biblical Institute, 1963], p. 8) sees it as qal passive. He takes the same approach to all three similar occurrences of this verb in the piel (see Song 7.13 [12] as well as Isa 48.8, on which see Goldingay and Payne, *Isaiah 40–55*, II, p. 131). The recurrence suggests that they should not be separately emended; more likely they instance intransitive piel (see GK 52k).

[32] 1QIs[a] has ולוא for MT לא and thus links the verb with the next line (Pulikottil, *Transmission of Biblical Texts in Qumran*, p. 84).

[33] Knobel (*Jesaia*, p. 483) sees נְהוּגִים as a noun meaning leaders (comparing GK 50f); Duhm (*Jesaia*, p. 410) suggests active participle נֹהֲגִים for נְהוּגִים. On the participial circumstantial clause, see *TTH* 159; *DG* 137b.

[34] For MT הַגּוֹיִם NEB 'wide regions' repoints הַגְּוִיִּם, apparently following Eitan, 'A Contribution to Isaiah Exegesis', p. 84 (and see *DCH*, II, p. 334).

[35] For the inf. חָרֹב Syr implies חֶרֶב '[with] the sword'.

13 The splendour of Lebanon[36] will come[37] to you,// juniper, fir, and cypress together,[38]
To glorify the place of my sanctuary,[39]// and so that I may make splendid[40] the place[41] for my feet.[42]

14 The[43] children of those who humbled you will walk to you bending low,[44]// all those who despised you will bow low at the soles of your feet.[45]
They will call you 'Yhwh's city,// Zion[46] of Israel's holy one'.
15 Instead of your being abandoned,// repudiated with no one passing through[47],
I will make you an object of pride forever,// a joy from generation to generation.
16 You will suck the milk of[48] nations,// suck the breast[49] of kings.[50]
You will acknowledge that I am Yhwh—I am your deliverer;// I, Jacob's champion, am your restorer.

[36] 1QIs[a] adds נתן לך [plus ו] from 35.2 (Kutscher, הלשון והרקע הלשוני של מגילת ישעיהו השלמה, p. 434 [ET p. 543]).
[37] Ehrlich (*Randglossen* 4.216) emends the qal to hiphil יָבִיאוּ 'bring'.
[38] 1QIs[a]'s change of יחדו to יחדיו may reflect concern to avoid any possibility of seeing the word as an occurrence of יחד, a term for the congregation at Qumran (Pulikottil, *Transmission of Biblical Texts in Qumran*, pp. 165-72).
[39] Oort ('Kritische Aanteekeningen', p. 475) omits the מ on מקדשי with LXX, suggesting the translation 'my holy place'.
[40] On the construction, see Mitchell Dahood, 'Ugaritic–Hebrew Syntax and Style', *UF* 1 (1969), pp. 15-36 (23), with his reference to *TTH* 118.
[41] For the repeated מקום Budde suggests מכון, with the same meaning ('Jesaia Kap. 40–66', p. 705). But the phrase מכון מקדשו comes in Dan 8.11, so we might rather make this change to the first colon. Julian Morgenstern ('Further Light from the Book of Isaiah upon the Catastrophe of 485 B.C.', *HUCA* 37 [1966], pp. 1-28 [22]) suggests הדום 'stool' (cf. 66.1).
[42] LXX omits v. 13bβ, perhaps not caring for the anthropomorphism or for the repetition.
[43] 1QIs[a] adds כול, 1QIs[b],כל perhaps based on and making explicit the parallelism in the second colon.
[44] For the inf. construct שְׁחוֹחַ used adverbially one would expect inf. absolute שָׁחוֹחַ (cf. Duhm, *Jesaia*, p. 410); but GK 118q accepts the usage.
[45] LXX omits v. 14aβ, again perhaps not caring for the anthropomorphism (so Fritsch, 'The Concept of God in the Greek Translation of Isaiah', p. 160).
[46] GK 125h sees such expressions where a proper noun seems to function as a construct as implying ellipse of a word such as עִיר, which here might carry over from the first colon. But *DG* 35 remark 6 simply asserts that place names can be put in the construct. Budde ('Jesaia Kap. 40–66', p. 707) suggests צִיּוּן 'monument' for צִיּוֹן; Klostermann (*Deuterojesaia*, p. 88) suggests רְצוֹן 'delight'.
[47] LXX 'helping' may imply עוזר for עובר.
[48] To avoid the repetition of the verb, Driver ('Hebrew Notes on Prophets and Proverbs', p. 165) emends to וְקָנִית חֵלֶב 'you will possess the fat of'.
[49] The pointing שֹׁד rather than שַׁד is unusual, though not unique (cf. Odeberg's puzzled remarks, *Trito-Isaiah*, p, 230); the occurrence of the homonym in v. 18 will explain it (cf. Payne, 'Characteristic Word-play in "Second Isaiah"', p. 226).
[50] 'Kingdoms' according to Dahood; see the translation note on v. 3.

17 Instead of the bronze I will bring gold,// instead of the iron I will bring silver.
Instead of the wood, bronze,// instead of the stones, iron.
I will make well-being your oversight,// faithfulness your bosses.[51]
18 Violence will not make itself heard any more in your country,// destroying or smashing in your borders.[52]
You will call deliverance your walls,// praise[53] your gates.

19 The sun will no longer be light for you by day,// for brightness[54] the moon will not be a light for you.
Yhwh will be for you lasting light,// your God your glory.
20 Your sun will no longer[55] set,// your moon will not withdraw,
Because Yhwh—he will be for you lasting light;[56]// your days of grief will end.
21 Your people, all of them, are the faithful ones// who will possess the country forever.
They are the shoot[57] I planted,[58]// the work of my hands,[59] to manifest glory.
22 The smallest will become a clan,// the least a strong nation.
I am Yhwh;// in its time I will speed it.

Introduction

MT and 1QIs^{b} treat Isaiah 60 as a unit, with no subdivisions; 1QIs^{a} also begins a new section at 60.1 but then has no major break until 61.10. Verses 1-3 constitute an introduction, with vv. 1 and 3 forming an *inclusio* for the three verses. Verse 19 returns to the theme of light, which thus completes an *inclusio* around the chapter as a whole. Within vv. 4-18, vv. 6, 9, and 16 bring sections to a form of climax or conclusion with

[51] On the idiosyncratic version in 1 Clement, see Craig A. Evans, 'The Citation of Isaiah 60:17 in 1 Clement', *Vigiliae christianae* 36 (1982), pp. 105-7.

[52] 1QIs^{b} sg. בגבולך assimilates to sg. בארצך (van der Kooij, *Die alten Textzeugen des Jesajabuches*, p. 121).

[53] LXX γλύμμα 'an engraving', perhaps a corruption of ἀγαλλίαμα, perhaps included in light of the image in 49.16 (*HUB*), perhaps influenced by 26.1-2; 54.12; Ezek 41.25 (see Ziegler, *Untersuchungen zur Septuaginta des Buches Isaias*, pp. 169-70).

[54] 1QIs^{a} adds בלילה '[by] night' (cf. LXX, Tg), a clarifying addition.

[55] 1QIs^{a} lacks עוד.

[56] 1QIs^{b} omits vv. 19bβ-20bα by homoioteleuton (van der Kooij, *Die alten Textzeugen des Jesajabuches*, p. 122); cf. also Syr.

[57] 1QIs^{b} omits.

[58] Q has מַטָּעַי 'my plantings'(cf. Syr, Tg, Vg); K implies מַטָּעוֹ or מַטָּעָו 'his planting[s]'; 1QIs^{b} has מטעיו 'his plantings'; 1QIs^{a} has מטעי יהוה 'Yhwh's plantings', perhaps suggesting an original מַטַּע יהוה 'Yhwh's planting'. LXX 'guarding the planting' implies נֹצֵר for נֵצֶר (Ottley, *Isaiah according to the Septuagint*, II, p. 367); Hanson (*The Dawn of Apocalyptic*, p. 51) emends to the pl. נצרי. Tg paraphrases 'my joyful shoot'.

[59] 1QIs$^{a, b}$ have third person suffix ידיו (cf. LXX). I. F. M. Brayley ('Yahweh is the Guardian of His Plantation', *Biblica* 41 [1960], pp. 275-86) reworks the whole line as third person in light of the textual evidence. Torrey (*Second Isaiah*, p. 452) sees MT as a composite reading combining first and third person.

a reference to the recognition of Yhwh, and vv. 13 and 18 do something a little similar. This suggests we could see vv. 4-6, 7-9, 10-13, 14-16, and 17-18 as sections. Yet whereas v. 4 has a 'proper beginning', none of these 'climaxes' are followed by a proper new beginning; vv. 7, 10, 14, 17, and 19 all begin resumptively, *in medias res*. Thus the whole chapter flows without marked breaks and there is only a little indication of logic or structure about its development. It may simply have a stream-of-consciousness nature, which would cohere with the way the poem expresses itself lyrically, imaginatively, and poetically. 'It seems as if the camels themselves are singing hymns. And as if the sheep and goats climb onto the altar to sacrifice themselves.'[60]

The chapter's lack of structure would neither imply nor preclude the possibility that it appears here in its original form, and there are various theories regarding its development, such as the following:

1. Vermeylen (first version): vv. 1-13 less v. 4b and 9aβ is the chapter's original form, with vv. 12, 14-18, 19-20, and 21-22 being later additions.[61]
2. Steck: vv. 1-9, 13-16 is the chapter's original form, with vv. 10-11, 12, and 17-22 being later additions.[62]
3. Koenen: vv. 1-18 less vv. 6bβ, 7b, 9b, 10b, 12, 13b, 17aβ is the chapter's original form, with vv. 19-20, 21, and 22 being later additions.[63]
4. Vermeylen (second version): vv. 1-14 less vv. 4, 6bβ, 7b-9, 10b-13, 14aβ is the chapter's original form, with vv. 15-22 being later additions.[64]

The variety of such theories encourages Childs's judgment that 'although I do not contest that the present text shows sign of growth, I question whether this complex process can be precisely reconstructed, and, even less, that such an alleged development provides the key to understanding the chapter in its final form'.[65]

The chapter comprises 22 verses, like an alphabetical psalm, and with some ingenuity it can be seen as 44 lines; these mostly come in pairs, though it would be a tour de force to turn it into 22 pairs of lines. Nearly all the lines are bicola, though v. 6a (or possibly v. 6b) is a tricolon, and one or two other lines might be understood as tricola. MT punctuates the rhythm of many as 3-3 (vv. 2b, 3, 4a, 4b, 5a, 6b, 7b, 9a, 9b, 13b, 15a, 15b, 16a, 17aγδ, 20a, 21a, 22a), but others are longer or shorter. Most

60 Koole, *Jesaja III*, p. 221 (ET p. 218).

61 *Du prophète Isaïe à l'apocalyptique*, II, p. 473-78.

62 *Studien zu Tritojesaja*, pp. 49-79.

63 *Ethik unde Eschatologie im Tritojesajabuch*, pp. 137-56.

64 'La lumière de Sion', in Camille Focant (ed.), *Quelle maison pour Dieu?* (Paris: Cerf, 2003), pp. 177-208.

65 *Isaiah*, p. 494.

lines are characterized by synonymous parallelism, though in vv. 4a, 9aγδ, 21a, and 22b the second colon completes the first, and in v. 10b the second contrasts with the first.

When one turns the page from chapter 59 to chapter 60 in Isaiah, the entire scene changes; the previous actors have disappeared and an unidentified voice now addresses an unidentified woman.[66] The poem changes from promises made with regard to the people, but framed in the third person, to an exhortation to a feminine singular addressee that is eventually explicitly identified as an entity that 'they will call "Yhwh's city, Zion of Israel's holy one"' (LXX and Tg make the point explicit in the first line by adding 'Jerusalem'). The second-person singular feminine suffix *-k* comes 51 times.[67] One might initially understand the exhortation as urging the city to 'rise and shine', to behave as people restored and perhaps thereby to find their restoration as they set about living as Yhwh's people and rebuilding Yhwh's city, but the exhortation makes a transition to declarations about Yhwh's splendour having begun to shine and promises that Yhwh's splendour will shine on the city and that its scattered people will return, and these suggest that promise and encouragement are the chapter's focus. On the stage, then, God exhorts the personified city; in the house, the people who actually live in the city overhear this exhortation and are intended to find encouragement in what Yhwh intends to do. The chapter is designed to transform the people's attitude, to move them from discouragement to encouragement.[68]

The way it does so may be analysed as involving the manner in which it envisages place. One aspect of this analysis involves working with the difference between place (definite, bounded) and space (open, undifferentiated). In theory Jerusalem is a place, the most emplaced place in all the earth; but what Judahites returning from Babylon would find is a ruin, unbounded and unrecognizable as the place that had existed in their mind and spirit. The vision in Isaiah 60 is of Jerusalem turned into the place that had existed in their dreams. Yet paradoxically, this transformation comes about by Jerusalem's becoming something more like space than place—an open city, open to the world bringing its resources. It is this process that brings Jerusalem as a city into line with Jerusalem as a symbol. 'The rhetorical purpose of Isaiah 60 is to sear an image of Jerusalem's restoration into its audience's retinas, so that, as they move about in its ruins, they are able to see its restoration superimposed above them'.[69]

[66] Croatto, *Imaginar el futuro*, p. 197.

[67] Cf. Fitzgerald, 'A Rhetorical Analysis of Isaiah 56–66', p. 196.

[68] Cf. Wells's comments on the background of Isa 60–62 in the laments of the exiles ('The Statements of Well-Being in Isaiah 60–62', e.g., pp. 125-28).

[69] Christopher M. Jones, in a paper 'What is the Light?' read at the Society of Biblical Literature meeting in San Francisco in November 2011, which this entire paragraph follows. Jones is taking up the work of Yi-Fu Tuan, *Space and Place: The Perspective of Experience* (Minneapolis: University of Minnesota Press, 1977), and Edward Soja, *Thirdspace* (Cambridge, MA: Blackwell, 1996).

The audience in the house is thus different from the one in Isaiah 40–55, if that house was located in Babylon. In the context of mid-sixth-century Babylon, one could imagine the pseudo-exhortation as designed to encourage the audience in the house to believe that they will have the opportunity to return to Judah and to encourage belief in a 'myth of the empty land', or at least an empty city. Indeed, chapters 60–62 have commonly been seen as the oldest chapters in Isaiah 56–66 and as the original kernel around which the section as a whole developed.[70] In their context in Isaiah 56—66, however, they presuppose that the audience in the house is in Judah. They presuppose that the city as a whole or the community within it envisaged by the prophecy is one that sees itself as desperately needing restoration and needing the return of people who once lived in the city. The three chapters do not indicate that they are heard only by people who have responded with penitence to the challenge about rebellion in preceding chapters.[71] The promise that returning people will bring resources for the city's needed restoration, and in particular for the restoration and beautification of its temple, suggests the beginning of the Persian period, and might imply the time between 537 and the temple's rebuilding in 520–516, though the period after 516 is also possible.[72] There are similarities between the portrayal of the restoration of Jerusalem and reliefs in the palace that Darius I began to build at his new capital, Persepolis, at the same time as the Second Temple was being built, which portray peoples bringing tribute to the king.[73]

The consistency and length of the encouragement that runs through the chapter makes for a contrast with what has preceded. Isaiah 56–59 has been more or less confrontational, though it was interspersed with promises and it closed on an encouraging note. Isaiah 59.15b-21 follow on what precedes but constitute a transition to the promissory nature of chapters 60–62, which are 'euphoric and upbeat'.[74] It has been said of Isaiah 60 in particular that 'this song is the gem of the book'.[75] Over against the confrontational moral and religious tone of much that precedes in chapters 56–59, in chapter 60 and what follows in chapters 61–62, God 'holds out to all the idolators, all the proudly defiant, all the unjust rebels in Zion, his prevenient grace, which takes the initiative in giving them abundant life, even if they do not deserve it'.[76]

[70] See the Introduction to this commentary, esp. sections 1 and 3.

[71] Against Darr, *Isaiah's Vision of the Family of God*, p. 74.

[72] Julian Morgenstern associates the latter part with a subsequent hypothesized destruction (see, e.g., 'Jerusalem–485 B.C.', *HUCA* 27 [1956], pp. 101-79 [153-55]; 'Further Light from the Book of Isaiah upon the Catastrophe of 485 B.C.' [see above], pp. 17-28).

[73] See Brent Strawn, '"A World under Control"', in Jon L. Berquist (ed.), *Approaching Yehud* (Atlanta: SBL, 2007), pp. 85-116. Paul also notes parallels with Sumerian and Neo-Babylonian inscriptions (ישעיה פרקים מ-סו, II, p. 471-72 [ET p. 516]).

[74] Blenkinsopp, *Isaiah 56–66*, p. 208.

[75] Briggs, *Messianic Prophecy*, p. 397.

[76] Achtemeier, *The Community and Message of Isaiah 56–66*, p. 82.

Associated with the difference between the audience on the stage and that in the house is the difference between the prophet's speaking *about* Yhwh (vv. 1-2, 6, 9b, 14, 19) and speaking *as* Yhwh (vv. 7, 9a, 10, 13, 15-17, 21-22). There is no reason to take this alternation as reflecting material from different hands; it is common for prophecies to move between these two ways of speaking. Rhetorically, the poem's abrupt transitions to first-person speech function to accentuate and call attention to the immediate presence of Yhwh.[77]

The poem develops and interweaves a small number of overlapping and interrelated images and themes. It begins with the image of light dawning on the dark city, which stands in contrast to the emphasis on darkness in 59.9-10 but takes up the language about shining, sun, and splendour in 59.19.[78] The replacement of the darkness of calamity by the light of blessing reflects the replacement of divine fury by divine compassion and issues in the city recognizing Yhwh afresh. Second, the power of light to attract makes possible a transition to talk of the nations coming to this light. They will recognize Yhwh as well as recognizing the city where the light now shines. The previous chapter's 'violence' and its 'destroying and smashing' (59.6-7) do reappear, but with a 'no more' attached to them, their point now being that the nations will not trouble Jerusalem as they have. Third is the gathering of the city's scattered sons and daughters whom the nations and kings bring with them. Fourth is these nations and kings also bringing their resources to build up the city and specifically its sanctuary.

In this connection the motif of glory or beauty is important; the verb *pāʾar* and related nouns appear five times (vv. 7, 9, 13, 19, 21; also in 61.3, 10; 62.3; 63.12, 14, 15; 64.10 [11]). It takes up a motif from 3.18; 4.2; 10.12; 13.19; 20.5; 28.1, 4, 5; 44.13, 23; 46.13; 49.3; 52.1; 55.5. Most of the occurrences of the root come in this book. Broadly, Isaiah 1–39 warns about false, alleged glory or beauty; Isaiah 40–55 emphasizes the glorifying or beautifying of the people; Isaiah 56–66 focuses more on the glorifying or beautifying of the city and the temple. 'Yahweh is the beauty of Zion, Zion is the beauty of Yahweh who shines light on it.'[79]

In expounding these overlapping images and themes, the poem takes up motifs, phrases, and whole cola from Isaiah 40–55 in order substantially and lyrically to develop them. The chapter's promises thus 'derive their main inspiration from Deutero-Isaiah'.[80] The author is a *schriftgelehrter Prophet*, a scribal prophet.[81] How would this relationship with the preceding chapters have worked? It is possible to imagine the prophet

[77] Cf. Lack, *La Symbolique du Livre d'Isaïe*, p. 203.

[78] See de Hulster, *Iconographic Exegesis and Third Isaiah*, pp. 173-76, and further pp. 169-229 on pictorial material which may provide background.

[79] Cf. Lack, *La symbolique du Livre d'Isaïe*, p. 207.

[80] Whybray, *Isaiah 40–66*, p. 229. Cf. Zimmerli, 'Zur Sprache Tritojesaja', pp. 222-23.

[81] Lau, *Schriftgelehrte Prophetie in Jes 56–66*, p. 65.

having access to a scroll bearing the content of Isaiah 40–55 or some earlier version of it, but the form of the allusions suggests that the inspiration more likely works by means of the recollection of lines and phrases than through transcription from a text lying in front of the prophet. The links are examples of the way memory is the force that keeps the world of texts alive and transforms it in light of the present.[82] This dynamic would explain the varied nature of the relationship with the earlier text. But further, the prophet's taking up of phrases regularly involves using them in a different sense from the one they have in Isaiah 40–55. Thus if the prophet's allusions to passages from Isaiah 40–55 'provide a warrant confirming the continuity' with the earlier prophet'[83] they also constitute a 'strong rereading' of the earlier text.[84]

The main correspondences are as follows:

1. Verse 4a corresponds to 49.18a. But whereas 49.18a is an indirect promise to exiles that they will be able to go back to Jerusalem, 60.4a is an indirect promise to people in Jerusalem that exiles will be coming back to join them.
2. Verse 4b overlaps with 49.22b, with the same difference in significance.
3. Verse 9aα overlaps with 51.5b. The difference is that in 51.5 the nations look to Yhwh because Yhwh's act on Israel's behalf will also benefit them; in 60.9 they look because they are impressed by what Yhwh has done for Israel.
4. Verse 9aγ overlaps with 43.6, some of whose wording also reappears in v. 4.[85]
5. Verse 9b corresponds to 55.5b except that it begins 'for the name of' rather than 'for the sake of', perhaps an unintentional difference rather than a calculated one.
6. Verse 10b overlaps with 54.7-8. The implication is that anger still needs replacing by compassion.
7. Verse 13a's second colon corresponds to 41.19; in addition, 'Lebanon's splendour' corresponds to 35.2. The difference is that in 41.19 and 35.2 the flourishing of the trees is part of a broader metaphorical transformation of nature; in 60.13 the trees provide resources and/or beautification for the temple.
8. Verse 14a overlaps with 49.23a. The implication is that this reversal is still needed.
9. Verse 16b combines phrases from 49.23b and 26b. The implication is similar.

[82] Roy D. Wells, '"They All Gather, They Come to You"', in Everson and Kim (eds.), *The Desert Will Bloom*, pp. 197-216 (201).

[83] Childs, *Isaiah*, p. 495.

[84] Harold Bloom's term in *The Anxiety of Influence* (revised ed., Oxford: Oxford University Press, 1997).

[85] See Nurmela, *The Mouth of the Lord Has Spoken*, pp. 109-10.

The links with Isaiah 49 cohere with the fact that Isaiah 60 is a proclamation of the transformation of the city rather than of the return of a people.[86] They might suggest that Isaiah 49 'provides the context' for Isaiah 60 as a whole;[87] promises that appear in seed thought form there do find full-length exposition here. Yet the taking up of lines and phrases is simply the taking up of lines and phrases; Isaiah 60 is not an exposition of Isaiah 49 but a poem that makes use of some of its language to formulate its own vision. It makes little reference to the idea of the city as a woman who is forgotten, bereft, and abandoned, which is a central feature of Isaiah 49.[88] This omission suggests that while Isaiah 60 is reaffirming the earlier promises, it does not imply a sense of being let down by God. The idea that promises have not been fulfilled is not overtly the background to the glorious restatement of the promises.

Isaiah 60 has further links with passages in Isaiah 1–39, especially 2.2-4; 9.1, 3 [2, 4]; 11.1.[89] These links also suggest that those earlier promises are being reaffirmed, but Isaiah 60 again nuances the ideas and phrases it takes up. One might see Isaiah 2 as 'inspiring' Isaiah 60.[90] Yet while the covert concern in Isaiah 2 lies with the city, the prophet's explicit focus there lies on the city's significance for the nations, whereas Isaiah 60 more overtly focuses on what their coming signifies for the city itself.[91] Its talk of light coming to the world through what Yhwh does in relation to Jerusalem has a very different focus from that of the Dogmatic Constitution *Lumen Gentium*.[92] In Isaiah 2 the nations come for instruction and conflict resolution. In Isaiah 60 they come to contribute to the city's wealth and worship. In Isaiah 2 they come freely and with head held high; in Isaiah 60 they come bending low (as in Isa 49). While one might wonder whether 'the nations are being made an offer they can't refuse',[93] it is not clear that they come involuntarily.[94] The chapter's focus is not the day of Yhwh but the day of Jerusalem.[95] While one might call this change a shift from a universal to a national point of view,[96] it does not imply that Isaiah 2 (or Isaiah 40–55) is universalistic and Isaiah 60 nationalistic. All these parts of the book are concerned with Yhwh's

[86] Cf. Hanson, *The Dawn of Apocalyptic*, p. 64.

[87] Childs, *Isaiah*, p. 496. Cf. Beuken, *Jesaja IIIA*, pp. 165-66.

[88] Cf. Torrey, *Second Isaiah*, p. 444. See further Wells, '"They All Gather, They Come to You"' (see above).

[89] Cf. Sommer, *A Prophet Reads Scripture*, pp. 80-82, 86-88; earlier, Fishbane, *Biblical Interpretation in Ancient Israel*, pp. 495-99.

[90] So Alonso Schökel and Sicre Diaz, *Profetas*, I, p. 365.

[91] See Gerhard von Rad, 'Die Stadt auf dem Berge', *EvT* 8 (1948-49), pp. 439-47 (444) (ET *The Problem of the Hexateuch and Other Essays* [New York: McGraw–Hill; Edinburgh: Oliver & Boyd, 1966], p. 238).

[92] See Steck, *Studien zu Tritojesaja*, pp. 80-96.

[93] Joseph Blenkinsopp, 'Second Isaiah—Prophet of Universalism', p. 93.

[94] Against Koenen, *Ethik und Eschatologie im Tritojesajabuch*, p. 139.

[95] E.g. Volz, *Jesaja II*, p. 239.

[96] Sommer, *A Prophet Reads Scripture*, p. 82.

commitment to Jerusalem and with encouraging its people; in all the parts of the book Yhwh's sovereignty over and interest in all the nations is an aspect of this encouragement. The point may be made by noting how the chapter combines the metaphors of pilgrimage and tribute.[97] To come as pilgrims to Jerusalem bearing tribute is a privilege extended from Israel to the nations.

The shoot that Yhwh is tending in Isaiah 11 is a descendant of David who will rule in faithfulness and wear faithfulness (or one who will be faithful, in Jer 23.5). In Isaiah 60 the people as a whole is the shoot and the people as a whole are faithful.[98] The same point emerges from the chapter's broader relationship with Psalm 72; its themes also overlap with Psalms 2; 46; 48, though its verbal links with these psalms are not as close. Isaiah 60 can thus be seen to 'depend' on Psalm 72, though it may 'omit any reference to the Davidic dynasty' because 'what happens to the king in the psalm provides the pattern for what happens to the people as a whole'. The nations bow down to the city rather than to the king.[99] Possibly this reflects the conviction that whatever fulfilment of 'messianic' prophecies might come in the future, they were not being fulfilled in this prophet's day, so that it was necessary 'to pass over in silence the references to a Davidic ruler' that appear in earlier texts.[100] Isaiah 56–66 continues the 'reconceptualization of the David covenant' that began in Isaiah 40–55; 'Trito-Isaiah presents a scenario in which the promises of Isaiah 11,1-16, and those of other texts from throughout Isaiah, are realized', but in a way that does not involve the restoration of the Davidic monarchy.[101]

Comment

60.1 Get up, be alight, because your light has come;// Yhwh's splendour has shone forth upon you.

Although the prophecy will be dominated by 3-3 lines, it begins sonorously with a long 5-4 line; we might read it as a 2-3-4 tricolon or reduce the stresses by linking 'because' with 'your light' by means of a maqqeph so that the line reads as 4-4 (but see further the comments on vv. 14a and 19a). However we construe its rhythm, the line comprises double imperatives followed by double qatal clauses, with the double

[97] Cf. Gary Stansell, 'The Nations' Journey to Zion', in Everson and Kim (eds.), *The Desert Will Bloom*, pp. 233-55.

[98] Cf. Sommer, *A Prophet Reads Scripture*, p. 87.

[99] Sommer, *A Prophet Reads Scripture*, p. 115; cf. Paul, ישעיה פרקים מ-סו, II, p. 470-71 (ET pp. 515-16).

[100] Sommer, *A Prophet Reads Scripture*, p. 154.

[101] See Marvin A, Sweeney, 'The Reconceptualization of the Davidic Covenant in Isaiah', in Ruiten and Vervenne (eds.), *Studies in the Book of Isaiah*, pp. 41-61 (55, 57).

imperatives applying to v. 1b as well as to the second half of v. 1a; thus v. 1b is parallel to the second half of v. 1a. The two qatal clauses work abb'a': 'Has come your light; Yhwh's splendour on you has shone'. At the same time, the middle two clauses are bound together by the double use of the root *ʾôr*, as verb and noun.

The chapter opens quite abruptly without identifying speaker or addressee; the prophet thus grabs the attention of the audience.[102] It is by reading in light of what has preceded in Isaiah 40–55 and what will follow in v. 14 that we know how to understand what goes on here. The opening verb 'get up' immediately advertises that the prophecy takes up the exhortations and promises to Jerusalem in Isaiah 40–55; this particular imperative came in 51.17; 52.2. There the woman city was pictured as lying on the ground after being poisoned by Yhwh. To mix the metaphor, she is lying prostrate in such a way that its victors may walk over her, and/or that they may rape her, and/or (to mix the metaphor yet again) as sitting in the dirt after being cast down from her throne. In each connection she is bidden to get up: to regain life, to regain freedom, to regain dignity, to regain power. The prophecy presupposes that the city still lies on the ground in these various senses or connections; it is the city's situation in the late sixth and fifth centuries. Nothing has changed very much in the decades that have passed since Yhwh issued that exhortation in the 540s. The prophet reissues it.

In contrast, 'be alight' is a new exhortation, though the image of light does come from Isaiah 40–55 (42.6, 16; 45.7; 49.6; 51.4), with its own background in Isaiah 1–39 (2.5; 9.1 [2]), and a foreground in Isaiah 56–59 (58.8, 10; 59.9).[103] (On the assumption that Isaiah 60–62 is older than the material on either side, then historically this usage is background to the one that came earlier; but for anyone reading Isaiah, Isaiah 58–59 is background to Isaiah 60.) In isolation one could understand it as an exhortation to take action to bring light, analogous to Jesus' exhortation to let our light shine so that people may see our good deeds (Matt 5.16). The prophets would affirm that idea,[104] but it is not a way the Old Testament uses the image of light. The only other occasion where the qal of *ʾôr* occurs in a metaphorical sense is 1 Samuel 14.27, 29 to describe Jonathan's eyes brightening. This idea fits well here, following on the exhortation or invitation to rise from a position of humiliation and subjection.[105] 'What the prophet has in mind is a beaming look on the face.'[106]

[102] Cf. Elliger, *Die Einheit des Tritojesaja*, pp 20-21.

[103] On the image of light in Isaiah, see Peter D. Miscall, 'Isaiah: The Labyrinth of Images', in D. Jobling and S. D. Moore (eds.), *Poststructuralism as Exegesis* (Semeia 54; Atlanta: Scholars, 1991), pp. 103-21. Clements ('A Light to the Nations') emphasizes the link between 9.1 [2], 42.6, and 60.1-3.

[104] Indeed, Park (*Die Gerechtigkeit Israels und das Heil der Völker*, p. 368) makes it the closing epigraph of his study of worship, temple, eschatology, and judgment in Isaiah 56–66.

[105] Cf. Rosenmüller, *Scholia in Jesajae Vaticinia*, p. 747.

It implies enjoying the brightness of restoration and blessing.[107] 'Be alight' is the kind of imperative that actually constitutes a promise (cf. 54.14),[108] 'not a mere admonition but a word of power which puts new life into her limbs'.[109]

The causal clause then explicates the point. The city will definitely shine out its light because its light will have dawned upon it. If the qatal has its usual past reference it will mean 'has set', as it does in the expression 'the sun will no longer set' in v. 20,[110] but this makes the line jerky and the usage is not otherwise paralleled with 'light', which does not 'come' and 'go' in the sense that the sun does each morning and evening. The idea of light 'coming' fits with the image of God sending it (Ps 43.3) and the qatal here and in the parallel colon refers to an event that is past in the prophet's vision. It signifies a projection into the future moment when that bright dawning can be literally spoken of as past; that projection is possible because the event is determined in the mind of God and is therefore effectively real and actual. So the city's being able to 'lighten up' is a response to light having shone out on it; a paronomasia is involved.[111] For 'your light' Tg has 'the time of your deliverance', which correctly interprets the image as it is used here and elsewhere in the book.[112] Whereas darkness suggests the gloom of defeat, loss, oppression, and disaster; light suggests deliverance, healing, restoration, and blessing (see, e.g., Isa 9.1 [2], an earlier passage that talks about darkness, light, and this light being bright—the noun 'brightness' comes here in v. 3).[113] The image also contrasts with 5.30 and reaffirms the theology disputed by Amos 5.18, which dissociates Yhwh's day from the shining of light and sees it as bringing darkness.[114] But there is no particular reason to link the prophecy with a new year festival.[115]

The second colon typically heightens and sharpens the point of the clause it parallels. 'God's splendour' suggestively heightens 'your light'. The light that dawns will be no ordinary light but something supernaturally bright, because it is not natural light but divine light. Only here are 'light' and splendour' in parallelism, though 58.8 brings them in close association. The city will mirror Yhwh's own shining brilliance. Its

[106] Westermann, *Jesaja Kapitel 40–66*, p. 284 (ET p. 357).

[107] See the discussion in Birgit Langer, *Gott als 'Licht' in Israel und Mesopotamien. Eine Studie zu Jes 60,1-3.19f.* (Klosterneuburg: Österreichisches Katholisches Verlag, 1989), pp. 22-24.

[108] See GK 110c; *IBHS* 34.4c.

[109] Delitzsch, *Jesaia*, p. 607 (ET II, p. 409).

[110] So Ibn Ezra, *The Commentary of Ibn Ezra on Isaiah*, p. 276.

[111] Cf. Lau, *Schriftgelehrte Prophetie in Jes 56–66*, p. 27.

[112] But see van Zijl, 'The root פרק in Targum Isaiah', on the way this reference to salvation fits in Tg Isaiah.

[113] Vermeylen, *Du prophète Isaïe à l'apocalyptique*, II, p. 472.

[114] B. Sanhedrin 98b-99a juxtaposes the two verses with an implication of this kind (cf. Beuken, *Jesaja IIIA*, p. 193).

[115] Against Volz, *Jesaja II*, p. 244.

restoration will not be something that can be humanly generated but something that issues from and reflects divine action. A promise that 'Yhwh's splendour' would appear came near the beginning of Isaiah 40–55; here it has different (but related) implications. There it pointed to a movement on Yhwh's part, a return to Jerusalem that reversed the departure of 587. Here it suggests a manifestation visible in something that happens in the city itself, or rather a manifestation of someone, of Yhwh's own person. Yhwh's splendour is the outward manifestation of Yhwh's holiness, Yhwh's supernatural deity, God revealed 'in the glow of holiness and the dynamism of being'.[116] In turn the final verb 'has shone forth', which closes the line, is much more unusual than the verb 'has come' and further heightens the parallelism. This verb, too, picks up from 58.10, where 'your light' is the subject. It denotes the sun's 'dawning' at the beginning of the day, though in northern climes 'dawn' is inclined to suggest something gradual that need not be very bright, whereas *zāraḥ* would suggest the bright bursting forth of the Middle Eastern sun. Whereas Isaiah 40.10 speaks of God coming in a way that locates this coming in a historical event, Isaiah 60 speaks in metaphor in terms of a star rising.[117] The coupling of *bā'* and *zāraḥ* parallels Deuteronomy 33.2, where it describes Yhwh's coming from Sinai, and that may also underlie the prophecy's use of the qatal rather than the yiqtol.[118]

The words in vv. 1-3 'point to a theophany'.[119] In connection with them, *Pesiqta deRab Kahana* relates a parable about a man who was walking at dusk. Each time someone lit a light for him it went out; so he concluded that henceforth he would simply wait for the dawn. The parable stands for Israel, which saw Moses' light go out, and Solomon's, but from now on waits only for God's light.[120]

60.2 Because there: the darkness will cover the earth,// pitch dark the peoples.
But upon you Yhwh will shine forth,// his splendour will appear upon you.

The formal structure of v. 2a follows that of v. 1, as 'Because there' is explained and spelled out by each of the two clauses that follow; they stand in parallelism, though the verb appears in only the first of the clauses and thus also applies to the second. To put it another way, the line works abcdb'd' (to ignore MT's maqqeph joining 'will cover the earth'). The first colon is another heavy one (three stresses in MT, but five words) but the second a brief one.

[116] Walter J. Burghardt, 'Isaiah 60:1-7', *Interpretation* 44 (1990), pp. 396-400 (396).
[117] Westermann, *Jesaja Kapitel 40–66*, pp. 284-85 (ET pp. 357-58).
[118] So Lau, *Schriftgelehrte Prophetie in Jes 56–66*, pp. 28-29. F. Schnutenhaus ('Das Kommen und Erscheinen Gottes im Alten Testament', *ZAW* 76 [1964], pp. 1-22 [9]) suggests that in both passages the imagery of the sun-god is being transferred to Yhwh.
[119] Sverre Aalen, *TWAT*, I, p. 180 (ET *TDOT*, I, pp. 165-66).
[120] *Pesiqta deRab Kahana*, II, p. 72.

The line offers a further explication, going behind the declarations in the first verse. Verse 1 raises the question 'Why is there a need for Yhwh's light to shine?' Verses 2-3 respond to this question with yiqtol verbs, which seems a little perverse in v. 2a because the darkness is already operative. We might translate the yiqtols as present (so TNIV); qatal verbs in v. 1 refer to the future, and yiqtol verbs in v. 2a refer to the situation as it is now but as it will also be on the eve of Yhwh's coming action. We have already noted that darkness suggests calamity, devastation, and loss, as light suggests blessing and fullness of life (cf. 58.10; 59.9; also, e.g., 5.30; 9.2 [1]; 45.7; 49.9).[121] 'Pitch dark' heightens 'darkness'; Sym nicely translates 'the darkness of Hades'. While *ʿărāpel* usually denotes the deep darkness that both indicates and mercifully conceals the presence of God, in the prophets it underlines the gloom of the trouble the people experience as Yhwh's day falls on them (e.g. Ezek 34.12).

In light of the way darkness has characterized Israel's experience, one might initially translate the first colon 'darkness will cover the *land*' (like a flood), as in Ezekiel 32.8 with reference to Egypt; v. 1 implicitly concerned Jerusalem in particular, and *ʾereṣ* referred to the land of Israel on its previous occurrences (57.13; 58.14) as it will in 60.18, 21. But the heightening in the parallelism in the second colon disambiguates the word. The word for 'peoples' (*leʾummîm*) is the rarest of the terms referring to the nations; it recurs in Isaiah, especially in chapters 40–55 (17.12-13; 34.1; 41.1; 43.4, 9; 49.1; 55.4). It indicates that *ʾereṣ* indeed denotes the world as a whole and not just the land of Israel. 'The peoples' can denote the worldwide imperial power in its waywardness as oppressor, and this would make sense; calamity has fallen on the empire, darkness has fallen upon it; the verse then 'contrasts disaster for the nations with salvation for Israel'.[122] But 'the peoples' can also denote the nations as the victims of the great imperial power, like Israel itself, and succeeding verses will suggest that this is the word's significance here. As the peoples of the world were once the victims of Babylonian power, now they are the victims of Persian power. 'Peoples' thus makes explicit that v. 2a also answers another question implicitly raised by v. 1. Why and where is the city's light to shine? It is to shine over the world and its peoples. Jerusalem and the world as a whole have darkness in common, and Yhwh's making light shine on and in Jerusalem will be an indirect means of bringing light to the world in its darkness (cf. 42.6-7). The rest of the chapter will further explicate what that means, though typically its focus lies on what it, too, means for Jerusalem itself. It is for the encouragement of the depressed people that the prophet pictures the difference its restoration will mean for the nations.

[121] See further Langer, *Gott als 'Licht'*, pp. 52-61.
[122] M. J. Mulder, *TWAT*, VI, p. 375 (ET *TDOT*, XI, p. 375).

Verse 2b thus focuses on the contrast between the unrelieved darkness that covers the nations and the dawning of bright light in Jerusalem. The line recycles words from v. 1 but the motif represents in heightened form an aspect of the exodus story, when Egypt lay in darkness but the Israelites had light (Exod 10.22-23 [E]).[123] It is the chapter's first regular 3-3 line, working abcc′a′b′ and continuing to express itself in yiqtol verbs that contrast with the earlier qatals. The prepositional expression opening the line and then recurring in the second colon immediately makes the point. Whereas the earth is in darkness and the peoples in pitch dark, 'upon you…upon you…' are shining and splendour; verb and noun reappear from v. 1. The line closes with the only new word.

60.3 Nations will walk to your light,// kings to your shining brightness.

Another neat 3-3 line (abcb′c′d) incorporates further recycling, in its reference to light and its inclusion of the noun shining (used adjectivally) related to the verb 'shine'. It makes explicit the way Yhwh's appearing is significant for the peoples. 'According to Isa. 40—66, the *kāḇôḏ* of Yahweh is delegated to his people and to Jerusalem; its purpose is to attract other nations and guide them in their darkness.'[124] The 'coming' of light finds a response in the 'going' of nations and kings. The idea of the nations being the beneficiaries of Yhwh's action in Jerusalem or through Israel, as well as being the objects of Yhwh's wrath, is familiar from earlier chapters in Isaiah (e.g. 2.2, 4; 25.7; 42.1, 6; 49.6; 52.15; 55.5). Isaiah 60 brings that idea into sharper association with the motif of light. It utilizes this motif in a different connection from that which appears in 42.6; 49.6, though the message of the chapter is similar to the message suggested by the motif earlier; one has to distinguish between the use of a motif and what the motif symbolizes. At the same time, the reference to kings also underlines how the coming event will be significant for Jerusalem and for the nations' attitude to God (as in 11.10, 12; 49.7; 52.15). In the second colon the rare word 'brightness' adds to the assemblage of linked expressions in vv. 1-3 (light, splendour, shine). The related feminine plural had appeared in 59.9, which already indicated how 'brightness' suggests the dazzling brilliance associated with the reversal of calamity and disaster. Thus the line once more affirms that Yhwh intends to do something that will transform the troubled state of the city with a brilliance that will draw the nations and their kings. The motif of light attracting compares with 2.5 as well as 2.2-4, where following on the description of the nations being drawn to Jerusalem, Jacob is urged to *walk* in Yhwh's *light*.[125] 'Jerusalem is the light of the world, as it says,

[123] Cf. the comment in Pisqa 21 in *Pesiqta de Rab Kahana*, II, p. 76.

[124] M. Weinfeld, *TWAT*, IV, p. 37 (ET *TDOT*, VII, pp. 35-36).

[125] See Gabriela Ivana Vlková, *Cambiare la luce in tenebre e le tenebre in luce* (Rome: Pontifical Gregorian University, 2004), pp. 163-86.

"Nations will walk to your light". But who is the light of Jerusalem? God, as it is written, "Yhwh will be for you lasting light"' (60.19-20).[126]

60.4 Lift your eyes around and look:// all of them have gathered, they have come to you.
Your sons will come from afar,// your daughters will support themselves on the hip.

So light will shine on the city in such a way as the nations will see it and be attracted by it; here the concrete implication for the city becomes explicit. The verse begins with another imperative that is an indirect promise, and another declaration using qatal verbs, concerning something that has happened in vision though not in literal reality. Verse 4a is another 3-3 line, as MT punctuates it, though it is 4-4 in words and thus perhaps draws attention to itself. There is no parallelism between the two halves; the line rather comprises two cola in which the second completes the first. One could say that the first raises a question ('What are they to look at?') which the second answers. Further, each colon manifests internal parallelism as it incorporates two verbs of comparable meaning. The effect of the first parallelism is to raise suspense. 'Lift up your eyes around' makes us want to know what people are to look at, but initially all we get is a repetition of the invitation. The effect of the second parallelism is again to raise a question that the second answers, though only partially, so that it again raises suspense. 'All of them have gathered': where, and who are these people? The answer to the first question comes in the last word. According to the regular rules of syntax, the answer to the second is, the nations and kings of v. 3, but more likely that apparent answer is a teaser. The 'them' is anticipatory; the true answer regarding its reference is held over until v. 4b.[127] Thus in translating 'all of them', LXX 'your sons' anticipates v. 4b to make clear that 'them' refers to the exiles not the nations and kings; Tg does this at greater length.

Admittedly, the rhetoric may work this way only for someone who has not recently read 49.18a, because 60.4a is a straight repetition of that line, and in that context the antecedent of 'them' is 'your children' in 49.17. There and here, the exhortation to lift up the eyes has two implications, which we may perceive by comparing and contrasting the use of this exhortation in 40.26. One is that there is something for people to see that they are ignoring. They are looking down instead of up and thus are not seeing things that could make them look at their situation in a different way. The other is that what the prophet wants them to see is as real as other things one might lift up one's eyes to see (like the heavens in 40.26). That is why, paradoxically, to see these things they are to look around as well as up. They are not to look up to the heavens but to look

126 Gen. R. 59.5.
127 Against Torrey, *Second Isaiah*, p. 444.

around and in their imagination see people—people whom the verse will go on to portray approaching the city. In the piel, in 40.11 'gather' describes Yhwh's collecting together the exiles to bring them home in the way a shepherd gathers sheep; the piel recurs in 43.5; 54.7; 56.8 without explicit reference to the shepherding metaphor. The niphal describes the sheep/people's own action; I take the niphal as intransitive rather than passive.

The declaration in v. 4b that makes clear who is gathering and coming speaks initially of *bānayik*, which in 49.17 denotes 'your children', as it does in 49.25 and elsewhere, but in 49.22 Yhwh declares that the nations 'will bring your sons...and your daughters'. Here, too, the appearance of daughters in the second colon makes the reader reconsider the first colon and realize that *bānayik* denotes specifically 'sons' not generically 'children'. The occurrence of 'bring' (*bôʾ* hiphil) in 49.22 also anticipates 'come' (*bôʾ* qal) here, but v. 4b more directly picks up the words 'will come from afar' from 49.12.[128] The expression connotes the remote places where people live in exile.[129] The use of the verb *ʾāman* (niphal) is unique but it also has its background in 49.22-23 and it is quite intelligible as a secondary denominative usage. The (rare) qal verb occurs only as a participle, denoting support or nourish, and it is thus used as a noun to denote a male or female nurse. Vg 'will suck', Aq 'they will be suckled' assume the latter, but in 49.23 the nursing was being done by kings, and here v. 3 has mentioned kings; it is likely that it is they who are nursing the daughters, though there is scope for reference to the nations, also mentioned in v. 3 and in this connection in 49.22. The kings are carrying them on their hip, not their shoulder, as in 49.23; that difference may reflect the influence of Ezekiel 34.21.[130]

The line is another 3-3 bicolon, abca′b′c′: the nouns for the sons and daughters stand in parallelism at the beginning of each colon, prepositional expressions in parallelism come in the middle, and the two verbs in parallelism close the cola. Masculine and feminine complement each other, different prepositions do so, then qal and niphal do so; in each case, a more familiar or common term is followed by a less usual one. Typically, the cola need interweaving to gain the line's prosaic meaning: 'Your sons and daughters will come from afar, supporting themselves on the hip'. In the background of the promise is the fact that not as many people have returned to Jerusalem as one might have expected from Isaiah 40–55; the accession of Cyrus did not make so much a difference. But the passage again does not explicitly agonize over this.

[128] Frederick W. Danker sees the words as then echoed in Mark 8.3 ('Mark 8 3', *JBL* 83 [1962], pp. 215-16).

[129] Peter R. Ackroyd, 'An Interpretation of the Babylonian Exile', *Scottish Journal of Theology* 27 (1974), pp. 329-52 (338-39), reprinted in Ackroyd, *Studies in the Religious Tradition of the Old Testament*, pp. 152-71, 282-85 (160).

[130] So Steck, *Studien zu Tritojesaja*, pp. 97-100.

60.5 Then you will revere and glow,// your heart will be in awe and swell.
Because the sea's multitude will turn over to you,// the might of the nations will come to you.

Yet another neat 3-3 line follows in v. 5a, each colon dominated by a pair of verbs in the manner of v. 4a. In other respects, the line is tantalizing.[131] The MT tradition is divided as to whether to read the first verb as from *rā'â* (see) or *yārē'* (fear/revere),[132] as was the case at 59.19. The first verb came in vv. 2 and 4, which pushes us in that direction, and earlier in the book the second verb almost invariably had the negative meaning 'fear', not the positive meaning 'revere'. The positive meaning is more frequent in the Torah, the Psalms, and Proverbs; the noun *yir'â* is used in the positive sense in 11.2-3; 29.13; 33.6; 63.17. The second verb *nāhar*, 'be bright, shine, glow', complements the other words with related meaning in vv. 1-3; it otherwise appears only in Psalm 34.6 [5]. But an almost as rare homonym appears in Isaiah 2.2, a promise whose theme is reworked in Isaiah 60. In Isaiah 2 the verb describes the nations 'flowing' to Jerusalem, and the prophet may well not have thought of these as different verbs.[133] Light becomes not only an objective feature of the city's life but a subjective sensation.[134] The third verb *pāḥad* has similar meanings to the more common *yārē'* and occasionally appears in parallelism with it (e.g. Ps 27.1). This suggests that the opening verb was indeed *yārē'*. Tg assumes that the city's awe has a negative significance, as the city will be in dread because of its 'dread of sins'; in contrast, Syr has 'rejoice' for 'be in awe'. The line works abcb'c'd, with the rarer *pāḥad* paralleling the more common *yārē'*. In turn the final verb (*rāḥab*) can suggest broadening in mind (1 Kgs 5.9; Ps 119.32) but also swelling with pride or confidence, which fits better here. Like the verbs for fear or revere, it can have a positive or a negative meaning; here the former makes sense. The heart swelling parallels the glowing of the first colon and contrasts with the idea of the breath being under constraint and anguish (*ṣar*; Job 7.11).[135] The line as a whole then expresses a response of awed amazement at what has happened, amazement of the kind that would make the city fall in submission to Yhwh as the one who made it happen.

131 Shalom M. Paul, 'Polysensuous Polyvalency in Poetic Parallelism', in M. Fishbane and E. Tov (eds.), *Sha'arei Talmon* (S. Talmon Festschift; Winona Lake, IN: Eisenbrauns, 1992), pp. 147-63 (157-58) sees the line as systematically ambiguous; cf. 57.18.

132 See the translation note.

133 Neither does L. A. Snijders in *TWAT*, V, p. 282 (ET *TDOT*, IX, pp. 262-63). Vg takes the verb as this other *nāhar* 'flow', as does Ibn Ezra (*The Commentary of Ibn Ezra on Isaiah*, p. 277) in the sense of running about, in association with his negative understanding of *yārē'*, but this requires considerable reading in. Sommer (*A Prophet Reads Scripture*, p. 81) sees Isaiah 60 as playing more broadly with both meanings of the verb.

134 Volz, *Jesaja II*, p. 245.

135 Marti, *Jesaja*, p. 382; cf. Ibn Ezra (*The Commentary of Ibn Ezra on Isaiah*, p. 277). Driver similarly suggests being 'care free' ('Notes on Isaiah', p. 48).

While this will denote a response to what has preceded, syntactically the basis for it comes in v. 5b, which rephrases what has preceded, in a 4-4 line comprising parallel cola working abcdc′d′a′b′ (or more broadly abb′a′). It speaks first of the *hāmôn* of the sea. LXX takes this word to refer to the sea's riches, which might suggest fish or might more plausibly refer to the wealth of (countries to) the west (so Tg; cf. 49.12). Vg even more plausibly gives *hāmôn* one of its more common meanings; etymologically it suggests noise, but it can thus denote the crowd that makes a noise (only in Eccles 5.9 does it clearly mean 'wealth'). In the parallel phrase, LXX paraphrases, while Tg takes *ḥayil* likewise to mean wealth (cf. 61.6), but it more often denotes strength (cf. Vg, Sym) and more concretely an army (cf. 43.17). All this suggests that the line repeats the point in v. 3. The vision once again describes the multitudinous forces of the nations, including those across the seas, turning to Jerusalem's light (which will be ironic if it is the case that Adam Smith's title for *An Inquiry into the Nature and Causes of the Wealth of Nations*[136] comes from this line).

60.6 A stream of camels will cover you,// dromedaries of Midian and Ephah;// all of them will come from Sheba.
They will carry gold and frankincense// and bring news of the great praise of Yhwh.

Eight lines now develop v. 5b in abb′a′ order: that is, vv. 6-7 give specificity to the nations that do not need to come by sea and approach Jerusalem from the south, and vv. 8-9 give specificity to the ones that do come by sea and approach Jerusalem from the west.[137] There is no reference to people coming back from the north and east, the direction from which people would come from Babylon or Persia; contrast 41.2, 25 and Zechariah 1–6. The sequence begins in v. 6a with a tricolon of parallel cola, 3-3-3; the second colon elaborates on the first, and the third elaborates on the first two. While we have concluded that v. 5b does not directly refer to the nations' riches, a major point about the nations coming to Jerusalem is what they bring. The desert regions to the south are one major direction from which resources for the city and the temple would indeed come, by camel train. In this 'pageant'[138] the camels come in such quantities, it will be as if they cover the city, like locusts covering the ground (Exod 10.5, 15) or clouds covering the land (Ezek 38.9, 16)—or perhaps with a look back to v. 1, like the darkness that currently covers

[136] 2 vols.; London: Strahan, 1776.
[137] Cf. Coffin, 'The Book of Isaiah: Chapters 40–66', p. 699. Pierre Grelot suggests that Isaiah 60 is here adopting and adapting a Middle Eastern motif illustrated in a prayer to Ishtar ('Un parallèle babylonien d'Isaïe lx et du Psaume lxxii', *VT* 7 [1957], pp. 319-21).
[138] Muilenburg, 'The Book of Isaiah: Chapters 40–66', p. 701.

the earth.[139] The Midianites were known as camel traders (cf. Gen 37.28), while the original Ephah was Midian's son and Sheba was Midian's nephew (Gen 25.3-4). Sheba (in south Arabia) is especially well-known as a place from which exotic and valuable things came to Judah, and as a trading people (e.g. 1 Kgs 10.1-2; Jer 6.20; Ezek 27.22-23; Ps 72.10, 15; Job 6.19). But the recurrence of this motif in biblical poetry issues a warning about being too prosaic in understanding the significance of the imagery, as if it offered a literal picture of nations coming from here and nowhere else.

Gold and frankincense (v. 6b) is the kind of freight one would expect such a camel train to be carrying (see 1 Kgs 10.2). While gold would be of wide significance for enriching the city and its palaces, frankincense points specifically to the temple and its worship (e.g. Exod 30.34 [P]; Isa 43.23; 66.3; Neh 13.5, 9). That is confirmed by the second of the two 3-3 parallel cola, at least indirectly. 'Bring news' (*bāśar* piel) is a rare verb but one that recurs in Isaiah 40–66 (40.9; 41.27; 52.7; 61.1). The noun *tᵉhillâ*, particularly in the plural, can point to praiseworthiness (e.g. 63.7; Exod 15.11; Ps 78.4). Thus LXX paraphrases 'salvation', though this might be a Christianized version affected by the reference to gold and frankincense.[140] But the idea of bringing Jerusalem news of Yhwh's praiseworthiness seems puzzling. One might ask whether the colon refers to the caravans taking home news of the praise offered in Jerusalem,[141] but the direction of movement in the line is towards Jerusalem. Rather the camel train is bringing news of the way Yhwh is recognized and praised in the faraway lands from which the camel train comes. The nations are recognizing Yhwh in the manner of Jethro or Rahab who heard what Yhwh had done and gave the news the appropriate response (cf. also 45.14).

Literally, it is the camels themselves who bring the news, which might seem implausible; Tg glosses the verse so as to indicate that it is the people who come with the camels who do so (cf. LXX, Vg). It is possible to understand the Hebrew in that sense by reading v. 6aγ as the beginning of the second line in the verse and translating 'All of the people from Sheba will come; they will carry…'. While v. 4 has illustrated how 'all of them' can anticipate the expression that identifies its 'them', there the words contain less ambiguity because the line itself contains no antecedent for the 'them', whereas here the camels and dromedaries provide the suffix with its antecedent. The line might involve a kind of metalepsis; the camels will give the news of Yhwh's praise by virtue of bringing the people who more literally convey that news. Yet v. 7 suggests that this is still too prosaic.

139 Cf. H. Ringgren, *TWAT*, IV, p. 274 (ET *TDOT*, VII, p. 261).

140 Cf. Seeligmann, *The Septuagint Version of Isaiah*, p. 28.

141 Cf. Julian Morgenstern, 'Two Prophecies from 520–516 B.C.', *HUCA* 22 (1949), pp. 365-431 (394-95).

60.7 All the flocks of Qedar will gather to you;// the rams of Nebaiot will minister to you.
They will come up for acceptance on my altar// and I will glorify my glorious house.

The first line (4-3) comprises parallel cola, in effect working abca'b'c. The two construct nouns stand in parallelism, as do the two place names, then the two verbs; standing outside this strict parallelism the first colon opens with 'all' (implicitly also applying to the second) and closes with a prepositional expression (equivalent to the one contained within the verb in the second colon). Flocks and rams are appropriate objects to be offered in worship; 'all' is a magnificent hyperbole (there are no flocks left in Qedar?!). Whereas the peoples mentioned in v. 6 are ones involved in trading by camel, Qedar and Nebaiot are more pastoral people. Nebaiot and Qedar were sons of Ishmael. The people of Qedar live in villages (42.11), though these are perhaps tent villages. They too lived south of Israel, though not as far south as the people mentioned in v. 6. Their rams will gather to Jerusalem. The niphal verb *qābaṣ* is a familiar one in Isaiah 40–55, applied to the nations (e.g. 45.20) as well as to dispersed Judahites (cf. v. 4); the piel also applies to both (e.g. 56.8; 66.18). The flocks and rams gather like human worshippers, then. They are not the objects that their owners offer in worship; they themselves gather and offer themselves. Indeed, the flocks and rams 'minister' to Jerusalem (*šārat* piel), like the Levites and the priests there (the verb can be used of ministering to Yhwh and of the Levites' ministering to the priests in doing the tasks that enable the priests to do their own work). Significantly, the word was used of foreigners who attach themselves to Yhwh as the objects of Yhwh's 'gathering'.

Verse 7b puts the point even more boldly and paradoxically as it pictures the animals climbing (*ʿālâ* qal) onto the altar in order to be killed. In the much more common usage, the priests cause the animals to go up (*ʿālâ* hiphil). Here they themselves go up. Alongside the unusual use of the verb is the unusual expression 'with acceptance [to] my altar' instead of 'for acceptance on my altar'.[142] The 3-3 line as a whole manifests a loose parallelism; the line is book-ended by its verbs, one third-person and one first-person, inside which are phrases with first-person suffixes referring to 'my altar' and 'my house'. They thus share a specific reference to the temple that contrasts with the address to the city that has characterized vv. 1-7a. The line further rounds off vv. 6-7 as its first colon picks up the significance of the animals in v. 7a while its second colon reverts to the significance of the goods brought by the camels in v. 6. When Ezra comes to Jerusalem, he comes on Artaxerxes' behalf 'to glorify Yhwh's house in Jerusalem' (Ezra 7.27), and in this context one can see glorifying the glorious house as adding beauty to a building that

[142] See the translation note; and for the rendering 'with', *DG* 118 remark 1 (see also *IBHS* 11.2.13e).

had already been restored and that people could already see as beautiful. In the context of 537–516, the expression would be a pregnant one. The house is not glorious now; it is a shambles. But in its inherent nature in the proper state to which it is destined to be restored it is glorious (cf. 64.10 [11]), and in Yhwh's mind and intention it is glorious. The double occurrence of words from the root *pʾr* announces the distinctive prominence it will have in these chapters (60.9, 13, 19, 21; 61.3a, 3b, 10; 62.3; 63.12, 14, 15; 64.10 [11]).The camels will bring materials that will contribute to that beautifying. It will be Yhwh who will do the beautifying, but the camels are Yhwh's ministers in this connection, as Artaxerxes will later be.

60.8 Who are these that fly like a cloud,// like doves to their holes?
9 Because for me distant shores wait,// Tarshish ships at the first,
To bring your children from afar,// their silver and gold with them,
For the name of Yhwh your God,// for Israel's holy one, because he has glorified you.

Verses 8-9 revert to the sea's multitudes in v. 5b, behind that line to v. 4, behind that to v. 3, and behind that to vv. 1-2, though it goes behind even what was stated there. In addition, the two verses utilize some suspense in revealing that this is their significance. They do so most overtly by means of their opening line asking a question. The question is not rhetorical in the sense that it lacks an answer or that the questioner is not really interested in the answer, but it is rhetorical in the sense that the questioner knows the answer but the audience cannot do so because it expresses itself in a pair of similes whose reference is not self-evident. Tg therefore provides the readers with the precise answer.[143] The line comprises parallel cola which MT punctuates as 3-2: 'Who are these that fly' applies to both cola, so that 'like a cloud' and 'like doves to their holes' are the two parallel expressions. The cloud is apparently a scudding one; an attentive reader might think of the camels covering the earth like a cloud, so that the cloud would suggest how many of them there were, and/or might remember that Hosea 11.11 has the Ephraimites fluttering from Assyria and Egypt like sparrows and doves to be settled in their homes. Elsewhere the flying of doves is an image for people flitting to safety, maybe in a place that is inaccessible but is nevertheless home, and finding it (e.g. Ps 55.7 [6]). 'Holes' (*ʾărubbâ*) can refer to many types of ways into and out of something. In light of etymology and usage it may suggest an opening with some form of fencing or lattice, and translations have words such as 'lattices' or 'dovecotes', but it is doubtful if we can be so precise about the word's meaning;[144] it may simply denote pigeon-holes.

[143] See the translation note.
[144] Cf. *HALOT*.

So what is the answer to the question in v. 8? While so far the lines have mostly come in pairs (and it would not be difficult to rethink vv. 1-3 as two pairs), here MT realistically divides these four lines as one and three. That reflects the fact that in v. 9a the prophecy does not answer the rhetorical question in v. 8, at least initially.[145] It may be that the answer comes in the second colon: it is the Tarshish ships that are cloud-like and dove-like. Or it may be that with typical poetic allusiveness the verse does not directly answer the question but leaves the reader to infer the answer from what it does say. In other words, notwithstanding the 'because' with which it opens, v. 9aαβ does not directly link with v. 8 at all but rather links to the answer that it never explicitly gives but that can be inferred most easily from v. 9aγδ. The straightforward answer is 'They are your children', but instead of saying so, 9aαβ refers to the people who bring the children. Even that reference is oblique, because the line actually speaks of the motivation that leads the people to bring the children, which goes behind the factors that led to their being drawn to Jerusalem (vv. 1-4). The people to whom it refers are the 'distant shores'. As in 59.18, Vg is most specific in turning the *ʾiyyîm* into 'islands' (cf. OL); LXX's and Tg's words are more open to denoting that it refers to areas that lie on the sea but need not be surrounded by water. Egypt, North Africa, and anywhere else around the Eastern Mediterranean would count. While the word recurs in Isaiah 40–55, the specific expression 'distant shores wait for me' comes in 51.5 (though 'to me' is *ʾēlay*, here *lî*). The prophet thus reaffirms the statement there that underlies promises of Yhwh's bringing people back to Zion. Judahites will come back to Jerusalem because the people among whom they live are waiting for Yhwh and themselves want to come to Jerusalem, having already been drawn into recognition of Yhwh and into praise of Yhwh (v. 6). 'Tarshish' might refer to places in India, Turkey, or Spain, but whichever might be geographically appropriate, Vg and Tg plausibly take 'Tarshish ships' to denote 'seagoing ships'. Earlier in Isaiah they were the object of critique as embodiments of human achievement (2.16; 23.1); they have become the means by which people seek and serve Yhwh. In Isaiah 40–55 '[at] the first' (*[bā]riʾšōnâ*) is another recurrent expression. This precise formulation came in 52.4 in a reference to the bad old days from which Yhwh is committed to rescuing the people. Here perhaps the idea is that the Tarshish ships are lining up to be first in facilitating this restoration.

It is then v. 9aγδ that provides the answer to the question in v. 8, though it does so by incidentally referring to the answer rather than directly stating it, as if to say 'I know you will have worked out the answer to the question, and knowing you will have done so, I make this further comment'. To put it another way, if the prophet worked prosaically (like Tg), v. 8 would indeed comprise two lines, the second of which would provide that answer and thus provide the antecedent to the

[145] Unless one emends the text; see the translation notes.

reference to 'your children' in v. 9aγδ. The actual antecedent for the line came in v. 4b. 'Your children from afar' exactly corresponds to the words in that line, though there *bānayik* was paralleled by *bᵉnōtayik* so referred specifically to sons; here there is no parallel reference to daughters and the word should presumably be taken inclusively. The verb is again from *bô'*, but whereas v. 4 used the qal, v. 9aγδ uses the hiphil in connection with its concern in the context with the people who bring the children home. Verse 6 has implied that it is they who will bring gold with them; v. 9aγδ adds that they will bring silver. Rhetorically it is thus unlikely that the gold and silver belong to the city's children.[146]

Verse 9b reveals the destiny of the gold and silver. NRSV and TNIV take the line as a tricolon, which would be appropriate at what is arguably the end of a subsection with a slight change of subject in v. 10, but MT's accents do not point in this direction; more likely the line is 3-4. There is a certain tension within it. Its parallel *lᵉ* expressions see the gold and silver brought by the city's offspring as destined to glorify Yhwh. But the glorifying of Yhwh comes about through the beautifying of the city (not explicitly the temple). This is a dangerous doctrine. The city could become important in its own right. The two cola have to be held together. Yhwh's glorifying does not come about without the beautifying of the city, but the beautifying of the city loses its point if it does not lead to the glorifying of Yhwh. In parallelism with the name Yhwh is the title 'Israel's holy one'.[147] The line repeats 55.5 except for the replacement of 'for the sake of' by 'for the name of'. This may be another way of saying the same thing (cf. the phrase in Ezek 36.22), but in 55.13 *lᵉšēm* has its common meaning 'for renown', and elsewhere the construct phrase suggests a recognition on the part of non-Israelites 'in connection with/ because of Yhwh's name/renown' (Josh 9.9; 1 Kgs 10.1; Jer 3.17), which fits here. The difference over against 55.13 (and 55.3-5) is that v. 9b applies the expression to the city of Jerusalem, and indirectly to its temple, rather than to the community that lives there.[148]

60.10 Foreigners will build your walls,// their kings will minister to you,
Because in my fury I struck you down,// but in acceptance I have had compassion on you.

Two more pairs of lines forget the temple for a while and elaborate on the significance of Yhwh's action for the city. Verse 10a (3-2) works abca′b′. In its parallelism, 'kings' sharpens the point made by 'foreigners', and 'minister' gives a new definition to the significance of 'build your walls'. Not only foreigners but even their kings will build the city's walls and

146 Against Torrey, *Second Isaiah*, pp. 449-50.

147 See the comment on v. 14.

148 Cf. Jacob Stromberg, 'The Second Temple and the Isaianic Afterlife of the חסדי דוד', *ZAW* 121 (2009), pp. 242-55.

thereby minister to it. The first colon presupposes that the walls remain in their demolished state, as they still were in Nehemiah's time. The way the chapter goes on to speak about gates and walls suggests that the promise does not have in mind the practical significance of walls as defences but their symbolic significance.[149] Demolished, they are a sign of defeat and humiliation; restored, they will be a sign of eminence and a reason for pride. More literally, the line promises that 'children of a foreigner will build your walls', which involves the paronomasia *banû bᵉnê*. The similarity of the words for 'children' and 'build' already features at least in the interpretation of 54.13.[150] More certainly, 49.16-18 promised that 'your walls' are continually before Yhwh, then in the next colon that 'your children' are hurrying home, and it goes on to urge the city to lift up its eyes and look around at the children gathering and coming; it is the exhortation repeated in v. 4a above. 'Children of a foreigner' thus compares and contrasts with 'your children' and also picks up from the promises in 56.6 about 'the children of the foreigner' who attach themselves to Yhwh, to minister to him', the verb that comes here in the parallel colon. This link points to the ambiguous relationship between the talk of foreigners in Isaiah 60 and in Isaiah 56, which parallels the ambiguous relationship between the promise that foreigners will build the city's walls and the earlier promise that Jerusalem's own people would do so (58.12). It reflects the general ambiguity about what is conventionally described as the relationship between universalism and particularism/nationalism in Isaiah 40–66. That very verb 'minister' expresses the ambiguity. To minister is an honour, but it also presupposes the subordination of the minister to the people ministered to, as is the case with the Levites ministering to the priests. The declaration does not offer any hint that the foreigners will perform forced labour.[151] If anything, it affirms that foreigners and kings will want and will be able to respond to seeing Yhwh's light shine in Jerusalem and will want to build its walls and minister to it, with foreigners putting aside their indifference to Jerusalem's fate or their hostility to it, and their kings willing to give up being people who are served, in order to minister. That prospect is good news for foreigners and kings; it is also good news for Jerusalem.

Verse 10b comprises a further neat 3-2 line, but with abcb′c′ parallelism that makes a contrast. The 'because' applies to both cola; there follow two *b-* expressions involving a noun with a first-person suffix, and two first-person verbs (one hiphil, one piel) with a second-person feminine singular suffix. The neat parallelism of form underlines the sharp contrast in meaning. The line takes up further formulations from previous chapters. There Yhwh had spoken of having been furiously angry (54.8; also the related verb in 47.6; 54.9), and within Isaiah 56–66 has already used

[149] Cf. Koole, *Jesaja III*, p. 238 (ET p. 238).

[150] See Goldingay and Payne, *Isaiah 40–55*, II, p. 356.

[151] Against B. Lang, *TWAT*, V, p. 5 (ET *TDOT*, IX, p. 429).

similar expressions and spoken of striking the people down (57.16-17). Yhwh has likewise spoken of fury being replaced by acceptance (49.8; also 56.7; 58.5; 60.7) and compassion (the same verb form occurred in 54.8, the noun in 54.7; cf. also 49.10, 13, 15; 54.10; 55.7). The coming of foreigners and their kings to build up the city's walls and thus minister to it will be an expression of the acceptance and compassion that replace fury and striking down. By implication, at the moment it seems that the people are still experiencing Yhwh's wrath.

60.11 Your gates will open continuously;// day and night they will not shut,
For bringing to you the might of the nations,// with their kings also being led along.

The 3-4 line works roughly abb′a′ in Hebrew as in English, with the piel verb complemented by the niphal and 'day and night' heightening 'continuously'. One would expect a city's gates to be open continuously in the sense of all day, then to be closed from dusk to dawn, but this will be impossible because of the line of camel trains queuing for admission. Strictly, 'open' indicates the act of opening not the state of being open, which would imply rather vividly that the gates keep having to open because new groups keep arriving.[152]

Whereas rhetorically the first line raises the question why the gates open, to which in general terms the answer will be clear, v. 11b goes on to make it explicit and concrete. The 4-2 line comprises parallel clauses, again roughly abb′a′ in Hebrew as in English. 'Their kings' gives sharpness to 'the might of the nations'; as in v. 5, Tg takes *ḥayil* to mean 'wealth', but the parallelism points rather to a reference to their military forces (cf. Vg, and this time LXX). 'To you' applies to the second colon as well as the first. The infinitival expression is paralleled by the participle in the circumstantial clause. There, the standard English translations of Tg[153] have the kings 'chained', but this likely gives a misleading impression of its verb *zᵉqaq*, which means something like 'bound', without usually having that specific sense. The Hebrew verb *nāhag*, 'lead', likewise reexpresses 'bring'. It is another expression taken up from chapter 49 (see 49.10, where it was piel; cf. 63.14). There it referred to Yhwh's leading Judahites back to Jerusalem, astonishing kings by restoring people who have been despised by nations; here it refers to Yhwh's leading the kings and the nations themselves, in their military strength, to Jerusalem.

In his *Libro de las profecías*, Christopher Columbus quotes the whole of Isaiah 60 and 62 (and parts of chapters 65 and 66), and in the introductory letter to the King and Queen of Spain explains the background of his

[152] On the piel, see the translation note.
[153] See Stenning, *The Targum of Isaiah*, p. 200; Chilton, *The Isaiah Targum*, p. 117.

voyage in his desire to bring the resources of countries across the seas so that they could be used for the restoration of Jerusalem, and adds that 'for the execution of the journey to the Indies I was not aided by intelligence, by mathematics or by maps. It was simply the fulfillment of what Isaiah had prophesied.'[154]

60.12 Because the nation and the kingdom that will not serve you:// they will perish, and the nations will become a total waste.

The line is unusually constructed and its *ʾăšer* is unexpectedly prosaic. Modern scholars do not care for its sentiment and commonly regard it as a gloss, perhaps based on Zechariah 14.16-19.[155] But it has no close verbal links with that passage, whereas the phrase 'the nation and the kingdom that will not serve' exactly repeats words in Jeremiah 27.8. Even if its prosaic elements mean it entered the text later than some other parts, it is part of the text; indeed, it has been called the chapter's 'dark pivot'.[156] But its prosaic nature reflects its origin as an allusion to the Jeremiah passage. The fact that the allusion ceases after the first verb also makes it possible to locate the division of the line after that verb, not after 'they will perish' (with MT) and thus to see v. 12 as a whole as a 4-4 line. The subject then occupies the whole first colon, being in terms of prosody extraposed, and the second colon completes the line rather than paralleling it except in the sense that 'the nations' summarizes the first colon. Within the first colon, 'nation' is paralleled by 'kingdom'. In this context, 'kingdom' as abstract for concrete will refer to the kings who rule these kingdoms and who have featured in vv. 3, 10, and 11 and will appear again in v. 16. Likewise 'serve' takes up the description of how the kings will 'minister' to you in v. 10, with the change in the verb coming about under the influence of Jeremiah 27.8.

At the centre of the line, at the end of the first colon and the beginning of the second, there sit two verbs whose similarity of sound contrasts with their contrast in meaning, *yaʿabdûk* and *yōʾbēdû*, 'serve or perish!'[157] Within the second colon, 'perish' is paralleled by the rarer 'become a waste', which is given further emphasis by the construction that precedes the finite verb by the cognate infinitive. 'Perish' came in 41.11, but more strikingly the parallel verb, though rarer, is nevertheless familiar from 49.17, whose words have already been taken up in v. 4 (cf. also 42.15; 44.27; 50.2; 51.10). There Jerusalem was the wasted one, but the prophecy promised that its wasters would leave it alone; here (the prophecy adds) they will either come to Jerusalem in a very different capacity, or will see the city's fate and their own fate reversed. The allusion to

[154] (Gainesville: University of Florida Press, 1991), pp. 110-11.
[155] So (e.g.) Duhm, *Jesaia*, p. 410.
[156] Motyer, *Isaiah*, p. 496.
[157] Polan, 'Zion, the Glory of the Holy One of Israel' (see above), p. 65.

Jeremiah 27.8 also likewise introduces a contrast, formally marked by the suffix on the verb *ya'abdûk*. Jeremiah spoke of nations (including Judah) serving the foreign king; Isaiah 60 reverses that declaration in envisaging foreign kings serving Jerusalem. Once again the prophecy implies an ambiguity about the destiny of nations and kings. One effect of it is once again to make us reconsider the way we construe and both nationalism and universalism.[158] Yhwh wants to draw the acknowledgment of both Judahites and foreigners, but the resistance of either means they fail to enter into the benefits of that acknowledgment.

60.13 The splendour of Lebanon will come to you,// juniper, maple, and cypress together,
To glorify the place of my sanctuary,// and so that I may make splendid the place for my feet.

In the further 4-4 line, v. 13a, 'the splendour of Lebanon', is spelled out in the second colon; at the centre, 'will come to you' applies to the second colon as well as to the first. While Lebanon featured only once in Isaiah 40–55, rather dismissively (40.16), and featured unfavourably on its first appearance in the book as a whole (2.13), 'the splendour of Lebanon' appeared in 35.2, the phrase's one other occurrence in the Old Testament. It is not clear whether historically Isaiah 35 antedates Isaiah 56–66, but within the order of the book, Isaiah 35 announces some key themes of Isaiah 40–66. A common reason for referring to Lebanon is its timber, and the second colon indicates that implication here. Yet it keeps readers on their toes by declining to refer explicitly to cedars, as a result of the fact that v. 13aβ is quoting from 41.19 (where 'cedars' had come in the previous line). LXX identifies the trees as cypress, pine, and cedar, Vg as fir, box, and pine, Tg as cypress, ash, and box; Aq, Sym, Th mostly transliterate the words.[159]

In what way will these trees be useful to the city? Verse 13b answers that question; the trees are destined to beautify the temple in particular, furthering Yhwh's project of doing so which was announced in v. 7. Admittedly, there are two ways in which they might fulfil this function. In 41.19 the point of mentioning the trees is their impressiveness over against the desert, and the Temple Mount would indeed be beautified by trees.[160] But these would be surprising trees to mention in that connection and more likely here the point about juniper, maple, and cypress (as of cedar) is that they are the kind of trees that would provide timber for a

[158] Cf. Childs, *Isaiah*, pp. 497-98.

[159] For the identification presupposed above, see Goldingay and Payne, *Isaiah 40–55*, I, pp. 184-85.

[160] Cf. E. Lipiński, 'Garden of Abundance, Image of Lebanon', *ZAW* 85 (1973), pp. 358-59; the expression in the article title comes from an Akkadian text which appears in *ANET*, pp. 109-10. See also Steck's discussion, *Studien zu Tritojesaja*, pp. 101-5.

project such as the rebuilding of the temple. While the last two trees come only in these two verses in Isaiah 41 and 60, juniper appears in connection with the temple's original building in 1 Kings 5–6. If the timber is needed for the restoring of the temple that had been burned in 587, the line confirms that the description of the house as glorious in v. 7 was a pregnant one; if it still needs its burnt timber replaced, the house is ugly at the moment.

LXX translates the opening phrase *mᵉqôm miqdāšî* 'my holy place', but for this one would expect *qodšî* (cf. Ps 24.3; Ezra 9.8).[161] Rather *miqdāš* has its usual concrete meaning 'sanctuary' (cf. Tg, and the similar phrase in Jer 17.12; also Dan 8.11, *mᵉkôn miqdāšô*; and *mᵉqôm ʾohŏlēk*).[162] The construct relationship is then a defining genitive not an adjectival genitive.[163] The parallelism between the two 3-3 cola (abcb′c′a′) does raise another possibility, that the construct relationship inolves an adverbial genitive,[164] 'a place *for* my sanctuary' like 'a place *for* my feet'. The phrase would then solemnly recognize that the 'place' is not really Yhwh's sanctuary at the moment. Yhwh has not yet returned there after abandoning it in 587; but Yhwh will do so. The parallel phrase then expresses the point more concretely, and too concretely for Tg, which paraphrases 'the place of the dwelling of my Presence [*šᵉkînâ*]'. Israelite thinking may commonly presuppose the idea that the sanctuary or the covenant chest is a stool for the feet of the Yhwh who is invisibly enthroned on the cherubim there, though the point is only occasionally explicit (e.g. Pss 99.1-5; 132.7; 1 Chr 28.2). Particularly significant for Isaiah 60 is Lamentations 2.1, which has Yhwh angrily throwing down Israel's 'glory' from the heavens to the earth and putting the footstool out of mind. Isaiah 60.13 promises a reversing of that throwing down (cf. Ezek 43.7). It does so without making any reference to Yhwh's being king or reigning, in the manner of Psalm 99 and related psalms, and also Isaiah 40–55. This omission is all the more striking in light of the chapter's four references to human kings (vv. 3, 10, 11, 16). Whereas Ezekiel preserves the kingship of Yhwh by exercising some restraint over the application of the word 'king' to a human monarch, at least of Israel, Isaiah 56–66 surrenders the notion of kingship to human rulers (along with the alleged king of Sheol, in 57.9).

The second colon goes beyond the first also in moving to a first-person verb at the close. Further, the verb 'make splendid' (*kābēd* piel) is usually one with a human subject and with God as object, suggesting 'honour' (e.g. 24.15; 25.3; 29.13; 43.20, 23; 58.13). It is a special promise that has God using this verb in the first person. Making the footstool splendid benefits God, but the promise presupposes that it benefits the promise's recipients.

[161] See the translation note.

[162] See *DCH*, V, pp. 457-59, 460-65.

[163] On this see, e.g., *DG* 35.

[164] On this, see *IBHS* 9.5.2.

60.14 The children of those who humbled you will walk to you bending low,// all those who despised you will bow low at the soles of your feet.
They will call you 'Yhwh's city,// Zion of Israel's holy one'.

So far the foreigners have been simply foreign people and powerful people such as kings. Verse 14a is another long parallel line (abca′b′c′, except that the 'to you' comes between the opening two verbs) with eleven actual words. MT makes it 5-4 (or perhaps 3-2-4); it would be simple to make it 4-4 by adding a maqqeph (as was the case with v. 1) so that 'the children of those who humbled you' had only one stress.[165] The line takes up another theme from Isaiah 40–55. When these people walk to you (a harmless enough beginning to the line), they will come 'bending low' (*šāḥaḥ*). The word has no background in Isaiah 40–55 but it plays a key role in Isaiah 2 in describing the way people who currently stand high will bend low (cf. also 5.15). The context there applies the warning to Jerusalem and Judah, but it is expressed in the general terms that recur later with broader reference (25.12; 26.5). Here Yhwh's words promise a reversal of the warning for Judah and/or an implementing of the words' more general implications. The verb 'bow low', similar in meaning and sound (whether understood as *šāḥâ* hitpael or *ḥāwâ* hishtaphel[166]) also occurred in Isaiah 2 to refer to people bowing low to images; once again the present usage makes for a telling contrast. But this second verb appears in Isaiah 40–55, too, sometimes in similar contexts to that in Isaiah 60 (44.15, 17; 46.6). It recurs even more significantly from 45.14 ('a perfect miniature of 60:3-16'[167]), where Yhwh promises how nations will bow low to Jerusalem; from 49.7, where Yhwh promises such bowing low on the part of people who had scorned and derided Israel; and from 49.23, whose significance we have noted in connection with v. 4; see also 51.23, where Yhwh promises the punishment of the people who told Jerusalem to 'bow low'. Yhwh here reaffirms these promises. Such bowing low is 'a gesture of submission or surrender'.[168]

In turn, 'the children of those who humbled you' is balanced by 'all the people who despised you'. These are people who put Jerusalem down, made it weak and powerless (*ʿānâ* hiphil); and 'despised' the city and treated it accordingly (the rarer *nāʾaṣ*). The 'all' that balances mention of the children suggests an emphasis on the totality of the obeisance rather than merely having in mind that they are the descendants of Jerusalem's original destroyers. Further, 'to you' is balanced and nuanced by 'at the soles of your feet', which makes for another link with 49.23, where the kings and queens are due not only to bow low to Jerusalem but to lick the dirt under its feet, beneath its soles. Tg glosses the expression in light of the plausible assumption that they will adopt this posture in order to ask

165 But concerning these long lines, see further the comment on v. 19a.
166 See Goldingay and Payne, *Isaiah 40–55*, I, p. 357.
167 Torrey, *Second Isaiah*, p. 445.
168 H. D. Preuss, *TWAT*, II, p. 788 (ET *TDOT*, IV, pp. 251-52).

for favour from Jerusalem. They will thus resemble Abraham bowing low before the Hittites in order to do so (Gen 23.7, 12 [P]); the expression does not imply abject self-humiliation.[169]

Verse 14b gives the verse's own specificity to the significance of the obeisance, though it is not incompatible with Tg's take on the question. In the 4-3 line the opening verbal expression applies to both cola; it is followed by two parallel descriptions of Jerusalem. It is 'Yhwh's city', the only occurrence of the phrase in Isaiah; indeed, it otherwise comes only in Psalm 101.8 (Ps 48.9 [8] refers to 'the city of Yhwh Armies',[170] while Pss 46.5 [4]; 87.3 refer to 'the city of God', and 'holy city' appears in Isa 48.2; 52.1; Dan 9.24; Neh 11.1, 18). The parallel expression 'Zion of Israel's holy one' comes here alone in the Old Testament, though 'Zion' and 'Israel's holy one' are favourite expressions in the book. Zion comes 49 times, while all but five of the Old Testament's uses of the latter title for Yhwh come in Isaiah, in all three major parts of the book, with the two in chapter 56–66 coming in 60.9 and 14. 'If there is any one concept central to the whole Book of Isaiah, it is the vision of Yahweh as the Holy One of Israel.'[171] The connotation of 'Israel's holy one' in this context will include that Yhwh once again undertakes to fulfil the promise that signifies a reversal in the implications of this title. Instead of its implying a warning of judgment by the holy one, it denotes that Yhwh's being the holy one *of Israel* implies that Yhwh must also be Israel's restorer. The people doing obeisance will acknowledge that God has indeed acted to restore the city. It is indeed God's city.

60.15 Instead of your being abandoned,// repudiated with no one passing through,
I will make you an object of pride forever,// a joy from generation to generation.

A 'because' could plausibly have opened v. 15; it provides the evidence for that recognition in v. 14. The two linked 3-3 lines are internally parallel and also similarly structured (abcc′ and abcb′c′): each begins with an expression that applies to the second colon as well as the first. The two 'a' expressions then parallel and contrast with each other in substance though not in form (one being a preposition, the other a verb), and the pair of parallel expressions in v. 15b (lasting pride, joy from age to age) parallel and contrast with the pair in v. 15a (abandoned, renounced with no one passing through).

[169] Paul (ישעיה פרקים מ-סו, II, p. 481 [ET p. 529]) also notes parallel formulae from Mesopotamian inscriptions.

[170] The prominent Isaianic title 'Yhwh Armies' does not come in Isaiah 56–66; Begg ('The Absence of *YHWH ṣebāʾôt* in Isaiah 56–66') associates this fact with considerations such as the chapters' avoidance of reference to David.

[171] J. J. M. Roberts, 'Isaiah in Old Testament Theology', *Interpretation* 36 (1982), pp. 130-43 (131). But see also the comments in section 6 of the Introduction to this commentary.

The first line, then, focuses on how things have been and are for the city. Abandonment (*ʿāzab*) is Zion's accusation of Yhwh (49.14), which Yhwh accepts (54.6-7, where the same participial verb form *ʿăzûbâ* occurs), while also promising not to abandon them but rather to restore them (41.17; 42.16). Here Yhwh again implicitly agrees that they had been abandoned and once again promises that it is not how things will always be. 'Repudiate' is *śānēʾ*, usually translated 'hate', but (like 'love') it commonly denotes an action of rejection and opposition, as much as a feeling. Here its resonances come from its being a term to describe a husband's rejection of his wife (Gen 29.31; Deut 21.15-17). The lack of people passing through is a motif from the description of a city upon which calamity has fallen so that it becomes like desert that no one can cross (e.g. Isa 34.10; Zeph 3.6).

While Yhwh was the unnamed agent of the passive verbs in v. 15a, in v. 15b Yhwh becomes the specific agent of their reversal. Like English 'pride', *gāʾôn* usually has pejorative connotations when applied to human beings; in Isaiah 2, again, the word belongs only to Yhwh. Human pride and things that human beings take pride in are thus to be put down; Zephaniah 3.11 sounds as if it offers rather a contrast with this promise. But there can be a proper taking of pride, as Zephaniah 3.20 goes on to imply (and cf. Ps 47.5 [4]). Jerusalem will be a place to take pride in forever, a place of honour (*yᵉqār*, Tg); to put it another way, it will be a place to rejoice in from age to age. Hyperbolically speaking, Jerusalem had been a reason for 'joy' (*mᵉśôś*) not only for its own people but for all the earth (Ps 48.3 [2]), but it ceased to be such (Lam 2.15). That will be reversed again. The motif will be a prominent one in chapters 60—66: 'one can view *śwś* and *māśôś* as programmatic terms within Trito-Isaiah, whose work contains nearly a fifth of all occurrences' (60.15; 61.10; 62.5; 64.4 [5]; 65.18, 19; 66.10, 14; the chapters also include five occurrences of *śāmāḥ*/*śimḥâ* and three of *gîl*). Yhwh intends a period of renewal 'with accompanying joy and jubilation—a motif unmistakably contrasting [with] the actual situation of the postexilic community'.[172]

60.16 You will suck the milk of nations,// suck the breast of kings.
You will acknowledge that I am Yhwh—I am your deliverer;// I, Jacob's champion, am your restorer.

Verse 16 goes on to reexpress the promises that have run through the passage so far, by means of yet another metaphor. It perhaps again picks up from v. 4 and from v. 6. Deuteronomy 33.19 pictures Issachar (literally) sucking from the abundance of the seas, which is slightly puzzling as it sits neither on the Mediterranean nor on Lake Kinneret, but perhaps the idea is that it profits from trade in things that come by sea or from

[172] H.-J. Fabry, *TWAT*, VII, p. 725 (ET *TDOT*, XIV, p. 53).

the sea; and this is what Jerusalem is promised. Tg thus puts the second colon more prosaically, 'you will delight yourself in the plunder of their kings' (cf. LXX 'the wealth of kings'). The 3-3 line works abcb′c′a′. The same verb (*yānaq*) is unusually repeated, though the first occurrence is *w*-consecutive, the second yiqtol. 'The milk of nations' is then paralleled by 'the breast of kings'. 'For as long as anyone can remember, Israel has paid imperial tribute to others—the Assyrians, the Babylonians, the Persians—all money going out. Now the process is reversed.'[173]

Verse 16b describes the consequences in a long 5-3 line. The aim or result 'that you should acknowledge that I am Yhwh' is another motif from Isaiah 40–55 (though it is more frequent in Ezekiel). The line in fact simply repeats phrases from 49.23b (you will acknowledge that I am Yhwh') and 26b ('all flesh will acknowledge that I am Yhwh; I am your deliverer, I, Jacob's champion, am your restorer').[174] EVV are inclined to translate 'know', but *yāda* ʿ commonly denotes recognition, in terms of attitude and will, rather than mere mental awareness.[175]

As is often the case, it is hard to turn the Hebrew noun clauses into English verbal clauses. EVV take 'I Yhwh' as an apposition, but there are many contexts where the words must be rendered 'I am Yhwh' (e.g. 42.6; 45.5, 6, 18); 49.23 (which has the full expression that recurs here) must be understood thus. Here, the appositional translation understates the significance of a phrase that has considerable inherent freight. Saying 'I [am] Yhwh' is a bigger statement than it sounds. It is not a mere self-announcement like 'I am John Goldingay'. It is more like a self-announcement such as 'I am Abraham Lincoln' when uttered by the U.S. President. The name implies reference to the position. Concealed behind the statement 'I am Yhwh' is the claim 'Yhwh is God'. The point is expressed paradoxically in the words 'I am Yhwh and there is no other' (45.5-6), which has similar implications to 'I am God and there is no other' (45.22) or the simple *ʾănî hûʾ*, 'I am the one' (e.g. 43.13). Here in 60.16, then, the initial point will be that as a result of Yhwh's action Jerusalem will acknowledge Yhwh as the only one who really deserves the title 'God'.

The content of that confession is spelled out in two parallel ways in the rest of the line. 'Your deliverer' and 'your restorer' are further familiar terms from other passages in Isaiah 40–55; it is clear enough that they are parallel and they would be part of the predicate of their sentences. 'Yhwh' and 'Jacob's champion', too, are parallel; the implication is that the expressions occur in abb′a′ order. The import of the sentence is then to declare something about the one whom Jerusalem will come to acknowledge as God, namely that this God is deliverer and champion. It therefore seems likely that the right way to represent this in English is in terms of two parallel statements. Yhwh is deliverer, one who rescues

[173] Brueggemann, *Isaiah 40–66*, p. 205.
[174] See the comments in Goldingay and Payne, *Isaiah 40–55*, on the passages.
[175] See the comment on 58.2.

people when they are in trouble, particularly under accusation. Jacob's champion is restorer, one who expends his efforts and/or resources on behalf of a member of his family when they are in need of someone to act to put the situation back to being level when it has got out of kilter.

60.17 Instead of the bronze I will bring gold,// instead of the iron I will bring silver.
Instead of the wood, bronze,// instead of the stones, iron.
I will make well-being your oversight,// faithfulness your bosses.

The prophecy likely returns to the resources that foreigners will bring. Copper or bronze (copper strengthened with a material such as tin so as to form an alloy) or brass (copper similarly compounded with zinc) was the material from which a number of the accoutrements of the temple (such as pillars, an altar, and lavers) were made or with which they were covered. In isolation it would thus seem that the two lines are concerned with the temple in particular rather than the city in general (for which one might have expected some reference to brick being replaced by stone). It is in this connection that 1 and 2 Chronicles make a number of references to the four elements mentioned in the first two neat 4-4 parallel lines. In the first, the preposition and verb are simply repeated. The structure of the parallelism recurs in the middle line, though here the verb is allowed to carry over from the first line. Wood and stone were major elements in the temple's construction; in exotic hyperbole, Yhwh arranges for a prestigious reworking of its raw materials.

The third line is another parallel bicolon, 3-2, working abcb′c′. The verb applies to both cola, concrete nouns with second-person feminine singular suffix follow (one feminine singular, one masculine plural), and more abstract nouns (one masculine, one feminine) close the cola. The gender order thus reverses in a way that expresses the reversal of which the line speaks.[176] The Hebrew word order puts the concrete nouns first and LXX most explicitly makes them the direct objects of the verb, understanding the promise to signify making the government peaceful and the bosses faithful. This understanding of the word order follows the common one when the verb *śîm* governs two accusatives (e.g. 54.12; 1 Sam 1.8).[177] Yet Psalm 66.2 instances the opposite order, and its understanding makes better sense in this context in that 'well-being' and 'faithfulness' sum up the nature and the significance of the gifts that Yhwh will bring through the nations and their rulers. Further, it corresponds to the way the Old Testament can personify what might seem abstract concepts.

[176] Cf. Watson, *Traditional Techniques in Classical Hebrew Verse*, pp. 210-11, 224, 351.

[177] It facilitates the understanding expressed in Irenaeus (*Against Heresies* 4.36) that the verse refers to presbyters and bishops; cf. Eusebius of Caesarea, *Der Jesajakommentar*, p. 377, with Hollerich, *Eusebius of Caesarea's* Commentary on Isaiah, pp. 181-82.

As a result of these gifts it will be *šālôm* and *ṣᵉdāqâ* (a formidable combination[178]) that are determinative for the temple's life, or for the city's life if we are to infer the broader reference here. While the preceding context suggests that *šālôm* has its broader meaning of well-being, the succeeding context may imply the narrower meaning 'peace'. 'Oversight' (*pᵉquddâ*) could apply to the temple (see, e.g., Num 4.16 [P]), but the 'you' to whom the prophecy speaks is the city. 'Bosses' (from *nāgaś*) is a more surprising word, which normally suggests authorities that behave rather oppressively (cf. 9.3 [2]; 58.3). It thus suggests a paradox; a tyrant who is called faithfulness 'would be no tyrant at all'.[179] Further, it more suggests the life of the city in general. All this may indicate that we should not confine the application of the rest of the verse to the temple (cf. 54.11-12). At the moment the city's oversight and its exercise of authority lie in the hands of imperial overlords who are not concerned for its well-being or for the exercise of faithfulness (in isolation the authorities might be national leaders, but v. 18 will support a reference to imperial overlords). Yhwh promises that they will be replaced by well-being and faithfulness, personified as Yhwh's agents as in passages such Psalms 23.6; 43.3.

60.18 Violence will not make itself heard any more in your country,// destroying or smashing in your borders;
You will call deliverance your walls,// praise your gates.

Verse 18 confirms the broader reference to the city, and to the land as a whole. A 4-3 line is followed by a 3-2 line, each internally parallel, and they are broadly parallel to one another. In each line the verb again comes first and applies to both cola, which is what makes the first colon longer.

Violently shed blood cries out from the ground (Gen 4.10 [J]), but no such cries will any longer need to make themselves heard in Judah. 'Any more' also applies to both cola, but here equality is preserved by the way the one word for violence is complemented by the two words for ruin and destruction. Each colon ends with a *b-* expression with second-person singular suffix, the nouns being feminine singular and masculine plural. Violence, destroying, and smashing recur from 59.6-7, but here the context suggests they are not characteristics of the country's internal life but characteristics of the action upon the country by external forces such as the imperial authorities: compare the violence of Jeremiah 20.8; 48.3; 51.35, the destroying and smashing of Isaiah 51.19, and more generally the promises of 54.14-17. The use of *šōd*, 'destroying', is rather droll after the use of the homonym meaning 'breast' in v. 16; its unusual pointing there (*šōd* not *šad*) underlines the link.[180]

[178] Cf. Brueggemann, *Isaiah 40–66*, p. 209.
[179] Whybray, *Isaiah 40–66*, pp. 236-37.
[180] See the translation note on v. 16.

In v. 18b double accusatives resemble those in v. 17b, though with variation in the word order; the line works abcc′b′, ‘you will call deliverance your walls, your gates praise’. Will they call divine deliverance and intervention the city’s means of protection, and its praise of God the means of keeping trouble out? Zechariah 2.5-9 [1-4] would cohere with this idea, as would the addition of the article on *yšwʿh* in 1QIs[a];[181] the second colon is then suggestive but rather subtle. Or will they call the city’s walls the means of its deliverance and its gates something that warrants its praise, which would at least be less mundane than Fish Gate and Dung Gate (Neh 3.3, 14)?[182] The first colon is then rather a statement of the obvious. Or might we follow the word order, mix the two significances, and have them calling divine deliverance its means of protection and its gates an object of praise? Vg has ‘deliverance will take hold of your walls and praise your gates’; Aq, Sym have ‘deliverance will come to your walls’. They thus assume that the verb is *qārāʾ* II ‘encounter’ and that ‘deliverance’ is the subject of the verb not the object.

60.19 The sun will no longer be light for you by day,// for brightness the moon will not be a light for you.
Yhwh will be for you lasting light,// your God your glory.
20 Your sun will no longer set,// your moon will not withdraw,
Because Yhwh—he will be for you lasting light;// your days of grief will end.

As it nears the end, the prophecy returns to where it began (see vv. 1-2) but tweaks and pushes the significance of its metaphor. It tweaks it in the sense that vv. 1-2 spoke of an event, the coming of light, whereas vv. 19-20 speak of a state, an ongoing blessing.[183] There it had Yhwh bringing light into the darkness of the community’s gloom with the brightness of the sun breaking into the darkness of night. So if Yhwh is shining like the sun, who needs either the sun or the moon? This way of pressing the metaphor thus compares and contrasts with the way 30.26 does so.[184] It also compares and contrasts with the way Psalm 72.5-7 works with the metaphor, underlining the absence of the king from the present chapter. I take v. 19a as one very long line (5-4, and twelve words); it might be taken as two parallel lines, but they do not make natural bicola:

The sun will no longer be for you// for light by day,
And for brightness the moon// will not be a light for you.

[181] Cf. Pulikottil, *Transmission of Biblical Texts in Qumran*, p. 91, though he does not draw this inference.

[182] Blenkinsopp, *Isaiah 56–66*, p. 217.

[183] Cf. Lau, *Schriftgelehrte Prophetie in Jes 56–66*, p. 62.

[184] See Vlková, *Cambiare la luce in tenebre e le tenebre in luce* (see above), pp. 187-209.

More likely the parallelism lies between two long cola, working abcc′b′a:

> No longer will be for you—the sun—for light by day,
> And for brightness—the moon—will not be light for you.

But the fact that this is the third such long line in the chapter (compare vv. 1 and 14a) may indicate that we should read all three as tricola, this one 2-3-4 (if we observe MT's maqqephs):

> No longer will be for you
> the sun for light by day
> and for brightness the moon will not be light for you.

The point of the line is not the prosaic one that Yhwh will reconfigure the cosmos so that sun and moon no longer shine because they are unnecessary. It again speaks metaphorically. For the community, the gloom that counts is the darkness of their political and physical circumstances; into these Yhwh will shine in a way that makes sun and moon seem unimportant. They will blush with shame at being outshone (24.23).

In a 4-2 parallel line, v. 19b then contrasts the sun's 'no longer' with the permanent nature of the shining Yhwh will bring, and contrasts the implied ugly awfulness of the city's state with the beauty that God's presence will bring, in restoring the city to the splendour that people cannot remember but have heard tell of and can imagine.

Verse 20 reworks the metaphor once again. Whereas v. 19 suggested that the literal sun and moon would not be there, or at least would have no role to fulfil, v. 20 promises that it will be as if sun and moon shine perpetually. In the 3-3 parallel line (roughly abcc′b′a′), the sun will literally not 'come'—but *bôʾ* is the regular expression for the sun 'setting'. Like English, Hebrew has no standard equivalent verb for the moon, perhaps because we do not need one since the moon does not disappear each day in the vivid way that the sun does; 'withdraw' (*ʾāsap*) thus provides a novel ending for the line in the second colon.

When Tg paraphrases v. 20a 'Your kingdom will no longer cease, nor will your honour pass away', this corresponds to the way the prophecy itself in v. 20b goes on to explain the sense in which that first line is true (which would otherwise be a puzzle), as a reworking of the figure. The first colon in v. 20b repeats v. 19bα except that the verb is yiqtol instead of *w*-consecutive and the subject is put ahead of the verb, represented in the translation by the extraposition. The second colon is parallel in substance but not in form; not surprisingly, in substance it also broadly corresponds to v. 19bβ. 'Grief' (*ʾēbel*) can refer to an anguish that follows calamity as well as one that follows bereavement, which fits here. It can also suggest the outward manifestation of grief or mourning such as the tearing of clothes and the adopting of a dishevelled appearance. Both these fit the parallel with the restoration of glory of which v. 19bβ speaks (and the recurrence of the word in 61.3). Yhwh's coming as a light and thus as restoration and blessing will permanently banish the appearance of grief that has been the city's lot.

60.21 Your people, all of them, are the faithful ones,// who will possess the country forever.
They are the shoot I planted,// the work of my hands, to manifest glory.
22 The smallest will become a clan,// the least a strong nation.
I am Yhwh;// in its time I will speed it.

The close of the prophecy becomes more literal though still lyrical. Verse 21 comprises two broadly parallel lines (3-3 and 3-2). While there is some internal parallelism within the second, in both lines the point is expressed only at the very end, and in this sense both are lines in which the second colon completes the first. In both lines, indeed, the first colon can be translated as a sequence of asyndetic phrases:

> Your people, all of them, the faithful ones, will possess the country in perpetuity,
> The shoot I planted, the work of my hands, to manifest glory.

But Hebrew poetry is inclined to cola that are grammatically self-contained, and readers would more likely take each first colon as a noun clause. In prose one would expect a pronoun functioning as copula at the end of each first colon, but this is less usual in poetry.

In speaking of 'your people', the prophecy reminds us that although it has been rhetorically addressing the personified city, the people who live there are its actual audience (the audience in the house as opposed to the audience on the stage). The prophecy continues to address the city itself; technically, the whole chapter is an apostrophe, a poem that 'turns away' from its literal audience to speak to an entity that is personified and addressed as if it were a person.[185] At this point it simply incorporates a third-person reference to the city's people who are its more literal intended audience. In what sense are they the 'the faithful ones' (*ṣaddîqîm*)? The reference does not seem to link very obviously with the isolated reference to 'the one who will show that he is faithful' in 53.11; this verse does not speak in terms of a promise of faithful offspring.[186] In 57.1 'the faithful person' was set over against the community as a whole, which 58.2 implies do not 'do what is faithful' (cf. 59.4). Here, then, are 'the faithful ones' set over against the faithless ones? The difficulty with that understanding is that 'the faithful' are identified as 'your people', the people of

[185] Cf. Blenkinsopp, *Isaiah 56–66*, pp. 203-18.

[186] Against Childs, *Isaiah*, p. 499; on the interpretation of the expression there, see Goldingay and Payne, *Isaiah 40–55*, II, pp. 325-28 (Childs translates *ṣaddîq* 'righteous' and we there translate it 'just', but this does not affect the main interpretative questions).

Jerusalem. Further, the addition of 'all of them' makes it the more difficult to reckon that the prophecy refers to a group within the population of the city as a whole who are identified as the city's people. Mishnah Sanhedrin 10.1 infers from the line that all Israelites have a share in the world to come.[187]

On the other hand, the prophecy will recognize that not everyone in the city is faithful, even that most are not. Perhaps it uses the term in an honorific sense, comparable to the term *ḥăsîdîm*, as in Psalms 68.4 [3]; 118.15; they are the people who share in salvation.[188] If so, it likely nevertheless issues an implicit challenge in keeping with the prophets' characteristic use of the term. It is then no coincidence that this side bar in chapter 60 comes in association with the reference to the 'people' who are the prophecy's actual audience. The city's community as a whole is destined to possess the country as a whole, and to do so on a permanent basis, but if they fail to live up to their name as 'the faithful', they cannot take that prospect for granted. In the second colon, then, as well as drawing attention to the city's population, the prophecy hints at the fact that there is a whole other question about the restoration of the people, beyond the question about the city. The common use of the verb 'possess' in connection with Israel's occupation of the promised land suggests that *ʾereṣ* must here refer to the country, not the earth as a whole.[189]

Verse 21b confirms that understanding of *ʾereṣ* as it initially returns to an image that specifically relates to Israel's relationship with its land. The term 'shoot' (*nēṣer*) is used of the people only here. We noted in the introduction to this chapter that in 11.1 it refers to a shoot from David's roots (it is one of a number of links with that chapter).[190] But it is a natural extension of the idea of the people as a vine or an olive. The verb 'plant' (*nāṭaʿ*) is used elsewhere in this connection (e.g. Jer 2.21; Ps 80.16 [15]), as is the related noun *nēṭaʿ* (Isa 5.7). The link and contrast with 11.1 also retrospectively confirms our understanding of the reference to the faithful in v. 21a, because 11.4 refers to the shoot's acting in faithfulness, while Jeremiah 23.5 refers to the branch from David's line being faithful. Verse 21a has democratized such statements in declaring that 'the people, all of them, are the faithful ones'. The image reappears as a self-description of the Qumran community (e.g. 1QS 8.5).[191] More prosaically than the talk of a shoot, the parallel phrase describes them as the work of Yhwh's hands; perhaps this expression qualifies the image and denotes that it was Yhwh's own hands that did the planting. But the line comes to its climax with a final reference to glory as Yhwh's purpose. In 44.23; 49.3 the

[187] Cf. Neusner, *Isaiah in Talmud and Midrash*, p. 4.

[188] So Volz, *Jesaja II*, p. 248.

[189] Against Beuken, *Jesaja IIIA*, p. 187

[190] Cf. Beuken, *Jesaja IIIA*, pp. 188-89. Berges (*Das Buch Jesaja*, p. 435) calls this an 'actualizing' of 11.1.

[191] See Blenkinsopp, *Opening the Sealed Book*, e.g., pp. 248-49; also *DCH* on מטעת.

hitpael referred to Yhwh's displaying splendour through Israel; the splendour is Yhwh's. Here that reference would fit the allusion to Yhwh's glory or beauty in v. 19. Yet Yhwh's glory becomes the city's glory (vv. 7. 9, 13), and here the verb may additionally refer to a manifesting of the people's splendour (as well as the city's).

Verse 22a stays with a description of the destiny of the whole people and implicitly with its destiny to occupy the whole country. To do so, it will need vastly to increase in numbers. The 3-3 parallel line works abca′c′, with the verb applying to both cola and the compound expression filling up the space unoccupied by a verb in the second colon. While 'small' and 'least' (*qāṭōn*, *ṣāʿîr*) commonly mean 'young', in the present context 'insignificant' is more the point (e.g. 1 Kgs 22.31; Jer 8.10; and Judg 6.15; Micah 5.1 [2]). LXX, Vg, Tg assume that *ʾelep* means 'a thousand', though the latter two passages (Judg 6.15; Micah 5.1 [2]) illustrate its meaning 'clan' and the parallelism with 'a strong nation' supports that understanding. The promise about becoming a strong nation recalls the promise to Abraham (Gen 18.18 [J]).

The closing line of this gargantuan composition (v. 22b) brings it to its culmination and closure by brevity rather than any further prolixity. The brevity could not be more pointed. I take the opening *ʾănî yhwh* as another noun clause and thus take the 2-2 line as a pair of clauses, rather than as a single statement 'I, Yhwh, will speed it in its time'. The noun clause initially provides backing for everything that has preceded. People may reasonably find all those promises unbelievable, but the one who speaks is Yhwh and is God (see the comments on v. 16b), and the promises should therefore be believable. This logic applies even if the line should be rendered as a single statement. Similarly, either way the statement about Yhwh in the first colon provides the backing for the verbal declaration that follows. The two words that comprise this declaration deconstruct. 'In its time' implies that the promise's fulfilment has its own timescale. The listeners could not be blamed for thinking that Yhwh's schedule left something to be desired, but they are warned not to expect it to conform to theirs. Yhwh might then go on to reassure them by saying 'I will bring it' (Tg) or 'I will gather them' (LXX), but instead says 'I will speed it' (*ḥûš* hiphil; cf. Vg, Aq).[192] Such speed is precisely what psalms ask for in situations of danger and abandonment (Pss 22.20 [19]; 38.23 [22]; 40.14 [13]; 70.2, 6 [1, 5]; 71.12; 141.1); Isaiah 5.19 has also noted the scornful encouragement to Yhwh to be a bit more speedy.[193] The tension in the closing line imperils the chapter's closure. It discourages people from settling down and expecting nothing in the future and

[192] Watts (*Isaiah 40–66*, p. 862) takes this as *ḥûš* II 'feel joy' but this occurs only in Eccles 2.25 and is of uncertain meaning there (see *DCH*). Comparing LXX's rendering of *ḥûš* at 5.19; 28.16, Troxel (*LXX-Isaiah*, p. 269) suggests that the translator did not understand the verb.

[193] Cf. Paul, ישעיה פרקים מ-סו, II, p. 486 (ET p. 535).

implies that they will surely not have to wait too long, but it locates the promise's fulfilment in its own time. They can be reminded that the resolution of the line's tension lies in seeing that the speed will come only when the right time has arrived. It does invite them to expect that they will not have to wait too long.

Conclusion

The promises in Isaiah 60 are often described as referring to the 'end time',[194] as eschatological;[195] 'what now lies ahead has become radically eschatologized' compared with the expectation in Isaiah 40–55, so that 'the new Jerusalem is not a rebuilt earthly city, but the entrance of the divine kingdom of God'.[196] The vision might even be described as 'apocalyptic'.[197] The contrast with the current age characterized by wickedness, which chapters 56–59 have described, implies that 'a righteousness in which everyone shares is far away'.[198] This seems an oversimplification on both sides, like that between nationalism and universalism.[199] The chapter indeed does not link Yhwh's new act with a specific historical event, in the manner of Isaiah 40–55. Whereas Isaiah 40–55 refers to places of present significance such as Babylon and to people of significance such as Cyrus, and explicitly has God's purpose being worked out in connection with these, the promises concerning the fulfilment of God's purpose in Isaiah 60 have no such references.[200] The all-transforming era which the whole world was to see was not initiated by the return from Babylon, and this prophet does not point to a definite historical event that is the initiation of this reality; in this sense God's coming is now more considerably dissociated from history.[201] But the dissociation does not issue from this prophet's lacking the insight to link Yhwh's coming with a definite historical event; whenever we date the prophecy, there was no Cyrus-like figure rampaging across the Middle East with whom to link Yhwh's coming.

[194] Cf. Jerome, *Commentariorum in Isaiam prophetam libri duodeviginti*, col. 597.

[195] Volz is especially fond of this word (e.g. *Jesaja II*, p. 239). On the 'eschatological' nature of Isaiah 56–66, see further the 'Conclusion' to the commentary on 66.18-24 below.

[196] Childs, *Isaiah*, p. 500.

[197] So Bernhard W. Anderson, 'The Apocalyptic Rendering of the Isaiah Tradition', in Jacob Neusner *et al.* (eds.), *The Social World of Formative Christianity and Judaism* (H. C. Kee Festschrift; Philadelphia: Fortress, 1988), pp. 17-38 (19).

[198] Koole, *Jesaja III*, p. 254 (ET p. 258).

[199] See further Sekine's discussion, *Die Tritojesajanische Sammlung*, pp. 72-74.

[200] Cf. Hanson, *The Dawn of Apocalyptic*, p. 62.

[201] Cf. Westermann, *Jesaja Kapitel 40–66*, p. 284 (ET p. 357).

On the other hand, as Isaiah 60 reworks material from Isaiah 40–55, Revelation 21 reworks Isaiah 60,[202] and the not-radically-eschatological nature of the chapter's promises is clearer when one compares them with that later vision. It is characteristic of prophecy to stand somewhere on a line between the promise or warning of a concrete event whose fulfilment can be seen on the earthly plane (e.g. Jer 28.16-17) and the promise or warning of an event whose fulfilment requires or presupposes the introduction of a new world order, such as has not yet arrived two and a half millennia after the prophet's day (of which Rev 21 provides an example). Isaiah 40–55 and Isaiah 60–62 stand on that line, the former nearer one end, the latter nearer the other. On one hand, it speaks of the actual city of Jerusalem and its temple, of actual Judahite exiles and contemporary peoples; on the other, it describes events that are larger than life. On one hand, the rebuilding of temple and city and the return of some exiles form a partial fulfilment of its promises; on the other, the larger-than-life nature of the promises is one reason why they stand open to reformulation in later contexts, as still instructive statements of God's ultimate intent. It resembles Ezekiel 40–48 in being imaginative and visionary without this characteristic implying that the prophets have no hopes or expectations regarding something to happen in the community's own experience. For this reason, it is risky to see the chapter as presenting Jerusalem as a 'metaphor for God's saving intervention'.[203] Nor is there a basis for seeing chapters 60–62 as reflecting 'internal discussion within a small marginal group which does not enjoy any public respect and which has largely lost all connections with historical and political reality'.[204]

The chapter is concerned with the restoration of both the city and the temple (and the land). 'Though a poem, Isaiah 60 tells a story', recounting a movement from lowliness to exaltation.[205] Whereas Persia expected its vassal states to pay tribute to its king, the prophet declares that they are destined to pay tribute to Yhwh.[206] 'The instruments of pagan commercial and technological strength will be absorbed or "gathered" into the city which God is preparing'.[207] It does not give much indication

[202] On the use of Isa 60–62 in Revelation, see Fekkes, *Isaiah and the Prophetic Traditions in the Book of Revelation*, pp. 264-76; also 'Isaiah and the Book of Revelation: John the Prophet as the Fourth Isaiah', in McGinnis and Tull (eds.), *'As Those Who Are Taught'*, pp. 125-43.

[203] So Ramis, *Isaías 40–66*, p. 289.

[204] So Albertz, *Religionsgeschichte Israels in alttestamentlicher Zeit*, II, p. 486 (ET p. 456).

[205] Gregory J. Polan, 'Zion, the Glory of the Holy One of Israel', in Lawrence Boadt and Mark S. Smith (eds.), *Imagery and Imagination in Biblical Literature* (Washington, DC: Catholic Biblical Association, 2011), pp. 50-71 (60, 70).

[206] Cf. Strawn, '"A World under Control"' (see above).

[207] Cf. Richard J. Mouw, 'What Are the Ships of Tarshish Doing Here?', *Crux* 17/2 (1981), pp. 20-26 (20-21); see further *When the Kings Come Marching in* (Grand Rapids: Eerdmans, 1983).

of what will happen in the restored city but it does allude to what will happen in the restored temple. In this sense it is worship-focused and it again corresponds to Ezekiel 40–48. It is characterized by both openness to the nations and rigour in relation to Judah and to the nations (whereas Ezekiel lacks much positive concern for the nations but explicitly envisages the restoration of Ephraim as well as Judah). When nations focus on their glorious heritage and their national honour, God determines to put them down, but this policy is an interim one. God then draws them to acknowledge and honour where true splendour lies.[208] The vision of the future in Isaiah 60 can be compared and contrasted with the stance of Chronicles–Ezra–Nehemiah as well as that of Ezekiel 40–48. Chronicles–Ezra–Nehemiah emphasizes the temple in a down-to-earth way. Ezekiel 40–48 focuses on the city, but does not name it, and speaks only of an imaginary city in a reshaped landscape; it is concerned for the temple and for its proper supervision by the Zadokites, and it may well (like the Qumran community) reject the actual temple. Isaiah 56–66 speaks of a new Jerusalem, but here 'Jerusalem/Zion functions…as a grand symbol' as the centre and possession of the whole reunited Israel.[209]

Christian lectionaries set the beginning of Isaiah 60 for Epiphany and thus link the chapter with the story of eastern sages bringing Jesus gold, incense, and myrrh (Matt 2.1-12). Cyril of Alexandria waxes lyrical on the way 'it is as though the promise that Israel will be saved had already been fulfilled' and adds that the prophet 'all but says that Christ, who was long ago predicted by the law and the holy prophets, was already present among them and now at the end of the age has shone on all who dwell on earth'.[210] While the recurrence of reference to gold and incense constitutes a link between the two passages, it does not work to think of Isaiah 60 as a 'prediction' of which that event is the 'fulfilment'; there is insufficient correspondence between the two. Indeed, the New Testament itself does not explicitly relate the prophecy and the event; it actually links the event with Micah 5.1-3 [2-4]. Further, while Cyril is typical of the Church Fathers in assuming that the chapter simply relates to the coming of Christ,[211] Theodoret of Cyrrhus sees it as relating simultaneously to three

[208] Cf. Mouw, *When the Kings Come Marching In*, pp. 18-19.

[209] Cf. Croatto, *Imaginar el futuro*, pp. 234.

[210] Ἐξήγησις ὑπομνηματική εἰς τὸν προφήτην Ἡσαΐαν, col. 1321, as quoted by Wilken and others (eds.), *Isaiah Interpreted by Early Christian and Medieval Commentators*, p. 462.

[211] E.g. Eusebius of Caesarea, *Der Jesajakommentar*, pp. 368-78; Cyril of Alexandria, Ἐξήγησις ὑπομνηματική εἰς τὸν προφήτην Ἡσαΐαν, columns 1321-50. Cf. Jerome, *Commentariorum in Isaiam prophetam libri duodeviginti*, columns 587-98; Hayman of Halberstadt, *Commentariorum in Isaiam libri tres*, columns 1051-52, with special reference to the beginnings of the church. Both start by denying that the prophecy suggests a millennial literal fulfilment for the Jewish people. But contrast Theodore of Heraclea, Ἐκ τῆς εἰς Ἡσαΐαν ἐξηγησέως, col. 1366.

subjects: the reconstruction of Jerusalem under Cyrus and Darius; the splendour of the holy church; and the celestial city.[212]

The explicit Christian juxtaposing of Isaiah 60 and Matthew 2 does do justice to the nature of Isaiah 60 better than does a reading that envisages Isaiah 60 as essentially a portrait of the way a prophet expects political events to unfold at the end of the sixth century or in the fifth. It is poetic, lyrical, and hyperbolic in its language. It is typical of Isaiah 56–66 in not relating its promises to specific political contexts or events. Like anything that anyone ever says or writes, it relates to a particular historical context in the sense that it emerges from such a context and reflects it. But both the attempt to see it as envisaging fulfilment in such a context and the understanding of it as a prediction of a particular event six centuries later miss the significance of its poetic nature. It is questionable whether establishing its historical context 'does very much at all to explain its character and intention'.[213]

Christian lectionaries further link the story of the eastern sages with Psalm 72, which also refers to the bringing of gifts and itself has a number of overlaps with Isaiah 60. Yet that comparison also draws further attention to a distinctive feature of Isaiah 60 over against the psalm, the story of the sages, and the earlier chapters of Isaiah with their recurrent focus on the destiny of Jerusalem. Isaiah 60 has in common with the rest of Isaiah 56–66 that it makes no mention of a king in Jerusalem. In this respect it takes on the stance of Isaiah 40–55 rather than that characteristic of Isaiah 1–39. It focuses on the community as a whole; unlike Ezekiel, it has no place for a Davidic ruler, for a Messiah. Alongside that fact, the nations' kings 'do not cease to be kings but exercise all their power for preserving the worship of God and administering righteous government'.[214]

212 *Commentaire sur Isaïe* 175b (III, pp. 238-41).

213 Ronald E. Clements, '"Arise, Shine; for Your Light Has Come"', in Broyles and Evans (eds.), *Writing and Reading the Scroll of Isaiah*, I, pp. 441-54 (446).

214 Calvin, *In Iesaiam prophetam*, p. 383 (ET IV, p. 287).

VII

ISAIAH 61.1-9

Translation and Notes

1 The breath of my Lord Yhwh[1] is on me,// because[2] Yhwh anointed me.
He sent me to bring news[3] to the afflicted,// to bind up[4] the people who are broken in spirit;[5]
To proclaim release to the captives,// the opening wide of eyes[6] to the prisoners;[7]
2 To proclaim the year of acceptance by Yhwh,// the day of redress by our God;
To comfort all the mourners,// 3 to provide for the people who mourn Zion// —to give them finery instead of ash,[8]

[1] LXX simplifies the double title to 'the Lord', as it does in (e.g.) 50.4-9 (so also Vg). 1QIs[a] simplifies it rather to יהוה. 1QIs[b] has יהוה אלהים (though the first part of יהוה is missing because of a gap in the ms). There are similar variations at v. 11.

[2] Donald E. Gowan ('The Use of *ya'an* in Biblical Hebrew', *VT* 21 [1971], pp. 168-85) notes that the use of יען here is very unusual; the conjunction normally occurs only on God's lips in connection with a declaration of what God intends to do because of some human action.

[3] The original text of 1QIs[a] lacks 'he sent me', so that 'to bring news' depends on 'he anointed me'.

[4] 1QIs[a] prefixes the infinitive with ו 'and', making explicit that being the anointed one implies two tasks—bringing good news and binding up or healing (cf. Pulikottil, *Transmission of Biblical Texts in Qumran*, p. 85).

[5] ל introducing the object is usually a mark of later Hebrew (GK 117n), but this verb is commonly used with a thing as direct object and the person as the indirect object (see BDB). Cf. J. Morgenstern, 'The Suffering Servant', *VT* 11 (1961), pp. 292-320, 406-31 (303).

[6] MT פקח־קוח (cf. 4QIs[m] פקח קוח) perhaps presupposes that קוח is a form from לקח, which can sometimes lose its initial ל and can refer to being taken into captivity (e.g. 39.7; 52.5); cf. Rashi, 'ישעיה'. Beuken (*Jesaja IIIA*, p. 201) calls this an 'étymologie savante'. A. S. Yahuda ('Hebrew Words of Egyptian Origin', *JBL* 66 [1947], pp. 83-90 [86-87]) rather suggests that קוח is a loan word from Egyptian, where *kḥ* means a prisoner's collar. But 1QIs[a, b] and many later mss lack the maqqeph and thus have a word that seems to be a reduplicated and emphatic form from פקח (cf. JM 59d). GK 84n suggests simple פקח as in 42.7 (dittog.). Ehrlich (*Randglossen*, IV, p. 217) suggests פתוח (cf. 45.1). Morgenstern ('The Loss of Words at the Ends of Lines in Manuscripts of Biblical Poetry', pp. 63-64) suggests פתח זקים 'the opening of fetters'.

[7] For MT אסורים LXX has 'blind people', perhaps implying סנורים (cf. Brockington, *The Hebrew Text of the Old Testament*, p. 197), but more likely translating in accordance with the context and in keeping with 42.7.

[8] On textual questions in this line, see the comment.

Festive oil instead of mourning,// a praise garment[9] instead of a flickering spirit.
So they will be called[10] the oaks of faithfulness,[11]// the plantation of Yhwh,[12] to manifest glory.

4 They will build up the lasting ruins,// raise up the desolations of the ancestors,[13]
Renew ruined cities,// desolations of many generations.[14]
5 Strangers will stand[15] and pasture your flocks,// foreigners will be your farm labourers and your vinedressers,
6 While you yourselves are called 'Yhwh's priests';// you will be termed 'ministers of our God'.
You will consume the resources of nations// and thrive[16] on their splendour.

[9] Gaster ('Notes on Isaiah', p. 106) derives from הלל I 'shine' rather than הלל II. LXX translates תהלה by δόξα, one a number of links between LXX Isaiah and LXX of Exodus 15, repeating the use of δόξα, which it uses three times in the verse, reflecting the translator's liking for the word (see Brockington, 'The Greek Translator of Isaiah and his Interest in δοξα', esp. p. 24; Olley, *'Righteousness' in the Septuagint of Isaiah*, pp. 81-82).

[10] With MT's וקרא (literally, 'it will be called [to them]', compare the passives in LXX, Vg. 1QIs[a] has the more common impersonal active וקראו 'and they will call [them]'. Hanson (*The Dawn of Apocalyptic*, pp. 52-53, 57) repoints as infinitive to conform to the infinitives that precede.

[11] There is some variation among manuscripts over whether to spell this word אילי or אלי. Klostermann (*Deuterojesaia*, p. 90) emends to אהלי 'tents of'. Scullion ('Some Difficult Texts in Isaiah cc.56—66', p. 117) emends צדק to צַדִּיק 'of the Faithful One', though he also notes that Roy A. Rosenberg ('The God Ṣedeq', *HUCA* 36 [1965], pp. 161-77 [170]) takes צדק itself as a divine title.

[12] P. A. H. de Boer takes this as an instance of the use of יהוה to denote the superlative, 'a majestic [plantation]' ('יהוה as Epithet Expressing the Superlative', *VT* 24 [1974], pp. 233-35 [235]).

[13] LXX, Vg, have 'the ancient desolations', but ראשנים should then be f. Rather, cf. Aq, Sym, Th. There is no parallel for the word meaning 'ancient times' (so, e.g., Julian Morgenstern, 'Isaiah 61', *HUCA* 40-41 [1969–70], pp. 109-21 [111]).

[14] 1QIs[a] repeats יקוממו from the previous line. Köhler (*Der Prophet der Heimkehr*, pp. 212-13) rather adds יַעֲמִידוּ 'they will cause to stand', adapted from v. 5a; Westermann simply moves that qal verb ('desolations of many generations will arise'): see *Jesaja Kapitel 40–66*, p. 293 (ET p. 368, but the translation contains a slip). But 'stand and pasture' in v. 5 seems to be a compound expression (see the comment).

[15] LXX 'come' translates loosely, following 60.6 (cf. 66.18, 23) (*HUB*).

[16] BDB takes תתימרו as a byform of תתאמרו, hitpael of אמר (for which see Ps 94.4); cf. 1QIs[a] תתיאמרו. BDB then takes it to mean 'glory in'; LXX has θαυμασθήσεσθε (cf. Vg *superbietis*, Syr *tštbḥwn*), though this verb 'has a tendency to occur in dubious passages' (Ottley, *Isaiah according to the Septuagint*, II, p. 370; he suggests that LXX, Vg, Syr imply תתמהו from תמה). The word looks more like one derived from a verb ימר, perhaps a byform of מור 'change themselves [into]' in the sense of change places with them (e.g. Saadia, 'Version d'Isaïe de R. Saadia', p. 64), or 'exchange' in the sense of trade with their wealth (Scullion, 'Some Difficult Texts in Isaiah cc.56–66', p. 118; cf. Duhm, *Jesaia*, p. 415). But this requires some stretching of meaning. *HALOT* more plausibly derives MT's form from a different אמר known in Mishnaic Hebrew and meaning 'thrive, prosper, exceed, get fat' (see *DTT*). This understanding fits the parallelism and could underlie 1QIs[a], LXX, Vg, Syr, and also Th ὑψωθήσεσθε, Sym στρηνιάσατε 'run riot',

7 Instead of your shame,[17] [there will be] double;[18]// [instead of] disgrace, they will resound[19] at their portion.

Therefore[20] in their land they will possess double;// lasting joy will be theirs[21].

8 Because I am Yhwh, one who loves the exercise of judgment,// one who repudiates robbery in oppression.[22]

I will give them their wages in truthfulness,[23]// seal a lasting covenant for them.[24]

Their offspring will come to be acknowledged among the nations,// their descendants in the midst of the peoples.

All who see them will recognize them,// that they are offspring Yhwh has blessed.

Tg תתפנקון 'delight themselves' (cf. Barthélémy, *Critique Textuelle de l'Ancien Testament*, II, p. 422). (Aq πορφυρωθήσεσθε 'be dressed in purple' may link the verb with another root אמר from which there are words to denote the fringe of a garment or the garment itself; see Talmon, 'Aspects of the Textual Transmission of the Bible in the Light of Qumran Manuscripts', p. 117 = p. 97; *DTT*, p. 51). Volz reaches a similar result by suggesting תתמריו or תתמראו from מרא = מרה 'graze, become fat' (*Jesaja II*, p. 254), while Albert Schultens suggests deriving the word from a word cognate with an Arabic verb *māra* meaning 'get provision' (see Alexander, *Isaiah*, II, p. 402) (and see *DCH* on these three verbs); cf. NEB 'be furnished with' on the basis of reading תִּתְמַיָּרוּ (cf. Brockington, *The Hebrew Text of the Old Testament*, p. 197). Ehrlich (*Randglossen*, IV, p. 218) emends to תתעמרו 'use as you wish', Torrey (*Second Isaiah*, p. 455) תתיקרו 'glorify yourselves', Klostermann (*Deuterojesaia*, p. 91) תתהדרו 'adorn yourselves', Kissane (*Isaiah*, II, p. 273) תתפארו 'beautify yourselves', Fischer (*Buch Isaias*, II, p. 181) תתעמרו 'gather for yourselves'.

[17] Budde ('Jesaia', p. 706) emends בשתכם to third person בשתם כי, in keeping with the rest of vv. 7-9; Kittel ('Jesaia', p. 692) reverses these two words, which makes it easier to translate 'because of'. Morgenstern ('Isaiah 61' [see above], p. 114) adds the possibility of reading simple בשת.

[18] Köhler (*Der Prophet der Heimkehr*, p. 213) emends משנה to משגה 'increase'.

[19] For MT ירנו Volz (*Jesaja II*, p. 255) reads רנה 'resounding [will be their portion]', NEB וָרֹן 'and an [abusive] shout [was their portion]' (cf. Brockington, *The Hebrew Text of the Old Testament*, p. 197), Klostermann (*Deuterojesaia*, p. 91) suggests וָרֹק '[disgrace] and spit [was their portion]', Dillmann (*Jesaia* [1890 edn], p. 513) יָרְשׁוּ or לָקְחוּ 'they will possess/take [as their portion]' (cf. v. 7b).

[20] In the sense of 'thus' (B. Jongeling, 'Lākēn dans l'Ancien Testament', in A. S. van der Woude [ed.], *Remembering All the Way...* [Leiden: Brill, 1981], pp. 190-200 [199]); see the comment.

[21] For 'theirs' LXX has 'on their head' as in 35.10; 51.11.

[22] For MT בְּעוֹלָה (cf. Vg), LXX, Syr, Tg may imply בְּעַוְלָה (cf. 59.3), though a similar pointing to MT's reappears in Pss 58.3 [2]; 64.7 [6]; 92.16 [15]; Job 5.16; Mitchell J. Dahood (*Ugaritic–Hebrew Philology* [Rome: Pontifical Bible Institute, 1965], p. 8) sees it as reflecting a Canaanite form. Torrey (*Second Isaiah*, p. 454) emends מעולם 'from of old', Knight (*The New Israel*, p. 58; cf. Koenen, *Ethik und Eschatologie im Tritojesajabuch*, p. 116) בְּעוּלָה as in 62.4.

[23] LXX readings vary between δικαίως 'righteously' (cf. Ziegler, *Buch Isaias*, p. 350) and δικαίοις 'to the righteous' (cf. Rahlfs, *Septuaginta*, II, p. 648); both perhaps simply make explicit an understanding of the implication of באמת.

[24] On 1QIs[a]'s second person suffixes in vv. 8-9, see the comment.

Introduction

MT and 1QIs[b] begin a section or chapter at 61.1 (1QIs[a] has a small mid-line space, and another after 61.7). MT and 1QIs[a] then begin a new section or chapter at 61.10 (the relevant part of 1QIs[b] is missing) which runs into chapter 62. The chapter as demarcated in EVV may presuppose that the 'I' of 61.10 is the same 'I' as that in 61.1 (the second 'I' uses the title 'my Lord Yhwh' as does the first).[25] The Hebrew division may presuppose that actually a different 'I' speaks at 61.10, which seems indeed to be so. I thus follow the Hebrew tradition in treating 61.1-9 as a unit, with a new unit beginning at 61.10. Verses 1-9 comprise eighteen lines, all bicola except vv. 2b-3aαβ (though this may have resulted from the conflation of two versions of the text).[26] Many are parallel bicola, though they manifest varying rhythms, with cola of two, three, or four stresses in varying combinations.

The first-person testimony in vv. 1-3 signals a marked new start after 60.1-22, while at the end vv. 8-9 stand apart as words of Yhwh that buttress and also summarize what precedes. These open as if Yhwh has already been speaking in what precedes, with which there is thus some continuity, and I take v. 7b as their introduction. Yet it is not explicit where we should see the transition from the prophet's testimony to Yhwh's words. It is usual to see a distinction between the more lyrical nature of the opening lines and the more down-to-earth speech of the lines that follow, but commentators vary over whether to close the first section after v. 3a or after v. 3b or after v. 4. Like the subsections in Isaiah 60, vv. 1-3 and 8-9 close with a formula suggesting recognition. I therefore divide the section into vv. 1-3, 4-7a, and 7b-9, while recognizing that they flow into each other in serendipitous or stream-of-consciousness fashion like the subsections in chapter 60.

It has been suggested that the prophecy was delivered in the context of worship[27] and further that chapter 61 as a whole is a liturgy, comprising an oracle (vv. 1-9) and a response (vv. 10-11).[28] The setting for the prophecy could then be the kind of fasting occasions referred to in Zechariah 7–8. But the evidence for such possibilities is very indirect. Indeed, the chapter is more mixed in form than the liturgical hypothesis implies. Verses 1-3 comprise a prophetic testimony, v. 4 a prophetic promise in the third person, vv. 5-7a a prophetic promise in the second person, and vv. 7b-9 a divine speech.[29] This diversity is not an indication that originally separate, formally diverse elements have been combined

[25] Fitzgerald ('A Rhetorical Analysis of Isaiah 56–66', pp. 222-23) argues for the English chapter division.

[26] See the comment.

[27] E.g. Jones, 'Isaiah—II and III', p. 532.

[28] Cf. Elliger, *Die Einheit des Tritojesaja*, pp. 24-26.

[29] See, e.g., Kellermann, 'Tritojesaja und das Geheimnis des Gottesknechts', p. 54.

in the chapter, but another marker of its serendipitous nature. Nor, therefore, can such diversity or unevenness be the basis for hypotheses regarding the redactional development of the chapter.[30]

While the section resembles Isaiah 60 in its content, themes, motifs, and words,[31] its first distinctive feature is its incorporation of the prophet's testimony in vv. 1-3. When it goes on to use second-person forms, these are masculine plural rather than second-person singular; they directly address people in general rather than doing so indirectly as they address personified Zion. Isaiah 62 will resume the latter address. The third-plural forms in 60.21-22 facilitate the transition to Isaiah 61; the testimony of an individual in 61.10-11 facilitates the transition to Isaiah 62.

The section's location at the heart of Isaiah 56–66 parallels the location of Isaiah 6 at the heart of Isaiah 1–12[32] (Ben Sira 48.24 simply assumes that Isaiah ben Amoz also speaks here).[33] In contrast, the difference between the linear arrangement of Isaiah 40–55 and the concentric structure of Isaiah 56–66 finds particular expression in the place given to prophetic testimony in these last two parts of the book. Isaiah 40–55 begins with an account of the prophet's summons to speak for Yhwh. In Isaiah 56–66 such an account comes at the centre of the chapters (90 verses precede it, 94 verses follow). Prospectively, 40.1-11 provides background and authorization for what follows; 61.1-9 fulfils this function retrospectively for what precedes and prospectively for what follows. In other words, what the prophet has been doing in chapter 60 is bringing news to the afflicted, comforting the mourners, and so on; 61.1-9 relates the way the prophet came to be doing so, while also reformulating the earlier message.

Thus the section is (or at least begins as) a prophetic testimony like those in passages such as Isaiah 6; 40; 49; and 50, and also in Jeremiah 1 and 11–20. Such testimonies fulfil two functions. One is to offer backing for the message the prophet brings. They provide the basis for heeding it and for taking it as a message that comes from someone who speaks for Yhwh, no false prophet.[34] But Isaiah 61 is more than merely an account of a prophet's commission.[35] The other function of such prophetic testimonies is that they are an indirect way of expounding the message itself. Isaiah 6 provides an example of a testimony where the two functions are nicely balanced; in Isaiah 61 the second function has the prominence, which links with the fact that the section represents an extraordinary

[30] For instance, Vermeylen (*Du prophète Isaïe à l'apocalyptique*, II, p. 478-83) suggests a process whereby sequentially vv. 1-3, 7b-9, 4-7a, 10, and 11 came together.

[31] See the detailed comparison in Paul, ישעיה פרקים מ-סו, II, p. 487 (ET pp. 536-38).

[32] Cf. Croatto, *Imaginar el futuro*, p. 288.

[33] Cf. Laato, *'About Zion I Will Not Be Silent'*, pp. 15-17.

[34] Cf. Margaret Dee Bratcher, 'Salvation Achieved: Isaiah 61:1-7; 62:1-7; 65:17–66:2', *Review and Expositor* 88 (1991), pp. 177-88 (177-78).

[35] Cf. Pauritsch's comments, *Die neue Gemeinde*, p. 107.

accumulation of key theological terms.[36] To put it another way, the testimony is not an account of a call like those in Isaiah 6 or Jeremiah 1 but something more like an account of 'the effect or the lasting endowment of the call'.[37] Verses 1-3a comprise 'the self-presentation of "the prophet"'; its focus lies on the effect of the call rather than merely the call itself.[38] 'The prophet not only claims divine authority for his announcement of well-being, but also presents his ministry as a crucial part of the imminent time of well-being which is to bring an end to the lamentation of the community.'[39]

The prophet's self-description has royal as well as prophetic features.[40] Yhwh's spirit comes on kings; kings are anointed; they proclaim release; they have responsibility for bringing comfort, for binding up, for comforting, and for making it possible for people to find transformation (e.g. Ps 72). The description of the speaker overlaps significantly with the description of a new David in Isaiah 11.1-10, upon whom Yhwh's spirit settles, who acts by speaking, who is girded in *ṣedeq* and *ʾĕmûnâ*, and who will draw peoples and nations.[41] The 'I' is that of a prophetic king, or rather of a kingly prophet.[42] The combination of features connects with the overlap between prophetic and royal features in the description of the servant of Yhwh in Isaiah 40–55, because a number of aspects of the self-description in 61.1-3 take up descriptions of Yhwh's servant. Admittedly, discussion of the relationship between this speaker and Yhwh's servant, and between this speaker and a coming new David, needs to avoid being confused by a failure to distinguish sense and reference in connection with both. The servant of Yhwh is not a person, so that one could then ask whether the speaker in 61.1-3 is the same person or thinks he is. The servant of Yhwh is a role. With the coming David, too, the role is to be distinguished from the person, as Isaiah 55 has made clear.

[36] So Hans-Winfried Jüngling, '"Die Eichen der Gerechtigkeit"', in G. Braulik, W. Gross, and S. McEvenue (eds.), *Biblische Theologie und gesellschaftlicher Wandel* (Norbert Lohfink Festschrift; Freiburg: Herder, 1993), pp. 199-219 (199). He goes on to note a number of links between Isaiah 61 and Isaiah 1–39.

[37] Childs, *Isaiah*, p. 503.

[38] Wim A. M. Beuken, 'Servant and Herald of Good Tidings', in Vermeylen (ed.), *The Book of Isaiah: Le livre d'Isaïe*, pp. 411-42 (415), taking up an expression of Peter R. Ackroyd, 'Isaiah I–XII: Presentation of a Prophet', in Emerton (ed.), *Congress Volume: Göttingen 1977*, pp. 16-47, reprinted in Ackroyd, *Studies in the Religious Tradition of the Old Testament*, pp. 79-104, 266-74.

[39] Wells, 'The Statements of Well-Being in Isaiah 60–62', p. 184.

[40] See Randall Heskett, *Messianism within the Scriptural Scroll of Isaiah* (New York: T&T Clark International, 2007), pp. 225-63.

[41] Cf., e.g., Morgenstern, 'The Suffering Servant' (see above), p. 412; Oswalt, *The Book of Isaiah Chapters 40–66*, p. 563.

[42] Cf. Martin Noth, *Amt und Berufung im Alten Testament* (Bonn: Hanstein, 1958), p. 26 (ET Noth, *The Laws in the Pentateuch and Other Studies* [Edinburgh: Oliver & Boyd, 1966], p. 248).

Related to this, 61.1-9 (in whole or in part) is not a servant song,[43] partly because there is no such thing as a servant song.[44] It is just as much a servant *passage* as the testimony in 50.4-9, though the voice that speaks here is not the same voice as speaks there; the identity of the servant figure can change as it changes within Isaiah 40–55, in connection with the fact that being Yhwh's servant is a role, not the identity of a single entity. Further, after Isaiah 53 the book ceases to use the word 'servant' in the singular and uses it only in the plural; this likely also means that we risk misapprehension and confusion if we think of the prophet as Yhwh's servant in the special sense that Isaiah 49, 50, and 52.13–53.12 do. One of the themes in Isaiah 61 is Yhwh's involvement with the whole people, who replace any David figure; they likely also replace any individual servant figure, in keeping with the original intent of that image (41.8-10). But this is not to say that that they are 'the servants of Yhwh' as opposed to 'the servant of Yhwh' or that they are the offspring of which 53.10 speaks;[45] at least, Isaiah 61 does not make this connection

To whom is the testimony in Isaiah 61 addressed? A feature of the section that recurs from other passages in the Prophets is that it moves between third-person plural verbs and pronouns (vv. 1-4, 7aβ-9) and second-person plural verbs and pronouns (vv. 5-7aα). The second-person forms refer to the prophet's Judahite audience. While some of the third-person forms refer to other nations (at least vv. 5-6), others also refer to the Judahites. Thus the reference of the second-person speech and of those latter third-person forms is the same or similar. The people referred to in the third person in vv. 1-4 and 7b-9 are the people who are listening to the prophet; the third-person references enable them to gain distance from themselves, to look at themselves from the outside. They are both the audience in the house and the audience on the stage; as the audience in the house they are invited to look at figures on the stage who represent them. Even the prophet's first-person speech has a related effect, in inviting them to identify with the prophet's message; it involves them.

One could thus hardly say that the community is less central in chapter 61 than it is in chapters 60 and 62.[46] Zion is not central, but it yields centrality not to Yhwh but to the people who mourn Zion.[47] Further, while

[43] Against, e.g., W. W. Cannon, 'Isaiah 61 1-3 an Ebed-Jahweh Poem', *ZAW* 47 (1929), pp. 284-88; cf. Robert Koch, 'Der Gottesgeist und der Messias', *Biblica* 27 (1946), pp. 241-68, 376-403 (396-400); H. A. J. Kruger, 'Isaiah 61:1-3(4-9) 10-11', *HTS Teologiese Studies/Theological Studies* 58 (2002), pp. 1555-76. See, e.g., Hans-Jürgen Hermisson, 'Gottesknecht und Gottes Knechte', in Hubert Cancik and H. Lichtenberger (eds.), *Geschichte—Tradition—Reflexion* (M. Hengel Festschrift; Tübingen: Mohr, 1996), pp. 43-68 (62-66).

[44] See Goldingay and Payne, *Isaiah 40–55*.

[45] Against Beuken, *Jesaja IIIA*, pp. 220-23 (cf. Beuken, 'Servant and Herald of Good Tidings' [see above], pp. 438-40).

[46] Against Volz, *Jesaja II*, p. 255.

[47] Cf. Sekine's comments, *Die Tritojesajanische Sammlung*, pp. 79-80.

Yhwh is not central, it is Yhwh with whom 61.1-9 begins and ends.[48] The section opens with a declaration concerning the commission of Yhwh which is what issues in the message of the verses and it closes with a declaration by Yhwh that confirms this message.

Like chapter 60, chapter 61 is in part inspired by the recollection of passages from Isaiah 40–55. This is especially so in the description of the prophet's commission in the opening lines, as the description of the earlier prophet's commission in 40.1-11 itself reflects that in 6.1-13. Indeed, this commission involves a reversal of that in 6.1-13.[49] A difference from chapter 60 is that here, the inspiration takes the form of a more systematic reuse of particular words and phrases rather than an occasional virtual quoting of whole cola. Thus the opening claim that 'the breath of my Lord Yhwh is on me' takes up words relating to Yhwh's servant in 42.1 '[I have put] my breath on him' and the recurrent use of the title 'my Lord Yhwh' in (e.g.) 48.16 (which also refers to Yhwh's breath) and 50.4-9, in prophetic testimonies. The verb 'anoint' used in a figurative sense takes up the use of related nouns in 45.1; 52.14[50] (this last is the only sign of the influence of 52.13–53.12 in the passage). 'He sent me' comes from 48.16 (see also 42.19). 'Bring news' comes from 40.9-10; 41.27; 52.7. For 'the afflicted', *ʿānāw* did not come in Isaiah 40–55, but *ʿānî* came in 41.17; 49.13; 51.21; 54.11. 'Bind up' did not come in Isaiah 40–55, though it did in 1.6; 30.26. 'Break' came in a similar connection in 42.3. Jerusalem's 'spirit' (literally, 'heart') is the object of comfort in 40.2. The testimony's form with its infinitival clauses (to bring news, to bind up, to proclaim…) also follows that of 42.7; 49.5-6.[51] The testimony has further points of contact with 21.1-12.[52]

Isaiah 61.1-3 is thus 'a key text for the phenomenon of scribal prophecy'. It is not in the traditional sense an account of a prophet's call but 'an apologetic legitimation of a scribal prophet'.[53] We have noted that accounts of a prophet's call regularly function as legitimation; this one does so in a new sense or a new way, by using phrases from earlier prophecy that imply a claim to continuity with it and to be its contemporary voice. The scribal prophet renews the message of his teacher.[54]

Admittedly the expression 'scribal prophecy' might seem to be an oxymoron. Its significance is on the one hand that the scribal can be prophetic and inspired; it is not mere rationalism, not merely the result of human thinking, of theological reflection. And on the other hand, prophecy can be scribal; it can be facilitated by reflection on what God

48 Cf. Beuken, *Jesaja IIIA*, p. 222, though he is referring to 61.1-11.

49 Cf. Francis Landy, 'I and Eye in Isaiah', *JBL* 131 (2012), pp. 85-97 (96).

50 On this passage, see Goldingay and Payne, *Isaiah 40–55*, II, pp. 290-94.

51 Blenkinsopp, *Isaiah 56–66*, p. 221.

52 See Bernard Gosse, 'Le "moi" prophétique de l'oracle contre Babylone d'Isaïe xxi, 1-10', *RB* 93 (1986), pp. 70-84.

53 Lau, *Schriftgelehrte Prophetie in Jes 56–66*, p. 72.

54 Kellermann, 'Tritojesaja und das Geheimnis des Gottesknechts' p. 63.

has said before. The prophetic testimony is one inspired by the words of the prophet's predecessor. The prophet has perhaps meditated and reflected on them in a way that has made them part of the prophet's mental and spiritual furniture such as then provides the formulation for a new individual, personal sense of divine vocation, and for an articulation of that sense of vocation. The implication is not that the testimony sees itself as an interpretation of the earlier prophecies or implies a claim to *be* the servant to whom those passages referred. It would be misleading to say that Isaiah 61 is the earliest interpretation of the servant songs, which it takes to refer to an individual.[55] The prophet is interested in using the servant figure in order to interpret and claim authority for the message that the chapters bring. The testimony is not interpreting the earlier prophecies but making use of them. It is in this sense that one might describe the chapter as midrashic.[56]

Comment

61.1abα The breath of my Lord Yhwh is on me,// because Yhwh anointed me.

In the absence of indications to the contrary, the first-person singular suggests that an individual speaks.[57] While a corporate entity such as Jacob-Israel or Zion speaks in the first person in passages such as 48.5, 7; 49.14, the prophet indicates that this is happening (vv. 10-11 will test this rule, but not in the end disconfirm it) and there is no indication that Jacob-Israel or Zion or a body within the community speaks here.[58] The fact that it is hard to see what would be the corporate entity to which such a corporate entity would speak and to which it would be called to minister heightens the implausibility of this interpretation, and justifies some expectation that the prophecy would have made it clear if the corporate understanding was right. We noted in the introduction to this section that the reference to anointing could make one think of a king, and the description of the speaker's role overlaps with that of a king.[59] But Isaiah 56–66

[55] Cf. Lau, *Schriftgelehrte Prophetie in Jes 56–66*, p. 70.

[56] E.g. Beuken, *Jesaja IIIA*, p. 220.

[57] Ulrich Berges ('Personification and Prophetic Voices of Zion in Isaiah and Beyond', in J. C. de Moor [ed.], *The Elusive Prophet* [Leiden: Brill, 2001], pp. 54-82 [74]) speaks of 'a sudden shift from "I" to "we" at this point' which 'shows that it is a group speaking here', but there is no 'we' in Isaiah 60–62, and the expression 'our God' in vv. 2 and 6 does not indicate that a group speaks, any more than it does in (e.g.) 1.10.

[58] Against (e.g.) Paul-Eugène Dion, 'Les chants du Serviteur de Yahweh', *Biblica* 51 (1970), pp. 17-38 (37-38); Smart, *History and Theology in Second Isaiah*, pp. 259-60; Vermeylen, *Du prophète Isaïe à l'apocalyptique*, II, p. 478; Hanson, *The Dawn of Apocalyptic*, pp. 65-69 (contrast *Isaiah 40–66*, pp. 223-24); Santiago Ausín, 'El Espíritu Santo en la comunidad escatolológica', *Estudios Biblicos* 57 (1999), pp. 97-124.

[59] See, e.g., John S. Bergsma, *The Jubilee from Leviticus to Qumran* (Leiden: Brill, 2007), pp. 200-2; Koole, *Jesaja III*, p. 263 (ET p. 270); Oswalt, *The Book of Isaiah*

does not otherwise speak of a king having a role to play. Tg begins the chapter, 'The prophet said, "The spirit of prophecy from before Yhwh God is on me"', correctly inferring the identity of the 'I'. R. N. Whybray's judgment on the first-person servant passages in Isaiah 40–55 also applies here: in a prophetic book, speech in the first-person singular when not Yhwh's is normally the prophet's.[60] If most of the prophecies in Isaiah 56–66 come from the same person, then this is that person's testimony. Whether they come from the same person or not, the arrangement of the chapters with this testimony at their centre invites us to see this prophetic commission as lying behind the whole of Isaiah 56–66.

The first line of the testimony (4-4) expresses itself entirely in words that go back to Isaiah 40–55.[61] The significance of this reuse of earlier words is twofold. Traditional words with authority help the prophet articulate the nature of the vocation and the nature of the ministry it commissions, and this helps the prophet's own reflection and self-understanding. Then when spoken or written they help the listeners or readers to understand the ministry and the words, and invite them to associate these with that authoritative tradition and thus to give them more credence. The opening claim that 'the breath of my Lord Yhwh is on me' takes up words that related to the prophet in 59.21 but go back behind that passage to words concerning Yhwh's servant in 42.1 '[I have put] my breath on him'. That statement speaks of Yhwh's servant in the third person and does not speak directly about the prophet, but the subsequent identification of the prophet as Yhwh's servant (most explicitly in 49.1-3) would make it reasonable to apply the words to the prophet, if justification were felt necessary (though such reapplication hardly feels the need to justify itself). But in the process they change their meaning. In origin the coming of Yhwh's breath on someone makes them do extraordinary things that indicate the activity of something other than their human capacity. In 11.1-9 that idea was stretched to apply to more regular but still extraordinary achievements on the part of the shoot to grow from the Davidic stump, who will see to the implementation of faithful decision-making in the community (*w^{e}šāpaṭ b^{e}ṣedeq*). In 42.1-4 it is further extended to apply to the role of Yhwh's servant (whom the previous chapter has identified as Israel) in relation to the nations. It is still a matter of action rather than words. It is stretched further in the enigmatic 48.16, which suggests the declaring of words. This implication is more overt in 59.21, and 61.1 picks up the idea. Varying views of the historical origin of 11.1-9; 42.1-4; 48.16; 59.21; and 61.1 will change the picture of the relationship between these passages, but not affect the fact

Chapters 40–66, p. 563; also 'Isaiah 60–62: The Glory of the Lord', *Calvin Theological Journal* 40 (2005), pp. 95-103 (100); Fitzgerald, 'A Rhetorical Analysis of Isaiah 56–66', pp. 226-29.

[60] Whybray, *Isaiah 40–66*, p. 135.

[61] On the interpretation of the passages referred to, see Goldingay and Payne, *Isaiah 40–55*; Goldingay, *The Message of Isaiah 40–55*.

that there is a move from Yhwh's breath as suggesting an event to Yhwh's breath as suggesting words.

The title 'my Lord Yhwh' also came in the prophetic testimony in 48.16 and then four times in the more extensive such testimony in 50.4-9. There are two explanations of the anomalous form *ʾădōnāy*. It may be construed as plural and understood by analogy with a word such as *ʾĕlōhîm* as an honorific plural, a plural of majesty; the suffixed form will then denote 'my Lord' or 'my supreme Lord'. But Ugaritic had a similar sufformative to the *-āy* on this word with an emphatic or intensifying sense; the sufformative then functions to intensify the meaning of the word itself and its meaning might be compared with that of English '*the* Lord'.[62] The Versions translate simply 'the Lord'. I have assumed that in this context the former connotation might apply.

The characteristic heightening in the second colon of the line attributes the presence of Yhwh's breath or spirit to Yhwh's anointing. The prophetic claim to anointing and the link between Yhwh's spirit and anointing is new, though it again takes up notes from Isaiah 40–55. Outside Isaiah, smearing someone with oil is a physical rite applied to priests and kings, as well as to objects. While the reference to anointing could make one think of a priest,[63] there is no specific indication that the speaker is a priest, and the idea stands in some tension with v. 6a.[64] The description of the speaker's role is not priestly except in the sense that it is pastoral, and Isaiah 56–66 does not otherwise emphasize the role of a priest. Anointing is a practice known among other Middle Eastern cultures and elsewhere, signifying the designation of a person or object for a task and a position, and the giving over of the person or object to God and to God's service. It thus also signifies the attributing of special status to them. Whereas anointing with the Holy Spirit came to be a significant Christian metaphor, the Old Testament does not speak of anointing with Yhwh's spirit. Yhwh's spirit does come on David after Samuel anoints him (1 Sam 16.12-13) and these two events might seem to belong naturally together insofar as a king is dedicated to Yhwh and equipped by Yhwh's spirit. David's 'Last Words' juxtapose his claim that those words are his utterance, his being Yhwh's anointed, Yhwh's spirit having spoken through him, and his commitment to being *ṣaddîq* (2 Sam 23.1-2). Only here is the rite of anointing and the coming of Yhwh's spirit brought into association.

Likewise there is little link elsewhere between anointing and the role of a prophet.[65] The exception that proves the rule is Yhwh's commissioning

[62] See Otto Eissfeldt, *TWAT*, I, pp. 66-76 (ET *TDOT*, I, pp. 62-70).

[63] So Pierre Grelot, 'Sur Isaïe lxi', *RB* 97 (1990), pp. 414-31; cf. Bernard Gosse, 'Sur l'identité du personnage d'*Isaïe* 61,1', *Transeuphratène* 5 (1992), pp. 46-48.

[64] Cf. J. Coppens's comments, 'L'oint d'Is., lxi, 2 [sic] et les prêtres d'Is., lxi, 6', *ETL* 53 (1977), pp. 186-87.

[65] But Paul (*Isaiah 40–66*, p. 539 [not in the Hebrew edition]) notes that some Qumran documents make this link.

Elijah to anoint Elisha (1 Kgs 19.16). The narrative does not record the fulfilment of this commission, which may indicate that Yhwh speaks metaphorically of Elijah's passing on his role to Elisha, on whom *Elijah's* spirit does 'settle' (the same verb as in Isa 11.2). If Elijah was to fulfil the literal commission, Elisha is the rare instance of someone who fulfils something like a prophetic office and is appointed as Elijah's successor in such an office. This parallel may put us on the track of an important aspect of the significance of the reference to Yhwh's spirit here. It parallels the development within Christian faith whereby the extraordinary endowment of the Holy Spirit is believed to continue in the expectation that the Holy Spirit comes on someone through the laying on of the bishop's hands at confirmation or at ordination. Linking the image of anointing with Yhwh's spirit perhaps encourages the assumption that the prophet's claim to being under the influence of Yhwh's spirit implies some routinization of that idea.[66]

The reference here to a prophet's metaphorical anointing takes up the use of related nouns in 45.1; 52.14. If Cyrus was literally anointed in Persia, he was also designated metaphorically 'my anointed one' by Yhwh. The prophet is claiming a role or position or vocation analogous to that attributed to Cyrus.[67] Likewise Yhwh's humiliated servant was destined to have his appearance 'anointed beyond that of anyone'.[68] Such anointing would be a sign of exaltation to special status. Tg's translation of this opening line continues, 'because Yhwh has elevated me'. Tg often uses 'elevate' (*r^ebāʾ* pael) to imply consecration by anointing.[69] So the prophet is indeed claiming Yhwh's designation to a special position or role.[70]

61.1bβγ He sent me to bring news to the afflicted,// to bind up people who are broken in spirit;

'The question is not, who is the speaker?' but rather 'what does it mean to be so endowed and commissioned?'[71] Two further bicola comprising v. 1bβγδε (both 3-2) are internally parallel and parallel to each other. In each, the opening verb applies to both cola (hence each second colon is shorter than each first colon), though it is also the case that the opening verb in v. 1bδε ('to proclaim') is subordinate to the opening finite verb in

[66] Cf. Blenkinsopp, *Isaiah 56–66*, p. 222.

[67] Cf. Williamson, *Variations on a Theme*, pp. 176-78.

[68] On the interpretation of 52.14, see Goldingay and Payne, *Isaiah 40–55*; Goldingay, *The Message of Isaiah 40–55*.

[69] See *DTT*.

[70] On the passage's relationship with Cyrus and Yhwh's servant, see Jacob Stromberg, 'An Inner-Isaianic Reading of Isaiah 61:1-3', in Firth and Williamson (eds.), *Interpreting Isaiah*, pp. 261-72 (262-67).

[71] Miscall, *Isaiah*, p. 138.

v. 1bβγ ('he sent me') and thus parallel to the two infinitives that follow in v. 1bβγ. Further, in substance the proclaiming in v. 1bδε is parallel to the bringing of news in v. 1bβγ and indicates the content of the news the messenger brings. Indeed, through vv. 1b-3a the prophet is not giving a list of discrete acts but describing one prophetic-pastoral ministry in a number of different ways.

'He sent me' is taken up from 48.16, where it was part of a brief prophetic testimony that also referred to Yhwh's breath and used the designation 'my Lord Yhwh'. It follows jerkily on the first line insofar as there was a kingly motif there in the reference to anointing, in that 'sending' suggests not a king but someone sent by a king; it belongs to the model of the prophet as an aide whom the king sends with a commission and with authority to announce and thus implement a decision. Jeremiah 26.12-15 instances a prophet's claim to be 'sent to...' followed by infinitives, as here.[72] In the Old Testament, however, kings do not send such aides with *news*; kings are the recipients of news rather than their sources (e.g. 2 Sam 18.19-20). The use of the verb 'bring news' derives from its appearance in Isaiah 40.9; 41.27; 52.7; 60.6. As was the case there, the prophet speaks in terms of 'news' yet refers to an event that has not yet happened. There, Cyrus might be on his way, but he had not taken Babylon and Yhwh had not begun to reign or returned to Jerusalem. But a contrast with the earlier use of the verb is that it exemplifies the way this prophet's proclamation does not speak of concrete events like Isaiah 40–55. The earlier passages that use the verb relate to an event (the fall of Babylon) of which news would indeed be transmitted around the empire. This prophet has no such event to latch onto. Isaiah 40.9 and 52.7 spoke of other people as the bringers of good news, though 41.27 likely designates the prophet as the news-bringer.[73] Yet the implication is not that the present prophecy has a different view of prophecy itself.[74] Whether or not the prophetic voice that speaks in Isaiah 40–55 sees itself as bringing news to the afflicted, binding up the broken, or undertaking the task that the rest of vv. 1-3 will go on to describe, it was what that voice was doing. Thus the prophet's proclamation constitutes an 'announcement...which also gives rise to that which is proclaimed'; it has an event-character.[75]

The recipients of the news are the *ʿănāwîm*, the afflicted, weak, or powerless. Most LXX manuscripts have πτωχοῖς, 'poor', but the term is not essentially an economic one; the poor will be weak and the weak may be poor, but the word itself refers to people's relationship to power and to power structures. An alternative LXX reading is ταπεινοῖς, 'lowly',

[72] Cf. Koenen, *Ethik und Eschatologie im Tritojesajabuch*, p. 104.

[73] See Goldingay, *The Message of Isaiah 40–55*, p. 146.

[74] Contrast Duhm's comments on the prophet changing the role of prophet for that of evangelist (*Jesaia*, p. 413).

[75] Josef Scharbert, *Heilsmittler im Alten Testament und im alten Orient* (Freiburg: Herder, 1964), p. 202; cf. O. Schilling, *TWAT*, I, p. 849 (ET *TDOT*, II, p. 316).

which can denote either a status or an inner attitude, while Vg has *mansuetis* 'meek'. Being afflicted and weak may make one meek (or it may not), but there is little evidence that the word denotes an attitude rather than a position in relation to the powerful. The word *ʿānāw* did not occur in Isaiah 40–55, but *ʿānî* (essentially a synonym) came in 41.17; 49.13; 51.21; 54.11, then in 58.7. In chapters 40–55 it referred to the community as a whole, in 58.7 to afflicted groups within the community. Succeeding verses here will suggest that the usage follows that in chapters 40–55 and coheres with this section's links with chapter 60.[76] The afflicted are the community as a whole, notwithstanding the possibility that there were a few powerful and oppressive people among them. The afflicted appear three times in Psalm 72 as the beneficiaries of the ministry the king is expected to exercise, and while the use of the verb 'bring news' is still innovative, in substance one can see how the psalm illuminates this colon. It is the king's responsibility to act on behalf of the afflicted, and if the king sends aides to announce action the king intends to take, they will indeed come as bearers of good news. The divine King likewise accepts the obligation to take action on behalf of the afflicted and sends this aide to announce the action. It is not based on their piety but on their need. The words about bringing good news to the afflicted recur in 4Q521, which has been variously described as a 'messianic apocalypse' or an 'eschatological psalm'; here, strikingly, it is God who brings the good news, though presumably it is assumed that God does so via 'his anointed' who also features in the text.[77]

The description of those to whom the good news comes contains many 'resonances and repetitions' of the description of the afflicted *within* the community in Isaiah 58. It would be an oversimplification to infer that 'eliminating the first, internal oppression is a condition of the second, external oppression ceasing'.[78] Rather the resonances and repetitions are an indication that the community in general is afflicted but that there are within it people who contribute to its oppression rather than sharing it, people with power and resources who live better than the vast majority and live off them.

By bringing news to the afflicted the prophet will bind up people who are broken in spirit. More literally their heart is broken, but talk of a broken heart in English gives a misleading impression. As usual *lēb* suggests not merely the emotions but the inner person as it engages in

[76] Against (e.g.) Volz, *Jesaja II*, p. 257; Ulrich Berges, 'Die Armen im Buch Jesaja', *Biblica* 80 (1999), pp. 153-77 (170-71).

[77] See John J. Collins, 'A Herald of Good Tidings', in Craig A. Evans and Shemaryahu Talmon (eds.), *The Quest for Context and Meaning* (Leiden: Brill, 1997), pp. 225-40. Christopher M. Tuckett, 'Scripture and Q', in Tuckett (ed.), *The Scriptures in the Gospels* (Leuven: Peeters, 1997), pp. 3-26, also discusses the influence of Isaiah 61 on 4Q521, which he calls 'On Resurrection' in light of its distinctive reference to raising people from the dead.

[78] Alonso Schökel and Sicre Diaz, *Profetas I*, p. 369.

thinking things through, forming attitudes, and making decisions. What has happened to the community has broken its morale and will. Here the verb for binding it up (*ḥābaš*) is one that does not occur in Isaiah 40–55 but does come in 30.26, which speaks of Yhwh binding up the people's brokenness (*šeber*), though there the noun (which also comes in 51.19; 59.7; 60.18) refers to a material and physical brokenness and destruction (compare the literal use of the verb in 1.6; 3.7). Ezekiel 34.4, 16 also speaks of binding up the broken. While the phrase that might be literally translated 'breaking of heart' does come in Psalm 34.19 [18] (cf. 51.19 [17]), the closest link with this colon comes in Psalm 147.3, which speaks of 'the one who heals those whose spirit is breaking, and binds up their hurts'.

61.1δε To proclaim release to captives,// the opening of eyes to prisoners.

The previous line did not specify the nature of the good news it promised; its second colon indicated what would be the effect of the event that the news related, but jumped over what it was. So it left us asking, 'What is this news about, then?' Here the answer comes, though it is expressed in metaphors. Indeed, one might say that it again indicates only the effect of the events, not their nature. 'Proclaim' is another word from Isaiah 40–55. It is the commission in 40.2, repeated (implicitly to a prophet) in 40.6. On the other hand, 'release' (*derôr*) comes only in Leviticus 25.10 [H] in connection with the release associated with the jubilee, in Jeremiah 34.8-17 in connection with Zedekiah's abortive proclamation of a seventh-year release of indentured servants, and in Ezekiel 46.17 in an incidental reference to the year of release. Both Leviticus and Jeremiah speak of 'proclaiming' this release. Its beneficiaries are not people in prison but people in servitude. Yet here they are not individuals in debt-servitude but a community in servitude to an imperial power. The practice of release provides a metaphor for the release of captives, though captivity, too, is here a metaphor.[79] The people to whom the proclamation relates are not captives in exile but people in Jerusalem whose lot does not seem much better than that of people in exile and who can hardly complain about that fact because they are not behaving any better than the people who were taken into exile. The image also recalls, in the broader Middle Eastern background, the idea of a royal proclamation of release, which took place on a one-off basis from time to time, notably on a king's accession.[80] It is such a one-off release that the divine King's aide

[79] Bradley C. Gregory ('The Postexilic Exile in Third Isaiah: Isaiah 61:1-3 in Light of Second Temple Hermeneutics', *JBL* 126 [2007], pp. 475-96 [485-88]) speaks in terms of typology rather than metaphor; cf. Barth, *Die kirchliche Dogmatik* III/2, p. 548 (ET p. 456).

[80] See Moshe Weinfeld, *Social Justice in Ancient Israel and in the Ancient Near East* (Jerusalem: Magnes; Minneapolis: Fortress, 1995), pp. 7-15.

proclaims. Its being a metaphor does not imply it is not a reality affecting needy people's lives in a practical way,[81] though it is an over-simplification to suggest that 'the prophecy...formulated the salvation which it promised predominantly as economic liberation'.[82]

Isaiah 40–55 provides the precedent for the way the parallel colon speaks of the opening of eyes and the freeing of the prisoner (*ʾassîr*, 42.7), and for the way it speaks of a proclamation to prisoners (*ʾăsûrîm* as here, 49.9). One might expect the prophet to promise either freedom for prisoners (so Sym) or the opening of eyes for the blind (so LXX); MT may seem to mix metaphors. This impression issues in part from the conflating of expressions that earlier came in parallel cola, 'to open blind eyes, to bring out prisoner from dungeon'. Both passages presuppose that leaving the darkness of prison for the light of freedom is like having one's eyes opened. Here Tg makes the point with its paraphrase '[proclaim] to prisoners, "Expose yourself to the light"'. At 42.7 it is likely that the infinitives should be understood as gerunds, of which the equivalent here would be 'by proclaiming'. That construction could then continue into v. 2a, but it would break down in v. 2b, and more likely the whole sequence should be understood as infinitives dependent on 'sent me'.

61.2a To proclaim a year of acceptance by Yhwh,// a day of redress by our God;

The infinitives thus continue in a further parallel line in which the verb applies to both cola; MT keeps a 3-3 rhythm by joining 'a year of acceptance' by means of a maqqeph. The line thus works abcb′c′. Proclaiming 'a year of acceptance' recalls 49.8, where Yhwh speaks of 'a time of acceptance', an acceptance expressed in the freeing of prisoners as here. In other words this is the moment when Yhwh accepts the people again instead of rejecting them. Once again the words presuppose that the situation on the eve of Babylon's fall has not changed much; it still seems as if Yhwh is rejecting the people. The prophet promises that this situation is going to change. Replacing 'time' by 'year' furthers the association with the 'year of jubilee' in Leviticus 25 or the year of release in Jeremiah 34 and thus tightens the metaphorical language of the lines. The year of release is a year of acceptance: the resonances of 'acceptance'

[81] Cf. the emphasis on the literal and practical significance of the reference in Walther Zimmerli, 'Das "Gnadenjahr des Herrn"', in Arnulf Kuschke and Ernst Kutsch (eds.), *Archäologie und Altes Testament* (K. Galling Festschrift; Tübingen: Mohr, 1970), pp. 321-32, reprinted in Zimmerli, *Studien zur alttestamentliche Theologie und Prophetie* (Munich: Kaiser, 1974), pp. 222-34; also Willy Schottroff, 'Das Jahr der Gnade Jahwes', in Luise Schottroff and Willy Schottroff (eds.), *Wer ist unser Gott?* (Munich: Kaiser, 1986), pp. 122-36; Henrique Pinto, 'Isaiah 61:1-2a in Liberation Theology', *African Christian Studies* 5/2 (1989), pp. 11-42.

[82] So Albertz, *Religionsgeschichte Israels in alttestamentlicher Zeit*, II, p. 487 (ET p. 457).

are increased by the appearance of the verb 'accept' (*rāṣâ*) in Isaiah 42.1 and perhaps by the appearance of the homonym meaning 'pay for' in 40.1. Yhwh has accepted the people and accepted that their suffering is enough. Yet *rāṣôn* has more active implications than 'acceptance' might imply. It suggests 'goodwill, favour';[83] 'the time of acceptance/favour/goodwill' stands in parallelism with 'the day of deliverance' in 49.8.[84] It is 'the year of restoration'.[85] While the prophet may attach the preposition *l*- to 'Yhwh' and 'our God' simply to avoid too long a construct chain, it does generate a slightly different meaning. It is a year or day *for* Yhwh to act or a year or day for the implementing of acceptance and redress *by* Yhwh.

It will thus not merely be 'a day of deliverance'; 'deliverance' in 49.8 becomes 'redress' here. The phrase 'day of redress' also comes in 34.8; 63.4; Jeremiah 46.10 ('redress' alone in Isa 35.4; 59.17). It recalls the expression 'day of Yhwh'. Traditionally people would expect Yhwh's day to be an occasion when Yhwh will exact redress of their enemies; in effect that expectation is the one Amos 5.18-20 reverses. This prophecy reverses the expectation again, reaffirming the traditional assumption about the day, like 60.1. It will be 'the day of Gog and Magog, when God will bring redress on them'.[86] The promise presupposes the logic that the freedom of the people depends on the putting down of their overlords, but its actual talk of 'redress' (*nāqām*) rather than merely putting down implies Yhwh's recognition that punishment is appropriate in light of the overlords' wrongdoing. On the other hand, perhaps it is significant that the prophet speaks of a *year* of acceptance and only a *day* of redress.[87] It is doubtful if we should see this as 'no particular event… but a new era',[88] though it does introduce a new era.

When Jesus quotes vv. 1-2 in Luke 4.18-19, he stops after v. 2aα, and exegetes have understood him to be deliberately distinguishing the year of acceptance from the day of redress;[89] this understanding coheres with modern dislike for the idea of redress.[90] But his quotation may simply involve his abbreviating of the prophet's parallelism (as he does in

[83] BDB.

[84] Cf. Delitzsch, *Jesaia*, p. 619 (ET II, p. 427).

[85] David Qimchi, 'ישעיה'.

[86] David Qimchi, 'ישעיה'.

[87] So Hitzig, *Jesaja*, p. 613.

[88] So Westermann, *Jesaja Kapitel 40–66*, p. 292 (ET p. 367).

[89] See, e.g., Peter Mallen, *The Reading and Transformation of Isaiah in Luke–Acts*. (London: T&T Clark International, 2008), p. 77.

[90] Whitehouse (*Isaiah xl–lxvi*, p. 290) comments that it 'stands in contrast with the spirit of the 'Servant-songs'. Zillesen simply emends to some form of *nḥm* 'comfort' ('"Tritojesaja" und Deuterojesaja', p. 270), Hugo Gressmann to *nōʿam* 'delight' (*Der Messias* [Göttingen: Vandenhoeck & Ruprecht, 1929], p. 205), Steck (*Studien zu Tritojesaja*, p. 117) to *yᵉšûʿâ* 'deliverance', as in 49.8. Hanson (*The Dawn of Apocalyptic*, p. 52) translates 'deliverance'. A. Joseph Everson's comments in 'Isaiah 61:1-6', *Interpretation* 32 (1978), pp. 69-73 (71), are more nuanced.

v. 2aα), in which the year becomes a day, Yhwh becomes 'our God', and acceptance becomes redress. In 11QMelchizedek, this passage fulfils an important role in providing scriptural warrant for expecting God's final implementing of deliverance and judgment on Belial and for the coming of the Messiah; 4Q521 takes up the passage in a comparable way.[91] A subsequent Christian exegete such as Theodoret of Cyrrhus, too, comments on the Lord's not only promising deliverance but warning of just judgment.[92]

61.2b To comfort all the mourners,// 3 to provide for the people who mourn Zion// —to give them finery instead of ash,
Festive oil instead of mourning,// a praise garment instead of a flickering spirit.

There is some jerkiness about vv. 2b-3a. Two successive cola refer to mourning; the verb in v. 3aα has no object; v. 3aβ begins resumptively with a further infinitive.[93] Verse 3aα could be omitted without disturbing the lines; the omission would turn vv. 2b-3a into two satisfactory bicola, though each second colon would be rather long (4-5). Possibly two versions of the line have been conflated. I have treated the present text of vv. 2b-3aαβ as one line in which the second colon parallels the first and begins to explain how the prophet is called to implement the comforting and also gives specificity to what people are mourning. The third colon is then parallel to the second in also beginning to explain how the prophet is called to implement the comforting. The further effect of the tricolon is to underline the wonder of the exchange it speaks of; v. 3aγδ will be another long line that will achieve the same effect in a different way.

[91] See, e.g., Merrill P. Miller, 'The Function of Isa 61 1-2 in 11Q Melchizedek', *JBL* 88 (1969), pp. 467-69; George J. Brooke, *Exegesis at Qumran* (Sheffield: JSOT, 1985), pp. 319-23; Bergsma, *The Jubilee from Leviticus to Qumran* (see above), pp. 277-91; Craig A. Evans, 'From Gospel to Gospel: The Function of Isaiah in the New Testament', in Broyles and Evans (eds.), *Writing and Reading the Scroll of Isaiah*, II, pp. 651-91 (659-62).

[92] *Commentaire sur Isaïe* 177b-78a (III, pp. 268-69). Cf. Peter Chrysologus's sermon 'De arbore ficulnea abscidenda', in *Collectio Sermonum* (Turnhout: Brepols, 1981), II, pp. 657-63 (661; ET 'On the Fig Tree to Be Chopped Down', in *Selected Sermons* [Washington: Catholic University of America, 2005], III, pp. 137-41 (141).

[93] LXX and Syr omit it, likely to simplify the redundancy. As another way of smoothing the unevenness, as object of the verb in v. 3aα Houbigant (*Notae criticae in universos Veteris Testamenti libros*, II, p. 408) adds *śāśôn* (joy, festivity), Perles (*Analekten zur Textkritik des Alten Testaments*, p. 91) and Elliger (*Die Einheit des Tritojesaja*, p. 24) *šālôm*, Morgenstern ('Isaiah 61' [see above], p. 112) *niḥumîm*. Volz (*Jesaja II*, p. 254) rather emends the verb *śûm* itself to *śammēaḥ* 'make [people who mourn Zion] rejoice', Kissane (*Isaiah* 2.273) to *šallēm* 'make whole', Ehrlich (*Randglossen*, IV, p. 217) to *šûb* 'return', Budde ('Jesaia', p. 706) to *māśôś* 'rejoicing'.

Comfort is another expression taken up from Isaiah 40–55. The chapters indeed began (40.1) with Yhwh's commissioning comfort for Jerusalem. There the verb 'comfort' (*nāḥam* piel) denoted words that bring comfort; it can also denote action that comforts (e.g. 49.13; 51.3; 52.9). In the present context, initially it might be unclear which form of comfort the prophet describes, but if so, the rest of these two lines makes clear that the reference is to words or signs of comfort. 'Mourners' is a natural object for 'comfort'; the root does not appear in Isaiah 40–55, though it is a recurrent feature of Isaiah 56–66 (three times in these two lines, also 57.18; 60.20; 66.10). In the middle colon, EVV take the genitive as partitive and referring to the mourners in Zion. But the expression is commonly used as an objective genitive (Gen 27.41; Deut 34.8; Jer 6.26; Amos 8.10) and this makes sense here. The prophet does not imply that only some people mourn Zion; the community as a whole does so.[94] This would again not exclude some of them being people with power and resources who were quite comfortable. Lamentations gives us an idea of what this mourning would look like (and cf. Isa 58.1-12).

In v. 3aα comfort is expressed by providing something. The verb *śîm* is vaguer than this translation implies; it can mean put, place, set, or make, and in isolation one could not guess what the action is or what kind of object the verb refers to. In the manner of parallelism, the third colon makes it possible to narrow the answer to that question; *śîm* and *nātan*, 'give', come in parallelism elsewhere (e.g. Josh 7.19; Ezek 20.28).[95] The objects of the providing and the giving are the objects that appear in the rest of v. 3a, each of which replaces something the mourners have at present. This providing and giving are again something the prophet effects by speaking; that is how a prophet acts. The prophecy promises action and events such as the chapter will go on to describe, but the prophet does not personally do anything to bring them about. The first exchange involves a paronomasia: *ʾēper* will be replaced by *pᵉʾēr*. The exchange of letters suggests the exchange of that to which they refer. The dominant significance of Old Testament references to ash is to suggest mourning, in connection with loss or humiliation or penitence; people rub ash on their head as an indication of such grief. Historically, *pĕʾēr* is a borrowing from Egyptian.[96] It refers to splendid headgear such as a priest's turban or a woman's millinery—or a groom's celebratory headwear (v. 10). But Judahites would likely associate it with the Hebrew root *pāʾar* and take it to imply something beautiful or splendid, which would fittingly replace the unsightly symbol of humiliation.

[94] Koole, *Jesaja III*, p. 269 (ET p. 276) thinks it is possible to hold both meanings.

[95] For this meaning of *śîm* earlier, see also the seventh-century silver plaque with a version of the 'Aaronic blessing' from Ketef Hinnom, transcribed as item 4.302 in G. I. Davies (ed.), *Ancient Hebrew Inscriptions* (Cambridge: Cambridge University Press, 1991), I, pp. 72-73 (GID).

[96] See *HALOT*.

The second line in v. 3a details two further substitutions. The sequence thus suggests a reversing of the negative substitutions in 3.24.[97] Both the verbs in v. 3aαβ govern both these parallel objects, though this does not stop the two cola being rather long (4-5); indeed, the three 'instead of' phrases are of increasing length, 3 stresses, then 4, then 5.[98] The length of the cola again underlines the wonder of the exchange the passage speaks of. In each case the thing being taken away is the reality the ash symbolizes. First there is the mourning; a third form from the root *ʾābal* appears. Then, whereas ash is an outward imposition, mourning is both an outward expression of loss and an inner sense of it, while conversely the final term 'a flickering spirit' suggests both the effect of that loss on the inner person and the way that sense of loss finds outward expression—because a person's spirit is their inner dynamism that finds such outward expression. The significance of 'a flickering spirit' is not so different from that of the breaking of the spirit (v. 1), but at this point the prophet returns to the language of Isaiah 40–55. Isaiah 42.3-4 spoke of Yhwh's servant as one who would not snuff a flickering wick and affirmed that this servant would not himself flicker until he had fulfilled his task. The irony was that whereas Jacob-Israel had the position of Yhwh's servant and thus the vocation to fulfil the role there described, Jacob-Israel was itself a flickering wick—or (as this verse now puts it) one whose spirit is flickering (here the word 'spirit' translates *rûaḥ*). In turn, 54.6 spoke of Zion as like a woman abandoned and grieved in spirit (cf. also 57.15). Here the prophet promises restoration to the one who is flickering in spirit.

The exchange the prophet promises is festive oil and a praise garment. The words again make clear that they do not refer to a mere inward transformation. Humanity and its spirituality is outward, bodily, and social, not merely inward, and Yhwh is the God of the outward, bodily, and social. 'Festive oil' (more literally, 'joyful oil') is the make-up that a man or woman puts on as an outward expression of rejoicing (cf. Ps 104.15). The phrase recurs in Psalm 45.8 [7] with reference to a bridegroom; again compare v. 10 here. It makes for a particular contrast with ash; ash is what people smear themselves with as an expression of mourning that other people can see, while oil is what people smear themselves with as an expression of joy that other people can see. In the context of this promise, a praise garment is likewise clothing that people can see and comment favourably on ('that's a fine suit'); compare the praise[worthy] city of Jeremiah 40.25. Yet the broader context in Isaiah would make it

97 Cf. Jüngling, '"Die Eichen der Gerechtigkeit"' (see above), pp. 210-13.

98 Cf. Koole, *Jesaja III*, p. 270 (ET p. 276). Elliger (*Die Einheit des Tritojesaja*, p. 24) reverses 'mourning' and 'garment' ('festive oil instead of a mourning garment, praise instead of a flickering spirit') and Hanson (*The Dawn of Apocalyptic*, pp. 52-53, 57) notes that the cola then conform better to the prosodic theory he advocates; but the change destroys MT's own pattern.

impossible for readers to avoid thinking of the praise of God, the significance of the word in 42.8, 10, 12; 43.21; 48.9; 60.6. The transformation of the people will surely lead to the praise of Yhwh. Verses 10-11 will make this connection as they speak further of joy, clothing, a garland, and praise.

61.3b So they will be called the oaks of faithfulness,// the plantation of Yhwh, to manifest glory.

As the promise expressed in the testimony continues, the imagery changes abruptly; so does the construction. It is a common idiom for a string of infinitives to give way to finite verbs without there being a change in the meaning[99] but here the changes signify that the line indicates the result or purpose of what has preceded. Literally, the 4-3 line begins 'so it will be called to them'. The two descriptions 'oaks of faithfulness' and 'plantation of Yhwh' are then parallel. We might see the verb at the end as balancing the one at the beginning and see the 4-3 line as working roughly abcb'c'a'. The pual verb *qōrāʾ* recurs from 48.8, with which it makes a nice contrast. Who are the people who will do the calling? The recurrence in 62.2 may provide the answer; the name will be bestowed by Yhwh, but it will be echoed and affirmed by the nations (cf. also 58.12).

There are several homonyms *ʾayil* with a masculine plural construct *ʾēlê* or *ʾêlê*; it is doubtful whether we can infer from the spelling which meaning a manuscript attaches to the word. One or other of the homonyms came in 57.5 (where see the comment). In 60.7 the word certainly meant 'rams', and here Aq, Sym, Th, Vg, Tg take it to be this word in its metaphorical sense 'strong ones' (LXX 'generations' may reflect uncertainty or unease about the word).[100] Reading the word in light of what immediately precedes might support that understanding, but the parallelism of this line itself implies the connotation 'oaks'; possibly the line plays with the two meanings (as may be the case at 57.5). In what sense are they oaks 'of faithfulness'? In 58.2, 8 'faithfulness' referred to the divine commitment to doing right by the community, and this is also the dominant if not exclusive use of the word in Isaiah 40–55. The parallelism supports it here, and it follows well on vv. 1-3a. The people will become strong as oaks as a result of the work of divine faithfulness that vv. 1-3a have been promising. But in 59.8 *ṣedeq* referred to a human commitment to doing right by one's community, and in 60.21 the related term 'faithful ones' likely both signified the people's status and pointed in the direction of their commitment; this might also be so here. The term might thus be understood 'both as gift and obligation'.[101]

[99] Cf. König, *Jesaja*, p. 510.
[100] See Baer, *When We All Go Home*, pp. 195-96.
[101] Mark Gignilliat, 'Oaks of Righteousness for His Glory', *ZAW* 123 (2011), pp. 391-405 (404).

Their being the plantation of Yhwh reexpresses the point; *maṭṭāʿ* is taken up from 60.21, though there it referred to the act of planting rather than its result.[102] The infinitive also recurs from 60.21[103] and states the object of the actions the line refers to. As in 60.21, the glory may be both Yhwh's and the community's.

61.4 They will build up the lasting ruins,// raise up the desolations of the ancestors,
Renew ruined cities,// desolations of many generations.

'Here begin the "good tidings".'[104] Two neat 3-3 lines describe the act of restoration in more down-to-earth terms. They are both internally parallel and parallel to one another. Verse 4a works abcb′c′a′; in v. 4b the verb applies to both cola, so it works abcb′c′. The two lines suggest something of what lies behind the demoralized spirit of the community, presupposed by vv. 1-3. Jerusalem and other Judahite cities have been ruined and desolated; the point is underlined by the repetition of the words for ruin and desolation in both lines. The problem is not merely the devastation in itself but the fact that the cities have been in this state for what seems like forever. In the last decades of the sixth century, virtually no one would be able to remember them in their intact state, and in the next century no one would be able to.

Verse 4aα repeats 58.12aα, at least in the order that we have these chapters, except for the omission of 'from you' for which there would be no antecedent here).[105] 'Raise up' also occurred in 58.12 (except that there the verb was second person singular), as did 'many generations' (literally, 'a generation and a generation'). Regular syntax would make one assume that the 'they' of v. 4 are the 'they' of v. 3b, and the use of a *w*-consecutive makes it the more natural to make this assumption. The mourners will have become so revitalized that they will be able to undertake the monumental work of rebuilding the cities of Judah that have lain devastated since the Babylonian invasion. On the other hand, 60.10 used the same verb form in declaring that foreigners would build the city's walls, and in Isaiah 61 the following lines also make it natural to think that foreigners will do this work. One could understand the syntax in v. 4 to allow this inference; the third-person plural verbs then become impersonal. Isaiah 45.13 spoke of Cyrus building the city (cf. 44.26, 28), which did not mean he would do his own labouring, and the verse might imply that the Judahites will get the work done, without implying that they personally undertake it.

[102] Cf. BDB.
[103] See the comment.
[104] Muilenburg, 'The Book of Isaiah: Chapters 40–66', p. 712.
[105] But Lowth (*Isaiah*, p. 385) adds it.

Isaiah 40–55 also spoke of Yhwh raising up ruins (44.26; cf. 51.3; 52.9), though it indeed goes on to indicate that Cyrus will be the means of doing so. Jeremiah 25.9 had warned that the land would become lasting ruins, and v. 4 (like 58.12) picks up this formulation and declares its reversal, in keeping with other promises in Jeremiah. Isaiah 40–55 likewise speaks of Yhwh restoring Jerusalem's 'desolations' (49.19) and it is fond of the word *riʾšōnôt*, 'former things', which can at least sometimes be associated with the events of the fall of Jerusalem (e.g. 41.22; 42.9; 43.9, 18; 46.9; 48.3). Further, Isaiah 40–55 sometimes sets the 'former things' over against 'new things' (42.9; 43.18-19; 48.3-6), which fits the present reference to 'renewing' ruined cities; 'cities' in the plural were the object of restoration in 44.26; 54.3. The masculine plural *riʾšōnîm* does not come in Isaiah 40–55. Here as in Leviticus 26.45 and Deuteronomy 19.14 it refers to earlier generations, and these will be specifically the 'former generation' that saw the desolation happen, the generation of the Babylonian conquest.

61.5 Strangers will stand and pasture your flocks,// foreigners will be your farm labourers and your vinedressers,
6a While you yourselves are called 'Yhwh's priests',// termed 'ministers of our God'.

Two sonorous 4-4 lines (they have even been seen as the highpoint of the chapter[106]) describe the ongoing situation in the community after the country's rebuilding. In v. 5, the 'strangers' are balanced by the 'foreigners'; the double verbal expression 'stand and pasture your flocks' is then balanced by the double nominal expression '[will be] your farm labourers and your vinedressers'. 'Standing' is the posture of respect and the posture of a servant, and the activities are those that the servants of a big landowner might undertake. The particular double expression 'stand and pasture' recurs in Micah 5.3 [4] and the significance of the verb here may derive from its being a description of a shepherd's posture as he sees that his flock get fed.[107] But in PBH the expression suggests more generally that a person is standing ready to perform a set task.[108] In the Prophets 'strangers' is inclined to suggest enemies, destroyers, aggressors, or occupying powers,[109] and these strangers may be the people who were responsible for the devastation presupposed by v. 4 (cf. Isa 1.7; Obad 11; Lam 5.2); 'foreigners' can appear in the same connection (cf. the similar parallelism in Obad 11; Lam 5.2). So here there is a reversing of their action; 60.10 spoke of foreigners being the people who would build

[106] So Zapff, *Jesaja 56–66*, pp. 389, 393.
[107] Cf. Oswalt, *Isaiah Chapters 40–66*, p. 568.
[108] Cf. Paul, ישעיה פרקים מ-סו, II, p. 493 [ET p. 543].
[109] So L. A. Snijders, *TWAT*, II, p. 559 (ET *TDOT*, IV, p. 54).

Jerusalem's walls. The foreigners might additionally or alternatively be the other client nations around Judah,[110] people whom Ezra–Nehemiah describes as often acting against Judah. Yet again, 'strangers' also appear frequently in the Old Testament as resident aliens who are close to being full members of Israel, and in Isaiah 56.1-8 foreigners were assured that they had such a position. Being a farm labourer or vinedresser does not imply slavery or even servitude. If anything it implies the opposite. Service associated with Judah and its service of Yhwh means freedom from servitude to the empire; it can no longer claim them.[111] Nor does it exclude making the offerings and prayers in the sanctuary of which 56.1-8 speaks. The ending of foreign domination over Israel does not mean its replacement by Israelite domination over foreigners.[112] So there is some ambiguity about what is said about the role of strangers and foreigners here; it can be read more positively or more restrictively. The following lines will point to some resolving of the ambiguity.

First, v. 6a both clarifies and reshapes the question in a neatly parallel line, working abcdb′c′d′a. 'You yourselves' at the beginning is balanced by 'of you' at the end. 'Yhwh's priests' is balanced by 'ministers of our God'. 'Are called' is balanced by 'termed' (more literally 'it is said of you'). The purpose of the strangers/foreigners' fulfilment of the role described in v. 5 is to enable Israel to fulfil the role described in v. 6a. The model is that of the Levites in relation to Israel; the other clans take responsibility for farming the land and thereby free the Levites to serve in the sanctuary. Here the whole community takes the priestly role, in keeping with Exodus 19.6 (D).[113] As the separating of Levi for its task implied no humiliation of the other clans, so the attributing of roles in accordance with vv. 5-6a implies no downgrading of the strangers/foreigners. But 56.1-8 has attributed a 'ministerial' role to foreigners and Isaiah 66 will be more positive in its description of their role. On the usual assumption that this chapter is part of the earliest core of Isaiah 56–66, then, 56.1-8 might be seen as an anticipatory modification of the expectation expressed here, though other differences between the passages point away from seeing 56.1-8 as exactly a correction of this passage—or at least suggest how the two passages might be seen as part of a coherent whole.[114] Isaiah 56.1-8 is concerned with individuals, with people who have attached themselves to Yhwh, and with practical policy in the community in the present. Isaiah 61 is a vision of something Yhwh will do in the future and it is concerned with communities; it is not

[110] So Brueggemann, *Isaiah 40–66*, p. 217.

[111] See Weinfeld, *Social Justice* (see above), pp. 231-43.

[112] Cf. Oswalt, *The Book of Isaiah Chapters 40–66*, p. 571.

[113] On the further development of what she calls 'The democratization of the priesthood in the literature of Second Temple Judaism', see Martha Himmelfarb, '"A Kingdom of Priests"', *The Journal of Jewish Thought and Philosophy* 6 (1997), pp. 89-104.

[114] Cf. Tiemeyer, *Priestly Rites and Prophetic Rage*, pp. 279-81.

concerned to work out the practical implications of the vision in terms of community policies for the present. The function of Isaiah 56.1-8 might well be to safeguard against mistaken practical inferences from Isaiah 61.

61.6b You will consume the resources of nations// and thrive on their splendour.
7a Instead of your shame [there will be] double;// [instead of] disgrace, they will resound at their portion.

Two further lines bring to a conclusion the verses' contrast between Judah and the nations, though the details are difficult. Verse 6b (3-2) is neatly parallel, aba′b′; the verbs come second in each colon. For *ḥayil* LXX, Vg have 'strength', as Vg in 60.5, but Aq, Tg, have 'wealth' (so LXX, Tg in 60.5), which fits here and is complemented by 'splendour' in the sense of wealth. The down-to-earthness of the first verb (literally, 'eat') is complemented by the unusual nature of the second verb.[115]

The second line, v. 7a, has seemed enigmatic for two reasons, and LXX omits it. First, it is elliptical. Initially, 'instead of your shame double' sounds as if the doubling refers to the shame. This will then recall 40.2, though more so in English than in Hebrew, where the word for 'double' is different (*kiplayim* not *mišneh*). Further, the second colon is then hard to construe, and the next line (v. 7b) will refer to double blessing not double punishment. The word for double is the one used in Job 42.10 to refer to a restoration from suffering that brings double blessing, which makes sense here. While the word can denote 'equivalent' rather than suggesting twice as much, like English 'double', in Job it means twice as much, and that fits the extravagant nature of the promises in these chapters. The colon is then a self-contained noun clause.

In turn, given the parallelism of the two cola in v. 7a (3-3, roughly aba′b′), the elusiveness of the second colon is clarified by the awareness that 'instead of' applies there as well as in the first.[116] The move from second person to third person within the line then corresponds to the move within vv. 5-6a, though it operates in reverse order, so that vv. 5-7a as a whole work abb′a′. On one hand, 'you', Judah, will experience double restoration to replace your shame. On the other, 'they', the nations, instead of experiencing shame will resound at their own lot. There is a sense in which the reversal of position between Judah and other peoples means the shaming of the latter as it means the exaltation of the former, and it might seem that becoming shepherds, labourers, and vinedressers is a humiliation. In fact (we have noted), this is not really so; it was as honourable a 'portion' for the majority of the Israelite clans to have those roles as it was for Levi's 'portion' to be in the position of priestly clan.

[115] See the translation note.
[116] Cf. GK 119hh. Syr repeats 'instead of' to clarify the point.

The nations' new 'portion' is thus not one that involves shame, and they can rejoice in it. For both Judah and the nations, shame and disgrace suggest both humiliation in relation to other peoples, their conquerors and spectators, and also inner mortification that takes away their own proper self-confidence and pride. There is none of that for either party. The 'daring' implication is that '*both* the returning exiles *and* the humbled "foreigners" might take possession of the land as compensation'.[117]

61.7b Therefore in their land they will possess double;// lasting joy will be theirs.

We noted that there are two reasons for which v. 7a has seemed enigmatic. The second is that v. 7b has naturally been read as a direct and syntactic continuation of v. 7a, which would mean that in v. 7b 'they' would be the nations, as was so in vv. 5-7. But in vv. 8-9 'they' are the Judahites, the 'you' of vv. 5-7a, which makes for a jerky transition between vv. 7b and 8-9. There are two usual ways of handling this jerkiness. One is to see it as an instance of the ease with which the Prophets do move between second and third person in referring to the same people.[118] The problem is that this instance seems particularly contorted. In instances such as 1.29-31; 5.8; 22.16; 31.6; 42.20; 48.1; 54.1 the move does not cause confusion; there are no other entities referred to in the context and thus there is no doubt that second- and third-person verbs and pronouns have the same reference.[119] In 61.5-9, there is confusion. It is not only modern Western readers[120] who find it difficult; 1QIs[a] changes many of the forms in vv. 7-9 and produces a much smoother text:

7 Instead of your shame [there will be] double;// [instead of] disgrace, they will resound at your portion.
Therefore in their land you will possess double;// lasting joy will be yours.
8 Because I am Yhwh, one who affirms the exercise of judgment,// one who repudiates robbery in oppression.
I will give you your wages with truthfulness,// seal a lasting covenant for you.
9 Your offspring will come to be acknowledged among the nations,// your descendants in the midst of the peoples.
All who see them will recognize them,// that they are offspring Yhwh has blessed.[121]

[117] Mark G. Brett, 'Unequal Terms: A Postcolonial Approach to Isaiah 61', in Katherine Dell and Paul Joyce (eds.), *Biblical Interpretation and Method* (John Barton Festschrift; Oxford: Oxford University Press, 2013), pp. 243-56 (251). The quotation marks around 'foreigner' reflects Brett's allowing for the possibility that the foreigners are Samarians.
[118] See GK 144p.
[119] On 52.14, see Goldingay and Payne, *Isaiah 40–55*, II, p. 290.
[120] See the translation note.
[121] Cf. Syr, which also continues the second-person version into v. 9b.

The idea of v. 7 as a whole in 1QIs[a] is then that the shame and disgrace of defeat, destruction, and ongoing subjection will be more than countered by the splendour of restoration such as previous verses have described, so that other people will resound with praise at what God now gives the Judahites.

In MT, however, whereas the lines preceding v. 7a suggest that 'they' are the nations, in the lines that follow in vv. 8-9 'they' must be the Judahites. Further, v. 8 will raise another question. It involves a move to Yhwh being the speaker, whereas from the beginning of the chapter the prophet was the speaker. While prophets can also move easily between speaking in Yhwh's name as 'I' and speaking about Yhwh as 'he', the suddenness of Yhwh's 'because I' in v. 8 raises a question about whether it actually is the beginning of Yhwh's direct speech. It opens up the possibility that v. 7b is the beginning of this direct speech and is in fact the beginning of a separate subsection from vv. 4-7a. In such a new subsection, it will not be surprising if there is a change in the reference of the third-person forms. Thus vv. 5-7a antithesize 'they', the nations, and 'you', the Judahites; vv. 7b-9 simply refer to the Judahites as 'they'. We might say that it is the Masoretic tradition that misleads our reading of the passage by making a single verse out of the two lines in v. 7 that belong to different subsections, and obscures the different reference of the third-person forms; 1QIs[a] avoids the misreading by its different formulation.

While changing the pronouns that refer to the Judahites, the first line of the new subsection manifests some parallelism with the last line of the previous one. Thus v. 7bα broadly reformulates v. 7aα. 'Double' recurs; here it certainly denotes blessing rather than trouble and denotes twice as much rather than equivalency, though the prophecy's capacity for rhetoric means one could not argue that this fact about its meaning adds to the arguments for taking 'double' in v. 7a to have that reference. The double restitution will come 'in the land' as the people enter into secure possession of it (it would be wooden to try to be mathematical about the 'double', as is perhaps also the case in 40.2). Another, prosaic way to express Yhwh's promise that the Judahites' shame will not only be ended but be replaced by something worth double is to make explicit that they will no longer be confined to the few miles around Jerusalem, but will possess much more. In substance the promises in these verses reformulate those in 54.3-4 and might be called the highpoint of the economic reordering of the people who mourn Zion.[122] Then the joy of the Judahites in v. 7bβ parallels the resounding of the nations in v. 7aβ; 'lasting joy' picks up from 51.11.

[122] So Berges, *Das Buch Jesaja*, p. 451.

61.8 Because I am Yhwh, one who loves the exercise of judgment,// one who repudiates robbery in oppression.
I will give them their wages in truthfulness,// seal a lasting covenant for them.

The two lines buttress the preceding promises both by their form and by their substance. They confirm that the beneficiaries of those promises are not a group within the community but the community as a whole. They recall that Yhwh's commitment underlies those promises, and they make the point by having Yhwh speaking in person (Syr underlines the point by repeating 'I' four times in v. 8a);[123] by implication the prophet has been the speaker through vv. 1-7. The change here is more rhetorical than substantial. The previous verses were Yhwh's words via the prophet; so are these. Making explicit that these are Yhwh's words heightens their force. As in 60.16, I assume that *ʾănî yhwh* is more likely a noun clause than a phrase placing the two words in apposition;[124] one might then take v. 8a as 3-2-3 rather than 5-3. Either way, the two participial phrases constitute parallel qualifiers of *yhwh* which provide a more precise basis for receiving the promises in vv. 1-7. As usual the verbs *ʾāhēb* and *śānēʾ* denote 'love' and 'hate' but also an active commitment and an active rejection.[125] And as usual, *mišpāṭ* points to the act of decision-making that is designed to implement what is right, rather than the abstract quality of justice (cf. Vg *iudicium*, Aq κρῖμα, Tg *dîn*, though they associate the decision-making with the processes of a court more explicitly than *mišpāṭ* does).[126]

Initially, one would read the phrase about affirming *mišpāṭ* as offering reassurance that Yhwh is indeed one who takes action of the kind that vv. 1-7 has promised, but the parallel phrase points in a different direction. 'Robbery' is a term for action taken within the community, including though not confined to the action of the powerful in relation to ordinary people. The immediately obvious significance of the double noun expression is 'robbery with a burnt offering'. That might imply people combining thieving with orthodox worship practice, the fault critiqued in passages such as 1.11-20; or it might imply offering something that you had stolen,[127] the possibility forbidden in CD 16.13 with possible reference to this passage. In the context of 56.9–59.8 this understanding would make sense, but it does not do so here. 'Robbery' (*gāzēl*) is not a term for the action of the devastators of v. 4. It could be a term for the oppressive exactions of the Persian authorities (cf. Neh 5.4). The second noun *ʿôlâ* might then refer to the way the Persian authorities supported

[123] Cf. van der Kooij, *Die alten Textzeugen des Jesajabuches*, p. 287.
[124] Cf. Beuken, *Jesaja IIIA*, p. 211.
[125] Cf. Beuken, 'Servant and Herald of Good Tidings', p. 429.
[126] On *mišpāṭ*, see the comment on 56.1.
[127] Cf. Ehrlich, *Randglossen*, IV, p. 219.

the worship of the temple (e.g. Ezra 6.8-10), or it might make one reconsider the word for robbery and be reminded of the references to a *mazlēg* in 1 Samuel 2.13-14, the means of robbing sacrifices,[128] or it might suggest that Yhwh is being robbed because the sacrifices are being offered to other deities,[129] or it might itself be the word for oppression, usually pointed *ʿawlâ*.[130] The preposition *b*- on the second noun presumably indicates that the phrase means something slightly more complicated than 'robbery *and* oppression'; perhaps the idea is that the violent wrongdoing of the authorities is the means or manner of their committing robbery. But the point about using the preposition becomes clearer when it recurs in the next line. If this is the reference of the closing phrase, then the *mišpāṭ* must also be that of the authorities. The line, then, describes Yhwh as one who approves the proper exercise of power but takes action when the authorities use their power to enrich themselves at the expense of their subjects.

The parallelism of v. 8b (4-3) also issues in the second colon clarifying the first and correcting a likely first impression. After v. 8a one might have thought Yhwh was paying the wages (*pᵉʿullâ*) that they deserved to people who are exercising their authority in an oppressive way (cf. the 'wages' of Ps 109.20), which would be an expression of Yhwh's truthfulness. But 'wages' is more often a positive expression and the second colon indicates that 'they' are actually Yhwh's own people. The word *pᵉʿullâ* came in 40.10 in a rather different connection in a line that will be taken up in 62.11, but the present occurrence has a greater substantial link with 49.4 where *mišpāṭ* and *pᵉʿullâ* came in parallelism. Yhwh's acting 'in truthfulness' contrasts with the authorities' acting 'in oppression'. Further, Yhwh will seal a lasting, perpetual covenant for them. The prophet takes up words from 55.3: 'I will seal [the form is cohortative] for you a lasting covenant'. Yhwh thus reaffirms the commitment that goes back to that context in Isaiah 40–55. In this new context, the lasting covenant is the basis for the lasting joy of v. 7. Literally, Yhwh will 'cut' this covenant; the background of the expression presumably lies in the practices described in Genesis 15.7-21 [J]; Jeremiah 34.17-20. It is a striking anthropomorphism in light of the very down-to-earth process that can apparently be involved in human covenants. Yhwh makes this covenant not 'with' them, which might imply a mutual commitment, but 'for' them; it is a one-sided sovereign divine commitment. 'Bᵉrit as "disposition" is efficacious foundation or renewing of the community of God and people.'[131] Describing a covenant as lasting or perpetual indicates not so much that it will necessarily last forever but that it is not made merely for a period of time, so that it would need renewing. As well

[128] Cf. Berges, *Das Buch Jesaja*, p. 452.
[129] So Tiemeyer, *Priestly Rites and Prophetic Rage*, pp. 215-17.
[130] See the translation note.
[131] Kraus, *Evangelium der unbekannten Propheten*, p. 216. The sentence is italicized.

as Isaiah 55.3, the expression parallels P's description of God's covenant with Abraham (Gen 17.7, 13, 19), and the reference to Yhwh's blessing which follows extends that link.[132]

61.9 Their offspring will come to be acknowledged among the nations,// their descendants in the midst of the peoples.
All who see them will recognize them,// that they are offspring Yhwh has blessed.

Two further lines (3-3, 2-5) extend Yhwh's promise in a way that issues directly from v. 8. The promise of a lasting covenant is one that is to hold beyond the present generation's lifetime, and thus it affects the destiny of the present generation's offspring. The parallelism in the two lines is complex and subtle. The first line is internally parallel, with the opening verb applying to both cola and the rest of the cola working abb′a′. The short first colon in v. 9b then parallels that first line, while the long second colon is not parallel to it but rather explains the logic of all three preceding cola.

'Offspring' and 'descendants' come in parallelism in 44.3; 48.19 (also 65.23, and in Job 5.25; 21.8; these are the only two books in which 'descendants', *ṣeʾĕṣāʾîm*, comes); further, 44.3 speaks of Yhwh's 'blessing' being on Jacob-Israel's offspring. 'Nations' and 'peoples' come in parallelism in 49.22 with reference to their bringing Jerusalem's sons and daughters to Jerusalem; it is a verse that underlies 60.4. Without there being close verbal links, Isaiah 40–55 also expounds the general theme of the world acknowledging Jacob-Israel or Jerusalem as a people in whom God has been active (41.20; 49.26; 55.5). The *kî* clause in v. 9b comprises an explanation of the preceding three cola; we might translate the *kî* 'because' or 'that'. The closing reference to blessing adds to the impression that the prophet is promising a fulfilment of Yhwh's commitment to Abraham, a theme underlying Isaiah 40–55. For the prophet's audience, declaring that peoples will acknowledge their offspring as blessed by Yhwh is an encouragement to the present generation itself.

Conclusion

Isaiah 61.1-9 promises the Judahite community that God intends to restore them. One presupposition of its reuse of motifs from Isaiah 40–55 is that their circumstances are not so different from the circumstances of the exile, either in Babylon or in Judah. They remain people who are

[132] Cf. Porúbčan, *Il Patto nuovo in Is. 40–66*, pp. 226-29, though I do not follow him in thinking that the prophecy is messianic or that it is concerned with salvation for the Gentile world.

afflicted and broken in spirit. Metaphorically speaking, they are captives, people sitting in the darkness of the prison. They are dressed in the garb appropriate to people who mourn the state of Zion. Their cities are in ruins. They live with humiliation and shame. The section does not show signs of being concerned with a group of needy people within the community but with the entire community, and the portrait matches one we might derive from Haggai and Zechariah or Ezra and Nehemiah. Its portrait of the community as a whole would not exclude the possibility that there were wealthy and powerful people within it who were doing well, as is commonly the case when a nation suffers. If there were such people, it ignores them. Its concern is with the afflicted state of the community as a whole. While it makes sense to assume that the section has its background in the circumstances of the late sixth or fifth century, it makes no specific reference to them and by its nature invites its readers in any such context to see its promises addressed to them.

To such people the section makes a series of promises. It brings news to the afflicted, though this is a rather paradoxical statement because it does not speak of anything that has happened that could as such be the subject of announcement. Bringing news is a means of bandaging the broken and comforting the people who mourn. This is so because (to change the image) the speaker's announcement is that the people in captivity are to be released. Slightly to change the image again, there is to be a time somewhat like the jubilee year when bondservants were released or somewhat like the day of Yhwh when Yhwh would exact recompense from oppressors and thus free the people they oppressed. The people characterized by mourning, exhaustion, and shame will be dressed in splendour and overcome by joy, looking like people in the splendour they would manifest at their marriage celebration. They will have the energy and resources to rebuild their cities or to supervise other people in doing so. They will realize their vocation to focus on serving Yhwh as a priestly people. They will thus know that Yhwh has turned them into a people who are confident and strong, as an expression of faithfulness to them.

The section gives a complex account of the destiny of foreign peoples. They are victims of redress (v. 2, cf. v. 8), people who undertake everyday work in the community (v. 5), people whose resources Judah lives on (v. 6), people who rejoice in their lot (v. 7), and people who come to recognize what Yhwh does for the community and its offspring (v. 9). At the same time, an aspect of its lack of specificity is that it contains no indication that the afflicted and broken in spirit for whom it is concerned need be limited to Judahites. Its message is not good news for people who afflict Zion, but it might be good news for anyone who mourns Zion.

Isaiah 61 'does not contain even one imperative, one call to action'.[133] It is not a commission to see that mourners are comforted, the broken are bound up, and the captives are freed. It is a series of promises concerning

[133] Donald E. Gowan, 'Isaiah 61:1-3, 10-11', *Interpretation* 35 (1981), pp. 404-9 (405).

what Yhwh is doing. To what do the promises refer? They make no allusion to specific events in the time of prophet or to people such as this prophet's predecessor's references to Cyrus, which is one implication of describing them as eschatological.[134] Once again, this lack of such allusion hardly implies that the prophet is to be seen as inferior to that predecessor; if there is no Cyrus to hand, this is God's responsibility, not that of God's representative. In the decades and centuries that followed, the Jewish people did not see these promises fulfilled, which was one reason why Jesus could take up 61.1-2. It was a favourite passage in his day,[135] 'a generative text for other later texts, especially in Judaism'.[136] Jesus' quotation from the Septuagint's translation in Luke 4.18-19 combines it with a phrase from Isaiah 58 (though possibly the two passages were already combined in a collection of testimonia, passages that had come to be linked). He omits the reference to binding up people who are broken in spirit and later adds from Isaiah 58.6 a reference to letting the broken go free, which in the Septuagint has a concrete point of contact with 61.1 in the recurrence of the term *aphesis*, 'release', the Septuagint's word for *d*[e]*rôr*.[137] Jesus' blessings in Matthew's version (Matt 5.3-4) as well as in Luke's also reflect these verses.[138]

134 Volz, *Jesaja II*, p. 257.

135 See James A. Sanders, 'From Isaiah 61 to Luke 4', in J. Neusner (ed.), *Christianity, Judaism and Other Greco-Roman Cults* (Leiden: Brill, 1975), I, pp. 75-106, reprinted in Craig A. Evans and James A. Sanders, *Luke and Scripture* (Minneapolis: Fortress, 1993), pp. 46-69; also on the use of the verb 'bring news', Evans, 'From Gospel to Gospel' (see above).

136 Tuckett, 'Scripture and Q' (see above), p. 22. See also the reference to 11Q Melchizedek in the comment on v. 2a above.

137 See, e.g. Patrick D. Miller, 'Luke 4:16-21', *Interpretation* 29 (1975), pp. 417-21; James A. Sanders, 'Isaiah in Luke', *Interpretation* 36 (1982), pp. 144-55 (151), reprinted in Evans and Sanders, *Luke and Scripture* (see above), pp. 14-25 (21); Rainer Albertz, 'Die "Antrittspredigt" Jesu im Lukasevangelium auf ihrem alttestamentlichen Hintergrund', *Zeitschrift für die neutestamentliche Wissenschaft* 74 (1983), pp. 182-206; Hubert Frankemölle, 'Jesus als deuterojesajanischer Freudenbote?', in H. Frankemölle and K. Kertelge (eds.), *Vom Urchristentum zu Jesus* (J. Gnilka Festschrift; Freiburg: Herder, 1989), pp. 34-67, reprinted in Frankemölle, *Jüdische Wurzeln christlicher Theologie* (Bodenheim: Philo, 1998), pp. 131-59; Martin Karrer, Ulrich Schmid, and Marcus Sigismund, 'Das lukanische Doppelwerk als Zeuge für den LXX-Text des Jesaja-Buches', in H. Ausloos, B. Lemmelin, and M. Vervenne (eds.), *Florilegium Lovaniense* (F. García Martínez Festschrift; Leuven: Peeters, 2008), pp. 253-74 (268-70). There is one deviation from the LXX version of 61.2, κηρύξαι for καλέσαι, and one from the LXX version of 58.6, the infinitive ἀποστεῖλαι for the imperative ἀπόστελλε.

138 Cf. Tuckett, 'Scripture and Q' (see above), p. 20, though the extent of the influence of Isaiah 61 is questioned in the same volume by Frans Neirynck, 'Q 6,20b-21; 7,22 and Isaiah 61', pp. 27-64; and see the references in both papers, e.g., J. Schmitt, 'L'oracle d'*Is*. lxi, 1 ss. et sa relecture par Jésus', *Revue des Sciences Religieuses* 54 (1980), pp. 97-108; Seccombe, 'Luke and Isaiah'; Robert B. Sloan, *The Favorable Year of the Lord* (Austin: Schola, 1977), pp. 111-53.

Pre-critical Christian commentaries naturally assume that Isaiah 61 is a prophecy of the Messiah. Theodoret of Cyrrhus comments that there is no need to offer much interpretation of the passage because Jesus has already done so.[139] This assumption then stimulates questions regarding what 61.1 implies about the Trinity and the person of Christ.[140] Even Jürgen Moltmann declares that here 'Trito Isaiah, finally, sees the coming messiah as quintessential bearer of the Spirit'.[141] Gerhard von Rad comments that, given Christian faith's orientation toward the inward, it is important that Isaiah 61 reminds its readers that 'even here in this life things can once again be put in order by God' even while itself also emphasizing the inward and spiritual.[142] This awareness links with the way Isaiah 61.1-2 became a key text for liberation theology.[143]

[139] *Commentaire sur Isaïe* 177b (3.264-65).

[140] E.g. Procopius of Gaza, Ἐπιτομή τῶν εἰς τὸν προφήτην Ἡσαΐαν καταβεβλημένων διαφόρων ἐξηγήσεων, cols. 2639-42; Irenaeus, *Against Heresies* 3.17.3; Barth, *Die kirchliche Dogmatik* I/1, p. 330 (ET p. 359; 2nd edn, p. 313). Since Barth is such a significant theological exegete of Scripture, I regret such an occasion when Homer nods.

[141] Jürgen Moltmann, *Der Geist des Lebens* (Munich: Kaiser, 1991), pp. 66-67; ET *The Spirit of Life* (Minneapolis: Fortress, 1992), p. 53.

[142] Gerhard von Rad, *Predigt-Meditationen* (Göttingen: Vandenhoeck & Ruprecht, 1973), p. 79; ET *Biblical Interpretations in Preaching* (Nashville: Abingdon, 1977), p. 93 (von Rad is working with the assumption that vv. 10-11 are part of the same section as vv. 1-9).

[143] See, e.g., Gustavo Gutiérrez, *El Dios de la Vida* (Salamanca: Sígueme, 2nd edn, 1994), pp. 31-42; ET *The God of Life* (repr., Maryknoll, NY: Orbis, 1996), pp. 3-9.

VIII

ISAIAH 61.10–62.12

Translation and Notes

10 I will rejoice fervently in Yhwh,[1]// my whole person will joy[2] in my God,
Because he has clothed me with deliverance garments,// he will wrap me[3] in a faithfulness[4] coat,
Like a groom who behaves priestly[5] in his finery// or like a bride who adorns herself in her accoutrements.
11 Because like the earth that brings forth its flourishing// and like a garden that makes its seed flourish,[6]
So my Lord Yhwh[7]// will make faithfulness and praise flourish// in the sight of all the nations.

[1] LXX (but not OL) has a third-person pl. verb and attaches this colon to v. 9.

[2] On the short yiqtol with future reference, see *DG* 62 remark 2.

[3] MT יְעָטָנִי looks like a qatal from a verb יעט, which would be a unique byform of עטה. Torrey (*Second Isaiah*, p. 455) sees the text as a composite of qatal עָטָנִי and yiqtol יַעֲטֵנִי. Following on the qatal in the first colon, it seems more likely that a yiqtol has been accidentally altered to a qatal than vice versa. M. Dahood ('Hebrew Lexicography', *Orientalia* 45 [1976], pp. 327-65 [333]) sees the form as a yiphil (cf. the translation note on 63.16).

[4] LXX has 'rejoicing', repeating the root that came twice in v. 10aα (the end of v. 9 in LXX).

[5] For MT יכהן Bredenkamp (*Jesaia*, II, p. 339) suggests יָכִין 'gets ready [finery]', but this would be an odd verb to govern פאר (Morgenstern, 'The Suffering Servant' [see above], p. 304, who suggests יחבש 'binds on'). LXX's version has one fewer verb and likely omits this one because of the unusual usage. Sym likewise paraphrases κεκοσμημένον, Vg *decoratum*. But Aq has ἱερατευμένον; cf. also Tg's expansive rendering. 1QIs[a] ככוהן shows it has something like MT's reading (cf. Kutscher, הלשון והרקע הלשוני של מגילת ישעיהו השלמה, pp. 247-48 [ET p. 322]).

[6] I follow LXX, Tg in assuming that כ each time has its regular prepositional meaning and thus that its noun is followed by an unmarked relative clause (cf. GK 155g); contrast Vg, which rather assumes כ functions as a conjunction (cf. JM174d). LXX omits the closing verb, which repeats the root of a noun in the first colon.

[7] For MT אדני יהוה (cf. LXX, where some mss have single κύριος, some double), 1QIs[a] has יהוה אלוהים (cf. Tg, Syr, which also had an equivalent expression at v. 1; and Vg, which had simple *Domini* there). It is difficult to say which of the witnesses has assimilated the text it received so that it corresponded to some other familiar or expected usage.

62.1 For the sake of Zion I will not[8] remain still,[9]// for the sake of Jerusalem I will not be quiet,
Until its faithfulness goes out[10] like brightness,// its deliverance like a torch blazing.[11]
2 Thus nations will see your faithfulness,// all kings[12] your splendour.
You will be called[13] by a new name// that the very mouth of Yhwh will determine.[14]
3 You will be a glorious crown in Yhwh's hand,// a royal turban[15] in your God's palm.
4 No longer will you be termed 'Abandoned',// no longer will your country be termed[16] 'Devastation'.
Rather you will be called[17] 'My Delight Is in It'[18]// and your country 'Possessed'.
Because Yhwh delights in you// and your country will be possessed.[19]

[8] 1QIs[a] has ולוא for MT's לא, which has the effect of linking 'for the sake of Zion' to 61.11 and thus makes a significant difference to the point made in 61.11 (cf. Pulikottil, *Transmission of Biblical Texts in Qumran*, p. 84).

[9] For MT אחשה, 1QIs[a] has the more common אחריש—rather oddly as it uses MT's verb elsewhere (e.g. 62.6; 64.11; 65.6; cf. Kutscher, הלשון והרקע הלשוני של מגילת ישעיהו השלמה, p. 180 [ET p. 239]). Talmon describes the two verbs as interchangeable (e.g. *The World of Qumran from Within*, p. 128).

[10] H. L. Ginsberg (*The Legend of King Keret* [New Haven: American Schools of Oriental Research, 1946], p. 45) sees this as an instance of יצא meaning 'shine'; cf. Mitchell Dahood, 'The Linguistic Position of Ugaritic in the Light of Recent Discoveries', in J. Coppens, E. Massaux, and A. Descamps (eds.), *Sacra pagina* (Paris: Gabalda, 1959), I, pp. 266-79 (274); Scullion, 'Some Difficult Texts in Isaiah cc.56—66', pp. 120-21; also *DCH*, IV, p. 265, though it does not refer to this passage.

[11] Vrs translate 'blazes like a torch', but the verb is m. and the word order suggests that the verb is an unmarked relative clause, virtually an adjective (cf. GK 155fg). 1QIs[a]'s f. verb suggests that it, too, did not recognize the relative clause (Kutscher, הלשון והרקע הלשוני של מגילת ישעיהו השלמה, p. 34 [ET p. 44]).

[12] 'Kingdoms' according to Dahood; see the translation note on 60.3.

[13] For MT's pual קרא 1QIs[a] has the more common impersonal qal קראו.

[14] The meaning of נקב is clear enough (e.g. Gen 30.28), though it is not clear how the word whose root meaning is 'pierce' comes to have this significance. If the link lies in the practice of engraving names, this background is evidently lost here, where it is Yhwh's *mouth* that does the designating. Mitchell Dahood hypothesizes a verb קבה 'pronounce' ('The Ugaritic Parallel Pair *qra//qba* in Isaiah 62,2', *Biblica* 58 [1977], pp. 527-28). LXX's paraphrase 'that the Lord will name' avoids the curious expression; it is not merely objecting to the anthropomorphic reference to Yhwh's mouth, for which see (e.g.) 58.14 (see Fritsch, 'The Concept of God in the Greek Translation of Isaiah', p. 158).

[15] K has צנוף (so also 1QIs[a]), possibly inf. abs., 'wrapping', possibly an odd form of the noun which usually appears as צניף (Q). See the comment.

[16] Duhm (*Jesaia*, pp. 417-18) deletes the repeated לא יאמר עוד and thus makes it possible to read vv. 4-9 as mostly bicola with two-stress second cola.

[17] Here MT has niphal יקרא while 1QIs[a] again has the impersonal qal יקראו, as in v. 2b.

[18] Blank (*Prophetic Faith in Isaiah*, p. 181) emends MT חפצי־בה to חפץ־יה 'Yhwh's delight' on the grounds that Yhwh is not speaking so that the first person is inappropriate.

[19] LXX lacks this line, which essentially repeats the previous line.

5 Because a young man possesses[20] a girl;// your sons[21] will possess you.
With a groom's rejoicing over a bride// your God will rejoice over you.
6 Over your walls, Jerusalem,// I have appointed guards.
All day and all night, continually[22],// they will not be still.
You who remind Yhwh:// no stopping for you.
7 Do not give him[23] stopping[24] until he establishes,[25]// until he makes Jerusalem an object of earth's praise.

8 Yhwh swore by his right hand,// by his strong arm:[26]
'If I again give your new grain// as food to your enemies,
If foreigners drink your new wine// for which you have laboured…'.[27]
9 Rather[28] its harvesters[29]—they will eat it,// and praise[30] Yhwh[31].
Its gatherers[32]—they will drink it// in my sacred courtyards.[33]

[20] For MT כי יבעל (cf. 1QIs[b]), 1QIs[a] has כיא כבעול (haplog./dittog.) and Syr, Tg, LXX have 'and as'. But Vg lacks the explicit comparatives; and on the omission of the comparative particle, leaving the comparison implicit, see *DG* 130; JM 174e. For the use of כי in a comparison compare 44.3 (Ehrlich, *Randglossen*, IV, p. 220; Goldingay and Payne, *Isaiah 40–55*, I, p. 323; Muilenburg, 'The Linguistic and Rhetorical Usages of the Particle כי in the Old Testament', p. 146).

[21] For MT בָּנָיִךְ Lowth (*Isaiah*, p. 386) suggests בֹּנַיִךְ (cf. Ps 147.2). But the pl. would usually signify 'your builders' and it is thus unexpected (though cf. 54.5 [Ehrlich, *Randglossen*, IV, p. 220]; Briggs ['An Analysis of Isaiah 40–62', p. 111] translates 'thy great Builder'). Oort ('Kritische Aanteekeningen', p. 475) suggests בֹּנֵךְ and adds that the verb needs to be not יִבְעָלוּךְ but יִבְעָלֵךְ; Torrey (*Second Isaiah*, p. 455) has יְבָעֲלֵךְ. LXX follows MT. For בניך, for metrical reasons Hanson (*The Dawn of Apocalyptic*, p. 58) suggests אדניך as in 51.22 (cf. Volz, *Jesaja II*, p. 250).

[22] 1QIs[a, b] omit תמיד.

[23] For לו 1QIs[b] has לכם, assimilating to the previous line; cf. LXX, though its version is more broadly different (see next note). Syr has 'them'.

[24] LXX eliminates the repetition in the last colon of v. 6 and the first of v. 7, and takes the word as from דמה I 'resemble' rather than דמה II 'cease'.

[25] 1QIs[a] reduplicates the verbs, עד יכין ועד יכונן, perhaps because the polel is no longer used, while in contrast, 1QIs[b] seems to lack one of MT's two עד clauses (a bit of the manuscript is missing and there is not enough space there for both) (van der Kooij, *Die alten Textzeugen des Jesajabuches*, pp. 103, 122). The verb's lack of an object stimulates the providing of one: e.g. דברו 'his word' (Kissane, *The Book of Isaiah*, II, p. 280).

[26] For the Leningrad ms's עזו, a Cairo Geniza ms has קדשו 'his holy' (cf. Sym), assimilating to 52.10 (also Ps 98.1).

[27] The 'if' clauses without an apodosis signify a strong denial; see the comment.

[28] Vg takes this כי to mean 'because' not 'rather' as in v. 4. In contrast, 1QIs[a] has כי אם, making specific the meaning 'rather'.

[29] On MT's form מְאַסְפָיו see GK20m; note the variants recorded by *HUB*.

[30] For MT's ו-consecutive והללו, 1QIs[a] has PBH-style conjunctive ו, ויהללו.

[31] For MT את יהוה 1QIs[a] has את שם יהוה 'Yhwh's name', the more common expression after הלל (so Pulikottil, *Transmission of Biblical Texts in Qumran*, p. 66). Thomas ('ספר ישעיה', p. 98) notes the proposal אותי 'me'.

[32] Resultative piel (Jenni, *Das hebräische Pi'el*, p. 159)? Paul (ישעיה פרקים מ-סו, II, p. 506 [ET p. 557]) implies that the unique use of the piel is intensive, reflecting the large number of gatherers because of the abundance of the crop.

[33] Günther Schwarz ('"…trinken in meinen heiligen Vorhofen"?', *ZAW* 87 [1975], pp. 216-17) suggests reordering the clauses in the verse; see the comments of Wilhelm

10 Pass through, pass through the gates,[34]// level the people's road!
Build up, build up[35] the ramp,// clear it of stones!
Lift high a banner over the peoples;[36]// 11 there, Yhwh has let it be heard[37]// to the end of the earth.
Say to Young Zion,// 'There, your deliverance is coming!
There, his wages are with him,// his recompense is in front of him.'
12 People will call them 'The holy people,// ones restored by Yhwh'.
You will be called 'Sought after,//a city[38] that has not been abandoned'.[39]

Introduction

MT and 1QIsa begin a new chapter or paragraph at 61.10, another at 62.10, and another at 63.1.[40] Given that 61.10-11 has themes, motifs, and words in common with 61.1-9,[41] the English chapter division suggestively points to the possibility of seeing 61.10-11 as a response to what precedes. Gerhard von Rad indeed comments that the crucial test for an exposition of Isaiah 61 is whether in its light people are driven to take the words of vv. 10-11 on their own lips.[42] Westermann suggests that 62.1-12 itself

Rudolph, 'Zu Jes 62 9', *ZAW* 88 (1976), p. 282; Gottfried Nebe, 'Noch einmal zu Jes 62 9', *ZAW* 90 (1978), pp. 106-11; Johann Maier, 'Ergänzend zu Jes 62 9', *ZAW* 91 (1979), p. 126. At the end 1QIsa adds אמר אלוהיך 'your God has said', making explicit that this part of Yhwh's message stops here.

[34] 1QIsa and LXX do not repeat the verb. More often than not, LXX Isaiah eliminates such repetitions (cf. 57.6, 14; also the elimination of parallel clauses in 59.6, 18; 60.13), perhaps because they seemed poor style in Greek (cf. Mirjam van der Vorm-Croughs, 'LXX Isaiah and the Use of Rhetorical Figures', in van der Kooij and van der Meer [eds.], *The Old Greek of Isaiah*, pp. 173-88 [186]); cf. the next note.

[35] LXX omits 'Build up, build up'. Vg has just one occurrence of the verb.

[36] For this colon 1QIsa has הנגפ אמורו בעמים. The first word belongs with what precedes, '[stones of] stumbling', an expansion from 8.14 (see further the comment); the subsequent change to 'Say among the peoples' simplifies a difficult line in light of the context. The sequence of changes in vv. 10-11a issues in quite a different reading of the lines as a whole (cf. Höffken, *Jesaja*, p. 13).

[37] For MT's qatal השמיע 1QIsa has imper. השמיעו, assimilating to the cola on either side. 'Here is Yhwh' then becomes the object of the proclamation (cf. Kutscher, הלשון והרקע הלשוני של מגילת ישעיהו השלמה, p. 299 [ET p. 394]).

[38] LXX, Vg link 'city' with what precedes, 'sought after city, not abandoned.

[39] Following MT's accenting the verb as qatal rather than as participle (GK 152a); cf. Tg but contrast LXX, Vg.

[40] Cf. the discussion in Johannes C. de Moor, 'Structure and Redaction: Isaiah 60,1–63,6', in Van Ruiten and Vervenne (eds.), *Studies in the Book of Isaiah*, pp. 325-46; also Olley, '"Hear the Word of Yhwh"', p. 28.

[41] Cf. Blenkinsopp, *Isaiah 56–66*, p. 230.

[42] Gerhard von Rad, *Predigt-Meditationen* (Göttingen: Vandenhoeck & Ruprecht, 1973), p. 83; ET *Biblical Interpretations in Preaching* (Nashville: Abingdon, 1977), p. 98 (von Rad is working with the assumption that vv. 10-11 are part of the same chapter as vv. 1-9).

then focuses on responding to the characteristic second-person statement in a protest psalm ('You have abandoned us'), whereas chapter 60 focused on the third-person statement ('Other nations have attacked us') and chapter 61 on the first-person statement ('We are afflicted and broken'). Yhwh is no longer being silent but has turned back to Israel. Further, the threefold 'until' of vv. 1 and 7 recalls the 'until when?' of a protest psalm (e.g. Pss 74.10; 94.3; also Isa 6.11).[43]

Yet 61.10-11 has as many concrete points of contact with what follows in 62.1-12 as it has with what precedes in 61.1-9, and especially with what comes in 62.1-5. These include the words 'rejoice', 'groom' and 'bride', 'praise', and 'nations', as well as 'finery (*pᵉʾēr*), which is related to the word translated 'glorious' (*tipʾārâ*), and other words that are more broadly characteristic of these chapters such as deliverance and faithfulness. Indeed, one might see 62.1 as confirming the statements of faith in 61.10-11 about deliverance and faithfulness. Further, 61.10-11 represents a change of speaker—not a reversion to the prophet's 'I' (as the English chapter division may suggest) but a transition to an 'I' representing the community. Read in isolation, 62.1-9 comes out of the blue, but read in connection with 61.10-11, it constitutes a response to that declaration of delight.

Isaiah 61.10–62.12 stands with 60.1-22 and 61.1-9 in comprising lyrical promises of Jerusalem-Zion's restoration. Each section goes about issuing its promises in a different way. The whole of chapter 60 directly addresses the city. In 61.1-9 the prophet reports a commission to undertake this encouraging ministry. In 61.10–62.12 there come a response to that report and further accounts of the divine intention to implement that restoration. Its particular similarity to 60.1-22 is reflected in its 19 uses of the second-person singular feminine suffix *-k*.[44]

In form, 61.10-11 begins as a thanksgiving that responds to Yhwh's acts. The identity of the speaker is left unstated. The thanksgiving links with what precedes in speaking of new clothing that points to Yhwh's faithfulness, and this suggests that it gives anticipatory thanksgiving for the promises incorporated in 61.1-9. In v. 11 it then makes a statement of trust and hope that continues a response to those promises. There is a sense in which the thanksgiving and statement of trust belong to the prophet; they are not yet being made by the people. But they are not personal to the prophet but prescribed by the prophet for the people. In other words, the first-person voice in vv. 10-11 is that of the personified community or of an individual representative of that community. Isaiah 62.1-9 constitutes a further response to that thanksgiving and statement,

[43] *Jesaja Kapitel 40–66*, p. 297 (ET p. 373). In turn, Otfried Hofius ('"Bis dass er kommt"', *NTS* 14 [1967–68], pp. 439-41) sees the 'until he comes' of 1 Cor 11.26 as taking up the 'until' of this chapter.

[44] Cf. Fitzgerald, 'A Rhetorical Analysis of Isaiah 56–66', p. 196.

one that takes up the image of bride and groom. The English chapter break thus does correspond to a change of speaker.

Verses 1-7 do not match any familiar forms of speech. In verses 1-5 the prophet more overtly speaks on Yhwh's behalf, using the divine first person in v. 1 and referring to Zion in the third person, but addressing Zion and referring to Yhwh in the third person in vv. 2-5.[45] This sequence is reformulated in vv. 6-7, which begin as Yhwh's words addressing Jerusalem and makes a transition to the prophet's words referring both to Yhwh and to Jerusalem. One might see vv. 1-7 as working abcb′c′a′. They open and close with reference to keeping silence (vv. 1, 6-7). Inside those references they speak of the city's new name (vv. 2, 4a) and of its new crown and marital splendour (vv. 3, 4b-5). With vv. 8-9 comes a transition to Yhwh's speaking to Zion, uttering an oath.

For vv. 10-12 the chapter reverts to the prophet's speaking, but now addressing unidentified road-builders. In the last two verses the prophet again reports Yhwh's words to Zion before making a final declaration concerning the nations' recognition. Before and after vv. 10-12 MT and 1QIs[a] have a chapter or paragraph divider (1QIs[b] only after v. 12). These division markers point us to the awareness that vv. 10-12 close off chapters 60–62 as a whole.[46] Elliger describes Isaiah 62 as 'quite a rich liturgy',[47] but this designation seems even less focused than is the case when it is applied to 61.1-9. The term does recognize the way the section represents more than one voice and that these are in some ways in conversation, though the nature of the section and the conversation does not point to a performance of some kind in the context of worship that has then been incorporated in a prophetic book, or to a section that has been composed for such a purpose.

Isaiah 61.10-11 and 62.1-3 are dominated by 3-3 rhythm, 62.4-5, 6-7, and 8-9 by 3-2 rhythm; these differences are interestingly at variance from the movement between human and divine speech in the verses. The rhythm in 62.10-12 is more mixed. After omitting some words and reworking the way MT links words, it has proved possible to understand 62.1-12 as more regularly metrical and to fit it with more than one understanding of a rhythm.[48]

[45] Michel ('Zur Eigenart Tritojesajas', pp. 183-85) sees v. 1 as the citation of an earlier prophecy and vv. 2-5 as an exposition based on this 'text'.

[46] 1QIs[a] underlines the sense of closure after 62.9 by adding 'your God has said' (cf. Oswalt, *Isaiah 40–66*, p. 583).

[47] *Einheit des Tritojesaia*, p. 26.

[48] See Sigmund Mowinckel, 'Die metrische Aufbau von Jes 62 1-12 und die neuen sog. "Kurzverse"', *ZAW* 65 (1953), pp. 167-87; Georg Fohrer, 'Über den Kurzvers', *ZAW* 66 (1954), pp. 199-236 (211-24); Volker Wagner, 'Jes 62—Der Bericht über eine Gebetserhörung', *BZ* 51 (2007), pp. 23-43 (40-43).

Comment

61.10 I will rejoice fervently in Yhwh,// my whole person will joy in my God,
Because he has clothed me with deliverance garments,// he will wrap me in a faithfulness coat,
Like a groom who behaves priestly in his finery// or like a bride who adorns herself in her accoutrements.

The transition to human first-person speech in v. 10 parallels that at v. 1 and one would initially assume that the speaker is again the prophet, but the content of the praise indicates that rather the speaker is a beneficiary of the restoration the prophet has promised. Perhaps 'the prophet speaks as the representative of Zion' so that 'her words are his words'.[49] Tg is again at least approximately right when it introduces v. 10 with 'Jerusalem said'; *Pesiqta deRab Kahana* also assumes that the speaker is Zion.[50] Jerusalem was not mentioned in 61.1-9 and in the context of 61.1-9 the 'I' that speaks might more likely be one of the captives or mourners to whom the prophet has been commissioned to speak. But if we associate 61.10-11 with what follows in 62.1-12, then the focus on Zion and Jerusalem running through the chapter retrospectively supports Tg's understanding. Yet the verse's not being explicit about the speaker's identity again puts us on the track of how the important point is the fact and the basis for the rejoicing, not the rejoicing voice.

The form of v. 10 is that of a thanksgiving or testimony psalm in which someone first declares a commitment to praising God (v. 10aαβ) then explains the reason for this praise (v. 10aγδb). The expression of commitment to praise (3-3) comprises parallel cola, working aba′b′. More precisely, it is not a commitment to praise but a commitment to joy. Indeed, while many psalms refer to joy, there are no examples of either of the verbs in this line at the beginning of a praise psalm. 'Rejoice fervently' is the verb *śûś* (the prophet uses the idiom whereby the finite verb is preceded by the infinitive of the verb), which comes eight times in Isaiah 56–66, more often than in the entire Psalter. The related noun *śāśôn* designated one of the fruits of the restoration the prophet promised in 61.3 (the expression 'festive oil' is more literally 'oil of joy'). In the parallel colon, the beneficiary of God's act uses an alternative way of making an intensive declaration: 'my whole person' (my *nepeš*) will 'joy' in my God. The verb, *gîl*, is less common than *śāmēaḥ*, the verb one might have expected to parallel *śûś*, though the combination of *śûś* and *gîl* recurs in 65.18, 19.

[49] Muilenburg, 'The Book of Isaiah: Chapters 40–66', p. 714.
[50] See Pisqa 22 in *Pesiqta deRab Kahana*, II, pp. 77-82.

As there are no psalms that open with reference to joy, so there are none that give thanks for a change of clothing in the manner of v. 10aγδ; the metaphor is another feature that rather reflects the language of Isaiah 40–55. The verb appears in a connection such as this in 49.18; 51.9; 52.1; 'garments' appears in 52.1. In effect this testimony declares that those promises in Isaiah 40–55 have been fulfilled. In general terms 61.3, too, was promising such a change of clothing; this rejoicing presupposes that its promise has been fulfilled. Likewise this particular word for deliverance (*yešaʿ*) was the promise in 45.8; 51.5; related words are common in Isaiah 40–55 and have already come in 56.1; 59.1, 11, 16, 17; 60.16, 18. At least as significantly, 59.16, 17 differ from 61.10 in that they speak of Yhwh's donning clothing. It is also those verses that are the background to the second colon's talk of being wrapped in a coat consisting of *ṣᵉdāqâ*; they spoke of Yhwh putting on *ṣᵉdāqâ* and 'wrapping on' passion as a 'coat'. In other words, each root that appears in this line has already appeared in 59.16-17, but the words have a new significance (once again, if 61.10-11 is older than 59.15b-21, this affects the direction of their relationship but not the nature of this difference). In the prophet's imagination, Yhwh put on the clothing that suggested deliverance and faithfulness, which signified taking on a commitment to act in faithfulness for the people's deliverance. Here in that same imagination and as a result of that action on Yhwh's part, people can testify to their own ability to put on this clothing in the sense that this action has transformed them; they are the beneficiaries of Yhwh's faithfulness in delivering. Further, for them (as the next line will indicate), their clothing will fulfil its regular function of marking their status and significance, now transformed. After the opening *kî*, the two halves of the 3-3 line work abb'a', with plural 'garments' complemented by singular 'coat', masculine 'deliverance' complemented by feminine 'faithfulness', and a qal qatal verb complemented by a hiphil yiqtol;[51] both refer to action Yhwh is going to undertake, which will in due course be the basis and reason for the joy in v. 10aαβ.

The neatly parallel v. 10b (3-3, abca'b'c') again picks up both from 61.3 and more closely from 49.18, but also adds its own new note which will be developed in 62.1-5. People in the community will put on the 'finery' that the prophet was bidden to proclaim. The expression elsewhere refers to headwear, and thus suggests something like a turban, though its similarity to the verb *pāʾar* perhaps once again made people think of a broader meaning. In putting on their finery they will be like a man getting married, but also like a priest. Elsewhere the verb means to fulfil the ministerial office of a priest; here the simile suggests a man dressing up in the way a priest dresses in order to undertake his ministry, and suggests that there is some overlap with the splendour of a priest's

[51] See the translation note.

headgear (his *pᵉʾēr* in Exod 39.28 [P]; Ezek 44.18).[52] The simile enfolding a novel metaphor is confusing; Tg in effect turns the line into three clauses comprising three similes, groom, priest, and bride.[53] The image of a bride is more familiar in Isaiah 40–66 as these chapters have already portrayed Jerusalem as a bride, though the actual word has come so far only in 49.18. There the prophet speaks of Zion putting on its adornment; here the prophecy speaks of a bride adorning herself with her accoutrements, such as her jewels. There would be no occasion when people were more spectacularly dressed up than on their wedding day, so the prophet takes up a significant second image for conveying the kind of rejoicing in which Yhwh's restoration will issue. People will be dressed like Yhwh, and they will be dressed like people in their wedding clothes. It makes sense to reckon that the construction of the second colon clarifies that of the first; both nouns are adverbial accusatives.

61.11 Because like the earth that brings forth its flourishing// and like a garden that makes its seed flourish,
So my Lord Yhwh// will make faithfulness and praise flourish// in the sight of all the nations.

It is common for prayer psalms to close with an expression of thanksgiving for the hearing of the prayer and for Yhwh's commitment to take action. The action itself has not yet materialized, and the thanksgiving may thus naturally be accompanied by a statement of confidence concerning what Yhwh will indeed do. The quasi-thanksgiving in v. 10 similarly leads into a declaration of confidence concerning the action that has been described as if it were already actual, though it is in reality still future. In other words, v. 11 describes the same action as v. 10 described, but does so in the yiqtol rather than the qatal, and does so in a further simile. It presupposes that people know from experience how the earth brings forth its growth and how a garden makes its seed flourish. One could sometimes get the impression that for the community in the Persian period the poverty of the harvest meant that this was far from being so; perhaps the prophet simply uses a familiar image. In its familiarity it presupposes a link between nature and the way God works in the community's experience. 'God's activity in nature is the image and the guarantee of his activity in history'; and the imagery of flourishing suggests not gradual and possibly imperceptible growth but the way rain suddenly transforms bare barrenness into lush growth.[54] Not surprisingly, God acts in a con-

[52] G. R. Driver suggests 'flaunts himself like priest' ('Studies in the Vocabulary of the Old Testament viii', *JTS* 36 [1935], pp. 293-301 [294]), but the pejorative connotation does not fit the context.

[53] Cf. Watts, *Isaiah 34–66*, p. 871. 1QIs^a also has 'like a priest' (*kkhyn*) for MT's verb (*ykhn*).

[54] Koole, *Jesaja III*, p. 286 (ET p. 296).

sistent way in creation and in dealing with Israel. The former is thus a guide to the latter and provides images for it. The first (4-3) line is neatly parallel; after the *kî* it works abca′c′b′. 'Makes flourish' is more vivid than 'brings forth'. 'Garden' makes 'earth' more concrete and speaks in a way that relates more to an individual family; it also recalls 51.3, though here the word is the less usual *gannâ* rather than simple *gan*. The parallelism also suggests that *ʾereṣ* means 'earth' in the sense of 'soil' rather than the land of Israel, and this is supported by the comparison with passages such as 45.8 and 55.10. The line recalls 55.10 more broadly. That verse expounds the same simile in a similar connection. It also speaks of 'seed' (compare 61.9 above, there translated 'offspring'), though again here the prophecy uses a much less common word, the very rare *zērûaʿ*. It also uses the verb 'make flourish' (*ṣāmaḥ* hiphil; cf. 42.9; 43.19; 45.8). One effect of choosing the different forms of the two nouns is to underline the fact that the line is indeed a simile; within the simile, their reference is more literal than usual in Isaiah 40–66.

1QIsᵃ reads the closing line as 5-3. Isaiah 61.1-9 had several five-stress cola, and this understanding makes it possible to see some slight parallelism in the line:

So my Lord Yhwh will make faithfulness flourish//
and praise in the sight of all the nations

But it is more natural with MT to take 'faithfulness and praise' as a phrase and then to read the line as 3-3-2, a tricolon closing the subsection; alternatively, given the total absence of parallelism, one could read it as a line of prose. 'Faithfulness' (*ṣᵉdāqâ*) picks up from v. 10 and will be taken up in 62.1 (*ṣidqāh*, the same consonants differently pointed). Yhwh's making praise flourish in the sight of all the nations will be taken up in Yhwh's making Jerusalem an object of earth's praise (62.7); Tg anticipates that note in making Jerusalem the object of praise here, in keeping with its emphasis on Jerusalem elsewhere.[55] In this connection, whereas the first four cola in v. 11 re-express the same reality as v. 10 but use different imagery, the closing colon goes beyond v. 10. Like 60.21-22, v. 11 links with the promise in Jeremiah 23.5 of a 'faithful branch/growth' (*ṣemaḥ ṣaddîq*), but it makes flourishing and faithfulness a promise applying to the people as a whole rather than simply to a new David. That promise is anticipatorily underlined by the link between v. 11a and 45.8, as the latter relates to what God would do through the anointed Cyrus.

[55] Cf Chilton, *The Glory of Israel*, pp. 25-28.

62.1 For the sake of Zion I will not remain still,// for the sake of Jerusalem I will not be quiet,
Until its faithfulness goes out like brightness,// its deliverance like a torch blazing.

Initially 62.1 gives no indication of a change of speaker. Its first line constitutes a particularly neat 4-4 parallel bicolon, abcda′b′c′d′. The second line works equally neatly abcc′b′a′, 'until emerges like the brightness its faithfulness, its deliverance like a torch [that] blazes'. The verse makes for comparison and contrast with the beginning of chapter 60, which directly addressed Zion but did not name it; chapter 62 names Zion but addresses it only indirectly. Further, chapter 60 suggested that the object of Yhwh's glorifying Zion is the honouring of Yhwh's own name (60.9), whereas here the promises begin by declaring that Yhwh will act 'for Zion's sake'; 'attention is immediately mobilized onto Zion'.[56] Within Isaiah 56–66, while 'Zion' came in 59.20; 60.14; 61.3, 'Jerusalem' comes here for the first time; the statistics will work the opposite way in Isaiah 62–66. Verses 6 and 7 will illustrate how 'Jerusalem' generally has more down-to-earth, material connotations, while 'Zion' is a more theological or religious term. But here in v. 1, one might attribute the presence of both words simply to the desire to let parallelism have its way.

In the address to Zion in chapter 60 Yhwh is indirectly the speaker, in chapter 62 directly so. In other words, I follow LXX and Tg in taking Yhwh as the 'I' and as the speaker throughout v. 1 (Tg actually has Yhwh not letting the nations be still until Jerusalem's comfort is achieved). This understanding is in keeping with the use of the verb *ḥāšâ* 'remain still' in preceding passages (42.14; 57.11) and subsequently (64.11 [12]; 65.6). The verb thus refers to the stillness of inactivity. It is a first indication of the way Yhwh's words take up the protests of Israel's prayers and respond to them (cf. Pss 28.1; and 83.2 [1] for the verb *šāqaṭ* in the second colon). Whereas Israel has had 'cycles of suffering imposed by the nations', Yhwh will not now continue to be silent 'but will intrude out of devotion to Israel'.[57] Those other occurrences of *ḥāšâ* further indicate that its use does not directly imply disappointment that promises in Isaiah 40–55 have not been fulfilled; it does imply a sense that the city is still in the same place as it was in the 540s. While 'be quiet' (*šāqaṭ*) is a more common word for resting, used especially in referring to the land resting from war, it is used in connection with God's inactivity in Psalm 83.2 [1] (see also Jer 47.6-7; Ezek 16.42).

If the prophet had been speaking in 61.10-11, it would be feasible to think that it was the prophet taking a vow to forgo silence here, but we have concluded that the prophet was not speaking there, and in the

[56] Lack, *La Symbolique du Livre d'Isaïe*, p. 211.
[57] Brueggemann, *Isaiah 40–66*, p. 220.

absence of some such hint to suggest that the prophet is speaking here, the background usage of *ḥāšâ* rather rules out that understanding (v. 6 will use the verb of the 'guards' whose appointment it reports, though however we identify these guards, this hardly retrospectively reworks the likely significance of the verb here).[58]

It is in the second line that LXX makes clear that it takes Yhwh as the speaker, by providing first-person pronouns that make the text read 'my faithfulness…my deliverance'. It thus assimilates to 51.5.[59] Vg has 'its righteous one…its deliverer', as it has in 51.5, making explicit that the promise is fulfilled in Jesus. Whereas the first line raised the question 'to what end is this activity to which Yhwh makes a commitment?', the second line clarifies the answer in another internally parallel 3-3 bicolon, abcc′b′d. Each of the two pairs of nouns comes in feminine–masculine order.[60] Letting the verbal expression carry over into the second colon makes room for the qualifier at the end of the line. Although the line is formally chiastic and could be described as abcc′b′a′, then, in substance it is not so; it does not describe the deliverance as blazing.[61] The parallelism of the two abstract nouns helps to nuance them. On one side, Zion's faithfulness (*ṣedeq*) is not the faithfulness shown by Zion but the faithfulness shown to Zion, expressed in its deliverance, so that in substance LXX is not wrong in taking the line to refer to 'my faithfulness' and 'my deliverance'. The use of *ṣedeq* thus corresponds to its regular usage (cf. especially 51.1-8; 58.8). On the other side, Zion's deliverance comes not because it deserves to be delivered but on the basis of the fulfilment of commitments that issue from Yhwh's relationship with Zion.

Talk of faithfulness and deliverance 'coming out' continues to take up the wording of 51.5, though here there is also a suggestion of metonymy, as it is the sun that 'comes out' at dawn (e.g. Judg 5.31; Ps 19.6-7 [5-6]).[62] Tg indeed takes *nōgah* to mean 'dawn', but the word denotes any kind of brightness (that of the moon in 60.19) and it is not elsewhere explicitly used to denote the dawn (though the Aramaic equivalent is so used in Dan 6.20).[63] It is the second colon that clarifies what kind of brightness the word denotes, the brightness of a flame (cf. Isa 4.5; also the use of the word to suggest the brightness of the fire that denotes Yhwh's presence, Ps 18.13 [12] and in Ezek 1). The brightness of Yhwh's faithful action bringing about Zion-Jerusalem's deliverance will be like that of a torch blazing. A link has been proposed between the reference to a torch and the lighting of torches at the celebration of Sukkot in later centuries,

[58] Against Blenkinsopp, *Isaiah 56–66*, p. 233.

[59] Baer (*When We All Go Home*, p. 72) notes the parallel with 57.12.

[60] Cf. Watson, *Traditional Techniques in Classical Hebrew Verse*, pp. 223, 350.

[61] Contrast Watson, *Traditional Techniques in Classical Hebrew Verse*, p. 373.

[62] See the translation note on the possibility that the verb here is a יצא II meaning 'shine'.

[63] Cf. Motyer, *Prophecy of Isaiah*, p. 506.

which might suggest the setting of the prophecy.[64] This possibility receives some support from the practice of raising of a torch when a Mesopotamian king made a proclamation concerning the establishment of just social order.[65] This more concrete image also points to the fire that suggests Yhwh's presence and coming (Gen 15.17 [J]; Ezek 1.13). The verb 'blaze' (*bāʿar*) appears along with the words for 'brightness' and 'torches' in Ezekiel 1.13, so it too suggests the blazing that reflects Yhwh's presence. The transformation of the city will testify to the presence and activity of God, as is implicit in its issuing from Yhwh's giving up silence and stillness. Elsewhere the verb often refers to Yhwh's own blazing, usually in connection with burning wrath or passion (e.g. Pss 2.12; 79.5; 89.47 [46]). An implication here could be the good news that Yhwh's energy is blazing on Zion's behalf against its foes.[66]

A further comparison and contrast with chapter 60 is that here, as sometimes happens in the Psalms (e.g. Ps 43.3), the prophet speaks of the coming of an aspect or expression of Yhwh's person rather than speaking generally about Yhwh's coming, as in 60.2. This way of speaking need not compromise the reality of Yhwh's personal coming; it answers the question what such a coming actually means or refers to and it brings out the concrete reality of that coming. While v. 1 compares with chapter 60 in the way it speaks of Zion and in its using the metaphor of light, the way it uses that metaphor is rather different. The way it talks about the nations in v. 2 will also compare and contrast with chapter 60.[67]

62.2 Thus nations will see your faithfulness,// all kings your splendour.
You will be called by a new name// that the very mouth of Yhwh will determine.
3 You will be a glorious crown in Yhwh's hand,// a royal turban in your God's palm.

Once again v. 2a comprises parallel cola, with the verb that opens the line applying to both cola so that the line works abcb′c′. Whereas Yhwh was implicitly the speaker in v. 1, with Zion as the subject of Yhwh's words and no addressee identified, here Zion is unmistakably the addressee, Yhwh is eventually the third-person subject of some of the verbs, and the prophet may therefore implicitly be the speaker. The fact that Yhwh is now named in the third person need not undermine the assumption that Yhwh spoke in the first person in v. 1 yet continues to speak here; third-person self-reference is common in divine speech. In theory one could

[64] So Volz, *Jesaja II*, p. 251.

[65] See Moshe Weinfeld, *Social Justice in Ancient Israel and in the Ancient Near East* (Jerusalem: Magnes; Minneapolis: Fortress, 1995), pp. 14, 73, 91.

[66] Cf. Vermeylen, *Du prophète Isaïe à l'apocalyptique*, II, p. 484; though this rather depends on taking v. 1 in isolation from the context.

[67] Cf. Lau, *Schriftgelehrte Prophetie in Jes 56–66*, p. 90.

take the change to mean that v. 1 was an oracle received from Yhwh that the prophet speaks in Yhwh's name, while v. 2 begins the prophet's commentary on the oracle which is spoken in the prophet's own name. Yet this is likely too prosaic an understanding. Prophets move easily between speaking as Yhwh's mouthpiece and speaking of Yhwh in the third person. The consistency with which Yhwh appears in the third person in vv. 2-5 may indicate that the prophet has slipped out of identifying with Yhwh; but if so, the prophet slips back again in v. 6. Verse 9 will see a move in the opposite direction between vv. 9a and 9b.

If Yhwh's faithfulness to Zion expressed in its deliverance is characterized by blazing brightness, presumably the point will include that it should be visible, and the people to whom it should be visible are nations and kings (cf. 60.3, 11, 16); only here does Isaiah 40–66 qualify 'kings' by 'all'. While the first colon repeats the reference to faithfulness in the previous line, faithfulness is here paired with splendour (*kābôd*). Once again this image reappears from 60.1-2, where it also occurred in connection with the verb *rāʾâ.* Yhwh's splendour will appear over the city; indeed, it becomes the city's splendour, which nations and kings will therefore see. Whereas kings are usually blinded by their own splendour and importance, they will now recognize Zion's.[68] As the splendour is Yhwh's and becomes the city's by Yhwh's action, so the faithfulness is again Yhwh's and comes to benefit the city by Yhwh's action.

Verse 2b (4-4) is the only non-parallel bicolon in vv. 1-5; the relative clause comprising the second colon simply qualifies the 'name' referred to in the first. The expression 'new name' comes here alone in the Old Testament, though the idea of the city's having a new name is taken up from 60.14 (and see 65.15). The presupposition is that a new name is not merely a new label but that it corresponds to and recognizes a new reality. Indeed, this is the point about the new name: 'The change is so immense that a new name must be coined for Jerusalem'.[69] The context in vv. 1-2 recalls specifically the talk of a new name in 1.26 and Jeremiah 33.16 (see also Jer 3.17; Ezek 48.35). When Revelation 2.17 takes up the notion of a new name (cf. Rev 3.12), it implies that this new name is a secret, and initially one might make that inference here, but v. 4 will reveal what the new name is. In the meantime, the relative clause anticipatorily underlines the certainty that this new name will become a reality, and presupposes the implausibility of what the new name will necessitate. The point is sharpened by the word order; the subject 'the mouth of Yhwh' precedes the verb. Indeed, this underlines the fact that another significance of the reference to giving a new name without revealing the name is that naming is an expression of sovereignty.[70]

[68] Calvin, *In Iesaiam prophetam*, pp. 391-92 (ET IV, pp. 321-22).
[69] Fischer, *Buch Isaias*, II, p. 183.
[70] Cf. Feldmann, *Das Buch Isaias*, II, p. 246.

In v. 3, before resolving the suspense over what the new name is, the prophecy first adds yet further to the implausibility of its promise. The 4-3 line again comprises parallel cola with an opening verb that governs both cola, so that it works abcdb′c′d′. 'Crown' is paralleled by 'turban' (both construct nouns), 'glorious' by 'royal' (both absolute nouns functioning adjectivally); in addition 'glorious crown' forms a rhyming expression, *ʿăṭeret tipʾeret*, and so perhaps does 'royal turban' in K if it should be read *ṣᵉnûp mᵉlûkâ*.[71] Finally, 'in Yhwh's hand' is paralleled by 'in your God's palm'. In 28.1-6 the Ephraimites are wearing a 'crown' that has a 'glorious' beauty that is superficial and temporary, soon to be trampled underfoot, while in due course (in a prose passage that may be later than its poetic context) Yhwh is a beautiful crown and a glorious coronet for the people. Yhwh is likewise the people's 'glory' (*tipʾeret*) in 60.19. The present passage thus reverses this symbolism in a distinctive image. Rather than receiving a crown, the city *is* a crown. The notion that a city with its battlements is its deity's crown is a familiar Middle Eastern and Greek idea. A prayer prayed by a priest at the New Year Festival in Babylon addresses Bel, the head of the Babylonian pantheon, 'your dwelling is the city of Babylon, your tiara is the city of Borsippa'.[72] This image suggests that *ʿăteret* here indeed denotes a crown rather than a celebratory wreath, which is its reference in contexts such as 28.1. As a crown it points to 'the establishment of the effective rule of God in Israel and in the world, encapsulated in the expression "the Kingdom of God"'.[73] In light of the wedding symbolism in the context, one could think of the crown as part of the dress for a wedding; 'Zion is the bride at a royal wedding', Yhwh being the groom.[74] Since Zion *is* a crown rather than *receiving* a crown, the crown must indeed be one for Yhwh to wear.

The surprise about the line is that the crown/turban sits in Yhwh's hand rather than on Yhwh's head. But to have something in one's hand is to have it in one's possession and in one's power and in a place of safety (or danger, if it is the wrong hand) (e.g. 43.13; 49.2; 51.16; Ps 31.6, 16 [5, 15]).[75] In the context, it could imply having it ready for showing to the

71 Cf. Watson, *Classical Hebrew Poetry*, p. 232.

72 *ANET*, p. 331; Borsippa is Babylon's sister city ten miles away. Cf. Stummer, 'Einige keilschriftliche Parallelen zu Jes. 40–66', p. 186.

73 Blenkinsopp, *Isaiah 56–66*, p. 236. Bernard Gosse ('Isaïe 28–32 et la rédaction d'ensemble du livre d'Isaïe', *SJOT* 9 [1995], pp. 75-82) sees the link with 28.1-6 as a reflection of the role of Isaiah 62 in the redaction of the book of Isaiah.

74 T. David Andersen, 'Renaming and Wedding Imagery in Isaiah 62', *Biblica* 67 (1986), pp. 75-80 (78).

75 So, e.g., Vitringa, *Commentarius in librum prophetiarum Jesaiae*, II, p. 980. See further Christl M. Maier, 'Daughter Zion as Queen and the Iconography of the Female City', in Marti Nissinen and Charles E. Carter (eds.), *Images and Prophecy in the Ancient Eastern Mediterranean* (Göttingen: Vandenhoeck & Ruprecht, 2009), pp. 147-62 (156-58).

nations of v. 2a[76] or ready for bestowal (cf. Zech 3.7)[77] or ready for donning when the moment comes of Yhwh's asserting kingship (cf. 52.7-10). As is the case with the reference to a new name, we cannot tell the answer to this question from the line where the expression appears; it is only v. 5 that will make things clearer. In a down-to-earth sense one might see the crown as the city's walls waiting for rebuilding (cf. the promise in 60.10, and earlier 54.11-12) and then see the promise fulfilled in a down-to-earth sense in the rebuilding of the walls under Nehemiah, which made the city once again look crown-like. The description combines the promise that the city will be splendid and impressive with the promise that it will be secure and safe, neither of these ideas being very plausible. The question regarding the head on which the crown will sit is not the point of the metaphor; the point is the crown's splendid nature.

62.4a No longer will you be termed 'Abandoned',// no longer will your country be termed 'Devastation'.
Rather you will be called 'My Delight Is in It'// and your country 'Possessed'.

At last we discover what the new name is, in what has been called the chapter's 'centrepiece'.[78] The two lines are neatly parallel, internally and mutually. The first (4-4) works abcdb'a'c'd', the second (4-2) abcdb'd'. The repetition of 'no longer will…be termed' makes the second seem prosaic, and omitting the repetition[79] improves the lines' mutual parallelism, but this fact does not imply that the repetition is not original.

A new name can signify a new reality without the content of the name being significant. Sarai's becoming Sarah simply marks the fact of her becoming a mother; no special meaning is attached to the name itself. Here, however, special meaning attaches to the names. Further, giving someone a new name need not mean people now literally address them by this name. Naomi did not in this sense change her name to Mara. Jerusalem's name was not previously Abandoned and it will not now change in that literal sense (any more than is implied by 1.26). The recollection of the city's being termed 'abandoned' specifically picks up from 60.14-15 and behind it from 49.14 and 54.6-7. In these earlier chapters 'abandonment…is the first word out of Zion's mouth'.[80] Yet further behind these promises are the community's protests: 'My God, my God, why have you abandoned me' (Ps 22.2 [1]); Mount Zion 'is devastated' (Lam 5.18).

[76] So e.g., Delitzsch, *Jesaia*, p. 625 (ET II, p. 435).
[77] So Bentzen, *Jesaja II*, p. 144.
[78] Paurisch, *Neue Gemeinde*, p. 117. It is close to being the actual centre of 61.10–62.9.
[79] See the translation note.
[80] Seitz, 'The Book of Isaiah 40–66', p. 515.

Zion is a wife abandoned by her husband. 'More painful than captivity or losing one's way is the mental anguish caused by the thought that those able to help have abandoned the search.'.[81] Isaiah 54.6-7 includes the participial form *ʿăzûbâ* which here becomes a name. Indeed, it was a real name (e.g. 1 Kgs 22.42), though it may have been linked to a different root *ʿāzab*.[82] The expression 'no longer' is also a motif that recurs from 60.19-20. The noun 'devastation' is a novelty in chapters 40–66, but it came twice in 1.7 and also in 6.11 (and 17.9). The present chapter is thus promising a reversal of the devastation described in the book's opening, introductory chapter, where the verse speaks of 'your country' as a 'devastation' as here (except that the pronominal suffix on 'your country' is plural). It is also promising a reversal of the devastation threatened in the further programmatic chapter 6. While the particular form of the noun *šᵉmāmâ* thus makes a link with those earlier chapters of the book, the verb *šāmēm* has recurred in chapters 40–61, especially in the form of the participle *šōmēmâ* (see especially 54.1, but also 59.8, 19; 61.4). That participle is nicely capable of being applied both to a place and to a person (e.g. 2 Sam 13.20; Lam 1.13, 16; 3.11), so that it applies to the city both literally and in terms of the figure of the abandoned wife. The country has a long history of being termed 'abandoned' and 'a devastation', and this description of it does not come merely from itself or from its enemies but from Yhwh in person. Thus Yhwh's own reversal of the designation is very significant. Jeremiah 4.27-29 also almost juxtaposes *šᵉmāmâ* and *ʿăzûbâ* in threats to Judah and Jerusalem, so that the present verse also constitutes a reversal of Jeremiah's threat.[83] Isaiah 6.11-12 juxtaposes *šᵉmāmâ* and *ʿăzûbâ* even more closely in a chapter that is of formative influence for the whole book of Isaiah, a fact that increases the likelihood that 62.4 is taking up Isaiah 6.[84]

'My Delight Is in It/Her', *ḥepṣîbâ*, is a real name (2 Kgs 21.1), but in this context it also takes up the import of the root *ḥāpēṣ* in Isaiah 40–66. The root has two kinds of significance in these chapters as elsewhere, and both connotations are significant here.[85] In passages such as 44.28; 46.10; 48.14; 53.10, the noun *ḥēpeṣ* suggests what Yhwh wishes to do; it refers to Yhwh's plans (cf. the verb *ḥāpēṣ* in 42.21; 53.10; 55.11). The first-person suffix might indicate that the prophecy has again switched to having Yhwh as the speaker, but equally the prophet may continue to speak and may simply be quoting the first-person expression that Yhwh would use. Here the verb *ḥāpēṣ* will point to a positive purpose Yhwh has

[81] Hanson, *Isaiah 40–66*, p. 226.

[82] Cf., e.g., *HALOT*.

[83] Cf. Baruch Halpern, 'The New Names of Isaiah 62:4', *JBL* 117 (1998), pp. 623-43 (629).

[84] Cf. H. G. M. Williamson, 'Isaiah 62:4 and the Problem of Inner-Biblical Allusions', *JBL* 119 (2000), pp. 734-39.

[85] Contrast, e.g., Odeberg (*Trito-Isaiah*, p. 262), who sees the word as having a 'quite different' sense here.

for Zion. A simple such reference to a positive purpose would make entire sense in this context. What will follow in the rest of vv. 4-5 will point in a further direction. In 54.10; 58.3, 13 the root suggests something emotionally pleasing (cf. the verb in 56.4; 65.12; 66.3-4). It gives an inkling of feelings Yhwh has for Zion. This hint need not be immediately conveyed by the declaration that Zion's country will be called *bᵉʿûlâ*, usually translated 'married'.[86] The passive participle comes from the verb *bāʿal*, which can indeed be translated 'marry' on a patriarchal understanding of marriage which pictures marriage as involving ownership and ruling; hence the above translation 'possessed' (LXX, Sym, Th, Vg, and Tg render this verb by words such as 'live with/in', here and in the next two lines).[87] The Old Testament only rarely uses the verb and its related nouns in connection with marriage; the usual words for 'my husband' and 'my wife' are simply 'my man' and 'my woman'. In connection with human marriage, the use of *bᵉʿûlâ* would not be very encouraging. But in connection with taking patriarchal marriage as an image for the relationship of Yhwh and the land, the logic works in an opposite way. The term reassures Zion that Yhwh regards the land as personal property with whose destiny Yhwh is involved. A master does not let his servant be neglected. It is not in the master's interests to do so. To be 'owned' is to be secure and protected. Verses 8-9 will work out the implications: the land will once again produce its fruit and its proper owners will enjoy it.

62.4b Because Yhwh delights in you// and your country will be possessed.
5 Because a young man possesses a girl;// your sons will possess you.
With a groom's rejoicing over a bride// your God will rejoice over you.

While in substance v. 4b adds nothing new, rhetorically it moves the argument forward over against the preceding line, as it makes Yhwh the subject of the verb *ḥāpēṣ* and directly addresses Zion itself in speaking of Yhwh's delight in 'you' not merely 'her'. Substantially the cola are again parallel (3-2, abcc′a′), though here a clause formulated in the passive stands alongside one formulated in the active.

The two lines in v. 5 comprise a double comparison, though the comparison is implicit rather than explicit; the terms involved in the comparison are simply juxtaposed. Both lines are both internally and mutually parallel. The first is 3-2, abca′b′; the three nouns all begin *b* and the repeated verb is the yiqtol of *bāʿal*. The second is 3-3, abca′c′b′, though in formal terms its parallelism is compromised by the use of the noun 'rejoicing' then the verb 'rejoice'.

[86] On the use of this image in William Blake, see Robert P. Carroll, 'Revisionings: Echoes and Traces of Isaiah in the Poetry of William Blake', in J. Davies, W. G. E. Watson, and G. Harvey (eds.), *Words Remembered, Texts Renewed* (J. F. A. Sawyer Festschrift; Sheffield: Sheffield Academic Press, 1995), pp. 226-41 (231-32).

[87] Cf. Christl M. Maier, *Daughter Zion, Mother Zion* (Minneapolis: Fortress, 2008), pp. 181-82.

Etymologically, the 'young man' (*bāḥûr*) is someone 'chosen', the kind of person you would choose for your team or your army or as your son-in-law, someone 'in the prime of manhood'.[88] 'Young man/men' and 'girl/girls' can form a pair (e.g. Deut 32.25; Jer 51.3), both suggesting teenagers, people of marriageable age. The word for girl, *bᵉtûlâ*, is often translated 'virgin', and the charitable assumption would be that she was indeed a virgin, but it is not clear that the word strictly denotes this; it means a girl who is not yet married.[89] As happened in the line about Zion as a crown, the metaphor arguably breaks down when the prophet comes to speak of the city's sons 'marrying' her, but the verb again suggests entering into possession. In substance the declaration makes sense; the city's inhabitants will live in the city and commit themselves to it. The city's sons are another important motif taken up from Isaiah 40–55 (see 43.6; 49.17, 20, 22, 25; 51.18, 20; 54.1, 13; also 60.4, 9).[90]

It is the second line that introduces a note of emotion into the prophecy, though even that note is less marked or less clear than it might be taken. In the Old Testament, rejoicing is essentially something one does outwardly; it denotes celebration and festivity. The words that refer to rejoicing denote more the outward expression of celebration than the inner feeling that goes with it. The groom is celebrating his marriage. But presumably the celebration does include emotion, so that this reference to emotion links with the references to delight in v. 4. Here, too, the prophecy reverses a threat in Jeremiah, and also confirms his reversing of that threat (Jer 7.34; 16.9; 25.10; 33.11). 'Your God' is the last expression in the line, as it was the last expression in v. 3, which suggests that v. 5b clarifies the answer to the question in v. 3 about the purpose of the crown in Yhwh's hand, or reworks the image. The image of a crown belongs in the context of the marriage motif running through 61.10–62.5; the crown is part of Yhwh's nuptial attire. A 'glorious crown' is part of a bride's dress in Ezekiel 16.12;[91] Zion is both part of Yhwh's nuptial apparel and Yhwh's bride.[92]

62.6a Over your walls, Jerusalem,// I have appointed guards.
All day and all night, continually,// they will not be still.

Yhwh speaks, perhaps continuing to speak, but the imagery changes and a new subsection begins. There is no parallelism about these two prosaic lines (2-2, 3-2). In general, a 'guard' (*šōmēr*) is someone stationed to protect something, such as sheep or baggage (1 Sam 17.20, 22). Some

[88] BDB.

[89] See Gordon J. Wenham, '*Bᵉtûlāh* "A Girl of Marriageable Age"', *VT* 22 (1972), pp. 326-48.

[90] Cf. Halpern, 'The New Names of Isaiah 62:4' (see above), p. 624.

[91] Cf. Koenen, *Ethik und Eschatologie im Tritojesajabuch*, p. 123.

[92] Lack, *La Symbolique du Livre d'Isaïe*, p. 214.

Levites functioned as 'guards' of the sanctuary (1 Chr 9.19), with the responsibility of ensuring that its sanctity should not be infringed, and there were musicians who had responsibility for their own work day and night (1 Chr 9.33). Psalm 134 describes the praise offered at night that also includes blessing from Zion,[93] and Psalm 130 speaks of guards waiting for the morning, which may imply that they are ministers waiting with anticipation for the dawn and thus for the time to offer sacrifice (so Tg). Psalm 127 speaks of guards that stay awake on their city's behalf, and Psalm 130 might have the same reference. A city's guards keep watch for the advance of enemy forces, or for movement on the part of a besieging army that suggests it is about to try to take the city (cf. Judg 7.19). Given that silence indicates inactivity, the sense the word had in v. 1, describing such guards as not being silent would affirm that they are doing their job properly. They are not asleep on the job. If we understand silence more generally, we might imagine the possibility of asking them what is happening and being sure of getting a reply. Or they might be offering regular reassurance, like a watchman who walks around the city checking for fires or other dangers and periodically reassures people with a cry such as 'Twelve o'clock and all's well'.

The Old Testament also refers to lookouts (*ṣōpîm*) who keep watch more generally. While they may thus warn of danger (e.g. 56.10; Ezek 33.1-7), they may also report the approach of visitors to the city or the return of the city's own army, and so convey good news (e.g. Isa 52.8). While we could wonder whether the 'guards' here in v. 6 are people keeping watch in that broader sense and continuously bringing good news to the city, that idea seems to require considerable inference about the verse and about the word's meaning. Guards are a subset of lookouts, or perhaps the two terms overlap (cf. their collocation in 21.1-12, though the passage is an obscure one);[94] it is not possible to infer that guards fulfil the broader role of lookouts. More likely they guard the city from danger.

Are they then guarding ruined walls? The verse might have in mind the city's rebuilt walls.[95] This would not establish that the prophecy dates from after the time of Nehemiah, when the walls have actually been rebuilt; the prophecy might be imagining the situation when rebuilding will have happened, in fulfilment of Yhwh's promises. The guards' activity is then a guarantee of the city's ongoing future security. Yet herein lies the problem in this interpretation. The lines on either side of v. 6a refer to the event of the city's restoration rather than to its ongoing situation, and v. 6a also more likely refers to this coming event. More likely, then, the posting of the guards relates to the city's situation as it

[93] Cf. Lowth, *Isaiah*, pp 386-87.

[94] Bernard Gosse ('Isaïe 21,11-12 et Isaïe 60–62', *BN* 53 [1990], pp. 21-22) connects these links between Isa 21 and Isa 62 with the role of Isa 62 in the redaction of the book of Isaiah.

[95] Cf. Rosenberg, *Isaiah*, II, p. 484, summarizing David Qimchi.

stands in need of restoration, and v. 6a compares with Yhwh's comment in 49.16, 'Your walls are before me continually'. The stationing of the guards could then promise the city's protection especially as it lacks proper walls. The prophet likely speaks of the guards as appointed 'over' the walls rather than 'on' them, given that the verb 'appoint' (*pāqad* hiphil) is commonly followed by *ʿal* meaning 'over'; see especially Joshua 10.18, where Joshua appoints men over a cave where people are hiding, and 2 Kings 7.17, where the king appoints someone 'over the gate' (see also Gen 39.4; 41.34; Num 1.50 [P]; 2 Kgs 25.22; Jer 1.10; 40.11; 1 Chr 26.32).[96]

Inferring that the guards are stationed over the walls, not on them, helps resolve the question of their identity. It makes it less likely that they are literal, down-to-earth city guards; it would in any case be prosaic to think of the poet-prophet describing these. It is more plausible to take them to be prophets. There are no other occurrences of the use of the word to describe them, as *ṣōpeh* is used with the negative sense in Ezekiel 33.7, but it would not be a stretch to use the word in this way. The prophets would then function as guards over the city by fulfilling the role Ezekiel 33.7 describes in continually warning the city about the way Yhwh will bring trouble to it because of its waywardness. While a promise of their thus having a continuous ministry would fit the promise of a continuous prophetic ministry in Isaiah 59.21, we have concluded that this verse more likely refers to the prophet's spiritual offspring than to 'sons of the prophets' in the sense of people who are themselves prophets, and there are no explicit references to such prophets in Isaiah 56–66. Further, the idea that these prophets act as guards by issuing continuous warnings to the city concerning its wrongdoing stands in tension with the otherwise promissory and encouraging contents of chapters 60–62. More likely, then, the guards are supernatural figures, who can be compared with the 'watchers' of Daniel 4 and later writings, though there the word is *ʿîr* not *šômēr* and their role is different. Here the guards' role will be to ensure that the city's restoration is not prevented by the opposition that the walls' rebuilding indeed met. Their non-silence will be like Yhwh's (v. 1), and will indeed be the implementation of Yhwh's non-silence, as they take the action that will ensure the city's interim safety and its proper restoration. Indeed, difficulty in identifying the guards raises the question whether focusing on this question misses the prophet's point. Whoever they are, they stand for protection, safety, and the completion of this work. The image of posting guards may be simply a metaphor[97] for a guarantee that this will happen, that Yhwh indeed will not be silent.

[96] Cf. Gunnel André, *Determining the Destiny: pqd in the Old Testament* (Lund: CWK Gleerup, 1980), p. 223.

[97] Cf. Penna, *Isaia*, p. 597.

62.6b You who remind Yhwh:// no stopping for you.
7 Do not give him stopping until he establishes,// until he makes Jerusalem an object of earth's praise.

These two further lines manifest little internal parallelism and can seem rather prosaic, though there is some parallelism between them in the form of stepping: 'stopping' in v. 6bβ recurs in v. 7a, and the subordinate clause in v. 7a (until he establishes) is resumed in v. 7b (until he makes). This suggests that seeing v. 7 as a 4-4 line is preferable to dividing it with MT after 'stopping' and seeing the line as a tricolon, 'Do not give him stopping// until he establishes, until he makes Jerusalem// an object of earth's praise'. Possibly we should read vv. 6b-7 in close association with v. 6a. If so, vv. 6-7 reduplicate the pattern in vv. 1-5; an initial first-person word of Yhwh's (v. 6a) is supplemented by comments that work out implications of Yhwh's words but speak of Yhwh in the third person. As was the case in vv. 1-5, one might understand this to involve a statement that came to the prophet from Yhwh which is then supplemented by the prophet's own reflections, or one might see this as an artificial distinction.

LXX and Vg understand v. 6b to refer to people who are mindful or make mention of Yhwh, as in 48.1,[98] but the parallelism in the form of stepping suggests that the hiphil of *zākar* here denotes reminding Yhwh. A *mazkîr* seems to have been an officer in a king's cabinet (e.g. 2 Sam 8.16; 2 Kgs 18.18).[99] The word is conventionally translated 'recorder', but one can imagine that the point about having records was so that the king and his cabinet could be reminded of things from time to time, in keeping with the regular meaning of the verb *zākar*. It is a plausible view that the *mazkîrîm* in v. 6b have this responsibility in relation to the heavenly king's cabinet, though the use of the participle with a direct object indicates that the word is not simply being used as a term for a position or post. Both the nature of the post and the use of this hiphil verb elsewhere would by no means imply it is good news when the earthly or heavenly king is reminded of things. A widow in Zarephat is worried that Elijah's relationship with her involves his ensuring that her waywardness is remembered in this way (1 Kgs 17.18), and Ezekiel uses the verb in the same connection (21.28-29 [23-24]). Here, the possibility that this reminding could have negative implications would link with the possibility that v. 6a refers to the role of prophets in warning people about their wrongdoing. Yet the context in which the present chapter sets both actions (guarding and reminding) implies that the reminding is positive. Any negative reminding (such as one that concerned a commitment to put down enemies), like guarding (against enemies), has a positive end. What

[98] See further Baer, *When We All Go Home*, pp. 72-74.

[99] See Joachim Begrich, 'Sōfēr und Mazkīr', *ZAW* 58 (1940–41), pp. 1-29, reprinted in Begrich, *Gesammelte Studien zum Alten Testament* (Munich: Kaiser, 1964), pp. 67-98.

follows in v. 7 likely implies that the reminding is inherently positive; it suggests reminding Yhwh of decisions the cabinet has taken to restore Zion, the kind of decisions chapters 60–62 focus on. There is thus an overlap between this reminding and what we would call intercession. The reminders bring to the king's attention people on behalf of whom he has a commitment to take action (see the use of the verb in Gen 40.14; 2 Sam 18.18). There is also an overlap with what we would call supplication, prayer for oneself (cf. the ironic occurrence in Isa 43.26; also the headings to Pss 38 and 70; and perhaps passages such as 1 Chr 16.4). The role of these reminders might thus as easily be seen as supplication as intercession. 'So what do they say?', the Talmud asks; and rabbis answer by quoting Psalms 102.14 and 147.2.[100]

As is the case with the guards of v. 6a, the image of people whose task is to act like recorders may simply be a metaphor, or the prophet may imply that there are such supernatural members of the heavenly cabinet, or that prophets function as such reminders. If the guards were prophets, and if the reminders are prophets, then v. 6b will mean that the prophecy moves from speaking about prophets in v. 6a to speaking to them.[101] The verse then covers the two roles of prophets, to speak to the people in Yhwh's name and to speak to Yhwh in the people's name. Nevertheless here, at least, their having this latter task derives from Yhwh's own charge. Like a king commissioning a servant to remind him of things to make sure he does not fail to do something to which he has made a commitment, Yhwh is commissioning them to make sure that no divinely announced intentions fail to get realized. Indeed, this applies whatever the identity of the reminders. The charge functions to reassure the community that Yhwh's declared intentions regarding Zion's restoration will get implemented.

Once more the fact that reminders are being commissioned is more significant than their identity. In the Old Testament the collocation of remembering and forgetting, especially when applied to God, does not refer merely to the way things can slip someone's memory and need to be caused to remain there. When Yhwh 'forgets' something it means Yhwh has put it out of mind and is therefore not doing something about it. When Yhwh 'remembers' something, it means being mindful of it and doing something about it. The issue that reminders thus handle is not that something may have slipped Yhwh's mind but that Yhwh has not taken action when we wished him to. This is the background to protests in the Psalms at Yhwh's having forgotten the suppliant—not 'seems to have forgotten' but has actually done so in the sense of not doing anything (e.g. Pss 42.10 [9]; 44.25 [24]). Yhwh has not merely 'apparently' failed

[100] B. Menahot 87a.

[101] But Koenen understands *mazkîr* to denote 'making mention' and as referring to a proclamation addressed to other people, as in Jer 4.16 (he surveys theories about the matter in *Ethik und Eschatologie im Tritojesajabuch*, pp. 124-26).

to do anything.[102] It is also the background to exhortations to 'remember'—in the sense of be mindful and do something (e.g. Pss 25.7; 74.2). The work of the reminders will express the 'splendid impatience' that characterizes this chapter.[103] 'Stopping' (*dŏmî*) looks like a form derived from *dāmâ* II 'cease', though the only other occurrence apart from Isaiah 62.6-7, in Psalm 83.2 [1], implies at least that it can also carry connotations deriving from *dāmam* 'be still'. So the reminders are urged not to stop undertaking their task or be still or silent.

Verse 7 then applies the stillness/silence image to Yhwh, in keeping with that occurrence in Psalm 83.2 [1], where it is used in parallelism with *ḥāraš* (the stillness Yhwh acknowledged in Isa 42.14) and *šāqaṭ* (the stillness Yhwh abjured here in v. 1). In other words, all three verbs suggest the silence or stillness of inactivity, which means Yhwh is doing nothing about delivering people. The task of the recorders, then, is to deny themselves any rest in order that they may deny Yhwh any rest from such activity. Insofar as *dŏmî* suggests silence, they are to deny Yhwh silence. Insofar as it suggests cessation, they are to deny Yhwh the right to stop before the work is finished; the 'until' takes up the 'until' in v. 1. Yhwh has declared the intention not to be still or quiet until the city's *ṣedeq* and *yᵉšûʿâ* have been achieved; v. 7 urges the recorders not to stop or to let Yhwh stop until that has happened. As Tertullian will comment, the community thus prays forcefully, and 'this violence is pleasing to God'.[104]

The work is then defined as establishing Jerusalem. The verb (*kûn* polel) can be applied to the initial founding of a city (Hab 2.12; Ps 107.36) but also to the confirming or strengthening of a city's position (Pss 48.9; 87.5).[105] Isaiah 54.14 used the hitpolel in a similar connection in a promise to Jerusalem.[106] The city of the day could indeed seem in need of such confirming or strengthening. On the basis of MT's division of the line one might take the second infinitive as nuancing the first; the aim is then that Yhwh should establish Jerusalem as the object of the earth's praise. If we read the line as 4-4, more likely the second infinitive adds a second aim to the first. The aim is that Jerusalem should be established, and thus made into on object of praise. This is rather an unusual concept in the Old Testament, though it recurs as a promise in Jeremiah 33.9; further, in Jeremiah 51.41 Babylon is the object of all the earth's praise. Jerusalem thus takes its place.

[102] Cf. Bonnard, *Second Isaïe*, p. 426.

[103] Herbert, *Isaiah 40–66*, p. 166.

[104] *Apology* 39; cf. Alexander, *Isaiah*, II, p. 409 (he also compares Luke 18.1).

[105] Since a city is a natural object for the verb, it is less likely that this is an instance of the intransitive use of the polel of *kûn*, as in 51.13 (against König, *Das Buch Jesaja*, p. 514).

[106] Cf. Beuken, *Jesaja IIIA*, p. 232 (but he gives the reference as 54.13); on the form, see Goldingay and Payne, *Isaiah 40–55*, II, pp. 356-57.

Tg reworks the meaning of vv. 6-7. The means whereby Yhwh is reminded about Jerusalem is the good deeds of the city's people in the past, which are always being recounted before Yhwh, and will be so until Yhwh makes Jerusalem an object of the world's praise.[107] Realistically, MT makes no assumptions about there being good deeds to remind Yhwh of.

62.8 Yhwh swore by his right hand,// by his strong arm:
'If I again give your new grain// as food to your enemies,
If foreigners drink your new wine// for which you have laboured…'.

In vv. 8-9, a subsection again introduces a first-person declaration that constitutes Yhwh's response to the prophet's 'bold call'.[108] It is later elaborated in v. 9 in words referring to Yhwh in the third person that might consciously be the prophet's own words. Here in v. 8 the divine word has an introduction that makes its nature explicit, though its point is hardly to indicate that this is Yhwh's word rather than the prophet's (no such need was felt in vv. 1 or 6a) but to indicate that it is an oath, and in this way to undergird the commitment expressed in the words. Swearing an oath and failing to fulfil it would jeopardize Yhwh's entire authority in Judah and in the world. The declaration concerning the oath (3-2) comprises parallel bicola, in which the subject and verb apply to the second colon as well as the first; strictly the parallelism appears in the expressions 'his right hand' and 'his strong arm'. Allusions to oaths sometimes refer to raising one's hand (e.g. Gen 14.22; Ezek 20.5-6); for a human being this is a way of calling on God as witness. But swearing *by* one's right hand or strong arm has a different significance. One normally swears by something more impressive than oneself, for instance by God or by God's name (that is, by the person God is, as revealed and reputed; Isa 48.1); God may then be expected to act in punishment of the sacrilege if one does not keep one's oath. Yhwh cannot swear by something more impressive, and thus swears 'by myself' (45.23), or 'by my holiness' (Ps 89.36 [35]). God's whole person undergirds the oath. Here, unusually, it is God's strength that undergirds it.

In accordance with common practice, in v. 8b the oath comprises only a protasis, 'If…'. The apodosis of the oath is left unstated; in a regular human oath it would implicitly take the form of a wish such as 'may I be torn limb from limb' (cf. examples in Job 31). The protasis of the oath thus stands as a strong declaration of intent, implicitly negative. The form is one especially applicable to God (for whom one would hardly be able to devise an appropriate apodosis). The implicitly negative aspect to the oath is expressed in two bicola (3-2, 3-3) that are mutually parallel

[107] On this motif in Tg, see van der Kooij, *Die alten Textzeugen des Jesajabuches*, p. 207.

[108] Paul, *Isaiah 40–66*, p. 556 (not in the Hebrew edition).

though not internally so; in each case the second colon simply completes the first. The experience of abandonment and devastation takes a different form over against those mentioned in connection with the fall of Jerusalem, when many people were transported. This community is back in Jerusalem but its life is not working out. New grain (*dāgān*) and new wine (*tîrôš*) appear in the company of olive oil and other blessings, not least in listing the loss of such blessings that will follow from failing to keep the covenant (Deut 28.51; also Hos 2), but they also often appear as a pair (e.g. Gen 28.28, 37; Deut 33.28; Lam 2.12). So they can sum up the fruits of the harvest. Both relate to the fruit of the harvest as recently gathered (thus 'new wine' is more strictly the unfermented raw material for wine-making—'grapes full of juice').[109] Foreigners such as the Persian authorities consume them in taxes; enemies such as Judah's neighbours might consume them when they invade the country.[110] Thus whereas 61.10–62.7 has focused on the once-for-all event whereby Yhwh will deliver and restore the city, vv. 8-9 look beyond that event to the ongoing life the community will then live, which will be more of a focus in Isa 65–66.[111]

> 62.9 Rather its harvesters—they will eat it,// and praise Yhwh.
> Its gatherers—they will drink it// in my sacred courtyards.

The positive aspect to the oath also occupies two lines (3-2, 2-2) that are mutually parallel, though not internally. The mutual parallelism is particularly close in the initial cola of each line. First the *kî* is taken up in the *û-*; there follows a piel participle plural with third person masculine suffix, the subject being in emphatic position, and each word having similar meaning; the colon concludes with a third person masculine plural qal yiqtol verb with third person masculine singular suffix, the words having complementary meaning. The two second cola are formally different but parallel in substance. Instinctively, the prophecy links the people's rejoicing in the harvest with the harvest celebration at the sanctuary, so that the rejoicing is an occasion when people praise Yhwh in the sanctuary courtyards (cf. Deut 12; 26).[112] The emphasis thus lies not on good harvests as opposed to poor ones but on harvests that the harvesters can partake of and rejoice in rather than watching them be used up by others.

[109] G. Fleischer, *TWAT*, VIII, pp. 645-46 (ET *TDOT*, XV, p. 655).

[110] Avrahami (*The Senses of Scripture*, p. 148) sees this expression as a metaphor for looting in general; but here the concrete depiction is worked out rather thoroughly without need to take it thus, or hint in this direction.

[111] Cf. Westermann, *Jesaja Kapitel 40–66*, pp. 300-1 (ET p. 378).

[112] Indeed, one might translate 'in the courtyards of my sanctuary'; but for this meaning the prophet could have used *miqdāš* (cf. 60.13, 18), and the adjectival use of *qōdeš* is very much more common (e.g. 57.13; 62.12; 64.9 [10]; 66.20).

Verse 8 might seem to have raised the question whether foreigners can join in celebrating before Yhwh in the way a passage such as 56.3-8 envisages. If anyone were to ask this question, v. 9 hints that such joining hardly counts as robbery, to which v. 8 refers. Foreigners are due to be people who facilitate the harvest (61.5) and they could be among the harvesters and gatherers who join in this celebration.

The move from speaking of Yhwh in the third person (v. 9a) and then again having Yhwh speak in the first person once more confirms that we should not be too wooden in seeking to separate the prophet's words and Yhwh's words. The move here happens in the opposite direction from that which has otherwise characterized the chapter, perhaps marking the close of 61.10–62.9 and preparing the way for a transition in vv. 10-12.

62.10abαβ Pass through, pass through the gates,// level the people's road!
Build up, build up the ramp,// clear it of stones!

The last subsection of the chapter closes off chapters 60–62 as a whole.[113] In vv. 11-12 there is a general consistency of theme with what has preceded, but the opening exhortation in v. 10 does suggest an ending. The plural imperatives parallel those in vv. 6-7. Who is being addressed? Initially one might think it is the harvesters of vv. 8-9, who are encouraged to come into the city or into the temple bringing the fruit of their harvest and/or arriving for the celebration v. 9 promised, but while this suits v. 10a, it hardly fits what follows.

In the second line, for MT's *ʾeben* 'stone' 1QIsᵃ has *ʾbn hngp* 'stone of hitting', that is, a stone on which one hits one's foot and thus falls. The expression comes from 8.14, where it came in parallelism with the phrase *ṣûr mikšôl*, an expression of similar meaning; 57.14 already took up the word *mikšôl* in urging, 'build up, build up, clear a road, lift high the obstacles from my people's road'. There the prophet was referring to a way for the people to tread as they take up the life journey which Yhwh wants them to be able to walk and which Yhwh is going to make it possible for them to tread; the term referred to God's dealing with the calamities that had tripped the people up, rather than to their obligation to clear them away. Here 1QIsᵃ implicitly reverses the judgment passed there.[114] It likely has in mind the community's need to remove the moral and religious obstacles that stand between it and God. Tg implies a similar understanding as it makes the prophets the addressees of the exhortations, which come to relate to the people's moral and religious preparation; the

113 Indeed, Steck (*Studien zu Tritojesaja*, pp. 20-27, 143-66) sees it as having a key place as the conclusion of the book of Isaiah in a form it reached in the Greek period; Vermeylen (*Du prophète Isaïe à l'apocalyptique*, II, pp. 486-89) suggests a variant on such a view of the origin of the verses.

114 See Koenig, *L'herméneutique analogique du Judaïsme antique d'après les témoins textuels d'Isaïe*, pp. 284-89.

exhortations encourage the people to turn to the right way as they look forward to Yhwh's comfort. This would be in keeping with a possible understanding of vv. 6-7, if the reminders were identified as prophets and were also identified with the guards whose task is to encourage people to stay on the right path. But all this involves some reading into the imagery.

It is a nice idea that v. 10bβ might refer to paving the road with stones,[115] but the piel verb's only other comparable occurrence (5.2) refers to de-stoning.[116] More likely the clue to understanding v. 10 lies in the relationship between these exhortations and previous similar ones, even though it is 'neither necessary nor possible nor even appropriate to reduce all the poems cited [40.3; 48.20; 49.22; 52.10] to a single referential denominator'.[117] In 52.7-12 a double exhortation to 'depart' followed up a declaration that God's deliverance was about to be seen in Jerusalem; the departure referred to the Judahites leaving Babylon.[118] A similar exhortation in 48.20 had the same significance. Here once more such an exhortation comes at the end of a section of the prophecy.[119] The language of v. 11 follows that of 48.20 and supports this understanding. In these chapters, however, the focus is on Jerusalem. The whole of 60.1–62.9, and the whole of 61.10–62.9 in particular, has focused on the city, and the verses have specifically referred to its walls and its sanctuary. Whether the addressees are to pass through the gates on the way into the city or on the way out of it, it is the city that the line refers to (not the temple), and the city to which it refers is surely Jerusalem. In isolation, v. 10aα might be addressed to exiles passing through the gates on their return to the city, but v. 10aβ rules this out; rather, the addressees are to go out through the gates to prepare a road whereby further returning exiles may come into the city, clearing it of the obstacles that make it impossible for people to come. Over against the exhortations whose wording it takes up, only this verse underlines its 'urgency'[120] by a double repetition of exhortations.

When 57.14 urged, 'build up, build up, clear a road, lift high the obstacles from my people's road', the addressees were Yhwh's heavenly aides. They were also the addressees in 40.1-11, though there the prophet spoke of levelling a road for Yhwh; the people came on Yhwh's coat-tails (or rather in Yhwh's baggage: see 40.10, to be taken up here in v. 11). Here the road is not cleared either for a divine King or for a human king

[115] E.g. Calvin, *In Iesaiam prophetam*, p. 394 (ET IV, p. 332)

[116] Cf. GK 52h.

[117] Lack, *La Symbolique du Livre d'Isaïe*, p. 214.

[118] Beuken (*Jesaja IIIA*, p. 225) sees 52.7-12 as the 'paradigm' for Isaiah 62 as a whole, though Lau (*Schriftgelehrte Prophetie in Jes 56–66*, p. 115) rather describes 49.14-26 as its background pattern.

[119] Cf. Delitzsch, *Jesaia*, pp. 628-29 (ET II, p. 440).

[120] Carol J. Dempsey, 'From Desolation to Delight', in Everson and Kim (eds.), *The Desert Will Bloom*, pp. 217-32 (228).

but explicitly for the people, though there are a number of links between 40.1-11 and 62.10-12. That passage, too, begins with a double imperative, goes on to commission the clearing of a route and the erecting of a ramp (*pannû, derek* and *mᵉsillâ* recur), and later urges a herald to 'raise' a voice with strength as here the prophet urges the addressees to 'lift high' a banner (both times *hārîmû*). Subsequently, 40.1-11 describes Yhwh's coming in those terms that will recur in v. 11.

The reuse of expressions from earlier chapters does not determine the sense in which they are used in a new setting; indeed, it is almost the rule rather than the exception for them to have different meaning in their new setting. But if we are to identify the addressees of v. 10, in this instance it makes best sense to infer that they are again Yhwh's heavenly aides, as was the case in 40.1-5. Nevertheless, uncertainty about the question of their identity may again indicate that we should not focus on this question. Perhaps they are again a metaphor, as the guards and the reminders may be. The point about Yhwh's or the prophet's exhorting someone to go out and prepare a way is to offer an indirect promise that a way will be needed and will be provided.

In v. 10abαβ the four cola are all to some degree parallel. The considerations just noted suggest that in the parallel cola in v. 10a, the second indicates the purpose of the first. The succeeding pair of parallel cola in v. 10bαβ restate that purpose, so that in substance they parallel v. 10aβ, but in form they overlap with v. 10aα in that the double imperative followed by a noun in v. 10bα parallels those in v. 10aα. The double bicolon comes to a close with the stone clearing, which thus has some emphasis. In turn this highlights the question raised by its further recollection, of 5.2; there the clearing of stones had a disastrous outcome.[121]

62.10bγ Lift high a banner over the peoples;// 11aα there, Yhwh has let it be heard// to the end of the earth.

The final, fifth colon of v. 10 moves in a new direction and stands isolated from the rest of the verse. It links with what follows rather than with what precedes. Indeed, even if we follow MT's division of the verses, in distinctive fashion v. 10bγ prepares the way for vv. 11-12, and by its isolation from what precedes it raises expectation and suspense concerning what will follow. But the first two cola of v. 11 turn out to stand in an unclear relationship with what follows them: while it is conceivable that Yhwh should be proclaiming to the end of the earth the commission to tell something to Zion, it is a little odd, and more likely this proclamation to the end of the earth relates to the lifting of a banner over the peoples. The combination of raising a banner and making something heard already appeared in 18.3, and in Jeremiah 51.27, with

[121] Cf. Miscall, *Isaiah*, p. 140.

the hiphil verb;[122] reference to raising a banner combined with reference to noise using some other expression appeared in 5.26; 13.2.[123] So vv. 10bγ-11aαβ form a tricolon leading into vv. 11aγ-12, with the second and third cola working in parallelism with the first. 'Lift high a banner' is paralleled by 'Yhwh has let it be heard'; 'over the peoples' is paralleled by 'to the end of the earth'.

Isaiah 49.22 spoke of 'lifting high a banner to the peoples'. There the banner raised *to* the peoples related to a commission for them to play their part in bringing exiled Judahites back to Jerusalem. While here the banner is raised *over* the peoples, what will follow in vv. 11-12 suggests that this difference is not significant. It does not suggest that the banner is raised *against* the peoples.[124] Whereas earlier promises in Isaiah 60–62 would make it not surprising if the banner were one under which the peoples themselves would come to Jerusalem,[125] the immediate context in vv. 11-12 suggests it rather relates to their facilitating the Judahites' own return, like the banner in 49.22.[126] The further two cola then re-express the idea that Yhwh is making a proclamation along these lines to the whole world. This might support the assumption that the entities raising the banner are Yhwh's heavenly aides, or alternatively that they should not be reified but again treated as a figure of speech. The two cola take up 48.20, 'Cause this to be heard...as far as the end of the earth'. Indeed, the threefold 'There!' in v. 11 might be seen as equivalent to a series of imperatives, also addressed to the aides.[127]

62.11aβ Say to Young Zion,// 'There, your deliverance is coming!
There, his wages are with him,// his recompense is in front of him.'

Once again, in the first line (2-3) the second colon completes the first rather than being strictly parallel to it; the second line (3-2) is internally parallel and also parallel to the second colon in the previous line. The two lines with their further plural imperative whose addressees are unspecified parallel the beginning of vv. 6b-7, v. 10abαβ, and v. 10bγ itself. Once again, the addressees might be prophets (for a prophet such as the present speaker certainly does deliver such a message) or might be Yhwh's heavenly aides, but most likely they are another figure of speech, for the

[122] Cf. Klaus Kiesow, *Exodustexte im Jesajabuch* (Göttingen: Vandenhoeck & Ruprecht, 1979), p. 134; he then sees the line as a later addition.

[123] Cf. Koole, *Jesaja III*, p. 308 (ET pp. 322-23).

[124] Against Steck, *Studien zu Tritojesaja*, p. 151.

[125] So Lim, *The 'Way of the Lord' in the Book of Isaiah*, pp. 123-30.

[126] Weinfeld (see the comment on v. 1b) links the banner with the blazing torch, on the basis of a link between banners/poles and torches in Mesopotamian texts, but here in a line rather different in content from v. 1 the significance of the banner seems to be different.

[127] So Alonso Schökel and Sicre Diaz, *Profetas*, I, p. 374.

certainty that the message with which they are commissioned will come true. MT's verse division points in the direction of taking the two lines as the content of Yhwh's proclamation in v. 11aαβ: what Yhwh bids them make heard is 'Say to Young Zion…'. But this seems laboured, and redividing the lines dissociates v. 11aα a little from these two lines. More likely 'Say to Young Zion' is a metaphorical commission rhetorically parallel to the commission and report in v. 11aαβ. Matthew 21.5 utilizes this colon to introduce a further quotation from Zechariah 9.9 about the arrival of Zion's king.

The expression 'Young Zion' is more literally 'Daughter Zion' (not 'Daughter of Zion'; the construct is a defining not a partitive genitive). The expression came in 1.8; 52.2; and elsewhere, though only here in Isaiah 56–66. Verse 4 has already linked with 1.7 in using the noun 'devastation'; 1.7 also spoke of strangers 'eating' the produce of the land (cf. vv. 8-9 just now), so possibly the parallel with 1.8 is significant. Parallel expressions are Daughter Egypt, Daughter Babylon, and so on, which all seem slightly odd until one recognizes that they regularly point to the (perhaps unexpected) vulnerability and helplessness of the people or city to which they refer (thus 'Daughter Zion' is a recurrent expression in Lamentations). The message 'There, your deliverance is coming' thus confronts and offers reassurance in connection with the helpless position that the city still presently occupies.

At least as significant is a link with 40.9-11, where Zion is the recipient of a message concerning its God's coming. There, the message indeed is 'There is your God. There, the Lord Yhwh comes in might.' Subsequently 51.5 declared that 'my deliverance has gone forth' and Isaiah 40–55 often describes Yhwh as 'deliverer' (e.g. 43.3, 11); here LXX, Tg, and Vg have 'deliverer' rather than 'deliverance'. One might argue that they are justified by the personal reference that reappears in the next line; the Old Testament can speak of Yhwh as 'my helper' or as 'my help', and 'my deliverance' might signify 'my deliverer'.[128] One can hardly suggest that this prophet sees Yhwh's deliverance or coming in less personal terms than the prophecies in Isaiah 40–55.

Verse 11b exactly repeats 40.10b.[129] As a result the line lacks antecedents for the 'his', though its reference is clear enough. The repetition underlines questions about the significance of material from Isaiah 40–55 when it reappears in Isaiah 56–66. In the context of Isaiah 40–55 and the 540s the prophet's promise reflects the awareness that Yhwh had left Zion in 587 and promises that Yhwh is about to return and will bring the exiled Judahites with him. This is good news both for the city and for the exiles. In the context of the beginning of the Persian period, especially

[128] Cf. John V. Chamberlain, 'Functions of God as Messianic Titles in the Complete Qumran Isaiah Scroll', *VT* 5 (1955), pp. 366-72 (370).

[129] See the commentary in Goldingay and Payne, *Isaiah 40–55*, and in Goldingay, *The Message of Isaiah 40–55*.

after the rebuilding of the temple, one would have thought that Judahites believed that Yhwh had returned to the temple, and many of the people themselves had returned from their exile. Yet this repeating of the promise presupposes limits to any sense that this is so. As the narratives in Ezra and Nehemiah show, people are simultaneously aware that Yhwh and former exiles are truly present in Jerusalem, yet also that the city still needs the kind of restoring that Isaiah 60–62 has been promising. In a sense, then, they still need Yhwh to return and to bring back the city's scattered peoples, and the prophet promises that Yhwh will do so.

62.12 People will call them 'The holy people,// ones restored by Yhwh'.
You will be called 'Sought after,//a city that has not been abandoned'.

The chapter and the major section Isaiah 60–62 closes with a further pair of bicola (3-2, 3-3) that are internally and mutually parallel. In each line the opening reference to calling applies to both cola, and these two references are then mutually parallel, with the variation that one is active and one niphal, while one uses the third-person masculine plural and one addresses a second-person feminine singular entity, and one refers to the people and one to the city; these differences then continue through the respective lines. Each line is completed by a double description of the entity to which it refers. With further subtlety of patterning, 'people' comes in the first colon in the first line, while 'city' comes in the second colon in the second line. The third-person formulation invites the audience to look at themselves from the outside and marvel; the second-person formulation invites them to hear themselves addressed and to respond in faith and hope.

The prophet's 'weakness for naming' finds further expression.[130] The two lines promise four descriptions of the people and the city, all to some degree innovative. This is the first occurrence of the precise expression for 'holy people'; it will recur in the Old Testament only in Daniel 12.7 (Isa 63.18 will have 'your holy people'; Deut 28.9 uses the similar expression involving an adjective; Isa 48.2; 52.1 did speak of the holy city). While liturgical texts can use *haqqōdeš* to refer to the sanctuary, the familiarity of phrases such as *ʿîr haqqōdeš* makes it doubtful whether people could be expected to understand *ʿam haqqōdeš* to mean 'people of the sanctuary'.[131] Rather the key to understanding the expression lies in the use of phrases such as *gôy qādōš* (Exod 19.6 [D]) and 'priests of our God' (Isa 61.6). Israel's being the holy people means it is Yhwh's special people, granted a special relationship with and by Yhwh; its being a holy people is not a statement about its inherent being, but a statement about

130 Berges, *Das Buch Jesaja*, p. 463.

131 So Beuken, *Jesaja IIIA*, p. 240. Contrast the use of *miqdāš* in 60.13, and the translation note.

something that comes about through Yhwh's association with it.[132] Likewise the expression 'ones restored by Yhwh' comes only here and in Psalm 107.2, though Isaiah 35.9; 51.10 did speak of 'the restored ones'. The reference to Yhwh parallels the reference to holiness in the first colon and thus suggests recognizing the people as a holy people implies recognizing that they are indeed a people belonging to the holy one.

The expression 'sought after' comes only here. The verb came in 58.2 in connection with seeking after Yhwh in order to get guidance or help, but it is less natural to speak of the city in these terms. Isaiah 60.15 noted that the city's abandonment meant no one passed through it.[133] Jeremiah 30.14 speaks of Israel as having no one to seek after it in the sense of seeking to look after its welfare; the observation in the parallel colon is that all its lovers have put it out of mind. Jeremiah 30.17 then uses the same verb of Zion in connection with noting that it is pillaged and in need of healing.[134] The declaration in Deuteronomy 11.12 that the land of Canaan is one Yhwh seeks after in the sense of looking after its welfare supports the implication that Yhwh is the implied agent of the passive verb.

Even the final verbal expression 'that has not been abandoned' is distinctive, though it is almost as if the prophet had to work hard to make it so. The qal passive participle of *ʿāzab* with this meaning came in v. 4, in 60.15, and earlier in 54.6, but here the prophet uses the niphal verb (it does come in related contexts in 27.10; Ezek 36.4). Other occurrences of this verb, too, make clear that Yhwh is the implied agent of the passive and niphal verbs. The last two lines as a whole thus implicitly focus on the relationship with Yhwh that the city and people's restoration will reflect and testify to.

To whom do the names refer? What precedes in v. 11b would make one think of people who will now return, but the prophecy presupposes that the people to whom its promises are given themselves already belong to the city and to the holy people. It seems implausible to imagine the prophecy disenfranchising or excommunicating them; the prophecy would surely then deconstruct. Rather the returners will come to count as among the holy people and among the ones restored by Yhwh. One can imagine that these new returners would be viewed as disenfranchised and excommunicated by some people in the city, both by some who had not gone into exile and by some who had come back and looked down on others who had failed to do so. By implication, the people in the city are thereby encouraged to take a positive rather than a negative view of others who will return. Indeed, their return will provide evidence that the

[132] Barth notes that the New Testament is very sparing in using equivalent phrases in respect to the church, with similar implications (*Die kirchliche Dogmatik* IV/2, p. 579 (ET p. 512).

[133] Cf. Bentzen, *Jesaja II*, p. 146.

[134] See further BDB.

city is 'sought after' and 'not abandoned'. The chapter thus ends with a litotes;[135] and the effect of v. 12 as a whole is to say nothing new but to say everything new.

Conclusion

Isaiah 61.10–62.12 opens and closes with declarations presupposing that Yhwh has brought about or is bringing about the city's restoration. The opening takes the form of an imaginary testimony to Yhwh's having acted; one might think of the city as the speaker, but the speaker is not identified, so the emphasis lies on the content of the testimony. The closing takes the form of a summons to clear the obstacles that would prevent its people returning to the city. Once again, the road-makers are not identified; I take them to be heavenly aides, but the emphasis once more lies on the fact that the obstacles are being removed and the city's people are returning. The intervening subsections (62.1-9) are more literal in locating the city in a time when it is looking forward to its deliverance and restoration, and it constitutes a series of divine promises that deliverance and restoration will come. Yhwh will indeed act in a way that brings about the city's transformation (vv. 1-5), has taken action to see to the city's protection and to the appointment of agents to issue reminders about what needs to be done (vv. 6-7), and swears that it will be able to celebrate the harvest in Yhwh's courtyards (vv. 8-9).

Volz sees the chapter as not very deeply religious because it does not talk about redemption from sin or of Zion's having a vocation in relation to the peoples.[136] To turn this comment on its head, the prophecy shows that God's concerns are down-to-earth as well as religious. God is concerned that people may have food to eat and wine to drink and that their city should be protected, established, and able to join in celebrating all this before Yhwh. It means there is some continuity between the community's past and present experience of Yhwh's involvement (or non-involvement) in its everyday life and Yhwh's act of transformation, rather than total discontinuity.[137] Further, as usual Volz sees the chapter as eschatological.[138] This designation usefully sets its perspective over against the idea that the prophecy has primarily political concerns; it is not setting forward a program. And the designation draws attention to the finality and radical nature of what Yhwh will do. On the other hand, the word 'messianic'[139] risks misunderstanding in that it easily suggests reference to a messianic figure, and there is no future messianic figure here or

135 Beuken, *Jesaja IIIA*, p. 242.
136 *Jesaja II*, p. 251.
137 Cf. Wells, 'The Statements of Well-Being in Isaiah 60–62', p. 256.
138 *Jesaja II*, p. 250.
139 Muilenburg, 'The Book of Isaiah: Chapters 40—66', pp. 716, 717, 719, 720.

elsewhere in Isaiah 56–66 (unless one counts the anointed prophet of 61.1). It is God who will restore the city, and God will relate to the entire people and treat the entire people as holy. Further, the word 'eschatological' should not be allowed to imply that the prophet is promising action that cannot be expected soon.[140] And while the events related in Ezra–Nehemiah do not constitute a final fulfilment of these promises,[141] they do constitute a first partial implementing of them. Nor should the word 'eschatological' be allowed to imply that the prophecy will bring an End after which there will be no ongoing life. The act of restoration will be the initiation of an ongoing life of harvesting and celebration.

[140] Cf. Kessler's remarks, *Gott geht es um das Ganze*, p. 70.

[141] Contrast Volker Wagner, 'Jes 62—Der Bericht über eine Gebetserhörung', *BZ* 51 (2007), pp. 23-43 (38).

IX

ISAIAH 63.1-6

Translation and Notes

1 ‘Who is this coming from Edom,// marked in clothes from Bosrah[1],
This person adorned in his garment,// stooping[2] in the greatness of his strength?’
‘I am speaking in faithfulness,[3] strong[4] to deliver.’
2 ‘Why red[5] as to your garment,[6]// your clothes like someone treading in a wine trough?’
3 ‘Because I have trodden the press on my own,// and from the peoples[7] there was no one with me,

[1] For MT מֵאֱדוֹם and מִבָּצְרָה, de Lagarde (*Prophetae chaldaice*, p. l) reads מְאָדָּם ‘made red’ (as in Nah 2.4) and מִבֹּצֵר ‘Who is brighter in his clothes than a vintager’. Duhm (*Jesaia*, p. 421) suggests that LXX Βοσορ supports this reading (Syr has *bwṣr*), but Βοσορ is commonly LXX’s rendering of בצרה. See further Sekine, *Die Tritojesajanische Sammlung*, p. 146.

[2] For MT צעה, Vg gradiens, Sym βαίνων might suggest צֹעֵד (cf. Michaelis, ‘Anzeige der Varianten in Jesaia’, p. 191) but might reflect assimilation to the similar context in Judg 5.4; Ps 68.8 [7], or might suggest סֹעֶה (Lau, *Schriftgelehrte Prophetie in Jes 56–66*, p. 282) or might be related to LXX βίᾳ (see de Waard, *A Handbook on Isaiah*, p. 209), which itself perhaps implies the metathesis עצה (Fischer, *In welcher Schrift lag das Buch Isaias den LXX vor?*, p. 66).

[3] For מדבר בצדקה Elliger (*Die Einheit des Tritojesaia*, p. 28) suggests מרבה צדקה ‘multiplying faithfulness’. 1QIs[a] בעדקה is apparently a simple slip (Kutscher, הלשון והרקע הלשוני של מגילת ישעיהו השלמה, p. 204 [ET p. 270]).

[4] For MT רַב from רבב (cf. Syr, Tg), LXX, Sym, Vg imply רָב from ריב, ‘contending’, which provides good parallelism; cf. J. W. Olley, ‘Notes on Isaiah xxxii 1, xlv 19, 23, and lxiii 1’, *VT* 33 (1983), pp. 446-53 (452-53). But on Sym’s use of the verb ὑπερμαχεῖν see van der Kooij’s comments (*Die alten Textzeugen des Jesajabuches*, pp. 240-42): it may suggest more than a mere verbal battle.

[5] אדם is usually an adjective, implying ‘Why [are you] red [as to your garment]’. Less commonly it is a noun, implying ‘Why [is there] red [on your garment]’. The first is more likely as the person was the subject through v. 1 and it is the more common usage.

[6] LXX, Syr, Vg ‘Why is/are your garment(s) red?’ suggest the omission of the preposition ל (dittog.). The Reuchlin ms of MT has pl. לבושיך, as do some medieval and post-MT mss (see *HUB*) and LXX, Syr.

[7] For MT עמים 1QIs[a] has עמי ‘my people’. Mitchell Dahood (‘Hebrew–Ugaritic Lexicography iv’, *Biblica* 47 [1966], pp. 403-19 [412]) sees MT’s ם as enclitic ם. In ‘Hebrew Lexicography’ (*Orientalia* 45 [1976], pp. 327-65 [347]) he attaches the ם to the next word to form the word מאין, an emphatic negative meaning ‘not one man’. The

I tread them[8] in my anger,// stamp on them in my rage,
Their spray[9] spatters on my clothes,[10]// I have stained[11] all my garments.
4 Because a day of redress was in my mind,// my year of restoration had come.
5 But I look[12]—there is no one to help,// I am devastated[13]—there is no one to support.[14]
So my own arm has effected deliverance for me,// my rage[15]—it has supported me.
6 I trample peoples in my anger,// make them drunk[16] in my rage,[17]// bring down their eminence to the ground.'

1QIs[a] reading might have a background in Ezek 25.14, which sees Israel as Yhwh's means of acting against Edom (Barthélémy, *Critique Textuelle de l'Ancien Testament*, II, p. 431; and see further de Waard, *A Handbook on Isaiah*, p. 210).

[8] For MT's simple *w*-yiqtols in this and the next line one would have expected *w*-consecutive. LXX, Syr, and Vg may imply this, but may simply be translating in accordance with the assumed sense. See further the comment.

[9] Sym, Th, Tg take this as נצח I 'eminence' (cf. v. 6) rather than נצח II.

[10] 1QIs[a] lacks v. 3aγδbα (the third to fifth cola in v. 3). Frederick C. Harding ('The Oracle against Edom', *JBL* 33 [1914], pp. 213-27), among other emendations, sees the entirety of v. 3aγδb as secondary.

[11] BDB sees אגאלתי as an Aramaic form; 1QIs[a, b] have the expected piel גאלתי, though Houbigant (*Notae criticae in universos Veteris Testamenti libros*, II, p. 409) suggests הגאלתי. More likely MT's form is a composite of qatal and yiqtol; Cyrus J. Gordon and Edward J. Young ('אגאלתי [Isaiah 63:3]', *WTJ* 14 [1951–52], p. 24) compare with certain Canaanite forms, suggesting it is an inherently composite form not one that results from the combining of textual traditions. Mitchell Dahood ('Some Aphel Causatives in Ugaritic', *Biblica* 38 [1957], pp. 62-73 [70]) rather sees the form as a Canaanite-style aphel. GK53p sees MT's initial א as comparable to the repointing of the ו on the three preceding verbs to make them refer to the future. Either way it compares and links with the way those three verbs may be *w*-consecutives that have been repointed as simple *w*-yiqtols.

[12] As in v. 3 we would expect *w*-consecutive verbs in v. 5a, and LXX, Aq, Syr, Tg might be taken to imply them; see the translation note and comment on v. 3aγ.

[13] As at 59.16, for 'I was devastated', LXX has 'I observed' (though the verb is now προσνοέω rather than κατανοέω), presumably again because of hesitation over the strong anthropomorphism; cf. Syr, also Tg 'it was known before me'; here, further, Vg has 'I sought'. But Aq has 'I was at a loss'.

[14] 1QIs[a] has תומך for MT סומך, with little difference in meaning; MT might be assimilating to the next line, where LXX, Sym, Aq use a different verb in their translation (cf. Kutscher, הלשון והרקע הלשוני של מגילת ישעיהו השלמה, p. 222 [ET pp. 295-96]).

[15] Two medieval mss and many post-MT mss have צדקתי (see *HUB*), as in 59.16; see the translation note there for the suggestion אמתי for MT חמתי.

[16] For ואשכרם one medieval ms, many post-MT mss, and perhaps the Leningrad Codex, have ואשברם 'I shattered' (see *HUB*); on Syr and Tg, see Barthélémy, *Critique Textuelle de l'Ancien Testament*, II, pp. 432-33. Gaster ('Notes on Isaiah', p. 106) rather suggests וָאֲכַשְּׁרֵם 'I crushed them' on the basis of a posited Arabic cognate. G. R. Driver ('Hebrew Scrolls', *JTS* n.s. 2 [1951], pp. 17-30 [29]) understands MT's verb in light of Akkadian *šukkuru* 'transfix'. MT's verbs in v. 6 are again simple *w*-yiqtols, as in v. 3.

[17] LXX lacks this colon.

Introduction

MT and 1QIs[a, b] provide a chapter or paragraph break either side of 63.1-6 (1QIs[b] is less clear at 63.6 because part of the manuscript is missing); the next break comes after 64.11 [12]. This provision corresponds to the nature of the material. At the end of chapter 62 the prophet was reporting Yhwh's words. In 63.1 the prophet asks a question that initiates a dialogue with Yhwh occupying vv. 1-6; by implication, the conversation presupposes a visionary experience, actual or imagined. In 63.7 the prophet begins a different kind of dialogue with Yhwh, which continues through to 64.11 [12].

In substance, however, the content of 63.1-6 links closely both with what precedes and with what follows. Both vision and conversation relate to the fulfilment of the promises in chapters 60–62, suggesting two links and contrasts with those chapters. First, Isaiah 60–62 focused on the positive aspect to the promises, the fact that Zion is to be restored; 63.1-6 focuses on the negative corollary, the fact that the peoples are to be put down. Admittedly we should not draw the contrast too sharply; the defeat of the nations is also integral to chapters 60–62.[18] This reflects the relationship assumed elsewhere in the Old Testament between Yhwh's defence of Zion, Yhwh's victory over the nations, and the nations' recognition of Yhwh. 'We should not be surprised, then, to find the nations streaming toward Zion in chaps. 60-62, having seen Yhwh's justice enacted both in Zion and abroad.'[19] Second, Isaiah 60–62 mostly portrays Yhwh's action as future, while 63.1-6 portrays it as past. Again, we should not draw this contrast too sharply. Chapters 60–62 use a number of past verbs and they portray Yhwh's restoration as so real in Yhwh's intent that in effect it is already actual and demanding of a response from the prophet's hearers, while 63.1-6 includes a number of *w*-yiqtol verbs that have traditionally been taken as having future reference.

In substance the section relates even more closely to the vision in 59.15b-21, the section preceding chapters 60–62, which more unequivocally combines past and future portrayal. In 63.1-6, once again Yhwh looks (though there the verb was *rā'â*). Once again what Yhwh sees is that 'there is no one (*'ên* occurs twice in both passages). Once again Yhwh is devastated at this fact. Once again Yhwh's arm effects deliverance for him; 63.5bα is identical to 59.16bα except for the person of the pronoun. Once again a quality belonging to Yhwh supports him; 63.5bβ is again identical to 59.16bβ except for the person of the pronoun and the

[18] Cf. Fredrick Holmgren, 'Yahweh the Avenger', in Jared J. Jackson and Martin Kessler (eds.), *Rhetorical Criticism* (J. Muilenburg Festschrift; Pittsburgh: Pickwick [1974]), pp. 133-48.

[19] Matthew J. Lynch, 'Zion's Warrior and the Nations: Isaiah 59:15b–63:6 in Isaiah's Zion Traditions', *CBQ* 70 (2008), pp. 244-63 (259).

substitution of 'rage' for 'faithfulness' (in 63.1-6 that word came earlier, in v. 1). Once again the prophet talks of Yhwh's clothing, using the nouns *bᵉgādîm* and *lᵉbûš* (59.17 had the related verb). Once again the prophet speaks of redress, fury, restoration, and of Yhwh 'coming'. The passages thus parallel each other and form an envelope around chapters 60–62, though in the manner of parallelism within a line, the second passage takes matters further. Views differ over whether 63.1-6 is based on 59.15b-21[20] or vice versa,[21] but the similarities and differences are significant whichever way the relationship worked. Like 59.15b-20, 63.1-6 can be described as a divine warrior hymn;[22] Volz again sees the prophecy against the background of the Sukkot festival, noting the focus on the grape harvest and on Yhwh's day of judgment.[23] This version of the divine warrior hymn emphasizes the element of threat and the need of effort on Yhwh's part, and again stresses the significance of the deity's victory for the community itself (faithfulness, deliverance, redress, restoration), but the most significant difference is that whereas 59.15b-21 was concerned with judgment on the community, 63.1-6 is concerned with judgment on the nations. Steck suggests that at one stage 63.1-6 closed off the book of Isaiah.[24]

The prophecy appeals to the hearers' imagination both visually and aurally; it invites them to create a scene in their minds, perhaps a variant on the scene when a lookout sees someone approaching a city. It is not a relatively realistic scene, like the one in 21.11-12 (located in Edom), since the person coming is a single warrior covered in grape juice or blood. Nor does it present itself as a vision. The visual element in the section is subordinate to the words of the warrior, who speaks in terms like those the prophecy elsewhere uses (see especially v. 1b). The section comprises a long question (v. 1a) with a short answer (v. 1b), then a short question (v. 2) with a long answer (vv. 3-6). The contrast in length derives from the way the first question actually functions to tell the hearers what they are to picture, while the first answer simply establishes the identity of the warrior/vintager and the relationship of the scene to what precedes and to the theme of the chapters in general. In contrast, the second question functions simply to give the warrior opportunity to speak further to the prophet's agenda. In other words, formally the two questions address the warrior, but substantially they address the audience, as do the warrior's replies. The conversation is thus artfully constructed, though the artfulness does not settle whether the prophet consciously constructed it or sensed receiving it from Yhwh. It is only superficially

[20] Bernard Gosse ('Detournement de la vengeance du Seigneur contre Edom et les nations en Isa 63,1-6', *ZAW* 102 [1990], pp. 105-10) speaks of 63.1-6 as inspired by 59.15b-21.

[21] So, e.g., Whybray, *Isaiah 40–66*, p. 226.

[22] See the introduction to 59.15b-21.

[23] *Jesaja II*, p. 263.

[24] See, e.g., *Studien zu Tritojesaja*, p. 30.

comparable with dialogues such as that in 21.11-12 or Psalms 24 or 118; it has more in common with the imaginative and imaginary dialogue in Song 3.6-11.

The passage gives no description of an act of slaughter. It confines itself to metaphorical language and describes the event only from a perspective set miles from any gory battle scene and in a time when the battle is long over. 'It is almost as though the Day of Judgment is too cruel, too painful to contemplate, and the exhausted, bloodstained victor is thankful that it is all over.'[25]

Comment

63.1a Who is this coming from Edom,// marked in clothes from Bosrah,
This person adorned in his garment,// stooping in the greatness of his strength?

Presumably the prophet speaks, but like a number of Old Testament accounts of visions and reports of conversations with a supernatural being, vv. 1-6 starts *in medias res*. A more prosaic account would have begun something like, 'In a vision I saw someone coming from Edom…'. I take the verb form *bā'* as a participle (as in 62.11), with LXX, rather than a qatal (as in 60.1), with OL, Vg.[26] It is part of the way the prophet pulls readers into the midst of the visionary account and of events as they happen rather than describing the vision in such a way that they stand outside it. It speaks as if we ourselves can see the figure the prophet refers to. In some sense the question is thus a rhetorical one. As far as we can tell, it is not addressed to anyone on the stage, unless to the prophet's own self. Nor is it answered by anyone except the person it refers to, who is not the person addressed. It functions to attract the attention of the audience in the house. It may also be a rhetorical question in the sense that it requires no answer. There is only one such person who would be coming from Edom. Yet the state of the figure points to the question's appropriateness. The figure must be Yhwh, but it does not really look like Yhwh.[27]

Verse 1a forms two 3-3 internally parallel lines (both abcb′c′, abcb′c′); further, the second line as a whole parallels the first. Taking the opening verb as a participle means that the first colon is a noun clause; the

[25] Sawyer, *Isaiah*, II, p. 196. On approaches to the passage over the past century, see Wolfram Herrmann, 'Die religiöse Signifikanz von Jesaja 63,1-6', in Markus Witte (ed.), *Gott und Mensch* (O. Kaiser Festschrift; Berlin: de Gruyter, 2005), pp. 533-40.

[26] Cf. Beuken's comments, *Jesaja IIIA*, p. 248.

[27] But Grotius, having referred Isaiah 60–62 to Cyrus, takes 63.1-6 to refer to Judas Maccabeus (*Annotationes in Vetus Testamentum*, II, pp. 129-30); Calmet (*Le Prophéte Isaïe*, p. 662) takes this as the literal sense, but takes the passage to refer spiritually to the ascended Christ.

parallelism of the two lines suggests that the force of the opening 'Who [is]' carries over into the second line, which is then also a noun clause. In each line 'this' is then qualified by two qal participles, active then passive in the first, passive then active in the second. The participles pair in meaning as well as in form: the active participles refer to the figure's movement, the passive ones to his appearance, and each of the latter is followed by a reference to his clothing. Each line includes a pair of prepositional phrases, two *min* phrases and two *b*- phrases. In the first line, Edom and Bosrah are parallel, as they are in 34.6 (and nowhere else in the Old Testament, though in Jer 49.22 they come in the same verse).

Edom is the territory of a people that lived to the southeast of Judah in the time of the monarchy; Bosrah is its capital. Israel saw itself and Edom as the descendants of two brothers, to whose brotherly history Malachi 1.2-5 refers back. In 553–552 the last Babylonian king, Nabonidus, invaded Edom and won a victory there.[28] It seems likely that this event was associated with the end of the Edomite monarchy and of Edom's existence as an independent state,[29] and in the next century Malachi 1.2-5 will be referring back to these events. Isaiah 63.1 can hardly be alluding directly to Nabonidus's acts, which would conflict with the statement Yhwh had to act alone,[30] but this present passage might have a less direct relationship with an awareness that Edom had hit hard times.

The brotherly relationship and tension between Israel and Edom might suggest one answer to the question 'Why does judgment begin with Edom and not with Moab or Ammon?'[31] Edom was always a people with whom Ephraim and Judah had an uneasy relationship, a relationship that seems to have become more uneasy in light of events associated with the Babylonian capture of Jerusalem (cf. Ps 137.7; Lam 4.21-22; also Ezek 35). The relationship no doubt became more uneasy as the Edomites, themselves under pressure from the Nabataeans, took over much of southern Judah in the Second Temple period. This might suggest another answer to the question 'Why does judgment begin with Edom and not with Moab or Ammon?' Isaiah 34, Jeremiah 49.7-22, and Obadiah speak at great length and in concrete (not to say gory) detail of Yhwh's judgment on Edom, without specifying the wrong for which redress is exacted. Isaiah 34 describes a great day of redress, a year in which Edom will be paid back in connection with a case that Zion has against it; overlapping phrases come here in v. 4. Possibly 63.1-6 presupposes Isaiah 34, as it

[28] See the Nabonidus Chronicle i.17 (A. Kirk Grayson, *Assyrian and Babylonian Chronicles* [repr., Winona Lake: Eisenbrauns, 2000], p. 105).

[29] See John R. Bartlett, *Edom and the Edomites* (Sheffield: Sheffield Academic Press, 1989), pp. 157-61.

[30] Cf. Koole, *Jesaja III*, p. 321 (ET p. 338).

[31] Max Haller, 'Edom im Urteil der Propheten', in Karl Budde (ed.), *Vom Alten Testament* (Karl Marti Festschrift; Berlin: Töpelmann, 1925), pp. 109-17 (115). Cf. Koenen, *Ethik und Eschatologie im Tritojesajabuch*, p. 86.

does in terms of its place in the book,[32] or possibly Isaiah 34 builds on this section if the order of composition is the reverse, or possibly (given that the overlap in phrasing is not extensive) the two passages are independent in origin.

Edom subsequently became a symbol for an oppressive superpower, a role Babylon plays in the New Testament, and Edom may play that role in Isaiah 34. The collocation of Isaiah 34–35 and Isaiah 60–63 might then suggest that judgment on Edom was a necessary concomitant of restoration for Zion.[33] Tg's very expansive version of 63.1-6, which makes explicit that Edom and Bosrah are the objects of God's judgment, perhaps makes Tg's usual assumption that Edom likewise refers to Rome here. In Isaiah 63 itself, however, there is no indication that Edom means anything other than Edom,[34] and we do not have evidence that in the historical context it would have had a symbolic significance that the prophet could have taken for granted.

At the same time, 63.1-6 has in common with Isaiah 34 that it concerns itself not just with Edom but with the destruction of the nations (34.4), the peoples (63.3, 6). Indeed, 63.1-6 does not say that Yhwh tramples on Edom in particular, only that this is the direction from which Yhwh comes to where the questioner is.[35] This fits with another connection in which Edom appears in the Old Testament. In Judges 5.4 Yhwh advances from Edom and Seir (mountain country commonly associated with Edom) in order to take action on Israel's behalf.[36] In Deuteronomy 33.2 Yhwh comes from Sinai and Seir. In order to act on Israel's behalf, Yhwh comes from Sinai and thus via Edom, as Israel had come by that route when it journeyed to Canaan (cf. also Ps 68.8-9 [7-8]). These parallels would suggest that in Isaiah 63 Edom is not an enemy or an object of judgment but simply a way station on Yhwh's journey to act against the peoples. Joel 4.12-13 [3.12-13] might provide another clue to the scenario the passage presupposes; there the 'Vale of Yhwh Judges' is the scene where Yhwh commissions a judgment of the nations, pictured as a harvesting and trampling of grapes. We do not know where Joel imagined the location of this visionary vale. It has commonly been assumed to be the Qidron ravine near Jerusalem, but that hardly counts as a 'vale' large enough to accommodate such a scene.[37] The Jordan Valley, between Jerusalem and Edom, would do so. Perhaps Isaiah 63 imagines Yhwh coming from Sinai/Edom for such a battle, which has now taken

[32] Cf. Seitz, 'The Book of Isaiah 40–66', p. 519.

[33] Cf. Claire R. Mathews's arguments in 'Apportioning Desolation: Contexts for Interpreting Edom's Fate and Function in Isaiah', in *Society of Biblical Literature 1995 Seminar Papers* (Atlanta: Scholars, 1997), pp. 250-66.

[34] Against, e.g., Volz; see *Jesaja II*, p. 262.

[35] Cf. Claire R. Mathews, *Defending Zion* (Berlin: de Gruyter, 1995), p. 79.

[36] It is here that the verb צעד occurs (see the translation note on v. 1).

[37] Cf. John Barton, *Joel and Obadiah* (Louisville: Westminster John Knox, 2001), p. 99.

place (34.4-5 envisages Yhwh first taking part in a battle in the heavens, but it is difficult to fit this into the scenario in Isaiah 63). On the other hand, the concrete reference to Bosrah might rather suggest that Yhwh comes after acting in judgment on Edom, so that on the basis of v. 1 in itself one can hardly decide whether Edom is victim or way station; it is vv. 3 and 6 with their references to the peoples that will tip the balance in the latter direction.

The description of the person as 'marked' (*ḥămûṣ*) is also enigmatic, and would likely be so for the prophet's hearers. There are two or three roots *ḥāmaṣ* from which the participle might derive. The most common one denotes 'be sour, leavened'. A less common one denoting 'oppress' may be related to *ḥāmas* 'violate', which can also refer to 'stripping' a person of clothes or a vine of its grapes (!).[38] A possible third root outside the Old Testament means 'be red' in the sense of blushing or being ashamed.[39] LXX, Sym, and Syr have 'reddened', Vg 'stained'; Tg is too paraphrastic to reveal how it understood the word. Does it signify that the warrior is soured or embittered? Or violated? Or embarrassed? How do his clothes reflect this? Are they 'sullied'?[40] Are they red with the stain of wine? Verse 2 will support this understanding. Until we reach its further question, however, all that seems clear at this point is that the word has negative implications.

The further passive participial phrase in the second line does not clarify the point, as it describes the person as adorned in attire that suggests honour. The verb (*hādar*) is again rare, but the related noun *hādār* denotes God's majestic splendour in passages such as 2.10, 19, 21, the king's in passages such as Psalm 45.4-5 [3-4], and the majestic splendour that the servant of 53.2 lacked. Psalm 104.1 declares to Yhwh, 'you are clothed in splendour and majesty', using the verb from which the word for garment comes (*lābēš*), and using for 'majesty' a noun related to the verb 'adorn'. So this person comes robed in royal and divine splendour. The parallel colon is again enigmatic, this time in connection with the final active participle (*ṣōʿeh*). The verb means 'bend over'; why is the person bending over? While one might speculate that he is straining forward like a runner, elsewhere such 'bending over' is negative (cf. Isa 51.14), which offers a parallel to the negative connotations of *ḥămûṣ*. It suggests that the person is exhausted by his journey or by the action whose nature we do not yet know. Given that the prophecy will turn out to refer to Yhwh, the anthropomorphism is bold, but not much more so than that in the parallel passage 59.15b-21 where Yhwh needed various

38 See *HALOT*.

39 See BDB; and for further suggestions, D. Kellermann, *TWAT*, II, pp. 1066-68 (ET *TDOT*, IV, pp. 492-93).

40 Corrine Carvalho's word in 'The Beauty of the Bloody God', in Chris Franke and Julia M. O'Brien (eds.), *Aesthetics of Violence in the Prophets* (New York: T&T Clark International, 2010), pp. 131-52 (142).

forms of armour in order to win deliverance, or than 42.13-14. After the participle with negative implications, the *b*- will imply 'despite' (cf. 47.9).[41] What the majestic figure has been doing has required and used up all his great strength.

63.1b 'I am speaking in faithfulness, strong to deliver.'

The figure responds to the question in another parallel bicolon (3-2, again abcb′c′) also comprising a double noun clause, with the 'I' applying to both cola as it responds to the 'Who?' that applied to both the preceding lines.

Although the line is a response, v. 1a was actually a rhetorical question and it was not addressed to anyone in particular, certainly not to the person who responds (so that one could call the line an interruption, not a response);[42] nor does the response strictly constitute an answer. 'It's me' is only an answer to the question 'Who's that?' if the questioner can be expected to recognize the person's voice. Here the answer lies not merely in the 'I' but in the words that qualify the pronoun. There is only one person who comes from Edom and who is characterized by speech that is faithful and by action that delivers. At the same time, for the indirect but real audience of the question (that is, the prophet's hearers), it is a real question not a rhetorical one. While there may be only one person who would be expected to come from Edom, and this person would indeed be of honourable appearance, in other respects the description in v. 1a did not match this implied answer to the question. So the answer is both unsurprising and surprising.

The self-designation as one who speaks in faithfulness recalls Yhwh's self-description in 52.6, 'I am the one who speaks: here I am'; in other words, I spoke, and my presence here means I am acting as I said I would (cf. the use of the qatal verb in 40.5; 45.19; 46.11; 48.15, 16; 58.14). Earlier, 41.26 had raised the question of who had announced ahead of time the rise of Cyrus (as Yhwh claims to have done) so that people would now have to say 'he is *ṣaddîq*', 'he is in the right' or 'he is faithful'. Here Yhwh declares that he indeed speaks in faithfulness, speaks as one who announces intentions and then fulfils them. LXX and Vg translate as if *ṣᵉdāqâ* were the direct object of the verb, as if Yhwh is speaking faithfulness. This is so, but it is not what Yhwh says; thus Tg, Syr, Sym, keep the preposition. The figure claims to be one who speaks in faithfulness in the sense of announcing action that will be a demonstration of faithfulness, an announcement that will find faithful fulfilment; in the context, in light of its use in Isaiah 56–62, *ṣᵉdāqâ* will have its fuller

[41] See BDB, p. 90b.
[42] So Croatto, *Imaginar el futuro*, p. 329.

implications (see especially 56.1; 59.9, 14, 16, 17). Isaiah 56–62 has been repeating and making even more glorious promises of the kind that already appeared in Isaiah 40–55; they will be fulfilled.

In the second colon, *rab* ('strong') picks up *rōb kōḥô* ('greatness of his strength') from the previous line. Yhwh's word can be fulfilled faithfully because Yhwh has the strength to 'deliver', another key word in the chapters: for instance, the same verb form came in 59.1, 'Yhwh's hand is not too short to deliver'; the same parallelism came in 56.1, 'my deliverance is near to coming, my faithfulness to appearing' and in 59.16, 'his arm has effected deliverance for him; his faithfulness—it has sustained him'; and earlier, 'I have declared and I have delivered', 43.12.

As well as being active in promoting *mišpāṭ ûṣᵉdāqâ* among his own people by putting down those who wrong the weak, a Middle Eastern king was expected to take similar action in relation to other peoples that wronged his people, in the way v. 1b describes. He was expected to speak with faithfulness about his intentions and to exercise his power to deliver his people by putting down their oppressors. Yhwh also accepts that moral obligation.[43] In one sense, then, the royal figure addressed in v. 1a has not answered the question. He has not said (for instance) 'I am Yhwh', as God might have done in Isaiah 40–55. But in substance he has made important declarations or claims in response to that question. That it is Yhwh might not need stating; it is the kind of person Yhwh is that needs reaffirming. The self-declaration has also provided an implicit answer to the question how Yhwh can be in the state that v. 1a describes, though that aspect of the question will now come into focus.

63.2 Why red as to your garment, // your clothes like someone treading in a wine trough?

The prophet asks a further question, in another 3-3 bicolon. This time it is a genuine one; it is addressed to someone, it asks a question to which the questioner does not know the answer (or purports not to know it), and it receives an answer from the person it addresses. It is parallel in content if not in syntax:[44] though the 'why' applies to both cola, there are two words for apparel with a second-person singular suffix (one singular, one plural), and 'red' is spelled out in 'like someone treading in a winepress'. The question in the first colon thus raises a further question: What kind of red does it refer to? The second colon clarifies this point: it is like the red of grape juice. The first colon also suggests a paronomasia, because 'red' is *ʾādōm*, which has the same consonants as Edom, the country from which the figure comes. The paronomasia is a familiar one (see Gen 25.30 [J]).

[43] Cf. Moshe Weinfeld, *Social Justice in Israel and in the Ancient Near East* (Jerusalem: Magnes; Minneapolis: Fortress, 1995), p. 189.

[44] LXX, Syr, Vg have versions that are more closely parallel: see the translation note.

The way the prophecy unfolds may imply another paronomasia, since 'blood' is *dām*; indeed Akkadian has a word *adamu/adamatu* meaning blood.[45] Yet a further paronomasia also remains implicit.[46] The name Bosrah comes from the verb *bāṣar* meaning 'cut off', specifically 'cut off grape clusters from a grapevine'. Thus a *bōṣēr* is a grape-gatherer and the vintage is *bāṣîr*. Though Edom had its share of vines (see, e.g., Num 20.17), and wine imagery appears in coins from Bosrah in the Roman period,[47] in the Old Testament there is no particular association of Edom with viticulture; the association is purely linguistic.

A winepress comprises two stone basins set or cut into the ground and linked by a conduit, one basin preferably being lower than the other. Grapes are stacked into the upper trough (*gat*) and are trodden (and/or in later times have other pressure applied to them) so that the juice flows into the lower vat (*yeqeb*; e.g. Isa 5.2; 16.10—reflecting the way both words can be used for the structure as a whole).[48] Although some passages refer to treading the wine trough (Lam 1.15; Neh 13.15; and the next line, with a different noun), the immediate object of the treading is the grapes in the trough (cf. Isa 16.10); hence the preposition here. It would be natural for the juice from the grapes to splash the clothes of the person doing the treading. Perhaps the implication here is that the stain is more extensive than one might ever have expected; v. 3 will then explain why this is so.

63.3 'Because I have trodden the press on my own,// and from the peoples there was no one with me,
I tread them in my anger,// stamp on them in my rage,
Their spray spatters on my clothes,// I have stained all my garments.

There are two surprising features of the wording in v. 3. The one often noted is the three simple *w*-verbs in the second and third lines, where one would have expected *w*-consecutive. MT may be referring the verbs to a future act of deliverance (cf. Tg), in association with the assumption that Edom refers to Rome.[49] The way 59.15b-21 combined past and future verbs would support MT's expectation that both would appear here, but it is hard to make sense of the particular way MT distinguishes between Yhwh's past and future action; the prophecy will originally have referred throughout to events that are past within its timeframe. On the other hand,

[45] Cf. Watson, *Classical Hebrew Poetry*, p. 29.

[46] But see the translation note.

[47] See, e.g., Cheyne, *The Prophecies of Isaiah*, II, p. 102.

[48] Cf. G. W. Ahlström, 'Wine Presses and Cup-Marks of the Jenin-Megiddo Survey', *BASOR* 231 (1978), pp. 19-49 (19).

[49] So G. Moore in a review of C. A. Briggs, *Messianic Prophecy* (*TLZ* 12 [1887], cols. 289-93 [col. 292]), following Luzzatto; cf. GK 107b; *TTH* 174.

instead of re-pointing the verbs it is possible to take the MT verbs as yiqtols with the same past time reference as the opening verb in v. 3 but as referring to the past in more vivid fashion.[50] The second surprising feature is the opening word order, where the object precedes the verb. One might then translate 'The press: I have trodden on my own; from the peoples there was no one with me'. But there seems to be no rhetorical point about this word order and more likely the significance is syntactical; it marks the clause as a circumstantial clause, specifically one providing a reason.[51]

We have noted that the first round of inquiry involved the prophet asking a two-line question and the figure giving a one-line answer, while in this round, the prophet asks a one-line question and gets an answer that occupies the rest of vv. 3-6. Its beginning in v. 3 is quite repetitive, with the implication that its content, though simple, is especially important. The three lines, each internally parallel, do make three different points.

The first (3-3) takes up from v. 2 but turns the simile into either a metaphor or a factual statement within the visionary conversation (it is thus still a metaphor in the broader context). Here the figure does speak of treading the press, using a noun (*pûrâ*) which comes elsewhere only in Haggai 2.16 and there implicitly refers to the vat; perhaps it denotes the whole structure and then can also be used either of the upper trough where the treading actually happens or of the vat.[52] So first, the figure confirms that he has been treading; but the last word in the first colon then makes a new statement, which is repeated and expanded on in the parallel colon. Within the picture, Yhwh has been treading the grapes alone. Grape treading was normally done in the company of other people;[53] the head of the family would not usually expect to undertake this task alone. So it is as if no one from the family was willing to help, which is one reason why the treader appears wine-stained and tired. In the second colon, reality pokes through. As one who is active in political events, Yhwh acted alone because no other people joined in the action. The destiny of the peoples did not inevitably involve their destruction. They had opportunity to side with Yhwh, but they did not do so. To put it another way, as usual the chapters presuppose that nations or peoples choose between alternative destinies. They can submit themselves to Yhwh, acknowledge that Jerusalem is Yhwh's city, support it, and enjoy the benefits of doing so; or they can insist on maintaining their stance of independence and resistance.

[50] So *DG* 85.

[51] For which see GK 156d; *DG* 125, 137.

[52] Carey Ellen Walsh (*The Fruit of the Vine* [Winona Lake, IN: Eisenbrauns, 2000], pp. 163-65) suggests it is larger than an ordinary *gat*.

[53] De Hulster, *Iconographic Exegesis and Third Isaiah*, pp. 235-36, provides pictorial material illustrating the point.

The picture of Yhwh fighting a lone battle might have more than one background. Isaiah 40.12-14 emphasized that Yhwh created the world without any help, and this line has resonances with the story of Marduk defeating Tiamat in putting down opposition and bringing about the world's creation, which belongs to the 'divine warrior hymn' genre. Once again God's bringing things about in history and/or at the End parallels God's bringing things about at the Beginning.[54]

Isaiah 44–45 presupposed a different framework. A common assumption in the Prophets is that Yhwh makes use of human agents in bringing about political change. The Assyrian king is the staff in Yhwh's hand in taking action against Judah (10.5), Nebuchadnezzar the Babylonian king is Yhwh's servant in a similar connection (e.g. Jer 25.9), and Cyrus is Yhwh's anointed in putting Babylon down and freeing the Judahite exiles (Isa 45.1). In these different historical contexts, there are agents Yhwh can thus conscript. In the context to which Isaiah 63 refers, there is no such agent among 'the peoples'. This expression can be used in a variety of ways. In Isaiah 56–66 it first appears with reference to peoples drawn into a relationship with Yhwh (56.7), then to peoples among whom Israel's offspring will be recognized (61.9) and to peoples who will hear of Yhwh's intention to restore Israel and are to facilitate the Judahite exiles' return to Jerusalem (62.10). Earlier in Isaiah it can also refer to the superpower (e.g. 8.9; 17.12) and to the victims of the superpower (e.g. 10.13, 14; 14.6). In light of the way the Prophets speak of the superpower as Yhwh's agent, in the present context reference to the superpower seems likely, and this will be confirmed by the next line. Yhwh cannot find a superpower to take action. The statement thus makes for a contrast with statements in earlier prophecy, in what has been called a move away from seeing Yhwh's hand in political events and towards an apocalyptic way of thinking.[55] The prophecy's own perception is that this is not a change in the way the prophets see things but a change in the way history is working out and/or in how Yhwh is working. In the terms of the former perspective (the one the prophet adopts), there is no superpower on the horizon to put (presumably) Persia in its place in the way Assyria, Babylon, and Persia itself had been present to be harnessed by Yhwh in earlier contexts. In the terms of the latter perspective, Yhwh declines to 'raise up' such an agent. It is not the prophetic perspective that has changed but the divine method. For this prophet, at least, the interaction between Yhwh's action and political events is indeed an interaction. The divine raising up of Assyria, Babylon, or Persia was not a miracle, one in which Yhwh makes things happen that cannot be understood in regular cause–effect terms, or in political and economic terms. In the present context there is no such development that can be harnessed.

[54] Cf. Westermann, *Jesaja Kapitel 40–66*, p. 304 (ET pp. 382-83).

[55] See Hanson, *The Dawn of Apocalyptic*, pp. 206-7. Cf. the 'Conclusions' to the commentary on Isa 59.15b-21 and on Isaiah 60, above.

The second line in v. 3 (2-2) is neatly parallel, aba′b′. Each colon begins with a *w*-yiqtol first-person singular qal verb with a third-person plural suffix. Thus in terms of their vowels the two verbs rhyme, and they have similar meaning. The first (*dārak*) takes up the verb from the preceding line (indeed, the preceding two lines); the second (*rāmas*) is the novelty. Both verbs are followed by nouns of similar meaning (though the second is more forceful and rarer), prefixed by *b*- and followed by a first-person singular suffix. What the line adds to v. 3aαβ is the reference to the vintner's anger or fury. The first noun is the one used (for instance) in connection with Yhwh's using Assyria against Judah in 10.5 and of Yhwh's action against Babylon in 13.3; 14.6. The second noun appears in association with the first in 42.25; 66.15 (also, e.g., Jer 7.20; 21.5; 32.31, 37; 33.5; 42.18; 44.6; Lam 4.11). It also appears three times in application to Yhwh in 51.17-23 and in 59.18. It is typical of such nouns to denote not so much the fury that Yhwh feels as the fury of Yhwh's action, and this fits the present context, where the fury of the vintner's action explains how so much juice has come to stain his clothes, though the implications in vv. 5-6 are different. Either way, Yhwh's furious anger is good news for the people who hear the prophecy. The verbs' third-person plural suffixes refer back to the peoples of the preceding line, and thus to the superpower. It is this reference that sways the balance regarding the significance of the allusion to Edom in v. 1; the peoples (cf. also v. 6) are the object of Yhwh's action and Edom is the direction from which Yhwh came after taking that action. Even if there is no indication of the rise of a power to put Persia in its place, this lack does not stop Yhwh acting forcefully. The prophet has seen Yhwh doing so.

Verse 3b (3-2) comprises two further cola that are parallel in substance though not so much in form; its opening and closing with verbs does bring the three-line statement to a close. 'All my garments' (the word is plural; it was singular in v. 1, though the evidence is a little mixed for v. 2) goes beyond 'my clothes'. Likewise 'stain' (*gāʾal*) goes beyond 'spatter' (*nāzâ*) though both are interesting verbs in the context. 'Spatter' usually refers to blood, though it can refer to oil or water; more consistently it suggests a religious rite, with 2 Kings 9.33 the only other clearly non-ritual reference. Further, except in that passage, spattering is elsewhere always a positive notion; it conveys cleansing or some other positive association. It thus has the opposite connotations to 'stain'. Although 'stain' also commonly has religious associations, all the references to stain come in the Prophets and the Writings, whereas all the other references to spattering come in the Torah except for the one just noted and Isaiah 52.15. Strikingly, 59.3 has noted that the community is stained with blood. The warrior's stain comes from shedding blood, but not with the pejorative associations that applied in 59.3. One reason for the prophet's using the word will emerge in the next line, when a homonym appears. Yhwh is stained in order to restore.[56]

[56] Cf. Paul, ישעיה פרקים מ-סו, II, p. 514 (ET p. 564).

For ‘spray’ (*nēṣaḥ*; the word comes only in this passage), LXX, Syr, and Vg have ‘blood’. Etymologically it seems to be something that splashes, and in this context the word’s usefulness derives from its ambiguity; it could refer to juice or blood, among other things. It also opens up the possibility of yet another paronomasia (see v. 6). Within the terms of the metaphor, it suggests the juice on the vintner’s clothes. In terms of the metaphor’s reference, it denotes the blood on the warrior’s clothes, though the prophecy never explicitly refers to blood. Thus, while there is some justification for the observation that ‘God returns from Edom like an Anat or an Ishtar covered in blood’,[57] the description is much less bloody than the one in the Anat story[58] and lacks such close parallels as need indicate a close connection.[59] Further, the passage illustrates a principle about the use of metaphor. Metaphor works because there is an overlap between something that needs to be understood and something that may help to understand it, but by definition there is not a one-to-one correspondence between these two, between the signifier and the thing signified. The prophet’s audience thus has to ask what aspects of the signifier aid the understanding and to perceive where the metaphor should not be pressed. Commonly, context aids that discernment, not least because it provides other metaphors, so that a group of metaphors helps one perceive the specific significance and the limits of any individual metaphor. Isaiah 56–66 as a whole, for instance, helps one not to over-interpret the metaphor of Yhwh the warrior. The particular point about the emphasis on the quantity of blood that Yhwh spills is to underline that Yhwh is a superlatively powerful actor, acting alone.[60]

63.4 Because a day of redress was in my mind,// my year of restoration had come.

Verse 3 answers the question in v. 2, but there is more to be said by way of explanation. After the opening *kî* the 4-3 line comprises parallel cola, abca′b′c′. Each begins with a construct noun denoting a time reference, followed by an absolute noun designating the time reference’s significance. ‘[Was] in my mind’ and ‘had come’ reveal that one cola is a noun clause, the other a verbal clause. In isolation one might give the line present time reference, translating ‘is in my mind’ and ‘has come’, but the context points to past time, and specifically suggests that it alludes to a time before the action reported in v. 3.

[57] Corrine Carvalho, ‘The Beauty of the Bloody God’ (see above), p. 149; cf. Paul, ישעיה פרקים מ-סו, II, p. 513 (ET p. 563).

[58] See, e.g., *ANET*, p. 136.

[59] Cf. John Day’s comments, *Yahweh and the Gods and Goddesses of Canaan* (Sheffield: Sheffield Academic Press, 2002), pp. 141-42.

[60] See Mark Zvi Brettler, ‘Incompatible Metaphors for YHWH in Isaiah 40–66’, *JSOT* 78 (1998), pp. 97-120 (103-6).

Solely by implication have vv. 1-4 concerned themselves with judgment and bloodshed. The word 'blood' has not appeared. Only the references to deliverance and to anger and rage and the 'like' in v. 2 have signalled that the prophet is alluding to anything other than a grape harvest. It is those words that point to there being something more to the picture, and the prophet's hearers could likely be assumed to be familiar with grape treading as a metaphor for judgment. Within the Old Testament, the image of grape treading is first applied to Yhwh's punishment of Judah (Lam 1.15); it is now applied to other peoples.[61]

The phrase 'day of redress' (*nāqām*) picks up from 61.2.[62] There the parallel phrase (though the two came in the reverse order) was 'year of acceptance' (*rāṣôn*), here it is 'my year of restoration' (*g*^{e}*'ûlay*). There are actually several ways of construing the latter word. LXX's 'year of release' suggests taking it as an abstract noun *g*^{e}*'ûlay* comparable to terms such as *šadday*. This seems least likely, as the ending that looks like a first-person suffix forms a parallel with the suffix on 'in my mind' in the first colon. Isaiah 62.12 referred to *g*^{e}*'ûlê yhwh*, 'ones restored by Yhwh', and the word here could be the same qal passive participle with a first-person suffix, suggesting 'a year of my restored ones'. But this does not make for a natural construction here. More likely it is a form from an abstract noun *g*^{e}*'ûlîm* meaning 'restoration', with the first-person suffix.[63] Whichever understanding is right, the word introduces a paronomasia with the use of *gā'al* II meaning 'stain' in the previous line. Yhwh's act of *g*^{e}*'ûlîm* in the first sense issued in *g*^{e}*'ûlîm* in the second sense.

Whereas in 61.2 the positive implications of 'redress' are anticipatorily spelled out in the parallel term 'acceptance', here they are thus spelled out in the word 'restoration'. The root is taken up from passages such as 60.16,[64] but the expression 'year of restoration' also suggests a more explicit link with the Jubilee year, the year when land was restored to its owners and when people who had to let themselves be employed as servants were restored to independence (see Lev 25 [H]). Here the idea of a year of restoration for a family's tract of land and for individuals becomes a metaphor for the whole land's restoration to the people and the whole people's restoration to independence from the control of a foreign power.

Verse 4 thus resumptively sums up statements from chapters 60–62. It declares that the action of the warrior/vintner constitutes the implementing of promises made in those chapters. Historically this action remains future, but it is certain. It was in Yhwh's mind or intention (*lēb*, anatomically 'heart') and thus it has in effect already arrived.

[61] Perhaps it is significant that Lamentations 1 itself ends with a plea for judgment on the enemy (GID).

[62] See the comment there on *nāqām* and on the alternation of 'day' and 'year'.

[63] Ludwig Köhler takes it to have temporal meaning, 'time of restoration' ('Jes 63 $_{4}$', *ZAW* 39 [1921], p. 316). Perles (*Analekten zur Textkritik des Alten Testaments*, p. 88) emends to גמולי (requital).

[64] See the comment there.

63.5 But I look—there is no one to help;// I am devastated—there is no one to support.
So my own arm has effected deliverance for me,// my rage—it supported me.
6 I trample peoples in my anger,// make them drunk in my rage,// bring down their eminence to the ground.

The final three lines in the section restate v. 3. Broadly, the two lines in v. 5 reformulate v. 3aαβ in reverse order, the two cola in v. 6a reformulate v. 3aγδ, and a last colon comprising v. 6b reformulates v. 3b. Verses 5a and 6a again use *w*-yiqtol verbs, which I understand along the same lines as the ones in v. 3. Each of the bicola in vv. 5-6a (3-3, 3-3, 3-2) is internally parallel.

While v. 5a reformulates declarations in v. 3a, in wording it is more closely a restatement of 59.16a, 'he saw that there was nobody, and he was devastated that there was no one intervening', though it still involves extensive and creative reworking. For the common verb 'see' (*rā'â*) this line has the much less common 'look' (*nābaṭ* hiphil), though it then simply repeats the parallel verb, while changing both verbs to first person. Whereas 59.16a has 'that' (*kî*) in each colon, this verse simply has *w*-. The line is thus harder to construe than 59.16a, and LXX, Syr, Vg, and Tg water down the second verb to something closer to a synonym of the first,[65] while some modern translations construe the second colon differently from the first.[66] More likely the two cola are to be construed in the same way.

Both versions follow with 'there was no' (*'ên*) as in v. 3 here, which indeed had the complete phrase 'there was nobody' which appeared in 59.16. The present verse has the stronger 'there was no one to help', a common expression in the Old Testament (e.g. Pss 22.12 [11]; 72.12; 107.12). Whether applied to God or to human beings, the image of a helper does not suggest someone who is essentially one's equal or colleague and who gives assistance, but someone who is more powerful and who acts as a deliverer when one is helpless. Thus the great 'helper' in the Old Testament is Yhwh (e.g. Pss 10.14; 54.6 [4]), and Yhwh is often the subject of the verb *'āzar* in Isaiah 40–55 (41.10, 13, 14; 44.2; 49.8; 50.7, 9). The point is underlined by the use of the participle from *sāmak* to parallel the participle from *'āzar*. Supporting implies holding up someone who would otherwise fall down; Yhwh is again the great 'supporter' (Pss 37.17, 24; 54.6 [4], in the same parallelism as here; 145.14). This verb replaces 'one to intervene' (*pāga'* hiphil) in 59.16a, which suggested that Yhwh was looking for someone who would take responsibility to act on Yhwh's behalf.

At first sight v. 5a might seem to be a lament that no one is acting as helper or supporter to Yhwh. It would be a strong anthropomorphism to

[65] See the translation note.
[66] See, e.g., Westermann, *Jesaja Kapitel 40–66*, p. 302 (ET p. 380); also TNIV.

describe Yhwh as needing and lacking help and support, and thus to suggest that Yhwh is not up to the task that needs accomplishing. It would be an ironic statement in light of the fact that Yhwh is the helper and supporter par excellence. While we could not assume that 63.5a has similar significance to 59.16a, here two considerations point in the same direction. Interpreting 63.5a in light of 59.16a avoids the attribution of an implausible meaning to 63.5a. The unstated object of help and support is not Yhwh but Israel, as in the other passages noted. In light of this usage of the two verbs and of the precedent in 59.16a, it is natural to expect that an Israelite would understand the line in this way. Yhwh had looked and been horrified that no one was acting as help and support to Israel.

Verse 5b then affirms that what political powers would not do, Yhwh determined to do. Again the line restates 59.16. The first colon is identical except for the necessary change in suffixes from third person to first person. The second colon involves the same change to two suffixes, but also the replacement of 'faithfulness' (*ṣ*ᵉ*dāqâ*) by 'rage' (*ḥēmâ*). The complementarity of these expressions compares with the complementarity of redress and restoration. Yhwh's rage against the community's oppressors energizes Yhwh in taking action against them in faithfulness to Israel. In this context, the reference to Yhwh's rage also anticipates the emphasis of the next line.

As v. 5 restates v. 3aαβ, then, v. 6 restates the declaration in v. 3aγδ and then the one in v. 3b. Verse 6a in itself is a straightforward bicolon whose cola begin with first-person *w*-yiqtol verbs and close with the same two expressions for 'in my anger/rage' as came in v. 3aγδ. The first colon has a different word for Yhwh's 'trampling' from the two in v. 3; its object is again 'peoples' (cf. v. 3aβ), which in the second colon is represented by the third-person suffix on the verb there (as in v. 3aδ). The novelty in the line is that second verb, 'make drunk' (*šākar* piel), which takes up the familiar prophetic picture of making someone drunk with a drink that is actually poisonous, which becomes an image for Yhwh making a people drink a cup full of Yhwh's wrath which causes them to collapse as if drunk, and die. The image came in 51.21, in a passage noted in connection with v. 3aγδ above because of its references to Yhwh's rage.

The bicolon in v. 6a would make a satisfactory close to the section; alternatively, one would not be surprised if there followed another line equivalent to v. 3b. What we actually find in v. 6b is one further colon, which makes v. 6 a tricolon. LXX omits the middle colon and thus ends the section with a more regular line, but with hindsight the tricolon to close the section is not a surprise; and this single colon is equivalent to v. 3b, though in a subtle way. Its opening first-person *w*-yiqtol verb parallels the one that precedes, and in substance makes for a suggestive sequence in the three verbs in the line. The first verb parallels the ones in v. 3. The second colon declines to maintain the imagery of trampling that appeared in both cola in v. 3 and instead takes the imagery in a new direction. The third verb (*yārad* hiphil) fits with that move as it describes the putting down of the peoples in power over Israel (cf. 10.13; 14.11; 43.14). The verb can be used for bringing people down to earth or down to death from their position of eminence (e.g. 14.11, 15; Obad 3), and if *ʾereṣ* can sometimes refer to the underworld, here the prophet may refer to Yhwh's bringing the peoples down to Sheol.[67]

The concrete link with v. 3b comes in the closing word, *nēṣaḥ*, which introduces yet another paronomasia. In v. 3 it meant 'spray', and in translating the word 'blood' here, LXX assumes it is the same word. But Aq, Sym, Th, Syr, Tg, Vg assume it is a homonym meaning 'eminence', which with this meaning is almost as rare as *nēṣaḥ* 'spray' (*nēṣaḥ* with the related meaning 'perpetuity' is much more common: e.g. 57.16). Indeed, perhaps the background of both meanings lies in the idea of brightness, and they are variant meanings of one word. For either meaning, the verb 'bring down' is unusual but possible; *yārad* hiphil is so used with liquids as well as with bringing people down to earth or death or Sheol.[68]

Conclusion

Isaiah 63.1-6 restates 59.15b-21, but the restatement has an extra level of significance as a result of its following on chapters 60–62, which have painted in more glorious colours the act of restoration Yhwh intends to bring about. The prophet's new vision of the process whereby Yhwh puts this act into effect begins more concretely by portraying Yhwh's approach to Jerusalem from the southeast, from the direction of Sinai. Yhwh's clothing is regal, but sullied. Metaphorically, Yhwh has been treading grapes; more literally (in a sense) Yhwh has been fighting a bloody battle. It is a battle that required much effort, and Yhwh is tired. The expenditure of effort derived from the fact that Yhwh had to fight this battle alone and had to summon up reserves of angry fury in order to do so effectively. But the battle has been won, and therefore Yhwh can come to Jerusalem as faithful deliverer, as one who speaks and does then act. The negative side of the task that was needed has been accomplished; Yhwh can now come to put into effect the positive side, the actual restoration of the city.[69]

The prophecy thus expresses the hope of a 'humiliated and marginalized people';[70] or rather, it expresses a prophet's response to the hope or to the lack of hope of such a people. The group whose views the

[67] So Scullion, 'Some Difficult Texts in Isaiah cc.56–66', p. 122.

[68] Cf. Paul, ישעיה פרקים מ-סו, II, p. 515 (ET p. 567).

[69] Contrast Lau's comment that in content 63.1-6 has nothing to do with Isa 60–62 (*Schriftgelehrte Prophetie in Jes 56–66*, p. 281); rather see Ruszkowski, *Volk und Gemeinde*, p. 49.

[70] Zapff, *Jesaja*, p. 402.

prophecy represents, 'uncompromising in its insistence upon the purity of the national cult, was just as uncompromising in its claim of Yahweh's lordship over the nations of the world'.[71] While the historical context of Isaiah 56–66 makes it likely that 'the peoples' whom Yhwh has been putting down are the Persian superpower, the effect of the anonymous nature of the reference to peoples is to make the prophecy more straightforwardly open to being claimed in different historical contexts, for instance by the community oppressed by the Seleucids in the second century, and subsequently by the Romans, and for that matter by subsequent peoples oppressed by superpowers. The prophecy has a 'clearly messianic character',[72] or rather a 'clearly eschatological character', since it does not picture the action of a Messiah but the action of God in person. While its opening question is rhetorical in the sense that it assumes the answer 'Yhwh', on the basis of a passage such as Psalm 2 we might have thought that the assumed answer was 'the king' or 'the Messiah',[73] but this understanding fits ill with the non-messianic thinking of Isaiah 40–66. Further, as usual we should not take 'messianic' or 'eschatological' to denote something that belongs to a future that might be centuries away. It presupposes that there is indeed no indication in terms of the political events of the day that the superpower is about to be put down; there is no new Cyrus within sight. But it promises that nevertheless—or rather therefore—Yhwh will intervene in events in person. Such an intervention is so certain it can be portrayed as actual, though the prophet does not say it is imminent.

The fact that the community experienced no such divine intervention did not stop it from preserving the prophecy as one in which it had heard God's promise; in other words, it indeed came to express the hope of a humiliated and marginalized people. Perhaps this people would have seen Alexander as a kind of fulfilment of the prophecy, even though this would hardly count as Yhwh's acting alone. More likely it would have seen the defeat of Antiochus IV in these terms. In turn, The Battle Hymn of the Republic sees God's involvement in the violent defeat of forces that supported slavery: 'Mine eyes have seen the glory of the coming of the Lord, he is trampling out the vintage where the grapes of wrath are stored'. It was a kind of anticipation of the final punishment of evil. On the way to this appropriation, within the New Testament 63.1-6 provides Revelation 14.17-20; 19.13-15 with an image for Christ's final judgment.[74]

[71] Hanson, *The Dawn of Apocalyptic*, p. 205.

[72] Feldmann, *Das Buch Isaias*, II, p. 256.

[73] See Ibn Ezra's opening remark, *The Commentary of Ibn Ezra on Isaiah*, p. 285; and Volz's remarks, *Jesaja II*, p. 263.

[74] On links with Jewish messianic interpretation of the passage (contrast Tg), see Pierre Grelot, 'L'exégèse messianique d'Isaïe, lxiii, 1-6', *RB* 70 (1963), pp. 371-80; and on the possible link between Revelation 19 and Isaiah 63 Tg, John L. Ronning, 'The *Targum of Isaiah* and the Johannine Literature', *WTJ* 69 (2007), pp. 247-78 (262-64).

A very different Christian appropriation of the passage is suggested by its traditional reading in Holy Week in association with Isaiah 52.13–53.12. Here Jesus becomes the one who has trodden the wine press, and the blood with which he is spattered is his own. The tradition is expressed in the work of commentators such as Jerome[75] and Cyril of Alexandria,[76] for whom 63.1-6 relates questions addressed to Christ that look back from the perspective of his resurrection and subsequent ascension to heaven. Indeed, the indications within the passage that the warrior-labourer has to pay a price in effort, self-sacrifice, and exhaustion provide some links with the idea of the Messiah's suffering.[77] In contrast, Calvin comments that 'This chapter has been violently distorted by Christians, as if what is said here related to Christ, whereas the Prophet speaks simply of God himself; and they have imagined that here Christ is read, because he was wet with his own blood which he shed on the cross'.[78] Luther agrees, though Edom (the assumed object of the judgment) then comes to stand for the Jewish people.[79]

In his commentary, Franz Delitzsch describes at length Edom's 'fierce, implacable, bloodthirsty hatred' of Israel,[80] though for information on this hatred we have only the Old Testament's testimony. Ironically, his son Friedrich Delitzsch in his foreword to a new edition of his second lecture on Babylon and the Bible comments on the 'political jealousy and passionate hatred' toward Edom expressed in 63.1-6 and other passages and adds that 'the more deeply I dive into the spirit of the prophetic writings of the Old Testament, the more I shrink from Yahveh'.[81] In effect it was what made him say goodbye to the Old Testament.[82] Subsequent scholars in Europe and the United States naturally also disapprove of the passage because we belong to imperial powers like those that are on the receiving end of Yhwh's grape-treading.

'This text is not for aesthetic, religious people.'[83] Corrine Carvalho comments, 'I read these texts as revealing something true about God's

[75] *Commentariorum in Isaiam prophetam libri duodeviginti*, col. 610

[76] 'Εξήγησις ὑπομνηματική εἰς τὸν προφήτην 'Ησαΐαν, col. 1382.

[77] So John F. A. Sawyer, 'Radical Images of Yahweh in Isaiah 63', in Philip R. Davies and David J. A. Clines (eds.), *Among the Prophets* (Sheffield: Sheffield Academic Press, 1993), pp. 72-82.

[78] Calvin, *In Iesaiam prophetam*, p. 395 (ET IV, p. 337). Contrast Zwingli, *Complanationis Isaiae Prophetae*, pp. 397-99.

[79] *In Esaiam prophetam enarraciones* 533-35 (ET pp. 352-55); cf. Cocceius, 'Curae majores in prophetiam Esaiae', p. 427.

[80] *Jesaia*, p. 630 (ET II, p. 442).

[81] *Zweiter Vortrag über Babel und Blbel* (Stuttgart: Deutsche, 2nd edn, 1903), p. iv (ET *Babel and Bible* [Chicago: Open Court, 1903], pp. 69, 70). See further Reinhard G. Lehmann, *Friedrich Delitzsch und der Babel–Bibel–Streit* (Göttingen: Vandenhoeck & Ruprecht, 1994).

[82] Cf. König, *Das Buch Jesaja*, p. 518. Fohrer similarly speaks of the 'misuse' of God's name (*Jesaja*, III, p. 246).

[83] Kraus, *Das Evangelium der unbekannten Propheten*, p. 224.

power and/ sovereignty. I experience this God as good, not evil, in the violence against enemies…. I find these portrayals appropriate, fitting, and satisfying…. I am attracted to this kind of god, not because I want to be the victim of divine violence, and not because I am secure in my own righteousness, but because at the end of the day I want a God who cares enough to be angry, involved enough to do something, and divine enough to accomplish what humans shouldn't even try.'[84] It is an important declaration that judgment is God's alone.[85]

[84] Corrine Carvalho, 'The Beauty of the Bloody God' (see above), p. 151.
[85] Cf. Leslie J. Hoppe, 'Jacob's Well', *The Bible Today* 23 (1985), pp. 103-4.

X

ISAIAH 63.7–64.11 [12]

Translation and Notes

63.7 I will recount Yhwh's acts of commitment,[1]// Yhwh's great praise,[2]
Because of[3] all that Yhwh bestowed on us,// the great[4] goodness[5] to the household of Israel,[6]
That which he bestowed on them[7] in accordance with his compassion// and the greatness of his acts of commitment.[8]
8 He had said, 'Yes, they will be my people,// children who will not be false'.
So he became a deliverer for them;// 9 in all their trouble it became troublesome for him.[9]

[1] LXX, Syr have sg. noun.

[2] MT תְּהִלֹּת is written thus defectively as in 60.6 and might be mis-punctuation for the sg. (cf. Vg, Syr).

[3] On the pleonastic compound preposition כעל (cf. the first occurrence of the expression in 59.18) see BDB, p. 455a; but I take its meaning to derive more from על than from כ (cf. Vg, Sym). G. R. Driver understands the על as another instance of על as a divine title, suggesting 'the praises of Yhwh are like those of the High One'; see 'Hebrew *ʿal* ("high one") as a Divine Title', *ExpT* 50 (1938–39), pp. 92-93, referring to H. S. Nyberg, *Studien zum Hoseabuche* (Uppsala: Lundequist, 1935), pp. 57-60, 89. Cf. the second of the two occurrences of the expression in 59.18.

[4] I take MT וְרַב־טוּב as adjective preceding its noun; there are other instances of this construction with רב (see *DG* 42 remark 1). BDB (p. 913a) rather takes רַב as a noun equivalent to רֹב (to which NEB emends MT [see Brockington, *The Hebrew Text of the Old Testament*, p. 197]), implying 'the greatness of goodness'; cf. Vg, Sym. Oort ('Kritische Aanteekeningen', p. 475) omits the ו, so that the phrase suggests רַב, 'great [in] goodness'; Ibn Ezra (*The Commentary of Ibn Ezra on Isaiah*, p. 287) takes MT itself thus. LXX κριτής implies רָב; compare 63.1 and the translation note on רַב there. Yhwh is then acting as judge on Israel's behalf.

[5] For MT טוּב LXX implies טוֹב 'a good [judge]' (see previous note), Tg (cf. Syr) טוּבוֹ 'his goodness [is great]'.

[6] Duhm (*Jesaia*, p. 423) omits 'to the household of Israel'; this regularizes the metre.

[7] MT's change from the earlier verb form with first-person suffix issues from the way reference to 'the household of Israel' has intervened. Syr repeats its earlier verb form, but this hardly implies that the Hebrew originally repeated גמלנו (so Duhm, *Jesaia*, p. 423; while LXX also has ἡμῖν, it has a different verb). Julius Morgenstern rather assimilates the first form to the second; see 'Isaiah 63.7-14', *HUCA* 23 (1950–51), pp. 185-203 (187). Mitchell Dahood (*Ugaritic–Hebrew Philology* [Rome: Pontifical Bible Institute, 1965], p. 34) sees the ם as enclitic.

[8] LXX, Syr have sg. noun, as earlier in the verse.

[9] On the text here, see the comment.

His personal aide—he delivered them;// in his own[10] love and pity he restored them.
He lifted them and carried them// all the days of old.
10 But they—they rebelled,[11]// they hurt[12] his holy spirit.[13]
So he turned into an enemy to them;// he himself fought against them.
11a But he was mindful of the days of old,// of Moses,[14] of his people[15].

11b Where is[16] the one who brought them up[17] from the sea,// the shepherds[18] of his flock,
Where is the one who put in its midst// his holy spirit,
12 Who made his glorious arm go// at Moses' right hand,
Who divided the water before them// to make for himself[19] a lasting name,
13 Who enabled them to walk in the depths,// like a horse in the wilderness,[20]// so that they would not stumble,
14 Like a beast in the vale that goes down,[21]// so that Yhwh's spirit would give it rest?[22]

[10] The pronoun suggests this emphasis; see Stephen A. Geller, 'Cleft Sentences with Pleonastic Pronoun', *Journal of the Ancient Near Eastern Society of Columbia University* 20 (1991), pp. 15-33 (31).

[11] Vg 'provoked to wrath'.

[12] The *w*-qatal is odd, since one would have thought that the hurting followed on the grieving; the two are treated as different ways of describing the same act.

[13] For MT קדשו 1QIs[a] has קודשיו, which might be equivalent to קדושיו and suggest '[the spirit of] his holy ones', implying that this holy spirit is a supernatural being who can be identified with the aide of v. 9.

[14] For MT משה Torrey (*Second Isaiah*, p. 463) emends to משיע 'the one who delivers', Ehrlich (*Randglossen*, IV, p. 223) מַשָּׂא 'the carrying'.

[15] For MT עמו Syr implies עבדו 'his servant', assimilating to the familiar expression (Barthélémy, *Critique Textuelle de l'Ancien Testament*, II, p. 438).

[16] LXX omits 'of Moses, of his people. Where is', perhaps because of difficulty in construing the words.

[17] 1QIs[a] has the easier המעלה without the pl. suffix (cf. LXX, Th, Syr) for MT המעלם, assimilating to Jer 2.6. Mitchell J. Dahood takes the ם as enclitic ('Northwest Semitic Notes on Genesis', *Biblica* 55 [1974], pp. 76-82 [77]). One might then take Moses as the implicit object (see next note) and take the 'sea' as a reference to the Nile (cf. Isa 19.5; Nah 3.8); so, e.g., Feldmann, *Das Buch Isaias*, II, p. 261. But for the MT expression, cf. Deut 8.14, 15, 16, explained in GK 127i (GID).

[18] For MT's object marker את Vg, Aq have 'with'; cf. Saadia, 'Version d'Isaïe de R. Saadia', p. 73. Tg perhaps implies a repeated איה 'where?' (cf. Ehrlich, *Randglossen*, IV, p. 223). Some MT mss and many post-MT mss have sg. רעה for רעי, 'the shepherd of his flock' (i.e. Moses; cf. LXX, Tg), while M. Dahood ('Proverbs 8,22-31', *CBQ* 30 [1968], pp. 512-21 [520]) sees MT's רעי itself as a Canaanite-style sg. participle. Combining either possibility with the 1QIs[a] reading of the preceding participle (see the preceding note) makes it possible to read the entire line with sg. reference.

[19] 1QIs[a] omits לו.

[20] Morgenstern ('Isaiah 63.7-14' [see above], pp. 189-90) suggests reversing במדבר and כסוס and reading כבמדבר.

[21] Scullion ('Some Difficult Texts in Isaiah cc.56–66', p. 124) suggests that the negative carries over, implying 'that does not fall down'.

[22] MT has a third-person m. sg. suffix on תניחנו, which can hardly apply to the beast (since the word is f.) but must apply to the people. Preceding lines have moved between

Thus[23] you drove your people,// so as to make for yourself a glorious name.

15 Look from the heavens,// see from your holy and glorious eminence.
Where are your passion and your acts of might,[24]// the roar from your heart and your compassion?
Toward me they have restrained themselves,[25] // 16 when you are our father.
If Abraham himself did not acknowledge us,//if Israel himself would not recognize us,[26]
You, Yhwh, are[27] our father;// ‘our restorer’[28] is your name of old.

17 Why, Yhwh, do you make us wander from your ways,// make our mind become hard[29] so that we do not revere you?
Turn for the sake of your servants,// the clans[30] that are your possession.[31]

sg. and pl., and sg. ‘your people’ will come again in the next line. The pl. in LXX, Syr, Tg implies this assumption. Vg suggests תַּנְחֶנּוּ ‘lead him’, LXX, Syr, Tg suggest תַּנְחֵם ‘lead them’, assimilating to the more common use of נחה in connection with the journey from Egypt to Canaan (see the comment). Tg and Syr also assimilate to their verb in the next colon. M. Dahood (‘Hebrew–Ugaritic Lexicography v’, *Biblica* 48 [1967], pp. 421-38 [437]) translates ‘your spirit, Yhwh you made rest upon him [Moses]’; but this requires readers to spot three less familiar usages (double duty suffix, non-construct relationship between רוח and יהוה, and datival suffix).

[23] 1QIs[a] has כיא ‘because’ for MT’s כן, modifying the logic (cf. Pulikottil, *Transmission of Biblical Texts in Qumran*, p. 149), perhaps because of not recognizing the unmarked relative clause (cf. Kutscher, הלשון והרקע הלשוני של מגילת ישעיהו השלמה, p. 187 [ET p. 248]).

[24] For MT’s pl. pointing, 1QIs[a]’s defective spelling גבורתך implies sg.; cf. Vrs.

[25] For MT התאפקו אלי LXX has ‘you have held back from us’ (a verb form influenced by 42.14?). Duhm (*Jesaia*, p. 426) suggests אַל־יִתְאַפָּקוּ, Oort (‘Kritische Aanteekeningen’, p. 475) תִּתְאַפָּק אַל, Marti (*Das Buch Jesaja*, p. 395) תִּתְאַפָּק אַל־נא (assimilating to 64.11 [12]?); indeed Berges comments, ‘The emendations are legion’ (*Das Buch Jesaja*, p. 488).

[26] For MT’s yiqtol 1QIs[a] has הכירנו (cf. Vrs); Mitchell Dahood takes this as evidence that MT’s form is a perfect yiphil (‘Ugaritic and Phoenician or Qumran and the Versions’, in Harry A. Hoffner [ed.], *Orient and Occident* [C. H. Gordon Festschrift; Neukirchen: Neukirchener, 1973], pp. 53-58 [56]; he refers to C. H. Gordon, ‘Marginal Notes on the Ancient Middle East’, *Jahrbuch für kleinasiatische Forschung* 2 [1951], pp. 50-61 [50]).

[27] 1QIs[a] adds הואה as copula, implying ‘You are Yhwh’ (cf. Pulikottil, *Transmission of Biblical Texts in Qumran*, pp. 108-9).

[28] LXX implies pointing גאלנו as imperative rather than participle (cf. Seeligmann, *The Septuagint Version of Isaiah*, p. 58).

[29] Or perhaps ‘make our mind turn away’; on קשח see Paul, ישעיה פרקים מ-סו, II, p. 527 (ET p. 578); cf. *DCH*.

[30] ‘Tribe’ is the conventional translation of שבט, but a tribe is an ethnic group, so this translation is misleading; see Aloo Osotsi Mojóla, ‘The “Tribes” of Israel’, *JSOT* 81 (1998), pp. 15-29.

[31] Vg ‘to the clans…’ recognizes that ‘for the sake of’ does not recur in the second colon. 1QIs[a] sg. שבט might refer to Judah (Kutscher, הלשון והרקע הלשוני של מגילת ישעיהו השלמה, p. 302 [ET p. 401]) or to the Qumran community (van der Kooij, *Die alten Textzeugen des Jesajabuches*, pp. 89-90).

18 As something small they dispossessed your holy people;[32]// our foes trampled your sanctuary.
19a Forever[33] we have been those whom you have not ruled,// over whom your name was not proclaimed.

19b Oh that you had torn apart the heavens and come down,[34] that mountains had quaked[35] before you,
64.1 Like fire igniting brushwood[36]// when fire boils water,[37]
To cause your name to be acknowledged by your foes,// so that nations might shudder before you.
2 When you did awe-inspiring deeds we were not expecting,[38]// you came down[39]—mountains quaked before you.
3 Of old, people had not heard[40], they had not given ear to,[41]// eye had not seen[42]

[32] Marti (*Das Buch Jesaja*, p. 396) reads לָמָּה צִעֲרוּ רְשָׁעִים ('why have the faithless despised'). For the verb, Frants Buhl (in his 1915 revision of Wilhelm Gesenius's *Hebräisches und aramäisches Handwörterbuch über das Alte Testament* [repr., Berlin: Springer, 1949], p. 453) suggests צָעֲדוּ 'marched on'; G. R. Driver ('Linguistic and Textual Problems', p. 405) suggests עָצְרוּ with the meaning 'trampled'; Klaus Koenen ('Zum Text von Jes 63,18', *ZAW* 100 [1988], pp. 406-9) suggests דשו 'threshed [to littleness]'. LXX 'so that we may soon possess your holy mountain' might suggest הר for עם, 'for a while they possessed your holy mountain' (cf. Klostermann, 'Jesaja Kap. 40–66', p. 18); but LXX is likely assimilating to passages such as 57.13 (cf. Seeligmann, *The Septuagint Version of Isaiah*, p. 114).

[33] For MT מעולם LXX, Sym, Vg imply כעולם 'as of old'; *HUB* suggests the influence of Jewish haggadic tradition.

[34] LXX 'if you open heaven' likely reflects unease with the forceful image, an unease that finds further expression in the cola that follow (see Baer, *When We All Go Home*, pp. 181-92).

[35] LXX, Vg may imply נָזְלוּ 'run down, dissolve' for MT נָזֹלּוּ.

[36] For המסים 1QIs[a] has עמסים, which Alfred Guillaume ('Some Readings in the Dead Sea Scroll of Isaiah', *JBL* 76 [1957], pp. 40-43 [42]) links with an Arabic word with this same meaning. Gutturals are subject to change in 1QIs[a]. LXX 'as wax melts from the fire' derives from Ps 68.3 [2].

[37] This second colon may also be influenced by the opening of Psalm 68. Before מים Torrey (*Second Isaiah*, p. 465) adds המון '[like] the thunder of water'. 1QIs[a] adds לצריכה (cf. LXX, Syr), anticipating v. 1b [2b] and interpreting v. 1a [2a]; Talmon ('Aspects of the Textual Transmission of the Bible in the Light of Qumran Manuscripts', p. 115 = p. 95) suggests that 1QIs[a] is a conflate reading.

[38] 1QIs[a] omits the negative, suggesting 'When you do awe-inspiring deeds, we hope' (cf. Rubinstein, 'Conditional Constructions in the Isaiah Scroll', pp. 69-70); LXX also omits the verb. Perhaps they did not recognize the unmarked relative clause (so Kutscher, הלשון והרקע הלשוני של מגילת ישעיהו השלמה, p. 342 [ET p. 431]).

[39] LXX omits this verb.

[40] For MT's third-person verb LXX implies שָׁמַעְנוּ 'we had not heard'; cf. later in the line 'our eyes had not seen'. LXX thus draws its audience into the text (Baer, *When We All Go Home*, p. 78).

[41] For MT האזינו Duhm (*Jesaia*, p. 428), partly on the basis of 1 Cor 2.9, reads אֹזֶן הֶאֱזִינָה 'ear had not perceived'. *HUB* notes that Vrs condense or expand on this line in varying ways.

[42] For לא־ראתה עין Torrey (*Second Isaiah*, p. 465) reads simply אין 'there is no'.

A God apart from you// who acts for the person who waits[43] for him.
4 You met with[44] the person who rejoiced[45] and acted[46] with faithfulness,// the people who were mindful of you in your ways.[47]

Now: you yourself got angry,// and of old we have offended in relation to them,[48] though we were delivered.[49]
5 All of us became like something taboo,// all our faithful acts like menstrual clothing,
And all of us have withered[50] like leaves;// our wayward acts, like the wind, carry us off.[51]
6 There is no one calling on your name,// stirring himself up to lay hold of you,
Because you have hidden[52] your face from us// and made us faint away[53] by reason of our wayward acts.[54]

[43] For MT's sg. Vrs read pl. למחכי 'those who wait'.

[44] Graetz (*Emendationes*, p. 36) suggests beginning the line with לוּ 'Oh that' (haplog.), as in 63.19b.

[45] LXX omits this word, perhaps by haplog. (*HUB*). Tg has pl.

[46] LXX, Syr, Tg imply pl. עשי for MT's sg.

[47] For MT בדרכיך יזכרוך LXX suggests וּדְרָכֶיךָ יִזְכֹּרוּ 'and those who were mindful of your ways'. NEB simply changes the verb to sg. to continue the construction from the first colon.

[48] For MT בהם עולם Volz (*Jesaia II*, p. 267) suggests בְּהֵעָלֶמְךָ 'when you hid'; NEB assumes בה מעולם 'in spite of it from of old' (cf. Brockington, *The Hebrew Text of the Old Testament*, p. 198).

[49] LXX has 'through this we went astray', which might imply וַנִּפְשָׁע or וַנִּרְשָׁע 'and we rebelled/were faithless' but more likely signifies uncertainty about how to understand the sequence in the Hebrew verbs.

[50] BDB (p. 117) takes MT ונבל as hiphil from בלל (or בול); to give the meaning 'fade' one would have to suppose that it is here not the usual בלל but a byform of נבל. 1QIs[a] has ונבולה, Tg ונתרנא; Dillmann (*Jesaia* [1890 edn], p. 525) reads וַנִּבֹּל from נבל. NEB margin 'are carried away' presupposes וַנּוּבֵל from יבל (cf. Brockington, *The Hebrew Text of the Old Testament*, p. 198).

[51] MT's pl. verb יִשָּׂאֻנוּ suggests that עוננו is pl. (cf. BDB, GK 91k); the Reuchlin ms of MT has ועונינו and 1QIs[a] has pl. ועוונותינו. LXX's sg. verb perhaps implies יִשָּׂאֵנוּ. Among the Vrs. there is considerable variation over sg. and pl. verbs and nouns in the context.

[52] Mitchell J. Dahood ('Ugaritic Lexicography', in *Mélanges Eugène Tisserant* (Vatican City: Biblioteca Apostolica Vaticana, 1964), I, pp. 81-104 (90) parses הסתרת as a form from סור 'turn' with infixed ת.

[53] For MT ותמוגנו, one medieval ms and many post-MT mss have the polel form וַתְּמוֹגְגֵנוּ (*HUB*), which is what one would expect; elsewhere the qal is intransitive. But 1QIs[a] has ותמגדנו 'you gave us [into the power of our wayward acts]; cf. Kutscher, הלשון והרקע הלשוני של מגילת ישעיהו השלמה, p. 190 (ET p. 252); also *DCH* on מגד. Cf. LXX, Syr, Tg, though their versions might imply וַתְּמַגְּנֵנוּ (e.g. Ehrlich, *Randglossen*, IV, p. 226), or might be making a link with the denominative verb מגן on the basis of MT; in connection with Tg, van der Kooij (*Die alten Textzeugen des Jesajabuches*, p. 178) speaks of word association. On the basis of comparisons with Arabic, G. R. Driver ('Literary and Linguistic Problems', *JTS* 38 [1937], pp. 36-50 [49]) suggests וַתְּמַוְּגֵנִי 'disquieted', and Mitchell J. Dahood ('Hebrew Lexicography', *Orientalia* 45 [1976], pp. 327-65 [347]) 'withdrawn from us' (he thus interprets the suffix datively).

[54] On עוננו see the translation note on v. 5.

7 But now, Yhwh, you are our father,// we are the clay, you are our potter,// all of us are the work of your hand.
8 Yhwh, do not be so very angry;// do not be mindful of our waywardness forever;[55]// now: do look at your people, all of us.
9 Your holy cities[56] have been a wilderness,// Zion has been a wilderness, Jerusalem a devastation.[57]
10 Our holy and glorious house,// where our ancestors praised you,
Has become something consumed by fire;// all that we valued[58] has become a ruin.
11 At these things do you restrain yourself, Yhwh,// remain still, and humble us so much?

Introduction

MT, 1QIs[a], and probably 1QIs[b] provide chapter or paragraph breaks that mark off 63.7–64.11 [12]. This corresponds to the way 63.7 makes a transition from the revelatory conversation in 63.1-6 to the praise and prayer that run through to the end of chapter 64.[59] There is a certain appropriateness to the way 1QIs[a] provides a small space after 63.14,[60] though it is doubtful whether the break at this point is sharper than others within 63.7–64.11 [12]. There is no obvious logic about the English chapter break that divides the section into two, though there is more logic about the English verse division which makes 63.19b a separate verse from 63.19a so that it becomes 64.1.

In 59.9-15a a prayer led into a vision of Yhwh's coming (59.15b-21) and then into the substantial promises concerning Yhwh's restoration of Zion (60.1–62.12); in 63.7–64.11 [12] a prayer follows on those promises of restoration and the subsequent vision of Yhwh's coming (63.1-6). The burden of this prayer corresponds to that of the earlier one in the sense that it acknowledges that the community's waywardness is the reason

[55] For MT לעד 1QIs[a] has לעת; cf. LXX ἐν καιρῷ. G. R. Driver suggests that MT is an example of עד meaning 'time' ('Hebrew Roots and Words', *Die Welt des Orients* 1 [1947–52], pp. 406-15 [412]); but see James Barr's critique, *Comparative Philology and the Text of the Old Testament* (Oxford: Oxford University Press, 1968), p. 247.

[56] LXX, Vg have sg, perhaps a Christian re-reading, but perhaps simply assimilating to the parallel colon (GID).

[57] On the text, see the comment.

[58] For MT's pl. מחמדינו (cf. LXX, Vg), Syr, Tg imply sg. מחמדנו, matching the verb.

[59] Lau (*Schriftgelehrte Prophetie in Jes 56–66*, p. 286) describes 63.1-6 and 63.7–64.11 [12] as linked only by the theme of judgment, a link he then calls 'banal'. In contrast, Cocceius begins his comments on chapters 63–64 by remarking that the two chapters 'hang together'; the praise that begins in v. 7 responds to vv. 1-6 ('Synopsis Prophetiae Jesaiae', on the passage); Conrad (*Reading Isaiah*, p. 107) also calls 63.7–64.11 [12] the response of the 'implied audience' to 63.1-6.

[60] Some commentators treat vv. 7-14 as a separate unit from what follows (see, e.g., Kraus, *Das Evangelium der unbekannten Propheten*, pp. 224-28; cf. Morgenstern, 'Isaiah 63.7-14' [see above]).

why it does not experience Yhwh's restoration, but there is no significant overlap in wording of the kind that appears in 63.1-6 over against 59.15b-21, and there is considerable disparity in the length of the two prayers. Thus there are no indications that 63.7–64.11 [12] was composed to pair with 59.9-15a in the way one is inclined to hypothesize that 59.15b-20 and 63.1-6 were related in their composition, one being dependent on the other. Further, in wording 59.9-15a overlapped with material on either side in its emphasis on *mišpāṭ*, *ṣᵉdāqâ* and *yᵉšûʿâ* and the imagery of light and darkness, while the wording of 63.7–64.11 [12] does not give these so much prominence and has a wide variety of other more distinctive concepts and images. Some overlap more directly with Isaiah 40–55. These include the verb *gāʾal*, especially the participle *gōʾēl* (restore, restorer), the reference to passion and to remaining still, the epithet 'holy', and the declaration that there is no god but Yhwh. The references to Yhwh as potter and perhaps to God as father also recall preceding material in Isaiah.[61] On the whole the section has rather few links with earlier parts of the book or with other parts of the Old Testament[62] and it does not rework material from Isaiah 40–55 in the manner of previous chapters, nor does it show as many links with other material within Isaiah 56–66 as other preceding chapters have done. There are enough links with Isaiah 40–55 and with the context in Isaiah 56–66 to make it implausible to suggest that the section is of independent origin from this tradition and might be even older than Isaiah 40–55. Yet one could not disprove the idea that its incorporation into the material in such a way that it contributes to the concentric shaping of Isaiah 56–66 as a whole is a later development than the development of the bulk of Isaiah 56.1–63.6. It is then in this eventual arrangement that Yhwh's subsequent statement beginning in 65.1 forms a response to the question with which 63.7–64.11 [12] closes.[63]

The section has a comparable dynamic to community prayers of lament or protest in the Psalter, particularly ones that incorporate some review of the people's history such as Psalms 74 and 79. It incorporates the kind of description of the community's desolation that characteristically appears in a protest psalm (e.g. Isa 63.18; 64.9-10 [10-11]), and it protests in the classic three directions, 'they' (the enemy), 'I/we', and 'you', with the pained stress on the last;[64] 63.7-13 holds back from addressing Yhwh but

[61] Cf. Johannes Goldenstein, *Das Gebet der Gottesknechte* (Neukirchen: Neukirchener, 2001).

[62] Cf., e.g., Odeberg, *Trito-Isaiah*, p. 19.

[63] See, e.g., Dillmann, *Jesaia* [1890 edn], p. 526, with regard to 65.1-25 (but contrast Dillmann and Kittel, *Jesaja*, p. 519); Kissane, *Isaiah*, II, pp. 288-89, with regard to 65.1-7; Steck, *Studien zu Tritojesaja*, pp. 221-25, with regard to Isaiah 65–66 as whole. Grotius sees the speaker in 63.7–64.11 [12] as Judas Maccabeus, to whom God then responds in chapter 65 (*Annotationes in Vetus Testament*, II, pp. 129-34).

[64] See Claus Westermann, 'Struktur und Geschichte der Klage im Alten Testament', *ZAW* 66 (1954), pp. 44-80 (50; ET *Praise and Lament in the Psalms* [Atlanta: Knox, 1981], p. 174).

in 63.14–64.11 [12] 'you/your' becomes pervasive.[65] As happens in some such psalms, the plea focuses on an appeal to Yhwh to pay attention to the suppliants and intervene (63.15, 17, 19; 64.1, 8, 11 [63.15, 17; 64.1, 2, 9, 12]), not on asking for any specific action. Yet while it begins as an act of praise in the manner of some protest psalms (63.7-9), it makes a transition not to simple protest at Yhwh's abandonment but into protest combined with confession of sin (63.10-14), though plea and protest do then become dominant for the remainder of the section (63.15–64.11 [12]). It thus also has a comparable dynamic to community prayers of lament and protest that incorporate confession of sin as well as review of the people's history and that are more characteristic of the exilic and postexilic periods, such as Psalms 78; 106; Nehemiah 9; Daniel 9—prayers that thus acknowledge a 'cycle of rebellion and deliverance'.[66] As a prayer of lament, protest, and confession, it also bears comparison with Lamentations, though Lamentations does not incorporate a review of the people's history.[67] And in its stress on its acknowledgment of the community's waywardness as a cause of its trouble, it has a broadly Deuteronomistic stamp.[68]

It thus manifests many features that commonly appear in Old Testament prayers, though many of these features appear here in distinctive forms. It begins with a confession of what Yhwh has done; 63.7-11a forms a variant on such confessions, and 64.2-4a [3-5a] resumes the confession. A protest follows in 63.11b-14 in the common form of a series of questions, about Yhwh's failure to act in accordance with the affirmations in this confession, and 64.4b-6 [5b-7] resumes the protest. A transition to plea comes in 63.15–64.1 [2]. It is first a plea for Yhwh to pay attention to the community's situation, commonly the first actual plea in a prayer psalm; it goes on to appeal for Yhwh to take action. The plea is resumed in 64.7-10 [8-11] before the prayer concludes with another question in 64.11 [12].

[65] Cf. Fitzgerald's comments ('A Rhetorical Analysis of Isaiah 56–66', p. 294) on 63.15–64.6 [7] in particular.

[66] H. G. M. Williamson, 'Laments at the Destroyed Temple', *Bible Review* 6/4 (1990), pp. 12-17, 44 (17). See further Williamson, 'Isaiah 63,7–64,11', *ZAW* 102 (1990), pp. 48-58 (56-57); Irmtraud Fischer, *Wo ist Jahwe?* (Stuttgart: KBW, 1989), pp. 205-56; Rodney Alan Werline, *Penitential Prayer in Second Temple Judaism* (Atlanta: Scholars, 1998); Judith H. Newman, *Praying by the Book* (Atlanta: Scholars, 1999); Richard J. Bautch, *Developments in Genre between Post-Exilic Penitential Prayers and the Psalms of Communal Lament* (Atlanta: SBL, 2003).

[67] See Blenkinsopp, *Isaiah 56–66*, pp. 265-66, with reference to 64.7-11 [8-12]. Fischer (*Wo ist Jahwe?* [see above], p. 255) links the prayer more generally with exilic passages rather than postexilic ones.

[68] Cf. Odil Hannes Steck, *Israel und das gewaltsame Geschick der Propheten* (Neukirchen: Neukirchener, 1967), pp. 110, 122-27.

As the prayer moves between recollection of Yhwh's past acts, questioning about the present, plea for attentiveness and intervention, and protest about how things are, these forms of speech do not come in either a logical or a consistent order so as to structure the prayer into orderly strophes. Their arrangement works approximately as follows:

63.7-11a	Recollection
11b-14	Questioning
15a	Plea
15b	Questioning
16	Protest
17a	Questioning
17b	Plea
18-19a	Protest
63.19b–64.1 [64.1-2]	Plea
64.2-4a [3-5a]	Recollection
4b-6 [5b-7]	Protest
7-8 [8-9]	Plea
9-10 [10-11]	Protest
11 [12]	Questioning

The subsections' lack of tidy pattern and logic expresses the lack of pattern or logic in the community's experience. Enjambment abounds and the language is prosaic.[69] At the same time, the imagery and ideas are innovative and distinctive, for instance in the description of the divine aide (63.9), the reference to Yhwh's holy spirit and to its capacity to be hurt (63.11), the description of the Reed Sea event and the time in the wilderness (63.12-14), the reference to Yhwh as father and to Abraham and Israel (63.16; 64.7 [8]), the declaration about Yhwh's making the people wander (63.17) and causing the people to sin through being angry with them (64.4 [5]), and the description of the people as like something taboo and like menstrual clothing (64.5 [6]). A number of words recur: for instance, be mindful (63.7, 11; 64.4, 8); name (63.12, 14, 16, 19; 64.1, 6); holiness (63.10, 11, 15, 18; 64.9, 10); glorious (63.12, 14, 15; 64.10).[70]

The prayer refers to the destruction of the Jerusalem temple, and the only such destruction that we know of before A.D. 70 is that in 587, so that proposals to relate the psalm to some other destruction of the temple have to presuppose an unrecorded destruction or onslaught, perhaps

[69] Hanson, *The Dawn of Apocalyptic*, p. 87.

[70] See further Fischer, *Wo ist Jahwe?* (see above), pp. 27-130. For analysis of the prayer's rhetoric, see Edwin C. Webster, 'The Rhetoric of Isaiah 63–65', *JSOT* 47 (1990), pp. 89-102 (89-96).

one associated with the more general news that reached Nehemiah (Neh 1.3).[71] If we assume that the destruction is indeed that of 587, the passage's speaking of the temple as still desolate suggests that it belongs prior to 520. Its lament over the destruction of city and temple might indicate that it belongs to the period not long after the destruction, like Lamentations; it has then been subsequently brought into association with the Isaianic tradition. This would fit with its not having as substantial links with other material in Isaiah as preceding parts of Isaiah 56–66 do, or with other parts of Isaiah 56–66 itself. It might alternatively come from the opening decades of the Persian period.[72]

Its overlap with other community laments might thus mean it was used in prayer gatherings in Jerusalem and that it has been adopted and/or adapted to make it part of a prophetic book, or that a prophet has adapted the form of such prayers. But its appearing in the context of a prophetic book suggests it has a different function from the one it would have in the Psalter or in a collection of liturgical texts such as Lamentations. One might compare the way earlier chapters of Isaiah include (for instance) a number of prophecies addressed to foreign nations. It is unlikely that most of these were designed for delivering to the nations they name; rather their form fulfils a rhetorical and theological function in relation to the Judahite community. One then has to distinguish between the literary form of a text and its rhetorical and theological function. While this prayer might once have fulfilled a liturgical function and/or might be one the prophet prayed on behalf of the community, in the context of a prophetic book it has a different function. It is not simply a liturgical text but something more like a 'sermon-prayer', which can be compared with the Deuteronomic/Levitical preaching of Chronicles.[73] As a prophetic composition it might be a passage telling the community how it needs to pray. In light of its links with preceding material in the book of Isaiah such as the reference to Yhwh's hardening people's heart,[74] the motif of the servant of Yhwh, and the promises in chapters 60–63.6, it has been seen as composed to close the book of Isaiah[75] and thus as the beginning of additions to the book that continue in 65.1–66.17,[76] possibly then dating from the fourth century.[77]

[71] E.g. Duhm, *Jesaia*, p. 427.

[72] So, e.g., Anneli Aejmelaeus, 'Der Prophet als Klageliedsänger', *ZAW* 107 (1995), pp. 31-50. Elliger (*Die Einheit des Tritojesaja*, pp. 94-99) takes it as a basis for dating Isaiah 56–66 as a whole in this period.

[73] Watts, *Isaiah 40–66*, pp. 897-99.

[74] On which see especially Uhlig, *The Theme of Hardening in the Book of Isaiah*, pp. 287-315.

[75] Cf. Steck, e.g., *Studien zu Tritojesaja*, pp. 233-42; Goldenstein, *Das Gebet der Gottesknechte*, pp. 152-231.

[76] Koenen, *Ethik und Eschatologie im Tritojesajabuch*, pp. 157-59.

[77] Cf. Cheyne, 'Critical Problems of the Second Part of Isaiah', pp. 104-10. See especially the arguments of Berges in *Das Buch Jesaja*, pp. 494-96.

Perhaps it did at one stage close the book and indicate the way the community prayed or should pray for the fulfilment of the book's promises; but if so, the relative paucity of these links and the novelty of much of its way of expressing itself does not suggest it was specifically written to round off the book. There are no indications that the prayer expresses the concerns of one group over against another in the community.[78]

There are various understandings of the process whereby the section might have come into being. Among these are:

Duhm:	(1) 63.7-16
	(2) 63.17–64.11 [12][79]
Marti:	(1) 63.7–64.8 [9]
	(2) 64.9-11 [10-12][80]
Pauritsch:	(1) 63.11b-14a, 15-19a
	(2) 64.4b-8 [5b-9]
	(3) 63.19b–64.4a, 9-11 [5a, 10-12]
	(4) 63.7-11a, 14b[81]
Sekine:	(1) 63.11b–64.3, 9-11 [4, 10-12]
	(2) 64.4b-8 [5b-9]
	(3) 63.7-11a, 64.4a [5a][82]

Comment

63.7 I will recount Yhwh's acts of commitment,// Yhwh's great praise,
Because of all that Yhwh bestowed on us,// the great goodness to the household of Israel,
That which he bestowed on them in accordance with his compassion// and with the greatness of his acts of commitment.

Verse 7 continues in first-person speech from v. 6 but the opening words make clear that the speaker is no longer Yhwh but someone who speaks about Yhwh. Tg appositely introduces v. 7 with 'The prophet said'; the words are those of an individual who speaks about Yhwh to some other people. MT divides the verse after 'bestowed on us', which suggests that the verse comprises two tricola, but three bicola[83] is an inherently more likely understanding, and the resultant three bicola manifest plausible

[78] Against, e.g., Watts, *Isaiah 40–66*, p. 907.
[79] *Jesaia*, pp. 423-31.
[80] *Jesaja*, pp. 399-400.
[81] *Die neue Gemeinde*, pp. 170-71. Fischer (*Wo ist Jahwe?* [see above], pp. 27-130) argues against redactional theories such as Pauritsch's, on the basis of the way various words recur throughout the section.
[82] Sekine, *Die Tritojesajanische Sammlung*, pp. 160-64.
[83] Cf. Volz, *Jesaja II*, p. 264.

parallelism. The alternation between 'I' and 'we' suggests the speaker's sense of identity with the people, while the threefold use of the name Yhwh suggests the reality of appeal.[84] In other words, as is often the case with the recounting of Yhwh's acts, the speaker may be formally speaking *to* people *about* God, yet be also *substantially* speaking *to* God *about* and on behalf of people.

When people are aware of God's abandonment, one might expect them to begin there in their prayer (as happens, for instance, in Ps 22). This prayer begins with the memory of God's acts of commitment; 'this orients the plea and gives it its divine bearings'.[85] While in general terms an undertaking to speak of Yhwh's acts recalls the Psalms, this particular expression of determination to recount Yhwh's acts is unparalleled in the Psalter except in Psalm 71.16 and in Psalm 77.12 [11], where the kethib has the same verb form (the qere has the qal 'be mindful', which also appears three other times in the psalm, and here in 63.11).[86] Psalm 71 is a prayer psalm that looks forward to being able to recount Yhwh's faithfulness when the suppliant has experienced it again. Psalm 77 presupposes a similar background, but its recounting relates to what Yhwh did in the past that contrasts with the present; it has other overlaps of language and theme with the prophecy. This link suggests the likely significance of the verb here, and helps to clarify that the community is the implicit audience of the recounting (Rashi adds 'Israel' as a first object of the verb).[87] In Psalm 77 the suppliant is mindful of and recounts Yhwh's acts in a context in which Yhwh is not acting now, and does so for two reasons. It is directly an act of self-encouragement, and indirectly a challenge to Yhwh with regard to the way Yhwh is not now acting in this way.

One implication is that from the very beginning of the section its nature as a prayer of protest is implicit, as is the discontinuity with what precedes in 63.1-6. To put it another way, the recounting parallels those in Psalms 44 and 89, though they do not use the verb 'recount'. Like this section of Isaiah and unlike Psalms 71 and 77, their recounting comes at the beginning of the psalm and makes them look like the opening to a praise psalm, whereas in reality it is the lead in to protest; and the stronger the recounting, the more forceful the protest. While Isaiah 63.7–64.11 [12] contains no explicit indication that its dissatisfaction relates to the way Yhwh has not fulfilled promises in Isaiah 40–55, it does indicate that it shares the dissatisfaction that lies behind those chapters and is expressed in Lamentations 5, that Yhwh's inaction has gone on too long, and it implies a dissatisfaction with the fact that Yhwh is not acting in the manner described in 63.1-6. To put it another way, it introduces an ironic

84 Cf. Volz, *Jesaja II*, p. 269.

85 Seitz, 'The Book of Isaiah 40–66', p. 530.

86 Ehrlich (*Randglossen*, IV, p. 222) also reads the qal here in 63.7.

87 'ישעיה', on the passage.

note into the reading of 63.1-6, whose vision has found no fulfilment. The form of address underlines this note, precisely because the recounting is not addressed to God. God is invited to overhear it and be affected by it. God is also indirectly invited to recognize the prophet's commitment to getting the community to note and affirm the nature of Yhwh's past acts even though doing so is painful (because of the contrast with Yhwh's inactivity now) as well as encouraging (because it reminds people that Yhwh has proved capable of so acting in the past).

In substance there is also some continuity between 63.7 and 63.1-6, as is reflected in the way English Bibles ignore the Hebrew section division. To Western thinking there is a sharp move from describing Yhwh angrily making peoples drunk to recounting Yhwh's acts of commitment, but in prophetic thinking this is not so. The action of Yhwh that vv. 1-6 have described constitutes an expression of what v. 7 also refers to. Verse 7 begins a description of how Yhwh has acted in the past in the way vv. 1-6 have portrayed, though this new description is of actual events not visionary ones. Related to this link is the fact that the description will indeed make a transition to lament at the way Yhwh is not acting in this fashion now, so that v. 7 will also turn out thereby to set up some tension with what follows. Its transition to a lament is anticipated further in the 3-2 rhythm of the first line, which works abca′b′. The verb comes in pivot position at the centre of the line and applies to both cola; on either side come two construct phrases that are its objects, the construct nouns being masculine and feminine plural and the absolute noun each time being the name Yhwh.

On the word *ḥesed* (commitment), see 57.1, which referred to human *ḥesed*. Applied to God, reference to *ḥesed* 'focuses on what Yahweh does for Israel and the individual worshipper. The history of Yahweh's people, past, present, and future, the life of the individual Israelite—in fact, the entire world—is the stage for the demonstration of Yahweh's *ḥesed*. Yahweh has decided in favour of Israel; he has promised life, care, alleviation of distress, and preservation,' and demonstrated it. And this act 'is characterized by permanence, constancy, and reliability'.[88] Its use in the plural to denote acts of commitment is much less common than its use in the singular; the occurrences at either end of Psalm 89 (vv. 2 and 50 [1, 49]) eventually make explicit the implicit protest here. To put it another way, this more specific parallel with Psalm 89 underlines for the attentive listener the suggestion that the opening of this section contains an irony. The statement of intent indicates an avoidance of the trap Israel could fall into (see Ps 106.7) while also implying a challenge to Yhwh that becomes explicit elsewhere (see Ps 25.6; both passages use the verb *zākar* as here). The plural of *tᵉhillâ* (praise) is also much less common

[88] H.-J. Zobel, *TWAT*, III, p. 69 (ET *TDOT*, V, p. 62). I have replaced Zobel's use of the word *Güte* [ET *kindness*] by *ḥesed* in the quotation.

than the singular. I take it as intensive, though LXX τὰς ἀρετὰς suggests taking *tᵉhillōt* to mean 'praiseworthy deeds', which is more plausible in this context than in 60.6.[89] Either way, the word makes for another parallel with the opening of Psalm 106, which in addition goes on to emphasize Israel's rebellion and thus adds a pointer towards another irony in this opening line of 63.7–64.11 [12].

The two further lines comprising v. 7aγb are both internally and mutually parallel. The repetition of the third singular qatal verb 'bestow' (*gāmal*) binds the two first cola, the words *rab* and *rōb* bind the two second cola, the preposition *k-* binds v. 7aγ and both cola in v. 7bβγ; in addition, the plural noun 'acts of commitment' forms an *inclusio* for the three lines as a whole and suggests the verse's completeness as an introduction to the section.[90] In each line the prosody combines repetition with variation: the preposition *k-* appears compounded with *ʿal* then alone, the verb appears with first-person then third-person suffix, the forms from the root *rābab* are an adjective then a noun, and 'greatness' comes to qualify 'acts of commitment'. Further, the entirety of v. 7bβγ qualifies the entirety of v. 7aγbα and thus resolves an ambiguity in that line. Speaking in terms of Yhwh's 'bestowing' could imply that the good things that Yhwh gave were rewards for the household of Israel's own deeds.[91] Verse 7bβγ makes explicit that they issued not only from Yhwh's commitment (as v. 7a already declared) but from Yhwh's 'compassion' (*raḥămîm*). The word comes in Isaiah 56–66 only here, in vv. 7 and 11 (elsewhere in Isaiah only in 47.6; 54.7). It constitutes another link with Psalm 77 (see v. 10 [9]). As the plural of the word for 'womb', it suggests that Yhwh's bestowing issues from Yhwh's mother-like strong feelings of care for the people. This might already be hinted by the link with the only previous use of the word *bayit* to mean 'household' rather than 'house' in these chapters, the reference to the sinful 'household of Jacob' in 58.1 (cf. previously 48.1 in its context). Yhwh's bestowal of good issued from Yhwh not from Israel's deserving. Succeeding verses will give some specificity to that bestowing of good. The expression thus compares and contrasts with the similar language in 59.18. In the parallelism within v. 7aγbα, the opening 'because of' also applies to 'the great good' in the second colon, which in turn gives precision to 'all' in the first colon, while 'to the household of Israel' also applies retrospectively to the first colon and restates 'us'. In the parallelism within v. 7bβγ, 'that which he bestowed on us' applies to the second colon as well as the first, and 'in accordance with the greatness of his acts of commitment' parallels and

89 Where see the translation note.

90 In light of the recurrence of 'bestow', Croatto (*Imaginar el futuro*, p. 351) sees the verse as a chiasm with 'the great goodness to the household of Israel' as its centre.

91 On the concrete, collective sense of *ṭûb*, see M. Mannati, '*Ṭûb-Y.* en Ps xxvii 13: *La bonté de Y.*, ou *les biens de Y.*?', *VT* 19 (1969), pp. 488-93 (491).

goes beyond 'in accordance with his compassion'. LXX's present verbs in the two lines mean that 'Israel's ancient history itself seems to have faded from view. What is left is a general statement about God's dealings with some present community'.[92]

63.8 He had said, 'Yes, they will be my people,// children who will not be false'.
So he became a deliverer for them;// 9 in all their trouble it became troublesome for him.
His personal aide—he delivered them;// in his own love and pity he restored them.
He lifted them and carried them// all the days of old.

In the parallelism of the opening 3-3 line, 'my people' is explicated by 'children who will not be false'; the relative clause explicates the implication of the pronominal suffix. The future reference of the second colon suggests the time reference of the opening noun clause, and in light of what follows suggests an assessment Yhwh made before the exodus. 'They/you are my people' and 'they/you shall be my people' are not common statements in the Old Testament, though the last is the commonest (Lev 26.12 [H]; Jer 7.23; 30.22; Ezek 36.28; cf. Isa 51.16; Hos 2.25 [23]; Zech 13.9). None precisely parallels the present passage as a declaration of what Yhwh intends. This distinctiveness links with the nature of v. 8a as a declaration of Yhwh's inner reflection; as is often the case, 'said' refers to saying to oneself, or thinking (cf. 56.3; 57.10). With some irony, the 'yes' (*'ak*) underlines the total certainty with which Yhwh had formulated the conviction expressed in this line; the irony is the stronger as the point is expanded in the second colon. In light of common belief about the nature of God, it might seem that this expression of God's apparently mistaken certainty cannot be literally meant.[93] The rarity of the verb 'be false' (*šāqar* piel) adds significance to the link it makes between this line and Psalm 44.18 [17] where the community insists that it has not been false.[94] Elsewhere, the noun falsehood/deceit (*šeqer*) is common in connection with duplicity in relation to God (e.g.

---

[92] Baer, *When We All Go Home*, p. 74.

[93] Ibn Ezra (*The Commentary of Ibn Ezra on Isaiah*, on the passage) describes the prophet as speaking 'according to the manner of a human being', anthropomorphically; cf. Cyril of Alexandria, Ἐξήγησις ὑπομνηματική εἰς τὸν προφήτην Ἡσαΐαν, col. 1388. Rashi ('יְשַׁחֵר' on the passage) has God making explicit the awareness that actually they would be false. Alexander (*Isaiah*, II, p. 417) sees the clause as jussive, '[my] children shall not lie'; but it is hard to find other examples of a third-person jussive with לֹא rather than אַל.

[94] Cf. Walter Harrelson, '"Why, O Lord, Do You Harden Our Heart?"', in David Penchansky and Paul L. Redditt (eds.), *Shall Not the Judge of All the Earth Do What Is Right?* (J. L. Crenshaw Festschrift; Winona Lake, IN: Eisenbrauns, 2000), pp. 163-74 (167).

Isa 57.4) and in relation to other people (e.g. 59.3, 13). It suggests someone who says one thing but means another or who claims the intention to act in one way but acts in another way or says that something is the case when actually something else is the case. The first two sorts of meaning are the key ones here. The link with Psalm 44 appears further in the fact that Yhwh's covenant is the object of the falsehood in that psalm (cf. also 89.34-35 [33-34]);[95] here, in v. 8, Yhwh had believed that the people would mean their word when they professed the covenantal-style commitment expressed in the other part of 'the covenant formulary' as they said 'you are my God' in response to Yhwh's saying 'you are my people', and would live by that commitment. But the language in v. 8 is not strictly covenantal, as is indicated by the move to the image of children in the second colon. This image will be taken up in the prayer's subsequent appeals to God as father and it might also recall the beginning of the book of Isaiah (1.2) with its reference to the children whom God brought up but who rebelled (though the verb is *pāšaʿ* not *mārâ*).[96]

It was in light of this conviction about the community that 'Yhwh became a deliverer for them' and thus lived up to the divine side of the covenant formulary. Whereas it was not because of their positive acts that Yhwh bestowed good things on them (see the comment on v. 7), it was on the assumption that positive acts would follow that Yhwh acted as their deliverer. While previous passages have spoken of Yhwh delivering (59.16; 63.5), describing Yhwh as deliverer (hiphil participle) suggests something about Yhwh's ongoing character, office, or commitment. Whereas Christian thought is often inclined to see the exodus as Yhwh's act of deliverance, it is the event at the Reed Sea that Exodus describes in these terms (Exod 14.13, 30; 15.2), and vv. 11-14 will confirm that it is the reference here.

The versification of the subsequent cola is difficult to discern, and the question is complicated by an uncertainty about text and translation in v. 9aαβ. MT's division makes v. 8 a tricolon and implies that v. 9a is another tricolon, and this may have to be the understanding if we follow K in v. 9aα (see below). I have followed Q, in light of which vv. 8b-9aα makes for a plausible 3-3 bicolon;[97] vv. 8-9 as a whole can thus be taken as four bicola. Yhwh's being affected by the trouble that came to the people then parallels and re-expresses Yhwh's becoming Israel's deliverer.

[95] Cf. Laurence E. Browne, *Early Judaism* (Cambridge: Cambridge University Press, 1920), p. 80.

[96] Cf. Goldenstein, *Das Gebet der Gottesknechte* (see above), pp. 49-50; Anthony J. Tomasino has pointed to further links between 1.2-9 and 63.7–64.11 [12] ('Isaiah 1.1–2.4 and 63–66', *JSOT* 57 [1993], pp. 81-98 [85-86], reprinted in Davies [ed.], *The Prophets*, pp. 147-63 [151-52]). Zapf (*Jesaja*, p. 407) also finds the influence of the Egyptian understanding of the god's father–son relationship with Pharaoh, which is here applied to Yhwh's people as a whole.

[97] Cf. Muilenburg, 'The Book of Isaiah: Chapters 40–66', p. 731.

While it would be natural to take v. 9aα as referring especially to (the exodus and) the Reed Sea deliverance, the 'all' suggests an ongoing involvement, which fits with *being* a deliverer.

The colon begins with the noun *ṣārâ* 'trouble' and closes with the word *ṣār*, which might be taken as the masculine noun with the same meaning.[98] But one would then expect the vocalization *ṣar*, and the move from the feminine to the masculine noun is odd; more likely *ṣār* is impersonal third-person from the verb *ṣārar*, which can be followed by *l-* (e.g. 2 Sam 13.2). Here the *l-* expression precedes the verb, which gives it extra emphasis; the trouble was *theirs*, but *to him* too it became troublesome. In what sense is it the case that Yhwh was troubled by the things that troubled Israel? Yhwh did not share experiences such as being ill-treated by the Egyptians. There is no parallel for the idea that Yhwh subjectively felt Israel's pain, as is suggested by the common translation 'distress' and some rabbinic and Christian understandings.[99] More likely the idea is that Yhwh 'took the trouble' to be involved in expending effort to bring Israel out of trouble. In Exodus 23.20-22 (D?) Yhwh promises that if the people pay heed to and do not rebel against the aide who guides them, 'I will be an enemy to your enemies *wĕṣartî ʾet-ṣōrĕrekā.* While strictly these words likely need to be related to *ṣārar* III 'show hostility to' rather than *ṣārar* 'trouble', the links with Exodus 23 in the context suggest that the prophet recognized the possibility of understanding Yhwh to be promising, 'I will trouble their troublers' and recalling how Yhwh became a troubler or enemy for them when they were in trouble or were experiencing enmity.

There are two other ways of reading the text. Whereas Q has *lô* 'to him' in v. 9aα, K has *lōʾ*, implying 'in all their trouble it did not become troublesome [to him]'.[100] It is quite possible to see how K could have issued from a reverential rereading of Q. Syr, Vg, Tg, and Th also presuppose *lōʾ*. 1QIs[a] *lwʾ* is ambiguous. LXX points in another direction in reading 'not an elder/ambassador', which suggests *ṣir* 'envoy' for MT's *ṣār*, and the translation 'in all their trouble not an envoy or aide, his face delivered them' (this also requires the repointing of *malʾak* to *malʾāk*).[101]

[98] Cf. BDB, p. 865.

[99] See M. A. Beek, 'Das Mitleiden Gottes', in M. A. Beek *et al.* (eds.), *Symbolae Biblicae et Mesopotamicae* (F. M. T. de Liagre Böhl Festschrift; Leiden: Brill, 1973), pp. 23-30; more generally, Ger Hoaas, 'Passion and Compassion of God in the Old Testament', *SJOT* 11 (1997), pp. 138-59.

[100] Rashi ('ישעיה' on the passage) understands 'it did not become troublesome to them [to the extent that they deserved]'. Yhwh's delivering them then links with that point; their sin did not mean Yhwh declined to deliver them.

[101] Cf. John Kelles, 'Note on Isaiah lxiii. 9', *ExpT* 18 (1906–1907), p. 384; also, on such expressions in haggadic traditions, P. Winter, 'ου δια χειρ πρεσβεως ουδε δια χειρ σεραφ ουδε δια χειρ αγγελου', *VT* 4 (1954), pp. 439-41; Judah Goldin, '"Not by Means of an Angel and Not by Means of Messenger"', in Jacob Neusner (ed.), *Religions in Antiquity* (E. R. Goodenough Memorial; Leiden: Brill, 1968), pp. 412-24; cf. Bonnard,

While Exodus 33.14-15 can speak of Yhwh's face 'going' (cf. 2 Sam 17.11), it would be a unique usage for 'face' to be the subject of a verb such as 'deliver.[102] More likely LXX, like K, issues from discomfort with Q's reading and/or from a reading in the light of Exodus 33.14-15.

The two subsequent cola comprising v. 9aβγ (3-4) close with parallel third-person singular verbs with third-person plural suffixes. The parallelism of the two root verbs is familiar (49.26; 60.16; Ps 106.10). Deliverance suggests the act of power that Yhwh alone can bring about; restoration suggests the relational context out of which that action comes. The agent of deliverance is 'his personal aide'. More literally it is 'the aide of his face', though the construct expression conveys apposition;[103] it is then comparable to expressions such as 'the maiden [of] the daughter [of] Zion'.[104] Although this double expression is unique, it compares with the common expression 'Yhwh's aide', which points to an entity identifiable enough with Yhwh to connote Yhwh's personal presence yet distinguishable enough from Yhwh not to be fatally electrifying. The exodus story often speaks of the activity of such an aide (Exod 14.19; 23.20, 23; 32.34; 33.2); it is often a feature of E. In the same context Yhwh declares that 'my face will go and I will give you rest' (Exod 33.14); Deuteronomy 4.37 has Yhwh bringing the people out of Egypt *bᵉpānāyw* ('with his face'). In other words, 'God's very self'[105] will be with them. It was Yhwh in person who delivered the people, in the person of the aide. It was he (*hûʾ*—Yhwh?) who thus restored them. The Exodus passages express themselves in such a way as both to declare that Yhwh in person accompanied the people and also to deny that this is so.[106] The need for the denial now issues from the people's waywardness as well as from their mere createdness, yet the reality of Yhwh's accompanying the people also needs safeguarding. Exodus attempts this by speaking in terms of Yhwh's aide and of Yhwh's face accompanying the people. This line in Isaiah combines the expressions.[107]

The additional phrase 'in his own love and pity' applies to the first colon as well as the second and is also a rephrasing of the reference to compassion and commitment in v. 7b. Love is a more general, everyday

Le Second Isaïe, p. 448. Torrey (*Second Isaiah*, p. 463) rather emends צר to זר 'strange [god]' (cf., e.g., 43.12).

[102] In Lam 4.16 it seems to be the subject of חלק piel, but the meaning is unclear. In Ps 34.17 [16] it may be the subject of כרת 'cut off', but the line may involve an ellipse with Yhwh as the implicit subject.

[103] Cf. König, *Das Buch Jesaja*, p. 518.

[104] Cf. GK 130e; JM 129r.

[105] Richard J. Clifford, 'Narrative and Lament in Isaiah 63:7–64:11', in Maurya P. Horgan and Paul J. Kobelski (eds.), *To Touch the Text* (J. A. Fitzmyer Festschrift; New York: Crossroad, 1989), pp. 93-102 (98).

[106] Sommer (*A Prophet Reads Scripture*, pp. 148-49) sees the prophet as agreeing with J (Exod 33.14-15) rather than E (Exod 23.20, 23).

[107] Cf. Fischer, *Wo ist Jahwe?* [see above], pp. 137-39.

word than commitment. Pity is also an everyday word; the noun comes only here and in Genesis 19.16.

Verse 9b comprises a 2-2 bicolon in which the second colon simply completes the first. Yhwh refers a number of times to having 'carried' Israel at the time of the exodus: see, e.g., Exodus 19.4 (D); Deuteronomy 1.31. The latter passage suggests the image of a father carrying his child, which was implied by Isaiah 46.1-4. That point about the exodus and wilderness journey is generalized by the second colon. In other words, through vv. 7-9 and on into vv. 10-11a, the prayer is recollecting both the particular events related in the Torah and the much longer line of events down to the prophet's own day. The story in the Torah encapsulates the dynamics of that longer story.

63.10 But they—they rebelled,//they hurt his holy spirit.
So he turned into an enemy to them;// he himself fought against them.

MT takes v. 10a as 3-2 'but they—they rebelled and hurt// his holy spirit', which is a more usual rhythm than 2-3 but seems less plausible than an understanding that ascribes one verb to each colon. MT's construal does put the emphasis on the object of the second verb and it thus highlights the extraordinary nature of the statement. Either way, the second colon again simply completes the first.

There is nothing novel or controversial about the idea that Israel had rebelled against Yhwh, though the syntactically unnecessary 'they' (*hēmmâ*) draws attention to the extraordinary nature of this rebellion following on the statements in vv. 8-9.[108] While the recollection expressed in those verses corresponds to that in prayers such as Psalms 44 and 89, the admission of guilt contrasts with such psalms and rather compares with Psalms 78 and 106, Lamentations, the narrative in 1 and 2 Kings, and the prayers in Ezra and Nehemiah.

In contrast, very striking is the extraordinary effect of this rebellion on Yhwh, not annoyance but hurt or sorrow (*ʿāṣab* piel). The usage compares with that in Psalm 78.40 (where the verb is hiphil not piel but follows on the same verb for 'rebel') and Genesis 6.6 (J) (hitpael). It is a neat reversal of the usage in Isaiah 54.6. Instead of using the cognate *ʿăṣab*, Tg uses the verb *rᵉgaz* which likely implies 'enraged' rather than 'hurt' (cf. KJV 'vex'). This makes good sense in the context, but it is doubtful whether *ʿāṣab* would have this meaning. Tg goes on to render the object of the enraging 'the Word of his holy prophets', which further reflects the provocative nature of the reference to hurting Yhwh's 'holy spirit' and suggests that the holy spirit refers to the spirit of prophecy.

[108] While Brueggemann calls v. 10 a 'disruption' (*Isaiah 40–66*, p. 230), R. Kuntzmann ('Une relecture du "salut" en *Is.* 63,7-14', *Revue des sciences religieuses* 51 [1977], pp. 22-39 [35-38]) sees it as introducing the central idea in vv. 7-14.

It corresponds to Tg's interpretation at 59.21 (and 40.13)[109] and fits the references to Yhwh's spirit in Nehemiah 9.20, 30, though the context of the repeated reference in 63.11b may point in another direction. Outside 63.10-11, the striking expression 'holy spirit' comes only in Psalm 51.13 [11]. Reference to 'Yhwh's spirit' (63.14) is more common. It does not occur in the exodus story but it does come in connection with reference to the exodus at Haggai 2.5, which suggests that it has become a way of conceiving of Yhwh's presence with Israel. Perhaps the holy spirit is to be identified with Yhwh's aide, as 1QIs[a] implies;[110] in Exodus 23.21 Yhwh warned about the possibility of 'rebelling' against the aide. In passages such as Psalm 89.6, 8 [5, 7] the holy ones are such figures.[111] Given the common association of Yhwh's spirit and Yhwh's extraordinary involvement with individuals such as kings and prophets (e.g. Isa 11.2; 48.16; 59.21; 61.1; also the Tg rendering here), one might see it as a kind of democratizing like that of the covenant with David. Indeed, such democratizing has already appeared alongside that of the Davidic promise, in 42.1.

In the book of Isaiah, the appearance of the word *holy* is hardly a surprise, and it carries connotations from 6.3.[112] The word comes five times in this prayer (63.11, 15, 18; 64.9, 10 [10, 11]) and it has been reckoned to locate the phrase 'holy spirit' within Isaianic speech.[113] Yet the point about holiness throughout the prayer is made by means of the adjectival use of the noun *qōdeš* (literally, 'spirit of holiness') not the adjective *qādôš*. It is the latter that is distinctive and characteristic of the book of Isaiah as a whole, mostly in the expression 'the holy one of Israel'. In contrast, the noun comes only five times in Isaiah 1–39 (all in passages commonly thought to be later than the eighth century), four times in Isaiah 40–55, but fourteen times in Isaiah 56–66;[114] comparable concentrations of occurrences come in P and H in Exodus, Leviticus, and Numbers, and in Ezekiel. In general, adding the word 'holy' suggests the connotation 'we are not talking about something or someone ordinary here'. This means that arguably the epithet 'holy' adds little to the noun 'spirit'. 'Spirit' denotes the dynamic presence of God, which contrasts with the relatively non-dynamic nature of humanity (cf. Isa 31.3). 'Holy' denotes the extraordinary, transcendent nature of the deity. The two terms thus reinforce each other. It was the holy one, the dynamic one, whom Israel hurt.

[109] Cf. Chilton, *The Glory of Israel*, p. 50.

[110] See the translation note.

[111] Psalm 106.33 refers to the people rebelling against 'his spirit', but the context suggests the suffix refers to Moses (see John Goldingay, *Psalms* [Grand Rapids: Baker, 2008], III, p. 234).

[112] Cf. Dillmann, *Jesaia* [1890 edn], p. 521.

[113] Cf. Aejmelaeus, 'Der Prophet als Klageliedsänger' (see above), p. 41.

[114] Cf. Beuken, *Jesaja IIIB*, p. 14

Christian interpretation is inclined to see an 'adumbration' of Christian thinking in this line,[115] but this understanding obscures the significance of the line more than it clarifies it. To say that the Israelites hurt Yhwh's spirit no more implies that Yhwh's spirit is a hypostasis than would be implied if someone spoke of hurting a human being's spirit.[116] Speaking of Yhwh's holy spirit does not imply any personification of the spirit as if it were a hypostasis in some way separate from Yhwh. 'Basically it is an emphatic expression for "him", as if to draw attention to God's presence and activity.'[117] While the phrase helped early Christians nuance their understanding of God, this is not to imply that the expression itself 'foreshadowed' the Holy Spirit as understood in Christian faith. The development of that understanding issued essentially from reflection on events that took place in the life of Jesus and subsequent decades, whose nature Old Testament expressions such as this one helped the early Christians to articulate. This does not mean that the connotations that come to attach to the phrase are somehow contained or implicit within the expression, and Christian interpretation consistently shows how this framework of thinking obscures understanding of the Old Testament by conforming it to the New.

The 3-3 parallel statement in v. 10b declares that even if v. 10a did not indicate that Israel enraged Yhwh, such enraging did happen. It reflects how hurt and anger sit close to one another, for God as for human beings (compare Gen 6.5-7 [J]). Given the combined resonances of 'holy' and 'spirit', both suggesting the transcendent and dynamic nature of God, it is not surprising that the divine reaction in v. 10b follows from the human rebellion. In other words, v. 10 expresses in different words the same understanding of God as Isaiah ben Amoz.[118] Only here is God described unequivocally as Israel's enemy (in Lam 2.4-5 he acts *like* an enemy). In the second colon, the syntactically unnecessary *hûʾ* ('himself') both pairs and contrasts with the *hēmmâ* at the opening of the verse and with the *hûʾ* in v. 9bα ('he was the one' who restored them). In turn, there is nothing scandalous about the declaration that Yhwh fights; what is scandalous is that Yhwh fights against Israel instead of for Israel (cf. the threat in Jer 21.5; and the further link with the language of Exod 23.20-22). In the parallelism, the suffixed prepositional expressions 'to them' and 'against them' thus form a pair, as do the two third-person niphal verbs.

63.11a But he was mindful of the days of old,// of Moses, of his people.

MT's verse division, associating this line with the two that follow, implies that these are the words of the people. One way of achieving this

[115] Childs, *Isaiah*, p. 524.
[116] Against Kraus, *Das Evangelium der unbekannten Propheten*, p. 227.
[117] Herbert, *Isaiah 40–66*, p. 176.
[118] Cf. Westermann, *Jesaja Kapitel 40–66*, p. 308 (ET p. 388).

understanding is to take 'his people' as the subject of the verb, 'but his people was mindful of the days of old, of Moses',[119] but this seems 'a little too ingenious'.[120] While a third-person singular can be used with indefinite subject,[121] suggesting 'people were mindful', it is hard to justify appeal to that usage in this context where a *w*-consecutive follows on the third-person verb in the preceding lines,[122] with which it stands in sequence quite satisfactorily.[123] Indeed, after a description of Yhwh's becoming angry with and taking action against Israel, one would almost expect to hear that Yhwh then 'became mindful' (*zākar*; cf. Gen 9.1 [P]; Lev 26.42, 45 [H]).[124] There has to be chastisement; there also has to be mindfulness. The asyndetic sequence of nominal expressions is then a sequence of objects for this verb, though in the parallelism the second and third expressions spell out the first. In a context such as that of the stories in Judges, when Yhwh fights against Israel, Yhwh is then mindful of the days of old to which v. 9b referred, and specifically of Moses and of 'his people' (more likely Yhwh's people than Moses' people). The asyndetic sequence of nominal expressions can be reduced to two by translating 'mindful of the days of old, of [or "as"] the one who drew his people out';[125] but this again looks too ingenious. The link with v. 9b hints at the more specific implications of Yhwh's mindfulness. Like other Old Testament prayers, in Exodus 32–34 (chapters whose themes vv. 7-10 have taken up) Moses himself urges Yhwh to be mindful, and there specifically to be mindful of past acts, the making of promises to Israel's ancestors. Moses also urges Yhwh not to give up on the project begun with the exodus and Reed Sea victory (for instance, because Yhwh will look pathetic). This suggests that here, too, Yhwh is being mindful of the need not to abandon this project with Moses and Israel in those days of old.

63.11b Where is the one who brought them up from the sea,// the shepherds of his flock,
Where is the one who put in its midst// his holy spirit,
12 Who made his glorious arm go// at Moses' right hand,
Who divided the water before them// to make for himself a lasting name,
13 Who enabled them to walk in the depths,// like a horse in the wilderness,// so that they would not stumble,

[119] So, e.g., Saadia, 'Version d'Isaïe de R. Saadia', p. 77; Rashi, 'ישעיה', on the passage.
[120] Ottley, *Isaiah according to the Septuagint*, II, p. 376.
[121] See GK 144d.
[122] Torrey (*Second Isaiah*, p. 463) implicitly recognizes this point in noting the possibility of emending to pl. ויזכרו. Elliger (*Die Einheit des Tritojesaja*, p. 29) and Volz (*Jesaja II*, p. 266) emend to first person ואזכור or אזכיר.
[123] Cf. Tg; also (e.g.) Lau, *Schriftgelehrte Prophetie in Jes 56–66*, p. 292.
[124] Beuken (*Jesaja IIIB*, pp. 10-12) sees vv. 10b-11a as completing a concentric arrangement in vv. 8-11a in which v. 11a corresponds to v. 8.
[125] Cf. JPSV.

14 Like a beast in the vale that goes down,// so that Yhwh's spirit would give it rest?
Thus you drove your people,// so as to make for yourself a glorious name.

The transition to questioning is sudden and may have contributed to the Masoretic verse division, which by associating v. 11 with what now follows provides the questions with an introduction. Yet the question in 63.1 had no introduction, nor did the succeeding statements in 63.1-6, nor do Yhwh's own next words beginning in 65.1. So there is nothing distinctive about the sudden transition to questioning in v. 11b. Verses 7-11a have formed a review of Yhwh's acts in the past; v. 11b begins the people's statements in light of them.[126] To put it another way, if vv. 7-11a were a Deuteronomistic-style sermon addressed to the people, v. 11b marks the transition to a protest prayer uttered by the people. While they accept the Deuteronomic logic (their trouble issued from their waywardness), this does not stop them protesting, and in that respect they speak in the manner of Lamentations. Their logic is that in the past Yhwh has moved on from justified abandonment and anger to mindfulness. So why is Yhwh not doing so in their present experience?

Verses 11b-14 comprise seven lines of which none is marked by parallelism; in each line the second colon simply completes the first. On the other hand, all seven lines are to some degree parallel with one another. Each of the first five has a participle in the first colon; the participles refer to Yhwh's acts (mostly or entirely associated with the deliverance at the Reed Sea), but the use of the participles suggests that these acts point to Yhwh's ongoing character,[127] an emphasis underlined in LXX.[128] They thus strengthen the protest about why Yhwh is not acting in this way now. They parallel the form of expression in confessions of faith such as Psalm 136 and in prophetic declarations in Isaiah 40–48 (40.22-23; 43.16-17; 44.2, 24-28; 45.7, 18; 46.10-11).[129] In effect they take up these statements and ask, 'What about these alleged truths concerning Yhwh that we affirm in our worship and that prophecy has assured us of? Why are they not evidenced in our experience? Torrey comments that the way these verses speak implies that the prophet 'knew of no "restoration" from Babylonia'.[130] Like prayers such as that in Nehemiah 9, they certainly imply that any restoration that had happened left much to be prayed for.

[126] Cf. Jerome, *Commentariorum in Isaiam prophetam libri duodeviginti*, col. 617.

[127] Cf. Oswalt, *Isaiah 40–66*, p. 601.

[128] So Philippe Le Moigne ('"C'est moi qui établis la lumière et fis l'obscurité, qui fais la paix et fonde les malheurs": théologie du choix des thèmes verbaux des participes [présent *vs* aoriste] se rapportant à Dieu, dans la Septante d'Ésaïe', in van der Kooij and van der Meer [eds.], *The Old Greek of Isaiah*, pp. 71-106), who understands the omission of the reference to Moses in v. 11a in this connection (pp. 95-96).

[129] Cf. Croatto, *Imaginar el futuro*, p. 361.

[130] Torrey, *Second Isaiah*, p. 463; Torrey italicizes the words.

The two lines in v. 11b (3-3, 2-3) are neatly parallel. Each time the second colon simply completes the first, but the two first cola are parallel, comprising the interrogative 'Where?', a participle (one piel, one qal, the first with a suffix[131]), and a prepositional expression (one *min*, one *b*-). The two second cola then comprise the object marker, a construct noun, and an absolute noun with third-person singular suffix.

We have noted that in Exodus the act of deliverance is the Reed Sea event, and v. 11b confirms this significance of the reference to deliverance in v. 8. In contrast, whereas Exodus speaks of Yhwh 'bringing them up' from Egypt and to Canaan (e.g. Exod 3.8, 17; 17.3; 33.12), v. 11b speaks of Yhwh 'bringing them up' from the sea. The specific reference to Yhwh's bringing up the shepherds follows on the reference to God being mindful of Moses (v. 11a); the shepherds might be Moses, Aaron, and Miriam (cf. Mic 6.4).[132] The parallel line then focuses on the flock itself, into whose midst Yhwh had put 'his holy spirit'; in turn this reference takes up the earlier allusion in v. 10a. Grammatically, one might translate 'in his [Moses'] midst', but the pronoun's immediate antecedent is the flock. Further, one might rather expect the prophet to speak of Yhwh's spirit being put *on* Moses, whereas Haggai 2.5 does speak of Yhwh's spirit being among (*b*ᵉ*tôk*) the people. Perhaps it makes little difference; the point about reference to Yhwh's spirit being in Moses would be that this means it is among the people. Tg's paraphrase, 'Where is the one who made the Word of his holy prophets dwell among them?', parallels its version of v. 10a and fits with the point. While the talk of Yhwh's putting the holy spirit *among* them might reformulate the idea that Yhwh 'put his Word in Israel's midst at Sinai when he gave his people the Torah',[133] more likely the idea is that Yhwh's spirit is *on* people such as Moses, Miriam, and the elders (see Num 11 [JE]), so that they all hear Yhwh speak (cf. Neh 9.20). The implication is hardly that in the prophet's own day there is no such prophesying; at least, Isaiah 56–66 as a whole presupposes that there is prophesying in the period to which the chapters as a whole belong. Rather, the community is not seeing the kind of events that should go with such prophesying and fulfil its promises. Given the fact that the earlier reference to Yhwh's holy spirit involved an admission that the community had hurt it, the plaint that asks where is the one who put this spirit in its midst involves some chutzpah.

As is often the case, a 'Where [is]?' question is rhetorical; it presupposes the answer 'Nowhere'. A comparison with the questions in 36.19; 37.13 (also Jer 17.15; Joel 2.17; Pss 42.4, 11; 79.10; 115.2) would be especially uncomfortable, though such usage of 'Where?' questions elsewhere indicates that they are more often an aspect of taunts than of

[131] But see the translation note.

[132] Cf. Cheyne, *The Prophecies of Isaiah*, II, p. 107.

[133] Knight, *Isaiah 56–66*, p. 77.

regular protest psalms. They do feature in a protest in Psalm 89.50 [49] and they are the question Jeremiah 2.6, 8 faults people for failing to ask,[134] though it is not clear whether Jeremiah implies that they will get an uncomfortable answer if they do ask it. In other words, it is not clear whether their turning to other deities led to trouble that should have generated the question or whether Yhwh's inactivity led to their turning to other deities instead of asking the question. Either way, here the people are not failing in this connection.[135] And either way, the question is rhetorical in that it is not designed to elicit an answer of the kind Elijah hypothesizes (1 Kgs 18.27) but to elicit action.

In vv. 12-14 the 'Where?' questions are taken further; in other words, syntactically the 'Where [is]' and the article on the participles carry over to the beginning of vv. 12a, 12b, and 13, and syntactically the question continues as an enjambment. Indeed, it continues to do so through to the end of v. 14a, though v. 14b is then an independent sentence marking the end of this subsection.

In isolation one might relate v. 12a (3-2) to the exodus, since elsewhere the exercise of Yhwh's arm is so linked (e.g. Exod 6.6 [P]; Deut 4.34; Exod 15.16 is more allusive), but in this context it likely refers to the Reed Sea. Only here is Yhwh's arm described as 'glorious', though the description corresponds to the way that arm is frequently described as great (Exod 15.16), strong (Isa 44.12; 62.8), or holy (Isa 52.10). 'Glorious' makes a link with the context here in Isaiah (60.7, 19; 62.3); the word will recur in this section (63.14, 15; 64.10 [11]). The Old Testament makes no other reference to Moses' right hand, though Moses' hand was an important means of Yhwh's acting both in Egypt and at the Reed Sea (e.g. Exod 10.12, 21, 22; 14.16, 21, 26, 27). The specific imagery of the right hand likely takes up the idea of Yhwh as support of a king or an ordinary person, at his right hand (Pss 16.8; 110.5; 109.31; 121.5). The second colon completes the first; more literally the line reads 'who caused to go at Moses' right hand his glorious arm', providing the verb with its missing object.

In v. 12b (3-4) the second colon again completes the first, though here the first colon is complete in itself syntactically. 'Dividing' (*bāqaʿ*) is the verb for dividing the Reed Sea in Exodus 14.16, 21 (P) (also Ps 78.13; Neh 9.11), but elsewhere it takes up the Middle Eastern way of picturing creation as involving the splitting of waters (Ps 74.15). The idea of God's name is not closely associated with the Reed Sea story but Nehemiah 9.10 speaks of Yhwh's making a name in this connection. The motif is

[134] William L. Holladay calls vv. 11-13 here an expansion on Jer 2.6 ('Was Trito-Isaiah Deutero-Isaiah After All?', in Broyles and Evans (eds.), *Writing and Reading the Scroll of Isaiah*, I, pp. 193-217 (198-99).

[135] Sommer (*A Prophet Reads Scripture*, pp. 224-25) sees the prophet as deliberately making this point, though it is not clear why the focus moves from the exodus itself in Jeremiah to the Reed Sea event.

another that makes a link with the language of the context in Isaiah (57.15; 59.19; 60.9; 63.14, 16, 19; 64.1, 6 [2, 7]).

Verse 13 comprises three short cola (2-2-2) whose form thus surprises the reader, and it uses the form to that end. The first colon is again a self-contained participial clause, but the second raises a question ('How on earth are they like a horse in the wilderness?'), which the third answers. The rhetorical false sense of security conveyed by the first colon is enhanced by its beginning with the same participle as v. 12a, though the participle now has a third-person plural suffix which marks the usage as different from the earlier one where Yhwh's arm was its object. It is then surprising to find that the Israelites are in the depths (*t^ehōmôt*), since really only the Egyptians are there, and that fatally (Exod 15.5). Presumably the Israelites might be reckoned to be in the depths in that they walked in their midst when the depths congealed on either side of their path (Exod 15.8). It is even more surprising to find that as they do so, they are like a horse in the wilderness (another *b*- expression). How so? Wilderness is not desert or hostile country. While it does not receive enough rain to make the land cultivable, it can provide pasturage for sheep. In Israel, it is specifically mountain country. A horse in such country does not stumble; it is sure-footed. Neither did Israel stumble as it walked between the walls of water. There is an irony about the simile. Exodus 14–15 refers to horses almost as often as any passage in the Old Testament, but these are horses that get overwhelmed by the sea. 'Stumble' (*kāšal*, here niphal) is not used in connection with that event, but it is a common image for the failure of enemies to overwhelm Israel and for Israel's own threatened or actual reversal (e.g. Isa 8.15; 28.13; 31.3; 40.30; 59.10).

The two cola comprising v. 14a (3-3) consist of a simile referring to an animal, followed by an asyndetic yiqtol clause, so that formally the two cola parallel the previous two cola, in v. 13bβγ. I take them as also similar in substance, with the asyndetic clause again indicating purpose. The line incorporates further reworkings of elements from previous lines. 'Vale' (*biqʿâ*) comes from the verb 'divide' (*bāqaʿ*). Formally 'vale' parallels 'wilderness', and possibly the two could be seen as set over against each other; wilderness is then harsher, more mountainous terrain with less rainfall, while a vale is greener, lower, and easier terrain. If so, the resonance of the root *bāqaʿ* is different, and the 'going down' likewise has positive connotations that contrast with its connotations in connection with the Reed Sea event (see Exod 15.5). The animal is going down in a good sense, to graze somewhere more pleasant (*b^ehēmâ* can denote a herd of cattle, but here the singular verb 'goes down' and the parallel comparison with a horse suggests the reference is to an individual animal). Or rather, the descent into the depths, which ought to be bad news, comes to be good news because Yhwh has a positive purpose to achieve through it, like the positive purpose a herdsman achieves in leading animals down into a vale. As happened in v. 13bβγ, the second colon abandons the simile. Here 'it' represents a masculine suffix, which has no proper antecedent, since the word for 'beast' (*b*ᵉ*hēmâ*) is feminine and the people have been referred to in the plural. But the switch from this plural to singular is easy enough ('people' will come in the singular in the next line). While it might be inappropriate to describe the colon as moving from simile to literal description, it does make a move to metaphor in seeing Yhwh's spirit as giving the people 'rest'.

This motif of God's giving rest (*nûaḥ* hiphil) links again with the motif of Yhwh's face/presence: 'my face will go and I will give you rest' (Exod 33.14). The dominant way in which the Old Testament speaks of God giving the people rest relates to its arrival in Canaan (e.g. Exod 33.14; Deut 12.9), which is the explicit horizon of Exodus 15.1-18. But Numbers 10.33-36 relates this image to the people's ongoing journey through the wilderness, and here in v. 14 it would be natural to relate it to Yhwh's giving the people rest by bringing them through to the other side of the Reed Sea. This understanding fits both the parallelism with 'so that they would not stumble' and the earlier association of the holy spirit with the people's passing through the sea, in v. 11b (once again Yhwh's Word is the agent of the leading in Tg). Similar considerations apply on the basis of Vg's reading 'lead' (*nāḥâ*) instead of 'give rest'; the verb can apply to Yhwh's bringing the people to Canaan (Exod 15.13; 32.34), to the stage-by-stage journey (Exod 13.17, 21; Ps 78.14; Neh 9.12, 19), and specifically to the passage through the sea (Pss 77.21 [20]; 78.53).

The final line in this recollection (v. 14b, 3-4) forms its one statement, announced by the 'thus' (*kēn*), and summarizing the recollection as a whole. 'Drive' (*nāhag*) is a more forceful synonym of 'lead', also commonly used of flocks, for whom driving is a friendly expression as they are being driven to pasture. While it is used (in association with 'lead') in connection with the exodus in Psalm 78.52, it is not elsewhere used of the journey to Canaan, though rather neatly it is used of the Egyptians' difficulty in driving their chariots at the Reed Sea (Exod 14.25; cf. also 10.13). Yhwh's driving of Israel thus contrasts with that driving. The closing colon repeats v. 12bβ except for a necessary change of pronoun and the replacement of 'lasting' by 'glorious' from v. 12a.

63.15 Look from the heavens,// see from your holy and glorious eminence.
Where are your passion and your acts of might,// the roar from your heart and your compassion?
Toward me they have restrained themselves,// 16 when you are our father.
If Abraham himself did not acknowledge us,// if Israel himself would not recognize us,
You, Yhwh, are our father;// 'our restorer' is your name of old.

After long subsections of recollection (vv. 7-11a) and questioning (vv. 11b-14), there come in brisker linked sequence the first plea (v. 15a), further questioning (v. 15bαβ), and the first explicit protest (vv. 15bγ-16). MT takes the plea as a regular 3-3 bicolon (which corresponds to the fact that the first colon forms a complete colon in Ps 80.15 [14]), but the collocation of two parallel verbs and two parallel *min* expressions suggests the line rather works 2-4. Like many Old Testament prayers, this prayer's initial concern is simply to gain Yhwh's attention. Following on the less common 'look' (*nābaṭ* hiphil), the familiar 'see' (*rā'â*) adds little (Tg has 'appear'), but this has the effect of underscoring the inherent emphasis in the compound expression 'your holy and glorious eminence' over against 'the heavens' (MT's division of the line has the same effect). Like the English word, 'eminence' (*zebul*) likely suggests both the literal elevation of the heavens above the earth (cf. Hab 3.11) and the honoured status of God's dwelling (in 1 Kgs 8.13 it denotes the earthly temple), but in any case the latter is brought out by the epithet 'holy' and also by the further recurrence of the epithet 'glorious' (cf. vv. 12, 14). The phrase simultaneously honours and challenges Yhwh. Given a dwelling in this elevated royal abode, Yhwh both should and can take an interest in what is happening on earth and resist the temptation simply to enjoy life in the palace.

The renewed 'Where?' question (v. 15bαβ) half-implies that the latter is exactly what Yhwh is doing. In the 3-3 line, 'Where?' introduces two pairs of parallel expressions. The word for passion (*qin'â*) can denote jealousy in particular, but here the more general reference is appropriate; the term denotes strong feeling that can issue in action. The reference picks up from 42.13 and 59.17 (also 9.6 [7]; see further the related verb *qānā'* in Zech 1.14; 8.2). Such passion issues in acts of might (*gebûrōt*): the word is especially associated with God's acts of faithfulness and grace, so that the English word 'might', with its moral connotations, is appropriate.[136] In addition, here the reference picks up the description in 42.13 of Yhwh's setting off as a *gibbôr*, a mighty warrior, to restore the people by acting powerfully (*gābar* hitpael). In such a linguistic context the roar (*hāmôn*) of the heart (*mē'îm*, literally, the 'insides') would naturally suggest the shout that issues from within such a warrior (cf. 42.13-14, though using different words). But the companion reference to compassion (*raḥămîm*) points in another direction. In 49.1 the 'insides' refers to the womb, and *raḥămîm* is the plural of the word for the womb. This suggests that the exclamation is a mother's, an expression of compassion that issues in action in the same way as does a warrior's passion. LXX's 'the multitude of your mercy' is thus not so far wrong (though contrast Aq, Sym, Th τῶν σπλαγχνῶν σου).[137] Once again that picks up

[136] See H. Kosmala, *TWAT*, I, p. 906 (ET *TDOT*, II, p. 370).

[137] LXX gives המון the meaning 'multitude' rather than 'noise'; cf. Tg 'the multitude of your good things'. LXX perhaps does not care for the anthropopathism (cf. Fritsch, 'The Concept of God in the Greek Translation of Isaiah', p. 161), though Orlinsky points out that LXX Isaiah is not generally averse to anthropopathism (see 'The Treatment of Anthropomorphisms and Anthropopathisms in the Septuagint of Isaiah').

references to a mother's feeling compassion in 49.15 (cf. also 49.10, 13; 54.8, 10; 55.7; 60.10; also the noun in 54.7). While it is questionable whether the idea that God suffers with Israel is conveyed by 63.9, something like this idea is present here.[138]

I take vv. 15bγ-16aα (2-2) as the next line in this subsection.[139] The pointer towards doing so is that vv. 15bαβ, 16aβγ, and 16b all work well as internally parallel bicola, which suggests that vv. 15bγ-16aα also belong together. The first colon sums up the implications of the rest of v. 15; the second colon introduces the motif that will be developed through the rest of v. 16. (The substance of the cola would thus suggest taking both v. 15b and v. 16a as tricola, and this understanding would make it possible to give the opening *kî* in v. 16 the more common meaning 'because', but would make it impossible to give appropriate weight to the internal parallelism just noted.) The problem with Yhwh's passion, acts of power, cry from the heart, and compassion is that they are restrained; once again the plaint picks up from 42.14 (the rare verb is used of Yhwh only in these two passages and in 64.11 [12]). The first-person reference 'from me' (literally, 'to me') takes up the first-person reference in the prayer's opening line.

In the second colon, the address to Yhwh as the people's father is very unusual in the Old Testament. The Old Testament thus distances itself from thr faith of other peoples and from the instinctive faith of Israelites themselves which they shared with other peoples.[140] In Deuteronomy 32.6, describing God as Father is a way of describing God as the one who brought the people into being (cf. Mal 2.10). Something similar is true of the appeal reported in Jeremiah 3.4, 19, where Yhwh as Father is the one who makes the crops grow and thus provides for his children. In Jeremiah 31.9 Yhwh is the Father guiding his son. In Malachi 1.6, conversely Yhwh as Father is one whom his son should surely honour.[141] In such passages the emphasis in the image lies not in the warmth of a personal relationship and care but in the mutual commitment the relationship implies. Bringing into being will be the connotation shortly in 64.7 [8].

[138] Cf. the emphasis on 63.15 in Kazoh Kitamori, *Theology of the Pain of God* (Richmond: Knox, 1965; London: SCM, 1966), pp. 151-67.

[139] See, e.g., Skinner (*Isaiah xl—lxvi*, p. 225) for the view that v. 16aα belongs with what precedes.

[140] Contrast Gottfried Vanoni (*'Du bist doch unser Vater' (Jes 63, 16)'* [Stuttgart: KBW, 1995], pp. 38-88), who suggests that 'father' is actually a kind of controlling metaphor, with which metaphors such as creator, redeemer, and king are closely associated. Lau (*Schriftgelehrte Prophetie in Jes 56–66*, p. 297) likewise sees the father-son motif as underlying the prayer as a whole.

[141] Hans-Winfried Jüngling ('Vatermetaphorik und Müttermemoria', in I. Fischer, U. Rapp, and J. Schiller [eds.], *Auf der Spuren der schriftgelehrten Weisen* [J. Marböck Festschrift; Berlin: de Gruyter, 2003], pp. 77-95 [78-84]) sees v. 16 LXX as influencing the Matthean version of the Lord's Prayer.

In a passage such as Psalm 103.13, however, fatherhood does imply warmth of personal involvement, and the present context in v. 15bαβ implies this connotation; 'compassion' is associated with fatherhood in Psalm 103.13 as implicitly here. Here, then, 'the primal relationship of trust' which is 'the relationship with God of family piety, conceived of in analogy with the creaturely relationship between parent and child which is ultimately inalienable, is now to help people get over the deep shattering of Israel's relationship with God' in the exile.[142] In neither way (either by fulfilling obligations or by showing warmth) is Yhwh behaving in the way expected of a father. In addition, the next line perhaps indicates that a reason for appealing to God as Father lies in the fact that the community's fathers in the sense of its ancestors would not view the community as their children.[143]

After the opening *kî* applying to both cola, the neatly parallel bicolon comprising v. 16aβγ (4-3, abcdb′c′d′) pairs Abraham and Israel. I take the line as leading into and dependent on v. 16b.[144] Each name comes before its verb, which suggests an emphasis on the names. The line follows each noun with the negative, then pairs similar third-person singular verbs with first-person plural suffixes—one qal qatal, one piel yiqtol, the two rhyming at the end of each colon. The second verb helps give precision to the significance of the first; the difference between qatal and yiqtol is stylistic.[145] 'Recognition' commonly signifies perceiving the identity of someone or something; a classic occurrence is its use in connection with Joseph's brothers failing to recognize him (Gen 42.8). The line's point, then, is that Abraham and Israel might not recognize the community whose prayer this passage expresses. Following on the reference to Abraham,[146] it would make sense to understand 'Israel' to refer to the ancestor Jacob-Israel, which would fit with the reference to Jacob in 58.13-14.[147] Abraham and Jacob would not realize that these are the

[142] Albertz, *Religionsgeschichte Israels in alttestamentlicher Zeit*, II, p. 415 (ET p. 401). Albertz thus sees this development as associated with the exilic and Second Temple period, though Richard J. Bautch notes that the other theological terms in the context suggest thinking that is otherwise characteristic of the preexilic period ('Lament Regained in Trito-Isaiah's Penitential Prayer', in M. J. Boda, D. K. Falk, and R. A. Werline [eds.], *Seeking the Favor of God* [Atlanta: SBL, 2006], I, pp. 83-99 [87-89]).

[143] Cf. Elliger, 'Der Prophet Tritojesaja', pp. 128-29.

[144] Cf. Blenkinsopp, *Isaiah 56–66*, p. 263, referring for the use of *kî* to GK 159aa, bb.

[145] Cf. Croatto, *Imaginar el future*, p. 348.

[146] Edgar W. Conrad argues that this last reference to Abraham in Isaiah, which merely leads into a reference to Israel, marks the low point in his diminishing importance in the book ('Isaiah and the Abraham Connection', *Asia Journal of Theology* 2 [1988], pp. 382-93 [390]).

[147] Cf. Thomas Römer, 'Abraham Traditions in the Hebrew Bible Outside the Book of Genesis', in C. A. Evans, J. A. Lohr, and D. L. Petersen (eds.), *The Book of Genesis* (Leiden: Brill, 2012), pp. 159-80 (171), who notes the contrast between the two references.

people descended from them, the multitude that Abraham was promised and the multitude Israel became. Alternatively, they might not be willing to recognize them in their waywardness.[148] In a discussion of this passage, b. Shabbat 89b has God pointing out to Abraham, Israel, and Isaac their descendants' waywardness. Abraham and Israel urge God to punish the people but Isaac urges God not to do so and offers himself as a sacrifice for them, in keeping with God's desire to forgive them as Father and Restorer. The expression suggests a broken relationship.[149] The wording does not give any indication that Abraham and Israel stand for one part of the community that is rejected by another part of the community that claims to be the real Israel.[150]

Verse 16b concludes the subsection by providing the main clause on which the *kî* clause depends. The 3-3 line is internally parallel in substance. 'You are our Father', it repeats from v. 16aα, adding the divine name Yhwh. It is presumably this name which it then takes up in the parallel colon with its reference to this name being 'of old', one that goes back to the time of the ancestors. There is some irony about this ascription, since literally the name Yhwh was likely not used in Abraham's day, though Genesis assumes it was indeed Yhwh whom Abraham acknowledged. More literally the colon attaches 'your name of old' to the epithet 'restorer' (*gōʾēl*), which is not actually a name. The implication is that the epithet 'restorer' spells out the implications of the name Yhwh. With similar irony, 'restorer' (*gōʾēl*) was not a term much used for God in the ancestors' day (but see Gen 48.16 [E]), though the Israelites knew God acting to restore them (e.g. Exod 6.6; 15.13) and this activity indeed spelled out the implications of Yhwh's actual name. The term came into its own in Isaiah 40–55 (see 41.14; 43.14; 44.6, 24; 47.4; 48.17; 49.7, 26; 54.5, 8; cf. also 59.20; 60.16).[151] The collocation of father and restorer is unique; the link perhaps lies in their shared association with the exodus.[152] For the previous line, Tg had declared that it was not Abraham or Israel who delivered the people, but this observation misses the point. Restorer is supposed to be Yhwh's name or nature as revealed; but Yhwh is not behaving that way.

[148] So Albert the Great, *Postilla super Isaiam*, p. 601.

[149] Cf. W. A. M. Beuken, *'Abraham weet van ons niet'* (Middelburg: Gihonbron, 2003), pp. 4, 6.

[150] Against Browne, *Early Judaism* (see above), pp. 70-86, who identifies the rejected with people who identify with the northern clans; also Hanson, *The Dawn of Apocalyptic*, pp. 92-93, who identifies them with a group within the Jerusalem community; cf. Williamson's critique, 'Isaiah 63,7–64,11' (see above), pp. 53-54.

[151] See Goldingay, *The Message of Isaiah 40–55*, pp. 114-16.

[152] So Paul Niskanen, 'Yhwh as Father, Redeemer, and Potter in Isaiah 63:7–64:11', *CBQ* 68 (2006), pp. 397-407 (400-404).

63.17 Why, Yhwh, do you make us wander from your ways,// make our mind become hard so that we do not revere you?
Turn for the sake of your servants,// the clans that are your possession.

The reversion to questioning suggests a new subsection, comprising questioning (v. 17a), plea (v. 17b), and protest (vv. 18-19a).[153] The question now takes the more familiar form of 'Why?' rather than 'Where?', though the query is again rhetorical. A satisfactory response would not be an explanation such as 'there is no convenient equivalent to Cyrus whom I can use to put Persia down' but an undertaking one way or another to act *now*. Whereas the question 'Why?' (*lāmmâ*) occurs only on Yhwh's lips in Isaiah 1–55 (40.27; 55.2; also 1.5; 5.4; 50.2 using other Hebrew words), here as in 58.3 it comes on the people's lips (a similar mixture appears elsewhere in the Prophets). Naturally enough, the statistics work the other way in the Psalms (e.g. 10.1; 22.2 [1]; 42.10 [9]; 43.2; 44.24, 25 [23, 24]; 74.1, 11; 80.13 [12]; 88.15 [14]; all *lāmmâ*).

As in v. 16a, this opening particle in v. 17a (4-3) applies to both cola, which then have parallel second-person singular yiqtol verbs (the first with a suffix, the second with an object which occupies the place of the vocative in the first) and parallel *min* expressions (literally, 'from your ways… from your revering'), each with a second-person singular suffix. Suggestively, Tg in effect takes the hiphil verbs as tolerative rather than causative:[154] it translates 'Why do you push us away, Yhwh, so that we wander from the ways that are right before you…? Our mind must not turn from reverence for you.' In other words, Yhwh took action that had these results, but it was not exactly the aim of the action (cf. *tāʿâ* hiphil in Gen 20.13 [E]). 'It is as if you make us wander.'[155] Writers such as Theodore of Heraclea rather suggest that the prophet speaks in this way in light of the fact that God is ultimately responsible for everything that happens; the implication is again that, more precisely, God permits this wandering rather than directly causing it.[156] In contrast, LXX and Vg translate by means of a bold causative, and it seems likely that Tg reduces the sharpness of the affront to Yhwh that is intended by the question, which is designed to provoke a response. The accusation makes for a comparison but also a strong contrast with pleas to Yhwh such as 'make me acknowledge your ways' (Ps 25.4). Only here does the Old Testament refer to Yhwh causing people to go astray morally or religiously (though Yhwh leads people astray more literally in passages such as Ps 107.40).

153 Contrast Beuken (*Jesaja IIIB*, pp. 20-21, 25) who sees v. 17 as balancing v. 15 in abb'a' order—a question followed by a plea.

154 See *IBHS* 27.5c.

155 D. Qimchi, 'ישעיה', on the passage.

156 Ἐκ τῆς εἰς Ἡσαΐαν ἐξηγησέως, col. 1369; cf. Hayman of Halberstadt, *Commentariorum in Isaiam libri tres*, col. 1060.

Elsewhere it is people such as prophets and kings who do so. The parallel reference to making their minds harden involves not the more familiar *qāšâ* (Exod 7.3; Deut 2.30) but *qāšaḥ*, which otherwise occurs only in Job 39.16. Whereas the use of *qāšâ* and more common related expressions (*ḥāzaq*, *kābēd*) allows for an interaction between phenomena ('his heart was hard'), personal responsibility ('he hardened his heart') and divine action ('Yhwh hardened his heart'), the use of *qāšaḥ* here is interested only in divine responsibility. Like a psalmist, the prophet will employ any means to goad Yhwh into a reaction, in charging Yhwh with the paradoxical intent of hindering people from revering the one who commands such revering, which is another way of referring to what the first colon called walking in Yhwh's ways (e.g. Deut 8.6; 10.12; 2 Chr 6.31). The verse has been seen as of central significance for the prayer's theology;[157] it is certainly central to its rhetoric. It is a common Old and New Testament assumption that God's judgment takes the form of such hardening.[158] While the prayer uses different language from Isaiah 6.9-10 in particular, the theological idea corresponds.[159] So perhaps does the line's rhetorical significance, except that it is here reversed, as happens with the question 'Why?' In 6.9-10 the prophet is seeking to provoke the people to respond to Yhwh; here the prophet is seeking to provoke Yhwh to respond to the people.

The challenge in v. 17b is as bold as the accusatory question. 'Turn' (*šûb*) is what Israel is supposed to do when it wanders from Yhwh's ways and fails to revere Yhwh. Here it is Yhwh who needs to turn. Once more the language takes up that in Exodus 32–34, where Moses urges Yhwh, 'Turn from your angry blazing' (Exod 32.12). But here the verb is used absolutely in the form that is commonly translated 'repent' (e.g. Jer 3.12, 14, 22), so that the plea almost urges Yhwh to repent. In the parallelism of the 3-2 line, 'turn for the sake of' applies to both cola, and the substantial force of the verb is then complemented by the force the motivation receives from the double description of the prophet's community. The basis for turning is that the people that Yhwh has been making wander and harden are 'your servants' and 'the clans that are your possession'. The change of image from father and restorer to master in relation to servants corresponds to the change of subsection with v. 17, but it also reflects the importance of the motif of 'servants' in Isaiah 56–66.[160] The parallelism suggests that 'your servants' is a term for the community as a whole, as in 54.17, not for a group within it that sees itself as Yhwh's real servants,[161] as it will be in 65.1–66.17[162] (56.6, where the term refers to

[157] So Zapff, *Jesaja*, p. 411.

[158] Cf. Kessler, *Gott geht es um das Ganze*, p. 79.

[159] See John L. McLaughlin, 'Their Heart *Was* Hardened', *Biblica* 75 (1994), pp. 1-25 (15-17).

[160] Cf. Beuken, 'The Main Theme of Trito-Isaiah', pp. 75-76; but see the comment on 56.6 above.

[161] Against Hanson, *The Dawn of Apocalyptic*, pp. 93-94.

foreigners, is also not so different in this respect). Misleading his servants so that they did not serve him properly is surely action that was not in Yhwh's own interests. Why would a master act thus? Why would a property owner abandon this property?[163] In a sense, 'plea' is the wrong word to describe this challenge in v. 17b. It cleverly argues not on the basis of the suppliant's need or rights but on the basis of the interests of the one addressed.

63.18 As something small, they dispossessed your holy people;// our foes trampled your sanctuary.
19a Forever we have been those whom you have not ruled,// over whom your name was not proclaimed.

Crucial to the interpretation of v. 18 is its opening word, *l^e^miṣ ʿār*. In a passage such as 1QH 14.8 = 6.8 *miṣ ʿār* denotes a short time, and lexica give it this sense here.[164] But 'for a little while they [our foes] dispossessed your holy people' makes poor sense in the context; portraying the exile as brief would weaken the prayer's argument. The reference to the way things have been or have seemed 'forever' in the next line expresses more appropriately how the community feels. It makes even poorer sense to translate 'For a little while your holy people possessed [your sanctuary]' (1QIs^a^ has a singular verb, *yrš*, and thus takes 'the holy people' as the subject, as does Tg). It would not be very realistic to attempt to portray the four centuries of the temple's existence under the monarchy as 'a little while'. The idea that 'our foes' is the subject of the first verb as well as the second is surely right, but Vg more plausibly gives *miṣ ʿār* the meaning it has on its other occurrences in the Old Testament (Gen 19.20; Job 8.7; 2 Chr 24.24); it denotes 'something small', with the implication of something trivial and insignificant.[165] Israel's foes have thought nothing of Yhwh's people in dispossessing them; or Yhwh is treating that dispossessing as if it is something insignificant. LXX and Syr are ambiguous but may imply the same understanding; LXX runs on the construction from v. 17b, 'so that for a little while we may possess your holy mountain' or 'so that we may possess a little of your holy mountain'. Given that we are 'your servants', 'your possession' (v. 17) and are also 'your holy people' (v. 18), it is very strange that you should allow us to be treated as of trivial significance. The line works abcdb′c′, with 'as something small' applying to the second colon as well as the first and 'our foes' applying to the first as well as the second (unless we should read the line as 4-2).[166] The second colon offers another angle on the

[162] Cf. Koenen's comment, *Ethik und Eschatologie im Tritojesajabuch*, p. 158.
[163] On *naḥălâ*, see the comment on 58.14.
[164] See BDB, p. 859; *DCH*, V, p. 452. *HALOT*, I, p. 624 emends the text.
[165] Cf. the comments in BDB, pp. 858-59, on related words.
[166] Cf. Fischer, *Wo ist Jahwe?* (see above), p. 3.

strangeness of Yhwh's action. The feet of people who worshipped alien gods have trampled the place that was holy to Yhwh; contrast the divine undertaking about trampling in v. 6. 'Holiness' (*qōdeš*) in the first colon is taken up in 'holy place' (*miqdāš*) in the second, both carrying the second-person singular suffix referring to Yhwh and underlining the nature of the problem in Yhwh's strange action in relation to 'your holy people' and 'your sanctuary' (cf. Lam 2.7, 20; also Pss 74.3-7; 79.1).

A further parallel bicolon (4-3) follows in v. 19a. Once again the first two words, 'Forever we have been', apply to both cola. It seems as if the present situation has obtained from of old (*mēʿôlām*). While the noun in the hyperbolic temporal expression is taken up from 58.12; 61.4, the expression itself is taken up from 57.11, but it has its significance reversed. There it referred to Yhwh's more-or-less eternal long-temperedness. Here it refers to Yhwh's more-or-less eternal absence, as it did in 42.14. More precisely, the ruling metaphor from the previous three lines continues into the parallel unmarked relative clauses that occupy the rest of the first colon and then the second. It is not merely that they *resemble* people whom Yhwh does not rule.[167] Yhwh actually does decline to rule over them; foreign kings rule them instead (cf. 52.5; Neh 9.37; Tg rather reverses the line's meaning in referring it to Yhwh's not ruling the nations by giving them the Torah). Ruling (*māšal*) denotes not merely an ongoing position as one with authority or sovereignty but an active assertion of power and command (in 40.10, JPSV translates the verb 'wins triumph').[168] Not ruling is expressed in other words by speaking of Yhwh's name not being proclaimed over them (contrast Jer 14.9 and Dan 9.19, though the implication is similar; also Jer 15.16; 2 Chr 7.14). The expression is also often used of the city and the temple. It is a sign of ownership and authority, as when David's rather than Joab's name is proclaimed over Rabbah (2 Sam 12.28) or a man's name is proclaimed over a woman (Isa 4.1). Once more, the implication is that the proclaiming of Yhwh's name over the people signifies an active assertion of ownership; it is thus a reason for nations to revere and/or fear them (Deut 28.1).

63.19b Oh that you had torn apart the heavens and come down, that mountains had quaked before you,
64.1 Like fire igniting brushwood// when fire boils water,
To cause your name to be acknowledged by your foes,// that nations might tremble before you.

The indirect plea in 63.19b–64.1 [64.1-2] begins a further subsection that goes on to additional recollection and protest in 64.2-4a, 4b-6 [3-5a, 5b-7]. In v. 19b (3-3) one can see the opening *lûʾ* as applying to the second

[167] So Westermann, *Jesaja Kapitel 40–66*, p. 311 (ET p. 391).
[168] Cf. H. Gross, *TWAT*, V, p. 75 (ET *TDOT*, IX, p. 70).

colon as well as the first, and in this sense the second is parallel to the first, but at the same time the second states the aim of the first, picturing what will follow from it. This understanding is also suggested by the absence of a *w*- to link the cola and by the word order; the verb closes the second colon. Strictly, *lû'* followed by a qatal verb expresses a wish relating to the past, though in this context the wish is not one now reckoned impossible of fulfilment; it is 'the more impassioned expression for, Oh that though *wouldst…*'.[169] The longing, then, is that Yhwh should first tear apart the dome in the sky so as to break through into the world's atmosphere and then descend to the earth itself. The verb 'tear apart' (*qāra'*) comes only here in this connection, though it compares with the language of spreading apart the heavens (*nāṭâ* hiphil) in Psalms 18.10 [9]; 144.5 (cf. also Mark 1.10).[170] It most commonly applies to tearing cloth, and the heavens can be pictured as tent curtains (cf. Isa 40.22; Ps 104.2), so the line may imply that the dome is conceived in this way. Naturally mountains would quake in their awareness that Yhwh has come. The created order thus shows itself sensitive to Yhwh's arrival and capable of responding in an appropriate way to it, as elsewhere it is assumed to be capable of praising Yhwh. I follow Tg in assuming that *zālal* is a synonym of *zûa'*; it has a byform *nāzal* which appears in Judges 5.5. LXX, Vg, Syr rather link it with the more common *nāzal* meaning 'flow/melt'; they may assume a byform *zālal* or may imply a repointing.[171]

Although the chapter break in English Bibles at 64.1 is inappropriate, to make v. 19b a separate verse from v. 19a and from what follows does correspond better to the way the text works at the level of lines and verses than does MT's verse division. Tg treats v. 19b as an appendage to v. 19a, understanding *lû'* as if it read *lō'*: 'not for them did you bend the heavens…'.

The simile in 64.1a [2a] (3-2) moves to a different aspect of the imagery for describing Yhwh's coming (cf. 30.27-33; 66.15-16; earthquake and fire are associated in 29.6). Brushwood is perhaps an alternative image for chaff or desert briars, and it could thus stand for Yhwh's foes (cf. 10.16-17; 33.11-14). The relationship of the second colon to the first is unclear. While each colon comprises a verb (the first prefixed by the preposition *k*-), a subject, and an object, the word order is abcc'a'b'; in the second colon the object thus comes first. I have assumed that the second colon is subordinate to the first (as is the case with the lines on either side) rather than that the *k*- applies to the second colon as well as the first ('like fire igniting brushwood, fire boiling water').[172] The line

169 *TTH* 140; cf. GK 151e.

170 See Ivor Buse, 'The Markan Account of the Baptism of Jesus and Isaiah lxiii', *JTS* n.s. 7 (1956), pp. 74-75, on the broader influence of Isaiah 63 there.

171 See the translation note.

172 So Paul, ישעיה פרקים מ-סו, II, p. 528 (ET p. 582).

then refers to the way a fire blazes up when someone is seeking to boil water. Tg refers fire boiling water to the Reed Sea.

The aim stated in v. 1b [2b] also belongs to the theme of Yhwh's appearing with earthquake and fire. Once again the 3-3 line comprises cola that can be read as parallel (abcb'c'a'), but with the second colon implying the further aim of the first. The first aim the plea has in mind is not that Yhwh's foes should merely know Yhwh's name; *yāda*ʿ has its common connotation 'acknowledge/recognize'. Thus Yhwh's people are those who acknowledge Yhwh's name (52.6). The implications of the expression are not very different from those of calling in or on Yhwh's name (12.4; 41.25), confessing it (25.1), proclaiming it (26.13), sanctifying it (29.13), trusting in it (50.10), dedicating oneself to it (56.6), or revering it (59.19). It is another way of referring to the idea of 'acknowledging Yhwh' or 'acknowledging that Yhwh is God' (e.g. 43.10; 45.3, 4, 5, 6; 49.23, 26; 60.16). Whereas the translation 'know Yhwh' or 'know Yhwh's name' raises questions about the nature of this knowing, a recognition that the prophet is concerned with the acknowledgment of Yhwh or of Yhwh's name sidesteps some of these questions. The plea is not concerned with Yhwh's foes coming to a personal acquaintance and friendship with Yhwh but with their recognizing and submitting to Yhwh. While this recognition might (or might not) have some benefit for the foes, the plea is not concerned with the foes but with Yhwh's name, and with the community itself that currently suffers because the foes do not recognize Yhwh. In connection with Isaiah 60 we have noted that 'the nations' can denote peoples that are under the not-very-beneficent control of the imperial power or can denote the imperial power itself. Here, where 'Yhwh's foes' will be the latter, the parallelism of a line such as this one could imply that the enforced recognition of Yhwh by the imperial power would be good news for other 'nations'. But 'trembling' (*rāgaz*) is usually negative, in Hebrew as in English. It is an apposite verb since it commonly denotes the earth trembling (e.g. Ps 77.19 [18]); the mountains' response to Yhwh's coming (v. 19b [64.1]) is appropriately mirrored in the nations' response. A more straightforward understanding of the line's parallelism would thus again refer the term 'nations' to the imperial power, which will acknowledge and therefore tremble before Yhwh. Once more, this understanding does not preclude the possibility that such awed submission will imply good news for the imperial power itself; it need not imply that the imperial power is being destroyed. But the focus of concern does not lie with that possibility but with the superpower's submission to Yhwh, which will mean good news for the community that it currently dominates.

64.2 When you did awe-inspiring deeds we were not expecting,// you came down—mountains quaked before you.
3 Never had people heard,// they had not given ear to,// eye had not seen
A God apart from you// who acts for the person who waits for him.
4a You met with the person who rejoiced and acted with faithfulness,// the people who were mindful of you in your ways.

Within 63.19b–64.6 [64.1-7], in 64.2-4a [3-5a] plea gives way to recollection. Verse 2 [3] (4-4) is another line in which the second colon simply completes the first. The first raises the question 'Oh, what happened then—what were these deeds?' and the second answers the question. In light of the stress on the Reed Sea event earlier in the prayer, the 'awe-inspiring deeds' (*nôrāʾôt* from *yārēʾ*) will be those associated with that deliverance (Exod 15.11; Ps 106.22), but the reference might also cover the acts associated with Israel's journey to Canaan (Deut 10.21) and its gaining possession of the land (2 Sam 7.23), or it might be taken quite generally (Ps 145.6). Expecting (*qāwâ*) such deeds is an obligation that rests on Israel (Isa 40.31; 49.23); one could say it is an aspect of acknowledging Yhwh. But Yhwh has not necessarily been inhibited from performing awe-inspiring deeds by the lack of that expectancy. Like the question of acknowledging Yhwh, the question of seeing such deeds does not ultimately relate to the needs or blessing of their immediate beneficiaries but to wider purposes such as the recognition of Yhwh by the world, and thus it is not ultimately dependent on whether or not Israel fulfils its obligation to be expectant.

The first colon reads more literally 'In your doing awe-inspiring deeds', so that its time reference is unclear. 'We were not expecting' is then yiqtol, and LXX and Vg thus take the colon as a whole as having present/future reference, 'When you do awe-inspiring deeds that we do not expect ', but this is hard to fit with the qatal verb in the second colon and with the broader context. Tg more plausibly takes the line as a whole to refer to the past; the yiqtol has past imperfect significance. The second colon then refers to Yhwh's coming down at the Reed Sea and perhaps on subsequent occasions in Israel's experience, with the literal or metaphorical accompaniments described. It repeats 63.19aβ, though with some subtlety, because now the verbs refer to actual events rather than merely desired ones.[173]

Verse 3 [4] comprises five 2-stress cola. MT divides them two and three; I divide them three and two, taking v. 3bα with the first line to form three parallel cola. This line then comprises all the references to hearing and seeing, while the second line simply contains the object of

[173] Contrast (e.g.) Dillmann (*Jesaia* [1890 edn], p. 524), who assumes that the words must have the same significance as they had in 63.19 notwithstanding the absence of *lûʾ*; but he associates this understanding with the hypothesis that the colon is a later addition to v. 2.

these verbs. Whereas *mē ʿōlām* in 63.19a covered a relatively short time span (since 587) that felt like 'forever', the *mē ʿōlām* that begins v. 3a [4a] refers to a much longer one. The first two verbs are then more or less synonymous, though the second (*ʾāzan* hiphil) is much rarer. It usually carries a more intrinsic connotation of listening and paying attention (thus its dominant usage is in the imperative), but it is doubtful whether that point can be pressed in this context. The third verb moves from ear to eye.

The content of the not hearing and seeing (v. 3b [4b]) is 'a God apart from you', an expression fitting Yhwh's own earlier claim that 'there is no God apart from me' (45.5, 21), addressed to Cyrus and then to people who escape Cyrus's campaigns[174] (cf. 2 Sam 7.22 = 1 Chr 17.20; Ps 18.32 [31]; also Isa 26.13; Hos 13.4). The first colon raises the question 'How is Yhwh unique?'; the second gives the answer. 'Waiting' for Yhwh (*ḥākâ* piel) is a synonym for 'expecting'. The line thus complements v. 2 in a paradoxical way. There Yhwh acts for people who do not expect it; here Yhwh acts (the same verb) for people who do expect it. Whereas this section has been especially resonant of the Reed Sea story, such talk of being expectant and of there being no God but Yhwh also recalls the context presupposed by Isaiah 40–55. By implication, the present subsection is challenging Yhwh both in respect of the acts that belong to the first context and in respect of the claims that belong in the second context.

In 1 Corinthians 2.9 Paul adapts v. 3 [4] to a point he wishes to make.[175] Calvin speaks of Paul seeming to 'torture' the text 'to a different purpose' from the one it has in its context; 'in this respect the Apostles were not squeamish; for they paid more attention to the matter than to the words and reckoned it enough to draw the attention of the reader to a passage of Scripture, from which might be obtained what they taught'.[176] Luther rather describes Paul as adapting a general statement to a particular context.[177]

In v. 4a [5a], 'rejoiced and acted in faithfulness' is a compound expression,[178] 'rejoiced to act in faithfulness [*ṣedeq*]', which suggests it is a 4-2 line, with the yiqtol clause in the second colon paralleling the participial expressions in the first. The participles in the first colon take their time reference from the opening qatal verb. The plural yiqtol verb in the second colon then provides variation from the singular participles; we might take the yiqtol as a 'true' imperfect or simply as instancing the way

[174] See Goldingay and Payne, *Isaiah 40–55*, II, p. 55.

[175] On the possible background to Paul's use of the text, see Hervé Ponset, 'D'Isaïe, lxiv, 3 à I Corinthiens, ii, 9', *RB* 90 (1983), pp. 229-42; also Koch, *Die Schrift also Zeuge des Evangeliums*, pp. 36-41; Pierre Prigent, 'Ce que l'oeil n'a pas vu, I Cor. 2, 9', *Theologische Zeitschrift* 14 (1958), pp. 416-29.

[176] *In Iesaiam prophetam*, p. 402 (ET IV, p. 364).

[177] *In Esaiam prophetam enarraciones*, pp. 544-45 (ET pp. 366-67).

[178] See Barthélémy, *Critique Textuelle de l'Ancien Testament*, II, p. 447.

a sequence of forms such as participles can give way to finite verbs. The more compressed expression in the second colon suggests walking in Yhwh's ways and thus expressing a mindfulness of Yhwh. The tricky question about the line concerns the first word. The verb *pāgaʿ* can suggest a meeting that is neutral, hostile, or friendly, though the last meaning is the least frequent. LXX, Vg, and Syr all translate with an equally ambiguous word. MT's verse division may imply a hostile meeting,[179] but Tg's paraphrase, 'the deeds of our faithful ancestors meet with you', suggests a positive understanding of the verb. This makes sense in the context as there is nothing to suggest a move in v. 4a [5a] from the positive statements about Yhwh's actions in vv. 2-3 [3-4], nor would a protest at Yhwh's hostile meeting that would apparently have been unfair fit with the recognition of waywardness that follows. The positive potential of the verb comes out most explicitly in its use to signify meeting with a person on someone else's behalf and thus interceding for them (cf. the hiphil in 53.12). Here, then, the verb denotes Yhwh's meeting people to deliver them, in keeping with preceding lines.

64.4b Now: you yourself got angry,// and of old we have offended in relation to them, though we were delivered.

5 All of us became like something taboo,// all our faithful acts like menstrual clothing,
And all of us have withered like leaves;// our waywardness, like the wind, carries us off.

6 There is no one calling on your name,// stirring himself up to lay hold of you,
Because you have hidden your face from us// and made us faint away by reason of our waywardness.

The opening of vv. 4b-6 [5b-7] suggests a transition from recollection to protest. All three verbs in v. 4b are easy enough to understand, but the relationship between them is a different matter; indeed, it has been argued that 'there is perhaps no sentence in Isaiah, or indeed in the Old Testament, which has more divided and perplexed interpreters'.[180] Whereas v. 4a [5a] contains no indication of a transition nor any grounds for protest, v. 4b [5b] begins *hēn* and is thus open to suggesting a contrast with what has preceded, and 'you yourself [the pronoun is expressed] got angry' confirms that impression, but there certainty ends. In its paraphrase Tg implies 'you yourself got angry because we offended'.[181] Yhwh's anger, then, is a response to the people's longstanding habit of offending against 'them'—the ways of Yhwh to which v. 4a referred. It would fit

[179] So Tiemeyer, *Priestly Rites and Prophetic Rage*, pp. 103-4.
[180] Alexander, *Isaiah*, II, p. 431; he is referring to v. 4 as a whole.
[181] So also Sym, according to Theodoret of Cyrrhus, *Commentaire sur Isaïe* 181a (III, pp. 306-7).

regular Old Testament thinking to take ‘we offended’ (*ḥāṭā*ʾ)[182] as providing the rationale for the change in Yhwh’s stance (though in this context the prayer’s protest would be compromised by such a recognition that Yhwh’s angry action was quite deserved); the *w*-consecutive would then suggest that the sequence in the verbs is one of thought and expression rather than time.[183] But this is by no means a natural way to read the sequence. As an alternative possibility, the verb does occasionally mean ‘incur guilt’ as a result of offending, or ‘be treated as guilty’ as if we had so offended (see Gen 43.9),[184] and on the latter understanding it might imply a claim to have been treated as sinners when they were not.[185] But the most obvious translation of the verbal sequence is ‘you got angry and [as a result] we have offended’ (cf. LXX, Vg). ‘The power of the verse’ then ‘lies in the unexpected sequence…and its literary function lies exactly in its outrageous formulation’.[186] Such a protest is consistent with 63.17, though even bolder and harder to parallel elsewhere, but v. 6b will support this ‘bold’ reading of the line. Its force lies in the claim that Yhwh has to accept some responsibility for the community’s being driven into ongoing (‘of old’) waywardness. Yhwh’s punishment is counterproductive. Therefore Yhwh should stop being angry and start taking the action urged in 63.19b–64.1 [64.1-2].

The final difficult question in the line is raised by the closing *w*-yiqtol verb. Vg again renders in the grammatically obvious way ‘and we shall be delivered’, but such a statement of conviction does not fit the context. EVV turn the statement into a question, but there is no indication that the verb is to be understood thus. Tg in its paraphrase interprets more plausibly in taking the verb to have past reference, like the verbs in vv. 63.3-6;[187] its paraphrase also develops the idea that it was because of the acts of the faithful ancestors that this deliverance came about. In effect the clause means ‘although we had been delivered’ or ‘when we had been delivered’. The acts of deliverance will be the ones that Israel had known in the past, beginning in Egypt and at the Reed Sea.

[182] On the verb, see the comment on 58.1.

[183] So *TTH* 76β.

[184] Cf. Delitzsch, *Jesaia*, p. 649 (ET II, p. 468); see BDB, p. 307.

[185] So Sheldon H. Blank, ‘“And All Our Virtues”’, *JBL* 71 (1952), pp. 149-54.

[186] Childs, *Isaiah*, p. 525.

[187] See *TTH* 84a for such use of simple *w*-yiqtol, though without referring to this verse as an instance. But perhaps the verb needs emending to *wayyiqtol*. With respect to v. 4bβ Lowth (*Isaiah*, p. 395) comments that ‘there is no doubt of the meaning of each word separately, but put together they make no sense at all’. He emends in the light of LXX and adds that ‘perhaps these may not be the very words of the Prophet’ but that risking such imposition is better than leaving nonsense or forcing sense on nonsense (compare James Barr’s remarks defending textual emendation in *Comparative Philology and the Text of the Old Testament* [Oxford: Oxford University Press, 1968], p. 191). See also the translation note on this verb.

In a 3-3 parallel line (abcb'c'), v. 5a expands on the reference to offences. Contact with death or sex, among other things, makes a person taboo in the sense that for a period one cannot go into Yhwh's presence, perhaps because there is too much clash between the effects of that experience or action and the being of Yhwh. The Old Testament sometimes speaks in terms of moral wrong having the same effect for the same reason, and the plea presupposes this assumption, in line with the pleas in Lamentations 1.9; 4.14-15.[188] The community, 'while ritually pure, does impure deeds';[189] the idea is not only that immoral behaviour coexists with ritual purity or that impurity is a metaphor for the consequences of immorality but that immorality conveys impurity and thus makes it impossible to approach Yhwh in the same way as follows from the infringement of ritual rules in the narrower sense. In themselves the words might imply that the community is being treated as if it were wayward and taboo when it is not, but the context indicates that rather it is being treated as wayward and taboo because that is what it is. Likewise, in themselves the words might be taken to indicate that even people's faithful acts were tainted by sin, but in the context this seems irrelevant. Again, in themselves the words might be read as a description of universal human sinfulness, but Calvin points out that this understanding, too, ignores the context, which makes clear that the words apply to Israel in a particular generation.[190] The reference to 'all of us' confirms the impression that the prayer speaks for the community as a whole that acknowledges its waywardness, rather than for a group that sees itself as in the right but as being oppressed, over against another group within the community. The point will be underlined by 'no one' in v. 6 [7] and by the 'all' in v. 7 [8].[191] It does not speak for a group that sees itself as in the right over against other elements in the community.[192]

The second colon makes the subject more concrete in speaking of our faithful acts (*ṣᵉdāqôt*). It thus takes up from the reference to acting in faithfulness (*ṣedeq*) in v. 4a [5a] and further suggests that the meaning of 'faithful acts' is not confined to purportedly faithful acts or to properly offered acts of worship, either or both of which might actually be compromised by wrong attitudes or wrong practices in other areas of life. They could hardly then continue to be termed faithful acts. The line refers to the speakers' having ceased to act in the faithful fashion to which v. 4a [5a] referred. Faithful acts have been replaced by acts that convey taboo and make it impossible for them to come into Yhwh's presence.

188 Cf. Fischer, *Wo ist Jahwe?* (see above), pp. 182-83.

189 Jacob Neusner, *The Idea of Purity in Ancient Judaism* (Leiden: Brill, 1973), p. 13 (cf. Bautch, 'Lament Regained in Trito-Isaiah's Penitential Prayer', p. 94).

190 *In Iesaiam prophetam*, p. 403 (ET IV, p. 369); cf. Jones, *Isaiah 56–66 and Joel*, p. 101.

191 Cf. Ruszkowski, *Volk und Gemeinde im Wandel*, p. 57.

192 Cf. Schramm, *The Opponents of Third Isaiah*, p. 155.

'Menstrual clothing' likewise makes the reference to taboo more concrete. The phrase is more literally 'clothing of periods/times' (*ʿiddîm*); the word occurs only here but the context and equivalents in cognate languages seem to make its meaning clear.[193] It lacks the pejorative connotations of translations such as 'a filthy cloth' (NRSV) or 'a filthy rag' (JPSV). It simply means clothing that is affected by and conveys a taboo, so that contact with it means one cannot come before Yhwh.

In turn, the effect of the acts of offence and their associated taboo has been to make people wither (v. 5b [6b]; 3-3). Prosaically put, 'our waywardness has caused all of us to wither like leaves which the wind carries off'. The line is a classic instance of the way a complex sentence can be conformed to the prosody of a bicolon. Here 'offending' is re-expressed as 'waywardness' (*ʿāwôn*); the two expressions came together at 59.2.[194] The result of waywardness is withering; it has an effect like that of the sun on foliage. In turn, withering is followed by being blown away. Alongside the personalist imagery of anger generating a personal action, implied by v. 4b [5b], is thus the imagery of natural cause and effect, a process built intrinsically into the way reality works. Waywardness naturally issues in withering, and further, the effect of waywardness is then like that of wind in the way it carries people away. Already, 57.13 declared that 'a wind will carry all of *them* off' (cf. 41.16). Here, the repeated 'all of *us*' comes in the same position at the end of the first colon as it came in the previous line. It underscores the way the whole community experiences these 'natural' consequences of offence and waywardness; the plea is not talking about one group or one class within the community. The expression suggests a sad contrast with other occurrences of 'all' in the context (e.g. 63.7, 9). There is also a sad contrast with the last occasion when 'all of us' recurred in successive lines (53.6, which also speaks of 'waywardness' and uses the verb *pāgaʿ* which came in v. 4a [5a] here), though vv. 7-8 [8-9] will shortly juxtapose a further pair of occurrences of 'all of us' that attempt to get Yhwh to complement the negative usage with a positive one in the way that 53.6 does.

Perhaps one should see v. 6a [7a] (2-3) as stating more literally the effect, or one aspect, of this withering. 'There is no' applies to both cola; each colon then comprises a participle (one qal, one hitpael) and an indirect object governed by a preposition (one *b*- plus a noun, one *l*- plus an infinitive with its own indirect object governed by another *b*-). 'Calling on someone's name' is literally 'calling by/in someone's name' (*qārāʾ bᵉšēm*) and it can denote simply addressing someone by name in a general sense or making a proclamation in someone's name, but it can also denote specifically calling upon someone to get them to do something, in the same way as 'calling on someone' (*qārāʾ b*-; e.g. 40.26;

193 See BDB, *HALOT*.
194 See the comment there.

42.6; 45.3-4). This makes sense here, though the verb indicates that the invocation happens out loud and the phrase 'by/in someone's name' suggests that the words are not simply addressed to Yhwh but are uttered in the hearing of other people.[195] The statement declares not merely that people have given up worshipping Yhwh but that they have given up pleading with Yhwh to intervene and act on their behalf. The line 'captures a loss of grace and human nerve in the milieu of divine abandonment'.[196] The point is made sharper by the parallel verbal expression in the second colon, which emphasises not so much the stirring of themselves up (which could be required for worship in general) but the laying hold of Yhwh in which it issues (*ḥāzak b-*; the verb is hiphil), like Yhwh laying hold of his servant or of Cyrus (42.6; 45.1), in order to get Yhwh to act on their behalf. But they are too discouraged by their awareness of having incurred Yhwh's wrath to be able to do so.

Verse 6b [7b] (3-2) makes that impression explicit. The reason they do not call on or lay hold of Yhwh is that they cannot. The opening 'because' applies to both the parallel cola, as does the closing 'by reason of our waywardness', which also picks up the word from the previous verse. The actually parallel expressions are thus 'you have hidden your face from us' and 'you have made us faint away'. The first expression throws back at Yhwh the admission in 54.8, though 59.2 has subsequently acknowledged that it is the people's offences that have had this result. The phrase recurs in protests in the Psalms (13.2 [1]; 27.9; 44.25 [24]; 69.18 [17]; 88.15 [14]; 102.3 [2]; 143.7).[197] The plea has asked Yhwh to look at what is going on (63.15) in the conviction that looking leads to action; how could it not do so? The only way for Yhwh to avoid acting on the community's behalf is to avoid looking. Yhwh has thus avoided looking, and people have therefore stopped calling on and laying hold of again, presumably Yhwh, because it is pointless. The parallel verb (*mûg*) literally means to soften; Psalm 65.11 [10] uses it in connection with the effect of rains on the earth, but it more often refers to the earth dissolving at Yhwh's appearing (e.g. Ps 46.7 [6]). It also applies to the effect of fear, danger, and disaster on people (e.g. Exod 15.15; Josh 2.9, 24; Jer 49.23; Ezek 21.20 [15]), which fits here. The community is demoralized by its trouble and by the way Yhwh stands by and does nothing, even though it knows it deserves everything that has happened. But Tg, LXX, Syr, Vg rather suggest linking the verb form with *māgēn*

[195] Cf. F. L. Hossfeld and E.-M. Kindl, *TWAT*, VII, p. 123 (ET *TDOT*, XIII, p. 114).

[196] Bautch, 'Lament Regained in Trito-Isaiah's Penitential Prayer', p. 95.

[197] Erich Bosshard works out a comparison of 63.7–64.11 (suggesting that it focuses on the problem of the spatial distance between God in the heavens and the people praying on earth) and Ps 102 (which focuses more on the problem of time—God's being lasts forever, our being does not) ('Ferne und Langzeitigkeit Jhwhs', in Thomas Naumann and Regine Hunziker-Rodewald [eds.], *Diasynchronen* [Walter Dietrich Festschrift; Stuttgart: Kohlhammer, 2009], pp. 39-55).

(cf. Gen 14.20) which produces the accusation 'you delivered us into the power of our waywardness'. Perhaps the prophet combines the connotations of the two verbs: 'you made us faint away into the power of our waywardness'.[198]

64.7 But now, Yhwh, you are our father,// we are the clay, you are our potter,// all of us are the work of your hand.

8 Yhwh, do not be so very angry;// do not be mindful of our waywardness forever;// now: do look at your people, all of us.

With v. 7 [8] the final subsection begins, comprising a plea with a long introduction (vv. 7-8 [8-9]), a protest (vv. 9-10 [10-11]), and a final question (v. 11 [12]). Rather extraordinarily, the two lines of the plea and the first line of the protest are all tricola; the subsequent two lines of the protest then comprise one sentence, which one might see as a quadricolon, if there is such a thing.[199] The use of these long lines brings the plea towards its climax, though it will actually reach this climax by reversing this aspect of the rhetoric and ending with a simple bicolon.

The three cola in v. 7 [8] are all parallel (4-4-3). The opening 'But now' marks the transition to plea (as happens in Neh 9.32);[200] it applies to all three cola, which in content at a macro-level work aba′b′ in the sense that they comprise statements about God, then about the people, then about God, then about the people. Another way to see them would be to link the first and third, which would form a pair, over against the middle colon, which is complete in itself. There is then parallelism between the first and third on one hand, and the second on the other. 'You are our father' resumes from 63.16, though pronoun and noun are reversed because 'you' is here set over against 'we'; placing 'you' at the end of the colon means the two pronouns come next to each other. In connection with 63.16 we noted that the imagery of fatherhood suggests one who brings things into being, and that governs the thinking here. 'God our Father means God our Creator.'[201] The way Yhwh acts as father of the community is by acting like a potter in relation to clay. This image takes up from 45.9-11, nicely turning back on Yhwh the appeal to the image there, where it is also juxtaposed with the image of fatherhood.[202] The implication is that Yhwh the potter is in the process of making a clay vessel and is hardly in a position to throw away the clay; the most the

[198] Cf. Barthélémy, *Critique Textuelle de l'Ancien Testament*, II, p. 451.

[199] David T. Tsumura so describes 1 Sam 2.8a (*The First Book of Samuel* [Grand Rapids: Eerdmans, 2007], p. 147).

[200] Watts sees the 'But now' introducing the prayer's climax as 'the critical turning point in the prayer' (*Isaiah 40–66*, p. 906).

[201] Barth, *Die kirchliche Dogmatik* I/1, p. 410 (ET p. 447; 2nd edn, p. 389).

[202] Cf. Goldenstein, *Das Gebet der Gottesknechte* (see above), pp. 130-34.

potter can do is compress the clay and start the shaping again. As we put it in connection with 63.11a, Yhwh needs to stay mindful of having begun a project that surely must not be abandoned. The point is then underlined by the third colon, with a further 'all of us' (cf. v. 5 [6]). Once more, the words refer to the community as a whole, not to one group within it. In light of the way the line turns Yhwh's own words back on Yhwh, one might see the same tactic in the 'but now' with which the line begins. 'But now' is the beginning of a word about judgment in passages such as 5.3, 5 (cf. Jer 7.13; Hos 2.12 [10]) but also of a word by way of promise in 43.1; 44.1 (cf. Jer 32.36).

This understanding of the relationship of Yhwh and the people is the basis for the renewed plea in the second tricolon comprising v. 8 [9] (3-3-4). Here the first two cola form a pair; the third colon forms the positive equivalent to the negative of the first two, while also pairing with the last colon in the preceding verse through the 'all of us' which again closes the line. In addition to this last link, 'do not be angry' takes up the verb from 64.4 [5]; 'do not be mindful' from 63.11; 'look' from 63.15. 'Waywardness' takes up from 64.5-6 [6-7], 'now' (*hēn*) from 64.4 [5], 'your people' from 63.14. Thus the only novelties in the line are 'so very' in the first colon, 'forever' in the second, and 'do' (the enclitic *nāʾ*) in the third. The rhetoric thus brings the plea towards its climax by repeating many terms from earlier in the prayer, but also underlines their significance by those three novelties. In this way it forms a new twist on the convention whereby pleas in Israelite prayers are not very specific. They seek to get God to act rather than to suggest what the action should be.

64.9 Your holy cities—they have been a wilderness,// Zion—it has been a wilderness,// Jerusalem a devastation.
10 Our holy and glorious house,// where our ancestors praised you—
It became something consumed by fire;// all that we valued became a ruin.

Moving one last time from plea to protest, in v. 9 [10] the prayer expresses itself first in a further tricolon. The three cola (4-3-2) are parallel, with the subject each time coming first; the entire predicate is repeated from the first colon to the second (with the necessary change of number) and then the verb carries its force over into the third, which has a different complement. Starting from the plural cities and then moving on to Zion contrasts with the order in 40.9; 44.26, though it corresponds to that in 1.7-8. Further, the order corresponds to the order in which the country was devastated (cf. 36.1-3) and also heightens the rhetoric; the line intensifies with the reference to Zion and then to Jerusalem. On the other hand, the expression 'holy cities', which comes only here, underlines their importance; it is not Jerusalem's devastation alone that matters. The whole land is the 'holy land' (Zech 2.12, the phrase's only occurrence in the Old Testament, from a period close to the one to which this prayer belongs).[203] Thus all its cities are holy. Their description as wilderness designates them as places where no one lives, though that is a hyperbole. Their designation as a devastation (*šᵉmāmâ*; cf. 62.4) heightens the point; they are not merely places that have never been developed but places that were once occupied and have been ravaged. Indeed, for *šᵉmāmâ* LXX suggests *qᵉlālâ* 'a curse', which MT might have toned down.[204] Either designation makes us reconsider the implications of the word *midbār*, which (like the word 'wilderness' in U.S. English) can have both positive and negative connotations; it can denote grazing land or suggest fearful wasteland.[205] In contrast, 1QIsᵃ softens the statement's harshness in reading 'like a wilderness' and 'desolate' (*šwmmh*).[206]

In v. 10 [11], the two bicola (3-3, 3-3) constitute one sentence; hence the possibility of seeing them as a quadricolon. The first line is the subject (again thus preceding the verb), with the opening colon in v. 10b [11b] its predicate. The last of the four cola then comprises a brief parallel to v. 10abα [11abα] as a whole. The entire verse also parallels v. 9 [10] and sharpens its point by talking not merely about the cities in general and about the capital city in particular, but about the temple. The beginning of v. 10 [11] particularly parallels the beginning of v. 9 [10], though with a noteworthy twist as 'the cities of your holiness' becomes 'the house of our holiness'. Indeed, the expression *qodšēnû*, 'our holiness', is almost an oxymoron; it comes only here. One might further have expected the pronominal suffixes to come in the opposite order, but the prayer's order emphasizes on one hand what the people's cities ought to mean to Yhwh and on the other what Yhwh's house means to the people. That point is underlined by the additional reference to the glory of the house (*tip'ārâ*), and further underlined by the adaptation of that phrase from the expression in 60.7, where Yhwh speaks of '*my* glorious house', and in 63.15, which speaks to Yhwh about 'your holy and glorious eminence' in the heavens; the word for 'glory' also came earlier in the prayer in 63.12, 14, and in 60.19; 62.3. The second colon in v. 10a [11a] then compensates for the description of the house as 'ours' by referring to it as the place where the ancestors praised *you* (though they too are 'our' ancestors'). The prayer is thus emphasizing the scandal of the temple's state.

In v. 10b [11b], as the first colon duly constitutes the predicate of the sentence begun in v. 10a [11a], the word 'became' (*hāyâ*) furthers the parallelism between v. 10 [11] as a whole and v. 9 [10], though it also modifies it. There, the verb was followed by a simple complement, suggesting 'was', whereas here it is followed by a pair of *l*- expressions,

[203] For other phrases implying the holiness of the whole land, see Isa 11.9; 65.25; Exod 15.13; Ps 78.54.

[204] Ziegler (*Untersuchungen zur Septuaginta des Buches Isaias*, p. 132) rather sees the influence of Jer 26.6 (LXX 33.6).

[205] See S. Talmon in *TWAT*.

[206] Cf. Rubinstein, 'The Theological Aspect of Some Variant Readings in the Isaiah Scroll', p. 190.

the usual construction when the verb means 'become'.[207] The term for 'something consumed' (*śᵉrēpâ*) can denote the process of burning or the end result of burning; either would fit here, but 'ruin' in the parallelism in the second colon suggests reference to the end result. Conversely, the parallelism further indicates that 'all that we valued' (*maḥmad*) also refers to objects in the temple, as it does elsewhere (e.g. 2 Chr 36.19). Likewise the term 'ruin' (*ḥorbâ*) is used of the temple in Ezra 9.9. That passage presupposes that by Ezra's day the ruin has been rebuilt, as Ezra 1–6 has described. The implication is that Isaiah 63.7–64.11 [12] comes from a time when the temple has not yet been rebuilt.

> 11 At these things do you restrain yourself, Yhwh,// remain still, and humble us so much?

For its closing line, the prayer abandons the expansive rhetoric of vv. 7-10 [8-11] for a simple 3-3 line articulating a final rhetorical question. The opening interrogative *ha-* applies to both cola, as does the vocative 'Yhwh' at the centre of the line. 'These things' looks back to vv. 9-10 [10-11] and perhaps more broadly to the protests in the prayer. The first verb 'restrain yourself' then picks up from 63.15 and behind that from 42.14 (where Yhwh was the subject, as here). Within the second colon, 'remain still' (*ḥāšâ*) directly parallels that first verb and also picks up from 42.14 (though there the verb was hiphil) and also from 62.1. Over against both these passages it confronts Yhwh with the fact that the action promised has not materialized. Yhwh has not given up remaining still. The final verb strikes off in a new and bold direction, though it also presupposes the opening 'at these things'. The verb 'humble' (*ʿānâ* piel) came in 60.14 but with human beings as subjects; Yhwh is the one who rescues the people from being put down. By letting Jerusalem stay in its devastated state, Yhwh is personally continuing to humble it. The verb is one with which the Psalms confront Yhwh (Pss 88.8 [7]; 90.15; cf. Lam 3.33). The 'so much' with which the prayer ends then recalls the ending of Lamentations, 5.22.

Conclusion

While the section pairs with 59.9-15a, its location after Yhwh's promises about putting down the superpower and restoring Israel gives it a different dynamic. It implies the conviction that in a situation in which Yhwh has not fulfilled these promises, an appropriate response to them is to urge Yhwh to do what they say. Its much greater length, complexity, urgency, and boldness cohere with this location.

[207] Cf. Alexander, *Isaiah*, II, p. 435.

The prayer is characterized by a deep poignancy over the relationship between God and the people, expressed in the extreme nature of what it says about the mutual relationship. The two parties resemble disappointed adoptive parents and children, each grieved over the other's attitude. The very opening of the prayer advertises this theme. In doing so, it locates the prophet in the place where a prophet regularly stands, between the two parties, identified with both. On one hand, the prayer recounts Yhwh's great praise, and implicitly seeks to draw the community into that praise. On the other, it expresses the community's bewilderment at Yhwh's total withdrawal from it.

On one hand, then, there is the commitment, goodness, compassion, love, and pity Yhwh showed to Israel in being willing to identify with its trouble. Yhwh personally acted as the people's restorer, in the manner of a member of its extended family with energy and resources he could expend on its behalf, and in carrying it behaved as its father. In acting thus, Yhwh naturally took for granted that Israel would respond like orphan children, grateful and obedient. Yet instead, the children rebelled against their father and hurt him. This left Yhwh torn between two attitudes, an inclination to punish because it is inappropriate simply to let children get away with waywardness, and a realization of the need to be mindful of the long-term intention expressed in that initial commitment. That dynamic has been a feature of Yhwh's ongoing relationship with Israel as it was a feature of its beginnings in the story told in the Torah.

On the other hand, however, from the community's angle the prayer confronts Yhwh with having given up on the tension involved in this dynamic. Yhwh is not behaving in the way that characterizes the story the Torah tells. They still see Yhwh as their father and restorer, but Yhwh does not behave thus; there is no compassion now, no presence of Yhwh's spirit now. This disparity of stance drives the community into extraordinarily bold words of confrontation; as in the Psalms, the prayer will say anything to provoke Yhwh to a response. So if Yhwh is supposed to be father and restorer, 'Why, Yhwh, do you make us wander from your ways, make our mind become hard so that we do not revere you?' Yhwh needs to 'turn'—the word commonly translated 'repent' when applied to humanity. At present (the closing verb in the prayer declares) Yhwh is simply humbling the community: the verb is *ʿānâ* piel, once used for the Egyptians' afflicting of the Israelites (e.g. Exod 1.11-12 [J]; and cf. Isa 60.14).

The prayer sees only a negative aspect to the people's relationship with their distant ancestors, whereas 41.8-9; 51.2 saw the relationship positively. The prayer sees the people as those over whom Yhwh's name has never been proclaimed, whereas 43.7 sees the exiles as people who can call themselves by that name. The prayer pleads with Yhwh not to be mindful of their waywardness as if Yhwh had not spoken in such terms in 43.25. It expresses puzzlement at Yhwh's self-restraint and remaining still, whereas in 42.14 Yhwh had already undertaken to stop doing so.

Indeed, 'it emerges that for those praying here all that has been said before in Isa 40:1–63:6 does not apply. Their situation is still that after Isa 1–39 yet before Isa 40:1.' Such elements in the petition 'show that the relationship between YHWH and his people is disturbed in a way unlike any earlier situation. As a result, enormous doubt is cast on the possibility that YHWH might answer this communal lament.'[208]

The community's own account of the history of the relationship is thus rather different from Yhwh's. Stage One involved Yhwh being in relationship with people who lived lives characterized by faithfulness and joy and were mindful of Yhwh. Stage Two involved Yhwh getting angry, for reasons the community discretely avoids explaining: was it because they deserved it and are not saying, or because Yhwh was just being capricious?[209] Either way, the community says, Stage Three came because it pushed us into behaving in ways Yhwh did not approve, so that Yhwh bears responsibility for the waywardness that brings about Stage Four and carries the people off. No one is calling on Yhwh, but that is because Yhwh's face became hidden. Thus the prayer contains some acknowledgments of waywardness; the prayer illustrates how 'ancient writers had no problems expressing both complaint and confession within the same text'.[210] But these acknowledgments are undermined by the emphasis on the fact that Yhwh at least shares in responsibility for this waywardness.

[208] Uhlig, *The Theme of Hardening in the Book of Isaiah*, with quotations from pp. 299 and 294-95.

[209] The negative interpretation of the first verb in 64.4 [5] (JPSV 'struck') would further strengthen this point.

[210] Werline, *Penitential Prayer in Second Temple Judaism*, p. 44; cf. Bautch, 'Lament Regained in Trito-Isaiah's Penitential Prayer', p. 99; Samuel E. Balentine, 'Afterword', in the same volume, I, pp. 193-204 (196).

XI

ISAIAH 65.1–66.17

Translation and Notes

1 I made myself available to those who had not asked of me,[1]// I made myself accessible to those who had not inquired of me.

I said, 'I'm here, I'm here',// to a nation that was not called by my name [*or* calling in my name].[2]

2 I have spread out[3] my hands all day// to a rebellious[4] people,

Those who are walking on a road that is not good,// following their own intentions.

3 The people are ones who are provoking me// to my face continually,

Sacrificing in the gardens// and burning incense on the bricks,[5]

[1] For MT שאלו 1QIs[a] has שאלוני which explicitly means 'asked of me' (cf. LXX, Syr, Tg). In MT the suffix on the parallel verb also applies to the first verb (cf. Ehrlich, *Randglossen*, IV, p. 227).

[2] For MT's pual קֹרָא 'was called', Vrs imply an active form such as קָרָא or קֹרֵא (read respectively by Kennicott 30 and 93, two mss thought perhaps to include extra-masoretic variants [*HUB*]). 1QIs[a]'s קרא likewise probably implies קָרָא (cf. Cook, 'The Orthography of Some Verbal Forms in 1QIsa[a]', p. 143). 4QIs[b]'s קורא could be pual or qal participle. The active participle might be assimilation to 64.6 [7].

[3] Resultative piel (Jenni, *Das hebräische Pi'el*, pp. 132-33; cf. *IBHS* 24.3.1b).

[4] LXX adds 'and contradictory', suggesting ומורה; 1QIs[a] has one verb like MT, but it is difficult to read and it might be either or might even be a composite reading (cf. Kutscher, הלשון והרקע הלשוני של מגילת ישעיהו השלמה, p. 203 [ET pp. 269-70]). Both are influenced by the association of the two verbs elsewhere (Deut 21.18, 20; Jer 5.23; Ps 78.8). LXX might have imported its extra verb from 50.5 (cf. Zillessen, 'Bemerkungen zur alexandrinischen Übersetzung des Jesaja', p. 248).

[5] In v. 3bβ, 1QIs[a] has וינקו ידים על האבנים, 'and they suck/emptied [depending on whether the verb comes from ינק or נקה] "hands" on stones', apparently a reference to a sexual rite; cf. 57.8. For the meaning of יד, see the comment on 56.5 (cf. Rubinstein, 'Notes on the Use of the Tenses in the Variant Readings of the Isaiah Scroll', pp. 94-95). If such a reference is original, it might not be surprising if it has been cleaned up in other texts (cf. Brownlee, *The Meaning of the Qumran Scrolls for the Bible*, pp. 234-35). The further suggestions that אבנים denotes either vagina (Joseph Reider, 'The Dead Sea Scrolls', *JQR* 41 [1950–51], pp. 59-70 [63-64]) or testicles (Brownlee, *The Meaning of the Qumran Scrolls for the Bible*, pp. 234-35) are more speculative, and Susan Ackerman (*Under Every Green Tree* [Atlanta: Scholars, 1992], pp. 171-72) takes the 1QIs[a] text to mean 'they empty [incense] tongs onto stones', a similar meaning to MT's. LXX adds 'to demons, which do not exist' (on this reading, see Seeligmann, *The Septuagint Version of Isaiah*, pp. 30-31; Hanson, *The Dawn of Apocalyptic*, p. 140; also Natalio Fernández Marcos, 'Is There an Antiochene Reading of Isaiah?', in M. N. van der Meer *et al.* [eds.], *Isaiah in Context* [A. van der Kooij Festschrift; Leiden: Brill, 2010], pp. 247-60 [256]).

4 Who are sitting in the tombs// and spending the night in hidden places,[6]
Who are eating swine's flesh,// with a broth[7] of profane things in their vessels,[8]
5 Who are saying, 'Keep to yourself,// do not come near[9] me, because I am too sacred for you':[10]
These people[11] are smoke in my nostrils,// a fire burning all day.
6 There—it is written before me:// I will not remain still;[12] rather[13] I am repaying.
I am repaying[14] into their bosom[15] 7 your waywardness// and your ancestors' waywardness,[16] all at once (Yhwh has said).

Tg adds '[gardens] of the idols', Vg has 'sleep in the shrines of idols'; these expansions relate to the critique in passages such as Lev 17.7; Deut 32.16-17 (*HUB*). There are several links between v. 3 and Deut 31–32 LXX (see Wagner, *Heralds of the Good News*, p. 202) though only the verb כעס corresponds to a feature of MT.

[6] For MT ובנצורים Ehrlich (*Randglossen*, IV, p. 227) redivides and repoints ובין צורים 'and between the crags'; Mitchell J. Dahood, 'Textual Problems in Isaia', *CBQ* 22 (1960), pp. 401-9 (408-9) renders 'within the mountains'. John F. Healey suggests that the word comes from נצר II 'mutter, chirp' ('Syriac *nṣr*, Ugaritic *nṣr*, Hebrew *nṣr* II, Akkadian *nṣr* II', *VT* 26 [1976], pp. 429-37 [433-34]) and denotes wailers or wailing in connection with mourning. NEB repoints וּבַנְּצוּרִים and translates 'keeping vigil' (cf. Brockington, *The Hebrew Text of the Old Testament*, p. 198).

[7] I follow Q מרק (cf. 1QIs[a], Vrs) rather than K פרק ('piece'), which Torrey (*Second Isaiah*, p. 468) defends for the sake of the paronomasia.

[8] One might see MT's כליהם as accusative of place (on which see GK 118d, g) or as the subject in a synecdoche: 'their vessels are a broth of desecrated things' (cf. Whitehouse, *Isaiah xl—lxvi*, p. 320). 1QIs[a] provides the expected ב, though LXX lacks it; מ has also been suggested (e.g. Torrey, *Second Isaiah*, p. 468), whose loss could be explained by haplog. (Driver, 'Hebrew Notes on Prophets and Proverbs', p. 165).

[9] For MT תגש 1QIs[a] and many rabbinic references (see *HUB*) have תגע 'touch'. Henoch Yalon ('נגש-גשש', *ZAW* 43 [1926], pp. 322-23) derives the verb from גשש 'touch' rather than נגש. The construction נגש ב is unusual (Kutscher, הלשון והרקע הלשוני של מגילת ישעיהו השלמה, p. 198 [ET p. 263]).

[10] The suffix on קְדַשְׁתִּיךָ apparently has quasi-dative force (JM1 25ba); cf. M. Bogaert, 'Les suffixes verbaux non accusatifs dans le sémitique nord-occidental et particulièrement en hébreu', *Biblica* 45 (1964), pp. 220-47 (242-43), instances other examples of such a quasi-dative use in comparisons. To regularize the construction, Abraham Geiger (*Urschrift und Uebersetzungen der Bibel* [Breslau: Hainauer, 1857], p. 170) suggested repointing קִדַּשְׁתִּיךָ ('I [will] have sanctified you'), but this does not fit the meaning of the line (see the comment) and the qatal is odd (cf. J. A. Emerton, 'Notes on the Text and Translation of Isaiah xxii 8-11 and lxv 5', *VT* 30 [1980], pp. 437-51 [446-51]).

[11] Following on the participles, אלה more likely refers to the people (cf. Vg) than the practices.

[12] The Leningrad ms of MT has אחשה, by a slip; other mss have אחשה.

[13] Or 'unless' (GK 163c; JM 173b). LXX, Syr have 'until'.

[14] LXX, Syh lack the repetition of the verb, though OL, Vg have it. I take the simple ו to indicate that the verb simply repeats the preceding one rather than that it is *w*-consecutive, though this makes little difference.

[15] For K על Q has אל (cf. 1QIs[a]). Along with the verb (see preceding note) Duhm (*Jesaia*, p. 433) omits the prepositional phrase, which recurs in v. 7.

[16] LXX, Syr have the expected third-person suffixes on the two nouns (Vg has second person).

Those who have burned incense on the mountains,// who have denigrated me on the hills:[17]
I am counting out their payment// first of all[18] into[19] their bosom.

8 Yhwh has said this:
As when juice can be found in a cluster// and someone says,[20] 'Don't destroy it, because there's a blessing in it',
So I will act for the sake of my servants,// so as not to destroy everything.
9 I will bring forth offspring from Jacob,// from Judah one who inherits[21] my mountains.[22]
My chosen ones will take possession of it;[23]// my servants will dwell there.
10 Sharon will become a pasture for flocks,// the Vale of Achor a resting place for cattle,// for my people who have sought me.
11 But you who are abandoning Yhwh,[24]// who are putting my holy mountain out of mind,
You who are laying[25] a table for Luck// and who are filling a mixing chalice[26] for Destiny,
12 I shall destine you[27] to the sword;// all of you will bow to the slaughter,
Because I have called but you have not responded,// I have spoken but you have not listened;
And you have done what was displeasing in my eyes;// what I did not delight in, you have chosen.
13 Therefore, my Lord Yhwh has said this:
Now:[28] my servants, they will eat,// but you people will be hungry.
Now: my servants, they will drink,// but you people will be thirsty.
Now: my servants, they will celebrate,// but you people will be shamed.

[17] *TTH* 123a takes this line as the extraposed opening to v. 7b.

[18] For MT ראשנה Marti (*Das Buch Jesaja*, p. 403) suggests בראשם 'on their head'. Ehrlich (*Randglossen*, IV, p. 228) adds the verb ושלמתי 'and I will repay' from v. 6.

[19] K has על as in v. 6. Q has אל, perhaps assimilation to Jer 32.18.

[20] For MT's *w*-consecutive ואמר, 1QIs[a] has *w*-conjunctive ויואמר, following PBH usage.

[21] For MT יורש, 1QIs[a] ירש and LXX imply qatal (cf. Wernberg-Møller, 'Studies in the Defective Spellings in the Isaiah-scroll of St Mark's Monastery', p. 264).

[22] For MT הָרַי Hanson (*The Dawn of Apocalyptic*, p. 142) reads הָרִי 'my mountain'.

[23] There is no antecedent for the f. suffix on MT's וירשוה; 1QIs[a] has וירשוהו with m. suffix, apparently referring to the preceding הרי understood as sg. Budde ('Jesaia Kap. 40–66', p. 715) suggests correcting to וירשם 'will take possession of them'. But see the comment.

[24] For MT עזבי יהוה LXX has 'those who forsake me'; the isolated third-person reference to Yhwh might issue from a false resolution of an assumed abbreviation of י taken to refer to Yhwh.

[25] For the Leningrad ms's הַעֹרְכִים, a Cairo Geniza ms has הָעוֹרְכִים.

[26] 1QIs[a] מסכה for MT ממסך may be another word with similar meaning (cf. Kutscher, הלשון והרקע הלשוני של מגילת ישעיהו השלמה, p. 196 [ET p. 259]); also *DCH* on מסכה.

[27] The qal וּמָנִיתִי elsewhere means 'number' (cf. Vg). One would have expected piel וּמִנֵּיתִי to convey the meaning 'destine' (cf. Ehrlich, *Randglossen*, IV, p. 228; LXX, Tg have 'give over'), but the qal makes the paronomasia with מני slightly closer. The *w*-consecutive arises from the extraposition of the verb's subject in v. 11.

[28] But perhaps here הנה is no longer a deictic particle but has become a conjunction, like הן, suggesting 'whereas' (cf. C. J. Labuschagne, 'The Particles הֵן and הִנֵּה', in C. J. Labuschagne *et al.*, *Syntax and Meaning* [Leiden: Brill, 1973], pp. 1-14 [13]).

14 Now: my servants, they will resound// from happiness of heart,
But you people will cry out// from pain of heart,// from brokenness of spirit you will howl.[29]
15 You will leave your name// as an oath[30] for my chosen ones,//
'So shall my Lord Yhwh kill you',// but for his servants[31] he will proclaim[32] another name,[33]
16 So that[34] the person who prays for blessing in the land// will pray for blessing by the God who says 'Amen',[35]
And the one who takes an oath in the land// will take the oath by the God who says 'Amen',
Because the former troubles will have been put out of mind,// and because they will have been hidden from my eyes.
17 Because here I am, creating// new heavens and a new earth.
The former things will not be recollected;// they will not come to mind.
18 Rather: rejoice and be joyful[36] forever// in what[37] I am creating.[38]
Because here I am creating// Jerusalem a joy, its people a rejoicing.
19 I will rejoice in Jerusalem,// be joyful in my people.
There will not make themselves heard in it again// the sound of weeping or the sound of a cry.
20 There will not be from there[39] again// a baby of a few days// or an old man who does not fulfil his days,
Because the youth will die as a person of a hundred years// and the sinner will be belittled[40] as a person of a hundred years.

[29] For MT תְּיֵלִילוּ, the original pointing may have been תֵּילִילוּ (see GK 70d). Torrey (*Second Isaiah*, p. 469) suggests the form is a composite of piel and hiphil.

[30] LXX 'fullness' implies שֹׂבעה for MT שׁבעה.

[31] For MT ולעבדיו some LXX mss imply ולעבדי 'for my servants'; cf. next note.

[32] For MT יִקְרָא LXX implies יִקָּרֵא 'will be proclaimed'. Aq, Sym follow MT.

[33] 1QIs[a] lacks v. 15b and most of v. 16a; the scribe left a space, suggesting his text was hard to read.

[34] For this meaning of אשר see GK166b; BDB, p. 83.

[35] For אָמֵן Dillmann (*Jesaia* [1890 edn], p. 531) suggests אֹמֶן, Klostermann (*Deuterojesaia*, p. 106) אֵמֻן. Either would imply 'the reliable God'; see the comment below. Shemaryahu Talmon rather emends בֵּאלֹהֵי to בֵּאלֹהַי 'by my God' ('Amen as an Introductory Oath Formula', *Textus* 7 [1969], pp. 124-29 [127], reprinted in Talmon, *Text and Canon of the Hebrew Bible* [Winona Lake, IN: Eisenbrauns, 2010], pp. 315-22 [p. 319]).

[36] For MT's two pl. imperatives שישו וגילו 1QIs[a] has שיש וגיל, which might be sg. verbs (difficult in the context) or might be nouns. The first would be a hapax but the two nouns would constitute an antecedent for the אשר that follows, which stands in uneasy relationship with what precedes (cf. Barthélémy, *Critique Textuelle de l'Ancien Testament*, II, p. 457). LXX also has two nouns; but on these, see Seeligmann, *The Septuagint Version of Isaiah*, p. 71. Ehrlich (*Randglossen*, IV, p. 229) emends to two nouns, מָשׂוֹשׂ וְגִילָה, which become further subjects for the verb in v. 17b. Vg has two statements about the future, as does Tg, but in the third person (cf. Syr).

[37] Grätz (*Emendationes*,p. 37) suggests adding על before אשר.

[38] LXX takes up its translation of this line from 51.3 (cf. Zillessen, 'Bemerkungen zur alexandrinischen Übersetzung des Jesaja', p. 252).

[39] Peter W. Flint ('Variant Readings and Textual Affiliation in the Hebrew University Isaiah Scroll from Cave One [1QIsa[b]]', in Donald W. Parry *et al.* [eds.], *Qumran Cave 1 Revisited*, pp. 33-53 [44]) sees 1QIsa[b]'s שם as 'the pristine reading' rather than MT's משם (cf. 1QIsa[a] משמה) even though he also recognizes that it is the easier reading.

21 People will build houses and live [there],// they will plant vineyards and eat their fruit.
22 They will not build and someone else live [there],// they will not plant and someone else eat.
Because the days of my people will be like the days of a tree;// my chosen ones will use up[41] the work of their hands.
23 They will not labour in vain// and they will not give birth[42] to dismay,
Because offspring blessed by Yhwh,// they and their descendants with them, will be.
24 Before they call, I myself will respond;// while they are still speaking, I myself will listen.
25 The wolf and the lamb—they will feed as one;// the lion like the ox—it will eat straw;// the snake—dirt will be its food.
They will not do harm or destroy// on all my holy mountain
(Yhwh has said).

66.1 Yhwh has said this:
The heavens are my throne,// the earth is my footstool.
Wherever[43] could be the house that you would build for me,// wherever the place that would be my abode,[44]
2 When all these things my hand made;// thus all these things came to be?[45]
(Yhwh's declaration.)
But toward this person I look, toward one who is afflicted,// struck down[46] in spirit, trembling at my word.
3 Someone who slaughters a bull is one who strikes down a person;// someone who sacrifices a lamb is one who strangles a dog.

[40] For MT יְקַלֵּל Volz (*Jesaja II*, p. 279) suggests qal יֵקַל 'will be swift/trifling', Driver ('Linguistic and Textual Problems', pp. 405-6) יְקַלֵּל 'will swiftly vanish' on the basis of the Aramaic usage of קַלִּיל.

[41] The verb בלה is used in an unusual, positive way, paralleled only by Job 21.13 and not recognized by LXX, which translates with the verb παλαιόω (cf. J. Gamberoni, *TWAT*, I, p. 652 [ET *TDOT*, II, p. 130]). Paul (*Isaiah 40–66*, p. 605 [not in the Hebrew edition]) infers from Syr *n'klwn* that the Hebrew originally read יאכלו 'consume'. Perles (*Analekten zur Textkritik des Alten Testaments*, pp. 56-57) emends to יכלה 'complete'.

[42] For MT's qal יֵלְדוּ, which usually applies to mothers, Thomas ('ספר ישעיה', p. 103) suggests hiphil יוֹלִדוּ, the usual expression for fathering.

[43] זה strengthens the interrogative אי twice in the line (see JM 143g).

[44] I take MT's מקום מנוחתי as a relative noun clause (see JM 158b), presupposing the אשר from the first colon and taking its time reference from that verbal clause. LXX's 'the place of my rest' (cf. OL, Tg, Vg, Syr) suggests construct מְקוֹם for MT's absolute; this corresponds to the construction in 1 Chr 28.2. LXX's use of κατάπαυσις is the first of a series of translations that are distinctive to Isa 66 over against Isa 1–65 in LXX and raise the question whether its translation history is different (cf. Ziegler, *Untersuchungen zur Septuaginta des Buches Isaias*, p. 42; David A. Baer, 'What Happens in the End?', in van der Kooij and van der Meer [eds.], *The Old Greek of Isaiah*, pp. 1-31 [5-6]).

[45] 1QIs[a] replaces *w*-consecutive ויהיו by *w*-conjunctive והיו.

[46] For MT ונכה some mss have ונכא, from נכא, the Aramaic equivalent to נכה which occasionally appears in Hebrew (e.g. 16.7) and here is likely assimilation to the related phrase in Prov 15.13; 17.22; 18.14. 1QIs[b] ונכאה is a more complete assimilation to that usage. On 1QIs[a]'s ונכאי see Kutscher, הלשון והרקע הלשוני של מגילת ישעיהו השלמה, p. 200 (ET pp. 265-66).

Someone who lifts up an offering—it is the blood of a pig[47];// someone who makes a memorial of incense is one who worships a bane.
They for their part—they have chosen their ways;// in their abominations their soul has delighted.
4 I for my part—I will choose caprices for them,// and their terrors[48] I will bring to them.
Because I have called and there has been no one responding,// I have spoken and they have not listened.
They have done what was displeasing in my eyes,// and chosen what I did not delight in.

5 Listen to Yhwh's word,// you who tremble at his word.
Your brothers have said—people who repudiate you,// who exclude you for the sake of my name[49],
'May Yhwh be severe[50], so that we may look[51] at your celebration',[52]// but they themselves will be ashamed.
6 The sound of uproar from the city,[53]// the sound from the palace,
The sound of Yhwh// paying back recompense to his enemies!

7 Before she labours, she has given birth,[54]// before pain comes to her,// she delivers a boy.[55]

[47] The structure of this colon does not match that of others in v. 3; for דם, among many suggestions, Volz (*Jesaja II*, p. 290) proposes חֹמֵד 'is one who delights in [a pig]', while Daniel Leibel, 'דם חזיר', *Bet Miqra* 8 (1964), pp. 187-97 (187), reads הֹדֵם 'is one who dismembers [a pig]' (cf. *DTT* for הדם, and Dan 2.5; 3.29 for the related noun).

[48] 1QIs[a] repeats the preposition ב, implying 'and their terrors, which I will bring to them'.

[49] MT accents link 'for the sake of my name' with the next line, but this is harder to make sense of.

[50] For MT יִכְבַּד LXX, Syr, Vg, Tg, Aq, Sym, Th have a passive verb, which might suggest niphal יִכָּבֵד but might simply be a loose rendering like KJV's 'be glorified'; it is not the only example of the Versions' translating כבד qal by a passive (cf. Exod 5.9; 9.7), and it is difficult to see why niphal should have been changed to qal but easy to see why qal should have been changed to or understood like niphal (cf. Volz, *Jesaja II*, p. 291).

[51] For MT נראה 1QIs[a] has יראה 'he will look', which might imply Yhwh as subject or might be impersonal third person 'one will look' (cf. LXX's passive; cf. Kutscher, *The Language and Linguistic Background of the Isaiah Scroll*, p. 562 [not in the Hebrew edition). Or it might be niphal, 'he will appear', taking MT's form as niphal third-person sg. qatal (or participle) rather than first-person pl. qal yiqtol; cf. OL, and KJV 'he shall appear to your joy', which takes MT's vocalized form as niphal. The subject of the clause will then be Yhwh and the brothers' words will be confined to 'May Yhwh be severe'. But Vg, Tg, Aq, Sym, Th have 'we will look', and the preposition ב is difficult; in other instances with ראה niphal, the preposition means 'in/at' or 'as'.

[52] Torrey (*Second Isaiah*, pp. 275, 473) emends MT בשמחתכם to read וְשִׂמַּחְתִּכֶם 'But I will make you rejoice'.

[53] For MT מעיר, 1QIs[a] interestingly has בעיר.

[54] To turn this colon into the expected bicolon matching the bicolon that follows and comprises v. 7b, Duhm (*Jesaia*, p. 440) suggests adding בן '[to] a son'. He also adds והיא 'but she' at the beginning of the line; Fohrer (*Jesaja*, III, p. 277) adds יֹלֵדָה 'the one who gives birth' after the first verb.

[55] בטרם is usually followed by a yiqtol verb, as in the two instances in this line, and such yiqtol verbs can refer to the past. This would make sense in v. 7a where the yiqtol verb is followed by a qatal, but in light of the *w*-consecutive in v. 7b I take the yiqtol

8 Who has heard of such a thing,// who has seen such things?
Can a country be brought through labour[56] in one day// or a nation be birthed in one moment?
Because she has laboured, also[57] given birth//—Zion, to her children.
9 Will I myself make a breach[58] but not bring to birth?// Yhwh says.[59]
Or am I the one who brings to birth but will close?[60]// your God has said.[61]
10 Celebrate with Jerusalem[62]// and be glad in her, all who love her.
Rejoice with her joyfully,// all who mourn over her.
11 So that you may nurse and be full// from her comforting breast,
So that you may drain out[63] and luxuriate// from her splendid bosom.[64]
12 Because Yhwh has said this:
Here I am, extending to her well-being like a river,[65]// like a flooding wadi the wealth of nations,
So that you may nurse[66] as you are carried on her side[67]// and you are dandled on her knees.

both times to have its more common present or future reference. 1QIs[a] simplifies the construction by omitting the ו. Mitchell J. Dahood ('*Ṣîr* "emissary" in Psalm 78,49', *Biblica* 59 [1978], p. 264) sees it as emphatic ו, for which see JM 177n.

[56] MT היוחל either implies m. verb with f. subject (not so unusual) or an impersonal construction, 'Can there be made to labour a country' (cf. GK 121a; *IBHS* 23.2.2e; JM 128; *DG* 95). 1QIs[a] התחיל not only corrects the verb's gender but changes hophal to hiphil, presumably 'labour [and bring forth]'; cf. LXX, Vg. But this makes poor sense in the context. Oort ('Kritische Aanteekeningen', p. 477) replaces MT ארץ by עָם; Duhm (*Jesaia*, p. 440) adds עָם before ארץ; McKenzie (*Second Isaiah*, p. 205) turns the m. verb into f. הֲתוּכַל.

[57] Mitchell J. Dahood ('Ugaritic Lexicography', in *Mélanges Eugène Tisserant* [Vatican City: Biblioteca Apostolica Vaticana, 1964], I, pp. 81-102 [p. 86]) sees this as an instance of גם meaning 'loudly' (cf. Ugaritic *gm*), for which see *DCH* II, p. 361.

[58] LXX 'I myself gave [you] this expectation' suggests it took the verb as שׂבר not שׁבר (Ottley, *Isaiah according to the Septuagint*, II, p. 384); cf. also Aq. LXX goes on, 'and you did not remember me', which may simply reflect uncertainty about the line or may indicate that LXX read some form of the Hebrew זכר referring to a male (child) (Seeligmann, *The Septuagint Version of Isaiah*, pp. 61-62) or may follow from the previous misunderstanding (Ziegler, *Untersuchungen zur Septuaginta des Buches Isaias*, p. 174) or may reflect unease with the verse's anthropomorphic language (Baer, *When We All Go Home*, pp. 156-59).

[59] Many mss have אמר 'said' for MT יאמר (cf. LXX); they may be simply assimilating to the next colon.

[60] For MT ועצרתי 1QIs[a] has ואעצורה, which might not be merely the replacement of ו-consecutive by *w*-conjunctive but indicate a cohortative, 'would I indeed close?' (cf. Rubinstein, 'Conditional Constructions in the Isaiah Scroll', pp. 78-79).

[61] One ms has יאמר 'says' for MT אמר; haplog. might explain the loss of the י (cf. Klostermann, *Deuterojesaja*, p. 111). Contrast and compare the note on יאמר in v. 9a.

[62] LXX 'rejoice, Jerusalem' ignores the את; cf. also Tg 'rejoice in Jerusalem'. Aq, Th correspond to MT.

[63] On the verb מצץ, see Harold R. Cohen, *Biblical Hapax Legomena in the Light of Akkadian and Ugaritic* (Missoula, MT: Scholars, 1978), p. 46.

[64] For מזיז, de Lagarde (*Prophetae chaldaice*, p. l) reads מְבִיז from the PBH word for breast used by Tg in v. 11a; see further the comment on this word.

[65] LXX 'I am inclining to them like a river of peace' takes the verb intransitively.

[66] MT links וינקתם with the preceding line (cf. Tg); I follow LXX in linking the word with this line. LXX's version 'their children will be carried on shoulders and comforted

13 Like someone[68] whom his mother comforts,// so I myself will comfort you.
You will be comforted in Jerusalem, 14 you will see[69] and your heart will rejoice,// your limbs will flourish[70] like the grass.

14b So Yhwh's hand[71] will cause itself to be acknowledged among his servants;// he will rage[72] among his enemies.
15 Because there: Yhwh will come with[73] fire,// his chariots like a whirlwind,[74]
To return[75] his anger with fury,// his rebuke with flames of fire.
16 Because with fire Yhwh is going to exercise authority,[76]// and with his sword,[77] among all flesh,[78]// and those pierced by Yhwh[79] will be many.

17 People who consecrate and purify themselves to go into the gardens// following after one[80] in the midst,[81]

on knees' may imply וְיֹנְקֹתָם (*HUB*) or וְיוֹנְקוֹתֵהֶם (Blenkinsopp, *Isaiah 56–66*, p. 304) or וְיֹנַקְתָּהּ (Ehrlich, *Randglossen*, IV, p. 231); cf. 1QIs[a], where the beginning of the word is missing but the end is תיהמה. In line with Ehrlich's view, Duhm (*Jesaia*, p. 441) also omits the ו on the two succeeding verbs in the line to make them sg.

[67] Vg 'udder' perhaps implies שד (cf. v. 11) for MT צד (cf. *HUB*).

[68] For the use of איש to denote a human being, even a baby, cf. Gen 4.1; 1 Sam 1.11 (Beuken, *Jesaja IIIB*, p. 122).

[69] Gaster ('Notes on Isaiah', p. 107) takes this as one of a number of places where ראה must be understood as equivalent to רוה 'drink one's fill'.

[70] On the basis of Arabic and the parallelism here, Eitan ('A Contribution to Isaiah Exegesis', pp. 87-88) hypothesizes here a different verb פרח meaning 'be cheerful'.

[71] Aloysius Fitzgerald ('Hebrew *yd* = "Love" and "Beloved"', *CBQ* 29 [1967], pp. 368-74 [371]) sees this as an instance of יד meaning 'love' (cf. *DCH* IV, p. 94), but notes that the f. verb is then odd.

[72] For MT's verb Duhm (*Jesaia*, p. 441) reads וְזַעְמוֹ 'and his rage'; cf. KJV.

[73] For MT ב two post-MT mss have כ; cf. LXX. Aq, Sym, Th have 'by fire'.

[74] For MT כ 1QIs[a] has ב.

[75] For MT להשיב Lowth suggests לְהַשִּׁיב 'to blow' (*Isaiah*, p. 404—though he seems to reverse the words in his comment).

[76] For MT נשפט 1QIs[a] has יבוא לשפוט (cf. Tg), as in Pss 96.13; 98.9 (Kutscher, הלשון והרקע הלשוני של מגילת ישעיהו השלמה, p. 435 [ET p. 545]); the niphal might be open to suggesting that Yhwh is judged (Rubinstein, 'The Theological Aspect of Some Variant Readings in the Isaiah Scroll', p. 190). LXX adds 'all the earth' as subject of the niphal verb, perhaps to balance 'all flesh' (Penna, *Isaia*, p. 626) as well as to safeguard the same point.

[77] For MT ובחרבו NEB readd בּוֹ וּבָחַר (cf. Brockington, *The Hebrew Text of the Old Testament*, p. 198), while Thomas ('ספר ישעיה', p. 104) suggests וּבָחַר בָּהּ, both meaning 'and by it he will test' (אש is usually f. but occasionally m.).

[78] Thomas ('ספר ישעיה', p. 104) adds an extra colon based on the first three words in v. 18.

[79] For MT חללי יהוה, 1QIs[a] has simple חלליו.

[80] Q has f. אַחַת (cf. 1QIs[a, b], Vg); K implies m. אֶחָד. There is some variation among other mss. Sym, Th, Syr 'one after another' might suggest אחד אחר אחד (haplog); cf. Tg 'company after company'

[81] For MT's absolute תָּוֶךְ (cf. Vg *intrinsecus*), Sym, Th imply construct תּוֹךְ (linking the word with the following phrase). LXX's 'in the porticoes' for the difficult 'after one in the midst' may be a guess based on this being an appropriate location for false worship (cf. Ezek 8.3, 14, 16; cf. Ziegler, *Untersuchungen zur Septuaginta des Buches Isaias*, p. 133). Klostermann (*Deuterojesaia*, p. 112) emends תוך to בַּתְּנֻךְ 'on the ear lobe',

People who eat the flesh of pig,// reptile,[82] and mouse:// all at once they will come to an end (Yhwh's declaration).

Introduction

Both MT and 1QIs^a provide a break at 65.1, where the speaker and addressees change. 1QIs^a then has a space at 65.8, and two MT manuscripts also have a break there. Both MT and 1QIs^a have further breaks at 65.13; 66.1, 5, 10, and 12 (MT's last in the book). MT has an additional break at 65.9a. 1QIs^a has other breaks at 65.5b, 10, 11, 16 (but this is associated with words being missing), 17, and 18b;[83] 66.6,[84] 15, 20b, 22.[85] 1QIs^b lacks much of chapter 65 but has breaks at 66.1, 5, 10, 15, 20b. In keeping with this odd collection of data, modern interpreters also differ in their understanding of divisions and interrelationships in the last two chapters of the book, which offer few indications of divisions and interrelationships. But it is the case that 65.1–66.17 focuses on the worship and life of Judah itself, while 66.18-24 also concerns itself with the nations as a whole and their worship.[86] Understanding 65.1–66.17 and 66.18-24 as the final sections in Isaiah 56–66 corresponds with the way the opening verses (56.1-8) relate to foreigners and their worship, while the subsequent major units (56.9–59.8) concern themselves with Judah itself, and with the way 65.1–66.17 follows on from the prayer in 63.7–64.11 [12] as 56.9–59.8 leads into the prayer in 59.9-15a. This understanding thus fits the section's relationship with the wider context in the broader stepped arrangement of Isaiah 56–66.

implying a reference to a consecration rite (see, e.g., Exod 29.20); Kissane (*Isaiah*, II, p. 320) to יִכָּרְתוּ 'will be cut off'; Fischer (*Das Buch Isaias*, II, p. 213) בָּתְרוּ '[one after another] they cut in two [their offering]'. J. A. Emerton ('Notes on Two Verses in Isaiah', in J. A. Emerton [ed.], *Prophecy* [G. Fohrer Festschrift; Berlin: de Gruyter, 1980], pp. 12-25 [21-24]) takes up a suggestion he attributes to D. Winton Thomas, that בתוך אחד אחר is a dittog. from v. 16.

[82] Syr *šrṣ'* (cf. Syh) for MT שקץ might suggest שֶׁרֶץ; but see the comment.

[83] In connection with these last, Olley ('"Hear the Word of Yhwh"', p. 37) notes an inclination to set apart references to the heavens and the earth.

[84] Olley ('"Hear the Word of Yhwh"', p. 31) notes that v. 6 refers to a heavenly voice calling, which is one of the criteria he identifies for the provision of such markers.

[85] 1QIs^a's distinctive reading at 66.17b, יחדיו אמר יהוה, may reflect the conviction that v. 17 is not the end of a section (so Pulikottil, *Transmission of Biblical Texts in Qumran*, p. 49); on יחדיו, see also the translation note on 60.13.

[86] W. A. M. Beuken (who himself takes a different view) notes that 'the majority of scholars' see the transition within chapter 66 as coming after v. 17 ('Isaiah Chapters lxv–lxvi', in J. A. Emerton [ed.], *Congress Volume: Leuven 1989* [Leiden: Brill, 1991], pp. 204-21 [207-8]); he mentions Delitzsch, Duhm, Skinner, König, Torrey, Volz, Köhler, Fischer, Penna, Westermann, Schoors, Bonnard, and Pauritsch. His own understanding links with his view that 'the servants of Yhwh' is the main theme in Isaiah 56–66; they make their last appearance in 66.14, which is where he sees the close of the section begun at 65.1.

I therefore take 65.1–66.17 as a self-contained section.[87] Like 56.9–59.8, it comprises a number of subsections of material that may be of separate origin, though there is enough unity of form and wording to make it possible to see the passage as a single composition.[88] Like those earlier long units, 65.1–66.17 turns to confront the community, though the confrontation again incorporates promises. Further, like those earlier long units, it presupposes that the community is involved in rites of worship directed towards other deities.

In the arrangement of the book, 65.1–66.17 constitutes a response to the prayer in 63.7–64.11 [12], and there are a number of verbal links between 65.1–66.17 and 63.7–64.11 [12].[89] Both readings in 65.1b (was not called by my name/was not calling in my name) and the recurrence of the verb in 65.12, 24; 66.4 resonate with the preceding passage (see 63.19; 64.6 [7]). 'I will not remain still' (65.6) takes up 'will you remain still?' (64.11 [12]). 'Your servants' came in 63.17; 'my/his servants' recurs in 65.8, 9, 13, 14, 15; 66.14.[90] This is not to reify the exchange or to see 63.7–65.25 as a liturgy.[91] Chapters 65–66 'do not present a close correspondence to the prophet's intercession yet there is sufficient *rough* correspondence to enable the editor to make them serve the purpose of an oracular answer',[92] a response that is 'at once caustic and comforting'.[93] In isolation, we might see 63.7–64.11 [12] as quite a reasonable prayer, but Yhwh's response suggests it is a prayer that 'discloses the hardness of the speakers'[94] or rejects the premise of the prayer, that Yhwh might restore the entire community despite its misdeeds; rather Yhwh will restore the faithful and judge the faithless.[95] It would be a mistake, however, to infer that this response is designed to be Yhwh's final word (any more than Yhwh's words in a passage such as 6.9-13, where telling the people that Yhwh is closing their minds is a way of trying to get through to them so that the declaration falsifies itself);[96] it is still open to the faithless to repent.

87 Cf. Smith, *Rhetoric and Redaction in Trito-Isaiah*, pp. 128-72.

88 See, e.g., Stromberg, *Isaiah after Exile*, pp. 42-63.

89 Indeed, Tiemeyer calls 65.1–66.17 'the purpose-written response to the lament in 63.7–64.11' (*Priestly Rites and Prophetic Rage*, p. 63).

90 See further Steck, *Studien zu Tritojesaja*, pp. 221-24.

91 See, e.g., Bentzen, *Jesaja II*, p. 149.

92 Jones, *Isaiah 56–66 and Joel*, p. 104.

93 Seitz, 'The Book of Isaiah 40–66', p. 539, summarizing Muilenburg, 'The Book of Isaiah: Chapters 40–66', pp. 744-73

94 Uhlig, *The Theme of Hardening in the Book of Isaiah*, p. 299; he capitalizes 'discloses' because he uses the word as a technical term.

95 Cf. David M. Carr, 'Reading Isaiah from Beginning (Isaiah 1) to End (Isaiah 65–66)', in Melugin and Sweeney (eds.), *New Visions of Isaiah*, pp. 188-218 (207). Judith Gärtner understands 65.1-7 and 8-12 as providing two answers to the prayer (see *Jesaja 66 und Sacharja 14 als Summe der Prophetie* [Neukirchen: Neukirchener, 2006], pp. 262-70; cf. '"…Why Do You Let Us Stray from Your Paths…"', in Boda, Falk, and Werline [eds.], *Seeking the Favor of God*, I, pp. 145-63 [151-56]).

96 See Goldingay, *Isaiah*, p. 61.

I understand the divisions of the material as follows.

(1) 65.1-7: whereas prophet or people speak in 63.7–64.11 [12], at 65.1 Yhwh begins to speak (and does so though 65.1–66.24). Verses 1-7 could constitute a complete unit comprising words of confrontation that lead into a warning of trouble to follow.

(2) 65.8-25: verse 8 starts with 'Yhwh has said this' which commonly suggests a new beginning, and in subject matter it signals a move from a declaration of judgment on the people as a whole to a declaration of intent to behave in a way that distinguishes between Yhwh's chosen servants and the people who have abandoned Yhwh. The question now is 'For whom is salvation effective?'[97] In vv. 8-25 there is an alternating movement between judgment on the people who have abandoned Yhwh and blessing for Yhwh's servants, with the blessing dominating vv. 16-25, but there are no clear markers within vv. 8-25 that suggest a movement from one subsection to another or from one separate prophecy to another. In particular, the formula in v. 13 (where MT and 1QIsª have a break) is usually a transition marker within a prophecy rather than an indicator of a new beginning.[98] It has been argued that there is a major division at v. 16b[99] or v. 17,[100] but formally it is hard to see a new subsection beginning at either of these points.[101] Such divisions issue from the conviction that the resultant two parts are different in content or themes and that the last third of the chapter is 'eschatological' or 'apocalyptic'. In the comment I argue that this is not so; the very difficulty in identifying the formal point of transition to material of an 'eschatological' or 'apocalyptic' nature points towards the fact that the distinction is not so real.

On the basis of content one could hypothesize that vv. 8-25 bring together a number of originally separate prophecies (e.g. vv. 8-12, 13-16, 17-25),[102] but if so, they have been provided with links that now make them part of a larger whole. It is more economical to suppose that vv. 8-25 is one composition.[103] There are verbal links between vv. 1-7 and 8-25. Both use forms of the word *ri'šōn* ('first of all/former things'; vv. 7, 16, 17); both use the verb *dāraš* ('made myself available/seek'; vv. 1, 10). These links might be a basis on which originally separate prophecies

[97] Kessler, *Gott geht es um das Ganze*, p. 82 (his comment applies to chapters 65–66 as a whole).

[98] Against J. T. A. G. M. van Ruiten, 'The Role of Syntax in the Versification of Is 65:13-25', in Talstra and van Wieringen (eds.), *A Prophet on the Screen*, pp. 118-47.

[99] E.g. Westermann, *Jesaja Kapitel 40–66*, pp. 323-24 (ET pp. 407-8).

[100] E.g. Fischer, *Das Buch Isaias*, II, pp. 198-207; Beuken, *Jesaja IIIB*, p. 59.

[101] Westermann recognizes that v. 16b cannot be the opening of a unit, and requires the transfer of an exhortation to rejoice such as appears in v. 18. Locating a new beginning at v. 17 requires us to understand its opening כִּי as purely asseverative, which no one would otherwise do.

[102] So Blenkinsopp, *Isaiah 56–66*, pp. 273-90.

[103] Hanson (*The Dawn of Apocalyptic*, p. 145) infers that this suggests literary rather than oral composition, which might but need not be so.

were brought together; they do not constitute a strong argument for an original linkage.

(3) 66.1-17. Chapter 65 closes with 'Yhwh has said' and 66.1 opens with 'Yhwh has said this'; the difference in the content of the message in 66.1-4 confirms that a new subsection begins here. A new bidding to 'listen to Yhwh's word' opens v. 5 and the theme changes once more. Another declaration that 'Yhwh has said this' comes in v. 12, though it is preceded by a 'because' and the theme does not change. On the other hand, the theme might be reckoned to change at other points in vv. 1-17 (e.g. vv. 3, 6, 7, 17). Overall, 66.1-17 compares with the previous two subsections in opening with critique, then moving to warning and promise, but the boundaries of (possible) units are not clearly marked, and it manifests more jumpiness than preceding chapters. A sign of this difficulty is the hypothesis that the subsection represents a liturgy, a recurrent scholarly hypothesis to explain unevenness.[104] In 1971 Karl Pauritsch commented that no other chapter in Third Isaiah has raised more questions about its unity and arrangement or structure.[105] Subsequent interest in the final form of the text has not changed that situation; scholars who approach the text with that focus also come to different conclusions. It may indeed comprise a collection of separate sayings, though links between the subunits again suggest that the collection has been deliberately arranged rather than assembled on a random basis. Perhaps the jumpy nature of the chapter 'testifies to the fractured and fractious character of the community addressed by these texts'.[106]

In seeking to analyse the subdivisions of chapters 65–66, then, and particularly here in 66.1-17, 'it is very difficult to demonstrate the sole legitimacy of one's reading', though resolution of this question may not be so important; 'the resonance set up from repeated themes' plays a more important role in conveying the passage's meaning.[107] As is the case with Isaiah 56–66 as a whole, however, a redaction-critical observation at least suggests a clue regarding one way to understand the structure of 66.1-17 as it stands. This observation is the view that the double promise concerning Jerusalem beginning in vv. 7 and 12 is the earliest material in the subsection.[108] In addition, both the opening and closing lines in the subsection, vv. 1-4 and 17, concern questions about worship; v. 17 takes us back to where vv. 1-4 started.[109] Immediately inside the bracket formed

[104] Cf. Elliger, *Die Einheit des Tritojesaja*, p. 37 (on vv. 5-16); see the introduction to 58.1–59.8 above.

[105] *Die neue Gemeinde*, p. 195.

[106] Brueggemann, *Isaiah 40–66*, p. 251.

[107] Childs, *Isaiah*, pp. 535, 534. Childs puts the second phrase in the context of a past-tense sentence concerning the 'ancient hearing and reading of scripture'.

[108] E.g. Westermann, *Jesaja Kapitel 40–66*, pp. 331-34 (ET pp. 417-21); Koenen, *Ethik und Eschatologie im Tritojesajabuch*, pp. 195-207; Lau, *Schriftgelehrte Prophetie in Jes 56–66*, pp. 126-34.

[109] Thus Volz (*Jesaja II*, p. 291) moved v. 17 back to follow v. 4.

by vv. 1-4 and 17, there comes in vv. 5-6 and 14b-16 material condemning the enmity of the permissive and promising their punishment. Thus the subsection as a whole outlines:

1-4 Critique of worship and promise of punishment (Yhwh speaks)
    5-6 Condemnation of enmity and promise of punishment (the prophet speaks)[110]
        7-11 Promise regarding Jerusalem (Yhwh speaks)
        12-14a Promise regarding Jerusalem (Yhwh speaks)
    14b-16 Condemnation of enmity and promise of punishment (the prophet speaks)
17 Critique of worship and promise of punishment (Yhwh speaks)

Beyond the recurrent observation that the verses making promises about Jerusalem constitute the oldest material, there are varying views as to the process whereby 65.1–66.17 reached the form in which we have it, as we have noted with preceding sections of Isaiah 56–66. Examples of these views regarding the stages of the subsection's growth are as follows:

Westermann:	(1) 65.16b, 17b-24; 66.7-14
	(2) 65.1-16a; 65.17a, 25; 66.3-5, 17
	(3) 66.6, 15-16
	(4) ?66.1-2.[111]
Sehmsdorf:	(1) 65.16b-19
	(2) 65.20
	(3) 65.21-22a
	(4) 65.22b-23
	(5) 65.24-25
	(6) 65.1-16a; 66.1-4
	(7) 66.17-24.[112]
Vermeylen:	(1) 65.8-10, 16-24
	(2) 66.7-14a
	(3) 65.1-2, 6-7a, 11a, 12-15, 25; 66.5-6, 14b
	(4) 66.1-2
	(5) 65.3-5, 7b, 11b; 66.3-4, 17
	(6) 66.15-16.[113]
Sekine:	(1) 65.16b-23, 25; 66.7-16
	(2) 66.1-4; 65.2-16a
	(3) 65.1, 24; 66.5-6, 17.[114]
Koenen:	(1) 65.16b-24; 66.1-2, 7-14a
	(2) 65.1-16a; 66.3-6, 14b-17
	(3) 65.25.[115]

[110] Except for the reference to 'my name'.

[111] *Jesaja Kapitel 40–66*, pp. 245, 316-35 (ET pp. 307, 398-422); there are slight inconsistencies between the introductory summary and the detailed commentary.

[112] 'Studien zur Redaktionsgeschichte von Jesaja 56–66'; he does not comment on the other material.

[113] *Du prophète Isaïe à l'apocalyptique*, II, pp. 492-501.

[114] *Die Tritojesajanische Sammlung*, pp. 43-65, 165-78 (summarized on p. 182).

[115] *Ethik und Eschatologie im Tritojesajabuch* pp. 157-240, with the text as laid out on pp. 254-57.

Lau: (1) 66.7-14a; 65.16b-25
(2) 66.1-4, 5-6, 14b-17; 65.1-7, 8-12, 13-16a.[116]

These scholars date the material in changing contexts; others locate the entire section in the early Persian period[117] or the time of Ezra and Nehemiah[118] or the fourth century[119] or the third.[120] The variety in the views concerning the chapters' development and dating suggests that the material lacks criteria that would enable us to trace any redactional history they have gone through.[121]

One consideration that feeds into suggestions regarding the date of the material is the indications in the chapters of a division within the Second Temple community. The Old Testament itself suggests several such tensions or divisions. There was tension between Judah and Samaria. There was tension between people who had been in exile and people who had stayed in Judah; each community might view the other as tainted. In the pre-exilic period there had been a division between people who followed the traditional religion of the country and people who believed that adherence to Yhwh precluded its practices. Isaiah 65–66 implies that the division to which it refers at least overlaps with this last. It implies that there are some people who worship Yhwh in accordance with the expectations expressed in the Torah and the Prophets, and others who continue in the traditional religious practices of the country. It is more difficult to relate these two groups to the ones of which we know from Ezra–Nehemiah or to groups we might hypothesize on the basis of insights from sociology and anthropology. One way of responding to this difficulty is to hypothesize that the prophecy speaks figuratively. The characterization of the group of which the prophecy disapproves is then a slur. It identifies these people as metaphorically indistinguishable from people critiqued by prophets such as Isaiah ben Amoz and Jeremiah; they are just as religiously reprehensible and just as much under Yhwh's judgment.[122] Another possibility is to leave the groups unidentified, rather than working against the texts' lack of definition. Instead of reifying the two groups, this approach sees their existence as primarily rhetorical.[123] The rhetorical strategy of the text then presses any community reading the prophecy to position itself in relation to its critique and its promises. To

[116] *Schriftgelehrte Prophetie in Jes 56–66*, pp. 118-202.

[117] Smith (*Rhetoric and Redaction in Trito-Isaiah*, pp. 187-88) argues that it 'forms an original and coherent poem'.

[118] E.g. Duhm, *Jesaia*, pp. 431-42.

[119] E.g. Fohrer *Jesaja*, III, p. 257.

[120] E.g. Steck, *Studien zu Tritojesaja*, pp. 217-28, 248-65.

[121] Smith, *Rhetoric and Redaction in Trito-Isaiah*, p. 171.

[122] So Hanson, *The Dawn of Apocalyptic*, p. 147.

[123] Contrast (e.g.) Joseph Blenkinsopp, 'The "Servants of the Lord" in Third Isaiah', *Proceedings of the Irish Biblical Association* 7 (1983), pp. 1-23, reprinted in Robert P. Gordon (ed.), *The Place Is Too Small for Us* (Winona lake, IN: Eisenbrauns, 1995), pp. 392-412, who seeks to identify the groups.

avoid begging too many questions concerning the identity of the groups, I shall refer to them as the purist (the view represented by the prophecies themselves) and the permissive.[124]

While the section has expressions in common with 63.7–64.11 [12], it also has many verbal links with Isaiah 1; indeed, Isaiah 65–66 has been called 'a gigantic *inclusio*' for the book as a whole.[125] Opinions differ as to whether the closing chapters are based on the opening chapter(s)[126] or whether the opening chapter(s) have been compiled and/or edited and/or supplemented in light of the closing chapters.[127]

(a) Comment: 65.1-7

In 63.7–64.11 [12] a human 'I' and then a human 'we' have been speaking. Here it soon becomes clear that the 'I' that speaks is Yhwh, as will be the case through the chapter. The chapter begins with a sequence of lines of increasing intensity and confrontation. A first pair of lines (v. 1) is hardly a protest at all, at least in MT; it simply speaks of people who had not made requests of Yhwh. A second pair (v. 2) express explicit protest; people were rebelling against Yhwh and going their own way. Then six lines (vv. 3-5) portray that rebellion in concrete terms and point to its implications. Verses 6-7 announce what will follow.

The subsection forms a prophetic indictment (vv. 1-5a) and warning of punishment (vv. 5b-7). The indictment accepts and underlines the self-assessment expressed in 63.7–64.11 [12].[128] The people have acknowledged that they have been a collection of rebels; the question their prayer raised is whether Yhwh has therefore totally abandoned them, whether punishment is to continue. The tough response in this indictment and warning is, 'Yes, it will'.[129] One could describe the prayer as lyrical, allusive, and aesthetically pleasing; the response is blunt, pointed, and

124 See further the Introduction to this commentary, especially section 2.

125 Alonso Schökel and Sicre Diaz, *Profetas*, I, p. 381. Cf. Lack, *La symbolique du Livre d'Isaïe*, pp. 139-41; Liebreich, 'The Compilation of the Book of Isaiah'; Sweeney, *Isaiah 1–4 and the Post-exilic Understanding of the Isaianic Tradition*, pp. 21-24; David M. Carr, 'Reading Isaiah from Beginning (Isaiah 1) to End (Isaiah 65–66)' (see above); also (for more complex theories) Judith Gärtner, *Jesaja 66 und Sacharja 14 als Summe der Prophetie* (see above); Beuken ('Isaiah Chapters lxv–lxvi' [see above]), suggesting more specifically that 66.7-14 is an epilogue to 56.1–66.6, while 66.15-21 is an epilogue to 40.1–66.14, and 66.22-24 to 1.1–66.21 (but see Blenkinsopp's comments, *Isaiah 56–66*, pp. 293-94). Jan Holman ('De kernboodschap van Jesaja', *Tijdschrift voor Theologie* 36 [1996], pp. 3-17 [13]) similarly works out a paragraph by paragraph relationship between 65.1–66.24 and 1.2-31; 2.2-4.

126 E.g. Schramm, *The Opponents of Third Isaiah*, pp. 161-62.

127 E.g. Stromberg, *Isaiah after Exile*, pp. 147-60.

128 Koenen works out in detail the links between vv. 1-7 and the prayer (*Ethik und Eschatologie im Tritojesajabuch*, pp. 162-64).

129 See Richard Nysse, 'Rebels from Beginning to End', *WW* 19 (1999), pp. 161-70 (165-67).

tetchy.[130] The sequence corresponds to that in passages such as Jeremiah 14.1–15.4 or Hosea 6.1-6. The confrontational nature of the prophecy is underlined by its speaking about the community in the third person through vv. 1-6 and again in v. 7aγb, rather than addressing it in a response to its prayer. The way the passage recalls 55.6-9 supports the impression that it speaks about the people as a whole, not just a group of unfaithful people within it, as 65.8–66.17 will do.

65.1 I made myself available to those who had not asked of me,// I made myself accessible to those who had not inquired of me.
I said, 'I'm here, I'm here',// to a nation that was not called by my name [*or* calling in my name].

Verse 1a comprises two perfectly balanced cola (3-3, abca′b′c′), incorporating two first-person singular niphal verbs of related meaning, the repeated expression *lᵉlô'*, and two third-person plural verbs of related meaning (one qal and one piel, with the second bearing a first-person suffix). While it would be quite possible for 'asked' to be used absolutely, I have followed 1QIsᵃ, LXX, and Syr in assuming that the subsequent suffix also applies to this first verb. Most of the occurrences of the verb (*dāraš*) in the niphal come in Ezekiel 14.3; 20.3, 31; 36.37, passages that make clear its inherent significance. It presupposes a situation where the community elders have come to consult Yhwh by consulting the prophet. Their consultation will relate to their desire to know what their future holds and also to plead with Yhwh about that future. The last passage makes explicit that pleading with Yhwh is their particular concern; it is also the only passage in which they do not receive a frosty response. If the stance Yhwh claims here in v. 1 involves looking back at a period such as the last decades of the sixth century or a later time, it contrasts with Yhwh's general stance in Ezekiel in the opening decades of the sixth century. In the second colon, the parallel verb (*māṣā'*) goes beyond the first in referring to finding and not merely asking, and it has a background in Isaiah 55.6 where (in the 540s) a prophet has urged people to consult Yhwh (*dāraš*, the first verb here) 'while he is making himself accessible'. Jeremiah 29.14 had made a promise of accessibility to people who inquire of Yhwh (*bāqaš* piel) or consult Yhwh, the last and first verbs in this line. This prophecy would then declare that Yhwh has fulfilled that promise.

First Chronicles 28.9; 2 Chronicles 15.2, 4, 15 take up from Isaiah 55.3 and Jeremiah 29.14 the combination of 'making oneself accessible' with one or other of those two verbs. In relation to these other passages, then, Yhwh's distinctive declaration is that people have not been consulting, asking, or inquiring about the their future as they are in Ezekiel and are

[130] Cf. Oswalt, *Isaiah 40–66*, p. 636.

encouraged to do in Isaiah 55.6 and Chronicles, even though Yhwh has been available and accessible to them.[131] In the arrangement of the book, this claim directly confronts the prayer it follows. On behalf of the people, the prophet has urged Yhwh to take note of the community and take action on its behalf instead of 'standing idly by and letting Israel suffer so much' (JPSV's rendering of 64.11 [12]). Yhwh snorts in response that the boot is on the other foot. In 55.6 Yhwh's self-offering takes place in the present and in other contexts one might ask whether the qatal verbs here are performative, 'I hereby make myself available',[132] but in 55.6 the present significance of these verbs is explicit. In the context of Isaiah 65, vv. 5-7 suggest that the die is cast (though we have noted that Yhwh's declarations of judgment—or promises of deliverance and restoration—are always open to being cancelled in light of the hearers' response). Further, the second verb refers to finding and not merely asking, which raises the question whether Yhwh's action is more than merely an unsuccessful offer of availability (compare LXX's 'I became manifest… I was found'). The 'tolerative niphal' denotes letting something actually happen, not merely being open to the possibility of something happening.[133] In MT the last verb in the verse will give readers cause to take up this question.

Meanwhile, Yhwh puts the point even more vigorously in v. 1b in the claim to have been saying 'I'm here, I'm here'. While elsewhere Yhwh can naturally use this expression followed by a verb, as an absolute expression it belongs on the lips of a servant indicating availability to a master. It comes first on the lips of Abraham when summoned by God (Gen 22.1, 11), and later on the lips of the young Samuel when he thinks his master Eli is calling him, and then when he realizes that Yhwh is doing so (1 Sam 3.4, 5, 6, 8). It recurs on the lips of Isaiah when he realizes Yhwh is looking for someone to send as his envoy (Isa 6.8). Yhwh has already used the expression in 58.9 to indicate availability to the community when it cries out in need, in the manner of a master who accepts the obligation to come to support his servant in such a situation. Here Yhwh claims to have offered to be in a position more like that of servant to Israel as the master, waiting to be summoned. The point is underlined by the repetition of the expression 'I'm here' (LXX and Tg reduce the line's force by omitting the 'unnecessary' repetition). In the 3-3 line the second colon completes the first, so that the line as a whole constitutes a parallel to either of the cola in v. 1a. Yhwh has been offering a servant's services to a nation (*gôy*). After the many references to the 'nations' in Isaiah 60–64 it would not be surprising if this is a slightly

[131] Cf. Stromberg, *Isaiah after the Exile*, pp. 87-91.

[132] So Beuken, *Jesaja IIIB*, p. 63.

[133] See *IBHS* 23.4fg; Allen A. Macrae, 'Paul's Use of Isaiah 65:1', in John H. Skilton, M. C. Fiser, and L. W. Sloat (eds.), *The Law and the Prophets* (O. T. Allis Memorial; [Philadelphia:] Presbyterian and Reformed, 1974), pp. 369-76.

pejorative term, but the singular was not so in 60.22, nor arguably in 58.2. The possible explicitly pejorative significance of Yhwh's words lies in the qualifying phrase involving the verb 'call', though there are two versions of it. MT has '[that] was not called by my name'; while the niphal is usual for this expression (43.7; 48.1), the pual is a plausible alternative. In 63.19 the people spoke of Yhwh's name not being proclaimed over them, but that phrase suggested Yhwh's disowning them, which does not fit here. Another possibility is the implication that the nation is called by Baʿal.[134] But more likely the statement relates back to the beginning of the prayer and the beginning of Yhwh's relationship with Israel or with its ancestors.[135] These were people who were not called by Yhwh's name, because Yhwh had not yet revealed that name to them (cf. Exod 3.13-15 [E]; 6.2-8 [P]). An allusion to people who did not yet acknowledge Yhwh follows on well from that use of the word 'nation'. Those to whom Yhwh became available like a servant were a nation who had no prior history with Yhwh. Another textual tradition, however, implies '[that] was not calling in my name/had not called in my name'. This expression can refer both to calling out in praise to other people in Yhwh's name (see 12.4; 41.25; Ps 116.13, 17) and to calling out in prayer to Yhwh in Yhwh's name (see Isa 64.6 [7]; Ps 116.4, 13, 17). The second significance is less common but would be more appropriate in the present context, and it takes up the use in the preceding chapter. Whereas one expects a master to call and a servant to respond by saying 'I'm here', this line implies a situation in which neither party has been calling but the master has been saying 'I'm here' as if someone had been calling. This second textual tradition could have the same reference as the first, to the situation of Yhwh's original entering into a relationship with Israel, when it was in no position to call on the name it did not know, or it could refer to the situation of the oppressed people in Egypt understood as one in which they were not calling on Yhwh. Or it could refer to the people's subsequent history, which the prayer summarized, as a period when they failed to call on Yhwh, and one that might be understood as a time during which Yhwh was always issuing the challenge expressed in 55.6-9.

65.2 I have spread out my hands all day// to a rebellious people,
Those who are walking on a road that is not good,// following their own intentions.

In the second pair of lines, v. 2a (3-2) parallels v. 1b and follows its structure in that the second colon completes the first. Indeed, v. 2aβ constitutes a close parallel to v. 1bβ: both begin with *'el*, which governs

[134] So Ibn Ezra, *The Commentary of Ibn Ezra on Isaiah*, p. 293.
[135] König (*Das Buch Jesaja*, p. 524) refers specifically to Abraham as someone who did not yet acknowledge Yhwh.

parallel words to designate the community (*gôy* and *ʿam*), which are then followed by terms to describe the community in critical fashion. In turn, the two cola in v. 2b (3-2) are mutually parallel phrases that are in substance further parallels to vv. 1bβ and 2aβ but in form work slightly differently. The preposition does not recur; rather the phrases qualify asyndetically 'a rebellious people', but involve a move from singular to plural.

Spreading out the hands, too, is usually the posture of a suppliant (e.g. 1.15; Exod 9.29, 33; 1 Kgs 8.22, 38; Pss 44.21 [20]; 143.6; Job 11.13; Lam 1.17; Ezra 9.5; 2 Chr 6.12, 13, 29). One may imagine that the phrase has its background in the posture a servant or subject adopts in relation to a master or king, but in the Old Testament it is used only of people's posture in relation to God, so that the line continues to describe Yhwh as behaving the way people properly behave in relation to God.[136] Yhwh has been turning things upside down, appealing to the people. While Yhwh's response is tetchy, one might argue that behind the tetchiness is also an implied vulnerability. 'Yhwh is one whose future lies in the hands of another. Issues of divine suffering loom large as Yhwh is daily exposed to the onslaught of rejection'.[137]

'All day' further underlines the point; Yhwh resembles a beggar who spends the whole day soliciting. Tg's explanatory version 'I sent my prophets' fairly interprets how Yhwh did so and thus presupposes that if v. 1 referred to the beginning of Israel's history with Yhwh, v. 2 begins to describe the ongoing history of this relationship, as the prayer did. As the first colon thus takes further each of the three phrases in the first three cola of v. 1, the second colon takes further the description of the people to whom God has been reaching out. They have not merely been people who had no prior relationship with Yhwh or even people who had been ignoring the suppliant God but people who had been actively resisting. The verb (*sārar*) is not so much a political term (as the more common *pāšaʿ* often is) as a family one. Isaiah 30.1 applies it to children (cf. Deut 21.18-21), but it also applies to animals (Hos 4.16; Zech 7.11; Neh 9.29). Through vv. 1-2 the language keeps intensifying the description of Yhwh's action and the people's action: being available, saying 'I'm here', holding out hands; not asking, not calling, rebelling.[138] Whereas 'a people' in v. 10 will be a term for those within the community who are faithful, here it denotes rebels, with no pointer to its referring to a group of rebels within Israel; previous usage of the term would suggest it denotes the community as a whole, as it did in the prayer (see, e.g., 63.8, 11, 14, 18; 64.8 [9]).

[136] Cf. Hitzig, *Jesaja*, p. 628.

[137] Michael J. Chan, 'Isaiah 65–66 and the Genesis of Reorienting Speech', *CBQ* 72 (2010), pp. 445-64 (448-49).

[138] Cf. Zapff, *Jesaja*, p. 418.

The two parallel phrases in v. 2b begin to explicate the nature of this rebellious life, which is continued in the 'catalogue of sins'[139] in vv. 3-5. 'Not good' involves a litotes; it is a terrible way.[140] A good road is one that is straight or direct (1 Sam 12.23) and also one that is safe and profitable (1 Sam 24.20 [19]). In many passages the expression could carry either connotation (1 Kgs 8.36; Jer 6.16; Prov 16.29; 2 Chr 6.27), perhaps with the implication that the straight road is the safe road. Here, too, both connotations might apply, though the second colon implies that the stress lies on the straightness of the road. An intention (*maḥăšābâ*) or thought or plan need not be bad and the word can apply to God's thinking, but the word often involves a contrast between God's thinking and human thinking, not least in 55.7-9. So the neutral translation in Tg, Aq, Th, Vg, is appropriate, but LXX's 'following their sins' brings out the implication.

Paul takes up vv. 1-2 in Romans 10.20-21, applying v. 1a to the way God has become available to peoples other than Israel in his day, and v. 2a to the way God has reached out to Israel in vain in his day. Ironically, while MT would have served his argument superbly in v. 1b, for both verses he follows LXX's wording (though he quotes the words in a different order),[141] and in LXX's version v. 1b adds nothing to v. 1a for him. Perhaps also ironically, the broader context of v. 1 in 65.1–66.24 does match the point Paul makes on the basis of v. 1.[142] Karl Barth generalizes Yhwh's statement in a different way. 'Is there anywhere or at any time a real human act of penitence for the sake of which it is worth while to God to spare men and to give them time and life?... Are there any genuine exceptions to what we read in Is. 65[1f.].'[143] But otherwise, taken up by Gentile Christians rather than Paul's fellow-Jews, his reapplication of v. 2a to the way God has reached out to Israel in vain in his day has unfortunate anti-Jewish potential.[144]

139 Beuken, *Jesaja IIIB*, p. 65.

140 Cf. Alexander, *Isaiah*, II, p. 438.

141 But on the complexities of LXX's reading(s) and of Paul's relationship to them, see Wagner, *Heralds of Good News*, pp. 206-11.

142 Cf. Shum, *Paul's Use of Isaiah in Romans*, pp. 226-31.

143 Karl Barth, *Die kirchliche Dogmatik* II/1, p. 467 (ET p. 415) (*sic*, without closing question mark).

144 Cf. Blenkinsopp, *Isaiah 56–66*, p. 270; and Sawyer's description of a church in Rome bearing this inscription, *The Fifth Gospel*, p. 100 (see also Sawyer, 'Isaiah and the Jews', in J. C. Exum and H. G. M. Williamson [eds.], *Reading from Right to Left* [D. J. A. Clines Festschrift; London: Sheffield Academic Press, 2003], pp. 390-401). Early Christian writers routinely follow Paul in applying these verses to Christ's preaching to the Jews (e.g. Justin, *First Apology* 35, 38, 49; Origen, *Against Celsus* 2.78). See further J. Ross Wagner, 'Moses and Isaiah in Concert', in McGinnis and Tull (eds.), *'As Those Who Are Taught'*, pp. 87-105 (89-97). Irenaeus is more even-handed in applying v. 1 to Gentiles and v. 2 to Jews (*The Demonstration of the Apostolic Preaching* 79, 92).

65.3 The people are ones who are provoking me// to my face continually,
Sacrificing in the gardens// and burning incense on the bricks,
4 Who are sitting in the tombs// and spending the night in hidden places,
Who are eating swine's flesh,// with a broth of profane things in their vessels,
5 Who are saying, 'Keep to yourself,// do not come near me, because I am too sacred for you':
These people are smoke in my nostrils,// a fire burning all day.

Verses 3-5 at first give the impression of continuing the enjambment in v. 2b, but the first and last lines form a pair describing the effect of the people's action on Yhwh and more likely they are parallel noun clauses. The intervening four lines take the description of the people's shortcomings from the general to the concrete.[145] Verses 3b-4a form a pair of 2-2 lines on the nature of their worship; vv. 4b-5a form a pair of 3-3 lines on the related implications for their purity status. The verses do continue from v. 2b in indicating what kind of road and what kind of intentions the prophet was referring to (namely, ones that relate to worship and to seeking contact with God), and what was the nature of the 'not good' in both senses.

In v. 3a (3-2) the second colon again simply completes the statement begun in the first. As was the case within v. 2, the corporate expression for the people is spelled out in a description of what 'they' were doing, by means of a participle. The verb 'provoke' (*kāʿas*) comes only here in Isaiah; it is a common one in Kings and Jeremiah to describe the people's provoking Yhwh to anger by serving other gods. The prophecy thus continues to confirm the perspective and follow the movement of the prayer, in describing a failure to respond to the exhortation in 55.6-9 that is analogous to or continuous with the community's failure before the exile. The prepositional expression and the adverb underline the point. Both 'to my face' (*ʿal-pānāy*) and 'continually' (*tāmîd*) could suggest provocation linked with the 'regular' offerings (*tāmîd*) to Yhwh in the temple,[146] though the compound phrase comes in Jeremiah 6.7 rather with reference either to violence in the city or to violence done to the city. Further, the regular expression used in connection with offerings in the temple is 'before Yhwh' (*lipnê yhwh*), literally, 'to the face of Yhwh' (e.g. Exod 28.29-30 [P]; Lev 24.3-8 [H]). The occurrences of 'to your/his face' in Job, using the preposition *ʿal* (1.11; 6.28; 21.31), suggest that the phrase implies brazen shamelessness. While *ʿal-pānāy* may 'bring to mind' the expression *lipnê yhwh*, these parallels with Job suggest that the former expression is not one that need suggest the context of worship, as the latter may;[147] certainly the two expressions are not synonymous.[148] The

[145] Cf. Croatto, *Imaginar el futuro*, p. 402.
[146] So, e.g., Cyril of Alexandria, 'Εξήγησις ὑπομνηματική εἰς τὸν προφήτην 'Ησαΐαν, col. 1407; D. Qimchi, 'ישעיה', on the passage.
[147] So Ruszkowski, *Volk und Gemeinde*, p. 93.
[148] As Hanson (*The Dawn of Apocalyptic*, p. 147) seems to imply.

occurrence of *ʿal-pānāy* with regard to God in the enigmatic final phrase in the first commandment (Exod 20.3; Deut 5.7) could suggest that the offerings that v. 3a denotes were indeed provocative because they were idolatrous. But vv. 3b-5a confirm that the line refers not to offerings in the temple but to other sorts of offerings. These were, however, made within yards of the temple, and the fact that Yhwh dwells there would mean that such offerings were made within Yhwh's sight.

Verses 3b-4a describe the practices implied by the reference to provoking Yhwh. The first bicolon comprises balancing participles (one qal, one piel) and prepositional phrases. The reference to worship in gardens takes up from 1.29 (cf. 66.17). Only here does the Old Testament refer to bricks in connection with sacrificing or the associated burning of incense (*qāṭar* piel). The Book of the Covenant (Exod 22.24-25) does envisage altars made of bricks, but Babylonian parallels suggest that the colon denotes offerings to celestial deities made on the roofs of houses (cf. Jer 19.13; 32.29), when offerings are made on bricks there.[149] Other Old Testament passages link offerings to celestial deities with the sacrifice of children in Tophet and with offerings to Molek (Jer 19.13; Zeph 1.5). Verse 4a makes more specific the likely implication of the preceding line. The gardens are graveyards and people are there with offerings in connection with making contact with their dead family members in order to consult them (instead of consulting Yhwh: see vv. 1-2). Thus while it is also possible to link the formulation in vv. 3b-4a with the worship of Asherah and with the discovery of many female figurines in Judah from the sixth as well as the seventh century, it is more likely that the lines refer to the kind of rites attacked in 56.9–57.21 in the corresponding earlier part of Isaiah 56–66.[150] LXX's 'who in tombs and in caves sleep for the sake of dreams' gives precision to the way people seek guidance (cf. Jer 23.25-32).[151] Here it is not explicit that the rites are consciously observed in honour of gods other than Yhwh, and no doubt some people making such offerings did not see them in this way, but that point will become explicit over coming verses. Here, too, the cola are parallel, comprising two verbs and two *b-* expressions, though (as is often the case) a finite verb succeeds the participle. This change and the abb′a′ arrangement of v. 4a also hints that the little unit comprising vv. 3b-4a is coming to an end. The word *n*ᵉ*ṣûrîm* in the second colon is of uncertain meaning. I take the passive participle to qualify 'tombs'. In light of its

[149] So Diethelm Conrad, 'Zu Jes 65 3b', *ZAW* 80 (1968), pp. 232-34; cf. Paul, ישעיה פרקים מ-סו, II, p. 539 (ET p. 593). Dahood offers an alternative archeologically based explanation ('Textual Problems in Isaia' [see above], pp. 406-8); cf. also Driver, 'Isaianic Problems', pp. 56-57; Ackerman, *Under Every Green Tree* (see above), pp. 173-85.

[150] Thus here as in 56.9–57.21 it is inappropriate to hypothesize reference to fertility rites (against Ackerman, *Under Every Green Tree* [see above], pp. 185-92). See further the discussion in Middlemas, *The Troubles of Templeless Judah*, pp. 81-96.

[151] Cf. Theodore J. Lewis, *Cults of the Dead in Ancient Israel and Ugarit* (Atlanta: Scholars, 1989), p. 159.

usual meaning it could naturally mean 'watched over', designating the cemetery as a place that was guarded. But we do not know that cemeteries were guarded, so 'hidden' in the sense of 'secret' is more plausible—not as strictly a description of the cemeteries but as a comment on the rites there.

Verses 4b-5a then form a second pair of lines describing the rebels' provocative behaviour. Not eating pork was a clear requirement of the Torah (Lev 11.7 [P]; Deut 14.8) on the grounds that the pig has a split hoof like a cow but does not chew the cud, so that it does not belong to a regular category of animals. Only here and in 66.3, 17 is there reference to Israelites eating pork. The collocation within v. 4 of eating pork with rites involved in contacting dead family members would support the theory that sacrificing pigs was related to such rites,[152] but the evidence for this theory is thin and the significance of the present passage in that connection is reduced if v. 4b pairs with v. 5a rather than with what precedes. The thinness of evidence for Israelites ever eating pork raises the question whether eating pork is purely a theoretical notion here. The possibility that the prophet is simply trying to formulate the most objectionable descriptions of theoretically possible actions is heightened by the phrase in the parallel colon. In Leviticus 7.18 [P]; 19.7 [H], 'profane things' (*piggullîm*) are parts of sacrificial offerings that have not been consumed the day after a fellowship sacrifice and are then consumed on the next day; the other allusion (Ezek 4.14) would likely have the same reference. The problem is that they are then being treated as ordinary food, in the way one might make a meal out of leftovers, when they had been made sacred.[153] Here, then, such an action has become more scandalous; the offerers are (allegedly) not just casually snacking but making soup out of these leftovers. But it may be chance that at least two of the only four occurrences of *piggullîm* have this reference, and that the word is a more general one for something abominable, as is the case when it occurs at Qumran.[154]

Verse 5a further supports the idea that this description involves hyperbole or caricature. The line incorporates some parallelism; one could characterize it as abb′c. The opening participle makes the line parallel with the preceding ones and applies to both cola. The two parallel imperatival phrases make identical statements in positive and negative form; one comprises a second-person singular imperative followed by an *ʾel* expression, the other a negative second-person singular yiqtol followed by a *b*-expression. The line then closes with a clause giving the

[152] See Walter Houston, *Purity and Monotheism* (Sheffield: Sheffield Academic Press, 1993), pp. 161-68; Ulrich Hübner, 'Schweine, Schweineknochen und ein Speiseverbot im Alten Israel', *VT* 39 (1989), pp. 225-36; G. J. Botterweck, *TWAT*, II, pp. 842-43 (ET *TDOT*, IV, pp. 297-98).

[153] Cf. Jacob Milgrom, *Leviticus 1–16* (New York: Doubleday, 1991), p. 422.

[154] See D. Kellermann in *TWAT*; also *DCH*; *HALOT*.

basis for the exhortation; again it applies to both cola. The exhortation raises questions in a number of ways. The first (*qārab*) is often used with *'el* to denote approaching God, and most interestingly with regard to approaching sacred offerings when in a state of taboo (Lev 22.3 [H]). There is thus some irony involved in the prohibition here; instead of drawing near to partake of an offering, draw near to yourself. The second verb (*nāgaš*) has similar meaning to the first[155] and is used in conjunction with it in Leviticus 21.16-23 [H]; Ezekiel 44.13-16. The rhetorical effect of the prophecy is thus enhanced by the use of language such as the priests in the temple might well use.[156]

All this helps resolve the significance of the closing verb, for which Tg and Sym properly presuppose the meaning 'I am sacred in relation to you' or 'I am too sacred for you', which comes to the same thing (LXX and Syr ignore the suffix and imply simply 'I am sacred', while Vg has 'you are impure). The people involved in the offerings are pictured as viewing themselves as holy and as viewing their offerings as holy, and are giving a warning about encroaching on them. They might be issuing this warning to other people, but the singular verbs rather point to its being addressed to Yhwh. The caricature fits with Yhwh's complaint in v. 1 and with Yhwh's use of the verbs *qārab* and *nāgaš* in passages such as 45.20; 48.16; 57.3.

Verse 5b (3-3) pairs with v. 3a in forming an envelope around vv. 3-5 in describing the effect of these rites on Yhwh, whether or not they are consciously offered to deities other than Yhwh. If the warning in v. 5a is addressed to Yhwh, this effect would be especially intelligible and the line especially forceful. The line again works abb′c, with 'these people' (or 'these things') applying to the second colon as well as the first, and 'all day' applying to the first as well as the second. 'Smoke in my nose' and 'a fire burning' are then parallel to each other. If the people who make these offerings, or the offerings themselves, are 'smoke in my nose', one might at first understand this to denote their causing anger (so Tg) or their having an unwelcome effect like smoke in the eyes (cf. Prov 10.26), but 'smoke in my nose' rather suggests Yhwh breathing angry and destructive fire (2 Sam 22.9; Ps 18.9 [8]; cf. Job 41.12 [20]), which is confirmed by the second colon. The line is thus a double exclamation or expostulation at what vv. 3b-5a have described. While the worshipers would think that the sacrifices they burn would please Yhwh, their smoke transmutes into something that will burn them up.[157] In this sense v. 5b begins the declaration of punishment that will be the focus in vv. 6-7 (hence 1QIs[a] not inappropriately has a space after v. 5a, associating v. 5b

[155] BDB (p. 620) describes it as a less frequent synonym.

[156] See further Hanson, *The Dawn of Apocalyptic*, pp. 147-49, though he assumes the language refers to the priests; cf. Lena-Sofia Tiemeyer, 'The Haughtiness of the Priesthood', *Biblica* 85 (2004), pp. 237-44.

[157] Cf. D. N. Freedman and J. R. Lundbom, *TWAT*, III, p. 848 (ET *TDOT*, VI, p. 273).

with what follows rather than with what precedes). 'All day' also makes for a grim comparison and contrast with v. 2a. Tg takes the line to refer to punishment in Gehenna.

65.6 There—it is written before me:// I will not remain still; rather, I am repaying.
I am repaying into their bosom 7 your waywardness// and your ancestors' waywardness, all at once (Yhwh has said).
Those who have burned incense on the mountains,// who have denigrated me on the hills:
I am counting out their payment// first of all into their bosom.

Verses 6-7 constitute the formal statement of that commitment to punish. MT's understanding of the prosody of vv. 6-7aα seems implausible; I have reworked it as two lines, 3-4 and 3-3, with '(Yhwh has said)' as a further colon that might be seen as extra-metrical.

The first line (v. 6abα) comprises two cola in which the second completes the first by telling us what it is that is written before Yhwh. 'There' (*hinnēh*) begins the declaration concerning punishment, as in 22.17; 1 Kgs 13.2).[158] This in itself makes it less likely that what is 'written' is a record of the community's sins,[159] and it is hard to find a precise parallel for this idea. Rather, things that are thus 'written' are commonly curses or declarations about punishment (e.g. Deut 29.19, 20, 26 [20, 21, 27]; Jer 22.30; 25.13; Ezek 2.10; Ps 149.9), and this is the significance of the prophet's reference to writing here. The distinctive addition 'before me' underlines the point; the declaration of judgment is not written but then filed away; rather, it sits there demanding Yhwh's attention. The line hardly need imply that the earlier words in Isaiah are literally in writing, though it might possibly do so. Indeed, if Isaiah 65–66 is designed to pair with Isaiah 1 as the opening and closing of the book, it might refer to the indictment and warning in that opening chapter.[160] Yet significantly, the parallel colon goes on to take up a phrase from earlier in these nearer chapters and then from the prayer. 'I will not remain still' is the undertaking in 62.1 (see also 42.14; 57.11). In the prayer, 64.11 [12] has asked whether it is really true, and v. 6 declares that it is certain in the way of something put into writing. But there is then some irony in the way the line takes up the verb; it declares that the undertaking is going to be true in an unpleasant sense, not the encouraging sense that held earlier. The precise verbal form for 'I am repaying' (*šālam* piel; I take it as instantaneous qatal) has not occurred previously in Isaiah in this connection, though it has come (as *w*-consecutive) in Jeremiah 16.18, and also in

[158] Pauritsch (*Die neue Gemeinde*, pp. 191, 193) gives a wider range of examples, but most involve *hinnēh* with a suffix, whose significance is rather different.

[159] So, e.g., Theodoret of Cyrrhus, *Commentaire sur Isaïe* 182a (III, pp. 314-15).

[160] E.g. Seitz, 'The Book of Isaiah 40–66', p. 543.

Jeremiah 25.14; 51.24 in connection with Babylon, with which one might compare Isaiah 59.18. Yhwh's set resolution involves treating the Judahite worshippers the same way as Babylon. The prayer had closed with an appeal for mercy; Yhwh denies the appeal, at the moment.

Verses 6bβ-7aα begin with a resumptive repetition of that verb and then with an indirect object and with its more necessary direct object, which is treated as the beginning of the next verse in MT's versification.[161] The verb and the indirect object also apply to the second colon; its parallelism adds a further direct object and an adverb, which also applies to the first colon. Thus the line works abcc′d. Anatomically, the word for bosom (*ḥêq*) covers a person's front from the chest downwards into the lap. Externally, it refers to the fold in the front of a garment in which one might carry something or hold a baby, the equivalent of a pocket; internally, it refers to the inner being that lies behind the person's front, which is vulnerable because the person's front gives access to it (e.g. Job 19.27). It is in this last connection that the Old Testament uses this word in speaking of Yhwh's punishment reaching a person's inmost being (Tg understands v. 6 to refer to the 'second death').[162] Here the prophet is taking up Jeremiah 32.18-19, which speaks of Yhwh 'repaying the waywardness of the parents/ancestors into the bosom of their children/descendants', itself taking up the formula that goes back to Exodus 34.7 (J). In effect, the prayer in 63.7–64.11 [12] has asked, 'Are you still going to punish our waywardness like the people who got taken into exile?' (64.8 [9] referred specifically to 'waywardness'). The prophet is replying, 'Yes, because you have admitted that you are still behaving like them, and Yhwh is treating you in the way of which Jeremiah (and Moses) spoke'. Admittedly, the prophet's version of this warning perhaps works more within a framework of thinking that sees wrongdoing finding its 'natural' result in calamity by a cause-effect process rather than as involving the (direct, interventionist) activity of the powerful creator, of which Jeremiah speaks.[163] Further, so far the prophet has been not directly addressing the wayward people but has been speaking of them; they overhear Yhwh talking about them. Suddenly in v. 7a the pronouns turn from 'their' to 'your'.

Admittedly the prophet might seem to be playing into their hands by describing them as experiencing redress for their ancestors' waywardness as well as for their own (cf. the protest in Lam 5.7). Yet in this respect the prophet is facing and expecting them to face the theological reality affirmed by Exodus 34.7. It simply is the case that children or descendants pay a price for the waywardness of their parents or ancestors. If the

[161] For this division of the lines, cf. Torrey, *Second Isaiah*, pp. 272, 468.

[162] This idea is then taken up in Revelation (e.g. 21.8); see Jacques van Ruiten, 'The Intertextual Relationship between Isaiah 65,17-20 and Revelation 21,1-5b', *Estudios Bíblicos* 51 (1993), pp. 473-510 (507).

[163] So Lau, *Schriftgelehrte Prophetie in Jes 56–66*, p. 192.

Second Temple community's ancestors had been less enthusiastic about the kind of practices Isaiah 56–66 condemns, these practices might have been less available to their descendants. In any case, the point about the polemic in vv. 3-5 is that the community cannot and does not claim it is itself blameless. Its punishment will take the form of redress for its own waywardness. This is underlined by the transition to second-person suffixes within the line, which seems odd to Western readers but can hardly be simply a slip. It is in any case the kind of transition of persons that is not unusual in the Prophets.[164] Here its effect is to make explicit that the warning in Jeremiah 32 is not one applying merely to the people on the eve of the fall of Jerusalem. It applies to 'you', the audience for this prophecy. The expression 'all at once' makes the declaration more solemn; it suggests something comprehensive and final. It use takes up a characteristic expression from Isaiah 40–55 (e.g. 40.5; 45.16; 46.2), but does so once again with barbed effect, because in Isaiah 40–55 the expression always underlines the prophet's good news, of the comprehensive and final nature of Yhwh's punishment of Israel's oppressors and of Yhwh's deliverance of Israel itself. Here it has the opposite significance. The addition '(Yhwh has said)' further underlines the solemnity of the declaration and in this respect forms an *inclusio* with the words that open vv. 6-7aα.

The *ʾăšer* opening v. 7aβ is an unusual feature of a poetic line. Rather than inferring the rare meaning 'because' (which would, however, simply make explicit a point that is implicit) and taking the line as an enjambment from the preceding lines, I understand the line as an extraposed phrase anticipating the third-person suffix on 'their payment', and thus take v. 7aβ as the first of a linked pair of lines comprising vv. 7aβb. Verses 6-7 therefore work broadly abb′a′, with Yhwh's declarations of intent to punish forming a bracket around the descriptions of the objects of punishment. Verse 7aβ itself then comprises a 3-2 abcc′b′ line in which the *ʾăšer* applies to both cola, which comprise balancing third-person plural qatal piel verbs (one with a suffix) and balancing *ʿal* phrases. The reference to burning incense resumes from v. 3b, but the *ʿal* phrases are surprising in light of the different account they imply of the location and nature of the wayward practices to which the passage refers; these are not rites on roofs or in cemeteries. The collocation of mountains and hills in connection with rites recurs from earlier prophets (see Jer 3.23; Ezek 6.13; 20.28; Hos 4.13), so perhaps the phrase is a conventional one and/or refers especially to the actions of the ancestors mentioned in the previous line. In the parallelism between the verbs, the reference to denigrating Yhwh (*ḥārap*) goes far beyond the reference to burning incense, in indicating the significance of the action, and also (by implication) of the actions referred to in vv. 3-5. To put it another way, the reason why Yhwh is provoked to anger is that the people's rites are such an insult.

[164] Torrey (*Second Isaiah*, p. 468) suggests that the line conflates two traditions.

They scorn Yhwh's importance. They imply that Yhwh cannot grant the blessings or deliverance or insights that people seek from other sources, and/or that Yhwh will take no action if they do have recourse to these other resources (cf. 37.4, 17, 23-24: these references comprise most of the uses with Yhwh as object). In effect the people's worship involves them in blasphemy.[165]

Verse 7b rounds off vv. 6-7 by restating v. 6. MT scans the line as 3-1, which suggests a translation such as 'I am measuring out their former work into their bosom'.[166] More likely the line scans as 2-2. Either way, the second colon simply completes the first. Read as 2-2, the line's first colon restates the repeated 'I am repaying' in v. 6. While the *w*-qatal might be a genuine *w*-consecutive following on the extraposed phrase, I rather take it as a further instantaneous qatal parallel to those in v. 6 and introduced by a simple *w*- like the second of those. In the second colon, the prepositional phrase repeats from v. 6, but the preceding word 'first of all' (*ri'šōnâ*) is more difficult in the context. It is hard to see why it should have the same meaning as *bᵉrō'š*, something like 'in full'.[167] But like 'I am repaying' in v. 6, it recurs from Jeremiah 16.18 (where also LXX omits it), which suggests that the difficulty in understanding should not be solved by emendation.[168] In the context in Jeremiah it draws attention to the fact that an act of punishment is to come 'first of all' before Yhwh's restoring of Israel (of which Jer 16.14-15 has spoken). Although it may be carried over somewhat mechanically from Jeremiah, this meaning will fit here.

(b) Comment: 65.8-25

The implication of vv. 1-7 was gloomy. The answer to the preceding prayer was that devastating judgment will continue because the speakers' assessment of themselves as people who have abandoned Yhwh is correct. Yet there was another aspect to the self-understanding expressed in the prayer. The people address Yhwh as 'your servants', 'your people'. It is a classic Old Testament conviction that Yhwh cannot simply cast off 'his people', even if they are rebels. Verses 8-25 thus constitute another response to the issues raised by the prayer.[169] They speak in a different way about judgment; it will not simply mean the annihilation of the entire community. In pre-exilic prophecy, judgment oracles and deliverance oracles commonly appear sequentially because these two experiences are to come sequentially to the people as a whole. This prophecy takes the

165 E. Kutsch, *TWAT*, III, p. 226 (ET *TDOT*, V, p. 212).

166 Cf. KJV; Bonnard, *Le Second Isaïe*, p. 458.

167 See NRSV; JPSV; TNIV.

168 Cf. Paul, ישעיה פרקים מ-סו, II, pp. 541-42 (ET pp. 595-97), though he translates 'in full' in both passages.

169 Cf. Koenen, *Ethik und Eschatologie im Tritojesajabuch*, p. 161.

form of one in which deliverance and judgment are combined, because these can be the interwoven destinies of different groups within the community.[170]

There is nothing so very novel about the notion of a judgment that will mean not the annihilation of the community but the preservation of a group within it, the nucleus of a new community.[171] From its beginning, Israel's story has spoken of a judgment that affects a small or large segment of the community rather than destroying the whole, sometimes on an apparently random basis, sometimes on the basis of eliminating the guilty (see, e.g., Exod 32–34; Num 13–14 [both JE, with developments from D and P]). Prophets have similarly spoken of a judgment that will either exempt a 'remnant' on a random basis for the sake of keeping Israel in being or will discriminate between the faithful and the faithless. Significantly, this motif appears in the opening chapter of Isaiah, with which these last two chapters pair (see 1.21-31; also, e.g., Jer 5.10; Amos 9.8-10). Indeed, the present community exists only because Yhwh acted in this way in preserving a number of Ephraimites and Judahites through the Assyrian and Babylonian destructions and transportations. Even the virtual division of the community into two categories is not exactly new; at least, Proverbs divides the community into the people of insight, who are the faithful, and the stupid people, who are the faithless.

What is distinctive in 65.8-25 is the way 'all of the traditional terms, such as "YHWH's people", "YHWH's servants" and "YHWH's chosen", are redefined'.[172] Like 56.9–59.8, with which 65.1–66.17 pairs in the structure of the book, 65.8-25 talks about two groups of people in the community, 'servants and renegades'.[173] A difference over against 56.9–59.8 is the application of those terms to one of the groups and thus implicitly not to the other. Only one is 'my servants, 'my chosen ones', 'my people'. The other is 'you who abandon Yhwh', 'who lay a table for Luck and fill a mixing chalice for Destiny', who have not responded when Yhwh called. The former are destined to take possession of the country and to live long and happy lives there; the latter are destined for punishment and death, hunger and thirst, anguish and shame. (In 57.14 'my people' may denote only the faithful, though in 58.1 it denotes the whole community; further, at the same time, 56.1-8 has also indicated that in another sense the definition of 'my people' is being broadened not narrowed.[174])

[170] Cf. Hanson, *The Dawn of Apocalyptic*, p. 150.

[171] Against (e.g.) Joseph Blenkinsopp, 'The Servant and the Servants in Isaiah and the Formation of the Book', in Broyles and Evans (eds.), *Writing and Reading the Book of Isaiah*, pp. 155-75 (168).

[172] Schramm, *The Opponents of Third Isaiah*, p. 155. Cf. Wallis, 'Gott und seine Gemeinde'; Paul, ישעיה פרקים מ-סו, II, p. 544 (ET p. 597).

[173] Roodenburg, *Israel, de Knecht en de Knechten*, p. 122.

[174] Cf. Obara, *Le strategie di Dio*, pp. 184-87.

65.8 Yhwh has said this:
As when juice can be found in a cluster// and someone says, 'Don't destroy it, because there's a blessing in it',
So I will act for the sake of my servants,// so as not to destroy everything.

The Old Testament, then, has to square the circle of how to envisage God both taking Israel's waywardness seriously and therefore punishing it, and also taking seriously an ongoing commitment to Israel that makes it impossible simply to destroy it or cast it off. A standard way to do so is to have God all-but destroying, but leaving leftovers from which new growth can come. Thus v. 8 declares the intention not to destroy the entire people. The introductory 'messenger formula', 'Yhwh has said this', appears for the first time since the opening line of Isaiah 56–66.[175] It thus underlines the truth claims of the declarations that follow and urges people to take them seriously. Yet the effect of the immediately following lines is to qualify the solemnity of vv. 1-7; thus the formula encourages people to pay attention to a note of hope.[176] The formula is likely extra-metrical, but the prosody of the verse as a whole is not very poetic. After the formula, in MT v. 8a scans 4-5 and v. 8b 4-3. In the main part of v. 8a the second colon is thus inordinately long. One might resolve this difficulty by seeing the line as a 4-2-3 tricolon, or by seeing the messenger formula as within the regular lines and thus scan v. 8a as 3-4 and 2-3, or one might rather infer that the five-stress colon requires a further maqqeph, probably linking *berākâ* and *bô* ('a blessing in it'). There is no parallelism within the lines, but the very nature of an 'As…so…' sentence involves some parallelism between them, and the verb 'destroy' (*šāḥat*) recurs. In isolation, one might not take the verse as poetic at all.

The background to v. 8 is either the practice of pruning grapevines, a particularly savage operation, or more likely the harvesting of grapes, as in 5.1-7; indeed, within the context of the book of Isaiah, v. 8 takes forward the promise of 27.2-6 that the threat of 5.1-7 will not have the last word.[177] The verse imagines a situation when pruning is due but there is a bunch of grapes on an otherwise poor branch, or harvest is due and there is a bunch of grapes that is not quite ripe. Either way, there is [the potential for] new wine on a vine that in general looks useless; the reason for the slightly odd use of the word for grape juice or new wine (*tîrôš*) instead of a word for grapes will appear in the next verse.[178] There is a blessing there: something good, fruitful, and profitable (cf. the use of the word in passages such as Gen 49.25; 1 Sam 30.26). It is therefore stupid

[175] See the comment on 56.1.

[176] Cf. Koole, *Jesaja III*, p. 398 (ET pp. 428-29).

[177] Cf. Elżbieta M. Obara, 'Dalla vigna al grappolo', *Rivista Biblica* 54 (2006), pp. 129-57.

[178] S. Naeh and M. P. Weitzman ('*Tīrōš*—Wine or Grape?', *VT* 44 [1994], pp. 115-20 [117-18]) argue that תירוש actually means 'grape' in passages such as this one; see also *TWAT* and the comment on 62.8.

to dismiss the vine or the branch in such a way as to lose the fruit. The recurrence of the verb *šāḥat* recalls Genesis 6.9-22 and 9.1-17 (P), where the verb comes seven times. Tg thus interprets the first line of Noah, who was found innocent in the flood generation, so that Yhwh said not to destroy him in order to establish the world from him. Tg then adds 'faithful' to 'servants' (so also in vv. 9, 13, 14, 15). It may thereby bring out an implication inherent in the line. While 63.17 used the term 'your servants' to denote the community as a whole, 65.13-14 will set 'my servants' over against other people within the community, which might already be the implication here. For the sake of these faithful servants Yhwh will not destroy the community as a whole. One might compare the comment with Genesis 18–19 (J), where the verb *šāḥat* comes even more times. Yet the immediately following v. 9 continues to give the term its general reference, suggesting the same understanding here. It is for the sake of the Israel that ideally comprises Yhwh's servants that Yhwh will remove the faithless. The linguistic ambiguity in the verse reflects an inbuilt theological ambiguity. Israel is a people chosen by God; yet the real Israel is the people committed to Yhwh. Ideally the chosen Israel and the committed Israel are the same; in practice this is not so. Whereas the *servant* in Isaiah 40–55 never refers to the true Israel, the term *servants* now comes to do so.

There is some overlap between the prophet's words and the idea of a remnant, which appears elsewhere, but the two ideas are not identical. The idea of a remnant is that Yhwh allows some of Israel to survive, even though none deserve to do so, so that the whole people does not die out. There is no implication that the leftovers are more faithful than the ones who die, though there is a subsequent challenge to these leftovers to become a remnant that is faithful. The prophet's idea here is that God will distinguish within the community between the faithless and the faithful, and preserve the latter.

65.9 I will bring forth offspring from Jacob,// from Judah one who takes possession of my mountains.
My chosen ones will take possession of it;// my servants will dwell there.
10 Sharon will become a pasture for flocks,// the Vale of Achor a resting place for cattle,// for my people who have sought me.

Whereas v. 8 relates only a negative (the vine will not be destroyed), three further lines now spell out a positive. Verse 9 comprises 3-3 and 2-2 lines that are both internally and mutually parallel. The first works abcb′c′: the opening verb applies to both cola, and two *min* phrases parallel each other. Within Isaiah, only in 48.1 do Jacob and Judah come together; there, too, the reference relates to offspring (*zeraʿ*) 'coming forth' from Judah (*yāṣāʾ* qal; the hiphil appears here). The combination reflects the assumption that the people of Judah after the exile *are* the embodiment of Jacob. 'One who takes possession of my mountains' then parallels 'offspring'; the singular participial phrase qualifies the collective noun. The line takes up the idea of blessing and suggests why v. 8 used this particular word (intelligibly, but slightly obscurely); when God blesses, this issues in fruitfulness (e.g. Gen 17.16 [P]). Blessing and offspring came in close association in 44.3, and offspring is an important motif for hope in 6.13; 41.8; 61.9. Yet the second colon takes the substance of the line substantially further, but it is again in keeping with the historical significance of God's blessing of Abraham, expressed in fruitfulness and in the possession of a land (Gen 12.1-3 [J]). In addition 'takes possession of' (*yôrēš*) makes for a paronomasia with 'juice' (*tîrôš*) in v. 8, also explaining why this particular word was used there (intelligibly, but slightly oddly, instead of a word for grapes). The idea of Judah's offspring entering into possession of the land recurs from 54.3, though the idea of entering into possession has recurred more broadly (57.13; 60.21; 61.7; 63.18). In particular, 57.13 spoke of people who take refuge in Yhwh taking possession of Yhwh's holy mountain. The plural here, unusual in this connection, picks up from v. 7; the places of blasphemous worship are reappropriated.

Verse 9b parallels v. 9a but takes its point further, and also resolves the ambiguity in v. 8b. In 63.17, 'your servants' were the community as a whole. In what sense will Yhwh be acting 'for the sake of my servants' in destroying most of the vine—most of the people? Likewise there was an ambiguity about v. 9a. Was the offspring of Jacob/Judah that was to take possession of Yhwh's mountains the very embodiment of Jacob/Judah? Rather, v. 9b makes clear, the offspring of Jacob/Judah is distinguishable from Jacob/Judah, as are 'my chosen ones' and 'my servants'. Plural 'chosen ones' comes in Psalms 105.43; 106.5, also in 105.6 = 1 Chronicles 16.13 in parallelism with singular 'servant'. In Isaiah 43.20 singular 'my chosen' describes the people, and also in 42.1; 45.4 in parallelism with singular 'my servant'.[179] Here the prophet is taking up those passages in Isaiah 40–55 but turning both into the plural. This again underlines the tension over the way 'chosen' and 'servant' are both designations of the status of the people and descriptions of its vocation, which only part of it fulfils. Given the nature of the promise expressed in v. 10, this ambivalence is telling. In 60.21 'your people, all of them, are the faithful ones who will possess the country forever'; it is no longer so.[180] The chosen servants who show promise of producing good fruit are the ones who will enter into possession of 'it' and thus dwell there on an ongoing basis. The odd verbal formation in which the 'it' has no antecedent reflects the fact that the verse as a whole is taking up Jeremiah 30.3. That earlier verse speaks of the restoration of Israel and Judah, the northern and southern nations; here v. 9a speaks of Jacob and Judah, on the assumption that Judah *is* the embodiment of Jacob/Israel.[181]

[179] Cf. Bernard Gosse, 'Le livre d'Isaïe et le Psautier', *ZAW* 115 (2003), pp. 376-87.

[180] Cf. Smith, *Rhetoric and Redaction in Trito-Isaiah*, pp. 141-42.

[181] Cf. Lau, *Schriftgelehrte Prophetie in Jes 56–66*, p. 195.

The tricolon comprising v. 10 (3-4-3) closes off the promises in 8-10, which will give way to threats in the following lines. The first two cola are neatly parallel; the third colon returns to the question raised by those ambivalent designations, and to a question raised by the very first line of the chapter. The two parallel cola work abcb′c′. The verb applies to both; it is followed first by its two subjects, each being a geographical term, then by two *l-* expressions. Neither geographical term is of very straightforward significance. There is a Sharon east of the Jordan (1 Chr 5.16); identifying the Sharon in this verse thus would make it possible to see the line as referring to land either side of the Jordan. But the Sharon on the coastal plain to the west is much better known. There is little basis for saying that its partly marshy nature would make Sharon as a whole not very useful and would make Sharon a negative image, though 33.9 has envisaged it dried up like the area around the Dead Sea, while 35.2 indicates how its flowers could mean it was described as glorious (cf. Song 2.1). Another possible significance of the image is that Sharon was not part of Judah and not part of the Persian province of Yehud, so that this promise might need to imply not the transformation of Sharon but simply its renewed availability. While the Vale of Achor west of Jericho was part of Judah or Yehud, Hosea 2.17 [15] likewise promises that it will become a door of hope; as the story in Joshua reflects, for people coming into Canaan from across the Jordan it is on the natural route up into the mountains and to Jerusalem.[182] So both geographical expressions could suggest entering into possession of the land. There is no more reason to think that the Vale of Achor is unfertile and needed transformation than is the case with Sharon. So if the prophet had wanted to make a point about transformation, then there are more obvious ways to do so, as is reflected in proposals to emend ‘Sharon’ to something that suggests desert.[183] The parallelism more likely implies that both flocks and cattle will pasture and rest in both Sharon and Achor; Sharon (as such a substantial plain in the west) and Achor (as such a key valley in the east) signify the country as a whole by a kind of merism.[184]

The final colon in v. 10 suggestively takes up the first word in the chapter and behind it the invitation in 55.6-9. It is insofar as the people relate to Yhwh in a different way from that suggested by v. 1 that they can expect to experience a fulfilment of Yhwh’s promises. The ambivalence attaching to expressions such as ‘my people’ is underlined by the use of the expression here.

[182] Cf. Frank Moore Cross, *Canaanite Myth and Hebrew Epic* (Cambridge, MA: Harvard University Press, 1973), p. 110.

[183] Ehrlich (*Randglossen*, IV, p. 228) emends to ישימון ‘Jeshimon’, Klostermann (*Deuterojesaia*, p. 104) to השרב ‘parched ground’ (cf. 35.7; 49.10); cf. the Reuchlin ms of Tg.

[184] Cf. Delitzsch, *Jesaia*, p. 658 (ET II, p. 481). Saadia (‘Version d’Isaïe de R. Saadia’, p. 79) omits the place names and renders ‘plains and valleys’.

65.11 But you who are abandoning Yhwh,// who are putting my holy mountain out of mind,
You who are laying a table for Luck// and who are filling a mixing chalice for Destiny:
12 I shall destine you to the sword;// all of you will bow to the slaughter,
Because I have called but you have not responded,// I have spoken but you have not listened,
And you have done what was displeasing in my eyes;// what I did not delight in, you have chosen.

For vv. 11-16 the prophet turns back to the people who are destined to experience punishment and makes a more longstanding transition to direct address, taking up the double 'your' of v. 7. The first five lines comprise 3-3 parallel bicola, except for v. 12aγδ which is 4-3. They comprise one sentence whose syntactical centre or main clause is their spatial centre, v. 12aαβ. The opening two lines form an extraposed description of the sentence's object; in substance they provide the rationale for the declaration in the main clause. The closing two lines form subordinate clauses expressing that rationale in a different way. Tg addresses vv. 11-12 to 'you household of Israel', which resolves a question left unresolved by the verses' actual words, but does so in a way that the context does not really support. It is the faithless over against 'my servants' who are addressed.

Verse 11a works abcb′c′. The 'you' applies to both cola, then a participle and an adjective complement each other, as do their two objects. In general, the line recapitulates vv. 1-7. The idea of 'abandoning' Yhwh (as opposed to Yhwh abandoning Jerusalem) has come in Isaiah only in 1.4, 28 (in the latter passage, the same participial expression as here), though it is more frequent in Jeremiah (e.g. 17.13 for the participle; also 2.13, 17, 19). The idea of putting out of mind (*šākaḥ*), specifically putting the temple out of mind, is a novel one. The parallelism reflects the fact that the verb suggests a deliberate action rather than an accidental forgetting. The designation 'my holy mountain' is taken up from 56.7; 57.13. The critique makes for a grievous contrast with Yhwh's intention for other nations (56.7) and for Israelites who trust in Yhwh (57.13). The description in this line makes explicit that the people the chapter critiques are not worshipping Yhwh in the temple in a way of which the prophet disapproves. They are not even worshiping in a way that they would see as worship of Yhwh but that the prophet would view as abandoning Yhwh. They have given up worship in the temple.

In describing their alternative practice, v. 11b works neatly abca′b′c′, participles (one qal, one piel), *l-* expressions, and direct objects. In the second colon, the words for fill, mixing chalice, and Destiny all begin with *m*. Laying a table was what priests did in the temple in connection with the worship of Yhwh, though the precise expression perhaps suggests something especially generous (cf. Ps 23.5; Prov 9.2). Likewise libations or drink offerings were an aspect of worshipping Yhwh (see especially Num 28–29 [P]), though the reference to mixing drinks again suggests something more exotic than the Torah speaks of; LXX takes *mimsāk* to refer to a mixed drink rather than to the mixing chalice. The mixing might be with a sweetener or with the blossoms of the vine.[185] More importantly, these people are laying a table for Luck (*gad*). While the name may appear as an element in some names (and see Gen 30.11), this is the only direct reference to such a deity in the Old Testament. Texts that equate *gad* with Greek *tuchē* and Latin *fortuna* (cf. Vg) confirm its meaning, though the word later acquired the more general meaning 'spirit'. Likewise this verse includes the only reference to a god Destiny or Fortune (*m*ᵉ*nî*), though other Middle Eastern and Greco-Roman texts confirm the significance of the name. LXX alone translates the name in accordance with its particular meaning; other translations are more general.[186]

The middle line, v. 12aαβ, declares judgment on these worshippers in two cola that are parallel in substance and work abcb′c′a′, though they manifest more formal difference than the average pair of parallel cola. In the aa′ element, one verb is first-person singular, one third-person plural; the second goes beyond the first in moving from the destiny to the implementation. Linking with this, in the bb′ element one expression is object, one subject, but both have a second-person plural ending; the second goes beyond the first with its reference to 'all of us'. It is the cc′ element that manifests regular parallelism, both being *l*- expressions, one more concrete, one more abstract. Strictly, the opening verb (*ûmānîtî*) denotes counting people out, but it makes for a paronomasia with the word for Destiny (*m*ᵉ*nî*), a paronomasia that makes a point of substance. The people are interested in destiny; they will find a destiny other than the one they are looking for. 'Bow' (*kāra*ʿ) in turn makes for a paronomasia with 'lay' (ʿ*ārak*) in the preceding line; laying that table will turn out to have a close link with bowing to slaughter. The verb appears in vivid contexts in similar connections to the one here, in 46.1-2 and Judges 5.27; it is a different kind of bowing from the ones this verb sometimes connotes (e.g. Ps 95.6), but it does point to an analogous submission, though one forced and fruitless rather than possibly willing

[185] See Carey Ellen Walsh, *The Fruit of the Vine* (Winona Lake, IN: Eisenbrauns, 2000), pp. 203-5.

[186] On the two deities, see van der Toorn, Becking, and van der Horst (eds.), *Dictionary of Deities and Demons in the Bible* (Leiden: Brill; Grand Rapids: Eerdmans, 2nd edn, 1999), pp. 339-41, 566-68; and on LXX's contemporizing renderings τῷ δαίμονι and τῇ τύχῃ, see Joachim Schaper, 'God and the Gods', in K. J. Dell, G. Davies, and Y. V. Koh (eds.), *Genesis, Isaiah and Psalms* (J. Emerton Festschrift; Leiden: Brill, 2010), pp. 135-52 (139-52), with Jerome's comments on practices in Alexandria, *Commentariorum in Isaiam prophetam libri duodeviginti*, col. 639; and W. F. Lofthouse's comments on modern equivalents, 'Isaiah lxv. 11', *ExpT* 49 (1937–38), pp. 102-5. KJV had understood מני etymologically as 'that number' (see C. H. W. Johns, 'Isaiah xlv.12 [sic]', *ExpT* 10 (1898–99), p. 423.

and constructive (e.g. Isa 45.23). 'Down on one's knees for Lady Luck? Down on one's knees for impending disaster, God's judgement!'[187]

Verse 12aγδ returns to the basis for this declaration of judgment, and expresses it more explicitly in a 'because' clause. After the opening 'because', the line works neatly abca'b'c'. Two first-person singular qatal verbs balance each other; *w^e^lōʾ* follows each time; then two further second-person plural verbs close the cola. The reasoning restates Yhwh's opening statement in v. 1, though it does so in different words and in its wording reinstates the proper relationship between God and people. Now Yhwh is the one who calls or summons (*qārāʾ*) and speaks in the way appropriate to a master, though the servants do not respond or listen in the way appropriate to servants. The pairing call–respond recurs from 58.9 (where see the comment). Tg makes explicit that v. 12aγδ refers to the work of the prophets, as is explicit in the context when this language comes in Jeremiah 7.13, 27; 35.17. A past perfect translation of the verbs is appropriate; they refer to action whose effect continues, as the participles in v. 11 suggest.

Instead of listening (v. 12b), the servants have done as they liked. The line works abb'a', signaling the close of this subsection. 'You have done' is followed by 'you have chosen', which emphasizes the decision-making to which servants have no right. 'What was displeasing or bad [*raʿ*] in my eyes' is followed by 'what I did not want [*ḥāpēṣ*]'. While present translation of the noun clause and of the stative verb would be possible, the past reference of the opening verb likely carries over into them, and this is confirmed by the past reference of the closing verb. Doing what is displeasing in Yhwh's eyes was a characteristic feature of the community's life before the exile (e.g. 2 Kgs 23.32, 37; 24.9, 19). Nothing has changed. The contrast with eunuchs who choose what I delight in (Isa 56.4) is especially marked.[188] Isaiah as a whole uses the verb 'choose' (*bāḥar*) in two contrasting ways, in connection with the divine choice of a people (14.1; 41.8, 9; 43.10; 44.1, 2; 48.10; 49.7; 65.9, 15, 22) and of the human choice of something illicit or inappropriate (1.29; 40.20; 41.24; 65.12; 66.3, 4); the book uses it once of the human choice of something good (56.4), twice of God's choice of a kind of human action (58.5, 6), and once ironically of a responsive divine choice (66.4). All these usages come in chapters 56–66, where the notion of choice is thus prominent.[189] Here, the interweaving of references to human choice and divine choice (65.9, 12, 15, 22; 66.3, 4) indicates that it is not the case that 'the old theme is transformed from one in which God chooses his people to one where his people choose him'.[190] The chapters preserve the ambiguity about the relationship between these choices.

[187] Koole, *Jesaja III*, p. 395 (ET p. 425).
[188] Cf. Croatto, *Imaginar el futuro*, p. 417.
[189] Cf. Obara, *Le strategie di Dio*, p. 237.
[190] So Stromberg, *Isaiah after the Exile*, p. 82.

65.13 Therefore, my Lord Yhwh has said this:
Now: my servants, they will eat,// but you people will be hungry.
Now: my servants, they will drink,// but you people will be thirsty.
Now: my servants, they will celebrate,// but you people will be shamed.
14 Now: my servants, they will resound// from happiness of heart,
But you people will cry out// from pain of heart,// from brokenness of spirit you will howl.

The resumptive introduction to Yhwh's words in v. 13aα again looks extra-metrical. It is a variant on the basic simple formulation 'therefore, Yhwh has said this' (e.g. 37.33), though the formulation commonly appears in a slightly expanded form (e.g. 10.24; 28.16; 29.22), underlining the backing it offers for whatever words follow. Here, it is the expression 'my Lord'[191] that adds this effect. While the formulation can constitute a bridge between comments on the community's predicament, so that the message it introduces constitutes a promise, it commonly forms a bridge between comments on the community's waywardness, so that the message it introduces constitutes a warning; vv. 11-12 have prepared us to assume this is so here. Like any such proclamation of judgment, the verses implicitly constitute an urgent challenge to turn.

A series of 3-2 bicola contrast the fate of 'my servants' and 'you people' (the prophet simply says 'you'; I add 'people' to make clear that the pronoun is plural). While the contrast Jesus warns of in Matthew 25.31-46 compares with these verses,[192] the contrast he warns of in Luke 6.20-26 does so more closely.[193] On the other hand, the passage does not make explicit that 'my servants' are currently any more hungry, thirsty, ashamed, pained, or broken in spirit than other members of the Judahite community, and while this may be so, there is no compulsion to infer it.[194] The translation represents the way the subject 'my servants' comes in emphatic position before the verb and the way the prophecy repeats the pronoun 'you', which does not need to be included in order to establish the phrases' reference but underlines the contrast in the lines. The repeated declaration 'my servants' suggests a connection with 'my Lord' in the introduction to these words. The master is declaring what will happen to the servants. In v. 13aβγδε, two lines first speak of eating and drinking over against being hungry and thirsty. In v. 13b a similarly constructed 3-2 bicolon contrasts celebration and shame; the verb *śāmēaḥ* suggests rejoicing, but a rejoicing outwardly expressed. 'Shame' (*bûš*) likewise suggests an awareness of disgrace that is felt in relation to other people and not simply in oneself. The background of the promises and warnings lies in the 'belittlings' in Deuteronomy 28.45-48; the verb

[191] Or 'the Lord': see the comment on 61.1.

[192] So, e.g., Herbert, *Isaiah 40–66*, p. 186.

[193] Cf. Croatto, *Imaginar el futuro*, pp. 423-25; see further J. Severino Croatto, 'El origen isaiano de las bienaventuranzas de Lucas', *Revista Biblica* 59 (1997), pp. 1-16.

[194] Contrast Blenkinsopp, *Opening the Sealed Book*, p. 69.

'belittle' (*qālal* pual) will come in v. 20. Deuteronomy speaks of people who do not 'serve Yhwh your God with celebration and with happiness of heart' and who will experience 'hunger and thirst'; here, vv. 13-14 speak of 'my servants' who 'will celebrate…from happiness of heart', while 'you people will be hungry/thirsty'.[195] In addition, this reference to shame is one of the links between the closing chapters of the book and the opening chapter (see 1.29).

The first colon of v. 14a looks as if it is going to continue the pattern, but it transpires that the final description of 'my servants' occupies the whole line as the second colon expands on the first by explaining the reason for 'resounding' (*rānan*).[196] The outer noise suggested by this verb reflects an inner happiness. As the fourth positive description of 'my servants' thus receives a whole line, so does the fourth description of 'you people' in v. 14b. 'Cry out' (*ṣāʿaq*) is a classic term for the expression of anguish under suffering, especially in connection with the community's suffering in Egypt. That was suffering from which Yhwh rescued the people; this is suffering Yhwh will impose. In 57.13 the prophet has already used the related verb *zāʿaq* in warning people that they will cry out but find that their alternative spiritual resources cannot deliver them. The inner reason for the outward expression again follows, so that v. 14bαβ as a whole parallels v. 14a. As 'cry out' parallels 'resound', 'from pain of heart' parallels 'from happiness of heart'. It is this parallelism of the lines that suggests we should read v. 14bα as a 2-2 bicolon rather than simply a 4-beat colon. Either way, the developing weight through vv. 13-14 comes to a climax with an unexpected further colon to close the subsection. Verse 14bβ essentially restates v. 14bα though it uses more extreme terms. 'Pain' (*kᵉʾēb*) 'denotes pain or suffering that afflicts the very heart of life, bringing the sufferer close to his final end and damaging or destroying his ties with the circle of the living',[197] which is bad enough, but it gives way to 'breaking'; 'heart' gives way to 'spirit'; 'cry out' gives way to 'howl'. Like the last colon in vv. 11-12, this last colon reverses the word order so as to close the line with the verb and thus mark the close of the subsection. As well as adding *ṣdyqyʾ* 'the faithful' to 'my servants' each time, Tg adds *ršyʿyʾ* 'the faithless' to 'you people' on its first two occurrences.

195 Cf. Smith, *Rhetoric and Redaction in Trito-Isaiah*, p. 143.

196 J. T. A. G. M. van Ruiten ('The Role of Syntax in the Versification of Is 65:13-25', in Talstra and van Wieringen [eds.], *A Prophet on the Screen*, pp. 118-47 [124, 127]) treats vv. 14abα as a further (though longer) instance of the pattern, by regarding these as two 4-beat cola. This involves viewing 'from happiness of heart' and 'from pain of heart' as having one stress each, whereas I have followed MT here as elsewhere. Further, it seems to ignore the role of v. 14bβ as a second, parallel statement of the fate of 'you' (GID).

197 R. Mosis, *TWAT*, IV, p. 11 (ET *TDOT*, VII, p. 10).

65.15 You will leave your name as an oath for my chosen ones,// 'So shall my Lord Yhwh kill you',// but for his servants he will proclaim another name.
16 The person who prays for blessing in the land// will pray for blessing by the God who says 'Amen',
And the one who takes an oath in the land// will take the oath by the God who says 'Amen',
Because the former troubles will have been put out of mind,// and because they will have been hidden from my eyes.

Verses 15-16 continue the contrast between the destiny of 'you people' and that of 'my chosen ones' or 'my servants' (cf. v. 9), though it expresses it in a different way. Further, whereas vv. 13-14 used the destiny of 'my servants' to highlight that of 'you people', here the emphasis is eventually reversed; the destiny of 'you people' highlights that of 'my servants'. In content or logic, vv. 15-16 follow from vv. 13-14, as the destiny of 'you people' will issue in the result described in v. 15abα; the prospects of 'my servants' will be very different, though the contrast is worked out in a different way.

The prosody of v. 15 is not clear. I have taken the verse as a 4-3-4 tricolon. The first colon again raises a question ('What is the oath?') which the second colon answers. The oath will be a curse on someone; 'So shall my Lord Yhwh kill you'[198] is an abbreviated form of the curse, which would be implicitly filled out by 'in the same way as Yhwh killed those other people', the 'you people' of vv. 13-14 (Tg takes 'my Lord Yhwh will kill you' to refer to the 'second death'; cf. v. 6). Jeremiah 29.22 exemplifies such a curse. Although one would expect a jussive verb in such an oath, one could hardly say that yiqtol is impossible given the diversity in the expression of oaths and wishes in Hebrew.[199]

TNIV moves back the midpoint of the verse and implies a 2-2, 3-4 arrangement of the line; in terms of the translation above:

> You will leave your name// as an oath for my chosen ones,
> 'So shall my Lord Yhwh kill you',// but for his servants he will proclaim another name.

The first three cola then simply follow from one another, and one could say that the first colon raises the question 'to what end is Yhwh leaving the people's name?', which the second colon answers while also raising the question 'what is this oath?', which the third colon answers. The whole of v. 15abα is then paralleled by v. 15bβ. But TNIV's own translation points rather to

> You will leave your name// as an oath for my chosen ones.
> My Lord Yhwh will kill you,// but for his servants he will proclaim another name.

[198] Again, or 'the Lord': see the comment on 61.1.
[199] On which see JM 165; *IBHS* 40.2.2

In other words, the third colon ceases to indicate the content of the oath and the second line becomes internally parallel. The prosody and parallelism are now more plausible, but the difficulty the translation conceals is that the 'you' in the second line is singular and is surely too sudden and isolated; all the second-person forms on either side are plural.[200]

LXX understands 'another name' to denote 'a new name', the expression that came in 62.2; both expressions, 'a new name' and 'another name' come only in these two passages in the Old Testament. The implication would be that the motif of the name is used in two different ways in v. 15. After the declaration concerning the use of one group's name, we would expect a declaration concerning the use of the other group's name, but LXX implies that instead the prophet makes a knight's move. MT rather implies that the otherness of the name stands not over against what the servants' name used to be but over against the fact that the name of 'you people' is a name to be used in curses. This other name will be one to be used in blessings, in the manner described in Genesis 12.2 (J).

Verse 16 indeed goes on to speak of praying for blessing, first in two lines (3-3, 2-3) that are mutually parallel, then in an internally parallel line (4-3) that provides the rationale for the first two. Verse 16aαβ takes the point about blessing in a different direction. The problem with 'you people' is that they serve other deities, and they will thus pray for blessing in the name of other deities, asking that Luck or Destiny may smile on them. The expression 'pray for blessing' or more literally 'bless oneself' (*bārak* hitpael) comes most famously in Genesis 22.18; 26.4 (JE), but there it refers to other nations praying for Yhwh's blessing on the basis of what they see in Abraham and Isaac (cf. Ps 72.17). The occurrences in Deuteronomy 29.18 [19] and Jeremiah 4.2 look more significant because they refer to Israelites praying for blessing for themselves, and praying to Yhwh rather than to other deities, and they refer to oaths and curses taken in Yhwh's name rather than by other deities.

In the other occurrences of *bārak* hitpael, the *b-* denotes the standard to which the prayer for blessing appeals or the means whereby the blessing comes. Here in v. 16aβ 'by the God who says "Amen"' involves the second possibility. One might expect that the opening phrase in the line, 'the one who prays for blessing *bāʾāreṣ*' would denote 'the one who prays for blessing by the land'; the land would then be means whereby blessing comes.[201] This notion fits the general context in Isaiah 65, but the relationship between the land and God as the standard or means is then unclear, and the jump from the way earlier verses have spoken, to the idea of the land or earth as a standard or means of blessing, is sudden. It

[200] Ehrlich (*Randglossen*, IV, p. 229) emends the suffix to pl. (actually he emends to בהמיתכם).

[201] So Anne Gardner, 'Ecojustice or Anthropological Justice', in Norman C. Habel (ed.), *The Earth Story in the Psalms and the Prophets* (Sheffield: Sheffield Academic Press; Cleveland: Pilgrim, 2001), pp. 204-18 (210-12); she actually translates 'the earth' rather than 'the land'.

was not spotted by the Versions, which assume that the land or earth is the place where blessing is experienced, a common usage of *bārak* piel (e.g. Deut 15.4, with *bā'āreṣ*). The same argument applies to 'takes an oath by/in the land' in the next line.

Elsewhere, the reference in v. 16aγδ to the taking of oaths might relate to giving testimony in court; the deity in whose name people take an oath is the deity whom they expect to be active in the world bringing trouble on a person whose oath is false. Following on v. 15, it more likely refers to the uttering of a curse, though this might still be a self-curse. LXX translates the expression *bē'lōhê 'āmēn* 'by the true God', implying that the exclamation *'āmēn* is being used in the construct expression as a noun equivalent to *'ĕmet* or *'ĕmûnâ* (though it is, indeed, adjectival in form). Vg and Sym simply transliterate the word, implying that it has its usual significance (cf. Syr, which transliterates into its equivalent, *'myn*, and Aq, which translates it adverbially, 'faithfully', as it does elsewhere). The context in talk of prayers for blessing and of oaths suggests it does have its usual significance as indicating an affirmation of someone's words.[202] God can be relied on to say 'Amen' to one's curses and thus to see that they get fulfilled. Whatever the right grammatical understanding of the word, it suggests the reliability of the God who answers prayers for blessing, vindicates those who take true oaths, and implements curses uttered in this deity's name.

Verse 16b indicates that this blessing will indeed come because the past is the past and Yhwh is now active in answering the community's prayers. The idea of the former things (*hāri'šōnôt*) and of their being put out of mind (*šākaḥ*) is familiar (e.g. 43.18; 46.9). The identity of the former things may vary in different contexts; they might be former blessings, or former calamities such as the fall of Jerusalem and the exile. It would be easy for the term to apply here explicitly to former troubles such as the latter. In 43.18 and 46.9 the community itself is bidden to put the former things out of mind, and it would be natural to take v. 16b as a promise that the community will have done so. If this is the right understanding, then the parallel colon takes the promise in a different direction. Whereas Vg here has the troubles being hid 'from our eyes', which makes for a close parallel with the first colon, and LXX has a looser translation with similar implications, 'and it [the former trouble] will not come up on their mind',[203] MT has the troubles being hid 'from my eyes', so that it makes a different point. With some irony, the reference to hiding (*sātar* niphal) parallels 40.27 but also recalls 59.2. In 40.27 Jacob-Israel complained that its way was hidden from Yhwh, and in 59.2 the

[202] Cf. Egon Pfeiffer, 'Der alttestamentliche Hintergrund der liturgischen Formel "Amen"', *Kerygma und Dogma* 4 (1958), pp. 129-41 (138-39); Alfred Jepsen, *TWAT*, I, p. 347 (ET *TDOT*, I, p. 322).

[203] See Baer, *When We All Go Home*, pp. 140-54, on the way LXX may have been disturbed by the possible theological implications of MT.

prophet declared that the people's offenses had hidden Yhwh's face from them, while Psalm 51.11 [9] appeals to Yhwh to 'hide your face from my offenses'. In v. 16b the point is that Yhwh will have let the troubles (and the offenses that led to them) be hidden. This second colon then makes one revisit the first. While the repeated 'and because' opening the second colon may prepare the way for it to make rather a different point from the first, so that the line declares that the past is the past both for the community and for Yhwh, alternatively the second colon might clarify that the first also refers to Yhwh. It is Yhwh who has put the past troubles and their causes out of mind. This would fit the promise in 43.25 and the appeal in 64.10 [9] that Yhwh would keep the people's offenses in mind no longer, using *šākaḥ*'s antonym, *zākar*. It would then be natural to translate both qatal verbs as straightforward past verbs; Yhwh has already put the troubles and their causes out of mind. Another possible nuance of the line, however, arises from the fact that both verbs are niphal rather than pual or hophal. In particular, the niphal of *sātar* as often means 'hide' in an intransitive or reflexive sense as 'be hidden' by someone (e.g. 28.15), and the present line may indicate that the former troubles will pass out of mind and hide from Yhwh's eyes; the question of agency is then not prominent.

65.17 Because here I am, creating// new heavens and a new earth.
The former things will not be recollected;// they will not come to mind.

The statement in v. 16b was a revolutionary one; vv. 17-18 provides the needed backing for it. I take v. 17a as a 2-4 line; the second colon simply completes the first, answering the implicit question 'creating what?' While one might translate the participle 'about to create', since it indeed refers to something that is future, the use of the particle 'here' (*hinnēh*) and the participle brings the action before the hearers' eyes as something that is in effect happening now, so certain is it in Yhwh's intention.[204] The notion of creation is taken up from Isaiah 40–55, where it had a prominent place (cf. also 57.19). There, Yhwh's coming creative activity denotes Yhwh's imminent sovereign activity in the historical and political events that will shape Jacob-Israel's imminent destiny (e.g. 41.20; 45.7, 8; 48.7), and the preceding context would suggest it has the same implication here; succeeding lines will confirm this. In other words, the line does not signify a transition to 'eschatological' or 'apocalyptic' thinking.[205] The prophecy is not referring to the creation of a new planetary system or implying that Yhwh is going back to square one of the process

[204] Muilenburg sees the combination *kî hinnēh* ('because here [I am]') as giving 'dramatic and climactic force to the oracle' ('The Linguistic and Rhetorical Usages of the Particle כִּי in the Old Testament', p. 137).

[205] So, e.g., Pauritsch, *Die neue Gemeinde*, p. 174; of course both words are capable of various meanings (see further the 'Conclusion' to the commentary on 66.18-24).

of creation and repeating the event described in Genesis 1 in order to improve on the results. While later thinkers may take the line's language in this direction (e.g. 1 Enoch 91.16;[206] Rev 21.1-5),[207] this is not the prophet's idea. Neither preceding material in the book of Isaiah nor other material in the Old Testament has suggested any reason for thinking in terms of the creation of a new cosmos; there is nothing wrong with the physical heavens and earth themselves, even according to 51.6.[208] New heavens and a new earth is an image for a transformation of the way life works out for the community, 'a powerful metaphor for the complete transformation of Jerusalem within history'.[209] Yet this use of the motif of creation to describe Yhwh's transformation of Jerusalem also indicates how the passage takes the idea of creation in a different direction from that which obtains in Isaiah 40–55; Zion is '*the* theme of Third Isaiah'.[210] To put it another way, the 'new things' of Isaiah 40–55 have become more radically new, as succeeding verses will indicate.[211]

Indeed, it is tempting to translate the phrase 'a new heavens and a new land'.[212] 'By these metaphors he promises a remarkable change of affairs'; God intends not only to restore the people 'but to restore it in such a manner that it shall appear to gain new life and to dwell in a new world. These are exaggerated modes of expression; but the greatness of such a blessing...could not be described in any other way.'[213] LXX's omission of 'creating' here and in v. 18 is puzzling (it includes it at 66.22), but its translation does give the right impression: 'because the heavens will be new and the earth will be new'. Indeed, the construction in v. 19 suggests

[206] Barker sees the dependence in the other direction ('Isaiah', p. 540).

[207] See Jacques van Ruiten, 'The Influence and Development of Is 65,17 in 1 En 91,16', in Vermeylen (ed.), *The Book of Isaiah: Le Livre d'Isaïe*, pp. 161-66, and 'The Intertextual Relationship between Isaiah 65,17-20 and Revelation 21,1-5b' (see above). But talk in terms of cosmic catastrophe and the creation of a new world continues at least sometimes to be used as an image for this-worldly transformation, and we should be wary of a literalist understanding of such language in any New Testament writings: see, e.g., Richard A. Horsley, *Jesus and the Spiral of Violence* (repr., Minneapolis: Fortress, 1993), pp. 157-60; cf. N. T. Wright, *Jesus and the Victory of God* (Minneapolis: Fortress, 1987), pp. 449, 513. Pilchan Lee comments on the close relationship between the new Jerusalem and the new creation in Rev 21.1-2 (*The New Jerusalem in the Book of Revelation* [Tübingen: Mohr, 2001], p. 272).

[208] On which see Goldingay, *The Message of Isaiah 40–55*, p. 427.

[209] Margaret Dee Bratcher, 'Salvation Achieved: Isaiah 61:1-7; 62:1-7; 65:17–66:2', *Review and Expositor* 88 (1991), pp. 177-88 (183). Cf. Ulrich Berges, 'Der neue Himmel und die neue Erde im Jesajabuch', in Ferenc Postma, K. Spronk, and E. Talstra (eds.), *The New Things* (Henk Leene Festschrift; Maastricht: Shaker, 2002), pp. 9-15, though he sees the promise as designed to benefit and encourage only Yhwh's 'servants'.

[210] Cf. Richard J. Clifford, 'The Unity of the Book of Isaiah and Its Cosmogonic Language', *CBQ* 55 (1993), pp. 1-17 (16).

[211] Cf. Stromberg, *Isaiah after Exile*, p. 94.

[212] Cf. Watts, *Isaiah 34–66*, p. 922.

[213] Calvin, *In Iesaiam prophetam*, p. 409 (ET IV, pp. 397-98).

translating 'creating the heavens anew and the earth anew',[214] though MT's conjunctive accents support the traditional translation.

Verse 17b spells out a corollary of v. 17a in a 3-3 parallel line, which works abca′b′. Each colon begins with 'And not'; 'be recollected' and 'will come to mind' are then parallel; and the subject 'the former things', which closes the first colon and thus occupies pivot position, applies also to the second colon. The line restates v. 16b, with 'the former things' restating 'the former troubles'. Like v. 16b, it might then imply reference to Yhwh's remembering or to that of the community; the next line will suggest the latter. Whereas Isaiah 40–55 spelled out that Yhwh's new act was something like a new exodus, here the subsequent context will make more explicit than v. 16b that the new act involves the creation of a new Jerusalem.[215] Even if Lamentations Rabbah's comment does not identify the new world with Jerusalem itself, its comment that v. 17 undoes the negative remembering of Lamentations 1.7 is striking.[216]

65.18 Rather: rejoice and be joyful forever// in what I am creating.
Because here I am, creating// Jerusalem a joy, its people a rejoicing.
19 I will rejoice in Jerusalem,// be joyful in my people.
There will not make themselves heard in it again// the sound of weeping or the sound of a cry.

The two lines of v. 18 (3-3, 3-4 or 3-2-2) confirm aspects of the interpretation of vv. 16-17. Once again the two lines are mutually but not internally parallel. They work abb′a′, with the references to rejoicing and joy (themselves in abb′a′ order) in the outside cola and the participle 'creating' in the inside cola. As a whole, then, v. 18 forms a chiasm.[217] This participle, and indeed the complete phrase 'here I am, creating', take up directly from v. 17. 'Jerusalem' and 'its people' replace 'new heavens' and 'new earth'; it is in them that the renewal of creation is to happen. It is not even that Jerusalem is at the centre of the new world; 'the new creation *is* Jerusalem'.[218] It will not be surprising if the appropriate response is then one that can last 'forever'. This responsive rejoicing and joy replace the community's mindfulness of the former troubles; in other words, Yhwh's promise is not merely that the negative awareness will be gone but that a celebratory awareness will replace it. Creating Jerusalem and its people [into] a joy and rejoicing (the first two nouns both feminine, the second two both masculine[219]) implies that they will become

[214] Elliger, 'Der Prophet Tritojesaja', p. 132.
[215] Cf. Lau, *SchriftgelehrteProphetie in Jes 56–66*, p. 135; also Elliger's comment on v. 9, *Die Einheit des Tritojesaia*, p. 100.
[216] Lam. R., commenting on Lam 1.2.
[217] Cf. Fitzgerald, 'A Rhetorical Analysis of Isaiah 56–66', p. 324.
[218] Kraus, *Das Evangelium der unbekannten Propheten*, p. 241.
[219] Cf. Watson, *Traditional Techniques in Classical Hebrew Verse*, p. 211.

a place and a people that are characterized by a celebratory joyfulness. In v. 18a, Vg's 'you will rejoice and be joyful' correctly interprets the imperatives as a form of promise.[220] The picture of transformation takes up and reverses the threat of Jeremiah 7.34; 16.9; 25.10, which speaks of an end to joy and rejoicing in Jerusalem. Jeremiah associates this joy and rejoicing with the celebration of a bride and groom, and an awareness of this connection would link with the promises that follow in vv. 20-23. But in addition, in light of the link between v. 21 and Jeremiah 29.5, we might note the reversal involved in the threefold occurrence of *gîl/gîlâ* in vv. 18-19a, which contrasts with the double occurrence of *gālâ/gôlâ* in Jeremiah 29.4: joy replaces exile.[221]

The two lines of v. 19 (2-2, 3-4) take up again the involvement of both Yhwh and community in reacting to the restoration of which previous lines have spoken. Whereas v. 18a spoke explicitly of the community's rejoicing and joy, v. 19a in its two parallel cola (aba′b′) speaks explicitly of Yhwh's rejoicing and joy, using the same two verbs. Conversely, whereas v. 18a thus encouraged the community to rejoice, v. 19b promises the removal of what counts as the antithesis of rejoicing and joy, though it does so following the formal structure of v. 18b in which the second colon comprises two phrases that are themselves parallel but complete the structure of the line as a whole—this time providing the verb in the first colon not with its object but with its subject. The end of crying (*zeʿāqâ*) recalls v. 14 (*ṣāʿaq*).

65.20 There will not be from there again// a baby of a few days// or an old man who does not fulfil his days,
Because the youth will die as a person of a hundred years// and the sinner will be belittled as a person of a hundred years.
21 People will build houses and live [there],// they will plant vineyards and eat their fruit.
22 They will not build and someone else live [there],// they will not plant and someone else eat.
Because the days of my people will be like the days of a tree;// my chosen ones will use up the work of their hands.
23 They will not labour in vain// and they will not give birth to dismay,
Because offspring blessed by Yhwh,// they and their descendants with them, will be.

Verses 20-23 move on to down-to-earth expressions of what this joy-bringing restoration will look like. The two parallel lines of v. 20 begin with its implications for people's length of life. I understand v. 20a as a 3-2-4 tricolon in which the first colon again raises a question, namely 'What is the subject of this verb?'; the second and third cola give two

[220] See further the translation note.
[221] Cf. Sommer, *A Prophet Reads Scripture*, pp. 41-43.

parallel answers. ‘A baby of a few days’ is literally ‘a baby of days’;[222] the complementary expression refers to a man who does not see out his expected lifespan. Christian writers come to assume that the line refers to the way everyone will enjoy eternal life,[223] but this assumption highlights the way the prophet is actually envisaging a full earthly life. The promise of Exodus 23.26 will come true.[224]

Verse 20b (5-4) re-expresses the point in two parallel cola, abcdeb′c′d′e′. Its first colon balances the first of the two previous parallel cola (v. 20aα). Not only will babies not die in infancy; even a person who dies in youth will live to a hundred before doing so. Verse 20bβ is more problematic. The structure of the colon is the same, and Vg and Tg are surely right to assume that the two cola have parallel meanings along the lines suggested in the translation above (contrast LXX). This also works against the idea that the sinner (*ḥôṭe*ʾ) is someone who ‘falls short’ of a hundred years, which involves giving the word an unusual meaning as well as compromising the parallelism of the line. Indeed, Tg assumes that the two cola have the same reference; the youth is the sinner: if someone dies at a hundred, he will be seen as a youth and his death assumed to be due to sin and to God’s curse.[225] In Deuteronomy 30.19 blessing and belittling (*qālal*), life and death, are set alongside each other, suggesting that here, too, being belittled is another way of describing death. The prophecy thus continues to make its point with extravagance in declaring that even a sinner will live to a hundred years, and only then will have the belittling that is associated with death descend on him. A ‘sinner’ will be not any ordinary human being but someone who has offended in noteworthy ways; even this person will still live out a hundred years. The presupposition is that in general, however, people will live the kind of life-spans that people lived in Genesis before the flood. In this sense ‘the world will at last be again as it was at the beginning’.[226] Yet there is no suggestion that death will have been abolished, as 25.8 may imply, another indication that the prophecy does not think in apocalyptic fashion.[227] In contrast to Daniel 12, the prophecy envisages a prolonging of earthly human existence not a compensation for its shortening.[228]

222 Francis S. North suggests that ‘days’ denotes a season, four months: see ‘Four-Month Seasons of the Hebrew Bible’, *VT* 11 (1961), pp. 446-48 (448).

223 E.g. Eusebius of Caesarea, *Der Jesajakommentar*, on the passage; Albert the Great, *Postilla super Isaiam*, p. 618.

224 Cf. A. Gardner, ‘Isaiah 65, 20’, *Biblica* 86 (2005), pp. 88-96 (93).

225 Cf. D. Qimchi, ‘ישעיה’, on the passage.

226 Ibn Ezra, *The Commentary of Ibn Ezra on Isaiah*, p. 298. Seitz finds a broader resonance with the opening chapters of Genesis in vv. 17-25 (‘The Book of Isaiah 40–66’, pp. 544-45); see also Odil Hannes Steck, ‘Der neue Himmel und die neue Erde’, in Ruiten and Vervenne (eds.), *Studies in the Book of Isaiah*, pp. 349-65.

227 Cf. Lau, *Schriftgelehrte Prophetie in Jes 56–66*, p. 138.

228 Cf. Robert Martin-Achard, ‘L’espérance des croyants d’Israël face à la mort selon Esaïe 65, 16c-25 et selon Daniel 12, 1-4’, *RHPR* 59 (1979), pp. 439-51. Irenaeus

Verses 21-22a (3-4, 4-4) put the point in a different way in a pair of lines that are mutually and internally parallel. In the first, abca′b′c′d, each comprises a *w*-consecutive third-person plural qatal qal verb, then a masculine plural noun as object, then another *w*-consecutive third-person plural qatal qal verb. While we might have expected something to follow the second verb in the first colon, the first colon does not satisfy our expectation (the Versions resist the temptation to provide something, but modern translations yield to it). Then the second colon maintains interest by providing an object at this point, a further object for its second verb. The second line, abcda′b′c′d′, is precisely parallel, comprising a negative (*lō'*), a third-person plural yiqtol qal verb (the yiqtol form of the verb from the previous line), the expression 'and someone else', and a further third-person yiqtol qal verb, now singular (again the yiqtol form of the verb from the previous line). Here even the second verb lacks the expected object, so that in this respect the line as a whole is more compressed. There are human activities that make sense only as an investment that may be expected to pay a dividend over a period of years or after a period of years. Building a house might take months or years but people hope to live in it for decades; yet a calamity such as the fall of a city to an enemy army may mean the house's destruction, or its builder may die young. Planting vines may take a shorter time (though the construction of terraces introduces a new factor into such calculations), but they take some years to reach fruitfulness, and they too are vulnerable to destruction by enemies invading the land, while their planter is vulnerable to death before his time. As was the case in v. 18, the prophet here reverses a threat fulfilled in the fall of Jerusalem (see Deut 28.30; also Amos 5.11; Zeph 1.13), which was itself an ironic reversal of a promise associated with the people's arrival in Canaan (Deut 6.10-11). Part of the background is the reality of war and especially siege, which did mean the destruction of people's homes and of the bases of their subsistence systems, which led to the incorporation of such threats in curses that are part of the more immediate background to the verse.[229] In turn this line reverses the command in Jeremiah 29.5, which constituted a warning that the exile was not to be over in a few years.[230] It thus also takes up a motif that appeared in 62.8-9, though here it is set in a broader context of the way human life commonly falls short of people's hopes and longings; there is no reference to enemies, as there was in 62.8-9. The section thus turns away from a concern with Israel's situation in relation to the nations, which was important through 60.1–64.11 [12], because of its

(*Against Heresies* 4.34) assumes that the fulfilment of the prophecy will come on earth after the resurrection.

229 See, e.g., Jeremy D. Smoak, 'Building Houses and Planting Vineyards', *JBL* 127 (2008), pp. 19-35.

230 Stromberg (*Isaiah after the Exile*, pp. 98-101) argues rather for a link with the similar wording in Isa 37.30.

focus on a division within Israel that leads to a different judgment.[231] The verses' presupposition is that 'the ideal life' is 'not one of idleness but of satisfying work',[232] and the notion of looking forward to retirement would be seen as odd. Further, the promises make for a suggestive contrast with 3.14-15, which note that the loss of one's house and vineyard in Judah has commonly issued from the deliberate oppression of the weak by the powerful. In the new Jerusalem, there will be no such oppression.[233]

The two cola in v. 22b (4-4) are parallel in substance, though not in form. They are also parallel in substance to the preceding lines, particularly v. 21, though they extend the argument in two ways. First, they move from the destiny of individuals to that of the people as a whole. 'My people' (cf. vv. 10, 19) is paralleled by 'my chosen ones' (cf. vv. 9, 15). Then they make a more far-reaching promise in comparing the lifetime of the people to that of a tree (LXX and Tg take this much further in rendering 'tree of life' and making the passage refer to eternal life).[234] Their audience will have known that this could be much more than a human lifetime, though they would likely not know how many centuries it could be. As the first colon parallels and exceeds the preceding promise about building a house, the second colon parallels and exceeds the preceding promise about the vineyard. Yhwh's chosen ones will have the chance to consume or use up or use to the full all the crops they work for. Declaring that it would be so got a pastor and political activist into trouble in the context of a strike in 1919.[235]

Verse 23 makes yet another restatement of the point, in two lines that are both internally and mutually parallel, the first negative, the second positive. The first (3-3) works neatly abca′b′c′: a negative *lōʾ* (the second prefaced by *w*-), a third-person masculine plural yiqtol qal verb, and a *l*- expression. First, people will not toil to no end. The word for toil or labour (*yāgaʿ*), like those English words, suggests the hard work that can be involved in farming or building; they can imply the weariness such labour induces, but they do not necessarily imply a negative attitude to it (see 62.8; Josh 24.13). In contrast, 'labouring in vain' (*lārîq*) is an inherently negative idea. The root idea of *rîq* is emptiness, and one can see this idea applying to work on the farm in a literal sense if the work produces nothing. Leviticus 26.16, 20 [H] speaks of farming that turns

[231] Cf. Jones, 'Isaiah—II and III', p. 534.

[232] Whybray, *Isaiah 40–66*, p. 278.

[233] See Park, *Die Gerechtigkeit Israels und das Heil der Völker*, pp. 330-31.

[234] In commenting on Gen 2.4a, Gen. R. 12.6 explicltly refers to v. 22b as implying the gift of immortality, while Justin Martyr (*Dialogue with Trypho* 81) seems to make a link between this line and the tree of knowledge (cf. Skarsaune, *The Proof from Prophecy*, pp. 404-5).

[235] See Walter Brueggemann, 'Five Strong Rereadings of the Book of Isaiah', in M. Daniel Carroll R., D. J. A. Clines, and P. R. Davies (eds.), *The Bible in Human Society* (John Rogerson Festschrift; Sheffield: Sheffield Academic Press, 1995), pp. 87-104 (98-100).

out to be 'in vain', and significantly speak of this failure as a punishment for declining to obey Yhwh. The more immediate background of the present verse is Isaiah 49.4.

The second colon returns to the subject of the birth of children. The qal verb *yālad* usually refers to a woman giving birth, but it can refer to begetting and it is here masculine in form. Zechariah 13.3 uses it to refer to fathering and mothering together, which might be the reference here. The expression for 'to dismay' (*labbᵉhālâ*) comes from a root that suggests the occurrence of something sudden, unexpected, and horrifying. Aq, Sym, Th have 'in haste'. But the cause of such 'dismay' is often sudden death;[236] the word is almost a euphemism. Once again the expression parallels Leviticus 26.16 as part of a warning about the consequences of disobedience that came true with the exile, but are now reversed. LXX has 'give birth for a curse' (cf. Syr), a rendering that makes for a contrast with the statements in the preceding line and the following line. The rendering reflects the difficulty of giving precision to what the cause of sudden dismay might be. Tg has simply 'death', which at one level must be right; the causes of dismay might include stillbirth or death in infancy, or losing one's children to sickness or war. OL's 'give birth in/with a curse' is less literal (the Hebrew preposition is *l*-) but might be closer in substance.

Verse 23b states the positive point. MT's accents suggest dividing the line after 'they' (*hēmmâ*):

> Because they will be offspring blessed by Yhwh,// and their descendants with them.

LXX implies the same understanding, though many manuscripts lack 'and their descendants will be with them'.[237] But the 5-2 division of the line would be unusual and more likely 'they and their descendants after them' is the subject and 'will be offspring blessed by Yhwh' is the predicate (so Tg). On the basis of MT, there is some parallelism in the pairing of 'they' and 'their descendants after them'; on my proposed division of the line, the first colon raises the question 'Who are we talking about?' and the second colon gives the answer. Either way, 'they' are the people who have been the subject of vv. 21-23a, Yhwh's people and Yhwh's chosen ones; their descendants are the children who issue from the birthing referred to in v. 23aβ. In v. 9 Yhwh's servants and chosen ones were identified as offspring Yhwh brought forth from Jacob; in light of vv. 21-23a, v. 23b adds that they can of course count among these offspring their own descendants (*ṣeʾĕṣāʾîm*; the word derives from the verb *yāṣāʾ* from which the term for 'brought forth' came). Vg takes

[236] Cf. Benedikt Otzen, *TWAT*, I, pp. 522-23 (*TDOT*, II, p. 5).

[237] Ziegler (*Buch Isaias*, p. 364) omits the words, Rahlfs (*Septuaginta*, II, p. 654) includes them.

'offspring' as construct and thus understands them to be 'the offspring of people blessed by Yhwh', the people blessed by Yhwh being Israel's ancestors: see, e.g., Genesis 12.2; 25.11. In light of Isaiah 65.9 we might think especially of Yhwh's blessing of Jacob (Gen 35.9). But in the light of Isaiah 61.9, more likely MT's accents, Tg, and LXX are right to take 'blessed by Yhwh' as in apposition to 'offspring'. That declaration fits with what precedes, insofar as the nature of blessing lies in fruitfulness, especially in having children. In substance Yhwh's chosen servants have been promised that they will be blessed, not merely that they will be the offspring of the blessed. So the line sums up vv. 21-23 by affirming that the present generation and their children will indeed experience Yhwh's blessing.

65.24 Before they call, I myself will respond;// while they are still speaking, I myself will listen.

From the immediately preceding verses, the transition of thought in v. 24 is sudden, but the prophecy is returning to a motif from the opening of the chapter, which referred to the fact that people were not calling on Yhwh. It is also returning to v. 12aγδ whose wording it takes up systematically; all four of that line's verbs reappear here. When Yhwh called and spoke in the manner of a master, Israel did not respond or listen in the manner proper to a servant. When Israel calls and speaks in the manner of a servant, Yhwh will respond and listen in the manner of a master.

While the length of the verse could suggest it comprises two parallel lines in each of which the second colon completes the first, with the *wᵉhāyâ* ('and it will be the case that') at the beginning of the verse applying to both lines, this latter feature makes it more likely that the verse is one internally parallel line. On MT's construal the verse's rhythm is then 4-5, whereas cola usually comprise two, three, or four stresses. It would be quite possible to understand *ʿôd hēm* ('they still') as sharing a stress and thus to link them by a maqqeph; for *ʿôd* followed by maqqeph, see Genesis 45.28; Ruth 1.11, while a maqqeph often links *hēm* to the preceding word. We can then understand the verse as a 4-4 parallel bicolon. While flexible attitudes to MT's understanding of the rhythm or metre of lines is inclined to issue in emendation of lines 'for the sake of the metre', and in general I prefer to play safe and stay with the Masoretes' understanding, in this instance I incline to suggest that we do add the maqqeph. The line thus works abcdb′c′d′. After the opening *wᵉhāyâ* applying to both cola, 'before they call' is balanced by 'while they are still speaking', a qatal verb balanced by a participial expression. The two temporal terms balance each other. If we are to be prosaic about the line's significance, the second presumably qualifies the first; either Yhwh will respond before they call, or if they get as far as speaking, Yhwh will listen and act before they have finished speaking. Following the phrases about calling and speaking, each colon begins its main clause with *wa'ănî*. The repeated redundant pronoun emphasizes Yhwh's personal involvement but also underlines the contrast with v. 12: *you* did not respond or listen, but *I* do so. Each colon then follows the pronoun by a first-person singular qal yiqtol verb. The sequence of 'responding' and 'listening' may seem odd. It reflects the fact that on one hand 'responding' a prayer is at stage one a matter of words, which will in due course lead to action; and on the other hand, 'listening' is not merely a matter of hearing but of responding to what one hears.

In the broad context of the chapter, then, v. 24 pairs with v. 1 and presupposes that the community will now call on Yhwh instead of calling on other deities. In the more immediate context of vv. 17-23, the line makes a different point, not one about the community but one about Yhwh. Weeping or crying out will not be heard, either because nothing that warrants them will happen, or because Yhwh will do something about them before people have chance to call on Yhwh or while they are still speaking their prayers.

65.25 The wolf and the lamb—they will feed as one;// the lion like the ox—it will eat straw;// the snake—dirt will be its food.
They will not do wrong or destroy// on all my holy mountain
(Yhwh has said).

The final verse closes off the promises in a more down to earth way. Verse 10 spoke of pasture for flocks and a resting place for cattle; v. 25 speaks of the meeting of the complementary need that their owners need to see fulfilled for them, the need for protection from other, dangerous creatures. The first line makes the point in vivid and concrete pictures, the second makes explicit the implication in a generalization, and the final extra-metrical colon provides backing for the statements.

Verse 25a (4-3-3) covers three especially dangerous creatures, standing for dangerous animals in general. All three cola are more or less parallel, though the first two are more so. Each begins with a predator and a potential victim, though in the first colon these are linked by *w*-, in the second by *k*-. The subjects appear in advance of their third-person plural yiqtol qal verbs (one plural, one singular), which have similar meaning and which now follow; the cola are completed by expressions that are parallel in position though not in substance, though the first (at least) applies to both cola. It is tempting this time to remove the maqqeph between *yō'kal* and *teben* ('eat straw') and render the cola a more perfect 4-4, abcda'b'c'd' pair.

Lion and wolf are the dangerous animals in Zephaniah 3.3 and the first two dangerous animals in Jeremiah 5.6; leopard follows. Wolf and leopard appear in Habakkuk 1.8; wolf appears alone in Ezekiel 22.27. Most comprehensively, wolf, leopard, lion, bear, cobra, and viper feature in Isaiah 11.6-8 in the company of lamb, goat, calf, yearling, cow, and ox, and the vision there leads into a promise in words identical to those in v. 25b. The use of the nominal expression 'mountain of holiness' is typical of Isaiah 56–66 and might suggest that Isaiah 11.6-9 (or at least v. 9a) is based on 65.25 rather than vice versa.[238]

The context in Isaiah 11 leaves open the possibility that the animals are metaphors for human beings, and Cyril of Alexandria refers it to harmony between Jews and Gentiles or between Christians and their persecutors,[239] but the context in Isaiah 65 suggests a literal understanding; the picture is of wolf and lion, lamb and ox eating together, rather than of wolf and lion eating domestic animals. Although at one level the prophecy makes a literal statement, farmers would perhaps be aware that wolves and lions cannot actually be imagined as living on a diet of straw, and the statement may be a hyperbole, or a metaphor for the complete safety of flocks and herds. Further, it implies the fulfilment of the creation intention of Genesis 1 (P).[240] The snake is a further danger to animals as to human beings, so it is not so surprising to see it included (though NEB omits this third colon). The description of its eating corresponds in content though not in wording with Genesis 3.15 (J), 'dirt you will eat', though the point about the words is different. In Genesis the words explain the way a snake lives its life crawling along the ground, apparently eating dirt. In Isaiah its habit of eating dirt is the reason the snake will not be seeking to eat other creatures.

In this context, the two cola in v. 25b (2-2) that correspond in wording to 11.9a refer to the safety of the animals on 'all my holy mountain', a term taken up from v. 11 but here denoting the holy land as a whole as in 57.13. Animals thus have a place in the region of the holy mountain; the divine inclusivity announced in 56.3-8 applies to them. 'God's sacred space welcomes all'.[241] Once again the second colon simply completes the statement begun in the first. The verb 'do harm' (*yārēʿû*) makes for a nice paronomasia with the verb 'feed' (*yirʿû*); feeding together rules out doing wrong. The verb 'destroy' (*šāḥat*) is taken up from v. 8.

[238] On the relationship of the two passages, see J. T. A. G. M. van Ruiten, 'The Intertextual Relationship between Isa 11,6-9 and Isa 65,25', in F. García Martínez, A. Hilhorst, and C. J. Labuschagne (eds.), *The Scriptures and the Scrolls* (A. S. van der Woude Festschrift; Leiden: Brill, 1992), pp. 31-42; also Stromberg, *Isaiah after Exile*, pp. 101-9; Nurmela, *The Mouth of the Lord Has Spoken*, pp. 127-28; Richard L. Schultz, 'Intertextuality, Canon, and "Undecidability": Understanding Isaiah's "New Heavens and New Earth" (Isaiah 65:17-25)', *Bulletin for Biblical Research* 20 (2010), pp. 19-38 (32-34).

[239] 'Εξήγησις ὑπομνηματική εἰς τὸν προφήτην 'Ησαΐαν, cols. 320-26.

[240] See David H. Wenkel, 'Wild Beasts in the Prophecy of Isaiah', *Journal of Theological Interpretation* 5 (2011), pp. 251-64.

[241] John W. Olley, '"The Wolf, the Lamb, and a Little Child"', in Habel (ed.), *The Earth Story in the Psalms and the Prophets*, pp. 219-29 (227). On the question as it arises in early Christian interpretation, see Vinzenz Buchheit, 'Tierfriede bei Hieronymus und seinen Vorgängern', *Jahrbuch für Antike und Christentum* 33 (B. Kötting Festschrift; Münster: Aschendorff, 1990), pp. 21-35.

Whereas 11.6-9 is set in the context of references to the root or stump of Jesse (11.1-5, 10), v. 25 does not take up this aspect of the passage. Insofar as it is set in the context of promises concerning David, this context is the application of such promises to the whole people (55.3-5). It is not the case that 'the editor of chapter 65 fashioned his vision of the eschatological hope to include, in some fashion, the messianic hope of First Isaiah along with the promises of Second Isaiah'.[242] This editor's work continues the 'strong rereading' of the attitude to David that appears in passages such as Isaiah 11; while his work focuses on the temple more than Isaiah 40–55 does, this focus does not carry with it an interest in David or an individual Davidic ruler.[243] 'The main point of chap. 11...is missing'.[244] But one could say that the book of Isaiah as a whole indeed embraces the 'messianic' and 'non-messianic' forms of hope and leaves them standing alongside each other.[245]

(c) Comment: 66.1-17

In 65.8-25 the prophecy spoke *to* the people who have abandoned Yhwh and spoke *about* the people who can be called Yhwh's servants (at least, rhetorically it did so; no doubt the prophet's words were meant for the latter, but in listening to them they are formally overhearing words spoken about themselves). In 66.1-17 it reverses the rhetoric.

Verses 1-6 major on critique. Verses 3-4 speak *about* the people who (from the prophecy's perspective, at least) have turned away from Yhwh. I take vv. 1-2 as speaking *to* the people who have not turned away; it does so in a fashion that is also initially confrontational, though eventually encouraging. Verses 5-6 continue that address. Verses 1-6 as a whole may be understood as working abcc′b′a′:

- 1-2a A proclamation about the temple
  - 2b An affirmation of the crushed, the people who tremble at Yhwh's word
    - 3a A declaration concerning people involved in wrong forms of worship
    - 3b-4 A declaration concerning people involved in wrong forms of worship
  - 5 An affirmation of the crushed, the people who tremble at Yhwh's word
- 6 A proclamation about the temple[246]

[242] So Childs, *Isaiah*, p. 539.

[243] Against Stromberg, *Isaiah after Exile*, pp. 183-205.

[244] Paul, ישעיה פרקים מ-סו, II, p. 553 (ET p. 607).

[245] Cf. Tremper Longman, 'Isaiah 65:17-25', *Interpretation* 64 (2010), pp. 72-73.

[246] Cf. Cf. Jill Middlemas, 'Divine Reversal and the Role of the Temple in Trito-Isaiah', in Day (ed.), *Temple and Temple Worship in Biblical Israel*, pp. 164-87 (178-79).

66.1 Yhwh has said this:
The heavens are my throne,// the earth is my footstool.
Wherever could be the house that you would build for me,// wherever the place that would be my abode,
2a When all these things my hand made;// thus all these things came to be? (Yhwh's declaration.)

Verses 1-2a belong together in content and are set off from what precedes and follows by the extra-metrical introduction corresponding to that in 65.9 and the extra-metrical conclusion like that in 59.20. The combination of these two expressions framing vv. 1-2a puts great emphasis on the declaration that comes between, which quite changes the subject in relation to what precedes. The declaration (vv. 1aβγb-2a) comprises three internally parallel bicola (2-3, 4-3, 3-2). In the first two, all the main clauses are noun clauses; the third then comprises verbal clauses.

The first (v. 1aβγ) works simply aba′b′, with 'heavens' and 'earth' forming a common word pair and 'throne' and 'footstool' forming a natural one, though not one that recurs. The second bicolon works abca′b′c′, with the interrogative repeated, 'place' balancing 'house' and the *'ăšer* applying to the second colon as well as the first. The collocation of 'you would build for me' and '[would be] my abode' shows more mutual independence in form, a verbal clause and a noun clause, and mutual interdependence in content, as the noun clause indicates the purpose of the verbal clause; prosaically put, 'that you would build for me as my abode'. Indeed, one could infer that the whole of 'that you would build for me' carries over into the second colon.

While the idea that Yhwh's throne is *in* the heavens recurs (e.g. Ps 11.4), only here does the Old Testament declare that the heavens *are* Yhwh's throne.[247] Likewise the idea that Yhwh has a footstool recurs, but elsewhere the footstool is Yhwh's covenant chest (Ps 132.7) or the temple as a whole (Pss 99.5; 132.7; Lam 2.1). These words in Isaiah 66 form a particular contrast with Yhwh's declaration in Ezekiel 43.7 that the temple is 'the place of my throne and the place for the soles of my feet, where I will dwell in the midst of the Israelites forever'. First Chronicles 28.2 refers to David's desire to 'build' an 'abode' (*mᵉnûḥâ*, as here; cf. also Ps 132.8, 14) for Yhwh's covenant chest, which is then identified as 'our God's footstool'. In building the temple, Solomon recognizes the illogic in the idea of building a house for the God who cannot be contained by the heavens (1 Kgs 8.27) but claims God's promise to put his name there. The declaring of the name 'Yhwh' brings home the reality of the person, as regularly happens when we declare someone's name.[248] Second Samuel 7.4-13 also illustrates the possibility

[247] Cf. Zapff, *Jesaia*, p. 431; Gärtner, *Jesaja 66 und Sacharja 14 als Summe der Prophetie* (see above), p. 63.

[248] Stromberg (*Isaiah after Exile*, p. 20) notes that 1 Kings 8 has a vision of the temple as a place toward which foreigners might pray as well as combining questioning of the

of questioning while affirming the idea of building a temple (whereas 2 Sam 7 plays with the fact that *bayit* can mean both house and household, it requires too much inference to take 'house' and 'abode' in Isa 66.1 to refer to Israel).[249] On the other hand, in the context of 65.8-25 perhaps we should infer that questions about temple-building need to be set in the context of Yhwh's intention to create a new heavens and a new earth in Jerusalem.[250]

Isaiah 66 thus begins by taking to its radical extreme the point Solomon makes. It portrays Yhwh in much bigger terms than happens when one speaks of a throne *in* the heavens and of the covenant chest as a footstool. In light of the fact that the whole cosmos is Yhwh's throne and the earth itself is Yhwh's footstool, the idea of building a house for Yhwh becomes a nonsense. One might see the prophecy as working out the logic of 40.12-26.[251] Where on earth or even within the cosmos, which are themselves Yhwh's footstool and throne, could you put a house for Yhwh to sit invisibly enthroned and for Yhwh's footstool to be located? Parallel within the second line to 'house', 'place' (*māqôm*) will have the specific connotation of 'worship place' (e.g. 18.7; 60.13). In referring to vv. 1-2, Acts 7.49-50 notes that David and Solomon indeed had no business attempting such a foolish project.[252] While the quotation there is approximate, it draws attention to LXX's taking up the other possible meaning of *'ê-zeh* as asking 'what kind of house?' (cf. Eccles 2.3; 11.6), and it follows LXX slightly less explicitly in asking 'what would be the place of my abode?'. While 'where' is much the more common meaning of *'ê-zeh*, both 'wherever' and 'whatever' fit here, the former in relation to the preceding colon, the latter in relation to v. 2a.[253]

Yhwh's declaration might be set over against Middle Eastern assumptions expressed in *Enuma elish* about the building of a temple for the deity, a project linked with creation and its celebration.[254] Its content does not suggest that it opposes the attempt of one party to control the temple, reflecting (for instance) the conflict between a prophetic group and a

temple and affirmation of the temple, and that this corresponds to emphases in the opening and closing chapters of Isaiah 56–66.

[249] So Edwin C. Webster, 'A Rhetorical Study of Isaiah 66', *JSOT* 34 (1986), pp. 93-108; 35 (1986), p. 121 (95-96).

[250] Cf. Ulrich Berges, 'Gottesgarten und Tempel', in Othmar Keel and Erich Zenger (eds.), *Gottesstadt und Gottesgarten* (Freiburg: Herder, 2002), pp. 69-98 (though I develop his point in a different direction).

[251] So Matthias Albani, '"Wo sollte ein Haus sein, das ihr mir bauen könntet?" (Jes 66,1): Schöpfung als Tempel JHWHs?', in Beate Ego *et al.* (eds.), *Gemeinde ohne Tempel* (Tübingen: Mohr, 1999), pp. 37-56.

[252] But T. C. G. Thornton's note on the possible midrashic background to 'Stephen's Use of Isaiah lxvi. 1' (*JTS* n.s. 25 [1974], pp. 432-34) perhaps implies a reduction in the level of the critique of David and Solomon there.

[253] Cf. Lau, *Schriftgelehrte Prophetie in Jes 56–66*, pp. 170-71. *Epistle of Barnabas* 16 already makes that connection.

[254] Cf. Croatto, *Imaginar el future*, pp. 445-46.

hierocratic group.[255] To judge from Ezra and from Haggai and Zechariah (as well as from other passages in Isaiah 40–66), Second Temple prophets were as positive as priests about the role of the temple.[256] Nor in the context of Isaiah 40–66 can the declaration be opposed to temple building in itself.[257] The same implication emerges from the reference to v. 1 in Pesiqta Rabbati, a collection of medieval homilies on the lessons for the festivals, which (not unnaturally) sees this verse as belonging to Isaiah's proclamation at the end of his life. Isaiah thus here speaks negatively about Manasseh's action in the temple, without implying opposition to the temple itself; Manasseh responds to his critique by ordering him to be seized, which leads to Isaiah's execution by being sawn in half.[258]

Verse 2a underlines the point in v. 1. In content this third bicolon links especially with the first (v. 1aβγ); 'all these things' are the heavens and the earth referred to there (rather than the temple itself, or the people involved in its building or its worship). The opening *w-* introduces a causal or circumstantial clause; the placing of the object at the beginning of the clause fits its being a subordinate clause, though it also appropriately puts 'all these things' (referring back to v. 1aβγ) in emphatic position, with the position of 'my hand' also before the verb further underlining the point. The fact that Yhwh created the heavens and the earth makes even more ridiculous the idea of humanity building Yhwh a house within the cosmos. In MT the line's abcc'a'd parallelism is less straightforward than those of the preceding lines, and its second clause, introduced by *w*-consecutive, is a little elliptical, but it restates the first clause, gives the hearers chance to draw breath, and thus signals that the declaration is coming to an end. While 1QIs[a, b], Vg, Tg, Aq, Sym, and Th correspond to MT here, LXX and Syr have 'all these things are mine', suggesting the addition of *lî*; the second colon then builds on the first and draws an inference. Yhwh's having made the heavens and the earth means they belong to Yhwh (cf. the argument of Ps 95.5). The *lî* would correspond to the *lî* in v. 1b: 'you plan to build a house *for me* but your proposed raw materials belong *to me*, because I made them'. Indeed, even on the basis of MT's text, the 'for me' in v. 1 implies a reversing of the relationship between God and people of the kind that Yhwh faults in 2 Samuel 7. People are pretending to build a house for God when God is all-powerful over the world that would have to provide the raw materials. The point about the statement concerning Yhwh's relation to the heavens

255 Against Hanson, *The Dawn of Apocalyptic*, pp. 172-73; he notes that Haggai the prophet, whom he sees as belonging to the hierocratic group, is close to the spirit of Isaiah 40–55 and 60–62.

256 Snaith ('Isaiah 40–66', p. 241) even sees the prophet as protesting that the people have *not* built Yhwh's earthly house.

257 Against, e.g., Volz, *Jesaja II*, p. 289. Cf. Bedford, *Temple Restoration in Early Achaemenid Judah*, pp. 283-85.

258 See Gary G. Porton, 'Isaiah and the Kings: The Rabbis on the Prophet Isaiah', in Broyles and Evans (eds.), *Writing and Reading the Scroll of Isaiah*, II, pp. 693-716 (706-7).

and the earth is not to say something in the realm of creation theology but to make a declaration concerning Yhwh's sovereign lordship.[259]

There are other buildings than the Jerusalem temple rebuilt by Zerubbabel and Joshua that could be the subject of polemic in the Second Temple period, such as the Samarian temple on Mount Gerizim and the Jewish temple at Elephantine, but the argument in vv. 1-2 does not concern the location of a particular temple outside Jerusalem.[260] Yhwh's words would apply to any temple, including the one whose rebuilding Ezra 1–6 recounts. The polemic might alternatively link with the development of synagogue-style worship in the Second Temple period and a related stress on Yhwh's being known through the Torah,[261] or to a project to enlarge the temple.[262] Once again, however, the prophet's view would then contrast not only with that presupposed by Ezra 1–6 and expressed in Haggai and Zechariah 1–8 but also with the view expressed elsewhere in Isaiah 56–66 itself. In this context, the prophecy can hardly have been understood to be simply dismissing the temple and its worship;[263] this view generates implausible tension with the assumptions expressed in 56.5-7; 60.7, 13; 63.18; 64.10-11 [11-12]; 65.11; 66.6, 20-21. While the first of these passages might suggest that the prophecy sees the temple as a place of prayer rather than a place of Yhwh's presence,[264] this hardly fits those other passages. It might more plausibly be seen as designed to console the community when it was unable to undertake the building project (see Ezra 4)[265] or to console people who were excluded from the project (cf. v. 5).

[259] Gärtner, *Jesaja 66 und Sacharja 14 als Summe der Prophetie* (see above), p. 21.

[260] Cf. Koenen, *Ethik und Eschatologie im Tritojesajabuch*, pp. 184-85.

[261] Cf. Westermann, *Jesaja Kapitel 40–66*, p. 328 (ET p. 413); Georg Fohrer, 'Kritik an Tempel, Kultus und Kultausübung in nachexilischer Zeit', in A. Kuschke and E. Kutsch (eds.), *Archäologie und Altes Testament* (K. Galling Festschrift; Tübingen: Mohr, 1970), pp. 101-16, reprinted in Fohrer, *Studien zu alttestamentlichen Texten und Themen (1966–1972)* (Berlin: de Gruyter, 1981), pp. 81-95; Koenen, *Ethik und Eschatologie im Tritojesajabuch*, p. 187.

[262] E.g. Berges, *Das Buch Jesaja*, p. 522.

[263] Cf. Anne E. Gardner, 'Isaiah 66:1-4', *Revue Biblique* 113 (2006), pp. 506-28. In *Anti-cultic Theology in Christian Biblical Interpretation: A Study of Isaiah 66:1-4 and Its Reception* (New York: Lang, 2007), Valerie A. Stein shows how anti-cultic instinct has affected interpretation of the passage and continues to do so; the very words 'cult' and 'cultic' are inclined to have negative connotations, and I avoid them. J. D. Smart ('A New Interpretation of Isaiah lxvi. 1-6', *ExpT* 46 [1934–35], pp. 420-24) sees the passage as opposing temple building insofar as the builders had a false idea of God and were not repenting.

[264] Cf. Jon D. Levenson, 'From Temple to Synagogue', in Baruch Halpern and Levenson (eds.), *Traditions in Transformation* (F. M. Cross Festschrift; Winona Lake, IN: Eisenbrauns, 1981), pp. 143-66 (159); David L. Petersen, 'The Temple in Persian Period Prophetic Texts', in P. R. Davies (ed.), *Second Temple Studies 1* (Sheffield: Sheffield Academic Press, 1991), pp. 125-44 (137-40).

[265] Cf. Menaḥem Haran, 'The Divine Presence in the Israelite Cult and the Cultic Institutions', *Biblica* 50 (1969), pp. 251-67 (266-67).

We have noted that a feature of Isaiah 40–66 is its lacking any expectation that Yhwh will eventually reestablish the monarchy; Cyrus and/or the prophet and/or the people as a whole will now fulfil David's role (45.1; 52.14; 55.3-5; 61.1). In a parallel way the prophecy questions the twin notion of building a temple, which like the monarchy entered Israel's story as a result of Israel's initiative rather than Yhwh's revelation. As the notion of human kingship makes no sense (because God is Israel's king), so the notion of an earthly temple makes no sense. One might also compare the way the way the prescription for the wilderness dwelling in Exodus 25–40 (P) suggests assumptions about a dwelling for God that stand in some tension with those implied by the temple. Similarly, Yhwh has no need to be fed by sacrifices; yet Yhwh is happy for Israel to offer sacrifices as a way of honouring its God (Ps 50.7-15, 23). Analogously, a recognition that building a temple is a theological oddity, like having kings, could coexist with building a temple or looking forward to having kings once again.[266]

66.2b But toward this person I look, toward one who is afflicted,// struck down in spirit, trembling at my word.

The formula at the end of v. 2a[267] would give the impression that Yhwh's declaration is complete, and for this reason alone v. 2b is a surprise following on vv. 1-2a. It is also a surprise in content, and not because it goes on to say that after all Yhwh affirms the idea of a temple. The rebuke implied by vv. 1-2a could have given the impression that contact between Yhwh and humanity is impossible because of Yhwh's exalted position, but v. 2b declares that in fact the opposite is the case. The possibility of such contact is not in question. Perhaps the prophecy implies that the problem lies in people's assumption that they have to make the contact possible, by building Yhwh a house. In reality the initiative in setting up such contact lies with Yhwh not with humanity. In making this point, Yhwh's words here overlap with those addressed to David in connection with his temple-building initiative (2 Sam 7), but also with a recurrent motif in the Psalms. The fact that Yhwh is in the heavens does not inhibit Yhwh from being involved with the earth. Yhwh looks from the heavens (*nābaṭ* hiphil; Pss 33.13; 102.20 [19]) in order to know what is going on and be able to act on people's behalf; the verb implies a more purposeful looking than *rāʾâ*, a taking notice that leads to action on behalf of the person at whom one looks. Lamentations 4.16 bemoans the fact that Yhwh no longer looks, and Isaiah 63.15; 64.8 [9] have pleaded with Yhwh to do so. The prophecy declares that it is logically impossible to build a house for Yhwh; yet it is this God who responds to the kind of cry

[266] Cf Justin Martyr's comments, *Dialogue with Trypho* 22.
[267] On which see the comment on 59.20.

uttered in 63.15.[268] The heavens are not merely God's dwelling but God's throne. 'God transcends [heaven] even though he also touches earth with his feet. Thus God comprehends all things with his presence but is not comprehended by any.' Yet 'precisely as the one who incommensurably transcends his creation, God is still present to even the least of his creatures'.[269]

In the 3-3 line, the initial prepositional phrase 'to this person' and the verb apply to both cola; the *'ê-zeh* ('wherever') of v. 1 gives way to the *'el-zeh* ('at this person') of this line.[270] The first colon is completed by a restatement of that opening phrase defining the characteristic of 'this person'. The parallelism in the second colon then provides two further phrases to describe the person. To whom, then, does Yhwh look? For the first two phrases, Tg has 'afflicted' and 'low in spirit', Th 'crushed' and 'wounded in heart', LXX 'lowly' and 'quiet', Vg 'poor' (so also Sym) and 'worn in spirit', Aq 'gentle' and 'stricken in spirit'. The versions thus take the person to be someone who is afflicted (*'ānî*) like the people described in 58.7 (or the *'ānāw* of 61.1); cf. also 3.14-15; 32.7; 41.17; 49.13; 54.11. It is someone broken in spirit; the adjective (*nākeh*) refers otherwise only to Mephibosheth who has broken feet (2 Sam 4.4; 9.3), though a related adjective (*nākē'*) refers to a brokenness of spirit. They are people of 'low social status'.[271] The point about Yhwh's attentiveness to people who are crushed has already been made in different words in 57.15. Yhwh's enthronement with earth as footstool makes possible Yhwh's involvement with the afflicted, rather than inhibiting it.[272] The transcendent God is also the immanent God.[273] Afflicted and broken in spirit would be a fair description of the exilic community and of the Second Temple community as portrayed in Ezra–Nehemiah; it might also be a fair description of a group within the community such as the people who see themselves as Yhwh's servants over against the people they see as having power in the community. The lines that follow will suggest that it here describes the latter.

Some of the Versions' words, such as 'lowly', 'quiet', and 'gentle', could be understood to point to commendable personality characteristics, suggesting that the people have the personal qualities that qualify them to be people whom Yhwh cares about. This is probably not indicated by Vg's *contritum spiritu*, 'worn in spirit', but English translations have

[268] Jones, 'Isaiah—II and III', p. 535.

[269] Wolfhart Pannenberg, *Systematische Theologie Band 1* (Göttingen: Vandenhoeck & Ruprecht, 1988), p. 445 (ET *Systematic Theology Volume 1* [Grand Rapids: Eerdmans, 1991], pp. 411, 412).

[270] Motyer, *The Prophecy of Isaiah*, p. 532.

[271] Joseph Blenkinsopp, 'A Jewish Sect of the Persian Period', *CBQ* 52 (1990), pp. 5-20 (9).

[272] Kraus, *Das Evangelium der unbekannten Propheten*, p. 246; cf. Beate Ego, '"Der Herr blickt herab von der Höhe seines Heiligtum"', *ZAW* 110 (1998), pp. 556-69 (566-69).

[273] Cf. Knight, *Isaiah 56–66*, p. 103.

commonly translated *nākeh* 'contrite', a derivative of *contritus* that came to have moral connotations. This translation gives a different cast to the line as a whole; the people Yhwh approaches are then humble or lowly in the moral sense, and contrite in spirit. They have repented and changed their stance to Yhwh, and this is why Yhwh looks to them. The initiative in the relationship between Yhwh and Judah then still lies with Judah, but Judah gets Yhwh to pay attention not by building a temple but by being humble and contrite. In contrast, MT's language rather suggests the assumption that recurs in the Psalms; people's claim on God is their neediness, not their personal qualities.[274] Yhwh's attention emerges simply from God's grace and mercy; it is not earned by the people's attitude. 'Though we appear to be wretched…, and although we appear to be unworthy of being beheld by men, yet we are truly happy; because the Lord looks upon us, and bestows on us his favour.'[275]

'Trembling at my word' is closer to having positive implications. Like *yārē'* and related words, the adjective *ḥārēd* and the verb *ḥārad* can denote a positive fear (being reverent and obedient) and thus a proper attitude to God, though their usage is predominantly negative (being afraid). Ezra 9.4; 10.3 are illuminating because they belong in a context of disobedience and faithlessness, where there is reason to be fearful of God's attitude.[276] Understanding humbleness and lowliness of spirit as positive moral qualities would suggest a positive spin on 'trembling at my word'. If (as seems more likely) the earlier expressions suggest a brokenness of spirit, the trembling is more ambiguous. It implies a recognition that the people have every reason to be fearful of Yhwh's word (the kind of word that appears in the Torah and the Prophets), the word that commands but has been ignored and/or the word that threatens punishment and has been experienced. Humbling, brokenness, and trembling are negative realities, but they are not reason for despair, because people who have such characteristics are people to whom Yhwh looks. While the trembling might be metaphorical, a way of suggesting fear (cf. 10.29; 17.2; 19.16; 32.11; 41.5?), the instinct of Old Testament worship to combine the outward and inward may make it more likely that the trembling includes a physical expression of awe or fear, like that of Quakers and Shakers; though it is noteworthy that physical trembling is not especially a marker of the modern orthodox Jews called the *haredim*.

The Judahite community as a whole, or the group within the community whom 65.8-25 has designated Yhwh's servants and Yhwh's chosen, people who are crushed and almost extinguished, yearn to build Yhwh a house, but their aim is strictly unrealistic and unnecessary. Yhwh is involved with them anyway. Like other Old Testament comments that question worship, sacrifice, and prayer, the prophecy does not necessarily

[274] Cf. Croatto, *Imaginar el future*, p. 447.

[275] Calvin, *Commentarii in Iesaiam prophetam*, p. 413 (ET IV, p. 414).

[276] A. Baumann (*TWAT*, III, p. 181 [ET *TDOT*, V, p. 170]) notes that in Isaiah 66 and Ezra חרד has lost the connotation of panic which commonly characterizes it earlier.

question the idea of building the temple in itself, though neither is it directly implying 'Get your attitude right and then you can build the temple'.

66.3a Someone who slaughters a bull is one who strikes down a person;// someone who sacrifices a lamb is one who strangles a dog.
Someone who lifts up an offering—it is the blood of a pig;// someone who makes a remembrance offering of incense is one who worships a bane.

The transition to vv. 3-4 is sudden; this fact in itself makes it unlikely that vv. 3-4 provide the reason for the polemic about the temple in vv. 1-2,[277] which in any case is there provided with its own rationale.[278] Yet the formal continuity from vv. 1-2 means it makes sense to assume that the prophecy continues to address the people who are broken in spirit; it now speaks to them about other members of the community, the rhetoric reversing that in 65.8-25 which spoke *to* the permissive group but spoke *about* Yhwh's servants. The first two lines in v. 3 are both 3-4 though they look like a classic case where Masoretic accentuation seems arbitrary; each line comprises eight actual words which could be naturally scanned as 4-4 or 3-3. All four cola are somewhat parallel in form and substance, and at least three comprise a series of noun expressions. Each colon begins with a participle, the two in the first line being qal, the two in the second hiphil. Each participle is followed by its object; these nouns have the article in the first line and refer to animals, but they are anarthrous in the second and refer to things. In three of the cola, the predicate begins with another participle; the exception is the third colon, which stands out from the pattern of the others and advertises that the second line works in a different way from the first. All four cola close with an anarthrous noun.

Vg takes the two lines as implying a series of comparisons, 'one who slaughters a bull *is like* one who strikes down a person' and so on. 1QIs[a] takes the first colon in the same way, reading *kmkh.* Tg takes the whole first line in this way; it paraphrases the second line, 'their offering of gifts is a gift of violence'. LXX makes a similar assumption but reworks the meaning of the lines more systematically, 'the lawless person who sacrifices a calf to me is like someone who kills a dog, and the person who offers fine flour is like [someone who offers] pig's blood. The person who has given incense as a memorial offering is like a blasphemer.' On the Versions' understanding, the lines could then be speaking *about* the same people as vv. 1-2 speak *to*. But MT's own form rather implies that they

[277] As Stromberg argues (*Isaiah after Exile*, pp. 18-26).

[278] Thus, while it is the case that only the opening and closing chapters of Isaiah incorporate a critique of Judah's worship (Tomasino, 'Isaiah 1.1–2.4 and 63–66', pp. 86-88 = pp. 152-54), the nature and basis of the critique here in vv. 1-4 is markedly different from the earlier one.

are regular examples of Hebrew noun clauses, which simply require the provision of a copula 'is' in English. The first line describes people who are involved in proper worship (slaughtering a bull for sacrifice and sacrificing a lamb) but also in improper worship (sacrificing human beings and dogs). The second describes people whose worship is inherently improper (offering pig's blood and making an incense offering in honour of gods other than Yhwh). The clauses may be seen as ironic versions of participial definitions in passages such as Proverbs 11.13; 12.1; 13.3, 24; 14.2, 21; 15.27, 32.[279]

'Slaughter' (*šāḥaṭ*) is a regular verb for killing an animal for sacrifice; 'bull' (*šôr*) is the object in passages such as Leviticus 17.3 [H]; 1 Samuel 14.34, especially in connection with a fellowship offering or voluntary offering. Sacrificing a lamb would likewise denote especially a fellowship offering. The grain offering accompanies other offerings. Incense also accompanies many offerings, but specifically the grain offering; the verb for 'make a remembrance offering of' (*zākar* hiphil) appears only here, but it will refer to the 'remembrance offering' (*'azkārâ*; Lev 2.2, 15-16; 6.8 [15] [P]; cf. 24.7 [H]). All four expressions thus refer to proper worship as described in the Torah. While the uniqueness of the last verb means we could not be sure who would be its subject, the first three verbs refer to actions undertaken by the people as a whole rather than by priests (e.g. Lev 1.5 [P]; Deut 27.6-7); it would be plausible to assume that the last action, too, could denote the action of the people bringing the sacrifice, over whose offering the priest then presided.[280]

It fits ill with the significance of all four actions in the context of the Torah that (first) the person who slaughters a bull also strikes down a person; *'îš* refers to an individual and could denote a man or a woman, though in the context a man is likely. The verb is a general one for murder; the actual phrase comes in the Book of the Covenant (Exod 21.12), but the use of a form of *nākâ* makes for a paronomasia with *nᵉkēh* ('struck down') in the previous line.[281] But in the context of reference to slaughtering a bull in connection with worship, the phrase could suggest human sacrifice, which is downgraded to murder, and this fits the cola that follow. There may likewise be some sarcasm about the reference to strangling or beheading a dog or breaking its neck; this action applies to a donkey or a heifer in other contexts when they are in some way offered to God in a non-sacrificial connection (Exod 13.3; 34.20; Deut 21.4, 6). Despite a passage such as Deuteronomy 23.19 [18], dogs are not despised. They are valued as watch dogs or sheep dogs (Isa 56.10-11; Job 30.1);

[279] Cf. Alonso Schökel and Sicre Diaz, *Profetas*, I, p. 391.

[280] Against Alexander Rofé, 'Isaiah 66:1-4', in Ann Kort and Scott Morschauser (eds.), *Biblical and Related Studies Presented to Samuel Iwry* (Winona Lake, IN: Eisenbrauns, 1985), pp. 205-17, who sees anti-priestly polemic here (cf. his essay 'The Onset of Sects in Postexilic Judaism', in Neusner *et al.* (eds.), *The Social World of Formative Christianity and Judaism*, pp. 39-49 (41-42).

[281] Berges, *Das Buch Jesaja*, p. 518.

but as sacrifices they are no more proper than donkeys. Pigs, on the other hand, have no positive significance. In the Old Testament one does not 'lift up' (*ʿālâ* hiphil) blood as an offering, though one can 'sacrifice' it (*zābaḥ*; Exod 23.18) or 'slaughter' it (*šāḥaṭ*; Exod 34.25), the verbs from the previous line here in Isaiah, and one can 'present' it (*qārab* hiphil). While reference to sacrificing dogs or pigs may be simply an insult of the kind that religious groups throw at each other, there is some evidence that both animals were sacrificed in the region.[282] Likewise pre-exilic precedent makes it quite reasonable to assume that Judahites were indeed worshipping other deities, as the final colon suggests, though it might be that they saw themselves as worshipping Yhwh when the prophet saw their worship as so affected by non-Yahwistic assumptions that it had ceased to be worship of Yhwh. While Ezra 1–6 makes no reference to such practices, the community's stringent attitude to people it sees as outsiders implies that it would have a sense of the danger of their being introduced; Ezra 9–10 implies the same concern, as does Malachi. 'Worship' is *bārak* piel, conventionally 'bless', but the verb needs to have rather a different meaning when God is its object than it has when created beings are its object and it connotes conveying the capacity to be fruitful. A 'bane' is *ʾāwen*, something deeply wrong (cf. 58.9; 59.4, 6, 7) but also deeply stupid (cf. 41.29);[283] the succeeding lines will bring out the latter connotation as well as the former. The two lines thus describe people as continuing the practices of the pre-exilic period (e.g. 2 Kgs 23.4-15; Jer 7; Ezek 8). In leading and taking part in worship in the temple and in its environs in Jerusalem, they combine worship of Yhwh in accordance with the Torah and worship that conflicts with the Torah. Comparison with the situation in the pre-exilic period also makes clear that there is nothing novel about tension within the community between people who are more permissive and people who are more purist in their religion.

66.3b They for their part—they have chosen their ways;// in their abominations their soul has delighted.
4 I for my part—I will choose caprices for them,// and their terrors I will bring to them.
Because I have called and there has been no one responding,// I have spoken and they have not listened.
They have done what was displeasing in my eyes,// and chosen what I did not delight in.

Whereas MT treats vv. 3-4 as a pair of three-line sequences, the first two lines (v. 3a) form a pair in structure and content. The middle two cola (vv. 3b-4aαβ; 3-3, 3-3), also form a pair, each beginning with *gam*

[282] See Blenkinsopp, *Isaiah 56–66*, pp. 297-98; Jack M. Sasson, 'Isaiah lxvi 3-4a', *VT* 26 (1976), pp. 199-207 (202-6); and the comment on 65.4 above.
[283] See Goldingay and Payne, *Isaiah 40–55*, I, p. 298

followed by a pronoun for emphasis (redundant for meaning) and then by a form of the verb 'choose'. The final pair (v. 4aγδb; 3-3) do not link with each other as closely, but could be seen as forming a further pair.

As a single *gam* commonly means 'also', repeated *gam* can suggest 'both…and', or in this instance in vv. 3b-4aαβ, a contrast.[284] The pronouns that follow indicate the contrast's subjects, and the repeated verb 'choose' indicates the contrast's nature. Thus the two lines are both internally and mutually parallel. Within v. 3b the motif of the people choosing without thought for God's wishes recurs from 65.12aγδb (see the comment), which indeed v. 4aγδb here repeats. As was the case in 65.12, the motif also recalls the opening chapter of Isaiah with which chapters 65–66 have many links (see 1.29). Talk of people's 'ways' in turn recurs from 57.18; 58.13, with some irony over against the references to Yhwh's ways in 63.17; 64.4 [5]. Verse 3b as a whole works abcc′a′b′. 'Their soul' corresponds to 'they for their part'. The expression underlines the involvement of their whole person in this choosing. 'Has delighted' (third person feminine singular) corresponds to 'have chosen' (third person masculine plural) but also heightens the point made by the earlier verb. As in 65.12, the stative verb could have present reference but the parallelism suggests reference to the past moment when they did their choosing; the parallelism also compares grievously with the contrast in 56.4. 'In their abominations' corresponds to 'their ways', which also began with the preposition *b*-. Further, it heightens the statement; the word comes only here in Isaiah.

Verse 4aαβ then works abcc′b′a′. 'To them' balances 'I for my part'. 'I will bring' balances 'I will choose'. 'Their terrors' balances 'caprices'. As significantly, we have already noted, 'I for my part—I will choose' balances 'They for their part—they have chosen'. 'Caprices' (*taʿălûlîm*) comes only here and in 3.4, where it describes Yhwh's judgment in the capricious or wanton or perhaps simply childish rule that will follow on Yhwh's removing Judah's proper rulers.[285] LXX, Vg have 'delusions'; Tg 'breaking'; Aq 'reversals of fortune'. It is a brave word to use of Yhwh, because while words from *ʿālal* can refer to deeds in general (e.g. 12.4), they more often denote wilful and unjustifiable acts (e.g. 1.16; 3.8, 10); Lamentations uses them to protest Yhwh's action in having Jerusalem fall (Lam 1.12; 2.20). For Yhwh to use the word is to underline the way the coming actions will seem excessive and objectionable to people. Further, they will be events that terrify the people. They might simply be ones that will cause terror, but earlier material in these chapters has implied that the people's religious practices are designed to guard against troubles that might come to them, so that Yhwh's point is more likely that

[284] Cf. *HALOT*, p. 196; BDB, p. 169.

[285] See H. G. M. Williamson, *Isaiah 1–5* (London: T&T Clark International, 2006), p. 233.

the experiences they are seeking to guard against by their 'abominations' will actually be hastened rather than prevented by them. LXX paraphrases the second half of the line 'and I will pay back [their] sins to them'. If they have tried to play games with God, God will play games with them.[286]

We have noted that v. 4aγδb repeats 65.12aγδb except that the verbs are changed from second person to third, in keeping with the rhetoric of vv. 1-4, and that the second colon uses the negative *'ên* instead of *lō'*. It thus closes off vv. 1-4 as 65.12aγδb closed off the accusatory subsection of 65.8-25.

66.5 Listen to Yhwh's word,// you who tremble at his word:
Your brothers have said—people who repudiate you,// who exclude you for the sake of my name,
'May Yhwh be severe, so that we may look at your celebration',// but they themselves will be ashamed.

Verse 5 explicitly speaks *to* the purist but continues to speak *about* the permissive. I understand the opening exhortation to attentiveness as a 2-2 bicolon, though (given its lack of parallelism) it might be another single extra-metrical colon like those that open and close vv. 1-2a, but with four stresses. It is the only exhortation to 'listen' in Isaiah 56–66 (there were fifteen in Isaiah 40–55) and the two references to Yhwh's 'word' are the only ones in the chapters except for the instance in v. 2. On the other hand, the exhortation does thus make for a striking *inclusio* with 1.10.[287] In the context, the unique exhortation links with the description of the addressees, which takes up words from the end of v. 2. There, trembling at Yhwh's word was the stance of the faithful person who is afflicted and struck down in spirit, aware of being under Yhwh's word of judgment. Here, Yhwh is about to declare a word that conveys promise, and the people who have that awareness are invited to pay attention to a different kind of word.[288] Trembling at Yhwh's word is now explicitly the attribute of a group, whom we may presumably identify with the servants of Yhwh of 65.13-15.[289]

The content of the word of promise comes in v. 5b, though it is only at the end of the two lines that the drift of the verse becomes explicit. The first 3-3 line, v. 5bαβ, works abcc'd, with 'Your brothers have said' also

[286] Zwingli, *Complanationis Isaiae Prophetae*, p. 407.

[287] See Se-Hoon Jang, 'Hearing the Word of God in Isaiah 1 and 65–66', in R. Boer, M. Carden, and J. Kelso (eds.), *The One Who Reads May Run* (E. W. Conrad Festschrift; London: T&T Clark International, 2012), pp. 41-58.

[288] Sekine (*Die Tritojesajanische Sammlung*, pp. 57-65) sees this as the word that welcomes foreigners (see 56.1-8), whom he takes as the addressees in v. 5; but this requires considerable inference and it depends on a particular redactional theory.

[289] Cf. Blenkinsopp, *Opening the Sealed Book*, p. 69.

applying to the second colon and 'on account of my name' also applying to the first. Thus the strict parallelism is confined to the two suffixed participles that are juxtaposed at the centre of the line. For the first time in Isaiah 56–66 the prophecy explicitly refers to actual conflict between the purist and the permissive[290] and explicitly indicates that the permissive are the people in power in the community. On one hand the permissive are 'your brothers', your kinfolk. This word likewise comes for the first time in Isaiah (it will recur in v. 20); it is frequent in Nehemiah (see esp. Neh 4–5), in a period not so far from that of this prophecy, as the basis for appeal to the community to support one another. The prophecy's point here is that, on the contrary, 'your brothers' have rejected or repudiated or opposed the people whom the prophecy addresses; the verb is *śānē'*, 'an attitude or action of social or political rejection'[291] (see 60.15; 61.8; and the comment). The implications are spelled out in the second colon; their kinfolk have excluded them. The verb (*nādâ*) occurs only here in the Old Testament, but in Mishnaic Hebrew it means 'excommunicate'. Perhaps the purists are indeed excluded from the temple and from citizenship in accordance with dynamics reported in Ezra–Nehemiah (see esp. Ezra 10.8) with the shoe on the other foot, or perhaps they are excluded from leadership or ministry. Either way, the power of the 'brothers' would make a specific reference to priests particularly plausible here.[292] As sometimes happens in such circumstances, the permissive do not act permissively towards people who disagree with them. Further, the people who do the excommunicating of course do not see themselves as the faithless but rather see the purists as themselves the faithless. They thus exclude them 'on account of my name'. This expression can be used in a weaker sense, to mean 'because of me'; the idea would then be that the permissive oppose the purists because of the latter's adherence to Yhwh. But the next line rather suggests that the expression has its more common, stronger sense; they see themselves as on Yhwh's side and excommunicate 'for the sake of Yhwh's name'.[293] The dynamics parallel those of the Reformation, when Catholics and Protestants took such a stance over against each other.

Perhaps LXX has difficulty in imagining this dynamic and this difficulty lies behind its version, 'Speak, our brothers, to the people who hate us and loath [us], so that the Lord's name may be glorified and seen in their rejoicing, and those people will be ashamed' (OL has 'hate you and loath you'; Syr has 'Say [or "they said"] to your brothers'; Aq, Sym, Th correspond to MT). Perhaps LXX wants to encourage

[290] Koenen (*Ethik und Eschatologie im Tritojesajabuch*, p. 204) compares 59.18; but I take that verse to refer to the enemies of the Judahites as a whole.

[291] Beuken, *Jesaja IIIB*, p. 106; cf. J. A. Thompson, 'Israel's "Haters"', *VT* 29 (1979), pp. 200-205.

[292] Cf. Tiemeyer, *Priestly Rites and Prophetic Rage*, pp. 267-70.

[293] Cf. Sekine, *Die Tritojesajanische Sammlung*, p. 48.

courageous declaration of Yhwh's teaching in a hostile environment.[294] Early Christian writers such as Tertullian can then read this line as an encouragement to loving one's enemies, 'Say "You are our brothers" to the people who hate you'.[295] On the other hand, it has been suggested that a homonym for *'aḥ* meant enemy, so that the prophecy's hearers could hear a paronomasia in the prophet's words, though there is no other evidence for this word in Hebrew.[296]

The content of what the brothers say occupies the first two-thirds of v. 5bγδ, which works 4-2 or 2-2-2 without any parallelism. Their words begin from the concern for Yhwh's name expressed in the preceding line, but they involve some mockery. The Versions take the opening verb *yikbad* to mean 'be glorious', 'be glorified', but this is a rare meaning for the qal (Job 14.21 is the only clear parallel) and it is not clear why the brothers would be expressing this wish; one would expect something more negative. But the verb usually signifies 'be heavy', and the Old Testament refers a number of times to Yhwh's hand being heavy on people (e.g. Ps 32.4).[297] The brothers are expressing the wish that Yhwh should come down heavily on the people whom they repudiate. They then go on to comment ironically on how that action will change the look on the faces of the faithful. They themselves will enjoy looking at the faithful. The expression *rāâ b-* can have various implications, like English 'look at'. While it can mean 'look at' without further implications, it can link with sympathy at someone's suffering (Exod 2.11; 1 Sam 1.11) or with satisfaction at someone's defeat (Obad 12-13).[298] The purists will not actually be celebrating when Yhwh acts in judgment, as their opponents expect (*śimḥâ* can carry the connotation of celebration in worship, like the English word). In connection with efforts to clarify the nature of the disagreement between the purist and the permissive, it has been suggested that the taunt 'makes clear that opposition to this group had something to do with their prophetic-eschatological beliefs',[299] which seems an

[294] Cf. Seeligmann, *The Septuagint Version of Isaiah*, p. 118; cf. Vande Kappelle, 'Evidence of a Jewish Proselytizing Tendency in the Old Greek (Septuagint) Version of the Book of Isaiah', pp. 144-46.

[295] *Against Marcion* 4.16. Cf. Theodoret of Cyrrhus, *Commentaire sur Isaïe* 184a (II, pp. 334-35); Cyril of Alexandria, Ἐξήγησις ὑπομνηματικὴ εἰς τὸν προφήτην Ἡσαΐαν, col. 1433; Eusebius of Caesarea, *Der Jesajakommentar*; pp. 401-2.

[296] See Perles, *Analekten zur Textkritik des Alten Testaments: Neue Folge*, pp. 77, 99 (he then sees 'people who reject' as an explanatory gloss); cf. Hempel, *Hebräisches Wörterbuch zu Jesaja*, p. 2; also Koenen, *Ethik und Eschatologie im Tritojesajabuch*, p. 200. *CAD* (I, Part I, p. 329) lists a word *aḫû* with this meaning in Akkadian.

[297] So D. Qimchi, 'ישעיה', on the passage, though he refers it to the heaviness of Yhwh's expectations of the people.

[298] But it is doubtful whether this usage carries the connotation 'gloat'; see J. A. Emerton, 'Looking on One's Enemies', *VT* 51 (2001), pp. 186-96.

[299] Joseph Blenkinsopp, 'Interpretation and the Tendency to Sectarianism', in E. P. Sanders, with A.I. Baumgarten and Alan Mendelson (eds.), *Jewish and Christian Self-Definition, Volume Two* (Philadelphia: Fortress; London: SCM, 1981), pp. 1-26 (8).

exaggeration; like other parts of Isaiah 56–66, this chapter makes clear only that the purist and the permissive disagreed on forms and objects of worship, not that they disagreed about proper expectations for the future except in the sense of disagreeing over who would be the beneficiaries when Yhwh's purpose was brought to fulfilment.

The closing colon at last brings the good news to the people who tremble at Yhwh's word. Their brothers have implied that the faithful will be ashamed; actually they themselves will be. The antithesis of celebration and shame recurs from 65.13 (and thus again compares with the declaration about shame in 1.29), so that the verse is reaffirming the point made there, with the rhetorical difference that 65.13 addressed the people who are abandoning Yhwh and spoke about the faithful, whereas 66.5 addresses the faithful and speaks about the people whose form of worship (v. 3) means that contrary to their own understanding, *they* are abandoning Yhwh. In 65.13 and here, and further in v. 6, declarations that elsewhere apply to the enemies of the community as a whole (cf. 59.18), or to Israel itself in its rebellion, apply to a group within Israel.

66.6 The sound of uproar from the city,// the sound from the palace,
The sound of Yhwh// paying back recompense to his enemies!

The two lines (3-2, 2-3) continue the good news for the faithful in the form of a declaration concerning Yhwh's action against the brothers, who are now further identified as Yhwh's enemies. The prophet speaks of the action as if it is actually taking place; it is doing so in the prophet's imagination, or rather in the experience the prophet has had of hearing something that is real because Yhwh is committed to it, but is not actual on the earthly plane. As was the case in a passage such as 40.1-11, the prophet's account (and presumably the experience it invites us to infer) is aural rather than visual; it relates sounds rather than sights. The term 'the sound' (*qôl*) thus compares and contrasts with the expressions *hēn* and *hinnēh*; the former urges us to pay attention by listening (almost 'hark!') as the latter two urge us to pay attention by looking (almost 'behold'). As the two lines unfold, the nature of the sound becomes more and more specific; the lines are internally parallel but also mutually parallel. In the first line, 'uproar' carries over from the first colon to the second, and 'palace' (*hêkāl*) gives precision to 'city'. Here alone in Isaiah 56–66 is the temple referred to as a palace rather than a house (cf. 6.1; 44.28; also, e.g., Hag 2.15, 18; Zech 6.12-15; Ezra 3.6, 10).[300] So the prophet is aware of hearing a sound of uproar from the city, then realizes that more specifically it comes from the temple. (There need be no implication that the temple has been rebuilt, any more than that the sound has yet become audible; but evidently the speaker of this prophecy is not one who could

[300] Cf. Beuken, *Jesaja IIIB*, p. 109. Or might היכל refer to the palace (GID)?

be totally dismissing the temple-building project.[301]) 'Uproar' (*šāʾôn*) commonly denotes the tumultuous noise of an army in battle (e.g. 13.4; 17.12), though it can also denote the noise of a party (e.g. 5.14; 24.8), which might add irony in this context where the brothers have been talking about celebration.

The second line removes any ambiguity and makes explicit that the uproar is one caused by Yhwh and that the scenario indeed compares with that in 13.4, where Yhwh Armies is mustering an army for battle. It is the noise of Yhwh battling that the prophet hears and invites the faithful to imagine they can hear. The final colon indicates why Yhwh is battling; it is to pay back recompense to his enemies. The promise thus compares with those in 59.15b-20; 63.1-6, where the precise language of 'paying back recompense to his enemies' indeed already appeared (59.18). But there Yhwh's enemies were other nations. Here the context indicates that Yhwh's enemies are the people who are the 'brothers', the people who have 'abandoned' Yhwh (65.11); the notion of 'paying them back' has already appeared in 65.6. The violent action Yhwh takes against his enemies will affect people within Israel, not just outsiders.

66.7 Before she labours, she has given birth;// before pain comes to her,// she delivers a boy.
8aα Who has heard of such a thing,// who has seen such things?

With v. 7, the prophecy suddenly takes a new direction. Perhaps a unit of independent origin begins here, though there is no indication of the close of a unit at the end of v. 6 or of the opening of a unit at the beginning of v. 7, except that a tricolon often marks a turning point. This invites us to treat the verses that follow as in some way continuing vv. 1-6; with vv. 10-17 it will become clearer how they do so. The sense of sudden transition is reduced by the prevalence of the motif of motherhood and birthing in the book of Isaiah as a whole (e.g. 3.25–4.1; 7.1–9.6; 13.5, 8; 26.17-18; 37.3; 54.1-7; 65.23).[302] But for a moment, the rhetoric makes the addressees forget about themselves and distance themselves from the prophecy. It points them as the audience in the house to something happening on the stage whose significance for them is not immediately explicit. Indeed, it does so in several steps, initially in vv. 7-8aα by means of a kind of riddle or a proverb. In the tricolon (3-4-2), the first

[301] Cf. W. A. M. Beuken, 'Does Trito-Isaiah Reject the Temple?', in S. Draisma (ed.), *Intertextuality in Biblical Writings* (B. van Iersel Festschrift; Kampen: Kok, 1989), pp. 53-66 (61); Park, *Die Gerechtigkeit Israels und das Heil der Völker*, pp. 311-17.

[302] See Darr, *Isaiah's Vision and the Family of God*, pp. 221-24; Sawyer, *The Fifth Gospel*, pp. 198-219; Marvin A. Sweeney, 'Prophetic Exegesis in Isaiah 65–66', in Broyles and Evans (eds.), *Writing and Reading the Scroll of Isaiah*, I, pp. 455-74 (468-69), reprinted in Sweeney, *Form and Intertextuality in Prophetic and Apocalyptic Literature*, pp. 46-62 (57-58).

clause within the opening colon is paralleled by the entire middle colon, and the second clause in the opening colon is then paralleled by the entire final colon. Given that 'give birth [to]' (*yālad*) normally has an object, the opening colon raises the question 'What did she bring to birth', which the final colon eventually answers. 'Deliver' (*malaṭ* hiphil) reflects the awareness that birth is a dangerous business for the child as well as a painful and dangerous business for the mother. Very many babies die in the process of birth, as many mothers die in giving birth; the Old Testament tells a number of stories that illustrate the fact. Actual birth does (usually) mean deliverance from the threat of death. Further, in this promise, not only will birthing be successful; it will be spectacularly easy. In the last colon Tg takes the boy to be the Messiah: 'her king will be revealed' (compare its introduction of the Messiah at 28.5). This understanding may also underlie 2 Thessalonians 1–2.[303] Certainly the passage came to be attached to the conviction that Mary gave birth to Jesus without experiencing the usual pain of childbirth.[304] But in contrast to passages such as 9.5 [6] and 11.1, 'the emphasis is on the birth itself, as an act of new creation, on the mother rather than on the child', and a noteworthy accumulation of terms related to giving birth appear in vv. 7-9: labour (three times), pain, deliver, birth (three times), make a breach.[305]

While the final colon in v. 7 clarifies the question raised by the opening colon, more significantly the line as a whole implies the question that becomes explicit in the second line. Giving birth is actually an inherently painful process and it regularly takes hours and hours; to say the woman gives birth 'before' experiencing any labour pains is a hyperbole that heightens the image. The 3-3 line takes a neat abca′b′c′ form: 'who' is repeated, 'has heard' is paralleled by 'has seen', and 'such a thing' is paralleled by 'such things'. Even more significant than the question who has heard or seen such a thing, however, is the question who is the mother to whom the two lines refer, whose experience has been so unprecedented.

[303] See Roger D. Aus, 'God's Plan and God's Power', *JBL* 96 (1977), pp. 537-53; also 'The Relevance of Isaiah 66 7 to Revelation 12 and 2 Thessalonians 1', *ZNW* 67 (1976), pp. 252-68. Charles C. Torrey takes this to be the meaning of the Isaiah passage ('The Influence of Second Isaiah in the Gospels and Acts', *JBL* 48 [1929], pp. 24-36 [27-29]).

[304] 'Because pleasure did not precede it, nor did pain follow it, in accordance with the prophet who says, "Before she felt pain, she brought forth," and again, "Before the time of her pain came, she was delivered and she brought forth a male"' (so the eighth-century Syrian monk John of Damascus, Ἔκδοσις ἀκριβὴς τῆς ὀρθοδόξου πίστεως 87 = 4.14 [*Die Schriften des Johannes von Damaskos* (ed. P. Bonifatius Kotter; Berlin: de Gruyter, 1973), II, p. 201]). Cf. Methodius, *Oration Concerning Simeon and Anna* 3, though in *The Banquet of the Ten Virgins* 7 he applies it to the church as it births its 'children'.

[305] John F. A. Sawyer, 'Daughter of Zion and Servant of the Lord in Isaiah', *JSOT* 44 (1989), pp. 89-107 (97). Indeed, H.-J. Fabry (*TWAT*, II, p. 717 [ET *TDOT*, IV, p. 189]) questions whether the idea of pain is central to *ḥēbel* and suggests that it rather denotes the beginning of labour with its anxiety.

66.8aγ Can a country be brought through labour in one day// or a nation be birthed in one moment?
Because she has laboured, also given birth//—Zion, to her children.

The next pair of lines provide the answer, though they do so in a way that continues to keep the audience in suspense until the last colon of the second line. Verse 8aγδ (4-4) first builds on the hyperbole in v. 7. Each of its neatly parallel cola begins with an interrogative (*hă-* and *ʾim* often introduce parallel questions, though these usually propose alternatives). Next comes a third-person singular passive verb (one hophal, one niphal), followed by its subject. There follows a time expression, and finally a form of the word for 'one'. The parallelism is enhanced by the way the nouns form a feminine–masculine–masculine–feminine sequence. It turns out that the riddle or proverb involved an allegory. The woman stood for a country or nation. In English the notion of the birth of a nation suggests its formation as a coherent political or cultural or social entity. Succeeding verses will make clear that the Hebrew image presupposes a more literal understanding. Birth means bringing people into being.

Verse 8b (3-2) begins by presupposing the unexpected answer 'Yes' to the question in the previous line, and explaining how this could be the right answer;[306] to put it another way, the use of *kî* parallels that following a negative clause and suggesting 'on the contrary'. There is indeed an example of someone who has with virtual simultaneity laboured and given birth. The virtual simultaneity is underlined both by the asyndeton and by the particle *gam*. The first colon thus provides part of the answer to the question explicitly raised by v. 8aγδ, but it also raises another question—who is the mother who has done what the first colon described, and who are the offspring? Suspense is thus further raised by using verbs whose subject and object remain unidentified until the second colon reveals them. Zion is the mother who has given birth with such speed. It would have been possible to express the content of the line by means of regular parallel cola: 'Because Zion has laboured, she has also borne her children.' But the rhetorical effect is heightened by holding back both subject and object until the second colon. The image of Zion as mother is taken up from 49.14–50.3 and 54.1-17; it appears here for the first time in Isaiah 56–66.[307] There is a sense in which the city exists as an entity semi-independent of the people who live there, who are its children. Tg gives a more specific twist to the declaration by paraphrasing, 'because Zion is about to be comforted and be filled with the people of her exiles'.

[306] Cf. König, *Das Buch Jesaja*, p. 531.

[307] While the reference to personified Zion also links the opening and closing chapters of Isaiah (Tomasino, 'Isaiah 1.1–2.4 and 63–66', pp. 88-90 = pp. 154-56), as is the case with the critique of Judah's worship in vv. 1-4, the way vv. 7-13 use the personification is quite different from that opening one and rather follows 49.14–50.3 and 54.1-17; see further Lau, *Schriftgelehrte Prophetie in Jes 56–66*, pp. 126-33.

66.9 Will I myself make a breach but not bring to birth?// Yhwh says.
Or am I the one who brings to birth but will close?// your God has said.

This further pair of lines recognize that v. 8b spoke prophetically even though they spoke in the past tense. The sound of the uproar in the city indicating Yhwh's action in judgment was a reality only in the prophet's imagination, or rather was a reality in God's intention revealed to the prophet but not a reality in this-earthly actuality. So it is with Zion's bearing children. It is a reality in God's intention, and thus it is as good as actual; hence the past tense. But v. 9 recognizes that it is not a reality in God's action, though the assumption likely is that Yhwh has initiated the process whereby Zion will give birth to children. If one is to try to reify the prophet's statement, it implies that Yhwh has indeed initiated the process whereby Zion-Jerusalem will once again become a city bustling with people, but has not completed it; the initiation would lie in the various arrivals and other events described in Ezra–Nehemiah, according to the date of the prophecy.

Here, it is the two lines that are neatly parallel. Each begins with an interrogative, on this occasion followed each time by a first-person singular pronoun that is unnecessary from a purely syntactical perspective (*ha'ănî* and *'im 'ănî*). In each line two verbs follow, the second verb in the opening line being taken up as the first verb in the parallel line. Each line closes with a declaration that these words are not merely the prophet's but God's, which guarantees that they will come about; the expressions for God and the tenses of the verbs complement each other.

The first of the verbs refers to the beginning of the birthing process, when the mother's waters 'break';[308] the prophet speaks of this breaking as Yhwh's first action in bringing about the birth. The double occurrence of 'bring to birth' takes up the verb (*yālad*) from vv. 7a and 8aδ but now uses it in the hiphil, again indicating that the process for which a mother is responsible is also one for which God is responsible. God breaches and brings to birth; 'in a sense, God plays the role of midwife who assists Zion in delivering her infants smoothly'.[309] Further, the God who brings to birth does not close (*'āṣar*); the implied object is 'the womb'. In the parallelism of the two lines, the second begins by generalizing by means of a participle the reasoning in the first. In one understanding of the second line, Yhwh is by nature one who brings to birth and therefore Yhwh will not put a woman through the experience of finding that her baby is unable to leave the womb. Of course women do go through that frightening and death-dealing experience, and in that sense Yhwh does close wombs, but in this case, at least, Yhwh will not do so. Whereas the act of deliverance promised in Isaiah 40–55 'had come to a stop half-way

[308] From the root שבר, the noun משבר denotes the mouth of the womb.
[309] Christl M. Maier, *Daughter Zion, Mother Zion* (Minneapolis: Fortress, 2008), p. 202.

along the road',[310] Yhwh will bring it to completion. Yet such a use of the verb would be unique; closing the womb elsewhere denotes preventing someone conceiving (Gen 16.2; 20.18 [JE]). This meaning is presupposed in LXX's loose translation, 'Lo, was it not I made the one who gives birth and the infertile?', and by Vg, 'Will I who make other people give birth not give birth myself?... As it is I who grant birth to others, will I be infertile?' More likely, then, v. 9b goes beyond v. 9a, or rather modifies the image. One who has brought Zion to birth (at the beginning or in restoring the city after the exile) would not then make Zion incapable of continuing to grow. Significantly, it is only the story of Sarah and Abraham that speaks of God closing wombs, and Sarah's then becoming the mother of multitudes provided 51.2-3 with a precedent and a model for what Yhwh could do for Zion. One might have thought that this mother was incapable of bearing more children, but the prophet promises that Yhwh will see that she not only does so, but does so with extraordinary ease. Tg provides the promise with a backing in Yhwh's being creator of and sovereign over the whole world, and also turns the allegory into literal terms: 'I God created the world from the beginning, Yhwh said; I created all humanity; I scattered them among the peoples; I am also about to gather your exiles, your God has said'. Its reference to gathering exiles corresponds to the language of Isaiah 56–66 elsewhere, but also reflects the sense expressed in other writings from the later Second Temple period that Israel still lives in exile.[311]

66.10 Celebrate with Jerusalem// and be glad in her, all who love her.
Rejoice with her joyfully,// all who mourn over her.
11 So that you may nurse and be full// from her comforting breast,
So that you may drain out and luxuriate// from her splendid bosom.

Four lines forming two pairs spell out the implications of vv. 7-9. The lines within each pair are mutually parallel, but each second colon for the most part simply completes the statement in its first colon. The four lines potentially imply an audience that is more generalized than that in v. 5. Those servants continue to be the audience in the house, while on the stage the prophet addresses this broader body. The way v. 11 speaks will imply that this audience can be identified with the children of vv. 7-9. The prophecy is thus not strict in its use of its metaphor; the children are people who are already in existence and they are characterized in two ways.

In the parallelism of the lines in v. 10 (2-3, 3-2), each line begins with an imperative, goes on to a 'with' expression, adds a second reference to rejoicing (here with the formal difference that the first line has another

[310] Westermann, *Das Buch Jesaja Kap. 40–66*, p. 333 (ET p. 420).
[311] Cf. Chilton, *The Glory of Israel*, pp. 28-33.

imperative while the second line has a cognate adverbial accusative), then has the word 'all', and closes with a participial expression to describe the addressees, in two contrasting ways—they are people who love and care about Jerusalem and people who thus mourn over her, because of her present state. Whereas 'comfort' is usually something Zion receives from Yhwh rather than something it gives, here the imagery of motherhood suggests that Zion is the giver of comfort, though theologically one could say that she is able to give comfort only because she has received it. The imperatives in effect collapse present and future; they invite people to start rejoicing with Jerusalem in light of what Yhwh is going to do, to behave as if Yhwh has already done it. To put it another way, these are more examples of the kind of imperatives that constitute promises (cf. 65.18).[312] They declare that the people who care for and mourn over Jerusalem are definitely going to be in a position to celebrate and rejoice with her when she gives birth to her children. The reference to their mourning takes up a note from 60.20, the first of several points in vv. 10-12 where the poetry takes up motifs from Isaiah 60 but applies it to 'you' in the plural rather than to the city in the singular. Rhetorically, the poetry thus moves to addressing its audience directly rather than inviting it to listen to an exchange on the stage, though it is doubtful whether the actual audience changes; it is not an invitation only to a circumscribed group of servants but an invitation to all who wish to listen.

The two lines in v. 11 (3-2, 3-2) then describe what can be the outcome of the celebration and rejoicing. 'The theology of Zion in the second half of the book of Isaiah here reaches its highpoint.'[313] The logic is similar to that in 40.31: the people who are looking expectantly for Yhwh to act are the people who gain new strength, both now and when Yhwh indeed acts. The image of birthing children returns in that the promise to the people who care for and mourn over Jerusalem and who will celebrate and rejoice with her is that they will be nourished by her like newborn babies. The image of nursing recurs from 60.16, though there the nations were the source of nourishment and the city as a whole was the entity taking nourishment; here it is its mourning children who do so. Part of the background is the picture in Middle Eastern texts of gods and kings suckling on the breasts of a goddess; as happens with some other images, Jerusalem takes on the position of the goddess.[314] The two 3-2 lines both begin 'so that', then go on to a pair of second-person plural yiqtol verbs; in each case the verbs in the second pair go beyond the first pair. Each of the second cola then comprises *min* plus a construct noun plus an absolute noun with a third-person singular suffix. The final noun *zîz* in turn goes beyond the one it parallels, though it has caused difficulties in the way it

[312] See GK 110c; *IBHS* 34.4c; *TTH* 57.
[313] Beuken, *Jesaja IIIB*, p. 120.
[314] Cf. Paul, ישעיה פרקים מ-סו, II, p. 566 (ET p. 619).

does so, as it is a word for teat or nipple but it does not otherwise occur in the Old Testament.[315] LXX 'entrance' might suggest a link with PBH *zûz* 'move' or *zîz* 'canopy' or with *m*^{e}*zûzâ*: cf. 1QIs^{a} *mzwz*.[316] Many later Hebrew manuscripts have *zîw*, an Aramaic and PBH word for 'splendour'; cf. Vg, Aq, Th (Syr has 'strength', Sym 'fat'; for the composite phrase Tg has 'the wine of her glory').

66.12 Because Yhwh has said this:
Here I am, extending to her well-being like a river,// like a flooding wadi the wealth of nations,
So that you may nurse as you are carried on her side// and you are dandled on her knees.
13 Like someone whom his mother comforts,// so I myself will comfort you.
You will be comforted in Jerusalem, 14 you will see and your heart will rejoice,// your limbs will flourish like the grass.

Once again the certainty of the promise that follows is anticipatorily underlined extra-metrically by the 'Because Yhwh has said this'. The usage follows the pattern in chapters 56–66 whereby the bare formula without a conjunction begins a section (56.1; 65.13; 66.1) while the formula preceded by a conjunction underlines a point or marks an transition within a section (56.4; 65.13; 66.12). Whereas v. 12 may mark the beginning of a prophecy that was originally separate from the context (*kābôd*, the last word in v. 11 which reappears in v. 12a, and the image of nursing, might then be links that encouraged the placing of the prophecy here), if so, it has been integrated seamlessly into the section. The substance of vv. 12-13abα comprises three lines that initially speak of Jerusalem in different imagery (v. 12aβγ; 4-4) then revert to the imagery of motherhood (vv. 12b-13abα; 3-2, 4-3) but with the difference that Yhwh is the one who is now spoken of in mother terms.

In the parallelism of v. 12aβγ (abcdc'd'), the opening deictic and the verb apply to the second colon as well as the first. 'Well-being' is then paralleled by 'the wealth of nations' and 'like a river' by 'like a flooding wadi'. The idea of well-being like a river takes up from 48.18, 'Your well-being would have been like a river' (there pointed as *kannāhār*, here anarthrously as *k*^{e}*nāhār*). The simile suggests the broader meaning of *šālôm* (as in 57.19, 21; 59.8; 60.17) rather than 'peace' as the absence of trouble and conflict (as in 57.2). The parallelism whereby 'the wealth of nations' spells out 'well-being' confirms the point; the idea of the wealth of nations recurs from 61.6. Over against 48.18 this line offers a significant reaffirmation that Yhwh is not finished with Jerusalem even though

[315] See *HALOT*, p. 268.

[316] Cf. Fischer, *In welcher Schrift lag das Buch Isaias den LXX vor?*, p. 68; Kutscher, הלשון והרקע הלשוני של מגילת ישעיהו השלמה, p. 192 (ET p. 254-55); Morrow, 'The Text of Isaiah at Qumran', pp. 164-65.

the city is no more faithful to Yhwh than it was when Yhwh expressed that regret in 48.18 (cf. 60.17). On the other hand, 59.8 has made clear that there is still no well-being if there is no faithfulness, and the context here also resembles that in 57.19, 21 with its warning that the promise of well-being carries with it the need for people to make a choice about whether they wish to belong to the community that will experience well-being. The further elaboration in the parallelism which compares the wealth of nations with a flooding wadi underlines the point and indicates that the comparison of well-being with a river is not just a formal allusion to the earlier chapter or a dead metaphor. '*The* river' is commonly a serious watercourse such as the Euphrates (e.g. 7.20). A wadi or wash is a watercourse that may be dry for much of the year but in the rainy season can become a raging torrent; hence 'a flooding wadi'. Flooding is therefore generally a negative image, suggesting an overwhelming force that will sweep away (e.g. 8.7-8;[317] 10.22; 28.2, 15-18; 30.28, where the phrase is the same as here;[318] 43.2; LXX 'like a wadi overflowing the nations' glory' apparently takes it this way here). 'River' can be a positive image (e.g. 33.21; 41.18; 42.15; 44.27; 50.2), though it has negative connotations in one other occurrence in Isaiah 56–66 (59.19), so that the two occurrences in the chapters nicely balance each other. Here abundant water suggests abundant well-being.

In v. 12b the image of nursing picks up from v. 11 but is here subordinate to another image from earlier chapters (see 49.22; 60.4), with Jerusalem being now the one who carries as it is now the one who suckles, and her children being the people who are carried. In the abcb′c′ parallelism, the opening verb[319] applies to both cola, with the *w*- in the second colon marking this point; each colon comprises an *ʿal* expression and a second-person plural yiqtol verb. As was the case in the previous line, whereas the first colon comprises an expression that could have been familiar from preceding chapters, the second colon reformulates the point in a more distinctive way, with a much rarer verb (*šāʿaʿ*) that comes with this precise meaning only here (but cf. 11.8).

Verse 13abα reverts to Yhwh's action (cf. v. 12aβγ). The parallelism involves an explicit comparison. Once again the prophecy takes up a familiar expression (40.1; 49.13; 51.3, 12, 19; 52.9; 54.11; 61.2) but does something different with it; the association of motherhood and comforting is new, as well as the association of the motherhood image with Yhwh rather than with Jerusalem. Yhwh will comfort in the way a mother comforts and Jerusalem will be the means or location of the comfort

[317] In light of verbal links with 8.6-8, Sweeney ('Prophetic Exegesis in Isaiah 65–66' [see above], p. 471 = p. 59) suggests that 'Isa 66:10-14 reverses the imagery of rape by the Assyrian monarch to the imagery of YHWH as the father who brings about the new birth in Jerusalem'.

[318] Gärtner (*Jesaja 66 und Sacharja 14 als Summe der Prophetie* [see above], pp. 105-12) analyses the links between v. 12 and 30.27-33 more broadly.

[319] On which see the translation note.

rather than the recipient or direct giver of it. Here, too, the prophecy reverses ideas that lie in the background. While preceding parts of the book of Isaiah have used motherhood imagery in a positive way, they have also used birthing language in particular in a conventional negative way (13.8; 23.5; 26.17-18); the prophet here reverses its significance.[320] Appropriating motherhood as an image for God parallels the use of fatherhood imagery in 63.16; 64.7 [8]; both are rare, and may have the same background, in the adapting of imagery from personal and family piety to refer to the relationship of the community as a whole to God. The appropriation of mother imagery may also have a specific background in people's belief in and prayer to a mother God alongside Yhwh.[321]

I take vv. 13bβ-14a (2-3-3) as a tricolon, which closes off vv. 7-14a; the verb 'comfort' picks up from v. 13abα but the tricolon forms a sequence of clauses in the second person.[322] After the resumptive reference to comfort, the second and third cola in vv. 13bβ-14a work abcc′b′: the opening verb applies to both cola and the two further verbs form a bracket around their parallel subjects. Given that the tricolon suggests the end of a subsection, the 'seeing' of v. 14a is more likely retrospective than prospective; that is, the line refers to seeing Jerusalem's restoration and well-being.[323] 'Rejoice' (*śûś/śîś*) is taken up from v. 10 but the idea of rejoicing at what one sees recurs from v. 5. It does so with some irony, as it takes up the mocking statement of the brothers about seeing the celebration of the faithful; it will now be the faithful who see and rejoice. The significance of their heart rejoicing is spelled out by and in turn explains the reference to their limbs flourishing like grass. The entire being of the people will rejoice and flourish, its centre (the heart) and its dispersed structure (the limbs, literally the bones). The collocation of rejoicing and flourishing takes up from 35.1. It is the obverse of the way the bones as well as the inner being are affected by trouble (e.g. Pss 22.15 [14]; 51.10 [8]; 102.4-5 [3-4]; Prov 14.30; 15.30; 16.23-24). Whereas the talk of comfort suggests a link with 40.1, the image of grass carries the opposite connotation to its point in 40.6-7. A negative image is again turned into a positive one, as in v. 12.

320 See Chris Franke, '"Like a Mother Have I Comforted You"', in Everson and Bloom (eds.), *The Desert Will Bloom*, pp. 35-56 (43-53); also Kessler, *Gott geht es um das Ganze*, p. 99.

321 Albertz, *Religionsgeschichte Israels in alttestamentlicher Zeit*, II, pp. 418-19 (ET p. 404).

322 Cf. Webster, 'A Rhetorical Study of Isaiah 66' (see above), p. 99.

323 Marvin A. Sweeney in 'On *ûmᵉśôś* in Isaiah 8.6', in Philip R. Davies and David J. A. Clines (eds.), *Among the Prophets* (Sheffield: Sheffield Academic Press, 1993), pp. 42-54, reprinted in Sweeney, *Form and Intertextuality in Prophetic and Apocalyptic Literature*, pp. 36-45, sees such description of rejoicing in 66.10-14 as based on the language and imagery of 8.6-8.

66.14b So Yhwh's hand will cause itself to be acknowledged among his servants;// he will rage among his enemies.
15 Because there: Yhwh will come with fire,// his chariots like a whirlwind, To return his anger with fury,// his rebuke with flames of fire.
16 Because with fire Yhwh is going to exercise authority,// and with his sword, among all flesh;// those pierced by Yhwh will be many.

Verse 14b marks a move back to talk of Yhwh's acting against his enemies, the topic of vv. 5-6. Another tricolon will close the subsection in v. 16. Once again, the subsection could have originally existed independently of the context, or have followed on vv. 5-6. Verse 14b (3-2) works abca′c′: each colon begins with a verb, the first colon alone having a subject for the verb. Each colon closes with a *ʾet* expression. The obvious way to take the second occurrence is to understand *ʾet* as the object-marker, but this can hardly apply to the first occurrence after the niphal verb, unless we take it as an unusual instance of its occasional diluted sense, meaning 'with regard to'. More likely the first occurrence of *ʾet* means 'with'. It then seems unlikely that the two occurrences involve one instance of the preposition, one of the object-marker, but the verb 'rage' (*zāʿam*) can be used intransitively (Ps 7.12 [11]; Dan 11.30), and more likely this is the usage here and *ʾet* has the same significance as in the first colon. The link with v. 14a implies that rejoicing and flourishing will come about because the faithful will recognize Yhwh's hand at work. LXX and Vg have 'will be known', but the niphal of *yādaʿ* likely has its more dynamic meaning (cf. 61.9). So Yhwh's servants will come to recognize Yhwh's hand. The prophecy reverts to speaking explicitly about two groups in the community, on one hand these servants and on the other hand Yhwh's enemies, in whose presence Yhwh will rage; the raging will be aimed at them. In light of the preceding lines, one might assume that Yhwh's hand making itself known and recognized would be a positive image, though the image commonly has negative implications for the people to whom Yhwh's hand is extended.[324] In v. 14b, the second colon makes clear that it has negative implications here; it will be the means of Yhwh's rage being expressed. But its extending will happen in the presence of Yhwh's servants, and it will therefore bring rejoicing and flourishing to the persons that at the moment are downcast through their oppression at the hand of Yhwh's enemies. LXX interestingly translates 'his servants' by 'those who revere him' (mss vary over whether they use σεβομένοις or φοβουμένοις), which suggests a different antithesis, between Gentiles who come to revere and Gentiles who do not; this antithesis would speak more directly to issues in the lives of the people for whom LXX Isaiah was translated.[325]

[324] Cf. Rashi, 'ישעיה', on the passage. See 59.1 and the comment.

[325] Cf. Baer, *When We All Go Home*, pp. 232-37. The rendering is a further example of the distinctiveness of LXX in Isaiah 66 over against earlier chapters. See Ziegler, *Untersuchungen zur Septuaginta des Buches Isaias*, p. 43; Baer, 'What Happens in the End?' [see above in the translation note on 66.1], pp. 19-21.

Verses 15-16 go on to explain what this raging will look like, with v. 15 working 4-2, 3-2 and v. 16 concluding the subsection with a tricolon 4-2-3 (indeed, one might take v. 15a as a 2-2-2 tricolon, 'Because there is Yhwh! He will come with fire, his chariots like a whirlwind'[326]). As 'comfort' recurred in each colon in v. 13, 'fire' recurs in each line in vv. 15-16. The two words sum up the implications of the prophet's message for the servants and for the faithless. The verses use the imagery traditional in descriptions of Yhwh's appearing to judge the world; they have specific links with Jeremiah 25.30-33. Like v. 6, however, vv. 15-16 apply this imagery to the prospect before people within Judah rather than that before Judah's external enemies.[327] 'Jerusalem's enemies are not foreign powers but the brothers, "the next-door neighbour".'[328] The expression for 'flames of fire' comes only here in the Old Testament using masculine *lahăbê* (the feminine equivalent comes in Ps 29.7), but it recurs in CD 2.5 to describe the judgment of people who do not turn from rebellion.

Each line in v. 15 comprises balancing cola. For v. 15a this understanding presupposes the assumption that the verb at the centre of the line applies to both cola rather than that the second colon (which recurs from Jer 4.13) is a noun clause. 'Because there…will come'[329] then applies to both cola; 'Yhwh' is paralleled by 'his chariots' (Yhwh's means of transport); and 'with fire' by 'like a whirlwind'. It is the first time any of these images have appeared in these chapters. They signify the frightening and destructive nature of Yhwh's rage. 'Return' is an odd verb; elsewhere *šûb* hiphil would imply pulling back anger. Here the context suggests another ellipse or condensed form of expression; Yhwh is repaying wrongdoing in a way that expresses anger. Yhwh's 'rebuke' (*gaʿărâ*) suggests 'the fearful and threatening voice of Yahweh, which he utters in the thunder, and which functions as a battle cry when he puts his various enemies to flight'.[330]

The tricolon comprising v. 16 takes the point further; Yhwh's action is an exercise of authority (*šāpaṭ* niphal), like that of a ruler punishing wrongdoing within his realm. But the line begins with another reference to this action as involving fire; this is no ordinary exercise of royal authority. The first two cola are parallel, in that 'by the sword' (a more predictable means of a ruler exercising authority) parallels 'by fire'. Near the beginning of this section Yhwh was simply destining people to the sword (65.12); at the end, the prophecy makes explicit that Yhwh is wielding the sword. 'Because Yhwh is going to exercise authority' applies to the second colon as well as the first, while 'among all flesh'

[326] Cf. Bonnard, *Le Second Isaïe*, p. 480.
[327] Cf. Smith, *Rhetoric and Redaction in Trito-Isaiah*, p. 166.
[328] Berges, *Das Buch Jesaja*, p. 520.
[329] On the force of כי הנה, see the comment on 65.17.
[330] A. Caquot, *TWAT*, II, p. 56 (ET *TDOT*, III, p. 53).

applies to the first as well as the second. LXX turns the first two cola from active into passive and thus makes 'all flesh' the victims of Yhwh's action, but the preposition *ʾet* has the same meaning as in v. 14bα, and 'all flesh' are not the victims of Yhwh's punishment but its witnesses (cf. 40.5; 49.26).[331] The parallelism between the first two cola means that v. 16a would make a quite satisfactory line on its own. The third colon is then a surprise, advertising that a subsection is coming to completion. 'Pierced' (from *ḥālal*) implies something more like 'slain' (Vg, Aq) than merely 'wounded' (LXX).

66.17 People who consecrate themselves and purify themselves to go into the gardens// following after one in the midst,
People eating the flesh of pig,// reptile, and mouse:// all at once they will come to an end (Yhwh's declaration).

For much of vv. 5-16 the explicit contrast between the purist and the permissive has gone underground, but the section closes by reaffirming that this contrast has underlain the section as a whole. Yhwh's enemies, the victims of Yhwh's fury and flame, are the people of whom v. 3 spoke. Only with some hesitation can v. 17 be construed as poetry (3-3, 3-2-3), and it may mark the transition to prose for most or all of the last eight verses of the book; its being prose might also draw attention to its discontinuity and its being of separate origin from the lines that precede.

The opening participles describing the permissive carry some irony. 'Consecrate oneself' (*qādēš* hitpael) is typically used to describe the action of priests, Levites, and people in connection with their worship of Yhwh or their meeting with Yhwh (e.g. Exod 19.22; 2 Chr 5.11; 30.3, 15, 17, 24), though also in connection with their broader maintaining of proper rules concerning what one eats (Lev 11.44 [P]). 'Purify oneself' (*ṭāhar* hitpael) is typically used in a similar way (e.g. 2 Chr 30.18; Lev 14 [P] is a concentration of instances). Purifying oneself denotes the removal of disqualifications for approaching God; consecration denotes the positive giving of oneself to God. Consecration or purification would presumably involve cleansing with water, washing one's clothes, and sexual abstinence (see, e.g., Exod 19.14-15 [JE]; Num 8.7 [P]). The terrible irony of the verse is that these people are consecrating and purifying themselves for actions that disqualify them from coming near Yhwh. They go into gardens, the kind of gardens to which 65.3 referred (see also 1.29)—that is, graveyards.[332] Their idea of sacredness is the one referred

[331] If on the contrary 'all flesh' are the victims, the term will refer to the faithless, who are to be subject to the judgment on all flesh of which vv. 18-24 will speak; see the discussion in Gärtner, *Jesaja 66 und Sacharja 14 als Summe der Prophetie* (see above), pp. 32-34.

[332] Francesca Stavrakopoulou (*Land of Our Fathers* [London: Continuum, 2010], p. 114) suggests that gardens would imply royal tombs.

to in 65.5. The picture of them going there '[following] after one in the midst' is elliptical; the one in the midst might be a god or goddess, or a worship leader, male or female (depending on whether one follows K or Q);[333] commentators routinely note the position of Jaazaniah 'in the midst' of worshippers in Ezekiel 8.11.

'Pig' reappears from v. 3 (also 65.4, which used the actual expression 'flesh of pig'). Like the pig, the mouse appeared in the Torah's list of creatures whose eating is incompatible with being 'pure' (Lev 11.7, 29, 47 [P]). 'Reptile' (*šeqeṣ*) recurs in that chapter to describe various creatures as 'abominations', but with this meaning the word's appearance in the midst of this little list of creatures is odd. In Mishnaic Hebrew it can denote a specific reptile,[334] and I assume this meaning here.[335]

To describe the permissive coming to an end, all at once, takes up two expressions from earlier in the section. In 65.7 Yhwh spoke of Yhwh repaying the waywardness of such people 'all at once'; the expression also came in the warning about judgment in 1.29-31 with its several parallels in chapters 65–66. 'Come to an end' (*yāsupû*) picks up 'whirlwind' (*sûpâ*) from 66.15; the words may or may not be etymologically related, but the verb's citation form and the noun are at least homonyms, and in the context the section's closing colon implies that the apostate will be swept away.[336] The final 'Yhwh's declaration' constitutes a concluding affirmation that it will really happen.[337]

Conclusion

It is possible to think of religion or faith as involving humanity's reaching out to God or trying to find God, and then to assume that one should validate all such attempts and all the convictions of faith in which they issue (or to repudiate them all). It is the journey of faith that counts. While Deuteronomy 32.8-9 may offer some support for that view in connection with the world in general, this section of Isaiah assumes that for Israel, at least, religion or faith is a response to God's making himself available and that the people's problem lies not in reaching out and

[333] Joseph Blenkinsopp argues for the feminine reading and a female officiant; see 'The One in the Middle', in Exum and Williamson (eds.), *Reading from Right to Left*, pp. 63-75.

[334] See *HALOT*; cf. Jacob Levy, *Neuhebräisches und chaldäisches Wörterbuch über die Talmudim und Midraschim* (Leipzig: Brockhaus, 1893), IV, p. 606a; Gustaf H. Dalman, *Aramäisch-neuhebräisches Wörterbuch zu Targum, Talmud und Midrasch* (Frankfurt: Kauffmann, 1901), p. 413b.

[335] Contrast Milgrom, *Leviticus 1–16*, pp. 657-58, who suggests that pig and mouse are synecdoche for categories of unclean animals, while in between them *šeqeṣ* is a general term for animals that defile only by ingestion.

[336] Cf. Beuken, *Jesaja IIIB*, p. 162.

[337] On the expression, see on 59.20.

failing to find but in failing to reach out or in reaching in wrong directions. Not all convictions of faith are valid. Consequently, whereas there is less reason for God to take action against other peoples, there is good reason for taking action against God's household; that is where judgment properly starts.

It is appropriate, however, for such action to allow for the possibility that the entire household does not deserve the same treatment. In this respect, the section does not suggest a distinction between First Temple and Second Temple ways of thinking. Both eras emphasized the importance of Israel's corporate commitment to Yhwh. Both emphasized the importance of individuals making their own commitment to Yhwh. Both recognized that this expectation could involve individuals being prepared to stand separate from the main body of Israel. Both recognized that sometimes this dynamic involved the community's being divided into at least two groups, which the Old Testament characterizes as a group that is faithful to Yhwh and a group that is unfaithful. If there is a difference between the eras, it lies in how far they make allowance for the notion of a discriminating judgment. In First Temple times and at the fall of Jerusalem, Yhwh's judgment fell on the whole community, on faithful as well as faithless. The judgment described in this section distinguishes between their destinies. The prophecies raise more explicitly than many the question whether God continues to relate to and restore Israel as an ethnic whole or whether God designates only part of Israel as the real Israel. Such 'a divine intervention at once bringing ruin upon one section of the nation and salvation upon the other cannot possibly be conceived in terms of history'.[338] The exchange between Abraham and God in Genesis 18 (J) perhaps confirms the point.

Meanwhile, it is still the case that 'the condemnation is uttered with the intention of summoning to repentance and salvation',[339] which reduces the force of that point (compare 66.24 and the comment). Dividing the community into two groups, so that final priority belongs with people's own decisions and with individuals and not the community, is not a great irreversible step forward, the prophet's 'final answer to the problem of how a God of righteousness is to fulfil his purpose through an unrighteous and rebellious people'.[340] The notion of a God-chosen community remains a key theme in the book, and a key theme in the Old Testament. It is also so for Jesus and Paul. Tertullian notes how Jesus confirms the prophecies' complex emphases; their warnings offer anticipations of Christ's warnings.[341] Jesus speaks of a judgment by means of fire (Matt 25),[342] as does

[338] Westermann, *Jesaja Kapitel 40–66*, p. 321 (ET p. 404).
[339] Herbert, *Isaiah 40–66*, p. 185.
[340] Smart, *History and Theology in Second Isaiah*, p. 275.
[341] *Against Marcion* 4.14.
[342] Cf. Haymon of Halberstadt, *Commentariorum in Isaiam libri tres*, col. 1081.

Hebrews 12.29,[343] and 2 Thessalonians 1.5-12 restates motifs from 66.4-5, 15 and makes its message more worrying.[344]

The prophecies continue to affirm that God is committed to transforming this-worldly life; it is neither the case that this transformation simply depends on our human effort nor that we must give up on hope for this world and look rather to a heavenly or spiritual fulfilment of God's vision.[345] Isaiah 65.18-25 in particular occupies a middle place between the expectation in Isaiah 1–39 of God acting in history in a way that is 'miraculous but nonetheless historically describable' and the expectation in Revelation 21 of God acting in a way so radically different that 'analogies to the reality of historical human life can be drawn, for the most part, only by denying their continued validity'. In 65.18-25 'the historic medium of God's re-creation is no longer in view' but 'the new world' is still one in which 'houses must be built and fields planted (v. 21), in which children are born (v. 23), and in which one will eventually die, albeit only at a ripe old age (v. 20)'.[346]

343 Cf. Jerome, *Commentariorum in Isaiam prophetam libri duodeviginti*, col. 663.

344 Cf. Bonnard, *Le Second Isaïe*, pp. 495-96; also Luther, *In Esaiam prophetam enarraciones*, p. 576 (ET p. 404).

345 Cf. John W. de Gruchy, 'A New Heaven and a New Earth', *Journal of Theology for Southern Africa* 105 (1999), pp. 65-74.

346 Ulrich Mauser, 'Isaiah 65:17-25', *Interpretation* 36 (1982), pp. 181-86 (182, 183, 182-83).

XII

ISAIAH 66.18-24

Translation and Notes

66.18 But as for me[1], given their deeds and their intentions:[2] the gathering
together[3] of all the nations and tongues is coming,[4] and they will come
and see my splendour 19 and I will set a sign[5] among them. I will send
off[6] from them survivors to the nations, Tarshish, Pul[7], Lud, the people
who draw the bow,[8] Tubal, Javan, and the distant shores far-off, which
have not heard report of me[9] and have not seen my splendour, and they
will declare my splendour among the nations. 20 They will bring all
your relatives out of all the nations as an offering to Yhwh, by means of
horses, chariotry, coaches, mules, and dromedaries, on my holy mountain[10], Jerusalem (Yhwh has said), as the Israelites bring the offering in a

[1] For MT ואנכי Michaelis ('Anzeige der Varianten in Jesaia', p. 222) reads אנכתי, a hypothesized denominative from אנך, implying 'I have applied the plummet to'; Klostermann (*Deuterojesaia*, p. 113) reads ואף כי 'And indeed when [their deeds and their intentions come about]'; Marti (*Das Buch Jesaja*, p. 412) reads כי הנה 'For there'.

[2] Volz (*Jesaja II*, pp. 294-95) moves מעשיהם ומחשבתיהם to v. 16, Torrey (*The Second Isaiah*, pp. 276, 473) to the beginning of v. 17 (along with the opening ואנכי), Duhm (*Jesaia*, pp. 442-43) to the end of v. 17.

[3] Resultative piel (cf. Jenni, *Das hebräische Pi'el*, pp. 193-99).

[4] For MT באה, 1QIs[a] has באו, assimilating to the preceding pl. nouns. LXX, Vg, Syr have a first-person verb, implying participial בא and assimilating to the opening 'I' (NEB presupposes ובאתי [Brockington, *The Hebrew Text of the Old Testament*, p. 198]). Marti (*Das Buch Jesaja*, p. 412) reads באה העת 'the time is coming'.

[5] For MT אות 1QIs[a] has pl. אותות, assimilating to the pl. nouns in the context (cf. Kutscher, הלשון והרקע הלשוני של מגילת ישעיהו השלמה, p. 300 [ET p. 397]); cf. LXX, but not OL.

[6] Resultative piel (cf. Jenni, *Das hebräische Pi'el*, pp. 186-88).

[7] For MT פול LXX implies פוט, as in Jer 46.9; Ezek 27.10. Vg has 'Africa', though Jerome (*Commentariorum in Isaiam prophetam libri duodeviginti*, col. 666) tells us that he reads Put or Pul, indicating that he knew the readings of MT and LXX (Barthélémy, *Critique Textuelle de l'Ancien Testament*, II, p. 464).

[8] For MT משכי קשת LXX Μοσοχ implies מֶשֶׁךְ (Lowth, *Isaiah*, p. 405), for which see Gen 10.23; Ezek 27.13; 38.2. MT's unexpected descriptive phrase might be a gloss, possibly based on Jer 46.9 (e.g. Volz, *Jesaja II*, p. 295). Duhm (*Jesaia*, p. 444) suggests rather that קשת is a corruption of ראש/רש 'Rosh' (Ezek 38.2-3; 39.1). De Lagarde (*Prophetae chaldaice*, p. l) reads מֶשֶׁךְ וְקֵדָר ('Meshech and Qedar'). 1QIs[a] has משוך קשת.

[9] For MT שמעי LXX has 'my name'; cf. passages such as Gen 29.13; Num 14.15. Thus it does not imply שמי.

[10] LXX has 'to the holy city', which might be designed to allow the Gentiles and their offering to come only to the city and not to the sanctuary itself (see Baer, *When We All*

pure vessel[11] to Yhwh's house. 21 Also from them I will take[12] some people as priests, as Levites[13] (Yhwh has said). 22 Because as the new[14] heavens and the new earth which I am going to make are going to stand before me (Yhwh's declaration), so your offspring and your name will stand. 23 New moon by new moon, Sabbath by Sabbath[15], all flesh will come to bow low before me (Yhwh has said). 24 People will go out and look at the corpses of the men who rebelled against me, because their worm[16] will not die and their fire will not go out, and they will be a horror[17] to all flesh.

Introduction

As the conclusion to Isaiah 56–66, 66.18-24 matches the chapters' preface (56.1-8) in broadening the horizon to incorporate reference to foreign people coming to worship Yhwh.[18] Further, it closes the book of Isaiah analogously to the way 27.12-13 closes Isaiah 1–27.[19] Like the preface, it constitutes both a promise to the Judahite community and warning about the consequences of unfaithfulness.

1QIs^{a}, ^{b} begin a new chapter at v. 20b; 1QIs^{a} does so again at v. 22, in each case following on 'Yhwh has said'.[20] Following on the further 'Yhwh has said', one might similarly think of v. 24 as a new beginning.

Go Home, p. 267, and the broader treatment [pp. 246-76] of v. 20 in the LXX as designed to safeguard the position of the Jewish community itself over against Gentile pilgrims).

[11] For MT בכלי טהור LXX has 'with psalms', following on its reading 'to the holy city' quoted in the previous note, which Adrian Schenker ('Dans un vase pur ou avec des Psaumes?', in van der Meer *et al.* [eds.], *Isaiah in Context*, pp. 407-12) views as original; but his suggestion that it cannot derive from Amos 5.22-23 because the reference there is negative (pp. 410-11) is surely mistaken, since LXX could be promising the restoration of offerings as they should be in light of Amos.

[12] 1QIs^{a} adds ליא 'for myself'; cf. LXX (but not OL).

[13] Many post-MT mss and Vrs precede ללוים by ו 'and'. Oort ('Kritische Aanteekeningen', p. 477) omits the first ל.

[14] For the Leningrad ms's הֶחֳדָשִׁים other MT mss have the expected הַחֲדָשִׁים.

[15] The expressions seem to combine or to be a variant on several separate idioms. שנה בשנה means 'year by year'. עלת שבת בשבתו (Num 28.10) means 'the burnt offering of each Sabbath'. מדי then suggests 'out of the sufficiency/requirement'. It appears in combination with שנה בשנה (e.g. 1 Sam 7.16; see BDB, p. 191b), perhaps the immediate model for the phrase here (GID). For MT בשבתו 1QIs^{a} has בשבתה; so also 4QIs^{c}.

[16] Tg has 'their breath'.

[17] For MT דראון, LXX 'spectacle' (cf. Vg, Tg) implies a reading such as לראוה or לראות (Klostermann, *Deuterojesaia*, p. 115).

[18] On the links between 56.1-8 and 66.18-24, see, e.g., Polan, *In the Ways of Justice*, pp. 79-89; Bernd Jørg Diebner, 'Jes 56,1-8 entsprechend Jes 66,18-24 und die prophetische Überbietung des Torah', in A. von Dobbeler, K. Erlemann, and R. Heiligentha (eds.), *Religionsgeschichte des Neuen Testaments* (Klaus Berger Festschrift; Tübingen: Franke, 2000), pp. 31-42.

[19] Willem A. M. Beuken, 'Yhwh's Sovereign Rule and His Adoration on Mount Zion', in Everson and Kim (eds.), *The Desert Will Bloom*, pp. 91-107 (102-7).

[20] But might the odd division before v. 20b reflect some Qumran doctrine? (GID).

Thus formally 66.18-24 differs from 56.1-8 in comprising a succession of short sayings that could be of separate origin.[21] Westermann sees the passage as issuing from the supplementing of vv. 18-19, 21 by vv. 20, 22-24;[22] Vermeylen sees the material as accumulating over four stages, vv. 18-19, 21; 23-24; 20; and 22;[23] Koenen sees vv. 18-22 as the original ending of Isaiah 56–66; vv. 23 and 24 are then two additions.[24] Further, Duhm suggested that the lists of places and of means of transport in vv. 19 and 20 were later additions to the text.[25]

I take the whole of this last section of the book as prose.[26] Admittedly it is possible to lay out vv. 22-24 in poetic lines:[27]

22 Because as the new heavens// and the new earth
Which I am going to make// are going to stand forever// (Yhwh's declaration)
So will stand// your offspring and your name.
23 New moon by new moon,// Sabbath by Sabbath,
All flesh will come// to bow low before me// (Yhwh has said).
24 People will go out and look// at the corpses of the men who rebelled against me,
Because their worm will not die// and their fire will not go out,// and they will be a horror to all flesh.

The lines are rhythmically plausible (4-2, 3-3, 2-2; 3-3, 2-2-2; 2-4, 4-3-3) but there is little regularity or parallelism or imagery about them, and their prosaic nature suggests we should treat them as prose. The same conclusion emerges with more force from any attempt to lay out vv. 18-21 as poetic lines.[28]

Comment

66.18 But as for me, given their deeds and their intentions: the gathering together of all the nations and tongues is coming, and they will come and see my splendour 19 and I will set a sign among them.

The opening of v. 18 is very jerky; I have remarked in the translation notes on some suggested emendations, but these are mostly matters of guesswork without support from the textual traditions. In MT itself I take

[21] Cf. Kellermann, 'Tritojesaja und das Geheimnis des Gottesknechts', p. 68.
[22] *Jesaja Kapitel 40–66*, p. 336 (ET p. 423).
[23] See *Du prophète Isaïe à l'apocalyptique*, II, pp. 501-3, 514-17.
[24] See *Ethik und Eschatologie im Tritojesajabuch*, p. 208.
[25] *Jesaia*, p. 443.
[26] Helen G. Jefferson ('Notes on the Authorship of Isaiah 65 and 66', *JBL* 68 [1949], pp. 225-30) notes that the use of the article, the object marker, and the relative are especially characteristic of 66.17-24.
[27] See, e.g., Thomas ('ספר ישעיה', p. 105) and NRSV.
[28] But see (e.g.) Edwin C. Webster, 'A Rhetorical Study of Isaiah 66', *JSOT* 34 (1986), pp. 93-108 (100-101); 35 (1986), p. 121.

the opening of the verse to involve a combination of extraposition or casus pendens[29] and anacoluthon[30] rather than ellipse or aposiopesis.[31] Aposiopesis implies incoherence that arises from passion or excitement, but 'there is no trace of passion or excitement in the context'.[32]

Ellipse would imply an understanding such as 'But I [know] their deeds and their intentions: [the time] is coming to gather all the nations and tongues'. The first ellipse is presupposed by 'I know' in some LXX manuscripts, though not OL (*HUB* compares Ps 94.11); compare Tg 'are revealed before me'. For the second ellipse, Ezekiel 21.12 [7] and 39.8 have been cited as parallels,[33] but in these passages the implicit subject of the verb 'come' is not a word for 'time' but rather the event that the previous lines have referred to; hence EVV there translate 'it is coming'.

More likely the extraposed 'as for me' anticipates and is taken up in the first-person suffix on 'my splendour' and in the first-person verbs in the next sentence; indeed, 'I' is the implied subject of the infinitive *l^eqabbēṣ*. The opening of the verse then signals a change of topic for what will follow in vv. 18-23, where the close of Isaiah 56–66 returns to the topic with which it began, the acknowledgment of Yhwh by foreigners. 'Their' in turn might anticipate and be taken up in 'all the nations and tongues';[34] 'their deeds and intentions' would then also be extraposed, and the phrase would refer to the nations bringing Judahites home. But it is easier to understand 'their deeds and their intentions' as taking up from the previous verse and as referring by anacoluthon to the faithless people mentioned there. The two nouns 'deeds' and 'intentions' have usually had negative reference earlier in Isaiah 56–66 (57.12; 59.6, 7; 65.2). The implication then is that their faithless deeds and intentions lead to Yhwh's decision to gather the nations,[35] while v. 24 will take up their destiny again. Either way, the coming actions of the nations will stand in contrast with those of the faithless within Judah.

I then understand the infinitive *l^eqabbēṣ* as the subject of 'is coming'.[36] Whereas earlier parts of Isaiah spoke of Yhwh gathering scattered Judah (11.12; 40.11; 43.5; 54.7), the opening section of Isaiah 56–66 already spoke also of Yhwh gathering people to Judah from the nations (56.8), and this closing section takes up that motif in declaring that Yhwh's gathering of the nations is coming. It is a 'coming' of a very different

[29] Cf. Young, *The Book of Isaiah*, III, p. 531.

[30] Cf. GK 167b.

[31] Cf. Vitringa, *Commentarius in librum prophetiarum Jesaiae*, II, p. 1102.

[32] Cheyne, *The Prophecies of Isaiah*, II, p. 128.

[33] See Barthélémy, *Critique Textuelle de l'Ancien Testament*, II, p. 463.

[34] So Rashi, 'ישעיה' on the passage.

[35] So D. Qimchi, 'ישעיה', on the passage; Ibn Ezra, *The Commentary of Ibn Ezra on Isaiah*, p. 305.

[36] So Friedrich Boettcher, *Proben alttestamentlicher Schrifterklärung* (Leipzig: Weidmann, 1833), pp. 36-37. For this usage see JM 124b. While the infinitive construct is more commonly treated as m., it can be treated as f. (e.g. 1 Sam 18.23).

kind from the one of which v. 15 warned. It is also a 'gathering' of a very different kind from that in passages such as Joel 4.2, 11 [3.2, 11] and Zephaniah 3.8 (and that in Zech 14.2, where the verb is *'āsap*).[37]

The expression 'all nations and tongues' comes only here, though Zechariah 8.23 speaks of individuals from 'all the tongues of the nations' attaching themselves to Judahites in order to come to Jerusalem to entreat Yhwh. In Isaiah, the 'nations' have often been referred to, while 45.23 has referred to 'every tongue' swearing by Yhwh. One can see Isaiah 56–66 in general, and this closing section in particular, as taking up the theme of 'universal' salvation in 45.22-25.[38] In what sense will the nations and tongues come to see Yhwh's splendour? In Isaiah 56–66 'seeing Yhwh's splendour' does not suggest a direct, unmediated vision of God's splendour of the kind that Moses was denied (Exod 33.18-33), nor the more mediated, less direct vision granted to Ezekiel ('the appearance of the likeness of the splendour of Yhwh', Ezek 1.28) nor the similar less direct appearance of Yhwh's splendour in the temple (cf. Ezek 43.1-4)[39] nor the manifestation of Yhwh's splendour in judgment on Israel (Ezek 39.21-24).[40] In this context it more likely suggests the splendour Yhwh will have manifested in bringing the Judahites home and restoring the city so that it shares Yhwh's splendour (v. 11; also 58.8; 59.19; 60.1-2; 62.2). The verse thus reaffirms the promise in 40.5 that all flesh would see Yhwh's splendour.[41] In the broader context of Isaiah 40–55 (see especially 42.8) one might think of the splendour that belongs to Yhwh alone and not to other deities such as the nations had once worshipped.

In turn, the 'sign' (*'ôt*) that Yhwh will set among the nations when they come to Jerusalem might be the sign of the Sabbath (cf. Ezek 20.12, 20); the nations' coming to observe the Sabbath will be a sign of their new status as people who belong to Yhwh (cf. v. 23; and 56.6-7). Or it might be the sign constituted by the restoration of Jerusalem (cf. the usage in 55.13, at the very end of Isa 40–55); this would be compatible with the idea that the word 'sign' refers to the same reality as the word 'splendour'.[42] Or it might be the punishment of the faithless and the vindication of the faithful of which the preceding section spoke.[43] Or it might be something that cannot be identified until it comes about.[44] Or it might be a standard to which the nations are to gather (cf. *nēs* in 11.12; 49.22; 62.10). Related to this suggestion is the idea that the sign is the

37 GID.

38 Cf. Beuken (*Jesaja IIIB*, p. 133).

39 Cf. Muilenburg, 'The Book of Isaiah: Chapters 40–66', p. 771.

40 E.g. Lau, *Schriftgelehrte Prophetie in Jes 56–66*, p. 144.

41 Stromberg (*Isaiah after Exile*, pp. 114-23) suggests further links in the closing part of Isaiah with 40.1-11.

42 Cf. W. A. M. Beuken, 'Isaiah Chapters lxv-lxvi', in Emerton (ed.), *Congress Volume: Leuven 1989*, pp. 204-21 (211).

43 Beuken's own view, *Jesaja IIIB*, p. 136.

44 Cf. Ibn Ezra, *The Commentary of Ibn Ezra on Isaiah*, p. 305.

very commissioning of missionaries that v. 19 goes on to describe.[45] It is likely not a sign like those given to Pharaoh (e.g. Exod 10.2), since in Isaiah 40–66 the 'gathering' of the nations always has a positive significance;[46] further, the signs in Exodus and in other such contexts are commonly plural (as here in 1QIs[a] and LXX, though not OL).[47] The sign set in Egypt that is promised in 19.20 would thus be a more plausible link. Whichever understanding is appropriate, the clause about a sign makes better sense in association with what precedes in v. 18 than in association with what follows in v. 19.[48] In other words, 'splendour' and 'sign' do refer to the same reality.

66.19aβb I will send off from them survivors to the nations, Tarshish, Pul, Lud, the people who draw the bow, Tubal, Javan, and the distant shores far-off, which have not heard report of me and have not seen my splendour, and they will declare my splendour among the nations.

It has been suggested that v. 19 goes on to explain how the gathering in v. 18 is effected,[49] but the 'from them' makes that understanding difficult. Further, if we were to treat v. 19 as a self-contained saying, then the 'them' from whom survivors are to be sent off could be the Judahites, and the idea that Judahites should be sent off to declare Yhwh's splendour would make entire sense. But set as it is in the context of vv. 18-19aα, the 'them' has to be the nations and tongues.[50] Apparently the 'survivors' are sent off from them. This makes sense in light of the fact that the word for 'survivors' is almost identical to one in 45.20 (the word there is *pālîṭ*, here the less common *pālêṭ*), where they are explicitly survivors *of* the nations. 'Survivors' is effectively a synonym for 'remnant' in the sense of a group of people who are preserved from a disaster and therefore have hope to enjoy new life—namely, to witness and in some sense share in the restoration of Judah and the fulfilment of Yhwh's purpose.[51] The context in 45.20 suggests that they are survivors in the sense that they are people who escaped the crushing of the nations by the Babylonians and/or the Persians,[52] with whom the Judahites have sympathy as fellow-victims (Jerome compares 1.9)[53] and for whom Yhwh has some concern

[45] So, e.g., Kellermann, 'Tritojesaja und das Geheimnis des Gottesknechts', p. 71.

[46] Cf. Koole, *Jesaja III*, p. 473 (ET p. 518).

[47] Cf. Koenen, *Ethik und Eschatologie im Tritojesajabuch*, p. 210.

[48] Bonnard, *Le Second Isaïe*, p. 480; cf. Theodoret of Cyrrhus, *Commentaire sur Isaïe* 185a (III, p. 344).

[49] So, e.g., Jones, 'Isaiah—II and III', p. 535.

[50] See the discussion in Stromberg, *Isaiah after Exile*, pp. 135-41, in the context of his examination of the relationship between 66.18-24 and 11.11-6; 49.22-23; and 62.10-12.

[51] See Giovanni Rinaldi, 'Gli "scampati" di Is., lxvi, 18-22', in *À la rencontre de Dieu : Mémorial Albert Gelin* (Le Puy: Xavier Mappus, 1961), pp. 109-18.

[52] Cf. Koenen, *Ethik und Eschatologie im Tritojesajabuch*, p. 211.

[53] *Commentariorum in Isaiam prophetam libri duodeviginti*, col. 669AB.

as well as for Judah, again because they are victims. So they are not people who have been allowed to survive Yhwh's judgment, like the Judahites themselves (the Judahites are a *pēlêtâ* in this sense in Ezra 9.8, 13-15). The nations are not under judgment in vv. 18-24 any more than in 65.1–66.17. These representatives of the nations are the kind of people who were prepared to put their hope in Yhwh's servant when he brings news of Yhwh's rule (42.4). The use of the verb *šālaḥ* (piel) makes this a rare example of what one could literally call 'mission' in the Old Testament,[54] and thus a new move in the vision of God's concern for the nations in the book of Isaiah. The nations are not merely welcome to come to Jerusalem; God intends to send out for them.[55] Yet the 'missionaries' are Gentiles not Israelites,[56] so that the prophecy does not go back on the awareness that it is not Israel's job to convert the nations; it is God's job to do so. Further, the prophecy is not any more universalist than other parts of Isaiah or of the Old Testament. From beginning to end the Old Testament assumes that Yhwh is Lord of the nations and it commonly refers to Yhwh's intention that the nations should come to acknowledge this fact (see, e.g., Pss 96–98). Further, here as elsewhere the reference to this theme is also Israel-focused.[57] Declaring that the nations will come to recognize the God of Israel and to recognize this God's restoration of the city of Jerusalem is expressed here because it constitutes good news for the people of Jerusalem themselves. Picturing the nations recognizing Yhwh's restoration of the city is another way of encouraging people to believe that Yhwh really will restore the city. In other words, the universalism of the prophecy continues to be combined with particularism. The prophecy does not assume a universalism that means all nations can find God in their own way. It assumes a universalism that means all nations can find the one God by recognizing what this God has done in Jerusalem.

So survivors *from* the nations are to go *to* the nations. The implication of the specific identification of the destination nations in v. 19 may be that the nations and tongues of v. 18 are more familiar ones that live nearer to Jerusalem (people such the Moabites, Ammonites, and Ashdodites, neighbours of Judah in the period after the exile). It is easy

[54] Cf. Westermann, *Jesaja Kapitel 40–66*, p. 337 (ET p. 425).

[55] Cf. Bernard Wodecki, 'Der Heilsuniversalismus bei Trito-jesaja', *VT* 32 (1982), pp. 248-51 (251); also '*šlh* [sic] dans le livre d'Isaïe', *VT* 34 (1984), pp. 482-88 (486).

[56] But contrast J. Blenkinsopp, 'Second Isaiah—Prophet of Universalism', *JSOT* 41 (1988), pp. 83-103 (98), reprinted in P. R. Davies (ed.), *The Prophets* (Sheffield: Sheffield Academic Press, 1996), pp. 186-206 (205).

[57] Contrast Begg ('Foreigners in Third Isaiah', p. 102), who portrays the attitude to foreigners sometimes rather negatively but sometimes in too selfless terms. J. Severino Croatto ('The Nations in the Salvific Oracles of Isaiah', *VT* 55 [2005], pp. 143-61) sees no place for a concern for the nations here or elsewhere in Isaiah; among the many passages he considers, 56.1-8 does not feature.

enough for news about Jerusalem to reach them. It is also easy enough for them to make pilgrimage to Jerusalem, and passages such as 14.28; 15.1-5 seem to envisage something of this kind. It is then their task to make it possible for nations that live further away to have opportunity to hear report of Yhwh and of Yhwh's acts.

The nations listed also appear in the broad context of a much longer list of nations in Genesis 10 (mostly in 10.1-7 [P]) and in Ezekiel 27.10-13 in the narrower context of a list of Tyre's trading partners.[58] In this context Tarshish might be Tarsus in Turkey or Tartessus in Spain (see further 60.9). Pul is usually assumed to be a variant for Put (the name that comes in Gen 10.6 and Ezek 27), that is, Libya. Lud might be Lydia in Turkey or might be a North African people; 'the people who draw the bow' seems to be an elaboration derived from Jeremiah 46.9, one of a number of parallels with Jeremiah in Isaiah 65–66, which encourages hesitation over reckoning it a gloss. Tubal is usually assumed to be the place of that name in Turkey suggested by its place in the lists in Genesis 10 and Ezekiel 28, though Vg's paraphrase of this list ('in the sea, in Africa, in Lydia people who hold the bow, in Italy, and Greece') implies reference to the tradition that Tubal was much further west, in Italy (or Spain).[59] Javan refers to the Ionian territory on the west side of Turkey. Thus these peoples are themselves examples of 'the distant shores', the countries across the Mediterranean from Canaan as opposed to the peoples around Judah. They will hear from those nearby peoples of how Yhwh's splendour has manifested itself in Jerusalem (cf. 60.2; 62.2).

66.20 They will bring all your relatives out of all the nations as an offering to Yhwh, by means of horses, chariotry, coaches, mules, and dromedaries, on my holy mountain, Jerusalem (Yhwh has said), as the Israelites bring the offering in a pure vessel to Yhwh's house.

The fact that the future declaration about the nations in vv. 18-19 is good news for Judah overlaps with the need to face the present fact that many Judahites remain scattered among the nations. The prophecy recognizes that even when Jerusalem has been restored and Yhwh's splendour thus been manifested, and nearby peoples have recognized this manifestation and taken news of it to nations further away, this scattering would continue to be a reality unless Yhwh also does something to restore the community in this further sense by bringing Judahites home in keeping with promises in earlier parts of Isaiah (e.g. 11.11-12; 49.8-12; 60.4-9). The response of the far-off nations to news of what has happened in Jerusalem will include their bringing with them to Jerusalem the

[58] Cf. Graham I. Davies, 'The Destiny of the Nations', in Vermeylen (ed.), *The Book of Isaiah: Le Livre d'Isaïe*, pp. 93-120 (95).

[59] See Jerome, *Commentariorum in Isaiam prophetam libri duodeviginti*, col. 667.

Judahites in their midst, the relatives of the Judahites in Jerusalem whom the prophecy continues to address. Indeed, this action comes first in the prophecy's account of their response; only in the verses that follow will there be reference to their action in coming to worship for themselves. The first significance of the proclaiming of the news about Yhwh concerns its importance for the Judahites listening to the prophecy.

The nations will bring Judahites as an offering to Yhwh. One might then translate 'Israelites will bring…', in keeping with the future reference of the rest of the verse, and this would be especially appropriate if the temple has not yet been rebuilt. The idea that people are an offering to Yhwh is novel. In isolation one might understand *minḥâ* as a political metaphor; this *minḥâ* is tribute offered to the divine King. But the verse's subsequent comparison with a *minḥâ* brought in a pure vessel suggests that the word indeed refers to an offering made in connection with worship. Exodus and Leviticus give prescriptions concerning the way people will 'bring' an 'offering' to 'Yhwh's house' and concerning the 'vessels' and the need to make sure that offerings are made in a 'pure' fashion (see, e.g., Exod 35 [P]; Lev 24 [H]). The prophecy combines this complex of ideas in a novel way. The Judahites themselves become the offering; appropriately, they are a *minḥâ*, a general word for an offering, not a sacrifice, which is an object that is killed. The survivors of the nations become the worshippers bringing the offering. The vessels by means of which they bring them become the means of transporting the Judahites. Their destination becomes Jerusalem as Yhwh's holy mountain; the notion of centrifugal mission combines with that of centripetal attraction. The reference to Yhwh's 'holy mountain' is another link with the opening section of Isaiah 56–66: see 56.7, which speaks of Yhwh 'bringing' foreigners to 'my holy mountain'. It also suggests a link with the immediately preceding section, which has described Judahites themselves putting Yhwh's holy mountain out of mind but has also promised that there will be no more harm or destruction on 'my holy mountain' (65.11, 25).

LXX rather compromises this point by rendering *minḥâ* 'gift' on the first occasion and 'sacrifice' on the second.[60] The idea of offering is thus not so much secularized as used with the implication that the whole life of the Judahites is given to Yhwh. The prophecy does not imply that literal sacrifices cease. It does suggest a link between literal sacrifices and the metaphorical giving of the whole people to God. To put it another way, it would close off from the Judahites themselves the idea that they can give literal sacrifices to God without giving themselves in their everyday life to God. The conviction that these two forms of giving are linked is implicit in the polemic concerning the tension between worship and everyday life in a passage such as 1.10-20.

[60] Cf. Daniel's comments, *Le vocabulaire du culte dans la Septante*, pp. 212-13.

Zechariah 14.15 includes a comparable list of animals to the one in v. 20, one of a number of links between the close of Zechariah and the close of Isaiah that point to some relationship between them.[61] The various forms of transport emphasize the honour conveyed on the Judahites by the people who arrange their return to Jerusalem. Horses belong to kings not ordinary people, and they are military transport, not everyday transport. The same is true of chariotry. The Old Testament otherwise mentions coaches (*ṣāb*) only in Numbers 7.3 in connection with the transporting of the covenant chest; BDB compares them with palanquins in which people such as kings were carried by porters. Mules are likewise a much rarer form of transport than asses; they are used by people such as royalty (see, e.g., 1 Sam 13.29; 18.9). The last word in the list, *kirkārâ*, comes only here, which itself hints that it, too, constitutes a rather exotic form of transport. The word may be connected with the roots *kārar* or *kûr*,[62] but this tells us little. Vg, Sym have 'carriages', and LXX implies that the word refers to some form of transport of this kind,[63] but Ibn Ezra and David Qimchi have 'dromedaries'.[64]

There is something both appropriate and paradoxical about the forms of transport being compared to a 'pure' vessel. Animals such as horse, mule, and camel are 'secular' animals in the sense that they are not categorized as either clean or unclean. An implication is that in the context of a metaphorical offering made in the city rather than in the temple, such animals can be like clean vessels. The cleanliness of the vessel contrasts both with the defiled and defiling nature of the worship of the faithless (cf. v. 17; also 65.4) and with the defiled and defiling nature of the context from which the worshippers come, brought about by its images (cf. Amos 7.17; Zech 3).[65]

66.21 Also from them I will take some people as priests, as Levites (Yhwh has said).

Grammatically, whereas the twofold 'them' in v. 19 must refer to the nations, 'them' in v. 21 might be either the people who are brought as an offering (the Judahites' relatives) or the people who bring them (the

[61] See, e.g., Gärtner, *Jesaja 66 und Sacharja 14 als Summe der Prophetie*; cf. Hanson, *The Dawn of Apocalyptic*, pp. 388-89.

[62] There is an Ugaritic verb *krkr* meaning 'roll' (cf. C. H. Gordon, *Ugaritic Textbook* [Rome: Ponitifical Biblical Institute, 1965], p. 421; Mitchell J. Dahood, review of Kutscher, *The Language and Literary Background of the Isaiah-Scroll*, *Biblica* 56 [1975], pp. 260-64 [262]).

[63] Kutscher (הלשון והרקע הלשוני של מגילת ישעיהו השלמה, p. 188 [ET p. 249]) suggests that 1QIs[a] invented its word כורכובות by combining the root כרר with the root רכב, with the same implication.

[64] Ibn Ezra, *The Commentary of Ibn Ezra on Isaiah*, p. 305; D. Qimchi, 'ישעיה', on the passage.

[65] Cf. Koole, *Jesaja III*, pp. 478-79 (ET p. 524).

nations). Deciding which understanding is right is complicated by the ambiguity of *lakkōhᵉnîm lalᵉwiyyim* as well as by the textual uncertainties attaching to that phrase. The phrase *lakkōhᵉnîm lalᵉwiyyim* comes only here. The phrase *lakkōhᵉnîm halwiyyim* occurs with reference to 'the Levitical priests' (Deut 18.1) and the phrase *lakkōhᵉnîm wēlalwiyyim* recurs with reference to 'the priests and the [other] Levites' (e.g. Neh 13.30; 2 Chr 31.2). Many post-MT manuscripts and Versions have this reading, surely an assimilation to that more familiar phrase. Grammatically, it would be possible for the phrase to mean 'take some people for the priests as Levites'—that is, take some people who are not from the clan of Levi to function as Levites, that is assistants, for the priests; this would fit with the reference to a shortage of Levites and to other assistants in Ezra 8.15-20. But such an interpretation is rather subtle. The same applies to the suggestion that the phrase means 'take some people for the priests, for the Levites'—as assistants.[66] More likely the phrase has the same meaning as *lakkōhᵉnîm halwiyyim* and means 'as Levitical priests'.

In itself 'take' could simply refer to bringing people back from exile; in this connection 'take' and 'bring' occur in parallelism in 14.2, while Ezekiel 36.24 refers to Yhwh 'taking' the exiles in the sense of bringing them back from exile. It would then be quite appropriate for the prophecy to speak of taking priests home in this sense. It would imply that the people who are brought back are Levites; since many priests and Levites were taken into exile in Babylon and came back to Jerusalem after the fall of Babylon, it would be quite possible to assume that there were also Levites and priests in other countries. The specific mention of Levites might then imply that they were not to be marginalized or neglected, in keeping with the concern with the Levites in the Torah (see, e.g., Deut 18.1-8).[67]

But taking people *lakkōhᵉnîm* implies turning people into something they were not before, and thus taking as priests people who would not otherwise be priests (cf. the use of 'take as' in Exod 6.7; also 'choose as priest' in 1 Sam 2.28). It might denote taking some members of clans other than Levi (specifically, no doubt, Judah) as priests: 'I will take some people as priests in addition to the Levites'. This would fit the form of expression in 56.8.[68] In effect these people would be adopted into Levi. But it is not clear why such a promise should be made, and the context rather suggests that Yhwh is going to take people from the other nations who have now received news of Yhwh and adopt them into Levi, so that they could then become Levitical priests. The placing of 'as Levites' after 'as priests' may then have its point here.[69] Levi is the clan into which they

[66] Cf. Dillmann, *Jesaia* [1890 edn], p. 542.

[67] See José Severino Croatto, 'La inclusión sociale en el programa del Tercer Isaías: Exégesis de Isaías 56, 1-8 y 66, 17-24', *Revista Bíblica* 60 (1998), pp. 91-110 (108-10).

[68] Cf. Klostermann, *Deuterojesaia*, p. 114

[69] Volz (*Jesaja II*, p. 295) thus sees it as a gloss.

will need to be adopted. The verse thus completes a suggestive sequence within Isaiah 56–66: in 56.1-8 the priesthood is broadened to include foreigners in Judah who have attached themselves to Yhwh, in 61.6 it is democratized to include all Judahites, in 66.21 it is globalized to include all the nations.[70] This is not to imply that the distinction between Israel and Gentiles has been abolished, any more than is the case when Paul speaks in similar terms to vv. 20-21 of proclaiming God's gospel to the Gentiles so that they might become an offering acceptable to God, sanctified by the Holy Spirit (Rom 15.16).[71]

66.22 Because as the new heavens and the new earth which I am going to make are going to stand before me (Yhwh's declaration), so your offspring and your name will stand.

As the reference to Yhwh's holy mountain in v. 20 took up the allusions to it in 65.11, 25, the reference to Yhwh's forming new heavens and new earth takes up the promise in 65.17-18; indeed, v. 22 has been called the 'quintessence' of chapter 65.[72] It does use the verb 'make' rather than 'create';[73] the sequence thus neatly corresponds to that in Genesis 1–2, and further, the present verse talks about people, about a new community, as 65.17 did not.[74] Thus Leviticus Rabbah 29.12 comments that when Israel comes before God to acknowledge their sin and depart pardoned, God views them 'as though today I have created you as a new creation', and notes that this is in line with 66.22. The resumed reference is apposite not least because of the way 65.17-25 explicates that it is the recreated city of Jerusalem that constitutes the new heavens and the new earth. Thus there is an intrinsic link between the new heavens and new earth and the offspring and name of the Judahites in Jerusalem whom the prophecy addresses. Yet the new context in which this new allusion to the new heavens and the new earth appears constitutes a reminder that the new Jerusalem is not merely a city, a place where people live or the capital of a nation, but that it is the location of a place of worship and/or that the temple itself is a symbol of the ordered cosmos.[75]

[70] See Tiemeyer, *Priestly Rites and Prophetic Rage*, p. 285.

[71] Against Walter Gross, 'Israel und die Völker: Die Krise des YHWH-Volk-Konzepts im Jesajabuch', in Erich Zenger (ed.), *Der neue Bund im alten* (Freiburg: Herder, 1993), pp. 149-67 (160-67).

[72] So Gärtner, *Jesaja 66 und Sacharja 14 als Summe der Prophetie* (see above), p. 52.

[73] Penna (*Isaia*, p. 629) notes that Vg takes *ʿōśēh ʿōmᵉdîm* as a periphrastic alternative to hiphil, 'make stand'; but this is hardly Hebrew usage.

[74] Cf. Anne E. Gardner, 'The Nature of the New Heavens and New Earth in Isaiah 66:22', *Australian Biblical Review* 50 (2002), pp. 10-27.

[75] Cf. Ulrich Berges, 'Der neue Himmel und die neue Erde im Jesajabuch', in Ferenc Postma, K. Spronk, and E. Talstra (eds.), *The New Things* (Henk Leene Festschrift; Maastricht: Shaker, 2002), pp. 9-15 (14-15).

Ezekiel 44.15 speaks of the Levitical priests standing before Yhwh to play their part in offering sacrifices (cf. also Deut 10.8; 18.7; Jer 15.1, 19; 18.20; 2 Chr 29.11), while other passages speak of the whole people as standing before Yhwh (e.g. Ezra 9.15; 2 Chr 20.13). They do so like a king's servants who stand before him in submission and/or in attendance (e.g. 1 Sam 16.21, 22; Dan 1.5, 19; 2.2). Thus here the point is not merely that the Judahites will remain before Yhwh, remain in existence as long as Yhwh is in existence.[76] Rather the new heavens and the new earth (that is, the transformed Jerusalem) will stand before Yhwh in a position of submission and service. The opening 'because' suggests that the prophecy's promise that Yhwh will bring Judahites back to Jerusalem from all over the world by means of the peoples among whom they live, and will take some of them as priests, is associated with a commitment to Jerusalem's being a place that Yhwh is going to renew and have serving him. So the community's offspring and its name will stand—that is, it will not merely stay in being, but will continue to stand before Yhwh. The reference to offspring takes up from 65.23, while the reference to the name recalls 56.5. The 'because' once again shows that the prophecy's underlying concern is with Judah. The nations' coming to acknowledge Yhwh and the taking of some of them as priests happens for Yhwh's sake, benefits the nations, and also benefits Judah. It does not mean Israel ceases to exist as a result of being assimilated to the nations.[77]

66.23 And new moon by new moon, Sabbath by Sabbath, all flesh will come to bow low before me (Yhwh has said).

The reference to standing before Yhwh is restated in terms of bowing low before Yhwh, an expression that superficially contrasts with bowing low but in substance refers to a similar expression of submission. The verb *hištaḥăwâ* has come once earlier in the chapters: the nations who had despised the Judahites will bow low at the Judahites' feet (60.14). Here once again the context suggests that 'all flesh' refers to the nations (as in 49.26) and not just to Judahites (as in v. 16). These foreign peoples do not come to Jerusalem as subdued and humiliated or as servants of Judah but as worshippers on a pilgrimage; it is now Yhwh to whom they are bowing low.[78] In respect of Judahites the point would hardly need making that they will so bow to Yhwh; on the other hand, in respect of the nations, the

76 Against Ehrlich, *Randglossen*, IV, p. 232.

77 See the discussion in Walter Gross, 'Israel und die Völker', in Erich Zenger (ed.), *Der Neue Bund im Alten* (Freiburg: Herder, 1993), pp. 149-67 (160-67).

78 Cf. Gary Stansell, 'The Nations' Journey to Zion', in Everson and Bloom (eds.), *The Desert Will Bloom*, pp. 232-55 (246). Joel Kaminsky and Anne Stewart ('God of All the World: Universalism and Developing Monotheism in Isaiah 40–66', *HTR* 99 (2006), pp. 139-63 [161]) see this worship as not implying conversion, or for that matter salvation, but making such distinctions seems to introduce foreign categories into the discussion.

parallel passage 56.1-8 has already emphasized the significance of observing the Sabbath in respect of foreigners who attach themselves to Yhwh; it is *the* sign of commitment to Yhwh. Thus v. 23 has been called the quintessence of 56.1-8 and 66.1-24.[79] A difference from 56.1-8 is that here the Sabbath is not a day for refraining from work but a day for bowing low before Yhwh and thus for worship, an unusual note since the Sabbath is not usually linked with worship. Indeed, the language of 'coming' could imply that it is an occasion for pilgrimage, which contrasts with the idea of refraining from journeying on the Sabbath.[80] The Sabbath and the new moon, the beginning of the month, are also associated elsewhere (e.g. 2 Kgs 4.23; Ezek 46.1-6; Amos 8.5). The one passage in the Torah that explicitly makes the link between Sabbath and worship is Numbers 28.9-10,[81] which specifies special offerings for the Sabbath, and significantly Numbers 28.11-15 then immediately follows this regulation with one concerning special offerings for the new moon. In another link between Zechariah 14 and this section, Zechariah 14.16-17 also has the people who are left of the nations who have attacked Jerusalem coming there to bow low before Yhwh, but has them doing so annually, at Sukkot, and with a sanction attached to non-attendance. The view of universal worship here in v. 23 is thus much more intense.[82]

66.24 People will go out and look at the corpses of the individuals who rebelled against me, because their worm will not die and their fire will not go out. It will be a horror to all flesh.

The closing verse of Isaiah reverts to the concern with the faithless which dominated 65.1–66.17, and works out the implications of the declaration that there will be no well-being for the faithless (48.22; 57.21).[83] It apparently describes a procession that would follow the worship of v. 23. The faithless are here described as people who 'rebel' (*pāšaʿ*), the verb with which the book of Isaiah started (1.2, 28). The talk of their fire not going out also takes up the last phrase in Isaiah 1.[84] 'Rebel' played a key role in Isaiah 40–55 in explaining the background to the exile of the people whose return Isaiah 66 is still concerned with (43.27; 48.8), and has described the behaviour of the exiles themselves (46.8; 53.12) and that of the Second Temple Judahite community (59.13). The noun 'rebellion' has also appeared in 43.25; 44.22; 50.1; 53.5, 8; 57.4; 58.1; 59.12, 20. We noted in connection with 58.1 that 'rebellion' is a more

[79] Gärtner, *Jesaja 66 und Sacharja 14 als Summe der Prophetie* (see above), p. 59.

[80] Cf. Lezek Ruszkowski, 'Der Sabbat bei Tritojesaja', in Huwyler and Mathys (eds.), *Prophetie und Psalmen*, pp. 61-74 (69-71).

[81] But behind Num 28.9-10 is Lev 23.3, though it is allusive (GID).

[82] GID.

[83] König, *Das Buch Jesaja*, p. 536.

[84] Cf. Liebreich, 'The Compilation of the Book of Isaiah', p. 277.

appropriate translation than 'transgression', because the term denotes flouting a person's authority rather than contravening a rule. The closing verse of the book called Isaiah affirms that people will not get away with such flouting, and other people need to be aware of that fact.[85]

In place of the last clause, Tg has 'the faithless will be judged in Gehinnam until the faithful say concerning them, "We have seen enough"' (cf. Vg). Mark 9.42-49 likewise applies the verse to punishment in Hell.[86] Westermann's comment is thus strange that in light of the New Testament we have to agree with vv. 18-19, 21 rather than with vv. 20, 22-24, even though he also notes that it is v. 24 that Jesus quotes with approval.[87] More apposite is Kessler's comment that 'the gospel is not the outworking of a harmless and feeble friendliness of God'.[88] Yet the verse hardly refers to Gehenna. As the talk of the restoration of Jerusalem in vv. 18-22 has related to the passage about the new Jerusalem in 65.20-25, the description of how the worm that eats up corpses will not die and how the fire that burns up bodies will continue to burn forms the other side to the coin of that earlier description of life in the new Jerusalem. The positive picture involved long life, enjoying the fruit of one's labour, and enjoying Yhwh's blessing. The book closes with a converse.[89] In both cases the prophecy refers hyperbolically to an enhanced version of what regularly happens in ordinary life, when bodies either rot or are burned in order to anticipate that rotting,[90] and not to something corresponding to the later idea of heaven and hell. As the prophecy refers to the literal Jerusalem, so it refers to the literal Hinnom Canyon outside the city, also referred to as the Canyon of the Son or Sons of Hinnom, variously identified as the canyon or valley west of the Old City of Jerusalem, or the one south of the city, or the one southwest of the temple.

David Qimchi says that the Hinnom Canyon was where people dumped rubbish and put unclean corpses and where a fire burned continually,[91] but there is no evidence for such practices nearer the time of

[85] John W. Olley ('"No Peace" in a Book of Consolation', *VT* 49 [1999], pp. 351-70) notes that the language of rebellion suggests that the verse refers to Israel rather than to foreigners; he incorporates a survey of Jewish interpretation in this connection. But Jewish tradition (e.g. Jerusalem Talmud Berakot 5.1) also notes that if the rebels are foreigners rather than Jews, this resolves the oddity of the book's ending on a down note (cf. Neusner, *Isaiah in Talmud and Midrash*, pp. 117, 365).

[86] Cf. Justin Martyr, *Dialogue with Trypho* 130; also Augustine's extensive exposition of this and preceding verses in Isaiah 65–66 in this connection, in *City of God* 20.21-22. On the relationship of Mk 9.42-49 to Tg, see Chilton, *A Galilean Rabbi and his Bible*, pp. 101-9.

[87] *Jesaja Kapitel 40–66*, p. 340 (ET p. 429).

[88] Kessler, *Gott geht es um das Ganze*, p. 101.

[89] Cf. Emmanuel Uchenna Dim, *The Eschatological Implications of Isa 65 and 66 as the Conclusion of the Book of Isaiah* (Bern: Lang, 2005), p. 238.

[90] Cf. Paul, ישעיה פרקים מ-סו, II, p. 577 (ET p. 632).

[91] 'תהלים' in מקראות גדולות, commenting on Ps 27.13.

the prophecy. It more likely builds on the notoriety of the canyon as the place where people sacrificed children and thus burned their bodies, and on the comments about this in Jeremiah 7.30-33. The passage implies that the place where the sacrifices were offered and the bodies thus burnt was either literally or in effect a graveyard, and declares that it will become just an ordinary graveyard, but one that will become so full that people will just have to dump bodies there where they will be eaten up. In the hyperbole of the description, the idea will not be that worm and fire are forever consuming the same corpses but that corpses for consuming will always be being added to the pile,[92] a converse of the way 65.20-25 pictures the ongoing positive life of the city. Theodore of Heraclea interprets the verse in the light of 37.36-38,[93] while Cyril of Alexandria sees a reference to the destruction of Jerusalem by the Romans.[94]

A second question raised by Tg is the aim or result of people's going to 'look at' the corpses. The expression *rā'â b-* could have various implications, like English 'look at'.[95] The description of the sight as a 'horror' may suggest that the procession was designed to motivate people to continue in submission to Yhwh rather than falling into rebellion. Their reaction of horror at what they see will surely make 'all flesh' determine not to fall into rebellion themselves. It might therefore be dangerous if eventually the faithful, too, stopped reminding themselves of the fate of the rebels. The word for 'horror', *dērā'ôn*, appears elsewhere only in Daniel 12.2, which may well be alluding to this passage, perhaps the prophet coined the word to express a unique disgust with the rebels.[96]

Further questions are raised by MT's instruction to repeat v. 23 after v. 24. In the text itself, the final verse makes for a link between the close of the book and its opening; Isaiah 1 puts before people a challenge to turn from rebellion, a warning about a fire that will not go out, and a promise of restoration. The close of the book does something similar. The implication of the final verse is thus not that 'in these last two chapters of Isaiah, there is no more room for forgiveness for unfaithful Israel'[97] or that Isaiah 65–66 'is not an exhortation to be on the right side of a division that is about to be made' but 'a pronouncement of the consequences of a choice that *has already been made*'.[98] Rather the contrast between vv. 23 and 24 lays before the readers of Isaiah two alternative commitments and two alternative destinies,[99] in the manner of 50.10-11, and also in that of Deuteronomy 28 (and Matt 25.31-46; Rev 21). 'Characteristic

---

[92] Gaster, 'Notes on Isaiah', p. 107.
[93] Ἐκ τῆς εἰς Ἡσαΐαν ἐξηγησέως, col. 1377.
[94] Ἐξήγησις ὑπομνηματικὴ εἰς τὸν προφήτην Ἡσαΐαν, col. 1448.
[95] See the comment on 66.5.
[96] So Miscall, *Isaiah*, p. 149.
[97] So Dim, *The Eschatological Implications of Isa 65 and 66 as the Conclusion of the Book of Isaiah* (see above), p. 229.
[98] So Carr, 'Reaching for Unity in Isaiah', p. 74 = p. 177.
[99] Cf. Coffin, 'The Book of Isaiah: Chapters 40–66', p. 773.

for the end of the book of Isaiah is the inseparability of salvation and judgment.'[100] The chapter as a whole treats 'exclusion as an extreme tactic of persuasion' in the course of seeking to bring into being 'the new people of God'.[101]

Conclusion

Isaiah 66.18-24 thus makes a fitting conclusion to the book called Isaiah. Willem Beuken has suggested that 65.1–66.14 closes Third Isaiah, 66.15-21 closes Second Isaiah and Third Isaiah, and 66.22-24 closes the whole book of Isaiah.[102] In contrast, Ronald E. Clements has questioned whether the contents of 63.1–66.24 enable it to constitute a proper ending to the book; it is really more like an epilogue.[103] Paradoxically, Peter Miscall sees Isaiah 66 as 'a fitting ending to the book because of its variety and because of its refusal to tie everything together, to leave no loose ends'.[104] I come to a conclusion somewhere between these views. The links between 66.18-24 and 1.1–2.4, 40.1–55.13, 56.1-8, and 65.1–66.17 are too numerous and significant to be treated as coincidental. The person who made 66.18-24 the closing section of the book called Isaiah surely did so aware of its resonances with earlier parts of the book. Yet the section's distinctiveness and jumpiness, and the jumpiness of the entire chapter, suggests that neither 66.17-24 as a whole nor the material within it was created in order to fulfil the function of closing the book. Rather the person who ordered the book in this way was able to use material that lent itself to fulfilling the function of closing the book in an apposite way.

Whatever its origin, it fulfils this function by reminding its readers that they have to take seriously the inclination on the part of the people of God to ignore Yhwh and turn to other resources; the possibility that God may therefore turn to other peoples in order to get the divine purpose fulfilled; God's intention to be recognized by other peoples; God's willingness to use other peoples to that end; God's intention that other peoples should see what God does in restoring Jerusalem and should respond to that awareness; God's promise to be faithful to Israel itself and to Jerusalem in drawing that response from other peoples; God's intention even to take some foreign people as priests, as if they belonged to Levi, as well as to have the foreign peoples take a regular part in worship in Jerusalem; and the seriousness of the fact that it will continue to be possible to ignore Yhwh and turn to other resources, and thus to open oneself to Yhwh's judgment.[105]

100 Park, *Die Gerechtigkeit Israels und das Heil der Völker*, p. 301.

101 Obara, *Le strategie di Dio*, pp. 373, 417.

102 'Isaiah Chapters lxv–lxvi' (see above), pp. 207-21.

103 'Isaiah: A Book without an Ending?', *JSOT 91* (2002), pp. 109-26 (113).

104 *Isaiah*, p. 146.

105 Cf. Smith, *The Book of Isaiah*, II, pp. 465-67.

> To speak of a Gentile mission does not, of course, mean that we are dealing with actual proposals and strategies. What these texts express are attitudes, even dreams and fantasies, entertained in one segment of post-exilic Judaism. That such attitudes can be self-deceptive, self-serving and self-defeating goes without saying. But it is also true to our experience to affirm that projections of a possible future, especially when emitted with the passion and power of conviction often attested in these chapters, can actually create a future, even if the reality is never quite the same as the projection.[106]

William R. Farmer has contended that for Tertullian, arguing against Marcion, the key significance of Isaiah is that it relates God's promises to save the nations, promises that would be fulfilled in the church's coming into being. Yet that implies faith in promises yet to be fulfilled, because the church is by no means yet what Isaiah promises. It is by such faith in the God of Isaiah that we live.[107]

Ulrich Berges offers a complementary argument.[108] Zion is the central theme in the book of Isaiah; it is the centre for worshippers both from Israel and from the nations. Zion occupies this central position in these closing chapters of the book. They declare that Yhwh made a lasting covenant with Zion; in this covenant, people who believe in Jesus the Jew gain a share. An understanding of the theological significance of the book, and in particular of its closing chapters, needs to hold together its testimony to Yhwh's commitment to Zion and its proclaiming of good news to other peoples.

In the context of Old Testament study over the past two centuries, such an understanding will also need to come to terms with the word 'eschatological'. We have noted the use of this word in connection with a number of passages in Isaiah 56–66,[109] but this final section is an appropriate point at which to reconsider the word. It has a number of meanings, and there is no basis for saying that one meaning is *the* correct one; we rather need to be clear what meaning attaches to the word in a particular context.

The End or the eschaton is the time when God's final or ultimate purpose is put into effect, when God's ultimate goal is definitively reached.[110] Understandings of the nature of that goal and the means of achieving it need to be understood in relation to several axes:

[106] J. Blenkinsopp, 'Second Isaiah—Prophet of Universalism', *JSOT* 41 (1988), pp. 83-103 (98-99), reprinted in P. R. Davies (ed.), *The Prophets* (Sheffield: Sheffield Academic Press, 1996), pp. 186-206 (206).

[107] William R. Farmer, 'The Role of Isaiah in the Development of the Christian Canon', in L. M. Hopfe (ed.), *Uncovering Ancient Stones* (H. N. Richardson Memorial; Winona Lake, IN: Eisenbrauns, 1994), pp. 217-22.

[108] See 'Sion als thema in het boek Jesaja', *Tijdschrift voor Thologie* 39 (1999), pp. 118-38; German version, 'Die Zionstheologie des Buches Jesaja', *Estudios Bíblicos* 58 (2000), pp. 167-98.

[109] See especially the 'Conclusion' to the commentary on Isaiah 60 above.

[110] Cf. Henk Leene, 'History and Eschatology in Deutero-Isaiah', in Ruiten and Vervenne (eds.), *Studies in the Book of Isaiah*, pp. 223-49 (226).

1. There is individual, communal, worldwide, and cosmic eschatology. Isaiah 56–66 has nothing to say about the first (about what happens at the end of an individual's life) beyond its references to death and Sheol, or about the last (about a new cosmos, other than the one to be created in Jerusalem). It focuses on God's ultimate purpose for his people and for the nations.
2. Eschatology may think in terms of an End after which there will be nothing, or in terms of historical experience giving way to an era of timeless blessing, or in terms of our era of flawed history and experience giving way to a new, wholesome era of history and experience. Isaiah 56–66 thinks in terms of the last; life (and death) will go on.
3. Eschatology can involve the belief that God is putting that ultimate purpose into effect now through events that can be seen in the world, so that it is already being actualized or realized, or the belief that God will do so at some time in the future by means that we cannot at the moment see. While the former perspective is characteristic of Isaiah 40–55 and the latter of Isaiah 56–66,[111] these later chapters nevertheless expect that what Yhwh intends to do will have some purchase in the present (e.g. 56.1-8).
4. While eschatology implies a radical distinction between this age and a coming age, it can see the coming of this new age as gradual, or as involving a dramatic transformation, reversal, or discontinuity. Isaiah 56–66 assumes the latter.
5. Eschatology can imply a future that is imminent or one that is far away. In Isaiah, there are explicit declarations that God's climactic action is 'near' in 13.22; 46.13; 51.5; 56.1. The first three relate to the fall of Babylon; the last restates the conviction expressed in the previous three, as a prelude to the prophecies in chapters 56–66. While otherwise the chapters give no indication that they expect the End soon, they give no indication that they envisage it only in the 'distant future'.[112]

[111] Cf. Hanson's distinction between prophetic eschatology and apocalyptic eschatology (*The Dawn of Apocalyptic*, pp. 11-12).
[112] Against Albertz, *Religionsgeschichte Israels in alttestamentlicher Zeit*, II, p. 486 (ET II, p. 456).

www.ingramcontent.com/pod-product-compliance
Lightning Source LLC
Chambersburg PA
CBHW050131240426
43673CB00043B/1633
9780567716941